EASTERN EUROPE

FODOR'S TRAVEL GUIDES

are compiled, researched and edited by an international team of travel writers, field correspondents, and editors. The Series, which now almost covers the globe, was founded by Eugene Fodor in 1936.

OFFICES
New York & London

FODOR'S EASTERN EUROPE:

Area Editors: GEORGE MADDOCKS, SYLVIE NICKELS

Editorial Contributors: ROBERT BROWN, RICHARD DAVY, LESLIE GARDINER, FRANCES HOWELL, IRA MAYER, DAVID TENNANT

Editor: RICHARD MOORE

Assistant Editor: THOMAS CUSSANS

Drawings: LORRAINE CALAORA

Cartography: C. W. BACON, KEN McCREITH, ALEX MURPHY, BRYAN WOODFIELD

FODOR'S

EASTERN EUROPE

1983

FODOR'S TRAVEL GUIDES
New York

All the following Guides are current (most of them also in
the Hodder and Stoughton British edition.)

CURRENT FODOR'S COUNTRY AND AREA TITLES:

AUSTRALIA, NEW ZEALAND
  AND SOUTH PACIFIC
AUSTRIA
BELGIUM AND
  LUXEMBOURG
BERMUDA
BRAZIL
CANADA
CARIBBEAN AND BAHAMAS
CENTRAL AMERICA
EASTERN EUROPE
EGYPT
EUROPE
FRANCE
GERMANY
GREAT BRITAIN
GREECE
HOLLAND
INDIA
IRELAND

ISRAEL
ITALY
JAPAN
JORDAN AND HOLY LAND
KENYA
KOREA
MEXICO
NORTH AFRICA
PEOPLE'S REPUBLIC
  OF CHINA
PORTUGAL
SCANDINAVIA
SCOTLAND
SOUTH AMERICA
SOUTHEAST ASIA
SOVIET UNION
SPAIN
SWITZERLAND
TURKEY

CITY GUIDES:

BEIJING, GUANGZHOU, SHANGHAI
CHICAGO
LONDON
LOS ANGELES
MADRID
MEXICO CITY AND ACAPULCO
NEW YORK CITY
PARIS

ROME
SAN DIEGO
SAN FRANCISCO
STOCKHOLM, COPENHAGEN,
  OSLO, HELSINKI, AND
  REYKJAVIK
TOKYO
WASHINGTON, D.C.

FODOR'S BUDGET SERIES:

BUDGET BRITAIN
BUDGET CANADA
BUDGET CARIBBEAN
BUDGET EUROPE
BUDGET FRANCE
BUDGET GERMANY
BUDGET HAWAII

BUDGET ITALY
BUDGET JAPAN
BUDGET MEXICO
BUDGET SCANDINAVIA
BUDGET SPAIN
BUDGET TRAVEL IN AMERICA

USA GUIDES:

ALASKA
CAPE COD
COLORADO
FAR WEST
FLORIDA
GRAND CANYON

HAWAII
NEW ENGLAND
PENNSYLVANIA
SOUTH
TEXAS
USA (in one volume)

CONTENTS

LKB June 21, '85

v

CONTENTS

HUNGARY

POLAND

CONTENTS

FOREWORD

There are not all that many voyages of genuine discovery left to be made in the course of taking a holiday, certainly not many that include the discovery of the everyday world seen through new glasses. It is all the more exciting, then, to find a region that lies, like Alice's Looking-Glass World, just beyond our own everyday life, touching it at many points; a region that was once an integral part of the Europe we know, part of its culture, thought, art and way of life, and yet never completely so; a region that for centuries lay halfway between the Occident and the Orient, sharing in the fascinations of both while preserving its own deeply ingrained character. This region we have called Eastern Europe and it includes Bulgaria, Czechoslovakia, Hungary, Poland and Romania, an area that stretched from the old Europe down into the Balkans.

The very nature of its isolation from the Western world over the last few decades has meant that Eastern Europe has preserved many of the qualities of charm and tradition that materialism and a more frenzied pace of life have to a large extent made things of the past in Western Europe. But, as we say elsewhere in this book, this sundering of Europe is a very recent phenomenon when looked at from the point of view of history. What are three-and-a-half decades of separation when it has been preceded by two thousand years and more of close correspondence? During those long, vibrant centuries Eastern Europe accumulated an enormously rich cultural heritage which can be seen today not only in the great baroque cities, but also in the churches, monasteries and castles that rise proudly throughout the countryside.

And what a countryside! The huge area covered by this book contains some of the most lovely and spectacular natural features anywhere on earth. Mountain ranges that thrust skyward between Poland and Czechoslovakia, providing summer outings and winter sports to rival anything in Switzerland; spas and beaches to delight everyone from a rheumatic sufferer to the most active skin diver; river trips through ancient landscapes, with spacious meadows for camping. What is more, Eastern Europe has been spared the worst excesses of modern motoring and its landscapes are virtually unspoiled. It is only when one visits such regions, hardly scarred by motorways, that one realizes just how much we have lost in the last, Gadarene decades of the automobile and how little we have gained in recompense.

A visit to Eastern Europe is not only fascinating for its discovery of the works of art and nature, rich and varied though those are, it can also be fascinating for its revelation of the people and their way of life, especially if such a journey can take in more than one country and thus provide the chance to compare life in neighboring lands. As we have tried to make clear in our background chapters, it is vital to approach such a trip with an open mind and in the ever-present consciousness that you are a guest, not an evangelist. Our popular concept of life behind the Iron Curtain has been out of focus for years. A lack of definition which was partially corrected when the Pope's visit to Poland, followed by the social upheavals of '81 and '82, shattered for a great many their long-held beliefs of a monolithic political and religious situation. It is a pity that the West has been mainly exposed to Eastern Europe through the medium of spy novels and espionage films, with the odd dash of Transylvanian wolves howling at a shrouded moon. You will not find yourself in a John le Carré novel come to life, but you may well meet attitudes and situations that are strange and, perhaps, even repugnant to your own beliefs. It is important that you should be sensitive to your surroundings and discreet in your behavior. With such simple caveats accepted, a tour of Eastern Europe, whether under your own steam or with one of the increasing number of package tours, can be both exciting and memorable.

* * *

We have been greatly assisted in our compilation of this book by many people, both here and in the five countries concerned. We would like to thank especially: Mr. A. Atanasov of the State Committee for Tourism in Bulgaria and his staff; Mr. V. Dvořak, Director of Čedok, the Czechoslovakia Travel Bureau, in London and his staff; Mr. Gábor Tarr, Managing Director of Danube Travel, the London representatives of IBUSZ, the official Hungarian Travel Bureau, for his courtesy and help in obtaining official information not otherwise easily come by; the Corvina Press in Budapest and its excellent publications for much valuable information and in particular Mr. László Boros, Corvina's chief English Language editor, for his constant help and interest; Mr. Rajmund Mendyka, Director of the Polish Tourist Information Centre in London and his staff; Mr. Nicolae Paduraru of the Ministry of Tourism in Bucharest and Mr. G. Mititelu, Director of the Romanian National Tourist Office in London, for their support.

We would like to make it very clear that any opinions expressed in this book are those of the editors and can in no way be attributed to any of the above mentioned people, for whose courtesy and kindness we are deeply grateful.

* * *

We are always grateful to readers of our Guides for their letters telling us of their experiences while using our books. Such comments often help us to correct errors that might otherwise escape the notice of our professional editors and revisors, who, naturally, see things from a slightly different point of view. This is especially important where service in hotels and restaurants is concerned. We would welcome letters from visitors to Eastern Europe, giving us their opinions of the tours they favored, pointers that they may have gleaned which could smooth the way for other travelers, estimates of hotels and restaurants they may have visited . . . in fact anything that might have a bearing on future editions of this book. Our two addresses are:

in the US—Fodor's Travel Guides, 2 Park Avenue, New York, NY 10016;

in Europe—Fodor's Travel Guides (UK) Ltd, 9-10 Market Place, London W1N 7AG.

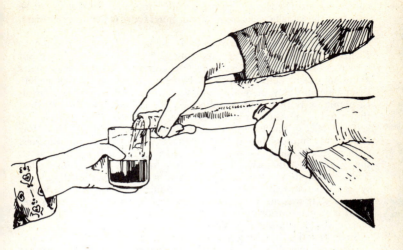

AN INTRODUCTION TO
EASTERN EUROPE

Pride of Place

by
RICHARD DAVY

It is easy to have erroneous ideas about Eastern Europe if you have never been there. Spy films and novels still tend to show it as a strange and rather sinister place 'behind the Iron Curtain' where men in dark glasses follow you down the street and arrest you for no reason at all. This view is now absurdly out of date. While there are certain things you have to be careful about, and we will come back to these later, you can have a perfectly normal holiday there. Western visitors are no longer the rare and suspect species that they were in the days of the Cold War. Hundreds of thousands of them stream in and out all the time. There are businessmen negotiating contracts, technicians servicing Western machinery, students and scholars, emigré natives returning to visit relatives, and very large numbers of tourists whom the authorities welcome with open arms for the hard currency they bring. The tourist industry is well organized and the main routes well trodden.

1

On the surface, at any rate, life is much more normal than the spy stories suggest. Provided you are a truly innocent visitor you can be sure that the knock on the door of your hotel room is the chambermaid, not the police.

There is also another erroneous idea that some people bring to Eastern Europe. They come expecting to find communism being put into practice. Right-wingers expect to confirm all their worst fears about socialism. Left-wingers look hopefully for a new type of society from which poverty, inequality and waste have been banished by socialist planning. Both will be disappointed. Reality is more complex than they think. Communism is still far over the horizon.

The Soviet system was imposed on Eastern Europe after World War II by local communists with the backing of Moscow. In some countries, such as Czechoslovakia, they had a fair amount of popular support, though never a majority. In most they had very little. During the Stalinist period, which continued even after Stalin's death in 1953, the system was imposed uniformly on all countries, by brute force where necessary. It was not a success. In spite of certain achievements and rapid industrialization it came nowhere near fulfilling early promises that it would overtake the West.

Since then the zeal has gone out of communist ideology. Officials and party newspapers have to take it seriously but most people do not think about it very much. They are too busy coping with the practical problems of life. Few seriously believe that Eastern Europe is demonstrating a revolutionary new way of managing human affairs. Human nature has proved stubbornly resistant to change, and national traditions surprisingly resilient. Each country has been stretching and bending the system to suit its own needs. Communist theory cannot be overtly abandoned but it is not the key to an understanding of Eastern Europe.

Old Empires and New States

It is best to start by putting current politics aside and looking at Eastern Europe in longer historical perspective. It is a very recent grouping together of countries with different histories and traditions. It has no reason to be treated as a single entity except that it happens to be the area which came under Soviet control as the Red Army marched out beyond its borders to defeat Hitler in World War II. It cuts across the old frontiers of the Roman Empire and the more recent division between the Turkish and Austro-Hungarian Empires. It has brought together old antagonists, such as Hungarians and Romanians, Poles and Germans. It includes very old nations and very new states—East Germany (which we cover in a separate book), was not created until after World War II, and Czechoslovakia became a state only in 1918. Altogether the area has had an extraordinarily rich and turbulent history, swept by wars, divided by empires, criss-crossed by national rivalries and constantly redefined by changing frontiers. It contains layers and layers of overlapping cultures and bitter memories of massacres and persecution. It has suffered terribly, but it has also been one of the richest sources of culture, learning and invention the world has ever known. It is, quite simply, an integral part of European civilization.

Against this background the political and military line that now divides Eastern Europe from Western Europe looks very recent and unnatural. Prague, Budapest, and Warsaw are closer to Vienna than to Moscow, both culturally and geographically. Indeed, Prague actually lies west of Vienna. Chopin traveled from Warsaw to Paris, Mozart from Salzburg to Prague, Goethe from Frankfurt to Weimar without any feeling that they were moving between 'east' and 'west' or from one ideological world to another. They were just moving naturally around the cultural heart of old Europe. Kings and princes might fight each other, nationalities might rise against the Emperor, frontiers might shift, but Europe was still Europe, at least until it merged eastwards into the Balkans and the areas that had been under Turkish rule.

The Iron Curtain

This cultural and economic unity was rudely interrupted by the Cold War. As Winston Churchill put it, an Iron Curtain came down across central Europe, cutting off the American from the Soviet sphere of influence. Stalin ruled in Eastern Europe, sweeping away the old order and stamping out dissent not only among the people but also among communists who wanted forms of communism that were less Russian and more European. Contacts with the West became dangerous. The upper and middle classes were mostly dispossessed. Prisons and labor camps filled up. Even communist leaders, often those of Jewish origin, became victims of rigged show trials designed to explain away failures and instil fear, especially of Western espionage. It was a period of terror, shortages and forced industrialization. Soviet tanks put down uprisings in East Germany in 1953 and Hungary in 1956, when they were also narrowly prevented from intervening in Poland where a new government was trying to throw off the worst aspects of the Stalinist system.

In the decade that followed liberalization began to seep slowly and unevenly through Eastern Europe, encouraged not only by the aspirations of the people, but also by the need for Western goods and the improving relations between the Soviet Union and America. Experiments were made with elements of the market economy; cultural expression became somewhat freer; contacts with the West began to open up.

However, it has not been smooth going since then. In 1968 Czechoslovakia tried to introduce a new form of democratic communism which was promptly crushed by Soviet invasion. In 1970 strikes in Poland toppled the leadership of Mr. Gomułka. While ten years later, amid deepening economic crisis, further strikes in Poland's Baltic shipyards led to the formation of Solidarity, Eastern Europe's first independent trade union. But after little more than a year of effervescent freedom, in December 1981 martial law was declared and Solidarity suspended.

Adaptable, yet Individual

Nevertheless, national traditions keep pushing their way through the system. Each state in Eastern Europe retains a very distinct individuality and national pride. Poland, for instance, has most of its farms in private hands and a very strong Roman Catholic Church, reinforced by the election of a Polish Pope. Culturally Poland looked mainly west, especially to Paris. Politically its history is one of playing off East and West with disastrous results, so that its powerful national spirit has been forged under the pressure of constant invasions, partitions and occupations. Even the post-war frontiers are new, with a chunk of eastern territory lost to the Russians and a chunk of western territory, including the Baltic ports, gained from the Germans. The Poles have emerged from all this as incredibly brave fighters, stubborn opponents of foreign domination, and prolific coiners of political jokes. A typical example is: 'What is the difference between capitalism and communism? Capitalism is based on the exploitation of man by man. Under communism it's vice versa.'

Bulgaria, in contrast, is a Balkan country that spent about five centuries under Turkish rule. Its church is Orthodox, its view more eastern, and its population still mainly rural, in spite of post-war industrialization. However, Balkan politics are never simple. Although it owes its liberation from the Turks to Russian help it aligned itself with Germany through most of both world wars, attempting a last-minute switch at the end of the second. Outwardly, it is now one of the most loyal allies of the Soviet Union. Its history has given it a certain eastern adaptability which spares it the worst stresses of opposition and dissent. Nevertheless, proud nationalism is never far beneath the surface. Having concentrated on developing its agriculture and smaller industries, it has avoided some of the worst problems of rapid industrialization and, aided also by an expanding tourist industry, has been doing comparatively well.

Romania is another contrast. An eastern outpost of the Roman empire, it was invaded by various barbarian tribes, which almost obliterated the original inhabitants. But its language is still as much Latin as Slav and it clings proudly to this distinction, seeing itself as a Latin island in a sea of Slavs. Culturally it looks west for inspiration, and in recent years its foreign policy has been conspicuously independent of the Soviet Union. It refused to follow the Soviet Union and break relations with Israel after the 1967 war, and it continued to cultivate relations with China when this was frowned upon by Moscow. Its internal system, however, is among the more tightly controlled in Eastern Europe and its standard of living among the lowest. Indeed Romania's economic difficulties have increased significantly of late, not least as a result of its headlong rush into industrialization at the expense of agricultural development, a step that was also taken in defiance of Moscow.

A Rich Cultural Heritage

Westwards to Hungary, and we are back in Central Europe. More than half the population here is Roman Catholic and the cultural traditions those of the Austro-Hungarian empire—though Turkish influence was not finally thrown off until the early 18th century. Under the rule of the Austrian empire the Hungarians developed strong national feelings, so they did not take easily to Soviet domination after World War II. Their uprising in 1956 was fierce and bloody. Since then they have developed a unique economic system which departs from the Soviet model in allowing more scope for market mechanisms and individual initiative. It has raised the standard of living to one of the highest in Eastern Europe and brought a fair measure of reconciliation between government and people. The Hungarians are a clever people with a taste for wine, women and song. The blue Danube, after all, runs through Budapest as well as Vienna.

Czechoslovakia has a tradition of gentler but skillful adaptation. It was created in 1918 out of two parts of the old Austro-Hungarian Empire. It embraces two distinct peoples and languages, the Czechs and the Slovaks, who have their regional capital in Bratislava. Czechoslovakia was a flourishing democracy before World War II, but it was betrayed by the Western allies and occupied by the Nazis. Resistance was nowhere near as active or bloody as in Poland, but when the country emerged from the War many people turned to Communism, only to be deeply disappointed. Since the Soviet invasion of 1968 most people have abandoned any interest in politics and concentrated on increasing their standard of living. It is a friendly, civilized and beautiful country, industrially advanced but saddened by political disappointments and the curbs on its rich cultural traditions.

Cities, Lakes and Mountains

These brief remarks cannot even begin to do justice to the rich variety that Eastern Europe can offer. It has, for instance, some of Europe's most beautiful old cities. Prague, once seat of the Bohemian kings, was scarcely touched by the war and remains a living museum of different architectural styles. It has a royal castle, intimate cobbled squares, lovely old restaurants and 113 churches, many of them of rare beauty. Budapest, too, preserves much of the atmosphere of old Europe, with its grand buildings rising beside the Danube, ubiquitous gypsy music, lively night life, and good food. Warsaw was cruelly devastated by the Nazis but the old center of the city and the Royal Palace have been rebuilt with loving accuracy using old paintings as guides. Poland also has Cracow, once the royal capital and more recently home town of Pope John Paul II. Its old square, royal castle and many of its old buildings survived the Nazi invasion. Sofia has impressive Orthodox churches and nearby monasteries. Bucharest, in spite of earthquakes, has areas of surviving elegance.

But Eastern Europe is not only cities. There are areas of great natural beauty, such as the Masurian lakes in northern Poland, the Tatra mountains, which divide Poland from Czechoslovakia, the great plains and wine country of Hungary, Romanian Transylvania, legendary home of Dracula, the mountains and Black Sea beach resorts of Bulgaria. There are castles, palaces, old battlefields, spas, lakes and country towns where the atmosphere of old Europe has still not been overwhelmed by motor cars, motorways and tower blocks.

East European tourism is geared for group travel under the auspices of state tourist offices and Western tour operators, but Western tourists are perfectly free to travel around on their own by car or public transport, and many of them do. The only problem is likely to be finding hotels if you have not booked in advance. Hotels tend to be full, especially during the tourist season. The big cities have hotels of all categories. Hilton, Hyatt, Holiday Inn and Intercontinental have been moving in, bringing standards comparable to those in the West, though there may be special problems, such as very limited supplies of Western newspapers. New hotels have also been springing up in many of the main tourist resorts. In remoter districts standards are likely to be lower than in the West. Camping sites are numerous and well organized and are good places to make friends. In many places it is also possible to rent rooms in private houses through the state tourist agencies. Sometimes you find yourself in cramped and noisy accommodations on the outskirts of town, but it is just as likely that you will be warmly welcomed into a friendly household and given a lot of help.

National monuments and old buildings are now lovingly cared for, in contrast to the early days of communism when every relic of the past, particularly if it had to do with religion, was supposed to be swept away. Tourism is not the only reason. National pride has long since broken through the bleaker doctrines of communism. The past is no longer all bad.

Avoidable Temptations

Although we said earlier that life in Eastern Europe is outwardly more 'normal' than many people expect, it is, of course, very different from Western Europe, and there are certain things that the visitor should be aware of. The governments of Eastern Europe are political, military and economic allies of the Soviet Union. They welcome Western tourists, but they remain careful about contacts with the West.

They cannot watch every tourist, but if you start doing anything outside the normal line of tourist activity you could find yourself attracting attention. You should not bring with you anti-communist literature or books by well-known dissidents. If you distribute bibles or literature which is not otherwise available, or if you insult the regime, you could be breaking local laws, which are stricter than in the West. If you visit well-known dissidents you could find yourself being questioned or even expelled from the country. You should also be cautious about photographing airports, bridges, trains or anything military. Be particularly careful near frontiers. Hobbies such as plane watching or writing down car numbers are not known in Eastern Europe and can arouse suspicion.

Probably the greatest temptation facing Western visitors to Eastern Europe is to change money on the black market. Outside the big hotels and indeed almost anywhere you go, you are liable to be offered several times the official rate. There is a big demand for Western currency. It can be used to buy goods in special hard currency shops, to pay for scarce services, and of course travel to the West. Sometimes it is very difficult to refuse a student who desperately wants hard currency for a trip to the West, or an acquaintance who needs a spare part for his car. Many Western visitors give in and do very well out of the bargain. Nevertheless, it is strictly against the law and it is a risky and foolish thing to do. If you want a relaxed holiday take local laws seriously.

Curiosity—About You

Making personal contact with the people of Eastern Europe is one of the more rewarding aspects of visiting the area. Mostly they welcome visitors from the West with genuine warmth and hospitality. Although many of them listen to Western radio, read Western books and see Western films, they are still much more cut off than they would like to be. For Romanians and Bulgarians, travel to the West is still a rare privilege. Czechoslovaks can travel a little more easily now, but they mostly need some kind of invitation from the West. Poles and Hungarians are the freest, but even their travel is rationed to certain intervals and they are allowed very little hard currency. Also, they can lose the privilege if they misbehave.

Thus most East Europeans, except those in sensitive official jobs, grasp eagerly at opportunities for contact with the West. You are liable to find yourself being questioned about your way of life, your income, the type of car you have, and so on, as well as about the broader aspects of life in the West, such as unemployment, poverty and the rights of minorities. Western shortcomings are much publicized in the communist press.

If you do make contacts of this sort you should be sensitive to the types of problem your friends may face. In some countries all contacts with foreigners are supposed to be reported, though this is rarely admitted and frequently ignored. The important thing is not to get people into trouble, as Western visitors have sometimes done through ignorance or carelessness. If, for instance, you draw people into a relaxed political discussion over drinks and they say things that are critical of the regime, do not talk about it afterwards in a loud voice or in your hotel where you may be overheard. Your friends could find themselves with problems long after you have gone safely home. So be discreet if people are frank with you and be understanding if they want to avoid politics. Their lives can be more complex than outsiders realize.

There is seldom a clear line between supporters and critics of the regime. People may be critical of some aspects while approving others. Some may be reluctant members of the Communist Party for the sake of their careers. Some may be just letting off a bit of steam. Things are not black and white in Eastern Europe, and the freedom with which people talk varies from country to country, place to place, and person to person. Tune in carefully. And incidentally, of course, if you yourself have a job that might interest the authorities, you will naturally be wary of certain types of approach.

An Easier Life—in Some Ways

Ways of life in Eastern Europe vary enormously. The urban industrial worker of Hungary or Czechoslovakia is worlds apart from the Bulgarian peasant. Even within one country, such as Poland, horse-drawn plows can be at work within sight of the most modern factories. Nevertheless, since all countries share variations of the same basic system they have certain ideas in common. Generally speaking, necessities such as bread, rent and public transport are kept cheap by means of massive subsidies. Luxuries, especially cars, are very expensive. Another political principle is that everyone has the right to work, so that very few people, except political dissidents, are totally deprived of jobs. Unemployment pay does not exist. Surplus workers are simply kept on the payroll, which anyway comes ultimately from the state budget. But since productivity is generally lower than in the West there is often a shortage rather than a surplus of labor.

Cheap necessities and secure jobs mean that is some ways life in Eastern Europe can be easier than in the West. Anybody who is not particularly able or ambitious can coast along with little worry. Welfare systems are extensive though often overburdened. Day care for small children receives fairly high priority, though there are never enough places. Maternity leave for working mothers is generally much more generous than in the West, partly because of the shortage of nurseries and partly to keep up the birthrate. There is very little severe poverty, though certain categories, such as pensioners on their own or single-parent families, may find difficulty making ends meet.

The stresses of life in Eastern Europe are mostly different from those in the West. The ladder of promotion can depend as much on politics as on ability, and because the system does not encourage delegation people who rise towards the top of the ladder can find themselves working very hard indeed, and worrying a great deal about their own security. Since the only employer is the state it is not a good thing to fall out with him, and since the party hierarchy can open the door to numerous privileges it, too, must not be offended.

For the ordinary family there are other problems, not shortage of money but shortage of quality goods, services and housing. Young couples may have to live with their parents for years before getting a flat of their own, and even then it will be small. Many authorities are now encouraging the trend towards privately-owned cooperatives because it takes some of the load off the state budget, mops up surplus purchasing power, and encourages better maintenance.

Distribution of food and goods to the retail shops tends to be unpredictable. Housewives can spend a lot of time standing in line if they want more than basic necessities. Alternatively they go to the vast grey 'parallel market' where goods and favors are exchanged informally. They pay the plumber in vodka or hard currency, and get to know a butcher who wants tickets to a football match, which their cousin can provide because his uncle helped the son of a sports official to get into university. Networks such as this proliferate and demand time, energy and skill, but they are one of the normal routes to the better things in life.

All this means that life in Eastern Europe has developed somewhat differently from communist theory and the hopes of early idealists. Private enterprise pushes its way through cracks in the system. People are as preoccupied with consumer goods as they are in the West, or even more so because the struggle is harder. Big cities encounter problems very similar to those in the West—traffic jams, pollution, restless young people, pop culture, and petty crime, though not yet at a Western level. The churches have not died, nor the appetite for wider sources of information. But standards of living have generally risen. At least, they rose rapidly in the late sixties and early seventies but higher costs of oil and raw materials and slower growth in Western markets are now bringing new headaches for the planners and slower improvements for the consumer. In this respect, as in most others, Eastern Europe is not an island. It is part of Europe and increasingly open to the rest of the world as well.

PLANNING YOUR TRIP

PLANNING YOUR TRIP

 HOW TO GO. Travel to Eastern Europe is by no means the uncertain, complex affair it once was. All the Eastern bloc countries are extremely eager to attract Western visitors, if for no better reason than to earn much-needed foreign currencies, and they consequently go out of their way to make life as easy and comfortable for visitors from the West as they can. Evidence of this desire to please is easy to find, from the impressive high-rise Western style hotels that now inhabit all the capitals and many of the principal cities of Eastern Europe to the extremely favorable exchange rates Western visitors are offered. But at the same time, it is very important to bear in mind that practically all foreign travel to Eastern Europe is organised by the State National Tourist Offices and that it is very much easier to work within the systems they have devised than to take on the countries entirely on your own. Essentially this means taking a group or package tour or at least taking advantage of the pre-paid voucher system. Though there are certainly no obstacles placed in the way of the independent traveler and anyone is free to travel at will within any given country, you will find that essential services such as hotels, restaurants, filling stations and the like, do not compare with those in the West. So if you have not made reservations in advance or bought vouchers before leaving, trying to find a hotel or restaurant, especially off the beaten track, can be both time-consuming and frustrating and you are liable to waste a good deal of time and money.

The first and most important step to take then in planning your trip, is to contact the office of the National Tourist Office of the country you want to visit, or one of the many travel agents officially accredited by them (these include many of the major and a good number of the lesser travel agents). They will supply details of the many hundreds of trips and deals on offer. For the independent traveler, these include vouchers mentioned above, which are good for restaurants, camp sites, filling stations and so on. Similarly, visas, as well as many of the other important regulations that must be complied with, can also be arranged. One of the other major advantages of pre-paid services such as these is that they overcome the necessity of changing a minimum amount of foreign currency for every day of your stay (this is usually around $15 per person per day), a regulation that is strictly enforced in every Eastern European country except Bulgaria, which also does not require visas.

As far as package deals are concerned, we give details of a few of the many that are available in the individual *Facts at Your Fingertips* sections later in the book. But you will find that the range is considerable and includes everything from hang gliding and bird watching to more every day pursuits such as coach trips, two or three center holidays, or simple sun, sea and sand holidays on the Black Sea. The State National Tourist Offices will also provide details of the special hard currency shops in every country.

The names and addresses of the State National Tourist Offices are:

In the US:
Bulgaria, Balkantourist, Suite 1501, 50 East 42nd St, New York, NY 10017
Czechoslovakia, Čedok, 10 East 40th St, New York, NY 10016
Hungary, IBUSZ, 630 Fifth Ave, New York, NY 10020
Poland, Polorbis, 500 Fifth Ave, New York, NY 10036

Romania, Romanian National Tourist Office, 573 Third Ave, New York, NY 10016.

In the UK:
Bulgaria, Balkantourist, 126 Regent St, London W1
Czechoslovakia, Čedok, 17–18 Old Bond St, London W1X 3DA
Hungary, Danube Travel Ltd (agents of IBUSZ), 6 Conduit St, London W1R 9TG
Poland, Polorbis, 82 Mortimer St., London W1.
Romania, Romanian National Tourist Office, 98–99 Jermyn St, London SW1.

For further details of travel to Eastern European countries, see *Facts at Your Fingertips* for the particular country you are interested in. Details of hotels and restaurants, as well as of prices, are also in the *Facts at Your Fingertips* sections.

 WHEN TO GO. The summer season in Eastern Europe lasts from May through September, or October on the Black Sea coast. The peak months are July and August, when the Black Sea and Lake Balaton resorts, in particular, are crowded with visitors from abroad and neighboring countries. There's much to be said for traveling in the less crowded months of spring and fall.

There is a thriving winter sports season lasting, in some centers, from November to May. The peak months are usually December to March. Winter is also a good time to visit the capitals, which offer a lively variety of cultural events. We give full details of the principal events that may determine when you take your vacation in *Facts at Your Fingertips* for each country.

 STUDENT AND YOUTH TRAVEL. From America. There are two main sources of information on foreign study opportunities and on student and youth travel abroad. The *Council on International Educational Exchange,* 205 East 42 St, New York, NY 10017, runs summer study, travel and work programs, travel services for high school and college students and issues a free booklet on charter flights. Their *Whole World Handbook* is the best single listing of both work and study possibilities abroad. The *Institute of International Education,* 809 United Nations Plaza, New York, NY 10017 can supply you with information on study opportunities abroad and scholarships and fellowships for international study and training. They publish *Vacation Study Abroad,* a complete directory of student study programs, and *US College-Sponsored Programs Abroad* gives details on foreign study programs run by American schools for academic credit.

From Britain. The *Central Bureau for Educational Visits and Exchanges,* 43 Dorset St, London W1, offers one of the most comprehensive sources of information on youth travel and study abroad. It publishes many useful booklets which are full of suggestions, including *Study Holidays, Sport and Adventure Holidays* and *Volunteer Work Abroad.* Complete details of their facilities can be obtained from the above address. Government-subsidized exchange visits for young working people are arranged every year to Romania. For details of this and visits to other Eastern European countries, contact the 'East Europe Interchange', *Educational Interchange Council,* 43 Russell Square, London WC1. Booklets and directories of summer jobs, voluntary work and adventure travel abroad are also published by *Vacation-Work Publications,* 9 Park End St, Oxford OX1 1HJ.

HANDICAPPED TRAVEL. Facilities for the handicapped traveler in Eastern Europe are extremely limited, to say the least. Those in wheelchairs in particular are liable to find few if any special facilities in hotels, public transport or places of interest. Where they do exist, they are skimpy at best. In Poland, for example, there are wheelchairs available at all airports and most trains have specially designated seats for the handicapped. Hungary has a *Society for Rehabilitation* at PO Box 1, H–1528, Budapest 123, and there is also a 12-page guide listing hotels in Hungary with facilities for the handicapped. But this is published in German only and is not available outside Hungary and Austria. Sadly, this is largely the extent of special facilities for handicapped people in Eastern Europe. You are also likely to find that the attitude of many officials toward handicapped travelers can be unhelpful, not to put too fine a point on it.

But if you do plan to visit Eastern Europe, your best bet would be to contact either the *Travel Information Center,* Moss Rehabilitation Hospital, 12th St. and Tabor Rd., Philadelphia, Pa. 19141, or the *Royal Association for Disability and Rehabilitation,* 25 Mortimer St., London W1 or *Mobility International,* 62 Union St., London SE1. The State National Tourist Offices may also be able to supply some information on handicapped travel within Eastern Europe, but it is liable to be of a rather negative kind. *The Society for the Advancement of Travel for the Handicapped,* 26 Court St., Brooklyn NY 11242, may also be able to provide information. In general, therefore, handicapped people wishing to visit Eastern Europe should have very good reasons for doing so.

TRAVEL DOCUMENTS. Visas. In addition to a valid passport (details of how to apply for a passport are given below), all Western visitors to Eastern Europe will require a visa for every country they intend visiting, other than Bulgaria. We give details of the specific requirements for visa applications in the *Facts at Your Fingertips* sections for individual countries, but in general it is as well to apply for your visa some weeks before your intended departure date as the process can sometimes be rather slow. Consulates, the National Tourist Office and many travel agents can all arrange visas. However, it is also possible to obtain visas for most Eastern European countries when you enter them, though this can often be a time-consuming business. Again with the exception of Bulgaria, transit visas are also required if you plan only to travel through an Eastern European country. There is usually a fee of around $15 per person for visas.

Passports. American Citizens. Major post offices and many county courthouses process passport applications, as do US Passport Agency offices in various cities. Addresses and phone numbers are available under governmental listings in the white or blue pages of local telephone directories. Renewals can be handled by mail (form DSP–82) provided that your previous passport is not more than eight years old. New applicants will need: a birth certificate or other proof of citizenship; two identical photographs two inches square, full face, black and white or color, on nonglossy paper, and taken within the past six months; $35 and proof of identity. US passports are valid for ten years and are not renewable. You should allow a month to six weeks for your application to be processed, but in an emergency, Passport Agency offices can have a passport readied within 24 to 48 hours.

British Citizens. You should apply on forms obtainable from your travel agency or local main post office. The application should be sent to the Passport Office for your area (as indicated on the form). The regional passport offices are located in London, Liverpool, Peterborough, Glasgow, and Newport (Gwent). The application must be countersigned by your bank manager, or a solicitor, barrister, doctor, clergyman or Justice of the Peace who knows you. Enclose two photos and a fee of £11.

Health Certificates. These are not required to visit any East European country.

MEDICAL SERVICES. Details of any reciprocal arrangements between the UK or USA and Eastern Europe are given in *Facts at Your Fingertips* for each country. However, it is highly advisable to take out a comprehensive insurance before you go. *IAMAT* (International Association for Medical Assistance to Travelers) offers you a list of approved English-speaking doctors who have had postgraduate training in the US, Canada or Gt Britain. Membership is free; office calls are $15, hotel and house calls $20, holiday and weekend calls $25. For details write in the US to IAMAT, 736 Center St., Lewiston, N.Y. 14092. A similar service is furnished by *Intermedic*, 777 Third Ave., N.Y. 10017. There is an initial membership charge of $6 per individual and $10 per family; thereafter, the fees for medical service are slightly higher than those of *IAMAT*. *Assist-Card*, 745 Fifth Avenue, New York, NY 10022, provides membership cards in packages ranging from 5 days ($25) to one year ($350). Should a medical emergency arise, call one of the company's toll-free numbers whereupon *Assist-Card* will make arrangements for all medical services plus pick up the tab on the spot. In Canada write to 123 Edward St, Suite 725, Toronto, Ontario M56 IE2. In Europe, Gotthardstrasse 17, 6300 Zug, Switzerland; in Australia, St Vincent's Hospital, Victoria Parade, Melbourne 3065.

In Britain, *Europ Assistance Ltd* is highly recommended and offers considerable help to its members (United Kingdom residents only). Multilingual personnel staff a 24-hour, 365-days-a-year telephone service, which brings the aid of a network of medical advisers to assist in any emergency. Special medical insurance costs £8.85 per person for a period of 13 to 23 days. Further information, plus details of their excellent insurance scheme for motorists, from 252 High St, Croydon, Surrey CRO 1NF.

WHAT TO TAKE. The first principle is to travel light. Airline baggage allowances on flights over the Atlantic and within Europe are based on size (over the Atlantic you may take two pieces of luggage free provided the length plus the height plus the width of both comes to no more than 107″; within Europe you may take one piece of baggage free provided the length plus the height plus the width comes to no more than 62″; in both cases you can also take hand luggage free provided its total dimensions come to no more than 45″ for Atlantic flights and 39″ for European flights). Penalties for excess baggage are very severe. But in any case, do not take more than you can carry yourself; it's a lifesaver in places where porters are thin on the ground. In practice, this means more or less everywhere these days.

It's a good idea to pack the bulk of your things in one large bag and put everything you need for overnight, or for two or three nights, in another smaller one so that you don't have to pack and repack at every stop. Motorists will find it advisable to be frugal as well. You should limit your luggage to what can be locked into the trunk or boot of your car when making stops.

Clothing. Informal dress is quite acceptable for Eastern Europe, though the smarter hotels and restaurants expect men to wear a tie for dinner. Pack light-weight clothes for summer visits, but take along a cardigan or sweater for cooler nights, also a raincoat. If traveling in winter you'll need thick woolens, heavy overcoats and boots or heavy shoes. Don't forget to leave some room in your suitcase for souvenirs and presents to bring back home.

Medicines and Toiletries. Take all the medicines, cosmetics and toiletries you think you'll need. Most items can be bought in Eastern Europe, but tampons in particular are difficult to find. If you wear glasses or contact lenses, take along the prescription.

Cameras and Film. Don't leave already exposed film in your pockets or in hand luggage when passing through airport X-ray machines. The process can sometimes fog the film and you may find a whole trip's photography ruined. It is worth investing in a product called *Filmashield,* a lead-laminated pouch. It stores flat when not in use and holds quite a lot of film—or, indeed, your camera with half-used film in it. It is available in many countries from photographic shops.

Getting to Eastern Europe

FROM NORTH AMERICA

BY PLANE. At the time of writing (mid-1982), there were only three direct air links between North America and Eastern Europe. All three are operated by Eastern European airlines. They are New York to Prague, oper-ated by *CSA* (Czechoslovak Airlines), New York to Bucharest, operated by *Tarom* (the Romanian National carrier) and Montreal to Prague, also operated by *CSA.* However, it is possible that by 1983 one or more of the North American airlines might be operating services to Eastern Europe, so ask your travel agent for details. The three services above all operate one or twice weekly according to season.

You may well, therefore, prefer to fly to one of the many European cities that are both well-served from North America and have good connections by West-ern airlines to East Europe. London, Paris, Vienna, Zurich, Amsterdam and Frankfurt are all good examples. An added reason for sticking to Western airlines is that all the East European airlines with the exception of Tarom use Russian-made airplanes which are both more uncomfortable and noisy than their Western counterparts. You will also find that the in-flight service on Eastern European airlines is poor and the cabin staff distant. For details of flights from Western Europe to Eastern Europe, see below.

The cost of flying from North America to Eastern Europe naturally depends on whether you fly direct or to Western Europe and continue on from there. In many ways, it can be less expensive to fly to London, for example, which has the greatest number of flights from the US and Canada and hence also the cheapest flights (either APEX or the increasingly popular charter flights are the least expensive) and then take a package tour from there or an APEX flight.

Flying direct to Eastern Europe from North America, the least expensive fares start at around $750 return (to Prague). But if you want to be sure of securing the best deal and unraveling the maze of fares currently bedeviling the airline business, ask your travel agent.

 BY SEA. The only direct sailings between North America and Eastern Europe are those operated by Polish Ocean Lines, who sail from Montreal to Gdynia in Poland via London and Rotterdam. There are some six sailings a year. For details, write McLeon Kennedy Inc., 410 St. Nicholas St., Quebec H2Y 2P5. March Shipping Passenger Lines has crossings between May and September from New York or Montreal to Leningrad in the Soviet Union. Details of these services are available from March Shipping, One World Trade Center, Suite 5257, New York, NY 10048, or Craig St. West, Montreal, Quebec H2Y 1K1.

If you prefer to travel rather more luxuriously, though indirectly, the *QE2* sails at regular intervals from New York to Southampton, England, from April to December. Details are available from Cunard, 555 Fifth Ave., New York, NY 10017. For details of onward travel from the UK to Eastern Europe, see below.

The only other sea routes from North America to Eastern Europe are on freighters. However, sailings are both infrequent and usually booked up far in advance and you may have to wait for as long as a year before being able to make your passage. However, the relative inexpensiveness, not inconsiderable comfort and informality of freighter life make the prospect appealing to a large number of enthusiasts.

To help you choose from the many lines available, consult *Ford's Freighter Travel Guide,* a national directory published twice a year from PO Box 505, 22030 Ventura Blvd., Woodland Hills, Calif. 91365; *Pearl's Freighter Tips,* 175 Great Neck Rd., Great Neck, NY 11201; *Air Marine Travel Service,* 501 Madison Ave., New York, NY 10022; or *Traveltips Freighter Association,* 163–09 Depot Rd., Flushing, NY 11358.

FROM WESTERN EUROPE

 BY PLANE. The two 'halves' of Europe have a very good network of air links uniting them and any good travel agent will be able to advise on the best services to suit your requirements. The national carriers of all the East European countries have services to most Western European capitals and main cities, some non-stop, the remainder through services. Similarly, the national carriers of most West European countries have frequent services to East Europe. Unfortunately, however, there are fewer low-cost tickets to Eastern Europe than to destinations in Western Europe as the bulk of travelers go either on charter flights or by rail. But the best bet is an APEX ticket; from London, these cost approximately £170 to Prague, £190 to Warsaw, £235 to Bucharest and £255 to Sofia.

 BY TRAIN. There are good train links between Western and Eastern Europe, several of which have connecting services from London. If you intend traveling around Eastern Europe by train once you arrive, it is always best to buy tickets before you leave. This will save many difficulties—standing in line, language problems and the need to pay supplements for fast/express trains. Always reserve seats and couchettes or other accommodations on trains well in advance. Reservations are in any case obligatory on many express trains within Eastern Europe. Details are available from travel agents and State National Tourist Offices.

To Poland. Warsaw is well-served by through trains from the West, and a wide choice of starting points is available. There are trains from the Hook of Holland, Ostend, Paris, Cologne, Frankfurt and Basle. The best services to use from Britain are those from the Hook, Ostend and Paris.

The train from the Hook is called the *Hook-Warszawa Express.* It runs daily throughout the year. There is a connecting service from London, Liverpool Street, which leaves at 0910 for Harwich, from where there is a ferry service to the Hook. This connects with the Hook-Warszawa Express, which leaves at 2000 and arrives in Warsaw at 1455 the next day. There are first and second class sleepers throughout and couchettes available as far as Berlin. A Polish buffet car joins the train at Berlin, reached at 0555.

The service from Ostend is called the *Ost-West Express* and is similarly convenient. There is a connecting service from London, Victoria, which leaves at 0930 and connects with the Sealink ferry from Dover. However, from May to September, it is possible to leave Victoria as late as 1130 and, by making use of the new Sealink Jetfoil, arrive in Ostend at 1600 in good time to catch the Ost-West Express which leaves at 1715. The train runs overnight to Berlin and arrives at 1615 in Warsaw the next day. There are first and second class sleeping cars for the whole trip and second class couchettes as far as Berlin. A Polish buffet car is provided from Berlin. Reservation is obligatory on this train.

If visiting Germany, there is a through train which leaves from Cologne at 1325. This is the *Leningrad Express.* It runs via Hannover and Berlin and arrives at Warsaw the following day at 0720. There is a West German buffet car (known as a Grill Express) as far as Berlin. First and second class sleepers and couchettes are available for the whole journey.

From Switzerland, there is a through train from Basle (from Berne in summer) to Moscow via Warsaw. Departure from Basle is at 1730 and arrival at Warsaw is at 1710 the following day.

To Czechoslovakia. There are similarly good services to Czechoslovakia from the West. Probably the most useful is the *Tauern Express* from Ostend. There is a connecting service from London, Victoria, which leaves at 1320 for the ferry from Dover. By using the Jetfoil service (summer only) you can leave London later (1600). The Tauern Express leaves Ostend at 2115 and arrives in Prague in the early evening at 1835. There are first and second class sleeping cars and second class couchettes. Light refreshments are available on the Belgian portion of the journey and from Stuttgart to Augsburg, while a Grill Express is attached from Munich to Villach providing a fuller meal service.

From Cologne, the *Donau Kurier* provides a daylight journey to Prague. Departure from Cologne is at 0720, and the train travels via Frankfurt, Nürnberg and Vienna, arriving at Prague at 2140 the same day. There is a Grill Express car from Dortmund to Vienna.

From Paris, there is a good service; this is the *Paris-Praha Express* (known in Czechoslovakia as the *Zapadni Express*). The train leaves from the Gare de l' Est at 2300 and travels via Frankfurt and Nürnberg, arriving at Prague at 1835 the following day. First and second class couchettes are available between Paris and Frankfurt, and second class couchettes are available throughout. A buffet car service is provided from Frankfurt to Prague.

To Hungary. There are four all year through services from the West to Budapest, plus a fifth in the summer. The most famous is the *Orient Express,* though do not confuse this with the privately-owned and highly-luxurious Venice-Simplon Orient Express. *This* Orient Express is the downgraded and truncated remnant of that made famous by Agatha Christie and others and which once continued on to Istanbul. Today, it peters out at Bucharest. However, its route is still of interest. It leaves from the Gare de l' Est at 2315 giving a daytime run through Bavaria (very dramatic) and along the mountainous Semmering line in Austria, arriving at Budapest at 2030 the following evening. First and second class sleeping cars and couchettes are available as far as Salzburg and there is a Grill Express car from Stuttgart to Vienna and a full restaurant car from Hungarian border to Budapest. During the summer, there is also a *Paris-Wien Rapide* which runs from Paris to Vienna, where it then combines with the Orient Express. This is an ideal train to use if you want to stop over in Vienna either for half a day, or perhaps a little longer. Leaving Paris at 2120, it arrives the following morning at Vienna at 1155. If you do only want to spend half a day in Vienna, it is then perfectly easy to catch the Orient Express which leaves the Austrian capital at 1625.

The *Oostende-Wien Express* provides a useful all year service from Ostend to Budapest. There is a connecting train from London, Victoria, at 0930 for Dover and Ostend. In summer you can leave Victoria at 1130 if you take the fast Jetfoil service. The train runs via Brussels, Cologne and Vienna, arriving at Budapest at 1425. There are first and second class sleeping cars and couchettes from Ostend to Vienna. A full restaurant car service is available from Ostend to Cologne; from the Hungarian border to Budapest a buffet car suffices. Reservation is obligatory.

The *Wiener-Walzer* connects Basle and Budapest, running via Zurich, Salzburg and Vienna. Departure from Basle is at 2030, and arrival in the Hungarian capital is at 1435 the following day. Reservation is obligatory.

Finally, there is a through train from Rome, the *Tisza Express Maestral,* which continues through to Moscow. The train leaves Rome at 1220 arriving in Budapest at 1415 the following day having traveled via Venice, Ljubljana and Zagreb. First and second class sleeping cars are included throughout, with first and second class day cars between Rome and Budapest. There is no restaurant or buffet car.

To Romania. Two of the international trains mentioned in the section on Hungary continue to Bucharest; the Orient Express and the Weiner Walzer. The Orient Express leaves Budapest at 2130 (on day two of its journey) to give a lunchtime arrival at 1330 in Bucharest (day three). Romanian sleeping cars, both first and second class, and second class couchettes are attached at Budapest, while a Hungarian restaurant car provides sustenance. During the summer, the Weiner Walzer terminates at Constanza on the Black Sea coast, stopping at Bucharest en route at 0825 (day three of its journey). It leaves Budapest at 1615 the previous afternoon. There are first and second class sleeping cars, but check the dates they are available when you book. A Hungarian dining car is provided for this section of the journey.

To Bulgaria. The Bulgarian capital Sofia can only be reached by one through service from the West. This is the *Istanbul Express* which runs daily throughout the year from Munich to Istanbul. The train leaves Munich at 1735 and travels via Zagreb and Belgrade, arriving at Sofia at 1955 on the second day. First and second class sleeping cars and couchettes are available from Munich to Belgrade. There are good connections from London to Munich.

BY CAR. Travel into Eastern Europe by car is still something of an adventure. Road conditions are not really comparable to those in Western Europe; filling stations, for example, are far and few between while facilities for dealing with breakdowns are naturally pretty scarce. Good preparation is therefore very important. It is a good idea to get in touch with one of the motoring organizations or the State National Tourist Office of the country concerned before you go. They are important sources of information.

Only Poland and Hungary now require you to have an International Driving License, but it is advisable to have one just the same. They are obtainable from motoring organizations. In the US, try the American Automobile Association, 811 Gatehouse Road, Falls Church, Virginia 22047. In the UK, both the AA, Fanum House, Basingstoke, Hants (or any of their regional offices) and the RAC, 83–85 Pall Mall, London SW1 (or any of their regional offices) can supply you with an International Driving License. There is a small fee.

Similarly, the Green Card, which gives full insurance cover abroad, is not strictly necessary, but it would be foolish not to have one. They are also good for Western Europe, but are not required in Western Europe for citizens of EEC countries. They are readily available from insurance companies and cost from £5. In the case of a rented car, the rental agency will arrange it for you. Ensure that it is valid for the countries you wish to visit (and signed by yourself). For a rental car you will also need written confirmation of your permission to use the vehicle and a copy of the vehicle registration document. This last is also required if you take your own car.

Apart from your visa for the country you plan to visit, check the requirements for transit visas for any Eastern European countries you may travel through.

It is possible to buy vouchers for petrol for Czechoslovakia, Poland and Romania. In the case of the last two, you can buy them at the frontier before entering the country. In the case of Czechoslovakia, you can buy them before you leave. But in both cases, check with the State National Tourist Offices as the situation concerning vouchers is in constant flux. It is also possible that they will be reintroduced for Hungary and Bulgaria.

Good maps to buy, which cover the above routes, are the *AA Road Book of Europe* (all countries except Northern Romania), *Europa* and *Kummerley & Frey AG*. These are available from any large map bookshop, where you can also buy individual country maps. Specific information on road routes and conditions can be obtained from the continental operations departments of your motoring organization.

Note that quite a number of frontier crossings between the socialist countries are only open to the nationals of these countries. Do not, therefore, be tempted by a less obvious crossing point without making sure first that you are entitled to use it, for you will only run the risk of being turned back. That said, it is worth avoiding major crossing points at the height of summer with their attendant queues. A slightly longer route is often rewarded by much lighter traffic and sometimes less spoilt scenery.

FERRIES FROM THE UK. The main ferry crossings that most conveniently connect with the principal highways through Western Europe are from Felixstowe, Sheerness, Ramsgate, Dover and Folkestone. These go respectively to the Continental ports of Vlissingen (Holland), Zeebrugge and Ostend (both Belgium), Calais and Boulogne (both France). Services are operated by Sealink, Olau Line, Sally Viking, Townsend Thoresen and P & O. Hoverspeed also operate hovercraft services for both cars and passengers between Dover and Calais throughout the year. There are additional 'flights' from Ramsgate to Calais in the summer.

Bulgaria. Bulgaria is usually approached via West Germany, Austria and Yugoslavia, particularly by motorists in transit to Turkey. There are also border crossings from Romania and Greece.

From Romania—(E20) Bucharest-Sofia; (E95) Black Sea coast road, Constanta-Varna. From Yugoslavia—(E27) Skopje-Sofia; (E5N) Niš-Sofia. From Greece—(E20) Thessaloniki-Sofia. From Turkey—(E5N) Istanbul-Sofia.

Czechoslovakia. The three principal routes are via West Germany, East Germany or Austria. From West Germany—(E12) Nürnberg-Plzeň. From East Germany (transit crossings only—not stopping or staying in Berlin West or East)—Leipzig or Berlin to (E15) Dresden-Prague. From Austria—(E14) Linz-České Budějovice-Prague; (E7) Vienna-Brno; (9) Vienna-Bratislava (A4 highway when completed).

Hungary. The main entry point to Hungary is via Austria and the Vienna-Budapest highway. From Austria—(E5) Vienna-Budapest; (16) Vienna-Sopron; (65, 307, 8, 84) Graz-(Lake Balaton)-(E96/M7) Budapest. From Yugoslavia (E96) Zagreb-(Lake Balaton)-Budapest; (E5) Belgrade-Novi Sad-Szeged-Budapest.

Poland. Poland is best reached through East Germany or Czechoslovakia. From East Germany (E8) Berlin bypass-Frankfurt an der Oder-Poznań-Warsaw; (E22) Berlin bypass-Wrocław. From Czechoslovakia (E14) Prague-Wrocław; (E12) Prague-Wrocław; (E7) Brno-Cracow; (E16) Vienna-Bratislava-Cracow.

Romania. The most direct route to Romania is via West Germany, Austria and Hungary. From Hungary, travel via Budapest-Szeged-(E15A) Arad-Bucharest. From Yugoslavia, travel via Belgrade-(E94) Craiova-Bucharest.

 BY BUS. The only bus service to Eastern Europe is that operated by Europabus, who offer a through service from London to Poznan in Poland. Travel is by ship and ferry from London, Victoria, (departure at 0930) to Ostend, from where the coach leaves. Arrival in Poznan is at 1530 the following day. The service operates only from June to September and you cannot leave the bus en route but must travel all the way to Poznan.

 BY BOAT. The only direct sailing to Eastern Europe is from London to Gydnia in Poland (via Rotterdam). This service sails six times a year from May to November and is operated by Polish Ocean Lines. For details, contact Stelp and Leighton Agencies Ltd., 238 City Rd., London EC1. In the US, contact March Shipping, One World Trade Center, Suite 5257, New York, NY 10048.

However, there are also a number of cruises along the Danube. These are operated by the Soviet Danube Line between Passau (on the Austro-German border) to Ismail in the USSR at the mouth of the Danube from April to September. There are usually stop-overs in the main cities through which you pass. The cruises last nine days in all and cost around £890 to £1,500 with return flights from London. Without flights, the cost is about £100 to £120 less. Full details from CTC Lines, 1 Regent St., London SW1

From May to September there is a regular hydrofoil service from Vienna to Budapest (daily on weekdays, additional service on Mondays and Thursday in peak season), taking about 4½ hours. Single fare is around $60. There is also a daily service each way between Vienna and Bratislava taking a little over one hour.

Staying in Eastern Europe

CUSTOMS. For details of Customs regulations, see the section on Customs in Facts at Your Fingertips for the country concerned.

 MONEY. There are a number of points to be aware of concerning money and financial transactions in Eastern Europe. The first is that unless you have pre-paid services of some kind (for example, if you are on a package tour or have reservations for hotels made and paid for in advance or have vouchers for hotels, restaurants, camp sites, etc.) you will be required to buy a minimum amount of local currency (usually around $15 per person) for every day of your stay in all Eastern European countries except Bulgaria. You must therefore be able to prove on entering the country that you have at least this minimum amount of foreign currency. If you do have pre-paid services, both Czechoslovakia and Romania offer very much more favorable rates of exchange than the official rates. All main frontier posts and points of entry have official bureaux de change, as do most major hotels and tourist shops.

Any amount of foreign currency may be imported into any Eastern European country and any left unspent may be exported, provided the original amount was declared on arrival. But no local currencies may be exported or imported from or to any Eastern European country. Major credit cards are accepted in most principal tourist resorts and in hotels, restaurants and tourist shops, as are traveler's checks.

Finally, be very wary of the thriving black market in currency exchange. You may be offered a rate of exchange several times better than the official one. But penalties for dealing in this black market are severe and unpleasant. The inside of any gaol is pretty nasty; the inside of an Eastern European gaol is very nasty.

 HOTELS. These are officially classified throughout Eastern Europe and in all countries you are strongly advised to book accommodations in advance, as there is a general shortage of hotel rooms, particularly in the high season. If you do turn up without having booked a room, there are accommodation offices, run by the state tourist organizations, who will help you, but obviously the choice will be limited.

There are not many hotels of the international super deluxe standard and these are usually confined to the capitals or major resorts. The Hilton and Intercontinental and other Western chains have been moving in, but elsewhere it is better not to expect the same standards of facilities and service as in equivalent hotel categories in Western countries.

Full details of hotel rates and other kinds of accommodations are given in *Facts at your fingertips* for each country.

YOUTH HOSTELS. Many youth hostels, or their equivalent, are open only during the summer, though a few are open year round. You should be a member of the International Youth Hostel Federation, which you can join through your national youth hostel association. For further information, in the US write to American Youth Hostels Inc., National Campus, Delaplane, Va. 22025; in Canada, Canadian Youth Hostels Association, 333 River Rd, Vanier City, Ottawa, Ont. K1L 8B9; in the UK, Youth Hostels Association, Trevelyan House, St Albans, Herts. AL1 2DY.

CAMPING. Many of the campsites in Eastern Europe are located in beautiful scenic settings and often have bungalows or cabins attached, which are also available for hire. All the countries, except Hungary, issue pre-paid camping vouchers and details of these are given in the individual *Facts at your fingertips* for each country. The national tourist organizations can supply you with maps marking the sites.

It's advisable to purchase an International Camping Carnet, which acts as a membership card in European camping associations and gives you certain privileges in some private sites. To obtain one before you leave, contact in the US the National Campers and Hikers Association, 7172 Transit Rd, Buffalo, NY 14221, in the UK the Camping Club of Great Britain and Ireland, 11 Lower Grosvenor Pl., London SW1W 0EY.

RESTAURANTS. Throughout Eastern Europe there is a wide variety of eating places, from expensive restaurants in the luxury hotels to sidewalk cafés. However, in some countries food supplies are erratic, with the best ingredients going only to top-class restaurants. Bulgaria and Czechoslovakia both offer a pre-paid meal voucher system by which visitors can vary the venue of their meals. You will invariably find that imported liquor, such as whiskey, is expensive, so try sampling some of the local brews, many of which are excellent. For details of regional cuisine, see the chapters and *Food and Drink* for each country.

TIPPING. Bulgaria is the only country that officially discourages tipping, though even here it is acceptable. Elsewhere, tipping is as prevalent as it is in the West. See *Facts at your fingertips* for details for each country.

ELECTRICITY. Most parts of Eastern Europe use 220 volt alternating current, though some older establishments, particularly in Romania, still use 110 volt, AC. A transformer can be attached to all kinds of electrical appliances you may take with you, but it will be satisfactory only where the appliance has no timing mechanism. The reason for this is that the current is 50 cycle instead of 60 cycle; an electric clock, for example, would run so slowly as to be worthless. Since there may be local variations you should always inquire in advance. Also note that most plugs are a different fit from both British and American plugs.

MEASUREMENTS. All the countries within Eastern Europe use the metric system, so throughout this guide we have given both imperial and metric measurements. The kilometer is 0.62 mile and an easy rule of thumb is that 8 kilometers = 5 miles. There are, of course, 1,000 meters in a kilometer and 100 centimeters in a meter. A meter = just over 3 feet and a centimeter = ⅜ inch.

Temperature is measured by the Centigrade (Celsius) system. We give a simple conversion chart below, but if you want to convert Centigrade to Fahrenheit, multiply by 9, divide by 5 and add 32. To turn Fahrenheit into Centigrade, subtract 32, multiply by 5 and divide by 9.

°Centigrade	°C or °F	°Fahrenheit
−18	0	32
−15	5	41
−12	10	50
−9.5	15	59
−7	20	68
−4	25	77
−1	30	86
2	35	95
4.5	40	104
7	45	113
10	50	122

If you are buying anything by weight, for example, fresh vegetables, you will find it marked in grams and kilograms; 1 kilogram = 2.2 lb. If you are traveling by car and are buying gasoline (petrol), you should remember that four liters are slightly over one US gallon and just under one imperial gallon. We give three useful conversion tables for motorists on pages 28–9.

PHOTOGRAPHY. Throughout Eastern Europe, it is forbidden to take photographs of military, industrial and transport installations (including trains and rail stations). There is a special international sign on roads where photography is forbidden—a camera in a red circle with a red line through the camera. Otherwise you can snap away when and where you like.

In some countries it can be difficult to obtain supplies of Western makes of film, though the foreign, or hard, currency shops usually stock a limited range. It's advisable to take your full limit of film with you.

Getting Around Eastern Europe

BY PLANE. The state-owned airlines in Eastern Europe operate an extensive network of services within the region and, other than in Hungary, within their own countries. All the capitals are linked by services at least twice daily. Most services are by jets (generally TU 124s and 134s, more or less like DC9s and Boeing 727s). Some services, however, are still operated by four engined turbo-prop Ilyushin 18 aircraft while Tarom, the Romanian airline, flies British designed BAC 1–11s (twin jet). On some longer routes such as Prague to Bucharest the larger four engined Ilyushin 62 jet is used. Flights are usually all one class, although you will sometimes find that a special section has been marked off for VIPs.

In addition to the capital linking routes there are services connecting main cities in neighboring countries, for example Cracow (Poland) and Bratislava (Czechoslovakia).

 BY TRAIN. The railways of Eastern Europe are all state-owned and are mainly standard gauge (although the broad Russian gauge penetrates into part of Czechoslovakia), with some narrow gauge services. Traction is electric or diesel, with the former rapidly expanding. There are still some steam trains left in operation, but they constitute only a very small part of the system.

Standards have improved in the last few years although on the whole they are far short of what is acceptable in the West. Trains are very busy and it is rare to find one running less than full or almost so. The design of carriages is similar to that in Western Europe (often they are indistinguishable, although the decor is more severe) and some of the crack expresses are quite luxurious.

All the countries operate their own dining, buffet and refreshment services. Always busy, they tend to open and close at the whims of the staff. Sleeping cars and couchettes for internal travel are directly operated by the railways, other than in Poland where they are operated by Orbis. Through sleeping cars from the USSR are all Russian owned and operated. Couchette cars are second class only.

Buying a ticket for internal travel within each country is comparatively easy though always time-consuming. Never leave it to the last minute. For international travel (unless you have already obtained your ticket outside Eastern Europe) it is not so easy. It is highly advisable to enlist the help of the nearest office of the State Tourist Organization. In most cases they will be able to issue the ticket or at least obtain it for you.

In those cities where there are several stations—Warsaw, Prague and Budapest are the best examples—be quite certain which station your train leaves from or arrives at. It is not always as logical as it might seem.

While as we have said trains are always busy in Eastern Europe we do recommend that you use them at least for part of your travel. You will almost certainly find that your fellow travelers (literally, not politically) are more than ready to enter into conversation, which is not always the case by any means at airports.

 BY CAR. With the exception of Romania the main roads of Eastern Europe are built to a fairly high standard in tarmac or concrete. There are few completed stretches of highway (motorway) in any of the countries, but a lot of road rebuilding work is being carried out. Some information on where the worst of the delays caused by roadworks occur is available from British motoring organizations. Off the main roads, and throughout much of Romania, surfacing is poor and care should be taken to avoid vehicle damage.

Particular road dangers to be wary of are—extremely slippy conditions on tarmac after light rain; sudden drastic changes in camber; the many slow agricultural vehicles (some animal drawn); the poor lighting of trucks, bikes and farm carts at night; and wandering livestock in rural areas. In towns the major public transport is by trams—treat them warily as they have the right of way over cars in many situations, people get off and on in the middle of the street (they have absolute priority) and at road junctions they can cut in unexpectedly from the left.

Gas stations are fewer than in the West, sited at intervals of about 30 miles (48 km) along main routes and on the outskirts of large towns. Very few stations are open after 9.30 P.M. At least two grades of petrol are sold in all countries—usually 90–93 octane (regular) and 96–98 octane (super). Hungary is unusual in that Western brands of fuel are available—Shell, BP and Agip. The supply of gas to filling stations is by no means regular, so that there are sometimes long lines and considerable delays. Try to keep your tank topped up. Tourists nearly always require Super for their Western-built cars, and some Eastern bloc countries will not sell anything else.

Rules of the road. In all countries of Eastern Europe traffic police have the power to make on-the-spot fines for minor motoring offences. In more serious cases the state can order the vehicle to be impounded and a cash deposit may be levied against future legal costs. After an accident, even a minor one, ensure that the police are called, summon medical assistance if necessary and remain with your vehicle if at all possible. In all countries it is necessary to inform the nearest office of the state's vehicle insurance company as soon as possible after an accident.

Throughout Eastern Europe it is prohibited to drink and drive—there is no fixed permitted alcohol level and heavy penalties can be imposed (prison terms are not unusual) on any driver proven to have taken alcohol.

Main road speed limits vary from 80 kph to 100 kph (50 mph to 62 mph) and up to 120 kph (72 mph) on the few stretches of motorways; these are advised by conventional speed limit signs. In towns speed limits are 50 to 60 kph (31 mph to 37 mph). Precise speed limit details are available from your automobile club. In Bulgaria main road parking is limited to lay-bys designated by 'P'; in Hungary only on the right-hand side; in Czechoslovakia it is forbidden on main roads.

On most main routes traffic has priority over sideroad traffic, but on anything other than the main international routes, unless otherwise indicated, traffic emerging from the right has priority. At roundabouts traffic entering has priority over traffic on the roundabout—except in Poland where the reverse of this system is operated, but in Eastern European countries nothing, but nothing, should be taken for granted by visiting motorists. The wearing of seat belts is compulsory.

In Bulgaria, border police have the power to inspect vehicles and insist that any repair work they deem necessary be carried out before the vehicle can enter the country. It is as well to recognize that crossing the frontiers of a communist country, even when all goes well, can be a very long business. For this reason it is essential that all your papers should be in order and that you can produce them instantly when requested. Border guards take their work very seriously and it is advisable to take them seriously, too.

Road signs in all the countries are the same international types used in Western Europe with a few local variations. In all countries, except Bulgaria, main route signposting is in Roman characters. In Bulgaria there are a few dual-language signs on major tourist routes, but the majority of signposts have Cyrillic characters. For reference to Western maps you will have to translate the destinations into Roman characters (use the conversion alphabet given on page 92).

For roadside assistance, help with any legal problems after accidents and tourist information, contact the following head offices of the automobile clubs in the relevant country.

Bulgaria. *Union of Bulgarian Motorists* (SBA), 6 Sveta Sofia St, Sofia (tel. 878801). Emergency service, tel. 146 in main town areas.

Czechoslovakia. *Ustredni Automotoklub* (UAMK ČSSR), Opletalova 29, Prague 1 (tel. 223547). Emergency service, tel. 154 in main town areas.

Hungary. *Magyar Autoclub* (MAK), Rómer Flóris Utca 4–6, H1277 Budapest (tel. 260268). Emergency service, tel. 260268.

Poland. *Polski Zwiazek Motorowy* (PZM), ul. Krucza 14, Warsaw (tel. 296252). Ring local offices for breakdown service.

Romania. *Automobil Clubul Roman* (ACR), Poligrafiei Blvd 3, Bucharest 1 (tel. 181649). Local office telephone numbers for breakdown emergencies are shown on road signs.

Car Hire. Both major Western car rental companies, *Avis* and *Hertz,* can make advanced bookings on rental cars in the Eastern bloc countries. Bookings are made through the normal international reservations system with associate companies in the particular country. Fly-drive packages ex-UK are available in most of the countries concerned. See **Facts at your Fingertips** for each country.

You can hire cars within Eastern Europe from major hotel reception desks or through the tourist offices.

Conversion Tables. One of the most confusing experiences for many motorists is their first encounter with the metric system, which is used all over Europe.

The following quick conversion tables may help speed you on your way.

Kilometers into Miles

This simple chart will help you to convert to both miles and kilometers. If you want to convert from miles into kilometers read from the center column to the right, if from kilometers into miles, from the center column to the left. Example: 5 miles = 8.0 kilometers, 5 kilometers = 3.1 miles.

Miles		Kilometers	Miles		Kilometers
0.6	1	1.6	37.3	60	96.6
1.2	2	3.2	43.5	70	112.3
1.9	3	4.8	49.7	80	128.7
2.5	4	6.3	55.9	90	144.8
3.1	5	8.0	62.1	100	160.9
3.7	6	9.6	124.3	200	321.9
4.3	7	11.3	186.4	300	482.8
5.0	8	12.9	248.5	400	643.7
5.6	9	14.5	310.7	500	804.7
6.2	10	16.1	372.8	600	965.6
12.4	20	32.2	434.9	700	1,126.5
18.6	30	48.3	497.1	800	1,287.5
24.8	40	64.4	559.2	900	1,448.4
31.0	50	80.5	621.4	1,000	1,609.3

Tire Pressure Converter

Pounds per Square Inch	16	18	20	22	24	26	28	30	32
Kilogrammes per Square Centimeter	1.12	1.26	1.40	1.54	1.68	1.82	1.96	2.10	2.24

Gallons Into Liters

U.S.		Imperial (British)	
Gallon	Liters	Gallon	Liters
1	3.78	1	4.54
2	7.57	2	9.09
3	11.36	3	13.63
4	15.14	4	18.18
5	18.93	5	22.73
6	22.71	6	27.27
7	26.50	7	31.82
8	30.28	8	36.36
9	34.07	9	40.91
10	37.85	10	45.46

There are 5 Imperial (British) gallons to 6 U.S. gallons.

Leaving Eastern Europe

 CUSTOMS ON RETURNING HOME. US residents may bring in $400 worth of foreign merchandise as gifts or for personal use without having to pay duty, provided they have been out of the country more than 48 hours and provided they have not claimed a similar exemption within the previous 30 days. Every member of a family is entitled to the same exemption, regardless of age, and the exemptions can be pooled. For the next $1000 worth of goods, inspectors will assess a flat 10% duty based on the price actually paid, so it is a good idea to keep your receipts.

Included in the $400 allowance for travelers over the age of 21 are one liter of alcohol, 100 cigars (non-Cuban) and 200 cigarettes. Any amount in excess of those limits will be taxed at the port of entry, and may additionally be taxed in the traveler's home state. Only one bottle of perfume trademarked in the US may be brought in. However, there is no duty on antiques or art over 100 years old—though you may be called upon to provide verification of the item's age. Write to US Customs Service, Washington, D.C. 20229 for information regarding importation of automobiles and/or motorcycles. You may not bring home meats, fruits, plants, soil or other agricultural items.

Gifts valued at under $50 may be mailed to friends or relatives at home, but not more than one per day (of receipt) to any one addressee. These gifts must not include perfumes costing more than $5, tobacco or liquor.

If you are traveling with such foreign made articles as cameras, watches or binoculars that were purchased at home, it is best to either carry the receipt for them with you or to register them with US Customs prior to departing. This will save much time (and potential aggravation) upon your return.

Canadian Residents may, after 7 days out of the country and upon written declaration, claim an exemption of $150 in Canadian funds a year plus an allowance of 40 ounces of liquor, 50 cigars, 200 cigarettes and 2 lb of tobacco. Personal gifts should be mailed as 'Unsolicited gifts, value under $25'. For further details, ask for the Canadian Customs brochure, *I Declare.*

British Residents, except those under the age of 17 years, may import duty-free from *any* country the following: 200 cigarettes or 100 cigarillos or 50 cigars or 250 grams of tobacco; 1 liter of spirits over 38.8% proof or 2 liters of other spirits or fortified wine, plus 2 liters of still table wine. Also 50 grams of perfume, ¼ liter of toilet water and £28 worth of other normally dutiable goods.

Returning from any EEC country, you may, instead of the above exemptions, bring in the following, provided they were *not* bought in a duty-free shop: 300 cigarettes or 150 cigarillos or 75 cigars or 400 grams of tobacco; 1½ liters of strong spirits or 3 liters of other spirits or fortified wines plus 3 liters of still table wine; 75 grams of perfume and ⅜ liter of toilet water and £120 worth of other normally dutiable goods.

BULGARIA

FACTS AT YOUR FINGERTIPS

Planning Your Trip

WHAT WILL IT COST. Costs in Bulgaria, as in most Eastern European countries, are generally low, and it is emminently possible to have a very reasonably-priced holiday here. But the country is cheaper still if you go on an inclusive package vacation or, if you prefer to travel independently, buy pre-paid vouchers for such as hotels, gasoline, camp sites and the like before you leave. Both have the additional advantage of entitling you to a very much more favorable rate of exchange than you would otherwise receive (approximately 50% above the normal rate). For details of package tours and pre-paid services, see *How to Go* below.

The unit of currency in Bulgaria is the lev, divided into 100 stotinki. There are notes of 1, 2, 5, 10 and 20 leva, and coins of 1, 2, 5, 10, 20 and 50 stotinki. You may import any amount of foreign currency and exchange it at branches of the Bulgarian State Bank, at Balkantourist hotels and offices, at airports and at all border posts. However, both the import and export of Bulgarian currency is forbidden.

The rate of exchange at the time of writing (mid-1982) was approximately 1 lev to the US dollar and 1.85 lev to the pound sterling. However, there is also an active black market in foreign currency, and you may be approached quite openly. However, illegal currency exchanges are strictly forbidden and the risk of penalties and the general unpleasantness that will inevitably result should you be caught far outweigh any small profit you might make (you are also quite likely to be cheated).

Major credit cards such as American Express, Diner's Club, Master Charge and so on, are accepted in larger stores, hotels and restaurants.

A day's basic costs for two people might be:

Hotel (Moderate), including breakfast	40 lev
Lunch, with wine	20
2 beers, 2 coffees	7
Transportation	2.50
Dinner, with wine	40
Total	109.50

Sample Costs. Theater seat (moderate) 6 leva; museum entrance 30–50 stotinki; coffee in moderate restaurant 1 lev; bottle of wine in moderate restaurant from 4 leva.

HOW TO GO. All foreign travel to Bulgaria is handled by Balkantourist, the Bulgarian National Tourist Office. They do not, however, actually organise tours to Bulgaria themselves (this can only be done by travel agents officially accredited by Balkantourist—these include many of the major operators), but they will be able to advise on all aspects of travel to and within the country. And indeed within Bulgaria, they own and operate a growing chain of hotels and restaurants and arrange tours of all kinds as well as being responsible for currency exchange.

The addresses of Balkantourist are:

In the US, Suite 1501, 50 East 42nd St., New York, NY 10017.
In the UK, 126 Regent St., London W1.

The cheapest and simplest way to visit Bulgaria is on pre-paid package tours which are available for groups and individuals. Thus independent travelers can also benefit not only from advantageous hotel rates, but also from such concessions as the currency bonus, while still retaining plenty of freedom of movement through the systems of accommodations and meal vouchers which have been devised to provide more flexibility for those who wish it.

In 1982 the cost of a two-week holiday (ex-London) in a popular Black Sea resort, at the height of the season, was from £245–£450, depending on the category of accommodations. This includes a return flight, full board, and an allocation of meal vouchers enabling visitors to eat at other Balkantourist hotels and restaurants (which means most of them). Prices drop by up to one-third for off-season holidays, when other extras, such as a free evening of folklore entertainment, are often provided. Reductions for children of 2–6 years can be up to 50% and from 7–12 years up to 25%; in some centers these concessions apply throughout the season. Families with small children are particularly well catered for in terms of child-minding services and entertainments for the young.

Other possibilities include the combination of a week on the coast with a week touring by coach throughout the country. In winter, skiing packages are arranged and, throughout the low season, weekend trips to Sofia and other short-duration arrangements are available.

Among less conventional arrangements are those devoted specially to Bulgarian culture and history, monastery tours, culinary tours (including possibilities of participating in cookery courses at Sunny Beach or Plovdiv), and attractive itineraries traveling by horse-drawn caravan. Pottery and embroidery courses are also featured, and sporting holidays include hunting and fishing. Arrangements can also be made by Balkantourist to cater for any special interest or study group; for example, those devoted to agriculture or different branches of industry. A special tour is organized for the Rose Festival, which takes place in the Valley of Roses during June. Excursions of one or more days in length are organized from main tours and resorts, ranging from local sightseeing to trips to neighboring Greece, Turkey, or even Moscow.

Those who do not wish to be tied by pre-arranged itineraries can obtain pre-paid vouchers for accommodations only, half or full board, enabling them to plan from day to day, though naturally at the height of the season they run the risk of finding hotels fully booked. Similarly, they can pre-pay for accommodations in camp sites or for the hire of a self-drive car. If they do not wish to plan even to this extent, freelance holidays are available through Balkantourist agents abroad, covering return air fare and currency voucher, which can be for any amount. This voucher can be exchanged for Bulgarian currency at the special bonus rate. It is very important, however, that individual travelers are prepared to exercise patience and perseverance since the package holiday-maker undoubtedly gets priority.

CLIMATE. Very warm, but not unpleasant even in summer when Black Sea resorts benefit from breezes and, inland, one can cool off in the mountains. Coastal areas get 2,240 hours of sunshine per year, nearly 30% more than southern England. Cold, crisp winters and with good snow conditions for skiing in mountain resorts.

Black Sea coast has a rather long season, from May to October. It's at its warmest and liveliest in July and August, but there is much to be said for the more temperate and less crowded months of spring and autumn. The coast is rather dry throughout the year, inland the wettest months are March/April. If you choose May or early June you will witness the fabulous harvesting of blooms in the Valley of the Roses (providing you are prepared to get up early). April/May are good times for fruit blossom, October for Fall colors. The main skiing season is January through March, and this is also the time when Sofia is enjoying a lively season of cultural events. Main festivities are listed below.

Average maximum daily temperatures in degrees Fahrenheit and centigrade:

Sofia	Jan.	Feb.	Mar.	Apr.	May	June	July	Aug.	Sept.	Oct.	Nov.	Dec.
F°	36	39	50	61	70	75	81	79	72	63	48	39
C°	2	4	10	16	21	24	27	26	22	17	9	4

 SPECIAL EVENTS. In 1981, Bulgaria celebrated her 1,300th anniversary and a full program of events has been launched in Bulgaria and abroad, that will continue through to 1985. Balkantourist can give the latest information. In addition, the following are among the most important regular annual festivals.

May: International Book Fair, Sofia; International Trade Fair, Plovdiv. **May-June:** Sofia Weeks of Music, an international event lasting four weeks. **June:** Golden Orpheus International Festival, Sunny Beach. **June-July:** Varna Summer International Festival and Varna International Ballet Competition. **July:** Neptune Carnivals, Black Sea resorts. **End of August:** International Folklore Festival, Bourgas. **September:** National Holiday (9th); International Chamber Music Festival, Plovdiv.

Many other events of a more local nature occur, and there is an especially lively program along the Black Sea coast throughout summer. If you're interested in Bulgaria's unique rose industry, the Rose Festival which takes place in the Valley of the Roses in June will have special appeal. Elsewhere there are all kinds of folkloric manifestations and it is best to get up-to-date information on these on the spot.

 VISAS. If you have any pre-paid services, you will not require a visa to enter Bulgaria. Otherwise, visas are obtainable from Bulgarian Embassies, the Bulgarian National Tourist Office and many travel agents, as well as at border points and airports. But it is best to obtain one in advance to avoid both delay and frustration. There is a fee of about $15.

HEALTH CERTIFICATES. These are not required to enter Bulgaria from any country.

MEDICAL INSURANCE. Emergency medical treatment in Bulgaria is free to all visitors, so medical insurance is not absolutely essential. But there are charges for all non-emergency treatment, though these are only modest. Medical insurance is therefore recommended.

CUSTOMS. You may import duty free into Bulgaria 250 grs. of tobacco products, plus one liter of spirits and one liter of wine, and 100 grs. of perfume. Gifts up to the value of 50 lev may also be imported duty free. Any amount of foreign currency may be imported; any that you have not spent during your stay in Bulgaria may be exported. Unspent amounts of lev can be exchanged at frontier posts on departure provided that counterfoils showing the lev were bought with foreign currency are produced.

The import and export of Bulgarian currency is not permitted.

Staying in Bulgaria

LANGUAGE. Bulgarian is a Slav language, closely allied to Russian and written in the Cyrillic alphabet. Though the Latin alphabet is increasingly common in tourist spots it is highly advisable, especially for independent travelers, to learn the Cyrillic letters, if only to identify *PECTOPAHT* as 'restaurant', to be able to read road signs away from the main routes and to find museums. Note too, that as yet very little tourist literature is available in English away from the main cities and Black Sea resorts. English is spoken by members of the travel industry and German is both spoken and understood fairly widely.

There is also the problem of the spelling of proper names in the Latin alphabet, which varies considerably from one source to another. The phonetic spelling has been chosen for this chapter, since that at least shows how words should be pronounced. On some maps however, a system of accents is used and the following examples may help in identifying place names spelt by this method:

Borovets - *Borovec;* Drouzhba - *Družba;* Zlatni Piassatsi - *Zlatni Pjašaci;* Slunchev Bryag - *Slunčev Brjag;* Turnovo - *Tărnovo.*

HOTELS. Hotels in Bulgaria are divided into four categories; Deluxe, First, Second and Third class. These correspond more or less exactly to our grading of Bulgarian hotels in the listings that follow as Deluxe (L), Expensive (E), Moderate (M) and Inexpensive (I). For an indication of prices, see below. In addition to these official gradings, there are about a dozen in the first two categories that are classified as Interhotels. In theory, this means that they conform to international standards expected of hotels of this type. In practice, however, this is by no means always the case. And you may well find that less expensive hotels are preferable if only because the human factor is liable to be rather more congenial than in larger and more expensive places. But as a general rule, standards of all hotels do not measure up to those of their Western counterparts; but then neither do the charges.

Most of the hotels used by Western visitors are owned by Balkantourist. In some of the coastal resorts there are sprawling modern complexes each consisting of several hotels of different categories, often with their own shops, hairdressers and entertainment facilities. The general impression can be rather clinical, but what they lack in local character, they make up for in convenience.

In addition, Balkantourist have self-catering accommodations in small villas or bungalows, especially near the coast. In many places, private rooms are also available, costing $4–7 per person per night for bed and breakfast, according to category.

Other hotels are run by the municipal authorities or by organizations catering for particular categories of visitor, usually in groups only. Examples are the establishments operated by Shipka for motorists, Orbita for young people, Pirin for hikers and Cooptourist.

Two people in a double room can expect to pay:

	Bed and Breakfast	Full Board
Deluxe (L)	$80–82	$100–110
Expensive (E)	$45–65	$ 65– 85
Moderate (M)	$30–45	$ 45– 60
Inexpensive (I)	$14–25	$ 28– 40

 CAMPING. There are over 100 camping sites throughout the country, many of them near the Black Sea beaches. These are classified as 'Special', I, and II, and in the top two categories will have hot and cold water, showers, electricity, grocery stores, and restaurants. A map showing their location is available from Balkantourist. Most have cabins for hire. Pre-paid (but non-refundable) camping vouchers may be purchased through Balkan Holidays in the UK. As an example, the cost of these in 'Special' sites in 1982 was as follows: £1.50–£2 per person per night, plus £1.50–£2 per car or tent, or £2.95–£3.60 per car with a trailer per night. Children under 12 get a 50% reduction, those under two are free. Note that there is a substantial service charge if vouchers are requested for less than four nights.

 RESTAURANTS. One of the very best, and least expensive, ways to eat in Bulgaria is to take advantage of the excellent pre-paid voucher scheme under which you can eat in a variety of different restaurants even if you have booked for full board in a particular hotel. These meal vouchers are issued on arrival in Bulgaria, the number of them varying according to the category of accommodations booked. They are valid in all Balkantourist restaurants throughout the country. They also have the advantage of allowing you to eat modestly on one occasion and gorge on another; or pay the difference and gorge every time. Unfortunately, in those inexpensive restaurants and cafeterias run by municipal authorities, vouchers are not valid.

An increasing number of attractive folk-style restaurants have been opened, not only in the resorts, but in towns and villages along the way. Quite often there is folkloric music, and sometimes dancing. The standard of food varies considerably, but has improved a great deal in the last year or so. Very often it is better in the smaller folk-style restaurants than in the main tourist hotels. Prices are very reasonable, and in the establishments listed in the following pages you can estimate as follows: Expensive (E) 15–20 leva, Moderate (M) 10–15 leva, Inexpensive (I) 5–10 leva. These prices are exclusive of strong drinks and are all per person.

TIPPING. Officially this is discouraged, but is nevertheless acceptable.

MAIL. Airmail letter to the US costs about 0.70 leva, postcard 0.39; to Great Britain a letter costs 0.42 leva, postcard 0.29 leva. But check before mailing.

TIME. Bulgaria is seven hours ahead of Eastern Standard Time and two hours ahead of Greenwich Mean Time. From early April to late September, the country operates on summer time which is eight hours ahead of Eastern Standard Time and three hours ahead of Greenwich Mean Time.

SPAS. Bulgaria has well over 500 mineral springs and some 130 spas. There are major spas at the following places: Velingrad, in the Rhodope Mountains, Kyustendil, in western Bulgaria, Sandanski, in the foothills of the Pirin Mountains, Hisarya, on the southern slopes of the central Gora Mountains. There are also a number of spas on the Black Sea coast. Cost of treatment is very low by Western standards, though more expensive on the Black Sea coast.

SPORTS. Facilities for water skiing, sailing and surfing exist in the Black Sea coastal resorts, along with tennis and mini-golf and possibilities for horse riding and cycling. Fishing and hunting tours are organized by Balkantourist who can make all the necessary arrangements regarding permits, guides, equipment and accommodation. Game includes various species of deer, wild boar, pheasant, duck and, on occasions, bear and wild goat.

In recent years, Bulgarian winter sports resorts have begun to make their impact on Western markets, the main centers being Vitosha just beside Sofia, Pamporovo south of Plovdiv, and Borovets south-east of Sofia in the Rila Mountains. Costs compare very favorably with those of Western resorts, but don't expect the variety and sophistication of après-ski or the same choice of ski runs that you would find in the established Alpine centers. Information on the winter sports tours currently available can be had from the Balkantourist offices.

MONASTERIES. There are a large number of monasteries in Bulgaria, some of which made a vital contribution to keeping the nation's cultural identity alive during the dark centuries of Turkish rule. Their secluded positions, often deep in the mountains and difficult to reach, largely protected them from the destruction that took place elsewhere. Nevertheless, battles and fires took their toll and many of the original buildings were rebuilt in the early decades of the 19th century, bequeathing their own testimonial to the vitality and talents of the National Revival movement. Older buildings and treasures that have survived are also to be found in these beautiful places. Quite a few of the monasteries provide very inexpensive accommodation for visitors. The best-known are those of Rila in the heart of the Rila Mountains south of Sofia; Bachkovo, in the Rhodopes south of Plovdiv; Troyan in the central Balkan Range; Dryanovo, in the Balkan Range between Veliko Turnovo and Gabrovo; Rozhen, near Melnik in the southwest corner of Bulgaria; and Preobrazhenski, near Veliko Turnovo. A leaflet describing these is available from Balkantourist.

Getting Around Bulgaria

 BY PLANE. The state airline *Balkan Bulgarian Airlines* (often known as *Balkanair*) have two internal routes linking Sofia the capital with Bourgas and Varna on the Black Sea coast. Flight times are between about 50 minutes (by turbo-prop) and 35 minutes (by jet). There are several services each way daily. Overbooking is not unusual. Get to the airport in plenty of time.

 BY TRAIN. From Sofia there are five main routes radiating to different parts of the country—to Varna on the Black Sea coast; to Bourgas on the same coast; to Plovdiv (the second city) and on to the Turkish border; to Dragoman and the Yugoslav border; and to Kulata and the Greek border. The route to Varna branches at Gorna Orjahovitza and goes to Rumania. Large sections of main line including the routes to Varna and Bourgas as well as to Plovdiv are electrified. Long-distance services have buffet cars; overnight trains to the Black Sea have sleeping cars and couchettes.

It is well worth ordering your tickets in advance from the appropriate rail bureau (see *Useful Addresses for Sofia*).

 BY BOAT. In addition to the Russian cruise vessels (see earlier) there are hydrofoil services along the Bulgarian stretch of the Danube linking a number of towns. From Vidin to Calafat there is a vehicle ferry linking Bulgaria with Rumania. Other hydrofoil services operate along the Black Sea coast in summer.

 BY CAR. Traffic drives on the right, and the usual continental rules of the road should be observed. Do not sound horn after dark and avoid using it at all in Sofia. Speed limits are 60 kph (37 mph) in built-up areas, 80 kph (50 mph) elsewhere except on motorways where it is 120 kph (80 mph). The limit for cars towing caravans is 10–20 kph (6–12 mph) less. The law concerning drinking and driving is very strict—no alcohol allowed at all. On-the-spot fines are imposed for offences.

At border points, be prepared for a delay while your documents are deciphered and duly stamped. A large-scale motorway construction program has begun which will eventually link all main towns on a circular route. Completed stretches include Kalotina (Yugoslav border)—Sofia and a section towards Plovdiv. Otherwise main roads are good, though some stretches of through routes are narrow for the weight of traffic they have to carry. The number of gasoline stations on such main roads is reasonable; elsewhere they may be few and far between. You will find them marked on the motoring map issued free by Balkantourist. Bring a spare parts kit with you.

Car hire. Self-drive cars can be hired through hotel reception desks. No fly-drive arrangements, as such, exist through airlines, but independent self-drive holidays can be pre-booked through Balkantourist agents abroad by which weekly rentals in 1982 were from $80 per week, plus 14 cents per km. or $200 per week with unlimited mileage.

BULGARIA'S HISTORY

A Nation in the Making

For a lot of people, Bulgaria means beaches and the Black Sea. The development of tourism along the Black Sea coast in the past 10 years or so has been quite phenomenal and, with the special emphasis that has been put on catering for children in particular and the young in general, it has become very much a coast with a youthful profile. Other things you will probably associate with Bulgaria are attar of roses, delectable fruits, colorful peasant costumes and crafts, spicy Balkan cooking, and some vague ideas of a history punctuated with bloody battles. Well, it's a start.

But first of all, there is a good deal more to Bulgaria than the Black Sea coast. The capital, Sofia, has some interesting things both above and below ground, and some of the most attractive surrounding countryside of any capital. The mountain ranges of the interior are very beautiful, and still for the most part little known; and a number of new and unusual ways are being devised for exploring them. Despite a good deal of industrialization, the pace of life in the rural areas—which still means most of the country—has a leisurely charm that has long been forgotten in most other places. Folk tradition, customs, and costumes still flourish in many areas as an integral part of life and not merely as a tourist show; and there is much of historical, cultural and architectural interest that has a refreshing 'difference' from more familiar western scenes.

Reasonable prices, attractive tourist rates of exchange, the easing of visa formalities and flexible arrangements for both package tours and independent travelers have all helped to remove some of the tiresome formality usually associated with holidays in this part of the world. All of which makes it a great pity that so few of Bulgaria's visitors manage to venture away from the sun-and-sand that probably lured them there in the first place.

You cannot be long in Bulgaria without becoming sharply aware of the very different cultural influences that have left their mark on its landscapes and its way of life. Orthodox domes compete with Moslem minarets, although the latter are much more in evidence in some parts of the country than others. There are many variations in local costume, and the architectural styles are strikingly different if you compare the villages close to the Greek border with those facing Romania across the Danube. A very chequered history has molded this country, and a little knowledge of it will contribute a great deal to your understanding and enjoyment. So let's start with a journey back through time, beginning with a very quick preliminary hop into the interior.

If you stand just about in the middle of the wobbly-shaped rectangle that defines Bulgaria on the map of Europe, you will certainly not be far from a small town called Kazanluk. The place itself isn't particularly attractive, but it is a significant point on the map from several points of view. First of all, it stands more or less at the crossroads of north-south and west-east routes linking Romania with Greece, and Yugoslavia (and western Europe) with the Black Sea and Turkey (and thence Asia). Mountains to the north of it separate it from the Danube Basin and to the south from the Thracian Plain. It becomes easy to see how this was a ready-made throughway for all-comers across a great many centuries.

Secondly, this is the main center of the Valley of Roses, producing what is probably Bulgaria's internationally best-known product (of which more later). Thirdly, it offers one of Bulgaria's oldest and finest historic monuments, impressive not for its size, but for its age and its beauty. It is a small domed and beautifully decorated tomb from the 4th to 3rd centuries BC (of which also more later). The original tomb is closed to the public, but the exact replica beside it can be visited and it is a fine memorial to the Thracian chieftain whose last resting place it was.

In the Beginning

The Thracians were Bulgaria's first known inhabitants and they have left quite a few relics scattered about the countryside (or now contributing to museum displays) to show how talented and artistic they were. These people were exposed to many outside influences, not least from the Hellenes whose civilization spread throughout the area. In due course Alexander the Great and his father, Philip II of Macedonia, absorbed it into the expanding Macedonian Empire that eventually penetrated far into Asia.

Around this time, far away in their homelands of the upper Rhine and Danube, the Celts were beginning to expand; and quite sensibly large numbers of them made use of the river as a natural, ready-made route which took them southeast through the heart of Europe and down to the Black Sea. Some settled on the way, but by the 3rd century BC others had spread as far as Greece and Asia Minor. Their raids aroused the kind of terror in antiquity that those of the Vikings were to do many centuries later in western Europe. Like the Vikings they settled, absorbed and were absorbed, many of them serving as mercenaries in the armies of Macedonia and later, Rome.

Those early centuries of Balkan history in general, and of Bulgaria in particular, are of a hideous but fascinating complexity. The winding 1,750 miles (2,816 km) of the Danube, (of which 300 miles/483km form the northern frontier of present-day Bulgaria) came in due course under Augustus and marked the northern limit of the Roman Empire, protecting it from the barbarian hordes. Military posts and forts sprouted along it, some of them eventually to tumble into ruins, others to provide the basis for medieval and modern towns. Along the Bulgarian section, two Roman provinces were established in the early decades AD: Moesia from the Danube south to the Balkan Range, and Thrace to the south of that. The Emperor Trajan (98–117 AD) was one of the greatest organizers of Roman rule in the Balkans.

The Birth of Christianity

But even as the Empire spread out and flexed the muscles of its growing strength, distant events of a very disparate nature were occurring that would turn the mighty architecture of Roman civilization to dust, and completely re-shape the map of Europe. In a remote village on the eastern rim of the Empire, the wife of a certain carpenter had given birth to a son whose followers were already spreading strange new teachings that reversed all the old beliefs. To the north and east, beyond the slender but strongly defended Danube boundary, wandering nomadic tribes roamed and marauded, occupied territory, attacked and were attacked, formed alliances and broke them. For a period, not of decades but of centuries, there unfolded a shifting kaleidoscope of humanity, building and destroying, ever fragmenting, overcoming or being overcome.

Among them were various Germanic tribes, including the Goths of whom the western branch—Visigoths—moved into the area north of the Bulgarian Danube in the 3rd century AD. The long and unwieldy northern boundary of the Roman Empire began to come under increasing external pressure, and within the Empire itself considerable changes were also beginning to take place. The followers of Christianity had grown considerably in number, and from being a source of irritation, mockery, and cruel sport, they had swollen into a moral and material force to be reckoned with. When Constantine the Great was converted to Christianity in AD 313, it became not only respectable but very rapidly spread to the far corners of the Empire. Constantine, born in Nis and very much a son of the Balkans, built a magnificent new capital city—Constantinople—on the site of the ancient Byzantium, the frontiers of Europe and Asia. It was completed in AD 330 and when the Empire split in AD 395 the city became the focal point of the Eastern half, from which Roman defense of the Balkans continued.

In the meantime, the Visigoths under Alaric, fleeing from the advancing Huns, had attacked and penetrated the northern frontier and had been allowed to establish settlements south of the Danube in return for the defense of this frontier from further barbarian attack. It was to prove a doubtful protection. The development of well-organized Visigoth and other barbarian kingdoms on Roman soil led to the disintegration of the Empire. It finally collapsed in the west in 476, and Constantinople was left as the capital of the troubled Roman territories of the east. From these ruins of Roman power eventually emerged the Byzantine empire.

Slavs and Bulgars

It was at about this time that the Slavs moved in from the north, and by the 6th century they had flooded the Balkans. In their wake came the Bulgars, a Turco-Tartar race originating in the steppes of Southern Russia from which they had been pushed out by another forceful people, the Khazars, who had moved in from the east. One branch of the Bulgars reached the Danube under Asparuch and now the stage was set. Providing the basis for the political organization of the embryo state, the Bulgars nevertheless adopted the Slav language and customs. From this fusion emerged the people we call the Bulgarians today. In AD 681 the Byzantines were forced to recognize this new state, controlled from its capital Pliska, and the First Bulgarian Kingdom was established.

Its rise was assisted by a decline in the Byzantine defense system and in one form or other the Kingdom survived until 1018. Early in the 9th century, a gifted leader led the young kingdom into victory against the Avars and attacked Byzantium, much extending Bulgarian territory. This was Khan Krum (802–14), known as the Terrible, no doubt because of his habit of drinking from goblets made from the skulls of slaughtered enemies. Perhaps it was some kind of retribution that he drank himself to death during his campaigns. Omortag, his successor, established a demarcation of spheres of influence with Byzantium, which brought a peaceful period in which Hellenic cultural influences and Christian missionaries made their mark. Under Boris I Bulgaria was converted to Christianity in 865.

About this time, an event occurred which was to have major repercussions on the Slav world in general and Bulgaria in particular. Two brothers, Cyril and Methodius, both later sanctified, created a new alphabet by which Christian and other writings could be read in a language understood by all Slavs. Thus the Cyrillic alphabet was born, sparking off a Golden Age of literature. Simeon, son of Boris, established a separate Bulgarian Patriarchate in his capital, Preslav.

For a period, Bulgaria's borders alternately expanded and shrank, at one time embracing parts of Greece and Albania and reaching to the Mediterranean coast. Twice in the 10th century, the armies of Simeon stood at the gates of Constantinople.

But Byzantium did not easily tolerate independent neighbors and, strengthened by victorious campaigns against the Arabs, turned her attention westwards. In 971 the eastern part of the country became a Byzantine province and Bulgaria lost both her political unity and the center of her national church. Under Samuel the western Bulgarian state retained independence for a while, with its capital at Prespa and later Ohrid (both now in Yugoslavia), where the Bulgarian church found a new focal point in the patriarchate of Ohrid. But a long drawn-out struggle with Byzantium ended horribly in 1014 when the Byzantine emperor Basil II took 14,000 Bulgarian prisoners, blinded them, and sent them back to Samuel as a ghastly insurance for future submissiveness. Not for nothing has Basil come down to us through the history books as 'Slayer of the Bulgarians'. Samuel, stunned by this unspeakable act, died soon after.

The Byzantine occupation lasted from 1018 to 1185, a period during which the Empire was under considerable pressure from all sides and growing political consciousness was stirring among the Balkan peoples. In Bulgaria it resulted in the uprising led by the brothers Peter and Assen, followed by the relatively short but, at times, shining period of the Second Bulgarian Kingdom from 1185 to 1396.

This was also a period that was both glorious and infamous for the Crusades, whose religious aims often became confused by the age-old lust for wealth and power. The Crusaders captured Constantinople and founded a Latin empire under Baldwin of Flanders, who then laid claim to former Byzantine possessions. The claim was violently and successfully contested by the Bulgarians under Kalojan at the Battle of Adrianople in 1205, and continued independence secured.

Turnovo became the new heart of the Bulgarian State and Church and, in the reign of Ivan Assen II, blossomed into a city of medieval wealth and splendor. For a while Bulgaria became the strongest power in southeast Europe, its territory reaching to the Black Sea, the Aegean, and the Adriatic. Alas, Ivan Assen's death in 1241 was followed by a succession of dynastic squabbles and rivalries that sapped the country's vitality from within and encouraged attack from without.

At about this time, not only Europe but most of the civilized world was reverberating with the expansionist activities of some fierce and highly organized newcomers—the Mongols under their fabled leader Genghis Khan. In Europe, Bulgaria was one of the first to come under attack. The combination of these pressures and a rapid succession of rulers led to the disintegration of Bulgarian unity into feudal territories. One of the main redeeming features of this period was a revival of literature among the circle of the last Bulgarian Patriarchate, Euthymius, in the latter part of the 14th century. His reform of the written language had considerable influence and, with his lives of the saints, he established a tradition in this type of literature.

After a brief period of glory, the neighboring Serbian Empire also began to suffer from dynastic feuds, and conditions in the mountain strongholds of the northern Balkans were ripe for further foreign aggression. Nor was there much doubt from which direction it would come.

The Ottomans and After

Ottoman power had been growing in strength and organization since the beginning of the 14th century. By the middle of it, they had crossed into Europe, and in 1389 there took place the great battle of Kossovo, which spelt doom for the Serbian empire and along with it, any hope of independence for her neighbors. Turnovo was destroyed in 1393 and three years later began a period of Turkish rule that was to last for over five centuries.

In terms of world history, Bulgaria disappeared from the scene for a very long time. Hers was the story of a backwater province of which few people had heard and to which even fewer went. The national church was put into the hands of the Greek Patriarchate. The two main broad effects of oppressive Ottoman rule on the evolution of the Bulgarian people was a general leveling of social classes, and an almost total cultural isolation from Western and modern influences.

But the Bulgarian spirit of survival was not so easily quenched, and slowly it was transformed into a spirit of revival and resistance. The monasteries in particular, which had kept close contact with the people, nurtured this spirit and emigrants abroad were active. The movement was given an enormous boost in 1762 when Païssi de Hilendar, in the seclusion of his monastic cell on Mount Athos, completed his *Slav-Bulgarian History,* which was not only a sketch of the nation's history but also contained a program for her reconstruction. Until it was printed in 1844, it existed only in manuscript form, but it was avidly read and circulated, and opened new vistas on the past on which to base the growing sense of national identity. A growing band of dedicated nationalists took to the mountains from which they harried the enemy, earning the undying admiration of every generation since. Songs, novels, and operas are dedicated to these *haidouti,* often described as the Robin Hoods of Bulgaria.

From 1835, schools began to teach in the Bulgarian language. Bulgarian literature, art, and architecture each developed and consolidated their own national forms of expression. From 1870, the Christian population was granted the choice between the Greek Church and newly-created Bulgarian Church, though the latter's independence was not to be officially recognized by the Greek Patriarch until the end of World War II.

On the political front radical revolutionary leaders—men like Vasil Levski, Georgi Rakovski, Ljuben Karavelov, Hristo Botev, and Stefan Stambulov—prepared the ground for the coming revolution. This culminated in the massive patriotic uprising of 1876 but, alas, it was too soon and insufficiently prepared. The reprisals were frightful and huge numbers of Christians were massacred in a bloodbath that aroused horror far beyond Bulgaria's boundaries. One of the loudest in Turkey's condemnation was Gladstone, who thundered about their 'fell satanic orgies'. Russia was more positive in her actions and, in her role as protector of the Slav peoples, took up arms yet again against the Turks in the Russo-Turkish War of 1877–78. Following Turkey's defeat, the proposed creation of various autonomous Balkan states by the

Treaty of San Stefano did not suit British and Austrian diplomacy, and the Congress of Berlin was called in 1878 to resolve this and other questions. The results for Bulgaria were hardly satisfactory, for she was now reduced to an autonomous principality between the Danube and Balkan Range, still under Turkish suzerainty, while Eastern Rumelia and Thrace to the south of the mountains were again lost to Turkey.

The Third Kingdom

Nevertheless, the Third Bulgarian Kingdom dates from 1879, with the adoption of the liberal Constitution of Turnovo and the election of a German prince, Alexander of Battenberg, to the throne. In 1885 Eastern Rumelia joined herself to Bulgaria, who declared herself independent of Turkey in 1908. Ferdinand of Saxe-Coburg took up the vacant throne following the abdication of Alexander in 1886. For some years there followed a repressive dictatorship under the anti-Russian Stambolov government; though Ferdinand later accepted Stambolov's resignation and relations with Russia improved.

In 1912, the Balkan Entente brought the combined strength of Bulgaria, Serbia, Greece, and later Montenegro to bear on waning Ottoman power and Turkey was finally ousted from the Balkans. Unfortunately, this rather unlikely band of allies could not agree between themselves on the division of conquered territory and, following the Second Balkan War, a defeated Bulgaria became isolated from her Balkan neighbors, also losing Southern Dobrudja to Romania.

Her dependence on Germany grew and in consequence she also suffered defeat in World War I, losing more territory to her Balkan neighbors. Some has been recouped, but these border areas are still a cause of controversy among nationalists on both sides of them. Ferdinand, faced with mounting rebellion, abdicated in favour of his son Boris.

In the years between the wars, hardship and discontent provided a natural breeding ground for the growing socialist revolutionary movement, assisted by the agitations of the Macedonian International Revolutionary Organization. Some kind of compromise between the extremes was found in the elections of 1920, resulting in a peasant dictatorship led by Alexander Stamboliiski who had greatly opposed the German alliance. But his assassination in 1923 was accompanied by a military coup, and the Fascist tendencies of the new government resulted in a clampdown on the strengthening Communist Party. A popular rising in September of the same year was followed by ruthless repression, the Communist Party was outlawed and, under Boris, Fascism now took its radical course, suppressing all the freedoms that had been granted by the Constitution of Turnovo.

Despite popular demonstrations and intellectual protests, Bulgaria came into World War II on the 'wrong' side yet again. An active resistance movement developed and the Fatherland Front was founded to unite all the opponents of Fascism. In September 1944 the Soviet Union declared war on Bulgaria, backed by resistance groups throughout the country, and the monarchy was overthrown. Thereafter Bulgarian forces fought alongside their Soviet comrades.

Subsequent events might be said to be fairly predictable. By a referendum in 1946, Bulgaria was proclaimed a People's Republic after the Soviet model, and Georgi Dimitrov became president of the Council. Dimitrov's colorful revolutionary career had brought him to the attention of the world in 1933 when, with others, he stood trial in Leipzig for setting fire to the Reichstag. The conduct of his own defense against Goering and others of like ilk was a masterly achievement after months of ill treatment. He was not, however, allowed to return to Bulgaria at that time, and found refuge in Russia, where he was able to put his political beliefs to practical use. Dimitrov died in 1949 and the multiparty Fatherland Front, now essentially Communist, gained 97 percent of votes.

Since then Bulgaria has firmly followed Soviet guidelines. A Western observer, secure in his long-established democracy, might too easily find cause for criticism. But remember that this is a country which has never had any real experience of democracy, and that the material benefits which have been gained in recent years (after centuries of foreign rule) are considerable. For a people who have stepped out of almost medieval bondage and into the atomic age in well under a century, it is no mean achievement.

BULGARIAN CULTURE

Cradle of the Arts

by
Leslie Gardiner

Many European nations trace a fairly pure and continuous artistic heritage; but not Bulgaria. Victim of her geography, vulnerable to powerful neighbors, a crossroads and battlefield of history, Bulgaria has known long periods of cultural desolation. Her native arts sparkled, died out and were rekindled from cold ashes.

Yet it is argued (chiefly by Bulgarians, but with some justification) that this land was a cradle of arts before Greece or Rome, possibly before Egypt. Recent discoveries in the Stone Age necropolis near Varna include golden artefacts of 3,500–4,000 BC, older than Troy and remarkable for the technical quality of their workmanship. A clay seal from Nova Zagora and a clay plaque from Vratsa, unearthed in 1971, caused a sensation among philologists. Were their pictographic scripts contemporary with, or the forerunners of, the oldest writings in the world? The debate continues.

During the excavations of Bronze Age sites, many bowls, cups, bracelets and cult figurines have come to light. In the museums of the Republic they are overshadowed by the wealth of Thracian objects

48

which superseded them. The Thracians, as mysterious and sophisticated a people as the Etruscans in Italy, flourished alongside the 'glory that was Greece' until crushed by the 'grandeur that was Rome.' They left no written history, but the Greek writer Herodotus said that Thrace, next to India, was the most populous land on earth; and they produced splendid artistic works.

The 2,300-year-old Thracian tomb at Kazanluk in the Valley of Roses is on UNESCO's list of monuments of world importance. The brick-built ante-chamber, tunnel and inner chamber, lime-washed and exquisitely frescoed, are a triumph of monumental building and of vivid painting.

Typical of the delicacy and imaginative treatment of Thracian domestic crafts is the golden treasure of Panagyurishte, a hill village of the Sredna Gora. This famous nine-piece wine set of the 3rd century BC is now to be seen in the archeological museum at Plovdiv.

The Thracians shared the Greek mythology. Dionysus and Heracles were Thracian gods borrowed by the Greeks. The Rhodopean mountains, where Bulgaria rises to its frontier with Greece, were traditionally the homeland of Orpheus, whose music charmed wild beasts. But the Thracians' revered deity was a mounted giant. Perhaps the Madara Hoseman, the huge bas-relief on a cliff-face near Shumen, is his portrait.

A Lamp of Learning

The Roman occupation lasted four centuries. Trade and the arts of war were brisk enough, but the Thracian culture was swept away. (What precious artefacts were plundered or destroyed on the surface of the land can only be surmised from the items dug out from underground, and dug out only very recently.)

The Romans brought circuses to Bulgaria. Summer shows are nowadays given in the ancient entertainment complex of Varna. Restaurants and city-center walkways line the top tiers of the amphitheater of old Philippopolis, modern Plovdiv. If native arts survived this period, they have still to be uncovered.

When Rome fell, the land we call Bulgaria became part of the Byzantine domains. Waves of Slavic tribes invaded her. Those who came from the lower Volga region and eventually set up the first Bulgarian state in AD 681 established a new artistic heritage. Excavations in the proto-Bulgarian capitals of Pliska and Preslav in eastern Thrace, and in the later 'old' capital of Turnovo are steadily confirming the existence at that time of advanced architecture, fine ceramics, jewelry and (after the adoption of Christianity in the 9th century) primitive schools of icon paintings—all of idiosyncratic character.

From the depths of turmoil and misery a Bulgarian language and a literature were born. The brothers Cyril and Methodius (9th century), inventors of the Slavonic alphabet, were not actually Bulgarians; they came from Thessaloniki in Greece. But they built the written language on a Bulgarian dialect; the earliest Slavonic inscriptions (10th century) originated in Bulgaria; and the so-called Glagolitic script and its later development Cyrillic (after Cyril) expressed in writing the Old Bulgarian tongue, which until the 12th century was the medium of an ecclesiastical literature common to all orthodox Slavs. Books and manuscripts written and decorated by the highly-literate monks of Turnovo spread far afield. Through its writings the 'Turnovo school' introduced most of the Slav nations to Christianity, including Russia. Old Bulgarian, or Old Slavonic as it is sometimes called, was accepted as the language of the liturgy, along with Greek, Latin and Hebrew. Seven centuries later, when the National Revival took place, Bulgaria's men of destiny turned again to Old Bulgarian, the sacred tongue, to seek the national character and its cultural identity.

The Arts in Hiding

For almost 500 years, the half-millennium of Turkish domination after 1396, Bulgarian culture went underground. The strong partnership between religion and the arts was intensified, because during those turbulent centuries the monasteries became refuges and centers of education for homeless natives. Great monastic fortresses like the Rila, Bachkovo, Dryanovo, Glozhen and Cherepish, remote and almost inaccessible, sheltered whole communities and kept the national spirit alive. In 1762 the monk Païssi returned to his native land from Hilendar on Mount Athos (Greece) with the manuscript of his *History of the Slav-Bulgarians.* Unable to print or distribute it, he wandered through Bulgaria, reading it to his enslaved countrymen. This work, written (said Païssi) in a language that 'the ploughman, the shepherd and the poor artisan' could understand, told Bulgarians to glory in their past, to protect their culture and to fight for their own schools, church and state. Païssi gave expression to a dormant patriotic dream, but much blood was spilled in realising it before the National Revival culminated in the expulsion of the Turks and the founding of modern Bulgaria in 1878.

Literary Heroes

The pioneers of modern Bulgarian literature were the educationists and historians who carried forward the torch Païssi had lit. Stoiko Vladislavov, also called Sophronius (1739–1814), Peter Beron (1797–1871) and Yuri Venelin (1802–1839) wrote textbooks and encyclopedias. In 1844 Konstantin Fotinov published *Lyuboslovie* ('Love of Speech'), the first Bulgarian periodical, and in 1846 Ivan Bogorov launched the first Bulgarian newspaper *Bulgarski Orel* ('Bulgarian Eagle'). The poet who most clearly reflected national aspirations was Hristo Botev (1848–1876). He lived and died a revolutionary and one of Bulgaria's highest mountains is named after him. Shortly afterwards came the best-known and most-translated of Bulgarian novels to this day: *Under the Yoke,* a tale of Turkish oppression by Ivan Vazov (1850–1921).

After independence, stories and poems were marked by less revolutionary fervor and more pointed satire—a foretaste of the wry needling wit and good-humored resignation which make Bulgarian literature so readable today. Outstanding short-story writers earlier this century were Elin Pelin (1878–1949) and Yordan Yovkov (1884–1937). Their works are available in English translation.

Social Realism

Social realism is the watchword today. Short stories are the popular medium (though Bulgarians are also great readers of long foreign classics, especially those of Dickens, Tolstoy and Dostoevsky). In the bookshops of Sofia and Plovdiv you will find English-language magazines with modern Bulgarian short stories in them, containing rather more condemnation of 'the way we live now' than one might have thought likely. A recent prize-winning tale, for example, describes the subtle revenge of a peasant after the tourist committee gave him notice to quit in order to turn his cottage into a folk museum.

Present-day writers of note (and whose works are available in English) include: Georgi Djagarov, born 1925, poet *(In Moments of Silence)* and playwright *(This Small Earth, The Prosecutor);* Yordan Radichkov, born 1929, satirical novelist *(Gunpowder Primer)* and playwright *(Attempt at Flying);* Pavel Vezhinov, born 1914, fiction writer *(At Night with the White Horses);* Dimiter Dimov, died 1966, an outspoken and original writer of short stories *(Damned Souls, Tobacco).*

Icons and Landscapes

Bulgarian painting is rooted in medieval religious ideals. Her chief contributions to world pictorial art are the icons, murals and miniatures from the ancient monastic schools. The large spreads of allegorical frescoes on the walls of the Preobrazhensky monastery near Turnovo and of the Bachkovo monastery south of Plovdiv are of indifferent quality. Religious paintings in the large city churches are sometimes quaint but rarely memorable. To see primitive frescoes of genius you must visit the dark little church of Boyana in Sofia's suburbs. (The place is often closed to keep the damp air out, so check in advance if you plan to visit.)

Around the monasteries you hear a good deal of Zahari Zograf, Hristo Dimitrov and Stanislav Dospevski, prolific icon-painting monks of the 18th and 19th centuries. Medieval artists were anonymous, and their works impersonal, but they produced the true mystical icons—not mere pictures of saints, but mirrors to the viewer's soul and a telescope into eternity. The best archaic works are now displayed in the crypt of the Aleksander Nevsky cathedral in Sofia and in the National Museum at the Rila monastery. They date from the 13th century.

Bulgaria is otherwise rather short on painting traditions, though there is much commemorative sculpture about, some of it impressive in a stark, granitic way. The national painter is Vladimir Dimitrov of Kyustendil, the centenary of whose birth was celebrated in 1982; but he is minor-league in Western eyes.

Some interesting new talent is developing. Landscapes and studies of country life are the favored subjects: 'Bulgarian' means 'farmer' and this nation remains close to the soil. The titles of recent award-winning pictures—*Mowers, In the Field, Yard, Young Orpheus, Spring, Child-*

hood, Country Musicians —indicate that modern artists find inspiration in the simpler life their grandparents knew.

At the picture exhibitions and *plein-air* (out-of-doors) paint-ins, frequently held in the summer months, look out for the canvases of Svetlin Roussev (born 1933, president of the Bulgarian Artists' Union), Boris Kotsev, Stoyan Venev, Daria Vassilyanska and Radi Nedelchev. They paint colorful, vigorous landscapes, childlike in pathos and innocence, clearly influenced by the icon masters of the distant past whose humanism and realism are said to have anticipated the Renaissance.

Spirit of Orpheus

The Rhodopean mountains, south of Plovdiv, gave birth to Orpheus and Eurydice. Not entirely for this is Bulgaria called the Land of Song, but rather because something in the climate produces great singers and great choral ensembles. She has given the world Boris Hristov (Christoff) and Nicolai Ghiaurov, arguably the finest basses since Chaliapin; Raina Kabaivanska, a magnificent prima donna; and a State Folk Song and Dance troupe which carries off grands prix all over the world. For a small country whose artists are not widely known, Bulgaria sustains an astonishing diversity of musical entertainment. Its cultural committees are tireless organizers of international festivals.

The National Opera season in Sofia runs from September to June. Performances, however, both of 'grand' and folk opera, are of approximately Italian provincial standard. Famous singers rarely appear.

Sofia's Philharmonic Orchestra is at home in the Concert Hall 'Bulgaria'—one of a dozen metropolitan orchestras which tour the country, playing not only in provincial culture halls but also in factories and on construction sites; as does the State Folk Song and Dance Company. The Children's Symphony Orchestra (Pioneer Palace, Sofia) and the Bodra Smyana Children's Choir are well worth hearing. They broadcast and their records are on sale. Visitors buying theater and concert tickets, books and gramophone records, find them remarkably cheap.

Throughout the country there are about 15,000 ensembles, amateur and professional, instrumental, vocal and dancing. The native ballet *Legend about a Lake,* by the composer and pianist Pancho Vladigerov (1899–1978) is often performed, as are the shorter works of Petko Stainov (1896–1977), an interpreter of folk traditions. The oldest ballet competition in the world is held every two years during the Summer International Music Festival (usually July) at Varna.

Bulgaria's biggest music feast is the Sofia Music Weeks, which takes place from the end of May to end of June. The programmes attract well-known foreign companies and soloists and include opera, symphony, cantatas and oratorios.

Music events and festivals run almost continuously from early May to early September in the Black Sea cities of Bourgas and Varna. Varna has its own State Opera, Theater and Philharmonic Orchestra and the *Varnensko Lyato* ('Varna Summer') brings musicians from all over Europe.

Every evening for two weeks in June, Sunny Beach stages the 'Golden Orpheus' popular-song festival and televises it in color to several countries. In these Black Sea resorts almost every bar, nightclub and folk restaurant offers music specialties—bands, jazz, folk, ballet, gypsy musicians, fire dancers, shepherd bagpipers—all adding up to a dazzling summary of the nation's folk heritage.

Craft and Cottage Industry

Bulgaria, essentially a peasant society, was once rich in crafts. Textiles, wood-carving and metalwork had their beginnings in early Slav cultures and the decorative needs of the churches. Crafts of the country districts were at first utilitarian, but as time went by Byzantine and Islamic influences crept in.

When Bulgaria entered her new nationhood 100-odd years ago, her merchants began to travel and make money. Retiring to their native villages, they built themselves houses of a splendor formerly unknown and employed local craftsmen to furnish and ornament the rooms. They were, after the medieval church, the first patrons of Bulgarian arts. Spacious, airy, conspicuous for their carved wooden balconies and ceilings, their woven fabrics indoors and garish frescoes on the facades (rustic painters' impressions of Venice, Ragusa etc. gleaned from the owners' descriptions), these mansions are now on the tourist circuit. Some, in fact, have become 'museum houses' and others are holiday self-catering apartments. The painted houses of Plovdiv are well known, but you can also find charmingly ostentatious merchants' and master-craftsmen's houses in the relatively isolated towns of Koprivshtitsa, Bozhentsi, Kotel and Zheravna.

The State encourages crafts and revives some obsolescent ones. But the old regional craftworkers, the carpet-weavers of Kotel and Pirdop, the rug-makers of the Rhodopean mountains, the wood-carvers of Samokov are all part of a State enterprise which spreads the product nationwide. Native craftwork must earn foreign currency and gift shops everywhere have the same range of goods to sell: the copper or leather rose-oil bottle, the brightly-striped 'peasant' tablecloth, the petal-patterned dark-oak carving, the old-fashioned coffee-pot and matching set of metal mugs.

Rationalization of cottage trades reaches its goal at the reconstructed 'craft villages' of Etur and Tryavna, both near Gabrovo. They are sensitively done and efficiently run, but are entirely tourist-oriented. Off the beaten track you may come across a village which has not been prettified to such an antiseptic conclusion. There is Bozhentsi, for example, in the northern foothills of the Balkan Range: a concise statement in stone of the history of rural crafts. In the 18th century its woodwork, wrought ironwork and woven goods found markets all over the Ottoman empire, and those comfortable-looking two-storied houses with roofs of heavy stone slabs and doors elaborately carved are memorials to an old prosperity. Then factory-made articles replaced handmade goods and Bozhentsi, depopulated, went into a 200-year sleep.

Within the past 20 years the culture ministry has restored and refurnished the houses of Grandma Raina and of Doncho the priest. The smithy, furrier's shop and candlemaker's house are open to visitors.

Painting holidays are offered, and *plein-air* painting contests bring in a few foreign amateurs. But Bozhentsi has not yet surrendered to tourism. It still breathes the authentic air of the past, the slow pace and tranquillity of village life in the golden age of folk art and cottage industry.

Pottery

The pottery of Bulgaria is largely Turkish in its decoration, although shape and form derive more from native traditions. The Turks in turn were influenced greatly by Persian traditions and the Persian style and spirit of innovation have been carried into modern Bulgarian techniques.

Typically, a red earthenware clay is formed on the potter's wheel into traditional shapes—plates, dishes and various bottle-shaped refinements of the narrow-necked jug, originally used for transporting oil, wine and water. These pots are then decorated with slips (mixtures of liquid clay and metal oxides) to produce colors of white, yellow, green, brown, terracotta, blue and black. The slips, brushed on or 'trailed' (squeezed out of a bulb) are often combed or incised to give distinctive geometric, floral or bird designs; finally a clear glaze is applied.

Bulgarian potters also fire white earthenware clay, glazing it over an incised pattern with copper green, yellow and white.

Nowadays there are special schools for the applied plastic arts; Troyan is particularly noted for its involvement with ceramics. The apprenticeship spirit is being regenerated. Pottery is prominent in the numerous exhibitions of crafts and in the various ethnographical museums and 'museum villages' where Bulgaria reconciles the past with the present.

Plays and Players

Bulgaria's first theatrical troupe set out from Plovdiv (then the capital) for Sofia (then a provincial town) not quite 100 years ago, passing, in the Maritsa valley, the stones of forgotten Thracian and Roman theaters. It is said that on their journey the players gave a performance in a small town. After it the audience remained silent, until an old man stood up and asked what the strangers were supposed to be doing. The leader explained what a play was and then the troupe went through it again, to hearty applause.

Even today, theater in Bulgaria is a minor cultural activity, although all towns and most villages have their theaters as part of the 'culture hall,' in pursuance of the policy of giving art to the masses instead of restricting them, as of old, to the 'top 10,000.'

The metropolitan theater of Sofia, the graceful pink-and-white building named after Ivan Vazov the novelist, offers sophisticated fare as well as the knockabout farces (generally based on incidents of the Turkish occupation, peasant cunning outwitting satrap pomposity) which Bulgarians still delight in. But Shakespeare and Ibsen are popular too, and Molière's sharp observation of human foibles appeals especially to the Bulgarian temperament.

Up to the present, no Bulgarian playwright, actor or actress has earned international renown. Modern plays worth seeing on their home stages, and more or less intelligible to non-Bulgarian speakers, include Djagarov's *The Prosecutor,* Radichkov's *January* and *Attempt at Flying* and the dramatisations of Dimiter Talev's epic tetralogy on the history of the Bulgarian minorities in Macedonia.

In mime, shadow-play and puppetry the Bulgarians are supreme. The top players are the Central Puppet Group of Sofia (they may be seen at the Ivan Vazov theater and they also tour the provinces in summer). Their short sketches, employing hands and fingers only, have tremendous pith and zest and their longer adaptations of Molière are quite memorable. Bulgarians are greatly in demand at mime and shadow-play festivals in other European centres.

The Seventh Art

What Bulgarians call the 'seventh art'—cinema—is also the youngest, barely 30 years old. The nation's first feature movie was made under State direction only in 1950. Now the catalogues lists 400 movies, to which Bulgarian Cinematography, the State organisation, adds about 22 annually. Film-makers are preoccupied with standard social and environmental themes: the drift to the towns *(Last Summer, A Tree without Roots, Peasant on a Bicycle);* rising consumerism *(Villa Zone, Fairy Dance);* growing up *(Boy Turns Man, The Pool, Boomerang);* and, inevitably, the war-of-liberation perspective *(Amendment to the Law in Defence of the State, On the Tracks of the Missing).*

There is nothing that could be called a star system so far as actors and actresses are concerned, but directors such as Hristo Hristov, Rangel Vulchanov and Binka Zhelyazkova are respected abroad and have gained prizes at international festivals. With the latest releases, notably *The Barrier, Illusion* and *The Unknown Soldier's Patent-leather Boots,* the Bulgarian cinema seems to be coming of age and moving confidently into wider areas of speculation about why people, whatever the political system under which they live, tend to behave like human beings.

BULGARIAN FOOD AND DRINK

The Home of Yogurt

Bulgarian food is hearty and good, its wines light and cheap, its world-famous fruits and vegetables delicious. Balkan cooking—which you find with various national and local variations in neighboring Yugoslavia, Greece, and Turkey—relies heavily on lamb, potatoes, peppers, aubergines, tomatoes, onions, carrots, and quite a few spices.

Meat Rolls, Hotpots and Soup

Soups are generally very good: for example the so-called Monastery Soup, which is made of well-soaked dried beans, and a variety of vegetables; and the nourishing *Shkembe Churba,* (beef offal and spices cooked in milk). *Kebapcheta,* which you can get in pretty well any restaurant as well as shops selling only these, are very tasty grilled minced meat rolls, usually veal or pork with lots of spice. *Gyuvech* is a kind of hotpot containing an astonishing variety of vegetables, including potatoes. Preferably, but not necessarily, it should have meat, and the real thing is cooked and served in an earthenware dish. *Kavarma* is another variation on this theme, with plenty of pork pieces, mushrooms, and vegetables. *Pile paprikash,* chicken in a rich sauce of tomatoes and peppers, can be delicious; alternatively a similar sauce can be used with fish. *Agneshki drebuliiki* is grilled liver, kidneys, and other offal of lamb, which tastes better than it might sound. *Meshana skara* is a Bulgarian version of mixed grill. *Sarmi* are cabbage leaves stuffed with meat: various other leaves and vegetables like peppers and aubergines, can be treated in the same way with very tasty results. *Imam bayalda* is a delicious cold vegetarian dish made from aubergines stuffed with finely-chopped onions, carrots, celery, and tomatoes. *Sirene po shopska* is a tasty baked cheese dish.

The True Taste of Yogurt

Bulgaria, of course, is *the* place for yogurt, for this is its original home. It's called *kisselo mleko* here and if you get the real thick, creamy homemade version, yogurt will never taste the same again anywhere else. It is partly to do with the milk—which should be sheep's—and the way it is fermented with a well-disposed bacteria whose name *Lactobacillus bulgaricus* confirms its national origins.

Kisselo mleko crops up in other guises, too, notably in *tarator,* a cold soup of finely chopped cucumber, ground walnuts, sour milk, dill and a dash of pure olive oil.

Vegetables and Fruits

The Bulgarians are deservedly proud of their reputation for high-quality vegetable and fruit produce. Apart from the vegetable dishes mentioned above, salads also come in for a number of variations. *Shopska* salad is available in nearly all restaurants and is composed of tomato, cucumber, sweet pepper, onion and grated white goat's cheese.

From spring through fall, the nicest way to round off a meal is with fresh fruit. Bulgarian fruits are in a class by themselves—and cheap. The first cherries and strawberries appear in May, reaching their peak in June and July, along with orange-red apricots and raspberries. Apples, pears and peaches are in abundance from June through October. Water and musk melons last from July to September and plums and rich, amber-colored grapes can be enjoyed from July through October.

What to Drink

When it comes to stronger drinks, *the* national pick-me-up is *Mastica,* with an aniseed base; you add a little water to taste, which makes it go milky.

There are plenty of wines with which to ring the changes. Look out for the reasonably dry white *Karlovski misket, Tamianka* and *Evksinograd.* Dry reds are *Gumza, Kaberne* and *Trakia.* If you prefer sweet, there's *Manastirska Izba* (white), or *Melnik* (red) comes sweet or dry. And like most Eastern European countries, Bulgaria has its own version of plum brandy. It's the national drink, and is called *slivova.* A typical Bulgarian meal invariably starts with a glass of *slivova* and one of the best brands is *Trojanskaia Slivova,* which comes from the Trajanskii Monastery. The most famous Bulgarian liqueur is the one made from flowers in the beautiful Valley of Roses.

A great variety of non-alcoholic drinks is available, including Coca-Cola. Bottled soft drinks made from 100 percent natural fruit juices are plentiful and very refreshing, as are the fruit-flavored mineral waters. Standard mineral waters include the well-known ones from Gorna Banya and Hisar.

Coffee, served in small cups in Turkish style, is thick and strong, but may be in short supply away from tourist spots. With it, you might eat *bánitsa,* a very sweet and sticky pastry that is also eaten with fruit or cheese.

SOFIA

City Beneath the Mountains

Two of Sofia's trump cards are its location and its climate. Situated at 1,800 feet (549 meters) pretty well in the center of the Balkan Peninsula, it lies on the high Sofia Plain ringed by mountain ranges of varying proximity: the Balkan range to the north, Lyulin Mountains to the west, Mount Vitosha to the southwest and part of the Sredna Gora Mountains to the southeast. Mount Vitosha is in fact on the city's doorstep, providing a marvelous natural playground for its inhabitants at all seasons. The city's setting contributes to summers that are relatively cool for these latitudes, and crisp winters, which provide excellent skiing.

The first general impression one gets of the city itself is neither of great age nor of great beauty, though in fact it is extremely old and has some delightful corners both above and below ground. The first thing to remember is that just about a century ago, it was a rather down-at-heel Oriental town, capital of the Turkish province of Rumelia. At that time, it had 3,000 houses and 15,000 inhabitants, living in narrow twisting streets punctuated by mosques and little churches, crouching half underground, for their roofs were not allowed to reach higher than a man on horseback. Two of the mosques and one or two of the churches remain, but otherwise most of central Sofia today has its origins in the first town plans drawn up in 1880 and later, and it was in the process of creating this new European capital that a number of sites of great antiquity were uncovered.

The area has been inhabited for about 5,000 years, but the first people about whom anything is known is the Thracian tribe of Serdi who gave Sofia its first name, Serdica. Then as now, it was on one of the main routes between east and west, and suffered regular harassment as a result. The Romans made it into the splendid capital of the province of Dacia and it seems to have been much favored by Constantine the Great. In AD 447 it was destroyed by the Huns under Attila, to be rebuilt in the 6th century by Justinian, who also added the Church of St. Sophia.

Soon afterwards the Slavs changed the city's name to Sredets, and by the end of the 14th century it had become Sofia. In the meantime, it had been subjected to pillage and attack by Pechenegs, Magyars, Serbs, Crusaders, and even in the Second Bulgarian Kingdom never retrieved its former importance. During the five centuries of Turkish rule however, Sofia was a major economic and cultural center within the Empire, until the 19th century, when there was a sharp decline in population.

Today, the streets are broad, the traffic light and there are spacious green parks and open-air cafés in which to join the people of Sofia in relaxation on warm summer days. The main sights of the city can be seen in a couple of days, and another day at least should be allowed for Mount Vitosha. But if you are interested in Bulgarian culture, you will want to stay longer, for there are a number of museums devoted to various aspects of the subject, and musical performances are of a high standard.

Exploring Sofia

Most of the city's main sights are centrally situated and can easily be visited on foot. If you take Ruski Boulevard and its continuation into September 9 Square as the main sightseeing arteries, most places can be found in relation to these. At one end is the Clement of Ohrid University and at the other Bulgarian Communist Party Headquarters, both pretty dominant buildings.

To the west of Communist Party HQ is Lenin Square with its monument to Lenin. At 1 Lenin Square you will find the main office of Balkantourist. On the same square is the Balkan Hotel, in whose courtyard crouches one of the oldest and most charming sights of Sofia. It is the little church of Sveti Georgi built in the 4th century on an even older site, possibly that of a pagan temple. The Huns destroyed it, Justinian rebuilt it, the Turks turned it into a mosque. It has now been restored, revealing frescoes from the 11th to 15th centuries.

Near by, in the middle of an underpass on Lenin Square, is another ancient church, built nearly a millennium later. It dates from the 14th century, and is particularly notable for the frescoes discovered during its restoration. Those from the 15th and 17th centuries are of special interest. This is the Church of Sveta Petka Samardjiyska and beside it in the underpass is an open air café and some shops, making this a pleasant oasis in the middle of the city bustle. The Central Department

Store is just across the road if you want to browse round one of Sofia's biggest shops.

North of Lenin Square on Georgi Dimitrov Street, Banya Bashi Mosque is one of the few major buildings left by the Turks. It dates from the 16th century and has rich interior decorations. Just across Georgi Dimitrov Street from here you will find the Central Market Hall, a good place to meet Sofia's housewives about their daily shopping. The big public mineral baths are also near the mosque, a reminder of the presence in and around Sofia of many hot and cold health-giving mineral springs.

From Lenin Square, head east now towards the Communist Party building. Right in front of it another underpass leads you back nearly 2,000 years—to the Serdica of Roman times. Here you will find quite substantial chunks of Roman walls, a stretch of Roman paved street and a collection of stone blocks and carvings from those times. There is also a model of the town as it probably was in Roman days.

The Communist Party building is in September 9 Square at the top of Ruski Street. On your right, with its entrance on parallel Alexander Stamboliiski Boulevard, is the National Archaeological Museum, housed in the former Buyuk or Great Mosque, a fascinating quadrangular building dating from the 15th century. The museum has four sections from prehistoric times to the late Middle Ages, plus a numismatic section. This is one of the most important of Sofia's museums. In the next block is the Georgi Dimitrov Mausoleum containing the embalmed body of this revered Bulgarian revolutionary leader, who died in Moscow in 1949. A changing of the guard ceremony takes place before it every hour on the hour. Across the road is the National Art Gallery in the former Royal Palace and, next to that, the ornate Russian Church of St. Nicholas, 1912–14.

At this point you enter Ruski Boulevard on or near which are several of Sofia's main hotels, as well as the building of the National Assembly. Before it is the Monument to the Liberators, dominated by the equestrian statue of Tsar Alexander II of Russia. Beyond the National Assembly, one of the city's most distinctive edifices stands beneath its glittering domes: the Alexander Nevsky Memorial Church. It is named after Alexander II's patron saint, a 13th-century Prince of Novgorod. This church was built in the early years of this century as a token of the gratitude of the Bulgarian people for Russian help in gaining their independence from Turkey. Its elaborate and ornate interior incorporates the work of many Russian and East European artists. The three altars, for example, are respectively the work of Russian, Bulgarian and Czechoslovak painters, and it is interesting to see the different styles in which the Virgin Mary has been depicted. Don't miss the museum in the crypt if you are interested in icons; it is an unusually fine collection.

The church and its adjoining square are on the site of a great Roman necropolis, the highest point of the city. But the most notable church in Sofia lies just across the square to the west. St. Sophia, in whose honor the city was renamed in the 14th century, dates back to the early 6th century. It was converted into a mosque in the 16th century, and was then partially destroyed by earthquakes, before being restored to

Hotel

SOFIA

STRUGA

STRUGA

KLOKOTNICA

HRISTO

DIMITROV

SLIVNICA

Pl. Lâvov

KIRIL i METODI

CAR

SIMEON

To Central Station

KIRKOV

To Central Station

PAISIJ

CAR SAMUIL

GEORGI

KNJAZ BORIS I

ANDREI

ŽDANOV

ANDREI ŽDANOV

①

OPÁLCENSKA

NAJČO

CANOV

HRISTO BOTEV

NAJČO CANOV

②

OTEC

Pl.
Vazrazdane

③

ALEKSANDÂR

STAMBOLIJSKI

Pl. Lenin

POZITANO

④

POZ ITANO

ALABIN

VITOSA

ANGEL KÂNCEV

1 Banya Bashi Mosque
2 St. Petka Samardjiyska
3 St. Georgi
4 Tourist Information
5 National Archeological Museum
6 Georgi Dimitrov Mausoleum
7 National Theater
8 Central Post Office
9 Sofia State Opera
10 Central Party Headquarters
11 Archeological Reserve
12 National Art Gallery
13 National Museum of Ethnography
14 Church of St. Nicholas
15 Alexander Nevsky Memorial Cathedral
16 Church of St. Sophia
17 Liberty Park

DONKOGLU

VASIL

KOLA

VLADIMIR

POPTOMOV

NEOFIT

PATRIARH

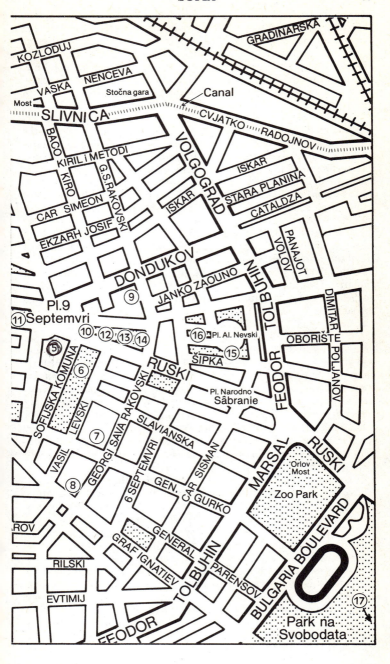

its original form. Lacking the ornamentation of its modern neighbor, the great age and simplicity of this three-nave church in mellow red brick are impressive. It is built in the form of a symmetrical cross beneath a central dome, typical of the basilicas of Asia Minor; but there are also romanesque features in the rounded arches of the vaulting. Traces of two older churches have been found in the course of excavations, and a mosaic from the second of these (5th-century) still survives. Just outside St. Sophia, a monument to the Unknown Soldier was unveiled in 1981.

Freedom Park (Park na Svobodata) with its lake and fountains, is the largest of several green areas in the city center—nearly 405 hectares (1,000 acres) of woods, lawns, and flowers; plus an openair theater, cinema, library, and other sources of entertainment. It also contains the main Vasil Levski Sports Stadium. To the north of Freedom Park, across Bulgaria Bulevard, is the zoo. As a recreation area, however, few capitals can boast anything on the scale of Mount Vitosha, a range of mountains whose highest point—Cherni Vruh—reaches 7,500 feet (2,286 meters). Mount Vitosha rises to the south of the city. From Lenin Square, follow Vitosha Street (recently rebuilt with all kinds of small shops and cafés) southwards, and you will be heading in the right direction. Soon you will come to the huge Palace of Culture, including Congress Hall and a theater which opened in 1981. South of this is Juzhen Park, which is to be developed into a continuous leisure area linked with Vitosha Mountain: in due course the zoo will also be transferred here.

On the way to the park you could include Boyana, only about six miles (nine km.) from the city center on the slopes of Vitosha. Here you will find one of Bulgaria's most precious historic monuments—the little church of Boyana—which dates from the Middle Ages and contains some exquisite frescoes, painted between the 11th and the 13th centuries. The best are from 1259, the work of an unknown artist, depicting scenes from the life of Christ, the Virgin, and St. Nicholas, with a remarkable display of individuality. Note especially *The Last Supper,* the *Annunciation,* the *Transfiguration,* the *Crucifixion,* and *Assumption.* It is a most peaceful spot and there are one or two rather nice folk restaurants in the vicinity.

From Boyana you can continue to the nearby village of Dragalevtsi. Above it in fine beechwoods is Dragalevtsi Monastery, its 14th-century church still surviving and decorated with 15th- and 17th-century frescoes. A chairlift from Dragalevtsi takes you up to the resort complex of Aleko on the northeastern slopes of Vitosha, also accessible by good road. From near here another chairlift takes you to the top of Malak Rezen, only a few hundred feet beneath Cherni Vruh.

On the northwestern slopes, reached by road and cable car from Knyazhevo, is the Kopitoto Hotel with a fabulous view over the city. A network of marked trails probe into many parts of the massif, among them the beauty spot of Zlatnite Mostove (Golden Bridges), with its foaming mountain waters. For the less energetic this can be reached by road, and there is a pleasant restaurant.

PRACTICAL INFORMATION FOR SOFIA

 WHEN TO COME. Spring is the time for blossom in the surrounding countryside; summer for the hottest weather, usually tempered by the city's altitude. Winter has the double advantage of being the best season for cultural programs and for the skiing, which is right on Sofia's doorstep. Music lovers should note the Sofia Music Weeks, end May to end June.

 GETTING AROUND SOFIA. By Train, Bus and Trolley. Work has begun on a new metro system, but for the moment you can use trams, buses, and trolleys, for which tickets can be bought in advance from special kiosks or on the vehicle: they cost 6 stotinki. If you already have your ticket you must get it punched in a machine after boarding the vehicle (watch how other people do it).

By Taxi. Taxis are inexpensive, but rather scarce; quickest is to order one from your hotel. Balkantourist arrange sightseeing tours of the city. Self-drive cars can be hired through hotel reception desks and Balkantourist.

 HOTELS. All the top hotels in Sofia are run by Balkantourist, the very best ones being classed as Interhotels. All the hotels listed below have restaurants unless otherwise stated and many have rooms in more than one category. Should you arrive in Sofia without reservations, there is an accommodations office at the Information Bureau at 37 Dondukov Blvd. (open 7 am to 10.30 pm) and at the Central Railway Station. Blankandtourist at Dondukov Blvd. can also help arrange private accommodations.

Deluxe

Vitosha-New Otani, 100 Anton Ivanov Blvd. 454 rooms, several suites and various restaurants (including a Japanese restaurant); plus nightclub, casino, indoor pool and sauna. The hotel is Japanese-designed and is the most luxurious in the country. It is on the south side of the city and is not central.

Expensive

Bulgaria, 4 Ruski Blvd. 72 rooms, very central, but quiet as this is now a traffic-free street.

Grand Hotel Balkan, Lenin Sq. 181 rooms, 35 suites; Interhotel, very central.

Grand Hotel Sofia, Narodno Sobranie Sq. 201 rooms, 3 suites, night club; Interhotel, very central.

Hemus, 31 Georgi Traikov Blvd. Over 200 rooms and suites.

Novotel Europa, 131 Georgi Dimitrov Blvd. 609 rooms, some suites. An Interhotel, and one of the French Novotel chain; near railway station and not far from center.

Park-Hotel Moskva, 25 Nezabravka St. 366 rooms, 34 suites, several restaurants (including Russian), nightclub. Interhotel in parkland setting, but not central. There is a scheme by which you can cook your own food using the hotel's ingredients and recipes!

Moderate

Pliska, 87 Lenin Blvd. Over 200 rooms, suites.
Serdica, Vladimir Zaimov Blvd. 2. 140 rooms; *Old Berlin* restaurant serving German specialties.
Slavyanska Beseda, 127 Rakovski St. 150 rooms, suites.
Slaviya, 2 Sofiiski geroi. 75 rooms, suites.

RESTAURANTS. In addition to the hotel restaurants, there is a growing number of eating places concentrating on local specialties, often with an attractive folkloric setting.

Expensive

Budapest, 145 G.S. Rakovski St. Hungarian food and music.
Berlin, 4 V. Zaimov Blvd. Bulgarian and German food.
Crystal, 10 Aksakov St. Restaurant-tavern.
Krim, 2 Dobroudja St. Russian food, summer garden.

Moderate

Boyana, about 6 miles from center, near historic Boyana church; folkloric program.
Chernata Kotka, about 8 miles south-east of city on E5N; folk music.
Gorubliane, attached to motel, about 6 miles out to south-east on E5N; folk program.
Koprivshtitsa, 3 Vitosha Blvd; folk music.
Shoumako, about 6 miles south of center on Simeonovo-Bistritsa road; folk music.
Strandjata, 19 Lenin Sq; folk music.
Vodenicharski Mehani, incorporating three old mills, at foot of Mount Vitosha above Dragalevtsi district; folkloric show.
Zlatna Ribka, about 15 miles south of city on road to Borovets; folk music.

MUSEUMS. Monday is usually, but not invariably, the day of closure, so it's best to check. Quite a few of Sofia's many museums are concerned with leading members of the country's revolutionary movement and a complete list can be obtained from Balkantourist. The following are the main museums and galleries of general interest.

Art Gallery, 6 Shipka St. Exhibitions of Bulgarian and foreign artists.
Boyana Church National Museum, about 6 miles (9.5 km) from the city center. An absolute must for its superb medieval frescoes, but it has just undergone major restoration, so check about reopening.
Crypt of Alexander Nevsky Memorial Church. A stunning display of icons and other religious works.
Ethnographical Museum, 6a Moskovska St. Displaying folk art, particularly costumes, from every region of the country. Housed in part of the former royal palace.
Georgi Dimitrov Mausoleum, 9th September Sq. Here lies the embalmed body of Bulgaria's revered leader. There is a changing of the guard ceremony every hour on the hour. A museum devoted to the life of Dimitrov is at 66 Opulchenska St.

Museum of the Revolutionary Movement in Bulgaria, 14 Ruski Blvd. Provides the answers to those curious as to the origins of Bulgaria's present-day socialist regime.

National Archaeological Museum, 2 Alexander Stamboliiski Blvd. Housed in a fine building, formerly a mosque.

National Art Gallery, 9th September Sq. Bulgarian art from medieval times to the present. Housed in another part of the former royal palace.

 OPERA, CONCERTS AND THEATER. The standard of opera is high in Bulgaria as is that of the folkloric performances, notably the excellent National Folk Ensemble. The standard of concerts is also high. The following are the main theaters and venues.

Bulgaria Hall, 1 Aksakov St. Regular concerts by leading Bulgarian and foreign orchestras and soloists.

Central Puppet Theater, 14 Gurko St. Puppet performances are very popular and of high standard.

Ivan Vazov National Theater, 5 Levski St, the country's largest.

Open-air Summer Theater, Freedom Park.

People's Army Theater, 98 Rakovski St.

Sofia State Circus, Hr. Botev St. Regular performances, except in the summer months.

State Opera House, entrance from 1 Yanko Zabounov St.

Stefan Makedonski Musical Theater, 4 Volgograd Blvd.

It is also well worth attending an Orthodox Church service, which can be both a musical and moving experience. The choir of the Alexander Nevsky Memorial Church is exceptional.

 NIGHTLIFE. Nightlife is not Sofia's strongest feature, but those who need their night club ration will find a night club with a floor show at the **Vitosha-New Otani Hotel,** the **Moskva Park Hotel** and the **Grand Hotel Sofia.** There is a disco in the **Novotel Hotel.** The **Orient Night Club** is at 2 Stamboliiski Blvd. *we stayed here*

 SHOPPING. The State commercial organization *Corecom* runs a network of shops in which goods—both Bulgarian and imported articles—are sold at favorable prices. In Sofia, the big central Corecom store is at 8 Kaloyan St., but there are several other branches, including some in most of the main hotels. *2 lb for cherry 20 c*

Some of the attractive items to look out for are replicas of antique jewelry, leatherwork, wood carving, embroidery, metalwork. Unusual are copies of some of the beautiful medieval frescoes. There is a good selection of arts and crafts at the shop of the *Union of Bulgarian Artists,* 6 Ruski Blvd, and a range of souvenirs at *Sredets,* 7 Legue St; *Souvenir Store,* 7 Stamboliiski Blvd.; *Prizma Store,* 2 Ruski Blvd. If you are interested in furs or leather, try one of the following—4 Slavyanska St, 7 Tsar Kaloyan St, or 2 Ruski Blvd.

All kinds of foodstuffs are on sale at the *Central Market Hall,* 25 Georgi Dimitrov Blvd, where you'll be able to choose from some of Bulgaria's excellent fruit and vegetable preserves as well as local wines and spirits.

Other countries' department stores are always interesting to browse through and the main *Central Department Store* is at 2 Georgi Dimitrov Blvd.

SIGHTSEEING. Balkantourist can arrange a wide selection of tours by car or minibus. These include sightseeing in Sofia by day and night, folklore evenings and day trips to Rila Monastery, Koprivshtitsa, the Valley of Roses, the mountain resort of Borovets. Also longer trips to different parts of the country.

USEFUL ADDRESSES (all in Sofia). Embassies: *USA,* 1 Blvd. Stamboliisky; *British,* 18 Blvd Tolbuhin. Tourist information and travel arrangements: *Balkantourist,* 37 Dondukov Blvd. (also in main hotels); *Interhotels Central Office,* 1 Lenin Sq.; *Balkan Bulgarian Airlines,* 12 Narodno Sobraniye Sq., (domestic services) 10 Sofiiska Komuna St.; *Rila International Railway Bureau,* 5 Gurko St.; *Domestic Railway Bureau,* 23 G. Dimitrov Blvd.; *Shipka Agency* (Union of Bulgarian Motorists), 6 Sveta Sofia St.; *Orbita Bureau for Youth International Excursions,* 45A Stamboliiski St.; *Pirin Tourist Bureau* (Union of Bulgarian Hikers), 30 Alexander Stamboliiski Blvd.; *Cooptourist Tourist Bureau* (Central Cooperative Union), 99 Rakovski St.

Emergency: telephone 150, motorists 146.

INLAND BULGARIA

Peaks versus Plains

Even a quick look at a relief map shows that Bulgaria falls quite readily into clearly defined topographical compartments, following more or less horizontal lines. In the north, the Danube forms the border and its plains soon merge to the south with the foothills of the Balkan Range of mountains, whose presence has played such an important part in Bulgarian history; they are marked as 'Stara Planina' (meaning 'old mountains') on most relief maps. Parallel with these are the lower heights of the Sredna Gora Mountains, with the famous Valley of Roses running between the two ranges. South of the Sredna Gora lies the fertile Thracian Plain, setting for Bulgaria's second largest city, Plovdiv. The southwest and south of the country is largely made up of a series of mountain groups: Rila, Pirin and the Rhodopes.

The three main routes linking Sofia with the Black Sea coast follow these three main latitudinal divisions: the northernmost passing through the ancient capital of Veliko Turnovo in the northern hills of the Balkan Range; the central one through the Valley of Roses; and the southern one through Plovdiv and the Thracian Plain. The central one can easily be combined with either of the other two for variety on a circular tour. It joins forces in any case with the southern route at Sliven. But if it is Bulgaria's past that particularly intrigues you, you'd

do well to include the northern route for, in addition to Veliko Turnovo, two even older capitals lie just off your way: Pliska and Preslav.

Danube to Balkan Range

LKB
June 23, 1985

Whether you are heading from Sofia to the Danube or the Black Sea
coast the road through the Iskar Gorge is the recommended one even
though, for the latter destination, it will add to your mileage. Through
this gorge, the Iskar river can claim to be the only Bulgarian waterway
cutting across the Balkan Range to flow into the Danube. The most
attractive section is the 42 miles (67 km.) to the north of Kurilo, near
which are the curious Kutino Earth Pyramids. About 25 miles (40 km.)
north of Kurilo are the precipitous rocks of Lakatnik, from which the
more intrepid enjoy dangling from ropes. There are also some caves in
the area. The Sofia-Ruse railway follows the Iskar for most of the way
to Pleven and provides some spectacular stretches.

The Bulgarian banks of the Danube are little visited by Western
tourists, but several places on or near them should be mentioned. In
the north-westernmost corner of Bulgaria, Belogradchik is another
place known for the extravagance of its red sandstone formations;
Romans and Turks incorporated them in their fortifications and, from
these, there are splendid views across the Danube plain and over the
extraordinary sculptures of this petrified forest of rocks. The area offers
scope for energetic rambling in remarkable scenery whose twisted
shapes have given rise to a host of legends. Some miles away are the
caves of Magura, among Bulgaria's biggest, whose most important
features are the primitive paintings created in bat guano by its Early
Bronze Age inhabitants. Birds and animals are depicted along with
hunting scenes and dancing ladies.

Bulgaria's section of the Danube is nearly 300 miles (483 km) long
and lavish in its complexities of islands and marshes. As part of the
northern boundary of the Roman empire, its importance both strategically and as a thoroughfare goes back into the dim mists of prehistory.
Fortifications punctuate its passage, starting in the west with the medieval ones of Vidin. Here, the Citadel of Baba Vida is the most impressive in Bulgaria from that period. With its massive walls and towers
rising almost out of the Danube, it is well worth visiting, and it is a
fitting setting for an annual Shakespeare Festival. In the vicinity two
historic buildings have been adapted as places of entertainment: the old
Turkish Post Office is now a café and disco and a Venetian warehouse
has been transformed into a night club.

Most of the others have vanished or been reduced to ruins. There is
not a great deal to see unless you would like to take to the water on
board one of the regular hydrofoils that link the riverside communities.
One of these is Kozloduj where the shipping station is two or three
miles west of the modern town. Beside the shipping station is a memorial to the poet and one of the great leaders of the anti-Turk uprisings,
Hristo Botev. His name is spelled out in trees on the hill above. One
of the most interesting sites lies a little inland from the mouth of the
Iskar river, near the village of Gigen. Here are the substantial remains
of the major Roman city of Oescus, in whose large palace a superb

mosaic was discovered. This fortified town once stood at a major crossroads, and during the 4th century a massive bridge spanned the Danube at this point. There is a substantial Turkish element in this Danube area, and they are even in the majority in some towns such as Nikopol, which has a dishevelled charm and a colorful small market by a very ancient church.

The two most interesting towns are Svishtov and Ruse, the latter also offering the only road connection across the Danube from Bulgaria to Romania; although there is a ferry from Vidin. Svishtov produced several major Bulgarian artists and writers, including Aleko Konstantinov to whom a museum is devoted. Ruse is Bulgaria's fourth city and rather new in appearance, though it stands on the site of the Roman fortress of Sexaginta Prista and was a bustling Oriental town in the 17th and 18th centuries. It's a lively town and port, with pleasant riverside walks. Several good museums include the house of Baba Tonka, who sheltered anti-Turk revolutionaries; the history museum; and the transport museum in the old railroad station. The Pantheon is a memorial to the revolutionaries in which an eternal flame burns, watched over by a team of young people.

The Levanta restaurant, housed in an 18th-century fortification on a hill overlooking the town, is made up of a series of attractive rooms whose decor represents the folkloric traditions of the eight countries through which the Danube runs. Up one of the branches of the Lom valley, in the vicinity of Ruse, there are a number of fascinating and little-known rock churches and monasteries. You will need a car and some detailed directions to find them, but head in the general direction of Cherven.

Further east, Silistra stands on the site of yet another Roman fortress, and beyond it the Danube turns away into Romania. There is an outstandingly good nature reserve in nearby Lake Sreburna; in fact, all along these Danube waters there is fascination for bird enthusiasts.

The road south from Ruse is the main E20 to Sofia, the new capital, and via E90 to Veliko Turnovo, the old. The former passes through the main town of Bulgaria's Danubian Plain: Pleven, with the usual long history but modern appearance. The Ottomans made it an important fortress, and it held out for five months against the Russians in 1877. A museum commemorates the event.

Early Cradles of Culture

On the whole though, it would be more rewarding to take the route via Veliko Turnovo, which is the most attractively sited of all Bulgaria's larger towns. It literally seems to spill down the hillside to converge on the river Yantra. Main roads from the four points of the compass twist through the mountains to meet at Veliko Turnovo.

Your best move is to find a vantage point above the town, drink in the view and pick out the landmarks. Thus you can see how the river pursues extravagant contortions through it, dividing it into three main hilly peninsulas. The oldest part is Tsarevets, so-called because it was the area where the tsar or king and the patriarch had their palaces. Thick walls, gates, towers and battlements surrounded it in those days and, as it is almost completely contained within a wild loop in the river, the only means of access is by a drawbridge. This fascinating area, including the Patriarchate and the royal palace, is under restoration, with paths and stairways being constructed for easier viewing of the extensive ruins. The ways are steep, but the setting is splendid, and you should allow at least an hour or two for this. One of the most prominent features is the tower known as Baldwin's Tower, because according to tradition, it was here that Baldwin of Flanders, Crusader leader and briefly the Latin Emperor of Constantinople, was imprisoned and died after being captured in the Battle of Adrianople in 1205.

Another of the peninsulas, Trapezitsa, was also fortified and it was here that the boyars or noblemen had their palaces and family chapels. The ruins of nearly a score of these can still be seen. The third peninsula is the wooded Sveta Gora on which there is a camp site, motel and restaurant offering a really splendid view over the town.

The year 1393 is important in Bulgarian history. That was the year that Veliko Turnovo fell to the Ottomans, and the year which marked the beginning of nearly half a millennium of lost liberty. Veliko Turnovo, captured after a long siege, was more or less razed to the ground, as well as damaged by subsequent attacks and an earthquake in 1913 so that what can be seen of the medieval city today is mainly restored ruins and scattered foundations. Three churches from that period, all in the Asenova district, or craftsmen's quarter, are 'musts'; although it is quite a long way from the center, and not yet included in official sightseeing tours. One is the Church of St. Dimitur, marking the place where the brothers Peter and Assen proclaimed the liberation of Bulgaria from Byzantine domination and thereby launched the Second Bulgarian Kingdom in 1185. The east part of the building is the best preserved. Then there is the Church of the Forty Martyrs built in the 13th century, subsequently used as a mosque, and with two interesting inscribed columns; one commemorates a victory over the Byzantines in 1230 and the other, very much older, of Khan Omortag from the 9th century contains the pious hope 'May it please God that he live a hundred years.' Thirdly, there is the church of SS. Peter and Paul from the 13th and 14th centuries, which suffered much damage in the 1913 earthquake, but still has very well preserved 14th-century and later frescoes.

During the centuries of Turkish rule, Veliko Turnovo by no means remained quiescent. There were a number of uprisings, and the city is dotted with monuments to these courageous if ill-fated bids for freedom. Making considerable impact from those days, which also saw the rebirth of a great new consciousness of national identity, are whole districts built in the National Revival style of which the self-taught master-builder Nikola Fichev (known as Kolyo Ficheto) was one of the greatest exponents. One of his finest buildings, Nikoli Han, is now a museum devoted to that National Revival Period. The style of these houses, with their red tiled roofs and jutting upper storeys, adds enormously to the charm of this city and a stroll through the steep, narrow streets of the old districts will be amply rewarded. An elegant church from this period is St. Constantine and St. Helena, designed by Fichev.

One could spend a lot of time in this area which has cradled the nation's culture over so many centuries. One of the sights that should not be missed is Preobrzhenski Monastery, the most interesting of the 11 monasteries in the area; superbly situated at the foot of limestone cliffs, looking out across a deep valley. It lies three miles (just over six km.) to the northwest, and was founded in the 14th century—although rebuilt in the 19th—the tower of the main monastery church being another of Nokola Fichev's designs, (he was responsible for the splendid iconostasis). The frescoes include a couple of rare portraits by the leading painter of the National Revival period, Zahari Zograf, and the one above the door of the inner church bears his signature. There is also a massive picture of the *Last Judgment*. The village of Arbnassi is another of the local sights; it was founded by Albanian immigrants in the 16th century. The ruins of the Roman city of Nicopolis ad Istrum are 11 miles (18 km.) to the north of Veliko Turnovo.

One of the most important areas in terms of Bulgaria's early history is as yet little known to Western visitors. The nearest main town is on the main road between Veliko Turnovo and Varna. Nowadays this is mainly an industrial center albeit with a well-developed taste for cultural activities. The first National Theater was established here in 1856, and it is the birthplace of several literary figures. The 18th-century Tombul Mosque is probably the largest and finest in Bulgaria.

A road leads south from Shumen to Preslav, which has the distinction of being Bulgaria's second capital from 893 to 972, in the distant Golden Age of the First Kingdom. The Turks made a pretty good job of destroying it down to its foundations, some of which can still be seen widely scattered over three square miles of the undulating countryside. Most interesting are the marble columns; chunks of sculptured stonework inlaid with colored stone fragments, and silver and gold decorations. They can be seen in the Archeological Museum here. John the Exarch, living in those times, described 'tall palaces and churches with countless tones, woodwork and painting, lined on the inside with marble and copper, silver and gold . . . '

A few miles east of Shumen at the junction with a minor road to Madara, you will see a copy of the famous Horseman of Madara. To see the original and much else, you must continue the few miles to the village of Madara and its backdrop of cliffs. Here there are remarkable remains from a whole tangle of cultures, going back to prehistoric times, the earliest from the 3rd millennium BC.

The famous Horseman of Madara itself was created by an unknown 8th-century chiseller high up on the cliff and continues to confound the experts. You can view it from a natural platform above the village, reached by 200 steps. Binoculars will be helpful. It depicts a horseman —perhaps Khan Omortag himself—slaying a lion with a lance and closely followed by a dog. There are some inscriptions in Greek, the earliest surviving examples of Bulgarian writing. The cliff face is also pitted with what were once the cells of a monastery. As you reach the top of the steps you will see footpaths leading off in both directions. If you follow the one to the right, in a few hundred yards you will come to the Small and Large Caves, in which have been found traces of habitation from prehistoric to medieval times. Nearby there is a medieval rock chapel. A footpath to the left of the steps leads to the foundations of a 9th- and 10th-century royal palace on the hillside, and eventually round the back of the cliffs to the plateau on the top. Here is the once great fortress of Madara. It probably dates from the 5th century, with later alterations, and was in use until its destruction by the Turks. The view from up here extends far over the valley and Balkan Range. Not far from the fortress are the remains of a Roman village. At the foot of the steps, near the coach park, is a museum. Just to the east of the present village of Madara are the remains of a considerable Roman Villa. Small wonder that Madara became known as the 'Bulgarian Troy.'

Pre-dating Preslav by two centuries was Bulgaria's first capital of all. You will find the well-organized remains of Pliska set in cornfields east of the Madara turning and a few miles to the north of the main road. Spread out over several square miles of the plain, the foundations of a triple line of fortifications as well as traces of the palace, temples and feudal residences have been uncovered. They are thought to date mainly from the reign of Omortag in the 9th century, although the earliest constructions are probably from the late 7th century. The second line of fortifications is being substantially reconstructed, as are the royal palace and nearby basilica. The museum has a lapidarium and various tools, trinkets and vessels on display. These are less sophisticated than those found at Preslav, the site to which the capital was moved after its conversion to Christianity as a result of its better natural defenses and the presence around Pliska of pagan tribes. It is worth pausing a moment to ponder that here around you was the seat of one of the first still surviving organized states in human history.

To the Valley of Roses

The main road south of Veliko Turnovo to Gabrovo winds attractively through limestone country, at times quite ravine-like in character. About half way you pass Dryanovo Monastery, huddled down in a hollow just below the road and scene of another desperate shoot-out with the Turks in 1876. A short distance north of Gabrovo, a minor road to the pretty village of Bozhentsi, a rural gem in unspoilt countryside. Gabrovo is a major industrial center on the upper reaches of the Yantra river. Indeed, it is known as the Pittsburgh of Bulgaria, although its backdrop of the Balkan Mountain Range gives it a certain scenic edge over its US rival; in fact the town is twinned with Aberdeen in Scotland. Gabrovo's inhabitants are famous for their sense of humor, to such an extent that the town features a House of Humor, and a festival of comedy and satire is held here every other year. The main square, the old bridges and the river banks are pleasant enough, but a place not to be missed is the museum-park of Etur, 5 miles (8 km) away. It is a living museum delightfully set in a mountain valley, its original houses grouped along a stream whose waters are used to power all kinds of activities from grinding corn to turning a roasting spit. Not only the architectural styles of the National Revival period are to be seen here, but also the way of life, arts and crafts, for each building is devoted to some end product: bakery, coppersmith, cobbler, potter, blacksmith, weaver, wood turner and so on. Some of the products can be bought. It is worth a detour. Eleven miles (17 km) east of Gabrovo the small town of Tryavna was once the center of a flourishing school of icon-painting and woodcarving, whose influence spread throughout the land.

South of Gabrovo, the road continues into the Balkan Range to cross the Shipka Pass before dropping down on to the Valley of Roses. The defense of the Pass was the reason for yet another epic battle in the Russo-Turkish war and a mighty monument, approached by a flight of steps, commemorates those who fell here in 1877. These monuments to battles and uprisings are very much part of any journey through Bulgaria; visitors who may begin to weary of them should remember that without the events that they commemorate Bulgaria would simply not exist. Some of the fiercest battles of all were fought against this mountain backdrop, so don't be surprised if you arrive in the village of Shipka to find it milling with Soviet tourists. For here, 20 years after the war was won, a large memorial church was built, honoring the 200,000 Russian soldiers and Bulgarian volunteers who perished here. The church is very colorful and ornate, and was designed by the same architect as the Nevsky Memorial Church in Sofia. Its bells were cast in metal which comes from bullets used in battle against the Turks.

We are now approaching the famous Valley of Roses, funneling between the Balkan Range and the hills of Sredna Gora. The rose-growing area extends along the valley floor from Kazanluk in the east to Klisura in the west, linked by one of the through routes between Sofia and the Black Sea. But if it is the roses and their harvesting that you are interested in, you should come in May or early June—and be prepared to get up early, as the rose pickers must be. The picking is done between dawn and about 8 A.M., for the good reason that once the sun gets too high in the sky the rose petals lose up to 50 per cent of their oil. Since between 3,000 and 6,000 kilos of rose petals are needed to make one liter of rose oil, a minor army of nimble-fingered pickers is at work while most tourists are still asleep. This fragrant harvest is then fed into giant copper vats; the precious attar is extracted still leaving a fragrant and useful residue of rosewater. In addition to the famous attar of roses, the blooms also contribute to the making of liqueurs, sweetmeats, jam and medicaments especially useful in treating skin complaints.

The production of attar of roses was begun in the 1830s under the Turks, who have always been partial to sweet smells and sweet flavors, and it is the oldest industry in Bulgaria. The Museum of Rose Production at Kazanluk traces its history and preserves some of the early tools and equipment used. Though unfortunately it lacks any explanatory text in English, it is fairly easy to pick up a general idea of what went on. Incidentally, the valley grows things other than roses—notably fruit crops, lavender, sunflowers, and vines, which add their own attractive blooms and fruit to the scene in due season.

The other great sight of Kazanluk, which otherwise has rather an industrial character nowadays, is a Thracian Tomb. The original is closed to the public for its better protection, but an exact replica has been constructed near it, so you can get an accurate idea of one of

Bulgaria's most impressive single monuments, demonstrating the high level of artistic taste of those original inhabitants of the land. The tomb dates from the 3rd or 4th century BC and was the last resting place of a local chieftain. The inner wall surfaces of the corridor and small domed burial chamber are decorated with frescoes depicting a scene from the burial feast, warriors on foot and on horseback, and a chariot race. They are finely drawn and full of movement.

West of Kazanluk, the road heads up the valley past the artificial waters created by Georgi Dimitrov Dam which drown the ruins of the ancient Thracian capital of Seuthopolis. The valley narrows as you proceed west, and soon after passing through the little town of Kalofer you cross a watershed and come to the upper end of the Valley of Roses; including Karlovo, Sopot, and Klisura. Kalofer is a picturesque little place, and Karlovo has its share of lovely old houses too. A road from Karlovo leads south over 16 miles (26 km.) to Hisarya, one of the best equipped of all Bulgaria's spas. Good use was made of its mineral sources by the Thracians and, even more, by the Romans who built an elaborate water system to feed their splendid baths. Part of the 4th-century walls are well preserved and there are remains of very early Christian basilicas.

At the village of Karnare, between Sopot and Klisura, a sinuous road leads north over the Balkan range to the attractive town of Troyan and, a few kilometers away, Troyan monastery nestling in the heart of the mountains, the third largest in Bulgaria. This can also be approached from the north, from the main Sofia-Veliko Turnovo road, but the road out of the Valley of Roses has the merit of providing wonderful views, not only over the valley and the Sredna Gora range, but beyond this to the rugged profiles of the Rhodopes. Troyan Monastery church, like so many others, was rebuilt in the 19th century, but it is extremely picturesque and its icons, wood carvings, and frescoes are fine examples of National Revival art. Zahari Zograf is among the artists.

Klisura huddles near the head of the valley and beyond it the road climbs up and over the Koznitsa Pass. Soon after this a minor road leads south in a few miles to one of Bulgaria's showpiece villages, Koprivshtitsa. Once again you see a veritable living museum of National Revival architecture, but this time adapted to a setting of mountain pastures and pine forests, at about 3,000 feet (915 meters) in the Sredna Gora range. Many of the houses are museums and can be visited, several of them belonging to poets and artists. There are courtyards behind studded wooden gates, broad verandahs and overhanging eaves, and nothing much has changed since the revolutionaries met in the pharmacy here to lay their plans for a free Bulgaria. The first shots of the tragic April uprising of 1876 were fired here and naturally there is a museum to tell you about this landmark in Bulgaria's history. This is a place of pilgrimage for many Bulgarians who come here to do honor to the first Bulgarian town briefly to taste freedom before the bloodbath of subsequent events, and it is also an increasingly popular destination for Western visitors who have heard of its picturesque houses and beautiful location.

South Bulgaria

Two main modern traffic arteries bore through the southern half of Bulgaria: E5N continuing southeast from Sofia into Turkey, and E20 linking Sofia with northern Greece. E5N basically follows the Maritsa River through the Thracian Plain, with the Rhodope Mountains and their foothills to the south. E20 mostly follows the River Struma which eventually empties itself into the northern Aegean as the Greek river Strymon. This road is your route for the mountains of Rila (the highest in southeast Europe) and Pirin.

Recreating history sometimes needs a fair dose of imagination and this will probably be the case when you find yourself part of a stream of tourist traffic and long-distance trucks heading southeast of Sofia on E5N in the general direction of Istanbul. However, it is worth exercising your imaginative talents a little to remember that you are following one of the oldest strategic routes in history. The Thracians and Macedonians, the Romans and Byzantines, the Slavs, Bulgarians, Crusaders, and Turks, all passed this way and the pity of it is that they were all so successful in destroying what went before. A few traces remain but nothing really worth stopping for—except perhaps the underground Church of the Holy Virgin at Pazardjik with its gloriously carved iconostasis—until you reach Plovdiv.

Plovdiv

As Bulgaria's second largest city, a major industrial center, and site of two of the most important trade fairs in the Balkans each spring and fall, it might seem unlikely that Plovdiv would have much in the way of character. But it most certainly does—and it has rather more to show for its extreme antiquity than most Bulgarian cities. Here stood the Pulpudeva of the Thracians, the Philippopolis of Philip II of Macedonia, the Trimontium of the Romans and the Filibé of the Turks. Here, too, was the scene of terrible slaughter after the 1876 uprising against the Turks.

The situation on several hills on the banks of the Maritsa River was one of the attractions, as noted by Lamartine when he traveled this way in 1833, for this is a truly commanding position from which to control the Thracian Plain. The old part of the town scrambles over the hillier southern side of the river and, on one of the three eminences that made up the Roman town of Trimontium, you will find Thracian foundations upon which Roman walls were superimposed. For other relics of those remoter times, you must visit the museums of which there are several worth attention. But of the Plovdiv of Ottoman times and, especially, of that famed National Revival period, there is plenty to be seen among the narrow twisting cobbled streets of the old district.

The bulging upper storeys of these old color-washed façades and their overhanging eaves come close to meeting over some of the narrower alleys. Some of the finest examples are: the Georgiadi House (now housing the Museum of National Liberation), the Koyumdjioglu House (now the National Ethnographic Museum), Nedkovich House and the Alphonse de Lamartine Museum (in the house in which that prominent French literary man recovered from an indisposition while journeying from Istanbul); and you will make plenty of other discoveries of your own. Two 15th-century mosques—Djumaya Djamiya and Imaret Djamiya—and a handsome clock tower are Ottoman legacies to note. The three most interesting churches—St. Constantine and St. Helena, St. Marina and the Church of the Virgin—are all from the 19th century, but again contain good examples of National Revival art. If this period seems to crop up rather frequently in these pages, it must be realized that there was no Bulgarian art prior to this, until you go back to the days of the Second Kingdom. The National Ethnographic Museum and the National Archaeological Museum are both rewarding, the latter housing especially fine treasures, including a fabulous wine set of nine pieces in solid gold known as the Panagurishte Gold Treasure; they date from the late 4th century BC and depict scenes from Greek mythology.

MISSED THIS

Mountains and Spas

The road east from Plovdiv leads across the Thracian plain, either via Stara Zagora and Sliven to the coast or, southeast, via Haskovo into Turkey. The roads south of Plovdiv take you right into the Rhodope Mountains. Beyond Assenovgrad—a tobacco and wine center—you pass through a fine stretch of the Chepelarska River gorge, its entrance dominated by the medieval ruins of Assen's Fortress and the well-preserved Church of the Virgin of Petrich. A few miles further on, a road to the left leads shortly to the second largest—and one of the finest—of Bulgaria's monasteries: that of Bachkovo, founded in 1083. Most of the buildings are from the 17th century or later, but in the oldest surviving Church of the Trinity, a short distance east of the monastery, some important frescoes from the 12th to 14th centuries have survived. National Revival art is also represented in the small church of St. Nicholas, the work of Zahari Zograf, including a notable *Last Judgment*.

The Rhodopes are dotted with spas and one of them, about 30 miles (48 km) further, is also a winter sports center whose reputation has spread far beyond Bulgaria's boundaries. This is Pamporovo, about 50 miles (80 km) south of Plovdiv at an altitude of 5,250 feet (1,600 meters). It's a lovely setting in summer too, even if you are perfectly healthy. Its advantage over its chief rival Borovets (in the Rila mountains) is its more open aspect, with wide meadows adding a dimension of spaciousness to the forested slopes. Walkers and climbers will find it a good starting point for their activities.

To the west of the Rhodopes are the two fine mountain groups which fill most of the southwest corner of Bulgaria: Pirin bordering on to northern Greece and, to the north of them, Rila which gives its name to Bulgaria's most famous monastery. The E20, which provides speedy access to them from Sofia, curves round Vitosha mountain on its way south and soon enters a rolling agricultural countryside, rich in orchards and misty with their blossoms in spring. Indeed, in the plains of the Struma valley to the west of here, the town of Kyustendil is the

heart of Bulgaria's main fruit-growing area. It has had the usual chequered history, stretching back as far as the Thracians. The Romans,
notably the Emperor Trajan, made good use of the warm mineral
springs, which have now made this one of the country's most popular
thermal resorts. You are aware of a strong Turkish influence here, and
though not on the usual tourist circuit, it has a pleasing atmosphere.
The Zemen Monastery, a circuitous drive to the north, has some unusually bold 14th-century frescoes, typical of the Macedonian school that
flourished in west Bulgaria at that time. You can also reach Zemen
more directly by train from Kyustendil through the impressive defile
carved out by the Struma river.

The latter flows southeast and the E20 soon joins it all the way to
the Greek border. By then it has already passed through industrial
Stanke Dimitrov, a main center for the production of tobacco, a crop
which is very much in evidence in these parts. In summer you will see
large quantities of that 'pernicious weed' drying on wooden racks along
the roadside and in every village. Wine is another important local
product.

A few miles east of Stanke Dimitrov, the spa of Sapareva Banya has
the distinction of producing the hottest and most sulphurous mineral
water in Bulgaria (over 100°C/212°F). Fifteen miles further east, Thracian and Roman traces are to be seen at Samokov, and a brilliantly
decorated mosque (now a museum). Above all, however, this small
town was a major center for the dissemination of National Revival art.
The Samokov school of painting, for example, is of great importance
in Bulgarian art history. It was founded by Hristo Dimitrov, whose son
Zahari Zograf was one of its most gifted exponents; his works embellish
monasteries and churches throughout the country. The Samokov
master woodcarvers acquired a considerable reputation; the iconostasis
in the monastery church of Rila is among their creations, as is the
splendid one in the Church of the Virgin in Samokov.

A Stronghold of Bulgarian Art

It is only a short drive from here to Borovets, the country's oldest
and most famous mountain resort, lying at about 4,300 feet (1,310
meters) on the northern slopes of the Rila Mountains. You can reach
it more directly (44 miles/71 km) from Sofia via the upper Iskar gorge
and lake to Samokov. On the way you pass Pancharevo, a small lake
with sports facilities, while lake Iskar (also offering water sports) is the
largest in Bulgaria. In Samokov there is a rather charming mosque,
rebuilt in the late 18th century in National Revival style; rather like a
private house with a minaret tacked on. This is the only sight of interest
in this small town, once famous for its craftsmen and painters. Prince
Ferdinand built three palaces and a hunting lodge in Borovets at the
turn of the century, and these were subsequently followed by the villas
of nobles and high officials, now mainly trade union holiday homes.
Together with the hotels they are scattered about the deep pine forests
that clothe these mountain slopes. It is an excellent walking center and
has now become well known in the West as a reasonably priced winter

sports resort. This is the most convenient point for the ascent of Mount Musala (9,564 feet/2,917 m), the highest in the Balkan peninsula.

To reach the Rila Monastery you must continue further south on E20, turning off for the village of Kocherinovo. The Rila Mountains soar into the sky ahead of you, making a really splendid backdrop to the tobacco fields and pasture-land that surround this village, which is also known for its prodigious population of storks, their nests adorning most of the village roofs. The approach to the monastery is through a steep, forested valley; watched over by its encirclement of mountains, it is easy to understand how the founders of Rila found the peace and beauty they sought for their spiritual pursuits, and also how, remote from the ravages of power struggles, it remained a stronghold of Bulgarian art and learning during the dark centuries of Ottoman rule.

The group of buildings, fortress-like in their compactness, stands at 3,760 feet (1,147 m). The monastery was founded in the 10th century by Ivan of Rila or Rilski. After damage by avalanche and fire, it was rebuilt on its present site in the 14th century by Hrelyu, a feudal overlord, who also built a church and a tower. Alas, the centuries took their toll. Rila may have been largely spared the onslaught of weapons, but it did not escape that ubiquitous destroyer of so many ancient buildings, fire. On several occasions the silent mountains witnessed the depredations of the flames and, in 1833, the greatest of them all destroyed virtually everything. A notable exception was the tower that Hrelyu built, which stands today, its rugged stonework contrasting with the arcaded elegance of the great complex that surrounds it. The money for the reconstruction of the monastery was collected from all over the country, coinciding with the potent impulses of the National Revival movement of which it is such a grand example. The foremost masters of the Samokov, Bansko and Debar schools of painting and woodcarving are represented in the monastery church, including the brothers Zahari and Dimitur Zograf. The monks had also established a printing press here, and the monastery library houses 16,000 volumes, many of great value, though at present it is open only to specialists.

Much of the rest of the complex, however, has been turned into a museum featuring old icons, frescoes, Hrelyu's 14th-century throne and tombstone, some ancient manuscripts, and a collection of objects in gold and silver. The monk's cells have been turned into guest rooms.

There are 14 small churches and chapels in the surroundings of the monastery with wall paintings from the 15th and 17th centuries. One of them is the little Church of St Luke, 2½ miles (4 km) east of the present monastery, close to the simple monastic cell first established by Ivan of Rila. The saint's tomb is also here. Rila Monastery is also an excellent starting point for a number of climbs to peaks 8,500–9,000 feet (2,592–2,745 m) high.

A Peaceful Backwater

Continuing south on E20 along the Struma valley you pass through the industrial town of Blagoevgrad, and soon the Pirin mountains replace those of Rila on your left. You won't find many tourist hordes around here, but there are some places to see towards the Greek border as well as some fine scenery. One is the spa town of Sandanski, just off the main road, whose Thracian and Roman origins have left a number of relics. Another is the little town of Melnik, a few miles east of the main road down towards the Greek border. It can claim to be Bulgaria's smallest town and, set amidst eroded sandstone cliffs, it is also one of its most picturesque. Many Greeks took refuge here in the Middle Ages. Once a fortress, then a feudal capital, later a major trade center, it suffered badly in the Balkan Wars and is now content to be a peaceful backwater that attracts an artistic set. A few miles up into the mountains to the east lies Rozhen Monastery. Founded in the 14th century, it retains a finely carved iconostasis from that period. The church dates from 1600, with mural paintings from 1732.

PRACTICAL INFORMATION FOR INLAND BULGARIA

WHEN TO COME. Late spring, summer and early autumn are the best times for these landscapes combining plains and mountains, remembering that summers can be very warm in the valleys and plains. There is much lovely spring blossom and, in the famous Valley of Roses, May and early June are the peak times for the harvesting of millions of blooms. Bulgaria's increasing winter sports amenities are attracting growing numbers to the mountains from January through March.

GETTING AROUND. Ideally by self-drive car. Otherwise, there is a selection of organized tours. Rail or bus services between them cover all parts of the country, if you can sort out the timetables.

HOTELS AND RESTAURANTS. The establishments listed below are classified according to price. An unusual form of accommodation is additionally offered by some of Bulgaria's lovely old monasteries, which have guest rooms available; a list may be obtained from Balkantourist.

ASSENOVGRAD. Assenovets (M).

BANSKO. Pirin (M)

BELOGRADCHIK. Belogradchishki skali (M).

BLAGOEVGRAD. Alen Mak (M).

BOROVETS. Musala, Bor (E); Edelweis (M); folk restaurant in Bor Hotel. A new Novotel with ski school and other sports facilities is under construction.

GABROVO. Balkan, Yantra (M).

HISARYA. Balneosanatoria Augusta (E).

KALOFER. Roza (M).

KARLOVO. Rozova Dolina (M).

KAZANLUK. Kazanluk (E), recent; **Roza, Zornitsa** (M).

KOPRIVSHTITSA. Barikadite, Koprivshtitsa (I). Rooms are also available
in some of the beautiful restored old houses, and there are several attractive folk
restaurants.

KYUSTENDIL. Pautaliya (E); **Hisarluka** (M).

MELNIK. Melnik (M).

PAMPOROVO. Mourgavets, Perelik (E); **Orpheus, Panorama, Prespa,
Rozhen, Snezhanka** (all M).

PAZARDJIK. Trakiya (M).

PLEVEN. Pleven (E); **Rostov-na-Don, Kailuka** (M).

PLISKA. Motel (I).   ✗ stayed here

PLOVDIV. Novotel Plovdiv (E), Interhotel, 319 rooms, 9 suites, night club,
indoor and open air pools, saunas, near Fair grounds and across river from city
center; **Trimontium** (E-M), Interhotel, 177 rooms, 4 suites, disco, very central;
Leningrad (M); **Bulgaria, Maritsa,** and **Leiptsig** are all (M-I).
   Restaurants. Attractive folk restaurants are **Pldin** (E), **Alafrangues,** and
Trakiyski Stan (both M).

RILA. Rilets (M); near the famous monastery, in the mountains of the same
name.

RUSE. Largest port on Danube. **Riga** (E-M), Interhotel, 178 rooms, 9 suites,
night club; **Dunav** (M), Interhotel, 111 rooms, 7 suites, disco.

SANDANSKI. Spartak (E, M).

SHUMEN. Madara (E); recently restored.
   Restaurant. Peti Kilometer (M); on the main road on the outskirts of town,
and good value.

SLIVEN. Sliven (M).

SOPOT. Stara Planina (I).

STARA ZAGORA. Bavaria, newer part (E), otherwise (M); **Vereya, Zelez-
nitsa** (M); **Moskva** (I).

SVISHTOV. Dunav, Kaleto (I).

TRYAVNA. Ralitsa (M).

VELIKO TURNOVO. Former capital and museum city in the mountains. **Veliko Turnovo** (E), Interhotel, 192 rooms, 9 suites, disco, pool, saunas, new; **Etur** (M), and **Yantra** (I), with a stunning view across river to Tsarevets; **Motel** (I).

VELINGRAD. Zdravets (E).

VIDIN. Rovno, Bononia (M).

VRATSA. Hemus (M); **Balkan** (I).

USEFUL ADDRESSES. There is a Balkantourist office in most towns and resorts. The following apply to the city of **Plovdiv.** Tourist Information, 39 Vassil Kolarov St; Motorists' Union, 129 Georgi Dimitrov Blvd; Railway Bureau, 13 Gurko St; Balkan Bulgarian Airlines, 4 Sasho Dimitrov St.

THE BLACK SEA COAST

Space to Spare

The Black Sea coast has been known to traders and invaders since the earliest days of recorded history. Thracians, Greeks and Romans were here; and the Vikings, who had reached the Black Sea a little further north via the river Dnieper, must have seen the self-same beaches from their vessels bound for Constantinople. The Bulgarians, Byzantines, and Ottoman Turks tussled over possession of the ports of this strategic strip. Exquisite churches were built in the name of less worldly conquests. Finally tourism arrived, a large, ever-growing, eminently peaceful kind of new invasion.

There is no denying that it is all very new. In the days before World War II those who found their way to these beaches were the adventurous or the privileged few. The latter would have had their own property here, since except in the ports there were no hotels. The great white modern buildings that you see now would have been as alien to the local people as the private villas of the rich. In those days too, the coast was also infested with snakes, although thankfully they are no longer a hazard. The problem was solved, so the story goes, by importing an army of hedgehogs which devoured them before being sold off themselves as pets!

From the point of view of sun, sand and scenery, the coast is well served. The resorts of Slunchev Bryag (Sunny Beach), and Zlatni Pyassatsi (Golden Sands), are both well named. When it comes to beaches, this is an ideal family coast and, visually, it lacks the flatness of neighboring Romania, for here the last hills of the Balkan Range and Strandja Mountains stretch down to the sea.

The Northern Section

If you come in via Romania from the north, you soon meet the mountains, and come to Shabla. Don't turn off for the coast here or you will find yourself in Bulgaria's only oil fields. A little to the south, the small resort of Ruzalka sits by the sea beneath the hills. The rocky peninsula of Cape Kaliakra, just to the south of it, has perpendicular cliffs pierced by caves and was made into a formidable stronghold in medieval times. The cape is also the home of Bulgaria's only colony of seals.

Back on the main road, Kavarna is the first small town in Bulgaria followed, a few miles later, by Balchik. Before the Second World War, this was still part of Romania and a fashionable resort. Romania's Queen Marie built herself a summer villa here, in Oriental style, its gardens sharply terraced into the natural cliffs. Nowadays, the villas that were once the holiday homes of the Romanian aristocracy provide a recreational setting for Bulgaria's writers, artists, scientists, and various trade unions and institutes.

Only a few miles further is the first and newest of the coast's modern resorts. This is Albena, and very modern it is, too, its pyramidical architectural styles recreating the National Revival style of the 18th and 19th centuries with a futuristic injection of the 1970s and 80s. Fine beaches are caught between the curving hillsides. It's a young resort—and has definite youth appeal.

Famous Zlatni Pyassatsi (Golden Sands) comes next, with 2 miles (3 km) of sands backed by wooded slopes—and a plethora of hotels of every shape and size. There are all the usual sports and entertainment facilities, but an 'extra' here is the natural warm water mineral springs which feed the public swimming pools. One of Bulgaria's oldest monasteries, the Aladja Rock Monastery, has been chipped out of the rocks only a few miles from here. It dates from the 6th century.

The next resort—Drouzhba (meaning Friendship)—began developing in the mid-1950s and can thus claim the distinction of being Bulgaria's oldest Black Sea resort, as well as having its most truly luxurious hotel. This is another place blessed with beneficial mineral springs and there is rather a nice story about their accidental discovery. In 1947 a search for oil was in hand on the principle that, since neighboring Romania was well endowed with the stuff, there seemed every good reason to anticipate sources here too. Instead of striking oil, they struck clear, natural warm mineral water. Not a great deal of attention was paid to it for some years until some Austrians, who had been making good use of it, spoke enthusiastically of the beneficial effects it was having on their rheumatism and announced that it was making their hair grow!

The luxury hotel mentioned is the Grand Hotel Varna. It opened in 1977, was constructed by a Swedish company and completely furnished and equipped by Scandinavian firms. Apart from its elegance, the Varna has some very sophisticated balnealogical equipment and can offer all kinds of hydrotherapy under medical supervision. Other facilities are listed in the hotels section, but even if you prefer a more modest holiday base it is worth having a look at the happy results of this piece of Balkan–Scandinavian cooperation. As a resort, Drouzhba benefits from the proximity of Golden Sands and its amenities while retaining its own calm and intimate character.

Varna

Only a few miles south of Drouzhba you come to Bulgaria's third largest city and major port: Varna (population, about 250,000), whose modern appearance belies its great age. Recent finds in the area include copper and superbly worked gold objects—perhaps the oldest in the world—dating back to around 4,300 BC, or 1,500 years older than anything comparable elsewhere. Later, as far back as the 12th century BC, a Thracian tribe of farmers and shepherds had their dwellings around the nearby lakes. Greek colonists from Asia Minor founded the city in the 6th-century BC and called it Odessos. Later it became a major trading center in this part of the Roman Empire. By AD 681, it was Varna—and Bulgarian.

Varna's medieval heyday came during the Second Bulgarian Kingdom in the 13th and 14th centuries and, if you give your imagination a polish, you might visualize the ships of those days setting off for Constantinople, Genoa, Venice and Ragusa (now Dubrovnik). In 1393, the city was captured by the Turks and for five centuries was a major Ottoman stronghold against periodical attack by Christian armies. In contrast, during the Crimean War, Turkey's allies—including Britain —had their headquarters here for a while.

Under the Turks trade flourished once more, and Varna's importance as a modern port was foreshadowed in 1866, when they opened the first railway of their still extensive empire linking Varna with Ruse on the Danube. It only needs a quick glance at the map of Europe to see the importance of this link between the Black Sea and central and western Europe. As a railway terminus, Varna has considerable significance and is not lacking in interest to railway fanatics and seekers of scenic travel. Two routes link it with Sofia, one through the Valley of Roses and the other across north Bulgaria, approaching the capital through the splendid Iskar Gorge. Regular hydrofoils serve the coastal towns and resorts, and this is a regular port of call on Black Sea cruise itineraries.

Present-day Varna has mainly been built since the turn of the century and most of its interesting historical items are contained in museums. These include the excellent Archaeological Museum whose four sections range from pre-history to the days of Ottoman rule; and the National Revival Museum, among whose most notable items are some original manuscript pages from Païssi's 18th-century Slav–Bulgarian history that played such a predominant role in prodding the Bulgarians into national consciousness. There are some interesting documents, too, relating to the Russo–Turkish War of 1877–78. Opposite the entrance to the port there's a Roman bath and, a few blocks away, Roman Thermae. Worth seeing is the Church of the Virgin by the market in the main square; its iconostasis dominates the tiny interior.

Of the modern city, the most pleasant area is around the verdant Marine Gardens from which you get fine views over the whole Bay of Varna. The gardens also contain a rather good aquarium devoted to the flora and fauna of the Black Sea and, not far away, the Naval Museum, which will appeal if you'd like to know more about the early days of navigation on both the Danube and the Black Sea. Finally, Varna is the main center for cultural and congressional activities along the coast, and there is good music and opera, especially during the annual 'Varna Summer' international music festival.

West of the city lies Varna Lake, linked by a canal to the sea, and in the same direction, 10 miles (16 km) along the road to Sofia is a fascinating curiosity aptly named Pobiti Kamuni (the Stone Forest). The first to ponder about this strange place was a British Officer by name of Captain Spratt, stationed in the area during the Crimean War, and well he might have wondered at these scattered groups of round stone trunks up to 17 feet (5 meters) high, and one to 10 feet thick. They are thought to be a kind of maritime stalagmite formed on the ancient sea bed in remote geological times when this was the bottom of the Lutsian Sea.

South of Varna

The stretch of coast immediately south of Varna has not yet been developed except for camp sites and small tourist complexes mainly catering for domestic tourism. There are splendid views of the city from the new bridge that carries the main road southwards out of Varna. The road curves inland initially, winding through the wooded hills that form one of the three terminal arms of the Balkan range, and crossing the Kamchiya river. A minor road leads to the mouth of this, and the fine adjoining beaches, which are now in the early stages of a major development program. The banks of this estuary, with its several arms, are almost tropical in their lushness, rich in flora and bird life. Ancient trees, some of them submerged in the water, weave dense curtains of foliage, reeds crowd the banks and water lilies drift on the surface. To get a full idea of this jungle-like profusion, allow time to take one of the boat excursions that are arranged throughout the area.

If you want to try Bulgarian yoghourt *(Kiselo mliako)* at its home-made best, there is a small restaurant called Poda specializing in it on the main road just north of the river. The main road returns towards the sea just before Ozbor, a small resort, popular among the Bulgarians, founded by the Greeks and still displaying the fragments of a Roman Temple of Jupiter. There are ruins of a Roman and a medieval Bulgarian fortress in the vicinity. Then the road crosses the bulge of Cape Emona (worth the short detour for the splendid views) before descending on to one of the most famous of all Bulgaria's resorts.

Slunchev Bryag (Sunny Beach) is the resort par excellence for families. It has wide, safe beaches, amenities with every kind of youngster appeal and, not forgetting the parents, offers various baby-sitting and child-minding services. The resort is spread out over a wide area, so those who are addicted to popping in and out of the sea at frequent intervals should make sure of a hotel with a beach-side location. There are plenty enough of these, as well as beach-side restaurants. Despite its size and popularity, the layout of Sunny Beach leaves no impression of crowding; hotels are well spaced out and there are plenty of gardens and green spaces. If your taste runs to the old and quaint, this is not a resort for you—nor indeed are any of the others. You would do better to find rooms in one of the small fishing towns.

An Ancient Trading Center

Sunny Beach does, however, have the advantage of being very close to Nessebur and it would be hard to find anything older and more interesting than this. Indeed, in terms of interest it is the sight of the Bulgarian coast. Clustered on a rocky peninsula just south of Sunny Beach and reached by a narrow causeway, this picture postcard of a place is peppered with ancient churches, of which the oldest is from the 5th century and the 'newest' from the 17th century. Greek colonists founded it as a trading center 25 centuries ago. They called it Mesembria and thus it was known throughout successive empires—notably the Romans under whom it became a backwater on the fringes of the empire, and the Byzantines who built the first of its churches and turned it into a fortified outpost of their Black Sea possessions. It was finally incorporated into Bulgarian territory by the redoubtable Khan Krum in 812. Happily, after falling to the Turks in 1453, Nessebur was granted a number of privileges, and allowed to keep its churches.

What the coastal resorts lack in antiquity, old Nessebur more than makes up for. You won't find any blocks of concrete and glass here, but houses mainly in the National Revival style huddled along the narrow cobbled streets and punctuated by the ancient churches in various stages of preservation. These can be divided into four groups. The earliest from the 5th and 6th centuries are the Old Metropolitan Church and the larger so-called Basilica on the Seashore. A second group dates from the 10th or 11th centuries and includes the rather well-preserved St. John the Baptist and St. Stephen's Church, also known as the New Metropolitan Church, in which there are some particularly good frescoes. The largest group dates from the 13th and 14th centuries and is characterized by cream-colored stone interspersed with layers and decoration in slim red brick—a typical artistic style of that period of Bulgarian–Byzantine architecture which reached its peak here in Nessebur. The five best churches in this group are those of the Pantokrator, St. John Aliturgetos (the best of all), Archangels Michael and Gabriel, and St. Paraskeva. The final group of less interest is from Ottoman times, the 16th and 17th centuries.

Inevitably, this is a popular sightseeing destination. The highrise buildings of modern tourism prod the sky just across the water and excursion buses come in droves from all along the coast at the height of the season. To see it at its best then, you want to be there early in the morning or, better still, rent a room in the old town.

Bulgaria's Salt Center

The next town, Pomorie, similarly clusters on a point and it, too, was founded very early as a Greek colony, Anhialo, which became a serious threat to neighboring Mesembria. Under the Romans it fared rather better and prospered as the administrative center of the area. In contrast to present-day Nessebur, it has little visual appeal, but it does have some extremely effective mud which is extracted from the adjoining lake for the relief of arthritis and sciatica. The local balneosanatorium is one of the largest in Bulgaria. Pomorie is also the center of a major wine-growing area (try the white *dimyat*) but, most important of all, it's the center for the nation's salt production. The local salt pans may be of interest to bird watchers, as indeed will be other salt-water stretches along this coast.

Bourgas comes next—Bulgaria's second main port on the Black Sea and the largest town on this southern section. It specializes in oil refineries and fast-growing industries of many kinds, and the wisest plan is not to get involved with it at all—though in fairness, it should be said that it has a very fine beach.

Little-Known Treasures

Bulgaria's southernmost section of Black Sea coast is, as yet, little developed though there are plenty of camping sites and private lodgings available. Well on the way to being discovered is the fishing port of Sozopol, on a small cape about 20 miles (32 km) south of Bourgas. Indeed, it is very picturesque with its old houses in the National Revival style and no modern architecture allowed to intrude. It's a popular haunt for Bulgarian and, increasingly, foreign writers and artists. This was the ancient Apollonia, oldest of all the Greek colonies founded in 610 BC and a great rival to Mesembria (Nessebur). A huge statue of Apollo was erected in honor of the sun god in 460 BC. Unlike Mesembria, Apollonia put up a fight against Rome and got sacked for its pains in AD 72. Apollo's splendid statue was part of the booty and, to see it, you must now go to the Capitol in Rome.

South of Sozopol, you come to the hills of Bulgaria's southern boundary range, the Strandja Mountains, that slip across the border into Turkey. The Ropotamo river flows down from these to the sea only a few miles south of Sozopol and has some of the same jungle-like qualities of the Kamchiya already mentioned, though on a smaller and less impressive scale. Boat trips are also available through its leafy waters.

Beyond, the coast continues in a series of rocky cliffs and sandy coves as yet untouched by mass tourism, though there are camp sites and some holiday homes and, most notably, the big international youth center of Primorsko. Near the small fishing and commercial town of Michurin, the main road turns inland to cross the hills into Turkey. A minor road continues along the coast to service a handful of communities such as Ahtopol, Bulgaria's picturesque southernmost town, and finally the village of Rezovo, facing neighboring Turkey, across the little Rezovo river.

PRACTICAL INFORMATION FOR THE BLACK
SEA COAST

 WHEN TO COME. In summer for the liveliest entertainments program and cultural events; spring and autumn for less crowds. Many hotels close in winter, but prices are very reasonable in those that don't. It can be very hot in high summer; winters are relatively mild and dry.

 GETTING AROUND. There are plenty of excursion possibilities by road or by sea along the coast, either organized or using regular services. Note the boat trips on the Kamchiya river. Self-drive cars are readily available and, in some cases, bicycles.

 HOTELS AND RESTAURANTS. An ambitious hotel construction program has equipped the main resorts with comfortable modern facilities ranging from deluxe through second class. Some hotels stay open year round, offering substantial reductions in winter. Rooms in private homes are available for those interested in closer contact with the local lifestyle. Small villas and bungalows are also for hire through Balkantourist.

The coastal resorts cater admirably for families; there are excellent discounts for children. As there is a large number of hotels in each resort, the following is only a selection. For the moment no more hotels are planned in existing resorts in order to avoid overcrowding, but older hotels are progressively being renovated.

ALBENA. Near the beach, **Orlov** and **Dorostor** are (E). Among those on the beach and all in a row are **Nona, Borvana** and **Elitsa** (M).

Restaurants. Slavianski Kt and **Neptun Tavern** are (M). Restaurants with cabarets include **Arabella** (E), on board a frigate, and **Gorski Tsar** (E).

BOURGAS. **Interhotel Bulgaria** (E) has 210 rooms and suites; **Primorets** is (M).

DROUZHBA. **Grand Hotel Varna** (L), Swedish-built Interhotel, is the best on the coast, with 296 rooms, 37 suites, night club, indoor and outdoor pools, saunas, varied sports facilities and full amenities. Not far from the beach, **Tchaika** (E); **Prostor** and **Rubin** (M).

Restaurants include **Bulgarska Svatba** (M), **Manastirska Izba** (I) and **Mehana Chernomorets** (I).

POMORIE. **Pomorie** (E) is a spa hotel.

SLUNCHEV BRYAG (Sunny Beach). Particularly well-equipped for children, the resort consists of a number of hotel complexes, each with several hotels, restaurants, shops, and other amenities. **Cuban, Tchaika, Bourgas, Nessebur,** and **Globus** are (E). **Amphibia, Fregata, Rila,** and **Sirena,** (M). **Astoria, Maritsa, Sozopol** and **Zornitsa** are classed as (I).

Restaurants include **Hanska Shatra** (about 3 miles/5 km. up in the hills with a folk and variety program); **Picnic** (about 8 miles/13 km. north, with fire dancing and barbecue); **Bchvata,** and **Vyatrna Melnitsa** (above the resort) are all (M). **Churchura** is (I). Restaurants with taverns are **Neptune, Strandja** and **Lazour** (on the beach), all (I). Several other beach-side restaurants include **Ribarska Hiza** (fish), and **Rusalka** and **Zlatna Jabalka,** both with disco.

VARNA. Historic Black Sea port. **Tchero More** (E), Interhotel, 220 rooms, 4 suites, night club, new and well-sited near Marine Gardens. **Odessa** (M).

ZLATNI PYASSATSÍ (Golden Sands). Resort with wide-ranging facilities. **International** (L-E), modern, night club, indoor pool, equipped for balneotherapy.

SPORTS FACILITIES. In addition to sea bathing, a number of hotels have swimming pools. Tennis, minigolf, horse riding, cycling, water skiing, sailing and surfing can all be enjoyed at one or more of the resorts.

USEFUL ADDRESSES. There is a Balkantourist Office in most towns and resorts. The following addresses apply to the city of **Varna.** Balkantourist, 3 Moussala St., 33 Avram Gachev St., 5 Tolbukhin St. and 73 Lenin Blvd; Balkan Bulgarian Airlines, 2 Shipka St., Shipka Agency, 10 Kliment St.

TOURIST VOCABULARY

Unlike the tourist vocabularies for the other four countries in this book, we have not included a column giving the phrases in original Bulgarian. This is because Bulgarian *(bulgarski)* is written in *Cyrillic,* an alphabet almost identical to that used in Russia, and we felt that it was better to give phrases intended for immediate use in their most assimilable form.

However, since you will see Cyrillic written in Bulgaria, here is the alphabet with the approximate English equivalent for each letter.

Bulgarian letter	transcription	Bulgarian letter	transcription
А, а	a	П, п	p
Б, б	b	Р, р	r
В, в	v	С, с	s
Г, г	g	Т, т	t
Д, д	d	У, у	u
Е, е	e	Ф, ф	f
Ж, ж	zh	Х, х	kh
З, з	z	Ц, ц	ts
И, и	i	Ч, ч	ch
Й, й	y	Ш, ш	sh
К, к	k	Щ, щ	sht
Л, л	l	Ъ, ъ	û
М, м	m	Ю, ю	yu
Н, н	n	Я, я	ya
О, о	o	ь	y ("soft sign")

Two points about the pronunciations below—the stressed syllables have been set in italic type; the 'a' is the same as the vowel in 'but'.

USEFUL EXPRESSIONS

Hello, how do you do	d*o*bur den
Good morning	dobr*o* outro
Good evening	d*o*bur v*e*cher
Goodnight	l*e*ka nosht
Goodbye	do vizhdane
Please	m*o*lya
Thank you	blagodary*a*
Thank you very much	mn*o*go
Yes	da
No	ne
You're welcome	ny*a*ma zasht*o*
Excuse me	izvin*e*te
Come in!	vl*e*ste
I'm sorry	sa-zhal-y*a*vam

My name is . . .   kazvam se . . .
Do you speak English?   govorite li angliyski?
I don't speak Bulgarian   ne govorya bulgarski
I don't understand   ne razbiram
Please speak slowly   molya, govorete bavno
Please write it down   molya vi se, napishete go
Where is . . . ?   ka-de e . . . ?
What is this place called?   kak se kazva tova myasto
Please show me   molya vi se, pokazhete mi
I would like . . .   bikh zhelal (a woman says bikh
                                              zhelala)

How much does it cost?   kolko struva

ARRIVAL

Passport check   pasporten kontrol
Your passport, please   molya, vashiya pasport
I am with the group   az sam-m s grupata
Customs   mitnitsa
Anything to declare   neshto za deklarirane
Nothing to declare   nishto za deklarirane
Baggage claim   bagazhna sluzhba
This suitcase is mine   tozi kufar e moy
A porter   nosach
  Transportation
  to the bus   na aftobusa
  to a taxi   taksito
  to the Hotel . . . , please   molya, vuh-f khotel-a

MONEY

Money   pari
The currency exchange office   bankata
Do you have change for this?   mozhete le da razvalite tova?
May I pay   mozhe li da se plashta
  with a traveler's check   sa-s chek
  with a voucher   sa-s-talon
  with this credit card   sus-s tazi kreditna karta
I would like to change some   bikh zhelal (zhelala) da smenya
  traveler's checks   nyakolko chekove

THE HOTEL

A hotel   khotel
I have a reservation   imam rezervirana staya
A room with a bath   staya sa-s banya
  a shower   dush
  a toilet   klozet
  hot running water   topla voda
What floor is it on?   na koy etazhe?
  ground floor   parter
  second floor   puh-rvi etazh
The elevator   asansyora
Have the baggage sent up, please   molya vi se, ispratete mi gore
                                              bagazha
The key to number . . . , please   klyucha na staya nomer . . .
Please call me at seven o'clock   sa-budete me vuf sedem chasa

Have the baggage brought down	donesete mi dolu bagazha
The bill	smetkata
A tip	bakshish

THE RESTAURANT

A restaurant	restorant
Waiter!	kelner
Waitress!	gospozhitse
The menu	kartata, menyuto
I would like to order this	bikh zhelal (zhelala) da pora-cham tova
Some more . . . , please	oshte malko
That's enough	stiga
The check, please	smetkata
Breakfast	zakuska
Lunch	obed
Dinner	vecherya
Bread	khlyap
Butter	maslo
Jam	marmelad
Salt	sol
Pepper	piper
Mustard	gorchitsa
Sauce, gravy	sos
Vinegar	otset
Oil	olio
Bottle	butilka
Wine	vino
Red, white wine	cherveno, byalo vino
Beer	bira
Water	voda
Mineral water	mineralna voda
Milk	mlyako
Coffee, with milk	kafe sa-s mlyako
Turkish	tursko kafe
Tea (with lemon)	chay (sa-s limon)
Chocolate	shokolat
Sugar	zakhar
Spirits	rakiya, slivovitsa (plum brandy)

(Further Bulgarian restaurant hints are given in the chapter on food and drink.)

MAIL

A letter	pismo
A postcard	poshtenska kartichka
An envelope	plik
A mailbox	poshtenska kutiya
The post office	poshtata
A stamp	marka
By airmail	vaz-dushna poshta
How much does it cost?	kolko struva
to send a letter	da se prati
a letter (a postcard) airmail to	pismo (poshtenska kartichka)
United States (Great Britain,	vazdushna poshta za

| Canada)? | suedinenite shtati (velikobritaniya, kanada) |
| to send a telegram, cable? | da se prati telegrama |

LOCATIONS

. . . Street	ulitsa
. . . Avenue	bulevart
. . . Square	ploshtat
The airport	letishteto
A bank	banka
The beach	plazh-a
The bridge	mosta
The castle	zamaka
The cathedral	katedralata
The church	cherkvata
The coffee house, café	kafeneto
The garden	gradinata
The hospital	bolnitsata
The movies, cinema	kinoto
a movie	film
The museum	muzeya
A nightclub	bar
The palace	dvoretsa
The park	parka
The station	garata
The theater	teata-ra
a play	piesa
The official travel bureau	Balkanturist
The university	universiteta

TRAVEL

| Arrival | pristigane |
| Departure | zaminavane |

The airplane	samolet
I want to reconfirm a reservation on flight number . . . for . . .	iskam da potva-rdya rezerviranoto myasto za . . .
Where is the check-in?	ka-de e kontrola
I am checking in for . . .	otivam za . . .
Fasten your seat belt	zakopchaite kolanuh

The railroad	zhepe
The train	vlaka
From what track does the train to . . . leave?	ot koi peron zaminava vlakat za . . . ?
Which way is the dining car?	na koya posoka e vagon-restorantat

Bus, streetcar	aftobus, tramvai
Does this bus go to . . . ?	otiva li tozi aftobus do . . . ?
trolley bus	troleibus
I want to get off at . . . Street at the next stop	iskam da sleza na . . . ulitsa na sledvashtata spirka

Taxi   tax*i*
I (we) would like to go to . . . ,   m*o*lya, *i*skam da ot*i*da (*i*skame da
    please   ot*i*dem) na . . .
Stop at . . .   spr*e*te na . . .
Stop here   tuk

NUMBERS

1	edin		20	dv*a*yset
2	dva		25	dv*a*yset i pet
3	tri		30	tr*i*set
4	ch*e*tiri		40	chet*i*riset
5	pet		50	pedes*e*t
6	shest		60	sh*e*yset
7	s*e*dem		70	sedemdes*e*t
8	*o*sem		80	osemdes*e*t
9	d*e*vet		90	devetdes*e*t
10	d*e*set		100	sto
11	edinayset		200	dv*e*sta
12	dvan*a*yset		300	tr*i*sta
13	trin*a*yset		400	ch*e*tiristotin
14	chetirin*a*yset		500	petstotin
15	petn*a*yset		600	sh*e*stostotin
16	shesn*a*yset		700	s*e*demstotin
17	sedemn*a*yset		800	*o*semstotin
18	osemn*a*yset		900	d*e*vetstotin
19	devetn*a*yset		1000	khil*y*ada

CZECHOSLOVAKIA

FACTS AT YOUR FINGERTIPS

Planning Your Trip

WHAT WILL IT COST. Despite recent increases in food prices, costs in Czechoslovakia are low by Western European standards. So however you choose to visit the country it should be possible to have a vacation for significantly less than in the West. But the least expensive way to visit, and in many ways the most convenient and sensible way, is to take a tour organized by Čedok, the Czechoslovak State Travel Bureau, or, if you prefer to travel independently, to buy vouchers before you leave for hotels, restaurants, gasoline etc. from Čedok or one of their accredited agencies. In both cases you avoid the necessity of having to comply with the minimum daily exchange regulations (currently 30 Deutschmarks per day or its equivalent in other foreign currencies), plus circumvent the problems caused by the acute shortage of accommodations. And if you take a package tour you will also be entitled to a very much more favorable rate of exchange, some 50% above the normal tourist exchange rate. But note that this does not apply to those with pre-paid vouchers only and that any Czechoslovak currency acquired at this special rate may not be reconverted to foreign currency. For further details of tours, pre-paid services and travel agents offering trips to Czechoslovakia, see *How to Go* below.

The unit of currency in Czechoslovakia is the crown or Koruna (Kčs) divided into 100 hellers or haléř. There are coins of 5, 10, 20 and 50 hellers and 1, 2 and 5 Kčs. There are notes of 10, 20, 50, 100 and 500 Kčs.

The rate of exchange at the time of writing (mid-1982) was about 10.30 Kčs to the US dollar and about 18.20 Kčs to the pound sterling. These rates will almost certainly change both before and during 1983. Foreign currency may be exchanged at all branches of the Czechoslovak State Bank, Čedok hotels and in Tuzex stores, but these last can only provide vouchers for use in other Tuzex stores.

You may import any amount of foreign currency into Czechoslovakia and export the balance provided the original amount was registered on arrival. The import and export of Czechoslovakian currency is not allowed. Traveler's checks and major credit cards are may be used to exchange currency and are accepted in the better hotels and restaurants.

All prices quoted are those of mid-1982. You should therefore allow for a slight increase for 1983.

A day's basic costs for two people might be:

Hotel (moderate), including breakfast	350 Kčs
Lunch, no wine	120
2 beers, 2 coffees	25
Transportation (2 bus trips, 1 taxi)	25
Dinner, with wine	200
Total	720

Sample Costs. Cinema seat 10–14 Kčs; good theater seat 30 Kčs; bottle of good Moravian wine 20–40 Kčs (in a store), 60–80 Kčs (in a good restaurant);

glass Scotch whiskey 35–50 Kčs; glass slivovice 12.50 Kčs; 20 cigarettes (best local) 12 Kčs, imported 25 Kčs (more in hotel kiosks and bars).

HOW TO GO. All foreign travel to Czechoslovakia is handled by Čedok, the Czechoslovak State Travel Bureau. Unlike the State Travel Offices of other East European countries, you may actually book tours to Czechoslovakia via Čedok as well as through the many travel agents officially accredited by them. A list of these travel agents is available from Čedok offices; they include many of the major agents both in the UK and the US. Both Čedok and travel agents are also able to supply pre-paid vouchers.

As well as the many offices they have within Czechoslovakia itself, Čedok has a number of offices overseas. Their addresses are:

In the US, 10 East 40th St., New York, NY 10016.

In the UK, 17–18 Old Bond St., London W1.

Sample costs for Čedok tours from the UK are: a 7-night stay in Prague with half board in a 4-star hotel, return flight, and a half-day sightseeing tour in high season is £255; in a 3-star hotel it is £239. A 14-night Grand Tour, with return flight, mostly full board in 3- and 4-star hotels, transport and entrance fees, is £459. A pleasantly flexible 6-night arrangement costing £163 ex-London (plus £10 in high season), covers return flight to Prague, a voucher to a local value of £48 towards the cost of accommodations and meals, and a half-day's sightseeing. This arrangement can be extended for up to one month at a cost of £7.50 per day, providing that it is booked prior to departure.

Within Czechoslovakia, Čedok owns and operates many hotels, organizes tours of all kinds, can arrange tickets for all kinds of transport, make reservations for cultural events, provide guides, and, in short, arrange more or less anything from a stay in a spa to a hunting trip. Among their tours are a 7-day Tour of Slovakia from Bratislava costing $300 with full board, transportation and guide services, and a 12-day Grand Tour of Czechoslovakia from Prague costing $585 for similar services. The cost of recommended tours depends on the number of participants, but possibilities include arrangements of varying duration to some of the lesser-known regions, as well as study tours catering for special interests or activities. There is also a series of recommended programs for motorists, either based on particular beauty or historic spots, or touring the countryside. Spa holidays with treatment are also arranged.

In addition to Čedok, a number of other travel organizations operate in particular spheres, but it is very important to realize that they are geared almost entirely to group travel and do not normally cater for individuals, except insofar as accommodations may be available in their establishments for independent travelers who happen to chance upon them when they are not fully booked. Their addresses are given under *Useful Addresses.* The principal organizations are:

Balnea caters exclusively for those following spa treatments and their companions, and runs a considerable number of sanatoria, some of them very modern and with highly sophisticated equipment. Many are in very beautiful settings. Balnea is concerned with spas in Bohemia and Moravia, and its counterpart, *Slovakoterma,* is concerned with those in Slovakia. Reservations at these sanatoria can be made through Čedok offices abroad.

CKM (Youth Travel Bureau) deals essentially with youth groups, runs its own hotels and rents other accommodation for such groups. A small percentage of this accommodation is reserved for independent travelers who are holders of

International Youth Hostels Federation cards and the most recent information on such accommodation may be had through your national YHA.

Sport-Turist, as its name suggests, concentrates on all kinds of sporting holidays, again for groups only.

Rekrea (Czech Union of Consumer Cooperatives) and *Tatratour,* its counterpart in Slovakia, collaborate with some overseas tour operators for individual travelers, but their main focus at present is arranging holiday or study tours of all kinds for groups.

CLIMATE. Czechoslovakia enjoys the extremes of a Continental climate: warm summers and cold winters, so conditions are ideal for outdoor activities appropriate to these seasons. May is a delightful month for fruit trees in blossom along almost every roadside, and blazing yellow mustard fields. This is also the time of the famous Prague Spring Music Festival. The fall offers the rewards of beautiful coloring in the many extensive woods. Since much of Czechoslovakia's fascination is historical, architectural and cultural, it can be enjoyed at any time. Though some monuments, especially castles, are closed in winter, this is a particularly lively time culturally in the cities.

Average maximum daily temperatures in degrees Fahrenheit and centigrade.

Prague	Jan.	Feb.	Mar.	Apr.	May	June	July	Aug.	Sept.	Oct.	Nov.	Dec.
F°	34	37	45	55	64	72	73	73	64	54	41	34
C°	1	3	7	13	18	22	23	23	18	12	5	1

SPECIAL EVENTS. Principal events are as follows. **April/May,** Flora Olomouc, flower show, Olomouc; **May,** Prague Spring Music Festival; Dvořák Music Festival, Příbram; Summer Theater in Castle grounds, Karlštejn and Konopiště (through August); **June,** Bratislava International Song Festival; Kmochův Kolín Festival of Brass Music, Kolín, Strážnice Folk Art Festival; **July,** International Puppet Festival, Chrudim; Brno Grand Prix Motor Rally; Karlovy Vary International Film Festival (biennial); **August,** International Festival of Dance, Telč; Flora Olomouc, flower show, Olomouc; **September,** Znojmo Wine Festival, Brno Music Festival, International Trade Fair, Brno; 'Dočesna' Hop Festival, Žatec; **October,** Bratislava International Music Festival; Pardubice Grand Steeplechase.

National Holidays. The principal national and religious holidays are Jan. 1; Easter Monday; May 1 (Labor Day); May 9 (Liberation Day); Dec. 25 and 26.

VISAS. In addition to a valid passport, residents of all Western European countries, North and South America and all Commonwealth countries require a visa to enter Czechoslovakia. These are not available at entry points and must be obtained in advance. Čedok offices, travel agents and Czechoslovakian consulates can all supply visas. It is advisable to apply some weeks in advance of your departure. Apart from the completed application form, you will be required to provide two passport sized photographs. There is a fee of approximately $12 for each visa application.

If you plan to stay with relatives or friends in Czechoslovakia, you must apply for your visa from a Czechoslovak embassy and must register with the police within 48 hours of arriving. Visas can be extended in Czechoslovakia.

HEALTH CERTIFICATES. These are not required to visit Czechoslovakia from any country.

MEDICAL INSURANCE. This is strongly advised for all travelers to Czechoslovakia. See page 16 in *Facts at Your Fingertips* for details of insurance schemes. Visitors from the UK benefit from a reciprocal agreement which insures a degree of free medical treatment, but they too are advised to take out medical insurance.

CUSTOMS. You may import duty-free into Czechoslovakia 250 cigarettes or the equivalent in tobacco; plus one liter of spirits and two liters of wine (for those over 18 only); plus ½ liter of perfume. You may also import any amount of foreign currency but must declare it on arrival or you will not be allowed to export the balance. You may neither import or export Czechoslovakian currency.

You are also permitted to import duty-free up to 600 Kčs worth of gifts and souvenirs. Clothing may be left duty-free. Purchases up to 300 Kčs may be freely exported. More valuable items, including articles from Tuzex (state-run stores that accept hard-currency only), may be exported duty-free, provided you have the bills. Note that crystal and cut glass items bought with local currency are subject to 100% duty and should be accompanied by an export permit.

Staying in Czechoslovakia

LANGUAGE. Czech and Slovak, both Slavic national tongues, are very similar. In Bohemia and Moravia, Czech is spoken by the Czechs and in Slovakia, Slovak. There are a lot of Hungarians in Slovakia and Poles in the northeast border regions who retain their national languages. Of western languages, German is the most readily understood and widely spoken. English is spoken by members of the travel industry, by staff at airports and leading city hotels; there is some French too.

HOTELS. Czechoslovakian hotels are officially classified from 5 to 1-stars. These ratings correspond closely to our gradings in the lists that follow as Deluxe (L) for 5-stars, Expensive (E) for 4-stars, Moderate (M) for 3- and 2-stars and Inexpensive (I) for 1-star. For indications of hotel prices, see the table below. Many hotels have rooms in more than one category, and only Deluxe, Expensive and Moderate hotels have rooms with private baths or showers. Bear in mind that in Moderate hotels these are likely to be the exception rather than the rule.

Older hotels are gradually being renovated to good effect, and it is quite possible that some of those listed in these pages will be undergoing this process at the time of your visit and either be temporarily closed or have improved their amenities. The best of these have great style and character. It is better however, not to expect the same standards of facilities and service as in equivalent categories in Western countries. The system is not usually geared to an army of bellhops or hovering waiters, and it can be difficult to get even a quiet cup of coffee after 10 P.M. in public rooms, even in some central Prague hotels. That said, prices compare very favorably with those of Western hotels.

Hotels are operated by various organizations, of which the most important from the tourist's point of view is Čedok. It cannot be emphasized too strongly that there is an acute shortage of accommodations in Czechoslovakia in the peak seasons and you will be very wise to pre-book.

Čedok's hotels are mainly in the top three categories and are known as Interhotels; they also run a number of motels similarly classified. In addition, they have an arrangement with municipal and other hotel/accommodation-operating organizations by which they can make reservations for their clients in their establishments.

Two people in a double room will pay approximately:

Deluxe (5-stars)	$88–154
Expensive (4-stars)	$40–74
Moderate (3- to 2-stars)	$28–62
Inexpensive (1-star)	$22–44

These prices include half-board and service. If you want a single room the price will probably be a little less than half those quoted above. Prices can be 15% higher in the peak season and as much as 40% lower in the off-season.

SELF-CATERING. Cottages or bungalows, usually with four beds, may be rented; cost per day is from $6.70–14.10. These are usually attached to motels or autocamps. Details from Čedok.

YOUTH HOSTELS. These do not exist in the western sense, but in summer, accommodations in various premises throughout the country are made available to youth organizations and a percentage of these are at the disposal of holders of International Youth Hostels Federation cards as listed in the IYHF handbook. Limited accommodations are available in student hostels, open summer only.

PRIVATE ACCOMMODATIONS. Availability is limited but bookings can be made through Pragotur, Staré, Město, U Obecniho domu, Prague 1.

CAMPING. A map marking and listing sites throughout the country, which are run by a number of organizations, is obtainable from Čedok, from whom pre-paid camping vouchers are also available. Otherwise the on-the-spot price range is from 15 Kčs per person per day in own tent or caravan, according to site category, plus a small charge per car or caravan in the better sites. These will have all the regular facilities, such as showers, cooking amenities, store, and in some cases small cabins for hire.

RESTAURANTS. The selection of restaurants is very wide, and there are some particularly attractive wine cellars *(vinárny)* and suitably down-to-earth beer taverns *(pivnice)* in some of which you can get snacks or even full meals, and in all of which you will find the Czechoslovaks indulging in their favorite pastime of talking. The self-service snack bar is an increasingly popular amenity in main towns and there is a scattering of small coffee bars where you can also eat at reasonable prices. Eating out is popular and it is wise to make reservations whenever possible; also check opening times, for some places close for part or all of the weekend.

We have divided restaurants in our listings into three categories: Expensive (E), Moderate (M) and Inexpensive (I). Prices for Expensive restaurants are from 120 to 200 Kčs, for Moderate restaurants from 60 to 100 Kčs and for Inexpensive restaurants from 20 to 50 Kčs. These prices are for one person only but include wine.

Hotel restaurants will mostly accept pre-paid meal vouchers which you can obtain before you leave. In Deluxe hotels these cost from $10 to 15, in Expensive hotels from $6 and in Moderate hotels from $3.50 to 4.50. These prices are also per person.

TIPPING. In popular restaurants, it is normal to round up the bill by 1–2 Kčs; 10% would be generous. In better restaurants add at least 10%. In restaurants, theaters and other public places there is usually a 0.40 Kčs cloak-room charge for leaving your coat and it is normal to give a little extra. For taxis add 1–2 Kčs to the fare; for hairdressers 5–10 Kčs. For porters at railroad stations, 2 Kčs per piece plus 1–2 Kčs. In theaters, round up cost of program to nearest Kč. Foreign currency or Tuzex vouchers would certainly be welcomed by anyone rendering you special service.

MAIL AND TELEPHONES. An airmail letter costs 6.60 Kčs, postcard 4.40 Kčs to the US; 3.60 Kčs and 2 Kčs to European countries. There is a 24-hour service at the main post office in Prague, Jindřišská Ulice 24, Nové Město.

In public phone booths (usually green with red windows) insert a 1 Kčs piece and dial. Long distance and international telephone calls are not something to be undertaken lightly in Czechoslovakia. They can be both time consuming and frustrating. Remember also that telephone calls from your hotel room will probably have a surcharge of between 200 and 300% added to them.

TIME. Czechoslovakia is seven hours ahead of Eastern Standard Time and two hours ahead of Greenwich Mean Time. In summer, the country is six hours ahead of Eastern Standard Time and one hour ahead of Greenwich Mean Time.

CLOSING TIMES. Shops generally open from 9–6, Mondays through Fridays (larger shops 9–8 on Thursdays), some closing on Saturdays, others open until noon and department stores until 4. Food stores open at 6 A.M. Banks are open 8–2, Monday through Friday. Museums, art galleries, and similar places of interest usually open from 9 or 10 to 4 or 5 and close on Mondays. Some museums and other monuments, especially castles, are open only in summer. Čedok can advise. It is also important to note that in recent years a considerable amount of restoration work has been in progress on buildings of historic interest, and it is possible that some places mentioned in these pages may be closed for some weeks or months, though where known, this has been indicated. Again Čedok can provide the latest information.

SHOPPING. For tourists in Czechoslovakia, shopping tends to center upon Tuzex where only hard currency or its equivalent in Tuzex coupons is accepted. The Tuzex head office is at Rytířská 13, Prague 1, and it has branches all over Prague, including in some main hotels, as well as all over the country, in large towns, spas, and resorts. In the larger shops you can buy all kinds of imported goods from the West, including liquor, cigarettes, and everything from tools to transistor radios; you will also find some of the best national souvenirs, such as Bohemian glass and crystal, peasant pottery, porcelain, wooden folk carvings, hand-embroidered clothing, and food items. Tuzex coupons will make a welcome gift to Czech friends or anyone who has been particularly helpful. An up-to-date list of Tuzex outlets can be obtained from the head office of Čedok.

In addition, there are a number of excellent shops specializing in glass and crystal, and various associations of Czechoslovak artists and craftsmen run their own retail outlets. In these you pay in local currency and some of their addresses are given under *Shopping* for Prague. Here, too, you will find the addresses of some of the main department stores where you can buy inexpensively the kind of everyday articles you may need.

In the provinces, look out for handmade pottery (at Kolovce and Strážnice in particular); folk ceramics in eastern Slovakia; china ornaments and geyser-stone carvings at Karlovy Vary; delicate lace and needle embroidery in many Moravian towns; wood carvings from Spišská Belá; blood-red garnets and semi-precious stones from Bohemia.

SPAS. The spas of Czechoslovakia are among the most famous in the world. Many an ailing body has sought treatment or relaxation at one of them, most notably at Karlovy Vary and Mariánské Lázně in the days when they were known as Karlsbad and Marienbad. The medical facilities are excellent. In some spas, a few of the older hotels have been renovated, and modern and sophisticated sanatoria have been built. The location of many is very beautiful, making them holiday resorts in their own right, as well as spas. All this, combined with a long-established tradition of caring for the sick has given the Czechoslovak spas a well-deserved reputation abroad. Western visitors are coming in increasing numbers, many of them appreciating the reasonable prices attached to these services and the emphasis that is put on health rather than high fashion. The spas may not be as chic as some of their western counterparts, but the suffering will find all the priorities are in the right direction, while their healthier companions will find plenty of amenities for entertainment, sports and sightseeing activities.

Altogether there are 56 spas and health resorts, about two-thirds of them in Bohemia and Moravia where the organization Balnea coordinates all the necessary services, and one-third in Slovakia, where the organization Slovakoterma is responsible. Both cooperate with Čedok and their agencies abroad.

An example of prices for a three-week arrangement ex-London, covering return flight, transfers, first-class accommodation in a double room with bath, medical examination and full medical care, full board with dietary meals where necessary and spa treatment according to doctor's prescription, is from £661–£761 in Piešťany, £780–£958 in Karlovy Vary; depending on season and standard of accommodations. Prices in some other spas are lower and, in all cases, accompanying adults without treatment pay less.

SPORTS. Though conditions in Czechoslovakia are excellent for a number of sports, arrangements mainly cater for groups. Those with their own equipment and prepared to make their own way, however, will usually find local sports clubs extremely willing to advise and assist if approached on the spot. The appropriate addresses can be obtained through Čedok.

Facilities for a variety of water sports, including water skiing, have been created in a number of the artificial lakes. Fast rivers provide excellent canoeing, for example, the Luznice or Ohre rivers in western Bohemia, the Hornád in Slovakia; or one of the country's principal rivers: the Labe (Elbe) and Vltava in Bohemia, the Morava and Dyje (Thaya) in Moravia, and the Danube, Váh and Hron in Slovakia. Walkers will find a very good network of marked trails in all mountain areas, and walking tours are arranged ex-UK by *Ramblers Holidays,* 13 Longcroft House, Fretherne Road, Welwyn Garden City, Herts. AL8 6PQ.

Two activities for which good facilities exist for foreign visitors are hunting and fishing. All arrangements for hunting, including permits, insurance, guides, and organized parties with accommodation and full board, are handled by Čedok. A permit to import your own gun and ammunitions must be obtained from a CSSR consulate before your trip, but equipment can be rented.

Čedok can similarly arrange for fishing permits and appropriate accommodation. The ponds of southern Bohemia are especially famous for their carp; sizable pike flourish in the artificial lakes; the sheatfish—largest of the European freshwater species—thrives in the Danube, where the very fortunate fisherman may also net a 40 lb salmon; trout and grayling can be caught in almost any mountain stream or lake.

WINTER SPORTS. There are first class skiing conditions in many parts of the country and a developing range of amenities with which to enjoy them. The best-equipped resorts at present are Špindleruv Mlýn in the Krkonoše (Giant Mountains) of northeast Bohemia, and Štrbské Pleso, Starý Smokovec and Tatranská Lomnica in the High Tatras range of Slovakia. These all offer ski lifts, ski instruction, and hire of equipment as well as good accommodations and some *après-ski* life. Winter sports tours are arranged by Čedok through some overseas agencies, but it is best to check for the latest details.

Getting Around Czechoslovakia

BY PLANE. Although not a large country, Czechoslovakia has a remarkably good internal air service linking ten cities and main towns. In addition to Prague these include Brno, Bratislava and the health resort of Karlovy Vary. Flights are by jet or turbo-prop aircraft. Prague's Airport (Ruzyne) is about ten miles from the city center with regular bus connections in addition to taxis.

BY TRAIN. There is an extensive rail network throughout the whole country. As with other Eastern European countries, trains are always busy and fares low in comparison to Western Europe, though a supplement is payable on almost all express trains. (If you have already purchased your ticket outside Czechoslovakia this does not apply). Long distance trains carry restaurant or buffet services and overnight trains connecting main centers have sleeping cars and second class couchettes.

 BY BUS. Although there is a good rail network Czechoslovakia also has an extensive bus system. However, much of this is complementary to the railway, although in some cases (eg Prague to Karlovy Vary, the health resort in Bohemia) it is in direct competition with the rail network. Fares are more or less parallel with rail fares. Buses are always busy and on long distance routes you should reserve seats wherever possible. Čedok is helpful in doing this.

 BY CAR. Czechs drive on the right and the usual Continental rules of the road are observed, except that a right turn is permitted on a red light if accompanied by a green arrow. There are speed limits of 110 kph (70 mph) on motorways, 90 kph (55 mph) on other open roads and 60 kph (40 mph) in built-up areas. Watch where motorway regulations begin as it is not always obvious, and if towing a caravan, never exceed 80 kph (50 mph). Seat belts are compulsory and drinking is absolutely prohibited, with no minimum intake of alcohol allowed.

Information on the documents you will need if you're taking your own car into the country is given on page 21. You can purchase gasoline coupons entitling you to about a 10% reduction from Cedok in London, from Zivnostenska Banka, 104–106 Leadenhall Street, London EC3 4AA, from the Tuzex Information Center, Rytířská 19, or Živnostenska Banka, Na Příkopě, both in Prague. It's best to purchase coupons in advance, to avoid tiresome waits. The coupons are available for Special (92 octane) and Super (96 octane). It has become easier to get the latter, but it is still wise to fill up when you can. Filling stations are quite often closed in the evenings.

In the case of accident or repair problems, get in touch with the Central Automobile Club, Opletalova 29, Prague (tel. 223547. It is sensible to carry a spare parts kit with you.

A number of main European (E) through routes cross Czechoslovakia. They include E12 from West Germany through Prague to Poland; E14 from Poland through Prague to Austria; E15 from East Germany through Prague, Brno, Bratislava to Austria and Hungary; E84 linking E15 from Prague with Vienna; and E85 heading eastwards via Žilina–Košice to the Soviet border. Main roads are usually maintained in good condition; secondary roads are mostly reasonable, and getting off-the-beaten track lets you in for some beautiful country and out-of-the-way finds. Except near main towns, traffic is normally light.

Car Hire. Self-drive cars may be hired through *Avis* and *Pragocar* at Ruzyně airport and Štěpánská 42, Prague 1, or pre-booked through Čedok and some of its overseas partners in all towns and resorts.

CZECHOSLOVAKIA OVER THE CENTURIES

Past and Present

If questioned about Czechoslovakia, most people would probably hazard a guess that Bohemia comes into the picture somewhere, that she has produced some exceptionally good musicians and rather fine glass, had a famous king called Wenceslas who trudged with his page through snow that was 'deep and crisp and even', and later revolutionized Europe with the liberal ideas of some people called the Hussites. Of her more recent story, they will remember her tragic role in the events that launched Europe into World War II and, with probably more clarity, recall the stark August days of 1968. All of which is as near true as generalizations can be.

Czechoslovakia is in central Europe. Indeed, one could say she *is* central Europe, for it would be difficult to be more centrally European than this. She is the center, the core, the heart of the Continent—and as in the case of so many hearts, the strains put upon it by the power struggles of the rest of Europe's anatomy make it a miracle that she continues to survive.

There is, of course, much more to Czechoslovakia today than old Bohemia in the west, which the Czechs call Čechy (the Czech Lands) and which contains the capital and jewel city of Prague. To the east of it is the central region of Moravia, with which Bohemia had long and numerous historical associations; today, these two make up the Czech Socialist Republic. Further east still is Slovakia, today the Slovak Socialist Republic, whose history from the 10th century until 1918, when the two were finally united, followed an entirely separate course. Together these form the federative state of the Czechoslovak Socialist Republic.

Liquid Assets

Before delving back into history, let's take a quick look at what the country has to offer the modern visitor. The answer is just about everything, except a sea shore. Ranges of hills and great mountains ring the land on almost every side, their presence responsible to a considerable extent for the course of history; only a quick look at a map of Europe is needed to see that no other Slav land bulges so far west into Germanic territory.

The highest ranges, such as Krkonoše (Giant Mountains) and Vysoké Tatry (High Tatras), lie along the northern borders, but the only really flat expanses are the plains of the Danube, a short stretch of which forms the southern boundary of Slovakia. Generally speaking, the rivers of the west drain northward into the Vltava and the Labe (Elbe) to empty eventually into the North Sea. But southern Bohemia opens out into the Moravian plain, drained by the Morava River and its tributaries, which flow, as do most of the Slovak rivers, eventually into the Danube and thence to the Black Sea.

The choice of river country is varied, from mountain torrents to the Danube itself, that mightiest of European waterways, and between them they offer fine waters for fishing, for canoeing, for bathing. Then there are the lakes—about 22,000 of them, many of them fish-filled; the greatest concentration is in the gentle southern Bohemian countryside. Modern man's contribution has been sinuous artificial lakes trapped behind great dams fulfilling another dual purpose—much-needed energy and new playgrounds for tourism.

Indeed, Czechoslovakia, despite her lack of sea, is an eminently watery place, and the fame of yet another of these liquid assets has echoed through pretty well every royal household of Europe at some time. We refer, of course, to the mineral springs of some of the world's best-known spas—Karlovy Vary (Karlsbad) and Mariánské Lázně (Marienbad) to name but two. Though the older spas date from the 16th century and some even earlier, their real heyday came in the 18th and 19th centuries. Today they are as busy as ever, if for good practical reasons rather than fashionable whim.

The Czechoslovak countryside has another delightfully ubiquitous feature—the fruit tree. Apples, pears, plums, or cherries stand sentinel along almost every country road, adding their mists of blossom to the spring scene, and in due course offering a rich harvest of fruit.

The villages vary enormously in style, from rather dull ribbons of squarish houses strung along a main street in the plains, to real medieval gems or, in mountain areas especially, timbered or half-timbered structures often gaily painted or decorated. They are fitting settings for age-old traditions that may manifest themselves in folk festivals, wedding ceremonies, or a particular talent in craftsmanship, all varying from region to region.

As for the towns, there are very few that cannot offer some treasure and many are stuffed with them, for they were the nerve centers of local power over the centuries, along with all the wealth and conflict that goes with it. A host of individual buildings, whole villages, and even towns are protected as national monuments, and have been or are being restored. Despite a struggling economy, much has been done, much is being done, and there is still much to do. When you notice peeling paint or cracking plaster, remember that destruction has always been a more rapid process than reconstruction and use your sense of vision to see what was and probably will be again.

But first back to history, without which little of what you see will have any meaning.

The Earliest Inhabitants

The Celts, whose homelands were around the Upper Rhine, spread east and southeast, some of them using the convenient waters of the Danube to lead them down into the Balkans. Among them was the tribe of the Boii and, from them, comes the name Bohemia. In the first century AD, Germanic tribes moved in, settling in the area north of the Danube which then provided the northern boundary of the Roman Empire. Unlike its Eastern European neighbors to the south, Czechoslovakia was little exposed to Roman influence and signs of their occupation are limited to southern Slovakia.

By the time the Roman Empire had divided and the Western Empire ceased to exist, Slavonic tribes were on the move and, in the 6th century, established themselves in the future Czechoslovakia. But, of course, they were not the only contestants for this territorial prize during those restless centuries. Among others were the Avars, who had pushed in from Asia in their flight from yet other conquering tribes. Under a Frankish merchant called Samo, a Slav union was formed to eject these belligerent rivals, but disintegrated after his death in 658.

From the early 9th century important conflicting influences began to infiltrate, both with the common aim of spreading Christianity. From the west came the German missionaries of the Frankish empire of Charlemagne and, from the east, those of Byzantium. The latter in due course included the famous Brothers Cyril and Methodius, bringing with them their new Slavonic or Cyrillic alphabet.

By then, the first Czechoslovak state had been established by Prince Mojmir I or Moravia, which grew into the Greater Moravian Empire stretching from Bohemia across Slovakia to western Hungary. In 880 an event with far-reaching consequences occurred; the Empire opted for the Church of Rome and, along with it, the influences of Western culture and the Latin alphabet. But, weakened by internal conflict, it was not long before the Empire broke up under pressure from the Hungarians, around the early 10th century. The resulting separation of Slovakia from Bohemia was to last for the next 1,000 years.

From Wenceslas to Charles IV

Bohemia, and its capital Prague, increasingly became the main pivot of influence under the royal dynasty of Přemyslides, including that famous ruler and devout Christian of Christmas carol fame, Václav or Wenceslas. Surrounded by Germanic power, Václav tried to find the best compromise for the protection of his people, but was murdered by his brother Boleslav, who then usurped the throne. The martyred Václav became a saint, venerated as the defender of the Czech lands.

Under the pressures of German political, cultural, religious, and commercial influence, Bohemia, together with Moravia, became increasingly entangled with their mighty neighboring Empire. As the economy strengthened, German settlers were invited to establish the first towns in Bohemia, in the 12th and 13th centuries, creating the basis for an influential German-oriented minority that was to have repercussions many centuries later. Under successive Přemyslide rulers, however, the land flourished and, indeed, expanded. Otakar II (1253–78) acquired Carinthia and expanded his territories to the shores of the Adriatic and thus, for a brief and unique period in her history, Czechoslovakia could claim a stretch of coastline. But Otakar was over ambitious and fell at the battle of Marchfeld against the German Emperor Rudolf I; his son Václav II retained only Bohemia and Moravia.

The Přemyslide dynasty came to an end with the assassination of Václav III, then only 17 years old, and for the first time the Bohemian Estates elected a quasi-foreigner to the throne from the House of Luxembourg. This was the son of the Holy Roman Emperor, Henry VII, Jan Lucembursky (John of Luxembourg). His wife, however, was the Přemyslide princess Elizabeth, and to this couple was born Karel IV, the famous Charles IV whose name features so prominently in the annals of Czechoslovakia.

Charles was sent to France for his general and political education and the frequent absences of his father abroad led to his early participation in Bohemian affairs. He was proclaimed successor to the throne in 1341. John, already blinded in an earlier battle, now flung himself and his small contingent of Czech knights into battle alongside the French against the English at Crécy. The little band was decimated, John was killed and Charles himself barely escaped with his life. It was fortunate that he did, for his reign marked the Golden Age of Bohemia.

In 1355, Charles was finally crowned Holy Roman Emperor in Rome and thus Prague became the proud head and administrative center, not only of Bohemia but of the Empire. In the 1340s, work began on the construction of St. Vitus Cathedral in Prague, the city expanded enormously, and the first university in Central Europe opened its doors. Painting, sculpture, architecture, literature, and the sciences were all encouraged and flourished. In buildings all over the land, but especially in Prague, the Gothic style with its developing and particular Bohemian character, reached its peak. Trade and agriculture developed as infertile land was reclaimed and such innovations as fish farming introduced.

Charles IV thus worked rigorously for the strengthening and growth of his ancestral dominion, achieving what the Přemyslide kings had vainly struggled to attain—the full sovereignty of the Bohemian state and its exclusive position within the German Empire. Charles died in 1378, and with him his dream of establishing an imperial dynasty. His incompetent son, Václav IV, faced with the rising phenomenon of Hussitism was unable to cope.

Hussites and Habsburgs

The reformist Jan Hus (John Huss), influenced by England's John Wycliffe, preached freedom of thought to a people increasingly aware of their national identity and increasingly burdened by a power-conscious church. His teachings aroused so much fervour in Bohemia that the church and the empire could not afford to overlook his existence. He was summoned to explain his position at the Council of Constance on a guarantee of free passage by Václav's brother and Holy Roman Emperor, Sigismund. The Council convicted Huss of heresy and he was burned at the stake in 1415.

Bohemia rose in revolt. For nearly 20 years, the Hussite armies under Jan Žižka and Prokop Holý defeated the crusading forces of church and emperor that were launched against them. Their successes became legendary and at last the church was forced to negotiate with the 'heretics' as equals.

A Hussite noble, Jiří of Poděbrady, was elected king by the Czech Estates, a fact that was hardly likely to please the Catholic crowned heads of Europe. Jiří of Poděbrady applied his reformist ideas to his foreign policies and even worked towards the establishment of a pan-European Christian confederation to unite against the Turkish menace. But there were too many factions, including an implacable papacy, against him. After his death in 1471, the Czech Estates were forced to look again for a king, this time for one who could command greater political support. They elected the son of the Polish king Casimir the Great, Vladislav Jagelowski. For nearly half a century the Jagellonian line ruled in Bohemia, and after the death of the Hungarian king, Corvinus, in 1490, over Hungary as well.

The union between Bohemia and Hungary was brutally broken by the Turkish thrust into the heart of Europe. In 1526, Vladislav's son and successor was killed at the Battle of Mohács. This crucial Turkish victory divided Hungary for two centuries leaving Slovakia in that part of the Hungarian Crown Lands which remained under Hungarian control. Ferdinand I, brother of the ruling emperor Charles V, was elected to the Bohemian throne and thus, consolidated by marriage and inheritance contracts, began 400 years of Habsburg rule, gradually depriving Bohemia of all the rights she had so arduously acquired in earlier centuries. It did, however, also bring strong government and a sophisticated administrative structure.

A counter-reformation was introduced by the Habsburgs, notably under Emperor Rudolf II. But though Rudolf resided in Prague and, indeed, turned it once more into a lively, cosmopolitan center of the arts, he left government to Czech court officials and in the end was forced to grant religious liberty. Thus, at the beginning of the 17th century, most of the Czech Estates were still Protestant and only a few of the Czech nobility were Catholic and supporting the Habsburgs. The question of whether Protestantism would survive in Bohemia now involved the position of Catholics and Protestants in the whole empire.

In 1617, Ferdinand II, nephew of the emperor Matthias, was elected King of Bohemia. Ferdinand was determined to bring the Czech Estates to heel. His intense recatholicization sparked outbreaks of violence and there occurred, in 1618, the first of the now famous defenestrations, when the imperial counsellors, both Czech Catholics, were hurled out of the windows of Hradčany Palace. The Imperial counter-attack that followed developed into the European power struggle of the Thirty Years' War. With the death of Matthias and the succession of the hated Ferdinand as Emperor in 1619, the war was on in earnest. The Czechs refused to recognize him as king and elected Frederick V Elector Palatine to the Bohemian throne instead, appealing at the same time to Frederick's father-in-law, England's James I. All James did was offer to act as mediator. The end came on November 8, 1620 when the Czech nobility was decisively defeated by the imperial forces at the Battle of White Mountain. In June of the next year, 27 of the principal initiators of the uprising were publicly executed in Prague's Old Town Square.

The significance of the Battle of White Mountain for Czech history cannot be too much stressed. Before the humiliating Czech defeat, despite differences between the Czechs and the Habsburgs, some sort of co-existence between peoples of two different religions and nationalities was still possible. After 1620, the situation irrevocably changed. The Habsburgs became a permanent symbol of oppression to the Czechs. A new foreign nobility, drawn from the ranks of the victor's bourgeoisie, confiscated the lands of the former Czech nobility, and what was left of the old Czech aristocracy intermarried and became Germanized. Many intellectuals were expelled from the land. Forcible Germanization and Catholicization, heavy taxes, and absentee landlords followed upon a people impoverished by the excesses of the Thirty Years' War.

In 1749 Empress Maria Theresa abolished the separate Czech Chancellery and placed Bohemia and Moravia under a central Vienna administration. At the same time, German was made the official language. There was nothing visibly left of the once proud Bohemian State, which now seemed to be no more than a place name on the map. Maria Theresa's son, Joseph II, continued the process of Germanization; yet oppression had one very positive result, giving stimulus to a rapidly growing Czech nationalism. It was during Joseph's reign, too, that freedom of worship was granted and serfdom abolished (1781).

The Czech and Slovak Revival

Germanization had rekindled rather than repressed national consciousness. The Czech national revival dates from the 1780s. It rose from the peasantry and lower echelons of society into the bourgeois class, who had come from the land to find work in the towns.

Cut off from their Czech neighbors by the boundaries of Hungary, the Slovaks also began to stir. The nationalist movement in Slovakia had its origins among the Protestant Slovaks, who had some contact with Hussitism and had later adopted Lutheranism from the German minorities in the towns. At the end of the 16th century, Slovakia was as Protestant as Bohemia. The memory of the religious affinity was to be an important factor in the national revival, but recatholicization in Slovakia broke the direct tie between Slovaks and Czechs. The advent of the Jesuits in Slovakia had serious linguistic consequences. In their effort to reach the common people they stressed the local dialect, thus reinforcing the growth of a separate Slovak language.

In Bohemia the glimmering spark of nationalism grew into an increasingly steady light as the 19th century progressed. A leading figure in its encouragement was František Palacký, historian and humanitarian, whose work contributed greatly to the sense of national identity and who strove hard to galvanize the Czech nobles into active support of democratic principles. But Czech attempts to regain political rights were unsuccessful. In 1848, a pan-Slav congress was held in Prague resulting in public enthusiasm, clashes with troops and a disorder that was finally quelled by artillery and martial law. Nevertheless, in due course some degree of liberalization followed and Czech nationalism became increasingly a political force to be reckoned with. Industrialization, too, altered the social structure and character of the country and, with a new awareness, the working classes became more active.

In their distrust of anything Slav, the Habsburgs created their own downfall, aligning themselves with imperialist Germany in World War I. Many Czechs and Slovaks went over to the Allied forces and Czechoslovak legions for this purpose were formed by a man destined to become the new leader of a new nation—Thomáš Masaryk.

Independence

Masaryk was just the man to undertake the formation of Czechoslovakia. He was born of a Slovak father and a Moravian mother. Receiving his doctorate at the University of Vienna, he started his teaching career there. In 1882, he went to Prague to become Professor of Philosophy and Sociology. He was passionately concerned with Czech politics, and ran and was elected to the Imperial Diet (1891–1893). At first, Masaryk was of the opinion that the monarchy was a good thing, but he soon changed his mind. When he was elected to the Reichsrat for the second time in 1907, it was as a member of his Realist Party, which stood for complete independence from Austria. Masaryk was convinced that a union of Czechs and Slovaks was essential for the independent existence of a new Czech State. He built his vision of the new republic on Hussitism and democratic philosophy, particularly that of England and the United States. His interest in the latter derived from his marriage to an American woman, Charlotte Garrigue. In his book, *The Making of a State,* Masaryk emphasized the specifically Czech mission to humanity—humanism.

Masaryk's chance to implement his theories came during World War. At its outbreak, he fled to Paris and proceeded, with Eduard

Beneš, to form the Czechoslovak National Council. Using his contacts in the United States, he raised funds for the Czech cause and in Russia he organized the famous Czechoslovak Legion, which was to harass the Bolshevik forces during the Russian Civil War. President Wilson's 'Fourteen Points' encouraged Czech and Slovak statesmen to meet in Philadelphia, Pennsylvania, to sign a treaty uniting the old Habsburg provinces in a democratic republic. On October 28 1918, independence was formally declared with Allied consent.

The First Republic was the great democratic experiment in Eastern Europe during the interwar period. To be fair, the intentions to make the First Republic a truly unified nation were good. Democratic freedoms were a fact. Industry and the economy boomed. Land reform was undertaken, although never completed. The social legislation was some of the most progressive of the time, and Czechoslovakia boasted one of the most advanced social security systems. Relatively speaking, the Czechs and Slovaks were extremely well-off, especially when compared with their neighbors.

But it was not long before the Slovaks under the leadership of Father Andreas Hlinka and his successor, Msgr Josef Tiso, were accusing the Czechs of having betrayed the Slovak national interest. At the same time, a rising Nazi Germany was encouraging dissent and revolt among the German minority, led by Konrad Henlein and his Sudetendeutsche Partei. Czechoslovakia tried to stabilize its position in the international arena by an alliance with France (1924) and the Soviet Union (1935), and a Little Entente with Yugoslavia and Romania. The country also firmly supported the League of Nations. But most of these alliances proved but pieces of paper when the real test came.

Munich and War

In September 1938, Hitler delivered an ultimatum of war or the cession of the predominantly German-inhabited Bohemian borderlands called the Sudetenland. The bankruptcy of French and British policy made tragedy inevitable. The Czechoslovak Army bravely mobilized, but Czechoslovakia was nonetheless invaded and dismembered. There was a systematic persecution of the Jews. Thousands of them were sent to concentration camps like that at Terezín. Czech national institutions, such as the Sokol and the Legionaries, were dissolved, and mass communications were strictly controlled. But the Czechs were past masters in the art of passive resistance and refused to bow. The man most responsible for trying to break the Czech spirit was Reinhard Heydrich. In June 1942 he was murdered by Czech resistance fighters, and the Nazis revenged themselves by literally wiping out the Czech town of Lidice.

A steady stream of Czech and Slovak emigrés and refugees joined Czech army and airforce units fighting with ferocious courage alongside the Allies. In Slovakia, the resistance movement was well organized. In August 1944, with Allied and Russian cooperation, the partisans triggered a national Slovak uprising against the Germans. The uprising was brutally crushed, but it had succeeded in pinning down eight German divisions when they could have been better used elsewhere.

Post-War Czechoslovakia

In view of its strategic position in Europe, the future of Czechoslovakia was a question of major concern to the Allies, Russia, and Czechoslovakia alike. Beneš evidently believed that his best course of action was to come to terms with the Soviet Union, and he completed a treaty of friendship with that country in 1942. By 1945, most of Slovakia had been liberated by Soviet and Czech troops and Beneš decided it was high time to return. The new government, composed of Communists, Communist sympathizers, and democrats, was formed in Kosice, in Eastern Slovakia during March 1945.

Beneš became the head of a four-party coalition government, which held power until 1948. In that year, a cabinet crisis brought on a takeover by the Czech Communist Party. Communist control of the police, the threat of Russian intervention, and their own divisions and unpreparedness tied the democrats' hands. In June Beneš resigned, and Communist leader Klement Gottwald became president of the republic. Stalinization of the country in all its manifestations inexorably followed.

The economic crisis and gradual striving for more political freedom culminated in the election of the Slovak leader, Alexander Dubček, as First Secretary of the Czechoslovak Communist Party in January 1968. For eight months, Czechs and Slovaks experienced a breath of liberalizing air, which they hadn't felt for 30 years. Then, in August 1968, combined Soviet, East German, Polish, Bulgarian and Hungarian forces entered the country. Since then the Czechoslovak Communist Party, under the leadership of Dr. Gustav Husak, has been in power. Perhaps all that is left to be said is that, for a visitor to gain the most from a trip to Czechoslovakia, he should go with a open mind.

Since the war, Czechoslovakia has been battling to restore her hard-hit economy. Apart from agriculture, in which a cooperative form of ownership is practised, all branches of the national economy are State owned. Fortunately, she enjoys rich resources and has no shortage of talent. The leading industrial branches are metallurgy and engineering, but the importance of the chemical industry is growing steadily. Traditional food, textile, leather, glass, ceramic, and wood-working industries continue to play their part.

The Czechoslovak economy is not currently in a happy state; foreign debts and low productivity being the major problems. Inevitably this has resulted in rising food prices and a shortage of some goods on the domestic market, although this affects Czechoslovaks rather than their visitors. Nevertheless, an improved standard of living over recent years is reflected in the rising number of cars on the road, and weekend cottages burgeoning in the countryside.

CZECHOSLOVAK CULTURE

Arts Unlimited

Politically, Czechoslovakia is a young country: born October 1918. Her cultural roots, however, go deep. Although her native artists and scientists had for centuries to look to Vienna and Budapest for recognition, although Germany, Hungary, and Austria claimed her talents for their own (Mendel, Freud, and Léhar were born in what is now Czechoslovakia), although Kafka had to write in German and Dvořák was ridiculed by sophisticated Viennese musicians whom no one remembers today, although an admixture of Saxons, Poles, Magyars, and Jews blurred the stream of indigenous culture . . . nevertheless the two nations, Czech and Slovak, could look back beyond the 10th century to their own empires and dynasties. In the stones and legends of Prague, old rusty city of the Bohemian kings, and in the forts and huts of the Váh Valley, the modern Czech and Slovak see the continuity of their generations and an unbroken tradition of arts, crafts, and folk customs.

Language and Literature

What strikes the visitor to Prague, Bratislava and Brno and many a smaller city is the high proportion of bookshops and stationers. Political parties, trades unions and social organizations all have their own publishing houses—there are 56 in all. Classical and contemporary literature is handled by Czech Writers in Prague, and Slovak Writers in Bratislava. Albatros publishes children's books and Artia (who are also responsible for musical scores, recorded music and the sale of postage stamps) put out some beautiful foreign-language picture books.

The Prague University Library, the Slav Library in the Clementinum complex in Prague and the University Library of Bratislava are well known to scholars. In the whole country there are more than 2,000 public libraries, and the number increases every year.

Czech literature began in the 9th century when the monks Cyril and Methodius devised Old Church Slavonic as a medium for spreading the Holy Writ. Jan Huss rationalized spelling in the 15th century and for another 200 years his followers, the 'Bohemian Brethren' developed the written language with their sermons and treatises. The counter-Reformation annihilated the Protestant literary tradition. The Catholic hierarchy re-established Latin and the inexorable process of Germanization of Czech literature began. Prose and poetry in succeeding dark ages was kept alive only by emigré scholars, chief among whom was Jan Komenský or Comenius (died 1670).

Present-day Czech and Slovak (the latter a separate language based on eastern country dialects and formalized by Latin-speaking priests) really date from the resurgence of nationalistic feelings from about 1850 onwards. The new literature made a slow start; it was hard to scale Parnassus with a language that only a few thousand people in the whole world could read. Tomáš Masaryk's *The Making of a State* was a landmark in political education, but of contemporary novelists the well-read foreigner may have heard of only two—Božena Němcová *(The Grandmother)* and Jan Neruda *(Tales of the Malá Strana)*—both writers realistic and gently satirical, foreshadowing that unique mixture of zany humor, delicate irony and sharp social comment characteristic of modern Czechoslovak novels, plays, and films.

To the same era (19th century) belongs the Byronic poem *May,* by Karel Macha, the one poem Czech schoolchildren learn and the only Czech poem likely to be found in a world anthology.

Kafka and his Contemporaries

Prague at the turn of this century was a hotbed of writers, a Bohemia in the Parisian sense, and she had already given birth to one of the most profound and original authors of all time—Franz Kafka (1883–1924). A cult figure in the West since the first translations of his major works began to appear, Kafka is now fully recognized in his native country. The birthplace (corner of Maislova and Kaprova streets, behind Old Town Square) has been pulled down for slum clearance, but his tomb in the great Olsány cemetery (far end of Vinohradská street) is well-signposted. You can go on a Kafka Tour in Prague that shows you houses and offices in and around Golden Lane associated with him and his friend and fellow-author Max Brod. *The Diaries of Franz Kafka* portray the literary life of Prague during his period. Newcomers to Kafka should read *The Trial, The Castle, America,* and *The Great Wall of China,* preferably in that order. Max Brod's novel, *The Kingdom of Love,* presents an account of their friendship.

Two contemporaries, proponents of the Czech genius that seems for ever to be smiling through tears, are Karel Čapek and Jaroslav Hašek. Karel Čapek is the playwright who, sometimes in collaboration with his brother Josef, achieved tremendous success with allegorical dramas of animal life *(The Insect Play, The War with the Newts)* and especially with *R.U.R. (Rossum's Universal Robots),* once a favorite with amateur dramatic societies everywhere. (Čapek invented the word 'robot'.)

Jaroslav Hašek found immortality with one work, *The Good Soldier Schweik.* The Schweik Tavern in Prague commemorates the 'Good Soldier', an old favorite in Bohemian folk-tale and legend: the peasant buffoon, sly, good-humored, forever bullied and pushed around. But he triumphs by pretending to be stupider than he really is, and to some extent he personifies the Czech national character.

Modern Authors

Up to the 1930's the poetry of Petr Bezruc and Pavel Országh Hviezdoslav reflected a spirit of national self-determination but—like all Czech and Slovak poetry until recent times—it had little impact on Europe.

After 1945 the Czech and Slovak Socialist Republics looked suspiciously at the world's favorite Czechoslovak writers and found decadence, flippancy, and undertones of subversion. Some writers drifted into exile, others bowed to political pressures. Literary history since 1956 has been a tale of censorship, repression, and revolt. Individual writers have been tempted to see how far they could go and some have gone farther than might have been expected. Josef Škvorecký showed the sordid side of the 1945 revolution in his novel of 1957, *The Cowards.* The Slovak writer Ladislav Mňačko published in 1967, both in Europe and the US, *A Taste of Power,* a reminder that ambition corrupts even Communists, or, perhaps, especially Communists.

Bohumil Hrabal's *The Pearls* deals surrealistically and symbolically with crime and prostitution and Martin Vaculík's *The Axe* plumbs the miseries that collectivization brings. On the other hand, Jan Otženášek (born 1924) writes sincerely from within the system and his novels, plays, and TV and film scenarios *(Lovers in the Year One, Citizen Brych,* among others) discuss the problems of people bewildered by the times in which they live.

There is today a good deal of experimental and enigmatic poetry which seems to move away from the 'socialist humanism' of the early post-war laureates: František Hrubin, Vitězslav Nezval and others. The young poets, like the young novelists, are preoccupied with the position of man at the center of revolutionary change. This is the spirit in which Ivan Skála, Miroslav Florian, and Vojtech Mihálik are currently writing.

Many of Czechoslovakia's most talented writers—some of them with long-established reputations—expend a great deal of energy on the creation of manifestos. From their *2000 Words* in the 'Prague Spring' of 1968 to *Charter 77,* which nine years later invoked the human rights clauses of the Helsinki Agreement, intellectuals have struggled for the artist's freedom to express himself. Like dissidents in the Soviet Union, these principled intellectuals are not only revered by like-minded campaigners abroad, but enjoy considerable support from the man in the street. Most readers, however, prefer the conventionally patriotic writers. Novelists who have risen to fame in the past few years include Jan Kostrhun, Petr Pavlik and Peter Jaroš. There is a vogue for science fiction, especially the highly imaginative tales of Ludvig Souček and Josef Nesvadba. Writers and illustrators of books for children have gained high honors abroad, none more so than Jiří Trnka and Bohumil Riha, both winners of the prestigious Hans Christian Andersen award.

A Museum of Czech Literature has been set up in the former Strahov monastery in Prague.

Music

The brightest and purest of Czechoslovak cultural streams is music and to music the nation has made a contribution over the past 200 years out of all proportion to its size.

In the late 18th century Prague was dubbed 'the conservatoire of Europe' (by the English traveler Charles Burney) because of its rich musical life. That was when Mozart, at the Bertramka villa where concerts and recitals are still held, composed *Don Giovanni*. He saw it premiered in Prague, but probably never dreamed that its arias (particularly the *Deh vieni)* would become theme tunes of the city.

Antonin Dvořák was born in 1841 at Nelahozeves, north of Prague, a pork-butcher's son. He became organist and violinist in the city and eventually became a popular composer with audiences both in the US and England. His opera *Roussalka* is a regular item in the State repertory and his museum on Ke Karlovu is a must for the tourist in Prague.

Best-loved of all Czechoslovak composers, however, is Bedřich Smetana whose *Má Vlast (My Country)*, performed at the newly-opened National Theater of Prague, gave Bohemian nationalism a strong impetus. Smetana died melancholy-mad in 1884; the theater was draped in black and the population followed his funeral from the Old Týn church to the Vyšehrad cemetery in 'a heavy cloud of smoking torches'. In the beautifully-kept Smetana museum on the Vltava bank in Prague he has a memorial that perfectly expresses the love and veneration Czechs feel for him. There you may listen, on request, to all the recorded music he wrote, from *The Bartered Bride* and the early quartets to the last opera, *Viola,* of which only fragments remain.

Leoš Janáček gains in esteem as his life and times recede (he died in Ostrava in 1928). Born in Hukvaldy, he first interpreted the vigorous harmonies of Moravian peasant communities. He quarreled with everyone and died an embittered man, but that aggressive temperament helped create pugnacious, provocative musical dramas. *The Clever Little Vixen* (from a strip-cartoon of the 1920's), and *The Macropoulos Case* (from a Čapek play) have the capacity to galvanize and disturb, and the song of human suffering by which he is best known abroad, *From the House of the Dead,* is a deeply inspirational composition.

Early 20th-century composers of world renown are Jaromír Weinberger and Bohuslav Martinu, and Josef Suk, better known in his lifetime as violinist and founder of the Czech String Quartet. Of more recent musicians, perhaps Alois Haba and the Slovak Jan Kapr, are most likely to become household names to posterity.

Among operatic composers, Jan Cikker and Eugen Suchoň are already established. The latter's *Krutnava* (The Whirlpool) has been premiered in a score of foreign capitals.

Music Today

There are 12 opera, 11 ballet and eight operetta companies in Czechoslovakia, all full-time and all busy from September to June at home and abroad. The most important opera theaters are the State Opera House and Smetana Theater in Prague. The Janáček Opera House in Brno is the newest and, architecturally, most adventurous building. 'Theaters of Music', sponsored by the State Gramophone Company, are found in Prague, Brno and Ostrava. They are informal concert halls, very cheap, where you listen to taped and recorded music. 'Theaters of Music' are also proposed for other cities.

Music-lovers do well to arrive in Prague in the second week of May, when the annual Spring Music Festival (established in Dvořák's time) takes place. Orchestras and soloists from many lands take part, but the top Czechoslovak names are missing. Suk and Hudeček the violinists, Václav Neumann the conductor, Lucia Popp, the latest in a long line of 'Bohemian Larks' (remember Emmy Destin ?), the Janáček and Martinu string quartets, the pianist Jan Panenka. . . . these great artists are usually busy performing abroad.

Jazz has an enormous following in the cities and on radio and television. Kamil Hála is the leading composer (and also conductor of the State Radio Jazz Orchestra) and fans of Count Basie, Stan Kenton, Gerry Mulligan, and even Igor Stravinsky will hear some imaginative arrangements of their works. The rapid spread of 'little theaters', cabarets, and nightclubs has boosted rock and other contemporary forms, as well as reviving the chanson and the blues. Today's adolescents worship singers like Karel Gott, Helena Vondráčková, and Hana Zagorová.

Architecture and Art

Stand upon one of the seven hills and look over Prague and an assortment of architectural styles meets the eye—romanesque, French Gothic, Italian renaissance, Czech renaissance, baroque, secession, art nouveau, art deco, socialist-monumental . . . a realization in stone of the confused history of Bohemia, ancient and modern. The upkeep of listed buildings, statues, and monuments is costly, but people do not complain.

The principal architectural treasures are well-documented and only a few examples are mentioned here. St. George's church in Prague, good romanesque with 12th-century frescoes; the Spišská Kapitula cloister at Spišské Podhradie in Slovakia, again romanesque; the romanesque fortress of Prague Castle; the bridge at Pisek on the Otava river, south of the capital, said to be the oldest stone bridge in Europe; the early-Gothic cathedral of St. Vitus in Prague, the middle-Gothic castle and chapel of Karlstejn and St. Barbara's cathedral at Kutná Hora; the Gothic churches of Znojmo and Brno in Moravia and St. Michael's cathedral in Bratislava; the carved altars of Master Paul at St. James's church in Levoča; the renaissance Belvedere in Prague, castles of Pardubice and Litomyšl east of Prague and of Topolčianky in Slovakia; the renaissance complex of Český Krumlov in Southern Bohemia. There are also innumerable baroque palaces, castles, and churches, of which the most impressive are Roudnice near Prague, Rajhrad monastery in Moravia and the archiepiscopal palace of Bratislava; the mock-tudor monstrosity on the Vltava called Windsorska; the frothy rococo of the spa towns Karlovy Vary and Mariánské Lázně.

Equally striking in their own way are some of the buildings and civil works of socialist Czechoslovakia. Jan Zázvorka's Memorial to Liberation on the Žižkov hill in Prague is outstanding among military monuments. Prague's new Palace of Culture designed by Czech Army architects, is the biggest and probably the most handsome cultural complex in Eastern Europe.

Painters and Photography

Picture galleries in Czechoslovakia are popular; the painter is an honored member of the community, but one looks in vain for a school that has influenced European art or an individual who has stamped his personality on it—unless it be the *fin-de-siècle* style of František Kupka or Alfons Mucha. Both men spent much of their lives in Paris, both died in the middle of this century. Kupka, pioneer of the abstract, was formerly in disfavor, but his works are on show again. Mucha, a master of art nouveau, is best represented by his monumental cycle of canvases in the castle of Moravský Krumlov, close to his birthplace at Ivančice.

More recent artists who have regularly exhibited abroad include Václav Rabas, the 'anti-impressionist' landscape painter Jiří Trnka, the puppet playwright, Vladimir Fuka and the sculptor Jan Štursa.

Photography is an art form in Czechoslovakia. Whole issues of magazines, and whole exhibitions, are sometimes devoted to the industrial studies of František Krasl and the photo-reportage of Dana Kyndrová, who works all over the world.

Folk Arts

Czechoslovakia, they say, was once a huge open-air museum. It is that no longer, but folklore and folk arts are undeniably closer to the surface of everyday life than might be expected in a land that has moved from peasant to industrial society in a very short time. Some remnants of regional costume still form part of most country people's wardrobes. Folk architecture flourishes, particularly in the baroque stone farmhouses of the Blata region of Southern Bohemia and the thatched wooden cottages (their beams colored with the blood of oxen) of Železný Brod in northern Bohemia.

Inhabitants of such places still paint Easter eggs and carve wooden birds and toys, which nowadays find their way to the tourist shops. Moravian country folk bake biscuits of such intricate shapes (cut out with tiny scissors) that it seems a pity to eat them.

Folk festivals actually increase in number and scope as forgotten feast days are revived. Východná in Eastern Slovakia has a great song-and-dance festival every summer in a large natural amphitheater. Strážnice in Moravia puts on an annual gathering with folkloristic symposia and craft exhibitions in June. The bagpipe festival at Strakonice in Bohemia revives memories of the legendary Švanda. Folk heroes of the old frontier forces are celebrated in the Chod festival at Domažlice on the German border.

Most country feast days fall on religious (Catholic) holidays and at the hop (in Bohemia) and the wine (in Slovakia) harvests. Easter and Pentecost (Whitsun) are commemorated everywhere and Christmas in Prague is the season when Good King Wenceslas comes into his own. (The English carol, by a 19th-century clergyman named J. M. Neale, is pure fiction, but the Czechs have latched on to it.)

The best concentration of folk art and architecture is seen at Rožnov pod Radhoštěm in the Beskyd Mountains, where a *skanzen* is reconstructed—a group of wooden cottages centered on a wooden town house of 1799 and a wooden ale house of 1660. Craftsmen live and work there. They even have an old-style Wallachian cemetery, where those who have helped preserve old folk customs are brought to be buried. Programs of folk activities run every weekend at Rožnov between early June and late August.

Tourist souvenirs, available in some unspoiled villages and from the special shops of Prague, Brno, and Bratislava, comprise wood carvings, glass paintings, straw dollies and baskets, pottery, lace, embroidery, hand-woven rugs, metalwork, and leatherwork; all distinctly typical of their region, often of their village. Pottery is the craft of the Bratislava area and Southwestern Slovakia, lace-making of Vamberk, wood-carving and rug-making of most hilly districts.

Stage and Screen

Czechoslovakia's 82 permanent theaters cover a repertory of classical and modern plays, from Molière to Shaw, and from Euripides to Brecht. Puppetry, ballet, and mime perpetuate the oldest dramatic traditions, while the well-known 'little theaters'—Viola, Rokoko, Ypsilon, Naive, Black, and others—are the envy of progressive theater groups the world over. Laterna Magika, to which all tourists in Prague are directed, is something different—though an interesting audio-visual experience as far as it goes.

Czech and Slovak drama stems from medieval mystery and marionette plays, but their theater did not exist in a serious sense until the Čapek brothers provided universally acceptable material. Experiment and shock have been its hallmarks every since. The 'Liberated Theater' of Voskovec and Werich lead the avant-garde of the 1930's.

The important State theaters are the National in Prague, the Slovak National in Bratislava and the Hungarian in Komárno, Southwest

Slovakia. Virtually every town has a municipal theater, and many are gems of baroque or renaissance architecture. (The Český Krumlov on the upper Vltava is believed to be the oldest theater in Europe.)

Irreverent satire and fantasy are what Czechoslovak audiences expect from their favorite playwrights, and contemporary figures like Václav Havel, Ladislav Smoček, and Peter Karvas supply it. Havel, spokesman of the Charter 77 human rights group, is known in the West for his dangerously symbolic play *The Memorandum.* Smoček's best-known work is *The Labyrinth.* Both plays attack the totalitarian bureaucracy, and both owe something to Kafka and to the Theater of the Absurd.

Foreign professionals admire Jiří Trnka's puppet plays with their clever blend of classical and modern. The outstanding theatrical producer, Janko Borodác, pupil of Stanislavsky, died recently in his native Bratislava.

The motion picture was always considered an original form of art in Czechoslovakia, and the screen attracted well-known writers like Karel Čapek. In what was once Marienbad (today Máriánske Lázně) and in Karlovy Vary, international film festivals are held. The first film studio, Barrandov, established in Prague in 1931, is still the most important; others include Koliba of Bratislava, and Gottwaldov (specializing in movies for the young) of Prague. Krátký Film, with Jiří Trnka and foreign partners, released two long puppet-and-cartoon hits in 1982: *Robinson Crusoe,* and *Mozart in Prague.*

Every year the list of feature films grows longer—81 in 1981. But most of the directors who swept the board at the international festivals of the 1960's—like Miloš Forman *(One Flew over the Cuckoo's Nest)*—are now in exile. A much-acclaimed director of the pre-1968 era, Vera Chytilová *(The Daisies)* has produced no recent work. The last great film of the 'New Wave' was *Closely Observed Trains,* adapted from Bohumil Hrabal's novel. Among the best of the latest batch of Czechoslovak films are *Great Wishes,* a study of idealism in the teaching profession; *One Hour of Life* (worker against industrialist in the 19th century); and *On the Whole We're Normal,* a comedy which ridicules the struggle for bourgeois living standards. For the rest, the titles say it all: *Liberation, Days of Betrayal,* and others in the same vein.

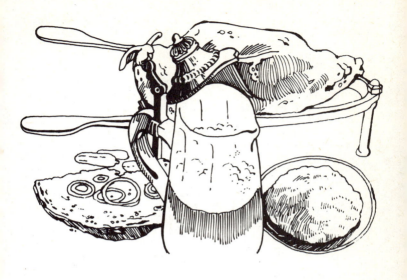

CZECHOSLOVAK FOOD AND DRINK

Pork, Game and Beer

Czech and Slovak cooking is living witness to the country's position as the crossroads of Europe. Many cultures contributed to the Czechoslovak cuisine. The Slav influence from the East brought the sour cream, vinegar, and sour vegetables, such as pickles. The goulash came from Hungary, the schnitzels from Vienna and the roast goose with sauerkraut and dumplings are German imports. The diet tends to be heavy, but the preparation of food is a tradition with Czechs and you will find eating out, especially in Prague, a thoroughly enjoyable gastronomic experience.

Starters

King of the cold table is the regal Prague ham, which sets a standard for hams everywhere. If you haven't tasted it, it could be said that you have never really eaten ham. The range of *hors d'oeuvres* is good, from eggs with caviar and smoked meats to Russian crabmeat in mayonnaise, and there is an excellent variety of salads in which pickles in an enormous number of guises are a recurrent theme. Herrings and sardines are other regular *hors d'oeuvres* items. When it comes to cheeses, some of the most interesting come from Slovakia and are made from sheep's milk.

Meat and Fish Dishes

The true Czech loves are pork, game, and goose. *The* Czech meal is roast pork with sauerkraut and dumplings; roast goose or duck similarly adorned are close seconds. Being a land where the art of conservation dates from the Middle Ages, the country abounds in game so hare, venison, and game birds are fairly common in season. Fish occupies a rather small place in the national cuisine; but the lakes of South Bohemia yield the Czech national fish, carp, served traditionally on Christmas Eve in several variations. The streams of Slovakia are abundant in trout.

Among other major meat dishes are variations on exotic stews. The goulash in Slovakia is particularly delicious, excellently seasoned with sweet paprika and slightly sharper than its Czech counterpart. But don't look for an accompaniment of fresh green vegetables with your meat dishes. The best you may do is pickled tomatoes or cucumbers, and canned peas and carrots. Fresh vegetables, particularly in winter, are extremely rare, and aside from tomatoes and cabbage, the Czechs simply don't know how to prepare them. An exception will be some of the most delicious-tasting mushrooms you have ever had. For some reason, these flourish in the Czechoslovakian fields and forests and a favorite weekend pastime is to take a trip out from the city to gather this delectable harvest.

The Ubiquitous Dumpling

Soups are another excellent feature, often with small dumplings floating in them. These can be made from just about anything. The basic Czech recipe is a mixture of slightly-dried bread cubes bound together with eggs, milk, and flour, but you can have potato dumplings, or a Slovak variation made from dough and cheese. There are also sweet dumplings, stuffed with plums or other types of fruit.

Pancakes and Pastries

The Czechs are not lacking a sweet tooth either, so on the whole it is best to put aside your diet altogether. From apple strudels and mouth-watering pancakes, you can pass on to the many different pastries and cakes, made from chocolate, almonds, or other nuts, and delectable combinations of eggs and flour. All are topped with cream icings and finished off with swirls of whipped cream.

What to Drink

A typical Czech meal needs something to wash it down. The favorite Czech drink is beer, and in recent years its popularity has spread in Slovakia, which otherwise is a wine-drinking region. In addition to the world-famous *Pilsen Urquell,* there is the *Budvar* beer from České Budějovice, and a number of ale houses produce their own brew.

Slovakia is the main wine-growing area, but there are some excellent Moravian reds. Bohemia's best wine comes from around Mělník. *Slivo-vice* or plum brandy is the national strong drink, the most famous brands coming from Moravia. Coffee is widely drunk, usually served in the so-called Turkish (unfiltered) style, without milk, and can be a bit gritty.

PRAGUE

The Golden City

Poets and artists, royalty and commoners down through the ages have praised the regal beauty of the capital of Czechoslovakia. Prague, like Rome, is built on seven hills and it spans the Vltava River (so graphically portrayed in music in Bedřich Smetana's tone poems *Ma Vlást*). Perhaps no other city in Europe possesses quite the same enchantment that lies in the perfect blending of nature and human achievement, of lush gardens with exquisite buildings. As in Rome, her varied architecture—Romanesque, Gothic, renaissance, baroque, 19th century, modern—exists together in serene harmony.

The visitor knows that history has been here a long time. Legend has it that The Lady Libuše, the prophetess of Czech tradition, stood on a rocky precipice overlooking the Vltava. Transfigured with inspiration she stretched forth her hands and cried, 'I see a great city, whose glory will touch the stars. The town you will build here shall be called Praha (threshold). Honor and praise shall be given to it, and it shall be renowned throughout the world.' She then dispatched her white horse to fetch her a consort and, when he returned with a certain Přemysl, a robust farmer, this rather unlikely pair founded the Přemyslide dynasty. So Prague came into being on the site where Slav tribes used to ford the river at its most shallow point, and where Charles Bridge stands today. Two fortresses, Vyšehrad and Hradčany, were built on

128

the heights above the river. Traces of romanesque Prague can still be seen in the Church of St. George at Hradčany and elsewhere, but the wooden houses of the common people have long since been destroyed.

Prague took the shape we know today during the 13th and 14th centuries. Much of the Gothic splendor of the city can be attributed to Charles IV, King of Bohemia and Moravia and Holy Roman Emperor, who made Prague the seat of his empire. During his reign (1346–1378), Charles University and Nové Město (the New Town) were founded, and Charles Bridge and other architectural monuments built.

The 15th century saw Prague torn by the religious and nationalist conflict of the Hussite Wars. For over 20 years, the Czech nation, noble and peasant alike, fought and defeated seven crusades mounted against them by the Holy Roman Empire and the Pope. The Czechs became known as the scourge of Europe and the word 'Bohemian' evoked the devil.

But the fighting was a tragedy for Prague. Trade could not flourish in the war-torn land and the ancient trading routes between the Baltic and the Danube were rerouted through German territory, never to return to Prague. The Czechs were eventually driven to defeat. Habsburg oppression caused the nation to rise once again in 1618, touching off the Thirty Years' War, which decimated the population of Central Europe. With the harsh reimposition of Habsburg rule after the defeat of the Czech nobility at the battle of White Mountain in 1620, Prague started to recover—albeit at a price. The favorite nobles of the Habsburgs confiscated the rich and fertile estates of the Bohemian aristocrats, and with the wealth acquired from their new lands, glorified their power in baroque monuments. Baroque was also the medium of the Jesuit movement of the counter reformation, which nowhere was more militant than in Bohemia. Thus, Prague was transformed by palaces and churches and made beautiful by landscaped, terraced gardens. The city also became a musical capital. Mozart walked her streets, claiming that no one but the Praguers understood him well.

With the coming of long desired independence in 1918, Prague became the capital of the newly-formed Czechoslovak democracy. During the inter-war period she was a commercial center for Central Europe while retaining her cultural primacy. Fortunately, Prague suffered little from the bombings of the Second World War. The city, which was liberated by its citizens between the 5th and the 8th May, 1945, was practically unscathed.

Exploring Prague

Prague, perhaps even more than other cities, is best seen on foot. But if you are going to spend only a day or so, the fastest way to see as many highlights as possible is to take one of the bus tours arranged by Čedok. If you are going to stay several days, your best move is to familiarize yourself with the map and the main districts of Prague, get an idea of the public transport system (you can buy a map with all the routes marked), and put on your walking shoes. You could start off by going to the top of one of the higher buildings, such as the Powder Tower

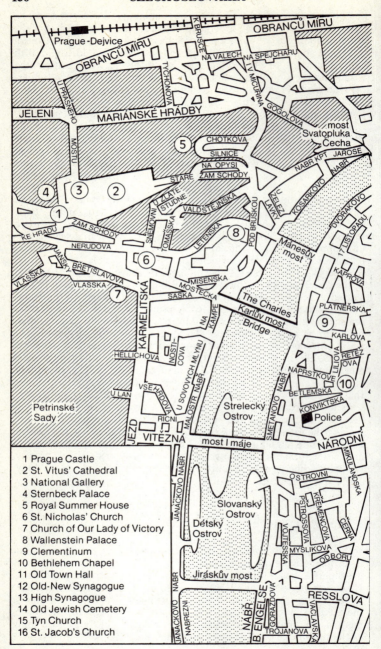

1 Prague Castle
2 St. Vitus' Cathedral
3 National Gallery
4 Sternbeck Palace
5 Royal Summer House
6 St. Nicholas' Church
7 Church of Our Lady of Victory
8 Wallenstein Palace
9 Clementinum
10 Bethlehem Chapel
11 Old Town Hall
12 Old-New Synagogue
13 High Synagogue
14 Old Jewish Cemetery
15 Tyn Church
16 St. Jacob's Church

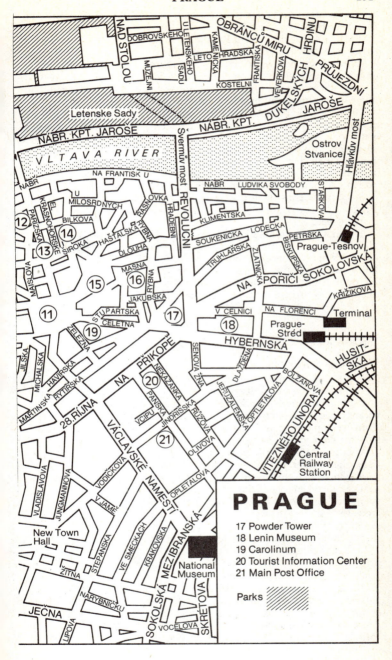

PRAGUE

17 Powder Tower
18 Lenin Museum
19 Carolinum
20 Tourist Information Center
21 Main Post Office

Parks

or Intercontinental Hotel, to sort out all the towers and spires and the layout of the city.

There are four districts of Prague which are your main concern. (1) Hradčany (the Castle area), the crowning glory of the city's skyline, perched above the river Vltava; (2) Malá Strana (Lesser Town) linking Hradčany with the river and Charles Bridge; (3) Staré Město (Old Town) across the river; and (4) Nové Město (New Town, founded in the 14th century!), an extension of the Old Town.

If you have a car, note that the center of the city is closed to private traffic, unless you are accommodated there. There is a comprehensive network of trams and buses, and the new subway system is clean, modern and very efficient; two of three lines are now open and both pass through Václavské Náměstí (Wenceslas Square), which is otherwise closed to public transport. One of the stations, Gottwaldova, is worth traveling to for its outstanding panoramic view alone.

Since Wenceslas Square is probably the best known landmark in Prague and you are likely to be staying in or near it, we may as well start off here.

The first thing to note is that Václavské Náměstí is not a square at all, but a long broad boulevard, sloping down from the National Museum to what was once the moat round the Old Town. The moat, which linked with the river at each end, is now occupied by the streets of Národní, Na Příkopě (which means 'at the moat'), and Revoluční, and once you have crossed to the other side of these you are in Staré Město, the Old Town.

Staré Město (Old Town)

The splendid buildings of Staré Město are far too numerous to mention them all; the most important are described, but you can hardly avoid making your own discoveries, whether it be some graceful piece of Gothic vaulting, some delicate renaissance doorway, or some exuberant piece of baroque carving. The best advice is to walk always with your eyes up, not down, and to probe into the tiniest alleys and the smallest courtyards.

At one end of Na Příkopě is a splendid remnant of the old fortifications, the Powder Tower, originally built by Matěj Rejsek in 1475 but rebuilt in neo-Gothic in the 19th century. Once you have passed beneath it, or taken any of the other streets into the Old Town, you will very soon come to its hub, Staroměstské Náměstí (Old Town Square). However, you may as well get there via Železná street since on it, and standing next to each other, are the Carolinium and the Tyl Theater. The Carolinium is the original Charles University building, founded in 1348 though much restored, and it was at the Tyl Theater that the first performance of Mozart's *Don Giovanni* was given in 1787, only four years after the building was completed.

Old Town Square, together with the adjoining Malé Náměstí (Little Square), is a delight. In the center is the statue (1915) of John Huss, or Jan Hus, whose humanistic teachings have made him both a religious and national symbol to the Czechs. In one corner is the famous 15th-century astronomical clock at the Old Town Hall, beneath which crowds gather every hour to watch Christ and the 12 Apostles show themselves at the little window above the clock face. Then comes Death, tolling for lost time and finally the Turk, the miser, the vain fool, and the cock.

The Old Town Hall was actually founded in 1338, built out of the proceeds of the wine tax, and rebuilt in late-Gothic style in 1470. The Nazis destroyed part of later additions in the Second World War, but the Gothic chapel, the tower and the splendid old Council Chamber remain. Opposite the Town Hall, the Týn Church is one of the gems of Prague Gothic to which later times have added an extravaganza of interior baroque decoration. The rococo building near it is the Kinský Palace, and there are a host of minor picturesque buildings famous for their Gothic, renaissance or baroque features.

If you take Pařížská or Maislová street out of Old Town Square, you will very soon be in the old Jewish Quarter, whose ancient buildings now comprise the State Jewish Museum. The Prague Ghetto is one of the oldest in Europe, dating back at least to the 10th century. By the 17th century, it had become a focal point for Hebrew culture in Central Europe. With the abrogation of the segregationist laws against the Jews after 1848, the Ghetto's autonomous existence ceased.

Built about 1270, the Old-New Synagogue is one of Prague's best examples of early Gothic, its wealth of sculptural decoration foreshadowing the naturalism of High Gothic. The Old Jewish Town Hall was restored in the 18th century, but is of less interest than the Klaus Synagogue and adjoining building now housing the Jewish State Museum, whose various collections graphically illustrate the tragic extinction of most of the 90,000 Czechoslovakian Jews during the war.

The final appalling chapter of the tragedy is told in the ancient Pinkas Synagogue, in which nearly 80,000 names are inscribed in rows on the interior walls—names of Jewish men, women and children from Bohemia and Moravia who were liquidated by the Nazis. It is a poignant memorial to the dead and a permanent reminder of man's cruelty to man.

The final astonishing sight of this district is the Old Jewish Cemetery, which seems unbelievably old and unbelievably crowded; it is both. With space restricted, graves were superimposed on each other—about 12,000 of them perhaps in 12 layers—and the ancient tombstones lean and joggle against each other in the resulting subsidence. The oldest preserved tomb dates from 1439; burials continued here until 1787, when a new cemetery was built elsewhere.

The cemetery makes up one corner of Náměstí Krasnoarmejců (Red Army Square) on which is also the elegant late 19th-century House of Artists, concert hall and home of the Czech Philharmonic. There is a splendid view from one angle of this square across the river to Hradčany. Another square with a splendid view across the river is Křižovnické Náměstí (Square of the Knights of the Cross), with the marvels of Charles Bridge in the foreground. From this square there is access to the huge complex of the Klementinum (1653–1722), which was originally a Jesuit College and now houses a major part of the State Libraries. The square, which is considered one of the finest in Central Europe, is bounded by the 16th-century church of St. Salvador, the baroque church of St. Frances (also known as the Church of the Crusaders), and the Gothic Old Town Bridge Tower (1357) dominating one end of Charles Bridge. The Smetana Museum is also near here.

Before taking this famous route to the Lesser Town, there is one more church to see. Only a short walk away on Betlémské Náměstí is the most revered of all the Hussite monuments in Prague, the Bethlehem Chapel. It was here that John Huss preached from 1402 until he left Prague to be martyred in 1415. The chapel was founded in 1391, later demolished and painstakingly rebuilt in its original form in the early 1950s. Its completion was marked by a massive attendance of the citizens of Prague who packed the church and the square outside in an atmosphere charged with emotion. Inside, note the wooden threshold of the pulpit, which John Huss used to cross on his way to preach over 500 years ago.

Charles Bridge and Malá Strana (Lesser Town)

Now it's time to follow the historic royal trail across Charles Bridge and the Vltava to the Lesser Town. The bridge itself was commissioned by Charles IV in 1357; its architect, Peter Parler of Grund, was then only 27 years old. Today it has been faithfully restored and measures 660 yards (603 meters) between the towers at either end. The wealth of statuary was mainly added in the 18th and 19th centuries, 26 of the 30 between 1706 and 1714. A few have been replaced, either by copies or later works, but most remain as powerful examples of the vitality of Prague baroque. Opinion generally concedes first place in artistic merit to the group around Saint Luitgarda (Matthias Braun, 1710), the 12th statue on the left as you go from the Old Town. The best loved is that of Saint John of Mathy, Felix, and Ivan with the Turk by F. M. Brokoff (1714), the 14th on the left.

As you approach Malá Strana, you cross the island of Kampa and Čertovka (Devil's Brook), the little arm of the Vltava that divides the Kampa from Malá Strana. The water is often lively with skiffs and canoes, and the island itself is a peaceful spot with a park and some lovely old houses.

Malá Strana is a most picturesque quarter of the city, full of winding streets, impressive palaces, fine churches, little taverns, and old houses with ornamental signs. The district developed rapidly from the middle of the 13th century, though a great part of it was destroyed in the disastrous fire of 1541. The wide spaces that were left were gradually filled by the renaissance and baroque palaces of the nobility, many of them today adapted as foreign embassies, museums or government departments. One of the grandest is the Valdštejn or Wallenstein Palace (1623–30), in whose riding school is an art gallery. Its spacious gardens sometimes provide a noble setting for open-air concerts.

The main way through Malá Strana is along Mostecká (Bridge Street) a continuation of Charles Bridge. Wander off to the left and you are in a maze of small streets around charming Maltézské Náměstí (Maltese Square) and Velkopřevorské Náměstí, both bounded by 17th- and 18th-century former palaces. Now head for Karmelitská street and the very early baroque Church of Our Lady of Victories (1611–1654), notable for its famous figurine of the Infant Jesus. This lavishly dressed Spanish renaissance wax effigy was the gift of Polyxena Lobkovič in 1628, and the miraculous powers associated with it started a vogue of replicas in churches all over the world.

The Petřin Gardens are in this part of town and contain the delightful collections of the Ethnographical Museum. From this you can walk up through the gardens to the Petřin Tower, a 197-foot (60-meter) copy of the Eiffel Tower, built in 1891, and a good place from which to check up on the city's layout.

The heart of the Malá Strana is Malostranské Náměstí (Lesser Town Square), dominated by the most splendid of Prague's baroque churches, that of St. Nicholas, yet another creation associated with the Dienzenhofers, father and son, who were responsible for so much of baroque Bohemia.

Hradčany (the Castle Area)

This district grew from Hradčanské Náměstí, the great Castle Square, rebuilt and expanded after the fire of 1541. On this square you will find the baroque Archbishop's Palace, and a passage leading to the entrance to the Šternberk Palace, with its magnificent art collections of the National Gallery. Also on this square is the Lobkovič Palace from the 16th century with its distinctive graffito decoration, restored in 1957. Today it houses the interesting Museum of Military History in whose courtyards tournaments are quite often held.

From here it is a short walk to Loretánské Náměstí, which is dominated by two imposing baroque buildings, the Černín Palace and the Loretto shrine and church. The latter takes its name from the Italian town to which, according to tradition, the Holy House of Nazareth, scene of the Annunciation, was miraculously transported in the 13th century to save it from the infidel. This version of it was donated by a Czech noblewoman in 1626, subsequently enlarged and provided with its baroque façade by the younger Dienzenhofer. The Loretto has a beautiful carillon from 1694, and a fabulous treasury of precious items whose crowning glory is the 'Sun of Prague', a glittering monstrance set with 6,222 diamonds.

A short distance to the south, you come to another religious foundation, the Strahov monastery, originating from the 12th century, rebuilt in the 16th to 18th centuries. It became known for its splendid collection of manuscripts and incunabula and so, fittingly, it is now in use as a Memorial to National Literature.

But now back to Hradčanské Náměstí (Castle Square) for the culminating point, in more ways than one, of your Prague sightseeing tour. The Přemyslide rulers moved here from their original seat a few miles upstream at Vyšehrad, and by the 12th century there was an extended stone castle. After damage by fire, it was reconstructed into an imperial palace for Karel (Charles) IV. Matthias of Arras and Peter Parler are two names closely associated with both castle and cathedral.

Charles' son, Václav (Wenceslas) IV, preferred to live in the Old Town, and it was under the Jagellonian king, Vladislav, in the late 15th century that significant building work was resumed, including the great

Vladislav Hall. The fire of 1541 did extensive damage, but reconstruction and expansion continued and, under Rudolf II, the castle became a center for the arts and sciences. Further damage was wrought by the troops of Frederick the Great in 1757 and, over the centuries of Habsburg rule, many choice items were dispatched to Vienna. Indeed, the later Habsburgs made infrequent use of the castle, though its baroque overlays date mainly from the reign of Maria Theresa, as does the present main gateway. It is through this gateway that you enter the Castle precincts and to get the best out of your visit you need a good plan of the area and plenty of time.

St. Vitus Cathedral and its towering spires rise out of the Third Courtyard, the creation of many centuries. Remains of earlier churches from the 10th and 11th centuries can be seen beneath the Cathedral, but interrupted by the Hussite wars, the fire of 1541, the Turkish wars, and general lack of interest on the part of some rulers, the present building spans nearly six centuries, from 1344–1929. Thus it is a blending of Gothic and neo-Gothic, the original work of Matthias of Arras and Peter Parler, finally completed by the architects and artists of the late 19th and early 20th centuries.

The main body of the church is soaring Gothic, the oldest parts being in the eastern half, round the high altar, with 11 of the cathedral's 19 chapels. They include the Chapel of St. Václav, its walls studded with semi-precious stones, containing the tomb and relics of the great Wenceslas. The tombs of the two architects, Matthias of Arras and Peter Parler, are in the Valdštejn Chapel. Two of the Přemyslide kings are buried in the Sternberg but the main 16th-century Royal Mausoleum is in the center of the Cathedral before the high altar and, in the crypt below, lie the remains of both great and lesser Bohemian kings.

Some of the truly fabulous Bohemian crown jewels (including the St. Wenceslas crown to which Charles IV added a thorn, supposedly from Christ's crown of thorns) are rarely on display; but there is a rich treasury in the Chapel of the Holy Rood in the Second Courtyard. The Cathedral's brilliant stained glass is modern.

Also reached from the Second Courtyard is the Castle Picture Gallery, displaying the very fine former collections of Rudolf II, which were thought lost for many centuries and only came to light in the 1960s; they include works by Titian, Tintoretto, Veronese, and Rubens. From this courtyard, too, you have access to the Powder Bridge with the Old Riding School beyond it, where temporary art exhibitions are held. This is also the way to the Royal Gardens, not usually open to the public, though you may and should visit the best renaissance building in Prague in the eastern part of the gardens. This is the Royal Summer Residence, or Belvedere, now another National Gallery exhibition venue, with its trim gardens and 'singing fountain'.

Across the square behind the Cathedral rise the towers of St. George's Church and Monastery, the earliest romanesque complex still in use today. The Monastery has been restored to provide a magnificent setting for the richest of all Bohemian art collections of icons, carvings, and paintings. Beyond here you come to Golden Lane, a most picturesque huddle of tiny houses built into the Castle walls in 1541 to house the royal goldsmiths and later the royal archers. At the end of the lane, Daliborka, the castle keep, contains some sinister dungeons and is named after its first occupant, the knight Dalibor of Kozojed; Smetana wrote an opera about his heroic story.

Many of the Castle's magnificent rooms are not normally open to the public, but you will be told which you can visit, and should not in any case miss the grandiose Vladislav Hall. Tournaments were also held here, hence the broad 'equestrian' staircase leading to it.

Whatever you do, don't leave the Castle area without strolling through the Gardens on the Ramparts. The views over the river and city are spectacular.

Nové Město (New Town)

Nové Město is, on the whole, where all the action is—most of the main museums, theaters, concert halls, hotels, commercial and office blocks, and the main shops. In the early 14th century a scattering of villages and hamlets existed in the countryside outside the walls of the Old Town. In the 1340s Charles IV founded the New Town that would weld them into a new district of his prospering and expanding city. Most of the grand plans died with him and what you see today is largely 19th and 20th-century Prague, but dotted among it are not a few buildings, especially churches, that still bring echoes of that Golden Age.

Most of them have been built, restored, and rebuilt again, and the most striking impression imparted by Nové Město is the neo-renaissance of the great buildings that went up at the end of the 19th and early 20th centuries. One such building is the National Museum dominating the scene from the top of sloping Václavské Náměstí (Wenceslas Square). This broad boulevard gets its name from the equestrian statue of that romantic and ill-fated ruler, who it is said will awake to lead his people again in their time of greatest need. Near the National Museum is Smetana Hall, beautifully restored within, and not far away the main railroad station.

The area south of the National Museum is peppered with churches founded at the time of Charles IV, though much altered since. A place you should seek out is one of K. I. Dienzenhofer's most charming secular buildings, a summer residence called Villa Amerika (1712–1720) on Ke Karlovu street, now housing the Antonín Dvořák Museum. This is another charming setting for summer concerts.

Very near is another building with a quite different cultural association—the inn of U Kalicha on Na Bojišti street, on the site of the one-time haunt of writer Jaroslav Hašek and his immortal Good Soldier Švejk (Schweik). Various paintings and other items commemorate this famous anti-hero.

If you go west from here, you will come to Karlovo Náměstí (Charles Square), the former hub of Charles IV's New Town. There is a lovely baroque arch (another of Dienzenhofer's creations), and one of the buildings has become known as Faust's house, due to a succession of owners who dabbled in the occult sciences. These included the English alchemist Edward Kelly, who lived here in the late 16th century. The oldest building on the square is the New Town Hall, on the north side, dating from 1367, rebuilt in 1561. This is where the Hussite revolution began.

North of Charles Square, Jungmannova street will bring you to the little square of the same name. Here, the Church of Our Lady of the Snows has the highest nave and the largest altar of all Prague's churches, and was one of the first churches in which Hussite services were held.

You are now only a stone's throw from Václavské Náměstí, and just round the corner from Národní Street. If you turn left down the latter, you will come to the river and the neo-Renaissance splendors of the restored National Theater. The island to the south of it is Slovanský Ostrov, Slavonic Island, with a park and another neo-Renaissance building still used for concerts and exhibitions.

Vyšehrad and Other Sights

There are still a few major sights that do not fit so easily into a particular area slot. One of these is Vyšehrad where the story of Prague first began, a couple of miles upstream from the National Theater and the boundaries of the Old Town. It stands on the top of an almost sheer rock face rising from the river bank, through which a tunnel has been built to accommodate the road. The early Přemyslides had their royal seat here. Under Charles IV a new castle was built and fortifications to link it with the New Town. The castle was destroyed by the Hussites and little remains except quite extensive fortification walls; but the view is lovely and the gardens within them are both scenic and peaceful. Among the later or restored buildings up here are the Church of SS. Peter and Paul and the 11th-century Rotunda of St. Martin, but, perhaps most important, is the old cemetery. This is the last resting place for some of Czechoslovakia's leading writers, musicians and artists, among them Smetana, Božena Němcová and Karel Čapek.

On the opposite bank of the Vltava is the Prague 5 district where, on Mozartova street, you will find lovely, peaceful Bertramka, the villa in which Mozart stayed on his visits to Prague. It belonged then to the Dušek family and is now the Mozart Museum—a most evocative place where you can listen to his music as you wander through the rooms, restored as far as possible to their original form and all of them packed with Mozart associations. Open-air concerts are held in the gardens in which you will also find a stone table at which Mozart is thought to have worked on his compositions.

Further out in Prague 6 district the summer palace of Hvězda marks the site of the Battle of White Mountain, now in the middle of a very fine park.

PRACTICAL INFORMATION FOR PRAGUE

WHEN TO COME. A year-round city, Prague is loveli-est in the spring, when its trees are blossoming and its parks and palaces resound with concertos and chamber music. The International Prague Spring Festival (May 12 to June 4) is the music lover's delight, attracting some of the world's out-standing soloists, ensembles and orchestras. If you come in summer, you can keep cool in one of Prague's many swimming pools (indoor ones in town, and open-air ones along the river), or head out of town to one of the waterside recreation areas. Winter is culturally very alive.

GETTING AROUND PRAGUE. By Subway. Two of Prague's three subway lines are now open; well designed and spotlessly clean, they provide the simplest and fast-est means of transport. Cost is 1 Kč for any distance; you drop your coin into a large collection box and don't need a ticket.

By Tram and Bus. One crown (1 Kč) also takes you anywhere in the city by tram or bus; prior to boarding, buy your ticket (you might as well get several) available from news-stands, tobacco shops, some stores or hotels. Each ticket entitles you to one ride and must be punched or validated as you get aboard—just watch how the other passengers do it.

By Taxi. Taxis are cheap, averaging about 3.60 Kčs per km, but can be difficult to get; best ordered from a hotel.

Car Hire. This can be arranged through *Pragocar* at Ruzyně airport and Štěpánská 42, Prague 1; or through Čedok.

HOTELS. The best hotels are under the management of *Interhotels,* a subsidiary of Čedok. They will be 5-star (Deluxe), 4-star (Expensive), and some 3 and 2-star (Moderate), though the latter will not have private bath or shower. Note that many establishments can offer rooms in different catego-ries. In most hotels which are 3-star or more, you can expect to find an exchange bureau, one or more bars, and hairdresser and barber services on or near the premises; all have restaurants unless otherwise stated. Some of the older hotels are showing their age, but they are gradually being renovated and can have a certain atmosphere that is lacking in some more recently-built premises. Though it is unwise to generalize, you may find that, as in many countries, front-desk clerks lack charm; others will take great trouble to be helpful.

Prague's hotels get very full indeed and if, unwisely, you have not pre-booked, go to Čedok's Department for Accommodation Services at Panská 5, Prague 1. Private accommodation is handled by Pragotur, U Obecniho domu, Prague 1, near the Powder Tower.

Deluxe

Alcron, Štěpánská 40, Prague 1. Central and an old favorite, with good restaurant. 150 rooms and suites with bath.

Esplanade, Washingtonova 19, Prague 1. Central, elegant, facing park. 55 rooms and suites, most with bath; famous Est Bar nightclub.

Intercontinental, náměstí Curieových, Prague 1. One of the American chain; splendid position on bank of river in Old Town. Over 400 rooms and suites with bath; ground-floor restaurant (M) and elegant top-floor Zlatá Praha restaurant (E) with superb view; also top-floor nightclub.

Jalta, Václavské náměstí 45, Prague 1. Very central; popular bar and restaurant. Nearly 90 rooms and suites with bath; nightclub.

Parkhotel, Veletržni 20, Prague 7. Fairly new, but not central. Over 200 rooms with shower, some (E).

Expensive

Ambassador, Václavské náměstí 5, Prague 1. Very central; old-fashioned, but with atmosphere. 135 rooms and suites, most with bath.

International, náměstí Družby 1, Prague 6. Not central, known to some as the Russian Ritz for its architectural pretensions. 375 rooms and suites with bath, some (M).

Olympik, Invalidovna, Prague 8. Modern, but not central. Over 300 rooms with shower.

Panorama, Centralní nám., Prague 4. 430 rooms and suites, folk-style wine cellar, disco, bar, pool, solarium, splendid views from upper floors. Brand new, near Vyšehrad Castle and subway station for quick access to center.

U Tří Pštrosů (Three Ostriches), Dražického náměstí 12, Prague 1. Magically located at Malá Strana end of Charles Bridge; 17th-century atmosphere and one of the most sought-after places in town. 18 rooms and suites with bath/shower.

Moderate

Adria, Václavské náměstí 26, Prague 1. Very central. Over 60 rooms without bath; no restaurant.

Flora, Vinohradská 121, Prague 3. Quite lively. Over 200 rooms, about half with bath.

Hybernia, Hybernská 24, Prague 1. Central. 70 rooms, a few with bath.

Merkur, Těšnov 9, Prague 1. Central. Nearly 70 rooms, a couple with bath.

Olympik II-Garni, Invalidovna, Prague 8. Opposite the Olympik. 275 rooms with shower; guests use Olympik's restaurant.

Palace, Panská 12, Prague 1. Very central, recently renovated. 32 rooms, most with bath.

Splendid, Ovenacka 33, some rooms with bath.

 RESTAURANTS. In addition to its hotel restaurants, Prague has a very wide selection of eating places. Look out for some of the characteristic ones, called *koliby,* usually with a folkloric décor and regional specialties; *vinárny* (wine cellars), which may have full restaurant service or simply serve snacks, but often in a cosy atmosphere; and *pivnice* (beer taverns) mostly offering inexpensive plain food and excellent beer, sometimes their own brew, in a more earthy and usually crowded setting. Quite a few places close for part or all of the weekend, or on one or two evenings of the week, and in many, advance reservations are advisable, so check first. The following are divided according to areas and categories for easier geographical reference. Some are in very quiet corners and not all are easy to find, so don't give up too readily.

Staré Město (Old Town)

Opera Grill, Divadelni 24 (E). One of the best in town, elegant décor with antique Meissen candelabra, French cuisine.

U Zlaté Konvice, Melantrichova 20 (M). Unusual underground Gothic labyrinth with tables set among huge wine barrels. Generous portions, but cold food only.

  Rotisserie, Mikulanská 6 (M). Excellent kitchen, always crowded for lunch.

  Klášterní, Národní 8 (M). Good wine restaurant in former Ursuline convent, for lunch or after-theater snack.

  U Golema, Maislova 8 (M). Good food, wine, intimate.

  U Zelené Žáby, U Radnice 8 (M). Medieval home of a legendary hangman, popular with young arty set. Cold snacks seem overpriced.

  U Zlatého Jelena, Celetná 11 (M). A restored ancient wine cellar.

  Železné Dveře, Michalská (M). Popular; specializes in Moravian wines.

  U Rudolfa II, Maislova 3 (M). Very small, intimate, excellent food.

  U Zlatého Hada, Karlova 18 (entrance from Liliová 17) (M). Good coffee and snacks in Prague's first coffee house from the early 18th century.

  U Medvídků, Na Perštýně 7 (I). South Bohemian and old Czech specialties in noisy, jolly atmosphere.

Malá Strana (Lesser Town)

  U Mecenáše, Malostranské nám. 10 (E). Wine restaurant in medieval setting; elegant, especially in back room.

  Valdštejnská Hospoda, Valdštejnské nám. (M). Pleasant; good food (international or Czech).

  U Malířů, Maltézské nám. 11 (I). 16th century, in lovely old part of town. Wine restaurant with relaxed Bohemian atmosphere.

  U Tomáše, Letenská 12 (M). Founded by Augustinian monks in 14th century; serves super 12° dark ale in ancient-style rooms; plain, honest food.

  Lobkovická Vinárna, Vlašská 17 (M). Wine restaurant with aristocratic origins, specializing in the fine Mělník wines.

  U Bonaparta, Nerudova 29 (I). Packed with the impoverished young, but lively.

Hradčany (Castle Area)

  U Labutí, Hradčanské nám. 11 (E). Exclusive dining in tastefully remodeled stables.

  Oživlé Dřevo, Strahovske Nádvoří 132 (E). Hidden away in gardens of a monastery; lovely view of city, but overpriced.

  U Zlaté Hrušky, Nový Svět 3 (M). Ancient setting; good atmosphere and food.

  U Lorety, Loretánské nám. 8 (M). Next to baroque church of the same name with its carrillon bells, an agreeable spot.

  Ve Zlaté Studni, U Zlaté Studně 4 (M). A steep climb through secret courtyards, but the view's worth it. Cold food only.

  U Zlaté Uličky Grill Bar, U Daliborky 8 (M). Snack bar grill in castle grounds; food served with care.

  Espreso Kajetanka, Kajetanske zahrady (M). Just under the castle ramparts, gorgeous view.

Nové Město (New Town)

Čínská Restaurace, Vodičkova 19 (E). Chinese décor and authentic recipes with emphasis on Canton and Szechwan regions. Good—but pricey.

Mayur, Štěpánská (E). Indian food is a rarity here, so you must pay the price; but the menu is good.

Jihočeská Restaurace, Na Příkopě (M). Down to earth South Bohemian food in down to earth setting.

Slovanský Dům, Na Příkopě 22 (M-I). Several restaurants and bars serving Czech food and snacks; central, handy and usually elbow room.

U Fleků, Křemencova 11 (M). Most famous of all Prague's beer taverns, brewing its own 13° caramel-dark beer. Several rooms and entertainment ranging from oompah brass band to light music. Convivial, but not as good as it used to be.

For a quick snack at rock bottom prices, go to the **Kõruna** self-service complex, very handy at the bottom of Václavské náměstí, near the corner with Na Příkopě. It's stand-up eating, except in the bar where you also can get coffee; but the range covers everything from soup and hot dishes to salads and sticky pastries. Also very handy is the new **Korunka,** just across the road in 28 října; here it's self-service from a small army of automats—open till late evening and useful if you're desperate.

Farther afield

Chalupa in Club Motel (M), 6 miles (10 km) south of town. Farmhouse atmosphere and country cooking.

U Kalicha, Na Bojišti 12, Prague 2 (M). Packed with associations with the Good Soldier Švejk (Schweik). Czech food.

Maxmilianka Koliba (M), in small town of Roztoky north of city. Attractive décor, good food, worth the ride.

U Pastýřky, Bělehradská 12, Prague 4 (I). Slovak setting; simple and good.

 HISTORICAL MONUMENTS. Whole areas of the city qualify as an historical monument; the following are the principal individual highlights. The most common opening hours are 9 or 10 to 4 or 5, but times vary according to season or a building may be closed for a period for some reason, so it is always best to check on the latest situation with Čedok or the Prague Information Service.

You should definitely take in **Prague Castle** (Hradčany), and its Gothic **St. Vitus Cathedral** and romanesque **St. George's Basilica,** both in the Castle grounds. Nearby is the former monastery **Loretto** (Loreta) with its distinctive carillon and magnificent reliquaries.

The **Church of our Lady Victorious,** Karmelitská 13, Malá Strana, houses the wonderfully attired statue of the boy Jesus, reputed to have miraculous powers. The churches of **St. Nicholas** on Malostranské nám. and **St. Jacob's** in Staré Město are grand examples of high baroque. The restored **Bethlehem Chapel** in Staré Město is a Gothic chapel in which Jan Hus preached. The **Powder Tower,** the **Old Town Hall** with its world famous **Clock,** and the **Old Town Bridge Tower** are all in Staré Město. So is the **Prague Ghetto,** the historic Jewish quarter, with its several ancient synagogues and other buildings. **Charles Bridge** from the 14th century, with its fabulous statuary, links the Old and Lesser Towns (pedestrians only). A couple of miles upstream are the cliff-top remains of **Vyšehrad Castle** (grand view), earliest of them all. Admittance into the churches is free; elsewhere there is a small fee.

 MUSEUMS. Prague's many museums contain note-worthy collections of every description. Most are open from 9 or 10 to 4 or 5 and closed Mondays, but check as there are seasonal variations and some of the smaller ones may close in winter. There is usually a small entrance fee. The following is a partial list of some of the most interesting ones.

Antonín Dvořák Museum, Ke Karlovu 20, Prague 2. The famous composer's memorabilia.

Bedřich Smetana Museum, Novotného lávka, Staré Město, Prague 1. The life and works of this grand old man of Czech music.

Bertramka, Mozartova 169, Prague 5. The delightful villa in which Mozart stayed on his visits to Prague. Concerts are sometimes held here.

Lenin Museum, Hybernská 7, Nové Město, Prague 1.

Military Historical Museum, Hradčanské nám. 2, Hradčany, Prague 1. Housed in part of the former Schwarzenberg Palace. Exhibits of European arms up to World War I. Medieval jousting tournaments staged here in summer.

Museum of Applied Arts, 17 Listopadu, Staré Město, Prague 1. There is also a huge glass collection, from Venetian and renaissance items to Czech and German baroque pieces.

Musical Instruments Museum, Lázeňská 2, Malá Strana, Prague 1. A charming collection.

National Museum, Václavské nám. 68, Nové Město, Prague 1. More of a landmark. Specializes in pre-historic, historic, natural science, zoological and numismatic departments. Its mineralogical collection is world famous.

National Technical Museum, Kostelni 42, Prague 7. For enthusiasts of old cars and locomotives. Exhibits from the field of cinematography.

Strahov Library Museum of National Literature, Strahov Courtyard, Hradčany, Prague 1. Beautifully preserved ancient manuscripts exhibited in lovely former monastery; bibles from all over the world.

State Jewish Museum, Jáchymova 3, Staré Město, Prague 1. Spread over several buildings, has a large collection of temple furnishings. Specializes in the history and customs of the Jewish community in Bohemia and Moravia.

 ART GALLERIES AND EXHIBITION HALLS. Prague has a traditional appreciation of the graphic arts. State galleries, often housed in beautiful palaces, keep excellent permanent collections and often supplement these with guest exhibits. There are dozens of small galleries offering works for sale by contemporary Czechoslovak artists, sometimes at quite reasonable prices. Opening hours of main galleries are similar to those of museums, with Monday the main closing day; but check the latest situation.

Château Zbraslav, originally a Cistercian monastery 7½ miles (12 km) south of Prague. Collection of 19th- and 20th-century Czech sculpture.

Convent of the Blessed Agnes, Anězska ulice, Old Town. Originally from the 13th century and recently restored to house 19th-century Czech art.

Kinský Palace, Staroměstské nám. 12, Staré Město, Prague 1. Collection of graphic art.

The National Gallery has the following collections: **Sternberk Palace,** Hradčanské nám. 15, Hradčany, Prague 1. A splendid collection of European art including all the main schools and the works of such masters as Canaletto, Goya, Ribera, El Greco, the two Brueghels, Rubens, Dürer and most of the French Impressionists. Well worth it. In addition, the National Gallery have exhibition halls in the **Riding School of Prague Castle,** in the Castle precincts; in the **Royal Summer House (Belvedere),** also in the Castle precincts; and in the **Wallenstein Riding School,** Valdštejnska 2, Malá Strana, all Prague 1.

Old Town Hall Cloister, Staroměstské nám., Staré Město, Prague 1.

St. George's Convent, Castle precincts, Prague 1. Beautifully restored to house an outstanding collection of Old Bohemian art from the 13th century onwards. The first floor concentrates on Bohemian baroque art from the early 17th to the late 18th centuries.

Prague Castle Gallery, Hradčany, Prague 1. Situated on the northern side of the second courtyard. Displays to full advantage the paintings which for 200 years were thought lost and were found by chance in an abandoned storeroom only in 1962. Originally they had belonged to Charles I of England, and while subsequent kings and queens sold off some of the paintings in this collection, the 67 that can be seen today are preserved intact. Restoration work, criticized by some as being too thorough, has brought these works by Rubens, Titian, Tintoretto and others, back to life.

NIGHTLIFE. Western-style nightlife is not one of Prague's specialties, but there are a number of bars with dancing, of which some also have cabaret: **Night Club,** Intercontinental Hotel; **Est Bar,** Hotel Esplanade; **Jalta Club,** Hotel Jalta; **Embassy,** Hotel Ambassador; **Park-Club,** Hotel Park; **Gruzia,** Na Příkopě 29, with Georgian atmosphere; **Lucerna,** Štěpánská 61. All (E). Others include the **Alhambra,** recently renovated and now a top night club; **Variete Praha,** an entertainment center with a more moderate night club; and the **International Hotel,** which puts on special programs, especially in the season.

OPERA, CONCERTS, THEATER. Prague has a sophisticated musical and cultural tradition and overflows with opera, ballet, stage plays, mime, puppet theater and concerts of everything from jazz to chamber music. The Prague Spring Music Festival from mid-May/early June is one of the great events on the European calendar.

Opera and Ballet. Opera especially is outstanding. Opera and ballet performances are held at the three following theaters—and remember that for the Czechs, these are occasions for dressing up: the **National Theater** at Narodni 2, has just reopened after major restoration; the **Smetana Theater,** Vitězného února 8, which has recently been superbly restored—now one of the grand theaters of Europe; and the **Tyl Theater,** Železná 11, also attractively redecorated.

Theater. One place where you won't need to know the language is **Divadlo na Zabradi** (Theater on the Balustrade), Anenské nám. 5. This is the home of the famous Black Theater when it is (rather rarely) in Prague; it is very difficult to get tickets, but if you're lucky you will find this skillful and artistic shadow-ballet an unforgettable experience. This theater is also the venue for the very talented mime Fialka—one of the best of its kind in the world, silently expressing the gamut of human qualities. Finally here, too, you can see performances of the famous chanson singer Hegerova. **Laterna Magika** (Magic Lantern),

Národní 40. Very popular with foreign visitors, this is an extravaganza combining live actors, mime, and very advanced cine techniques.

Concerts. These are held at the **House of Artists,** Dvořák Hall, Krasnoarmejců nám. and **Smetana Hall** (not to be confused with the Smetana Theater), nám. Republiky 5, an extravaganza of turn-of-the-century design. The Czech Philharmonic is first rate, as is the Smetana Quartet. There are literally dozens of talented ensembles and performers, and you can hardly go wrong. Sunday afternoon music sessions are held in a hall of the **National Museum,** where one sits on steps of the grand staircase, and in the rooms of the **National Gallery,** thereby making the experience a visual treat as well. **Bertramka,** Mozartova 169, the lovely villa where Mozart used to stay, is a lovely setting for the music of Mozart and his contemporaries. Not to be missed are the marvelous organ recitals in the magnificently appropriate settings of **St. Jacob's** (Old Town), **U Křižovníku** (near Charles Bridge) and **St. Nicholas** (Lesser Town). Military and other brass bands are very popular and there are rousing open-air concerts including on the terraces of the **Castle Gardens,** beneath the castle.

Puppet shows. These are brought to a high art form at the **Spejbl and Hurvínek Theater,** Římská 45, which provides a unique opportunity to observe the actual skills of puppet manipulation on stage. Note also the **Jiří Wolker Theater** at the Comedy Theater, Jungmannova 1. The **Central Puppet Theater** performs at Loutka, nám. M. Gorkého 28, and Sluníčko, Na Příkopě 15.

 **SHOPPING.** *Tuzex,* the government chain authorized to deal only with hard currency export items, has a network of shops throughout the country where one can purchase quality goods of foreign and local production for Tuzex vouchers or directly in exchange for hard currency. Prices can be advantageous so don't change all your shopping money into local currency.

For the latest information on Tuzex outlets, their information center is at Rytířská 11, Prague 1.

 GUIDED BUS TOURS. A good choice of these is arranged regularly by Čedok, with English-speaking guides provided. There are city sightseeing tours by day and by night, and trips out into the surrounding countryside, ranging from wine-tasting in Mělník to various one-day tours of different parts of Bohemia. Longer arrangements include a 5-day itinerary in Bohemia, and a 12-day Grand Tour of Czechoslovakia.

 USEFUL ADDRESSES. Embassies. These are all in Prague: *British,* Malá Strana, Thunovská 14; *USA,* Malá Strana, Tržiště 15; *Canadian,* Mickiewiczova 6.

Travel Organizations. *Čedok,* Na Příkopě 18, Prague 1 and (for their Department for Accommodation Services) round the corner at Panská 5; other Čedok addresses are given under individual centers. *Prague Information Service,* Na Příkopě 20, Prague 1. *Balnea* (for spas in Bohemia and Moravia), Pařížská 11, Prague 1. *Slovakoterma* (for spas in Slovakia), Radlinského 19, Bratislava. *Youth Travel Bureau (CKM),* Žitná 12, Prague 2. *Autoturist* (Central Automobile Club of ČSSR), Opletalova 29, Prague 1. *Rekrea* (Cooperative Travel Office for Bohemia and Moravia), Revoluční 13, Prague. *Tatratour* (Cooperative Travel Office for Slovakia), Bajkalska ul., Bratislava. *Sport-Turist* (for physical training and sport in Bohemia and Moravia), Národní tř. 33, Prague 1; *Slovakoturist* (for physical training and sport in Slovakia), Škovrančia 9, Bratislava.

Transport. *ČSA* (Československé Aerolinie), Staré Město, Kotva Building, Revoluční 1 (for tickets), Vltava Building, Revoluční 24 (air terminal). *British Airways,* Nové Město, Štěpánská 63. *Railways,* Main Railway Station. *Buses,* Central Bus Station. All in Prague.

Emergency telephone 155 (first aid); 333 (ambulance). There is a clinic catering especially for foreigners, for payment in hard currency only. The address is Fakultní poliklinika, Karlovo náměstí 32, Prague 2, and here there are English-speaking doctors on call from 8 a.m. to 4 p.m. In case of an emergency ring 155, or to call an ambulance, ring 333. There is an all-night drug store at Na Příkopě 7, Prague 1.

BOHEMIA

A Stormy Heart

Bohemia should be approached with caution. So many rulers and noble families of greater or lesser stature have built so many castles, palaces, and churches, that there is a grave risk of seeing too much and remembering very little at all. In the following pages a selection of the more important and attractive sites has been made, to which you can add your own discoveries according to the time available.

Broadly speaking, you head north or northeast of Prague for the grandest scenery, and south or southwest for the historic-cultural sights. Naturally, this is a very general guideline and, in fact, you can be sure of a good deal of history and a lot of fine scenery whichever way you go. Since many places can be visited on half- or full-day trips out of Prague, we shall deal first with the highlights of central Bohemia.

Central Bohemia

Starting in the south we come to the first of many castles encircling the capital: Zbraslav, less than 10 miles (16km.) away. It was founded by Václav II as a Cistercian monastery and burial place for the Czech kings, but what you see now is an 18th-century château, which now houses the National Gallery's excellent collection of modern Czech

A ruined Byzantine church at Nessebur, on the Bulgarian Black Sea coast.

Deep forest encircles this beautiful lake in the Low Tatras of Slovakia.

The magnificent memorial to Jan Hus in the Old Town Square of Prague.

Winter on the River Vltava, subject of Smetana's famous tone poem.

Baroque statuary on Prague's Charles Bridge, with St. Vitus Cathedral beyond.

Some of Esztergom's lovely architecture reflected in the Danube.

East and West meet in Eger, Hungary, where both mina-
ret and steeple point to heaven.

murdered). The castle has some very good renaissance and baroque sections, and houses a wine restaurant.

Southwest of here, Veltrusy castle is particularly notable for its beautifully landscaped park and, nearby, the rather austere renaissance Nelahozeves castle broods over the village of the same name. The house of its most famous son—Antonín Dvořák—is now a museum.

A few miles northwest of Prague is the mining village of Lidice, where one of the great abominations of World War II was perpetrated on June 9th 1942. Following the assassination of Reinhard Heydrich, the ruthless Nazi Protector of Bohemia and Moravia, Lidice was selected for reprisals. The town was razed to the ground, its population executed or deported, mostly to die in concentration camps. A new village has been built, but old Lidice remains as a poignant memorial, now garnished with rose bushes sent from all over the world.

About an hour's drive west of Prague is the Castle of Křivoklát, a favorite hunting ground of Czech rulers from time immemorial. The present building dates from the end of the 15th century, with 19th-century alterations; but the castle's great feature is its wonderful woodland setting. From here you can drive via the Berounka river valley to Koněprusy, and the largest underground Karst grottoes in Bohemia. These were certainly inhabited in prehistoric times, but also provided a hidey-hole in the 15th century for forgers of counterfeit Hussite money.

So we return to the Berounka river and follow it through its rocky valley to come to one of the sights of Bohemia: the castle of Karlštejn built by Charles IV as a magnificent repository for his crown jewels, important documents of state and the holy relics of which he was such an avid collector. Founded in the 14th century, it was restored in Gothic style in the late 19th century. The crown jewels are no longer there, but you must on no account miss the Chapel of the Holy Rood, in which they were once kept. This truly sumptuous place makes a great impact with its 128 Gothic panel and wall paintings by Master Theodorik, and walls encrusted with over 2,000 gems.

Southern Bohemia

This is the right direction to head for charming old towns, Hussite history, and gentle, lake-strewn, wooded countryside, gradually rising to the substantial heights of the Šumava mountains along the West German border.

Tábor, 55 miles (88 km) south of Prague, is the first place to go, founded by the Hussites in 1420, near the castle of Kozí Hrádek where their leader had spent the last years of his life. Its founders were convinced that the Czech nation was chosen by God to destroy the temporal power of the church and state, and usher in a New Jerusalem. The people called themselves Taborites after their town, and adopted a patriarchal constitution.

Tábor is a very different town today, but the old part is well worth seeing, with its twisting streets built to prevent the enemy gaining easy access to the center. On Žižka Square is the Taborite church and the Town Hall from 1520 containing a museum to Hussitism. Note the invention of one of its greatest leaders, Jan Žižka—an armored wagon, forerunner of the modern tank. Beneath the museum is a labyrinth of tunnels and cellars used by the Taborites as both living quarters and as links with the outer defenses of the town.

South Bohemia is strewn with old towns of which part or all have been declared urban reservations because of their architectural value. Some restoration work has been done, much more is still to be done, but the basic shapes and structures are there, evidence of a prosperity that began to burgeon in that distant golden era of Charles IV, and sometimes even earlier. In most cases, their focal point is the main square, usually bounded by arcaded houses that show an infinity of variations on Gothic, renaissance and baroque themes. One such town is Jindřichův Hradec, which also has a landmark of a castle terraced above the Nezárka river on one side and reflected in a lake on the other. About 9 miles (15 km.) away, the deep pink renaissance castle of Červena Lhota is another South Bohemian gem.

About half way between here and the South Bohemian capital of České Budějovice is the small town of Třeboň, another architectural jewel still partially surrounded by 16th-century walls. Třeboň has a severe castle with an interesting museum, and is also a spa, but above all it is the heart of pond and fish country. There are literally thousands of ponds in South Bohemia, created by aristocratic and ecclesiastic landlords in the 14th to 16th centuries, partly to drain the land and partly to provide fish farms for breeding the highly-prized carp, which is a major delicacy of Czech gastronomy. The Rožmberk family peppered the countryside with both castles and ponds, many of which qualify as lakes and the largest of which bears their name just north of Třeboň.

The main sight of České Budějovice is the massive main Žižka Square (you will find there are an awful lot of Žižka Squares in this South Bohemian Hussite country), said to be one of the largest in Europe and certainly one of the most handsome, with arcades all the way round and a fine baroque fountain with a statue of Samson in the middle; this was once the town's only water supply. Hluboká is an attractive little place in more pond country with a castle that may look curiously familiar; it is in fact a mini replica of Windsor Castle.

Hluboká is near and České Budějovice is on the Vltava river, which is born in the Šumava mountains near the southwest border with West Germany and then pursues a great twisting curve, first southeast, then north through the heart of the region towards Prague. Below Lenora, the Vltava soon swells into a twisting, elongated lake, trapped by another great dam, the Lipno. This, too, has become a popular recreation area, equipped with camping and sports facilities amongst excellent walking country in which it is not difficult to lose your fellow tourists. There is good fishing in and sailing on the lake, and sightseeing trips by steamer.

You can reach Lipno from České Budějovice via Český Krumlov, one of the most delectable old towns of all, with the Vltava snaking right round it. The Old Town Square is a delight, and so are the narrow lanes twisting away from it. Here, too, is yet another castle which is also yet another Rožmberk pile, well worth visiting for its collections, its 18th-century theater (one of the oldest in Europe) and the adjoining Masquerade Hall with extraordinary life-like murals. The town also has an open-air theater with revolving auditorium.

You could return to Prague or continue into West Bohemia via Prachatice, once on the Golden Trail along which salt was brought from the Bavarian mines to Bohemia as early as the 9th century. Husinec, the birthplace of John Huss, is three miles (five km) north of it. Further north still is Písek whose seven-arched stone bridge over the Otava river is even older than Charles Bridge in Prague and is similarly adorned with statues from the 18th century. An interesting event each June in this area is the Schweik Walk, which follows the route taken by that unwilling Good Soldier whose admirers now come from far and wide to participate in it. Zvíkov Castle stands a few miles to the north of Písek above the confluence of the Otava and Vltava rivers, now swollen to lake-size proportions by the dams downstream. From here northwards, these man-made lakes stretch almost continuously to within a few miles of Prague. Orlick Castle, is magnificently placed beside them.

Liquid Assets

As a region, West Bohemia has a lot of particularly 'liquid' assets; notably the mineral springs that feed some of the world's oldest and best known spas, and the beer which flows from the breweries of Plzeň (Pilsen) to the furthest corners of the earth.

The story goes that around 1347, Charles IV (no less) stumbled by chance upon the spring of Vřidlo during a hunting expedition; or rather his dog did for, as the harried stag turned suddenly in a last-ditch stand, the poor hound fell into boiling water and was scalded. Charles investigated the matter and, familiar with health cures in Italy, ordered baths to be established here in the village of Vary. Thus was Karlovy Vary (Karlsbad) born. It reached its heyday during the 19th century when kings, princes, and dukes came from all over Europe and, in their wake, the fashionable sets of the day. The colonnades, baths, pensions, sanatoria, and luxurious hotels date from this period, though new ones of course have been built.

The colonnades, punctuated by the health-giving springs, follow the curve of the little Teplá river through the resort beneath the wooded hills. This is the place to stroll, sip the waters in traditional-shaped cups, nibble rich Karlovy Vary wafers *(oplatký)* and, finally, sample the water from the '13th spring', a liqueur called Becherovka made from Karlovy Vary water and herbs.

Both Karlovy Vary and Mariánské Lázně (Marienbad) have a well organized cultural life to entertain both the fit and the ailing, and they have the two best golf courses in the country. Mariánské Lázně is younger, and its waters have quite different and more varied properties than those of Karlovy Vary. It is also more spacious, though smaller, with its lovely parks and homogeneous architecture. Indeed this was the spa much favored by Britain's Edward VII but, from all accounts, he did not waste too much time on strict diets or rigorous treatment.

The third well-known spa in West Bohemia is Františkovy Lázně (Franzenbad), but the place that really revolutionized medical science is Jáchymov, north of Karlovy Vary. This originally made its living from mining silver ore and here were struck the famous Maria Theresa 'thalers', from which the American dollar derives its name. The silver was exhausted, and the town might have died, if the Austrian government of that time had not sent to a certain M. and Mme Curie two railway cars of local pitchblende (uranium ore) to help in their research. From this, in 1898, they isolated two new miracle elements. One they named polonium after Mme Curie's native Poland; the other they called radium. The mining of uranium ore for the production of radium was started in 1908. The mining of the ore for the uranium itself was a post-World War II development.

All roads from the west lead through Plzeň, which is mainly a large industrial town nowadays, though there is some dignified architecture from Gothic and later times in and near the main Republic Square. You will no doubt want to sample the excellent beer in the restaurant adjoining the famous brewery.

One rather lesser-known area of West Bohemia lies to the southwest of Plzeň, towards the border with West Germany. This is the region of Chod. For centuries the Slav Chods were traditionally the guardians of Bohemia's frontiers for which they were granted special privileges. Domažlice is the main town of the area and very charming it is, too, with some original fortifications and a lovely arcaded square. Chod folklore is particularly interesting and very much alive, the dancing especially contagious with its accompaniment of the Chod version of Scottish bagpipes. Pottery, painting, and distinctive local costumes are other Chod specialties. There is a host of attractive old towns and villages in this area, and some wonderful view points for you are on the edge of the Český Les and Šumava mountains here.

Charming and Rural

The most spectacular scenery in all Bohemia is undoubtedly in the northeast, in the Krkonoše (Giant Mountains) bordering Poland. Not only is the scenery beautiful, but the local architecture is refreshingly rural, the steep-roofed timber houses painted in warm colors that look just right against sunlit pinewoods or snowy pastures.

The area was known long before the days of vacationing. Through its mountain passes the Protestant exiles fled across the frontier to escape persecution. To assist the fugitives on their way, a 'bouda' or wooden hut was built in Bilá Louka (the White Meadow) in 1620. In memory of that historic first hut, many hostels and hotels are called 'bouda' today.

The principal resorts are Harrachov, Pec pod Sněžkou, Janské Lázně (another spa) and Špindlerův Mlýn, this last being the most sophisticated in its accommodation and facilities. It is most attractively placed astride the rippling young river Labe (Elbe), here in its early formative stages. If you're feeling energetic, a good trip is to take a bus from Špindlerův Mlýn via Janské Lázně to Pec pod Sněžkou, there embark on the two-stage chair lift to the top of Sněžka (highest of the range at 5,290 feet (1,611 meters) and right on the Polish border), then walk the seven miles (11 km) down, eventually through deep, silent pine-woods, to Špindlerův Mlýn again.

Vrchlabí is a quaint old town of leaning old wooden houses. Of the other towns in East Bohemia, little Nové Město nad Metují is one of the most remarkable renaissance monuments in Central Europe with its one arcaded square and its exquisite renaissance castle. Litomyšl in the foothills of the Bohemian-Moravian highlands is another worthy little place, its main square considered to be one of the most beautiful in the country. It has, of course, a castle and, close to it, a baroque brewery notable for being the birthplace of Bedřich Smetana in 1824. East Bohemia's capital is Hradec Králové, which combines old and new architecture rather well. Its red brick Cathedral of the Holy Ghost on the main square (where most of the historic monuments are) is early Gothic.

Traveling west from the Giant Mountains you come to the Lusation range (Lužické Hory). To the south of them lies the heart of Bohemia's famous glass-making industry. Its most important center is Nový Bor, whose crystal tableware, painted glass and chandeliers have graced the halls of Europe's greatest crowns and princes. Other major centers are Železný Brod (cut and engraved glass) and Jablonec (glass jewelry). All have museums.

Two areas of unusual natural interest are the Bohemian Paradise (Český Raj, main town Turnov) and Bohemian Switzerland (Děčinskí Stěny, best visited from Děčín). Both are remarkable for their ravines and strangely eroded rock formations of Cretaceous sandstone. These areas—and especially the latter—are really walking and scrambling country, but those less energetic may take boat trips through some of the gorges of the Kamenice river from Hřensko in Bohemian Switzerland, right on the East German border.

Two other places should be mentioned for very different reasons. One is Teplice, Czechoslovakia's oldest spa, near the East German border. The other is Litoměřice, a beautiful old town on the Labe (Elbe) river. Very close to it is Terezín where the Nazi concentration camp of Teresienstadt is now left as a poignant memorial to the countless numbers who did not survive its horrors. It is yet another reminder of how Bohemia has paid the price for being the stormy heart of Europe.

PRACTICAL INFORMATION FOR BOHEMIA

WHEN TO COME. Spring (especially lovely for fruit blossom), summer and early fall are all good times for touring and sightseeing. January through March is the season for the Giant Mountains (Krkonoše) resorts. Note that some monuments, especially castles, close in winter. Spa treatment is available year round.

GETTING AROUND BOHEMIA. Čedok have various tours. Touring by car gives the greatest freedom. Rail and bus connections between them cover the region and are inexpensive, if you can sort out the timetables.

HOTELS

All hotels listed below have restaurants unless otherwise stated.

BEROUN. Český Dvůr (I), 11 rooms.

ČESKÉ BUDĚJOVICE. Zvon (E, M), 50 rooms, a few with bath; **Slunce** (M), 30 rooms, two with bath; **Malše** (M), 34 rooms, a few with bath; **Vltava** (M), 70 rooms, a few with bath or shower.

ČESKÝ KRUMLOV. Krumlov (M), 35 rooms, some with bath; **Vyšehrad** (M), 50 rooms, most with bath or shower.

DOMAŽLICE. Chodský Hotel (M), 20 rooms, a few with bath or shower; **Koruna** (M), 10 rooms.

FRANTIŠKOVY LÁZNĚ. Bajkal (M), 46 rooms; **Slovan** (M), 23 rooms.

HARRACHOV. Hubertus (M), 17 rooms, half with bath or shower; **Diana** (M), 10 rooms.

HLUBOKÁ. Parkhotel (M), 50 rooms, several with bath.

HRADEC KRÁLOVÉ. Černigov (E), 230 rooms and suites with bath or shower; **Alessandria** (M); **Bystrica** (M), 80 rooms, a few with bath or shower; **Avion** (M), 28 rooms.

JABLONEC. Corso (M), 40 rooms, some with bath or shower; **Praha** (M), 17 rooms; **Zlatý Lev** (M), 15 rooms, 3 with bath.

JÁCHYMOV. Klinovec (M), 47 rooms, snack bar.

JANSKÉ LÁZNĚ. Horský (M, I), 50 rooms, a few with bath or shower; **Praha** (M), 19 rooms.

JINDŘICHŮV HRADEC. Grand (M), 26 rooms; **Vajgar**, 30 rooms, a few with shower, no restaurant.

KARLOVY VARY. Grand Hotel Moskva-Pupp (L, M), 170 rooms, most with bath or shower; **Parkhotel** (E, M), 110 rooms with bath or shower; **Central** (M), 70 rooms, some with bath or shower; **Slavie** (M), 58 rooms with bath or shower; **Adria** (M), 40 rooms with shower; **Otava** (M), 70 rooms, a few with bath; **Sevastopol-Hornik** (I). The **Terminal Spa Sanatorium,** with 533 rooms, is very central, modern and extremely well equipped for those following treatment and their companions. Its fine open-air thermal pools are available to everyone.

KARLŠTEJN. U Nádraží (I), 7 rooms.

KONOPIŠTĚ. Myslivna (M), 30 rooms, some with bath; **Motel** (E), 40 rooms with shower.

KUTNÁ HORA. Mědínek (M), 90 rooms, nearly half with bath.

LIPNO. Lipno (I), 88 rooms with shower.

LITOMYŠL. Slezák (I), 14 rooms.

MARIÁNSKÉ LÁZNĚ. Golf (L), 30 rooms with bath, newly renovated and upgraded; **Palace Hotel Praha** (E), 45 rooms, most with bath, plus annexes; **Esplanade** (M), 60 rooms, half with bath; **Excelsior** (M), 70 rooms, most with shower; **Corso** (M), 28 rooms, some with bath; **Crystal** (M), 95 rooms, a few with bath.

MĚLNÍK. Ludmila (M), 70 rooms with shower; **Modrá Hvězda** (I), 7 rooms.

NOVÉ MĚSTO NAD METUJÍ. Metuje (I), 50 rooms.

NOVÝ BOR. Grand (M), 35 rooms.

PEC POD SNĚŽKOU. Horizont (M), modern, 126 rooms, excellent facilities; **Hořec** (M), 18 rooms, a few with shower; **Děvín** (I), 15 rooms; **Kolinská Bouda** (I), 28 rooms.

PÍSEK. Otava (M), 28 rooms; **Bílá Růže** (M), 26 rooms; **Tři Koruny** (M), 17 rooms.

PLZEŇ. Ural (E), 85 rooms and suites with bath or shower; **Continental** (M), 50 rooms, most with bath or shower; **Škoda** (M), 80 rooms and suites with bath; **Slovan** (M).

PODĚBRADY. Hubert (M), 20 rooms, a few with bath; **Praha** (M), 22 rooms, a few with bath.

PRACHATICE. Narodní Dům (M), 14 rooms, half with bath.

ŠPINDLERŮV MLÝN. Montana (E), 60 room and suites with bath or shower; **Alpský** (M), 20 rooms; **Labská Bouda** (M), 55 rooms with shower; **Savoy,** 28 rooms, a few with bath; **Davidova Bouda** (I), 25 rooms; **Jeleni bouda** (I).

TÁBOR. Palcát (M), 68 rooms with shower; **Jordán** (M), 60 rooms.

TŘEBOŇ. Bilý Koniček (M), 12 rooms with shower; **Svět** (M), 50 rooms.

VRCHLABÍ. Krakonoš (M), 18 rooms; **Labuť** (M), 18 rooms.

ZBRASLAV. Vltava (M), 10 rooms with bath.

ŽELEZNÝ BROD. Cristal (M), 45 rooms, several with bath.

USEFUL ADDRESSES. Most towns and resorts have a Čedok office. The principal ones for the region are as follows: **České Budějovice** Hroznova 21; **Hradec Králové** Leninova třída 63; **Karlovy Vary** Tržiště 23; **Kladno** nám. Revoluce 4/5; **Liberec** Revolučni 66; **Mladá Boleslav** třída Lidových milicí; **Plzeň** Sedláčkova 12; **Trutnov** Gottwaldovo nám. 120/21; **Ústí nad Labem** Hrnčířská 9/3.

MORAVIA

Forests and Furnaces

Moravia is separated from Bohemia by the Bohemian–Moravian highlands and, from Slovakia, by the Little and White Carpathian mountains. In the north of it is the industrial and coal-rich area that was once part of the historically much-disputed region of Silesia. Central Moravia is a series of valleys watered by the Morava River and its tributaries, opening into Austria in the south.

The Moravians will still energetically argue that temperamentally they are quite different from the Czechs of Bohemia. Indeed, within Moravia there are a number of quite distinct groups whose separate ethnic development is reflected in dialect, costume and folk culture. So it is perhaps not surprising that Czechoslovakia's most colorful annual folkloric event occurs on Moravian soil; at Strážnice, near the southeastern border with Slovakia.

Moravia also produces most of the country's best wines, offers some very fine grottoes, lovely river valleys, and one or two mountain areas of note. It can also claim to be the earliest nucleus of the future Czechoslovak state.

South Moravia and the Approach to Brno

Brno is Czechoslovakia's second largest city (population 340,000) and the capital of Moravia. If you have been exploring South Bohemia your approach is fortuitously through one of Czechoslovakia's most exquisite towns: Telč whose long rectangular square, almost surrounded by arcades, must be the dream of any architectural historian. On the lowest levels are beautifully-vaulted Gothic halls, then some renaissance floors and, last but not least, baroque gables, the whole complex gleaming in white and pastel tones. Overlooking the square, part of the original battlements adjoin a high watchtower from which trigger-happy photographers will be in their element snapping splendid perspectives of the arcaded square. At the other end is the impressive Gothic-renaissance castle. Baroque statuary is another feature of this astonishing little town. And to round off the scene, the surrounding countryside is lovely, too, studded with fish ponds, like that of neighboring South Bohemia.

Eastwards towards Brno, Třebič is a pleasant highland town with the romanesque-Gothic Church of St. Procopius retaining its character and a lovely Gothic entrance despite later reconstructions. The town is especially known for its production of Christmas cribs many of which can be seen in the local museum.

An alternative route to Brno from Telč would be the more devious one south through Znojmo, on the threshold of the great Moravian wine-growing region. Despite its industrial appearance, Znojmo has retained sections of medieval ramparts, and a variety of monuments. The most important is the 11th-century rotunda of St. Catherine near the castle displaying a rare cycle of frescoes (restored) from which you can see what various members of the Přemyslide dynasty looked like, at least to a contemporary artist. While you are here, it is well worth following the upstream meanderings of the river Dyje. These will bring you to the artificial lake of Vranov, a popular holiday area overlooked by a very fine baroque castle near its eastern end. It perches on top of a rock cliff and, seen from one of the pleasure boats on the waters below, looks for all the world like a great ocean liner about to take to the skies.

The whole vineyard area adjoining Znojmo echoes its long associations with the Liechtenstein family who started cultivating the grape almost as soon as they arrived here in medieval times. They also dotted the scene with castles. One of these, which they subsequently sold to the Dietrichsteins, is at Mikulov near the Austrian border and you should certainly seek it out. The castle, restyled in baroque, houses a simple hotel, a wine restaurant, wine cellars, and a museum; a remarkable possession is a wine cask made in 1643 with a capacity of over 22,000 gallons! They don't make them like that nowadays, but the products of the modern winery on the outskirts of the town are still among the local attractions.

Valtice, to the southeast of Mikulov, has another Liechtenstein castle (now largely baroque) with 365 windows, painted ceilings, and much exuberantly ornate woodwork. Between here and yet another Liechtenstein pile at Lednice to the northwest, this family of avid builders peppered the pleasant countryside with neo-classical temples and follies in the 19th century.

So man has moulded and made his marks on the countryside over the centuries, unaware and probably uncaring that very, very much longer ago his early ancestors had done just the same. At Dolní Věstonice, only a few miles from Mikulov, one of the most exciting excavation sites revealed, in 1950, traces of a settlement, graves, and a load of ivory and mammoth bones left by hunters over 20,000 years ago. Some of the first ceramics in the world were discovered here, too, among them a most curvaceous female statue of ash and clay, which has become known as the Věstonice Venus.

If your approach to Brno is from East Bohemia, your route will take you right through the Bohemia–Moravian Highlands via Žďár, near the source of the Sázava river and a starting point for trips into the northern part of the Bohemian–Moravian Highlands.

A somewhat circuitous route from Žďár would bring you most pleasantly down the lovely Svratka River, starting with Vír artificial lake, and proceeding via Pernštejn Castle and the old mining town of Tišnov. Pernštejn Castle, perched on a rocky headland above the Svratka River looks every inch the fortress it was, and is one of the best preserved late medieval structures in Moravia. The residential palace within it, with a stunning late Gothic façade, is of particular interest.

Brno

No one would claim this industrial metropolis is Czechoslovakia's most beautiful city but, as visitors to its regular international trade fairs will know, there is more to it than initially meets the eye. Two of its sights, however, cannot fail to meet the eye very rapidly. One is Špílberk Castle sitting up on its hill. Its dungeons and torture chambers are its macabre main sights, having witnessed horrors from the time of the Habsburgs to the Nazis. They do not leave too much to the imagination and it is a relief to escape to the pleasant restaurant and enjoy refreshments-with-a-view. The other hill-top sight is the Cathedral of Saints Peter and Paul on Petrov hill. Its Gothic look dates from the early 20th century and there is some good interior baroque.

Around these two monuments is the old part of town. You can follow steps down from the cathedral to the market place, whose stalls are to one side of the baroque Parnassus Fountain in the middle of the square.

The Dietrichstein Palace, now the Moravian Museum, is on one side of the square, its courts decorated with renaissance arcades. The museum possesses a good art gallery and, in a separate building, exhibits of Moravian folk art and ceramics. The Old Town Hall is worth seeing for its exquisite Gothic stone portal. The busy hub of Brno is Freedom Square (Náměstí Svobody), which has one or two fine renaissance and baroque buildings, one of which is the interesting Ethnographic Museum. A short distance away is one of the best Gothic buildings in Brno, the Church of St. James, with a splendidly austere simplicity and a tower 91 meters (300 feet) high. If you prefer baroque, the Jesuit

Church on Jesuitská street has some memorable statuary and restored paintings. After which you can refresh yourself in one of the cafés in the pleasant gardens off Rooseveltova street. On Malinovsky Square, the modern Janáček Opera House is a tribute to that composer's close association with Brno. His *Symphonietta* is dedicated to the city.

One more Brno 'must' lies on the way to the attractive Brno Exhibition Grounds—the Augustinian Monastery, whose brick-built church is virtually untouched since it was first erected in 1322. Among famous men who worked at the Monastery were the aforementioned Janáček and Gregor Mendel whose research on heredity led to the Mendelian Laws. The Exhibition Grounds themselves have some eye-catching modern architecture and are open all the year as a cultural and recreation park.

Border Country

Only a couple of dozen miles or so, to the east of Brno lies the site of one of the great battlefields of European history: Slavkov, better known to us as Austerlitz, where the armies of Napoleon met and defeated the combined forces of Austrian Emperor Francis I and Russian Alexander I. If you happen to have Tolstoy's *War and Peace* handy, you will find no better account of it. There is a museum, a landscaped garden, and the memorial chapel of the impressive Cairn of Peace a few miles away and, in the town of Slavkov itself, the baroque château houses more memorabilia from the battle.

Further east still you reach the Morava valley, with its many links with the days of the Great Moravian Empire of the 9th century. Remains from those and earlier days have been found on the outskirts of Uherské Hradiště and near Břeclav, but the most dramatic are at Mikulčice, a few miles south of Hodonín where remains (6th to 10th centuries) of defenses, a fortress, palace, several churches and many graves have been uncovered, some containing jewelry, weapons, coins and crucifixes. The whole provides a well-planned natural archeological museum.

In this border country with Slovakia, known as Moravian Slovakia, you will find Strážnice, where the top annual folklore festival is held each summer. The Institute of Folk Art has its museum in Strážnice Castle, which was most recently reconstructed around 1850. Near the town is a growing open-air museum of dwellings and workshops brought together to create a community of living history.

If it's scenic tourism you want, however, you should head north from Brno up the Svitava valley and into the Moravský Kras. This Moravian Karst is an area of limestone formations, underground stalactite caves, rivers, and tunnels. The most interesting part is near Blansko and includes Kateřinská jeskyně (Catherine Cave), Punkevní jeskyně (Punkva Caves), and the celebrated Macocha abyss, the deepest drop (over 400 feet, 120 meters) of the Karst. Boat trips can be made on the underground river through some of these remarkable limestone formations.

BRNO

1. Špilberk Castle
2. The Cathedral of SS. Peter and Paul
3. Moravian Museum
4. Old Town Hall
5. The Church of St James
6. Jesuit Church
7. Janáček Opera House
8. Central Station
9. Tourist Information Center

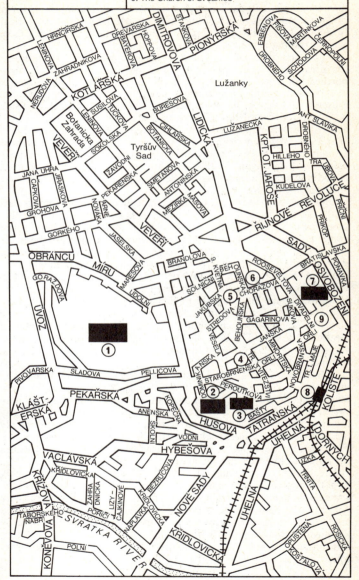

Northern Moravia

Industry and agriculture are two major themes of North Moravia. Here, near the northern border with Poland, lie the rich coalfields of former southern Silesia, which gave impetus to the major mining towns of Opava and Ostrava, Czechoslovakia's fourth largest city. Historically Opava is particularly important as the one-time capital of Silesia on a main trading route between the Baltic and Italy.

To the southwest of them lies Olomouc. It sprawls in the middle of the great granary of the Haná Plain, only about an hour's drive northeast of Brno, a region of formerly rich farmers that has produced its own folklore; this folk culture is particularly well represented in the museum at Litovel. To get a better idea of this fertile countryside, however, you would do better to take a route via Kroměřiž still in South Moravia. Much of it was destroyed during the Thirty Years' War, but subsequent reconstruction—mainly baroque—has left it with a main square splendidly bounded by patrician houses and a great palace, with an elegant English park and a splendid art collection that includes works by the Brueghels, Veronese, Van Dyck, and a particularly notable Titian.

Olomouc, despite its industry, retains its historic core from its days as the Moravian capital. The Town Hall has very attractive Renaissance features, although the present clock is modern. The best Gothic building is the Church of St. Maurice, whose colossal baroque organ is said to have 2,311 pipes, should you not feel like counting them. The town is famous for its superb flower exhibitions, held annually.

You now have the choice of North Moravia's two main mountain ranges: the Hrubý Jezeník (High Jeseníks) to the northwest and the Moravskoslezské Beskydy (Moravian-Silesian Beskydy) to the east. The High Jeseníks certainly offer tempting walking country, with plenty of marked trails, mountain chalets and inns, and a number of pleasant little spas. The Beskydy have a wilder, more primeval quality, and contain some of the most dramatic areas of virgin forest in Central Europe.

The composer Leoš Janáček was born in the village of Hukvaldy and must certainly have wandered in the woods of Beskydy. Only a few miles away, Příbor produced its own famous son, Sigmund Freud, only two years later in 1856. Štramberk is a charming little town of largely timbered houses. Much larger, Nový Jičín's arcaded square and mainly renaissance and baroque architecture qualify it as an urban reservation. The castle's collections include a most unusual museum; it illustrates the hatter's craft through the ages.

The Beskydy Mountains and the neighboring Javorníky roughly form the boundaries of Valašsko (Wallachia). This is the domain of the wooden cottage and the wooden church, and the valleys and hills are dotted with them. Valašske Meziříčí is the main gateway. If you haven't time to go further, go at least to the open-air museum at nearby Rožnov pod Radhoštěm with its splendid collection of folk architecture and folk activities. If you do have time, follow the Bečva valley from which you branch off for Velké Karlovice, a jewel of a Wallachian village. You can rejoin the main road to cross the forested ridge of the Javorníky Mountains into Slovakia.

PRACTICAL INFORMATION FOR MORAVIA

WHEN TO COME. The seasons are the same as for Bohemia, though the early fall has the added advantages of vintage time in some of the country's best wine-producing regions, and is also the time for Brno's major international trade fair.

GETTING AROUND MORAVIA. Čedok arrange sightseeing in and from Brno, and Moravia is included in more general tours of Czechoslovakia. Most people combine Moravia with Bohemia, and the same comments apply as for Bohemia.

HOTELS AND RESTAURANTS

All hotels listed below have restaurants unless otherwise stated.

BRNO. International (E), Husova 16, nearly 300 rooms with bath or shower; **Continental** (E), Leninova 20, 230 rooms with bath or shower; **Grand** (E), Tř. 1. máje 18/20, 110 rooms and suites, most with bath or shower; new **Voronez** (E), Křížkovskeho 47, over 1000 beds; **Slovan** (M), Lidická 23, 110 rooms, most with bath or shower; U Jakuba, Jakubské nám. 6, 38 rooms with bath or shower; **Metropol** (M), Dornych 5, 55 rooms, some with bath or shower.

 Restaurants. U Kralovny Elisky, a restored ancient wine cellar in former cloister with fireplace grill; **Castle Špilberk,** period decor, folk band, good wines; **Myslivna,** in outskirts, good views of city.

BŘECLAV. Grand (M), 20 rooms; **Slavia** (M), 30 rooms, some with bath.

GOTTWALDOV. Moskva (E); **Družba** (M).

HODONÍN. Grand (M), 24 rooms; **Sportklub** (M), 12 rooms.

HUKVALDY. Hukvaldy (M), 25 rooms.

JESENÍK. Slovan (M), 32 rooms.

KARLOVA STUDÁNKA. Džbán (M), 13 rooms.

KROMEŘIŽ. Hana (M), 65 rooms, some with bath or shower.

MIKULOV. Zámecká Vinárna (I), 12 rooms, part of castle.

NOVÝ JIČIN. Praha (M), 32 rooms, a few with bath.

OLOMOUC. Flora (M), 170 rooms with shower, new; Národní Dum (M), 65 rooms, some with bath or shower; Palác (M), 55 rooms, half with bath or shower; Morava (M), 60 rooms, a few with bath or shower.

OPAVA. Orient (M), 65 rooms, a few with bath; Zimní Stadion (M), 12 rooms.

OSTRAVA. Imperial (E, M), 125 rooms, most with bath; Palace (M), over 200 rooms, half with bath or shower; Odra (M), 50 rooms, a few with bath; Moravia (M), 33 rooms.

PŘÍBOR. Letka (M), 40 rooms with shower.

STRAŽNICE. Čemý Orel (I), 11 rooms.

ŠUMPERK. Grand (M), 57 rooms with shower; Moravan (M), 38 rooms, a few with bath.

TELČ. Čemý Orel (M), 23 rooms, a few with bath.

TIŠNOV. Květnice (M), 18 rooms, a few with bath.

TŘEBIČ. Zlatý Kříž (M), 25 rooms, half with bath or shower.

UHERSKÉ HRADIŠTĚ. Grand (M), 34 rooms, half with bath or shower; Morava (M), 56 rooms.

VALAŠSKÉ MEZIŘIČI. Apollo (M), 66 rooms with shower.

VELKÉ KARLOVICE. Razula (M), 40 rooms with shower.

ZNOJMO. Družba (M), 68 rooms with bath; Nádražní (M), 7 rooms; Znojmo (M), 26 rooms.

ŽDAR. Bílý Lev (M), 40 rooms with shower; Tálský Mlýn (M), 19 rooms with shower.

USEFUL ADDRESSES. Most towns and resorts have a Čedok office. The principal ones for the region are as follows: Brno: Divadelní 3; Gottwaldov: Kvítkova 80; Olomouc: nám. Míru 2; Ostrava: Dimitrovova 9.

SLOVAKIA

Mountains and Medieval Castles

The predominant ethnic group of this second half of the Czechoslo-vak federated state is of course Slovak, but there are important minori-ties of Hungarians along the southern borders and a number of Ukrainians in the east. Geographically, Slovakia is separated from Moravia in the west by the White Carpathians. It has a rich folklore and great contrasts of scenery, including some of the most spectacular in Europe. In the south are the fertile plains of the Danube and its tributaries—a major Czechoslovakian granary—but these give way to hills and mountains, rising sometimes quite suddenly from the plains, in the north. They reach their greatest height (8,730 feet, 2,760 meters) in the High Tantras.

Although they speak a language closely related to Czech, there is a strong force of Slovak nationalism and, indeed, the two Slav groups developed quite separately. Though united in the 9th century as part of the Great Moravian Empire, a century later the Slovaks were con-quered by the Magyars and remained under Hungarian or Habsburg rule until 1918.

Bratislava

Bratislava (population 306,000) is the third largest city of Czechoslovakia and capital of Slovakia. Its history goes back to Roman times. The Slavs settled here in the 5th century under their leader Břetislav, but the city came under the rule of Hungary who called it Pozsony. Its many German-speaking settlers called it Pressburg and only in 1918 did it regain its Slavic name. It lies on the banks of the Danube close to the frontiers of Austria and Hungary and thus its three names reflect the racial confusion of this meeting place of cultures. From the restaurant in the tower of the elegant modern bridge spanning the Danube, you get superb views of the city and its mighty waterway.

After the capture of Buda by the Turks in 1541, Bratislava became the capital of Hungary in 1536 and many monarchs were crowned in the Cathedral of St. Martin. A university was founded here in 1467 and Bratislava was the seat of the Hungarian Diet until 1848. The old parts of the city have great charm. Bratislava Castle dominates the city, massive and square but with corner towers later added to relieve its heaviness. From its walls are splendid views over three countries. It has been restored in renaissance and baroque styles and, after a disastrous fire in 1811, has been reconstructed in recent times. The Habsburg queen Maria Theresa in particular took a fancy to the place and her presence attracted noble families whose patrician houses add much charm to the narrow streets of the old town below the castle. The Cathedral of St. Martin is the most beautiful and historically interesting church of the city, built in the 14th and 15th centuries. On top of the high tower, which was part of the town's fortifications, is a carved cushion and a replica of the crown of St. Stephen.

Central in the Old Town is the 4th April Square (Námestie 4 Aprila) and, at one end of it, the Old Town Hall, also 14th to 15th-century, now housing part of the city and wine museums. In the fine courtyard, with its renaissance arcades, concerts are held in the spring and summer. Close by is the baroque Archbishop's Palace (Primatial Palace), 1778–80, in whose Hall of Mirrors the historic Peace of Pressburg was signed after the Battle of Austerlitz (1805) by Napoleon and the Austrian Emperor Francis I. The Municipal Gallery is housed here. It includes six magnificent tapestries depicting the classical story of Hero and Leander, created by Flemish weavers in Mortlake, England, in the 17th century.

The Old Town is the historical heart of the city and currently a good deal of restoration work is in progress. Approached from a Gothic chain bridge is October Square (Októbrove Nám). Here is Michael's Gate, with its 15th-century tower; this is the best preserved part of the town's fortifications and offers excellent views. Built into the barbican of the gate is a baroque building now housing the Pharmaceutical Museum in what was the city's first apothecary, once known as the Red Crayfish (U Červného Raka). Nearby is Băstova street, narrow, old world and charming, which leads into Klariská street where you'll find one of the oldest Gothic buildings in Bratislava, the Church of the

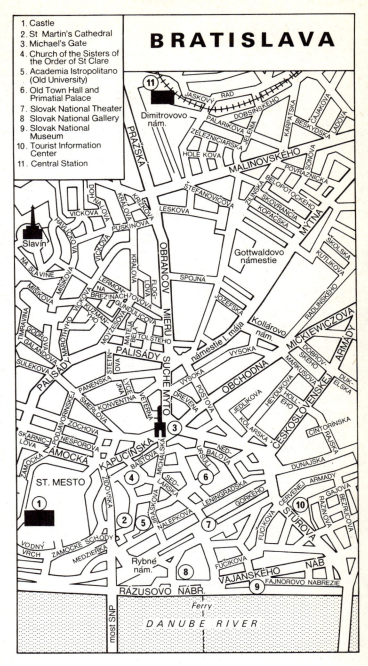

BRATISLAVA

1. Castle
2. St Martin's Cathedral
3. Michael's Gate
4. Church of the Sisters of the Order of St Clare
5. Academia Istropolitano (Old University)
6. Old Town Hall and Primatial Palace
7. Slovak National Theater
8. Slovak National Gallery
9. Slovak National Museum
10. Tourist Information Center
11. Central Station

DANUBE RIVER

Sisters of the Order of St. Clare (early 15th century). A section of the Municipal Gallery is here.

From Michael's Gate a walk down Michalská street, which leads into Jiráskova street, gives sight of some of the loveliest buildings of the city. There is the Segner House (Segnerova Kuria) with renaissance bay windows and a finely decorated façade; and the University Library which was the former Royal Chamber (built 1753–56) and the seat of the Hungarian Diet from 1802–48. Further along in Jiráskova street are the renaissance buildings of the 15th century Bratislava University (Academia Istropolitana).

South of the Old Town and nearer to the Danube is the business section of the city where are also the best hotels. Here, too, are the Slovak National Theater, the National Gallery and, further down the Danube, the Slovak National Museum.

West Slovakia—Little Carpathians

Just outside Bratislava, where the Little Carpathians slide down to the Danube, the majestic castle ruin of Devin (closed) stands high on a rock promontory at the confluence of the Morava and Danube rivers. The castle, destroyed by Napoleon's Army, dates from the 9th century and the days of the Great Moravian Empire. A few miles to the north, Stupava is a good starting point for walks into the southwest part of the Little Carpathians, and offers the remains of a Roman camp—something of a rarity here, since most of this land stood beyond the fringes of the Roman Empire. Recent excavations indicate that this was also an early Slav settlement.

The southeastern slopes of these hills are wine-growing country and Pezinok is one of its attractive towns. Its renaissance castle is now a Museum of Viniculture, a wine bar and restaurant. The earliest building is the 14th-century Gothic church, but there are also remains of 17th-century fortifications. Close to Pezinok is the village of Slovenský Grob, famous for folk crafts and painted peasant cottages.

Jur pri-Bratislave is another early wine-growing town in this area, its town museum containing exhibits relating to its Turkish occupation. If you continue along the road from here through Pezinok, you will come in a few miles to Modra, a small town at the foot of the wooded peaks of the Little Carpathians, notable for its wines and crafts.

One of the castles you should seek out in the Little Carpathians is Červený Kameň, originally a frontier fort on the old 13th-century trade route from Hungary to Bohemia. It has been restored as a museum of Renaissance and baroque artifacts from the whole of West Slovakia. A little further north are the villages of Smolenice and Jahodnik, both typical villages of the Little Carpathians. While you are in this direction one of the richest archeological sites in Czechoslovakia is at Skálica, on the Moravian–Slovak border, east of the Moravian town of Hodonín. Here you will find late Stone Age settlements as well as a Slav burial ground from the 8th and 9th centuries. There is a Jewish cemetery constructed from the old castle moat and its 18th-century tombstones recall the days of the former ghetto.

West Slovakia—The Váh Valley

If you head northeast from Bratislava, you will soon come to the Váh valley, on the way passing one of the oldest towns in Slovakia. This is Trnava, raised to town status in 1238 and, from 1635, a university town. After the occupation of Buda by the Turks it was for nearly three centuries the see of the Archbishop of Esztergom and the silhouette of the town bristles with towers and spires. The large Gothic Church of St. Nicholas dates from 1380; the Church of St. Elizabeth is even earlier as is the hospital adjoining it.

Northwards up the broad Váh valley you will come to Piešťany, ranking in fame with the best known spas of Bohemia. The therapeutic use of its mineral waters and mud for relief of rheumatism and other disorders goes back to very early times and is well documented in the town's well-arranged Balneological Museum. Most of the spa installations are in the town's park-like island of Kúpelný Ostrov. Nearby Slňava dam lake offers boating and water sports, and bird-watching enthusiasts will find many small inlets and islands that provide a haven for water fowl.

The next major town is Trenčín, originally a Roman fort and, indeed, the site of the most northerly situated Roman military settlement in Central Europe. There is an inscription on the castle rock proclaiming the victory in AD 179 of Emperor Marcus Aurelius over the Germanic tribes then residing in these parts, but to see it you will need to visit the Hotel Tatra; here, next to the dining room, a window faces the inscription only a few feet away. The Gothic castle, part of which is now a museum, dominates the town. A few miles away is another very well known spa, Trenčianske Teplice, with a natural thermal swimming pool called the Green Frog (Zelena Zaba) cut into the rock. The facilities are excellent and the setting particularly attractive.

In due course, the Váh curves eastwards and passes through Žilina, one of the most industrialized towns in Slovakia. Nevertheless, its Dukla square goes back to medieval times and is graced with arcaded houses, mostly in renaissance style. The most historic building is the late romanesque St. Stephen Church with wall paintings from the 14th century. South of Žilina, you can follow the valley of the Rajčianka to the medieval town of Rajec; here and in the surrounding villages, folklore is still very much alive.

East of Žilina and on the north side of the Váh, a road will take you to the lovely old village of Terchová, starting point for the Vrátna Dolina, one of the most beautiful valleys of Czechoslovakia leading into the heart of the Malá Tatra mountains. This is wonderful walking country and, in winter, there is some of the best skiing in the country.

Further east along the Vah, this great Slovak river is joined by one of its major northern tributaries, the Orava. A short drive upstream, Dolný Kubín is the starting point for climbs into the Oravska Magura range and the Chočské Pohorir. Podbiel gives access to the Roháče massif. Trstená, nearer to the Polish border, is another good center, close to the artificial lake of Orava where there are recreational facilities. The area is notable for woodcarving and folk architecture.

The Upper Váh valley falls more naturally into the eastern half of Slovakia and we shall deal with it later.

West Slovakia—The Danube and its Plains

The route from Bratislava to Komárno is through one enormous island, contained between the so-called Little Danube and the main river. As well as being a rich agricultural area, its considerable watery areas provide one of Europe's richest natural habitats for waterfowl and game birds. It is a veritable paradise for fishermen and naturalists, and, as one might expect, a popular hunting ground. For full information on these passive and active pastimes, you should enquire locally for there are a number of important reservations. In future years, however, there are likely to be many changes as major hydro-electric projects in co-operation with Hungary take shape, raising the level of the Danube and flooding considerable areas. Zlatná-na-Ostrove is an old gold mining center. Komárno itself lies at the confluence of the Váh and the Danube and is an important river port, as well as an official crossing point for Hungary (Komaron) to which it is linked by road bridge. The underground fortifications, first built after the Turkish occupation of Hungary, are of interest.

Among the many rivers that flow down from the Slovak mountains into the Danube basin is the Nitra. The important town of Nitra itself lies about an hour's drive north of the Danube and today is mainly industrial despite its ancient origins. Of particular interest, however, is the Episcopal Cathedral consisting of three churches in different architectural styles, and the baroque Bishop's Palace, which houses the Archaeological Institute. In the old Franciscan Monastery, there is an Agricultural Museum. East of Nitra is the Mlyňany Arborétum, open to the public throughout the year, and outstanding of its kind with its 2000 different species of tree. Only a few miles to the north, Topol'čiany has an old château which is now a museum of period furniture and local arts and crafts. It is also known for its stud farm, breeding Lippizaners, Arab stallions and English thoroughbreds.

East Slovakia—Upper Váh Valley and the Low Tatras

Now we come to the region of soaring landscapes, of peaks that seem suspended in their own remoteness, of deep valleys ribbing their flanks: these are the mountain landscapes par excellence of the Nízke Tatry and Vysoké Tatry (the Low and the High Tatras). The Upper Váh has its source in both, for two main streams meet to form it, the Čierny (or Black) Váh from the Low Tatras, and the Biely (or White) Váh from the High Tatras.

But before we reach them, we come to Ružomberok. Originally founded as a German mining town, it is a good starting point for the tourist centers in the Great Fatra and Low Tatras ranges to the south of the Váh, and Chočské mountains to the north. There is skiing and walking to suit all grades. A few miles east and to the north of the road is the great lake created by the Liptovská Mara dam, which is being developed as a tourist area with all kinds of water sports. After this you reach Liptovský Mikuláš; starting point for excursions into the loveliest parts of the Low Tatras. One of the oldest (but restored) Gothic churches in Slovakia is here: the Church of St. Nicholas. Worth visiting in the vicinity is the splendid 18th-century wooden church of Paludza.

South of the town is the Demänovská Dolina, the most beautiful valley of the Low Tatras. This leads to Demänovská ice cave and the Demänovská Jaskyňa Slobody (Freedom Cave), both part of a massive cave system whose known caverns and passages cover 12 miles (19 km.) on nine levels. Liptovský Ján is a summer resort and a starting place for ascents of Ďumbier, the highest peak in the Low Tatras. Another resort a little further east is Liptovský Hrádok. The nearby villages of Východná and Važec are rich in folklore; indeed the annual folklore festival at Východná in July is one of the highlights of the Slovak calendar.

From near Liptovský Hrádok, a road heads south right across the Low Tatras range to Banská Bystrica in the upper Hron valley. This industrial and historic town has a splendid situation with hills and mountains in all directions. From the 14th century, and for 200 years, it held an important position in the copper trade, mined near the town. It has many handsome renaissance mansions, the best being around the main square. Surviving from the old castle complex are the gate, the Gothic Royal Palace, the Praetorium, and two Gothic churches. The nearest recreation areas are just west of the town in the Kremničke Pohorie mountains with skiing facilities, chalets and many paths. Indeed, all these mountain ranges of Slovakia are provided with an extremely good network of marked trails. A few miles to the south Zvolen is another ancient town, much restored, but still with a Gothic concept. The castle now contains part of the collection of the Slovak National Gallery.

West of Banská Bystrica is another beautifully situated Slovak town, dominated by a castle complex in the heart of the Kremnice Mountains. Kremnica's days of glory were in the 14th and 15th centuries when it minted gold ducats which became a standard of currency in Europe. The mint has been in operation ever since and a museum is devoted to its activities. The heart of the Old Town has some of the best-preserved Gothic burgher houses in Slovakia, contrasting with the miners' charming little houses with their wooden balconies.

East Slovakia—the High Tatras

But the region that most people have come to see is the Vysoké Tatry, the High Tatras, Czechoslovakia's highest mountains and some of the finest in the world. Their best point of entry is the road and rail junction of Poprad (it also has an airport), a major tourist and industrial town. The most beautiful part is the suburb of Spišska Sobota, with its steep, shingle-roofed Renaissance and baroque buildings.

A few miles northeast is Kežmarok, where there are fine examples of the typical local style of architecture: steep shingled roofs, high timber-framed gables, and brick-arched doorways. The old Evangelical Church, now a museum, is built entirely of wood with no stone foundations and no nails.

In the mountains to the northeast of here, you can visit villages which seem quite untouched by the passage of time. One of these is Jakubany, a Ukrainian–Ruthenian village, where the clock seems to have stopped a century ago. The villagers still produce the raw materials for their folk costumes and their old way of life has been preserved almost intact. Further north you come to the Pieniny National Park and to Červený Kláštor near the Polish border, one of the most beautiful natural beauty spots in Slovakia.

But the main purpose of a visit to Poprad is to wallow in the magnificent scenery of the High Tatras. The best possible way is on foot, remembering that these are mountains to be reckoned with and you should not embark on any major walk without proper clothing and footwear, and clear directions. Many marked trails make it quite easy to explore some of this exciting area. The highest mountain is Gerlachov Štít (Gerlach Peak), 8,730 feet (2,660 meters), and the whole area is the nature preserve of the Tatra National Park.

A chain of High Tatras villages and resorts are connected by the Freedom Road. Traveling northeast on this road, you come first to the well-equipped ski resort of Štrbské Pleso, site of many an international ski event; then the health resorts of Vyšné Hágy and Tatranská Polianka. A little way beyond is Smokovec, the largest of the tourist centers and the most important starting point for many of the mountain excursions. Another excellent center both for summer or winter is Tatranská Lomnica from which there are cable railways to Skalnaté Pleso (Rock Lake), at 5,250 feet (1,600 meters). Further north, Ždiar is an enchanting little place with its timber-built folk architecture; and it's the only farming community in these parts.

The Easternmost Corner

To the east of these grandiose mountain ranges are yet more mountains which, though of rather lesser stature provide a setting for some of the most charming folk architecture and folkloric traditions. This easternmost section of Slovakia is still relatively little known to Western visitors.

Either Poprad or Rožňava would be a good place from which to start. Rožňava is a medieval gold mining town and, as in so many other towns, the best and oldest architectural gems are concentrated round the main square, built over the former passages and shafts of the gold mines. The Cathedral, originally a Gothic church of the 13th century but enlarged and restyled, has an altar piece of scenes from the working life of miners. The town museum is devoted to the same theme. Hill-top Krásna Hôrka castle 3 miles (5 km) away, is one of the most beautiful in Slovakia.

South and east of Rožňava is the region of Slovenský Kras (Slovak Karst) with more caves and natural limestone features. There is the Domica cavern which was inhabited by Neolithic man, where visitors can now go by boat along the aptly named river Styx. North of the road to Košice is the Zádielska valley, a long and narrow limestone gorge. Nearby is the Jasovská cave.

Košice is the second largest town in Slovakia. Again the best historical features are spread around the original medieval square. The most important building is the Gothic cathedral of St. Elizabeth completed in 1508; the high altar is a monumental piece of wood carving by an unknown genius. The Miklušova prison in a remnant of the old walls and its torture chamber are genuine pieces of pure medieval horror.

One of the unusual sights of the neighborhood is the Herl'any Geyser, 20 miles (30 km.) to the north-east in the Slanke hills. As it has an eruption interval of 28 to 36 hours you should first check with the Čedok office in Košice. The display, shooting up to nearly 130 feet (40 meters), lasts for about 20 minutes. East of Košice at Dargov, a Victory Memorial and rose garden mark the site of a battlefield where 22,000 Soviet soldiers died in the winter of 1944/45.

Although now a fast growing industrial town, the heart of Prešov has quite a lot of interest. Its center is the long spindle shaped square with ornate burgher houses and arcades. The three churches—the late Gothic St. Nicholas, the renaissance Orthodox and the baroque Evangelical Churches—represent three different Christian sects and three different styles. Prešov is also of interest as a cultural center for the Ukrainians of East Slovakia.

Another interesting town of this Šariš area of Slovakia is Bardejov, which has well preserved medieval fortifications. The cobbled square is a veritable outdoor museum of Gothic and renaissance architecture, many buildings with a characteristic sign above the door. The monumental late Gothic Church of St. Egidius (St. Giles) has Gothic aisle altars, with complex decorations in their original 15th-century state. The Šariš Museum contains a valuable collection of icons dating from the 16th century.

This is Orthodox Christian country, echoing the work of Byzantine missionaries a millennium ago, and an area of enchanting wooden churches. At Hervatov (just a few miles southwest) is one of the earliest, but the best area for these charming structures is east of Bardejov in the villages around Svidník. They are built in Byzantine style and date from the 17th and 18th centuries. The oldest is at Kružlova.

Svidník itself is a completely new town, having been destroyed in the fighting of World War II. There are more reminders of the last war at the Dukla Pass, on the Polish border, scene of ferocious fighting. It was here in the winter of 1944 that Russian and Czechoslovak troops fought for many weeks seeking to break through the pass into Slovakia. The battlefield has been turned into an outdoor museum with all the paraphernalia of war.

West of Prešov lies the mountainous region of Spiš, many of whose towns are prefaced by the word 'Spišský'. It was originally settled by German immigrants who came to work in the mines and act as a defense against eastern invasion in medieval times. For 300 years from the 15th century, much of the area was under Polish jurisdiction. Levoča, founded in 1245, was the former seat of the Spiš district. The main square is lined with the impressive façades of the houses of the rich Levoča merchants; the Gothic church of St. James, completed in 1400, is the second largest Gothic church in Slovakia and its massive main altar is said to be the largest in the world. Note *The Last Supper* carved in limewood. The 12 disciples are portraits of Levoča merchants.

Levoča is only a short drive from Poprad and the High Tatras, but there is one more mountain area deserving attention. This is Slovenský Raj, the Slovak Paradise to the southwest, to which the inhabitants of the Spiš towns fled during the Tartar invasion of 1241–42. It is a wild and romantic region of gorges and cliffs, caves and waterfalls. The main tourist center is at Kláštorisko (2,445 feet/745 meters), best reached from Spišská Nová Ves.

PRACTICAL INFORMATION FOR SLOVAKIA

WHEN TO COME. Wonderful hiking in late spring and summer, the best time for general touring and sightseeing. Winter brings the crowds to the splendid skiing grounds of the High and Low Tatras and elsewhere. Spring and Fall are good for blossom or wonderful colors. As in Bohemia, spa treatment is available year round.

GETTING AROUND SLOVAKIA. Čedok arrange tours in and around Bratislava and also have a 7-day tour of Slovakia starting here. Otherwise your own car gives the greatest freedom. Rail and bus services cover the region.

HOTELS AND RESTAURANTS

All hotels listed below have restaurants unless otherwise stated.

BANSKÁ BYSTRICA. Lux (M), 150 rooms with bath; **Národný Dom** (M), 40 rooms, most with bath or shower; **Urpín** (M), 60 rooms, most with bath or shower, snack bar.

BARDEJOV. Minerál (M), 60 rooms and suites with bath or shower; **Dukla** (M), 37 rooms, a few with bath.

BRATISLAVA. Devín (L), Riečná 4, over 100 rooms and suites, most with bath or shower; **Carlton** (M), Hviezdoslavovo nám. 7, 120 rooms, most with bath or shower; **Kyjev** (E), Rajská 2, over 200 rooms with bath; **Motel Zlaté Piesky** (E), Senecká cesta, 40 rooms with bath; **Bratislava** (M), Urxova 9, over 300 rooms and suites with bath; **Krym** (M), Safárikovo nám. 6, 50 rooms, some with bath or shower; **Clubhotel** (M), Odborjárov 3, 30 rooms with shower; **Dukla** (M), nám. Lud. milicí 1, 52 rooms with bath; **Palace** (M), Poštová 1, 75 rooms, a few with bath; Botel **Javorina** (M), 55 rooms.

Restaurants. Nearly 300 wine-cellar restaurants include the recently opened **Hradná vináreň** (Castle Wine Cellar) tastefully arranged in the Bratislava castle complex. Among others are **Velkí Františkani**, Diebrovo nám.; **Kláštorná vináreň**, Pugacevova, in 300-year-old monastery; **Pod Bastou** and **Ribársky Cech. Slovenska Restauracia** is one of the best for Slovak specialties. In the main square of Slovak National Uprising is **Polom**, an attractive new complex of coffee houses and small restaurants (open air and indoor). There's a rotating café atop the new TV tower and the **Bystrica Café** perched on a pylon above Slovak bridge; both offer outstanding views. **Koliba Expo,** farther out, has gypsy music and heady wines in a lovely setting of wooded hills.

DOLNÝ KUBÍN. Severan (M), 45 rooms, many with shower.

KEŽMAROK. Štart (M), 32 rooms, many with bath or shower.

KOMÁRNO. Europa (M), 60 rooms with bath or shower; **Spoločenský Dom** (M), 50 rooms.

KOŠICE. Slovan (E), over 200 rooms and suites with bath; **Imperiál** (M), 45 rooms and suites with bath or shower; **Hutník** (M), 200 rooms and suites with bath or shower; **Club-Vsž** (M), 56 rooms, half with shower.

KREMNICA. Veterník (M), 26 rooms.

LEVICE. Rozkvet (M), 60 rooms, half with bath.

LEVOČA. V Domě Služieb (M), 12 rooms with shower; **Družba** (M), 22 rooms, no restaurant.

LIPTOVSKÝ HRÁDOK. Smrek (M), 17 rooms.

LIPTOVSKÝ MILULÁŠ. Jánošík (M), 68 rooms, half with bath; **Europa** (M), 11 rooms; **Lodenica-TJ** (M), 14 rooms.

MODRA. Modra (M), 16 rooms, a few with bath or shower; a few miles away **Zochovo Chata** (M) in charming traditional style.

NITRA. Nitra (M), 135 rooms, new; **Zobor** (M), 50 rooms, a few with bath; **Tatra** (M), 11 rooms, cafe.

PEZINOK. Grand (M), 110 rooms, most with bath; **Horský** (M), 50 rooms.

PIEŠŤANY. Magnólia (E), 120 rooms and suites with bath; **Eden** (M), 50 rooms, some with bath or shower; **Klas** (M), 40 rooms; **Lipa** (M), 47 rooms.

POPRAD. Európa (M), 73 rooms; **Gerlach** (M), 120 rooms, over half with bath.

POVAŽSKÁ BYSTRICA. Spoločenský Dom (I), 25 rooms with shower.

PREŠOV. Dukla (M), 90 rooms and suites, many with bath or shower; **Verchovina** (M), 18 rooms, 1 with bath; **Motel Stop,** 9 rooms.

RAJECKÉ TEPLICE. Velká Fatra (M), 52 rooms, 1 with bath.

ROŽŇAVA. Kras (M), 60 rooms and suites, most with bath or shower.

RUŽOMBEROK. Hrabovo (M), 20 rooms and suites with bath; **Kulturný Dom** (M), 40 rooms; **Savoy** (M), 7 rooms.

SMOKOVEC. Really three resorts in one. In *Starý Smokovec:* **Grand** (E), 100 rooms and suites, most with bath or shower; **Udernik** (M), 34 rooms, café. In *Novy Smokovec:* **Park** (M), 96 rooms with bath; **Tokajík** (M), 13 rooms, half with bath; **MS** (M), 10 rooms; **Bystrina** (I). In *Horný Smokovec:* **Bellevue** (E-M), 110 rooms, indoor pool, most comfortable; **Sport** (M-I), 59 rooms.

SPIŠSKÁ NOVÁ VES. Metropol (M), 90 rooms, most with bath or shower.

ŠTRBSKÉ PLESO. Patria (E), 157 rooms and suites with bath; **Fis** (M), 50 rooms with shower; **Panoráma** (M), 65 rooms and suites with bath or shower.

SVIDNÍK. Dukla (M), 26 rooms.

TATRANSKÁ LOMNICA. Grandhotel Praha (E, M), 110 rooms and suites, most with bath; **Slovan** (M), 80 rooms with bath; **Lomnica** (M), 16 rooms, a few with bath; **Motel Eurocamp FICC** (M), 100 rooms with bath.

TERCHOVÁ. Boboty (M), 140 rooms, many with shower.

TOPOL'ČIANKY. Národný Dom (I), 12 rooms.

TRENČÍN. Laugaricio (M), 100 rooms, nearly half with shower; **Tatra** (M), 68 rooms, some with bath.

TRNAVA. Karpaty (M), 100 rooms, some with shower.

TRSTENÁ. Roháč (I), 7 rooms.

VAŽEC. Važec (M).

ŽILINA. Metropol (M), 51 rooms; **Polom** (M), 65 rooms, 1 with bath; **Dukla** (I), 24 rooms.

ZVOLEN. Polana (M), 80 rooms and suites, most with bath.

USEFUL ADDRESSES. Most towns and resorts have a Čedok office. The principal ones for the region are: **Banská Bystrica** nám. Červenej armády 26; **Bratislava** Štúrova 13; **Košice** Rooseveltova 1; **Nitra** Leninova 72; **Piešťany** Pavlovova 50; **Starý Smokovec** Starý Smokovec 33; **Žilina** nám. Budovatelov 1.

TOURIST VOCABULARY

Most letters in the Czech alphabet are pronounced approximately as in English but here are the basic variations, with their corresponding English sounds italicized in brackets. All vowels are pronounced long if provided with an accent; thus á (*al*mond or *bar*), é (*a*rea or c*a*re), í (*ea*sy or s*ee*m), ó (*o*rchestra or d*oo*r), ú or ů (*Ou*se or s*ou*p). The letter ý is pronounced like the í.

Other letters are pronounced as follows—a (*A*lbert, never as in case, share, etc.), c (Be*ts*y or titbi*ts*), č (*ch*arter or bit*ch*), dě, tě, ně (*Di*ego, *Ti*entsin, *Nye*rere), e (s*e*t, *e*nd, etc., even at the end of a word!), g (*g*ame or bo*g*ey, never as in ginger!), ch (a Scottish lo*ch*, symbolized in our pronunciation by kh), i (*i*nk, Map*li*n or bu*s*y), j (*Y*ank, pa*y*, never as in jam), o (*O*scar, b*o*ss), ou (kn*ow* or *ow*n, never as in thousand or now), ř (pronounced roughly like the middle group of consonants in cou*rg*ette, it is symbolized in our pronunciation by rzh), s (*s*alt, bo*ss*, never as in easy), š (*sh*ine or cu*sh*ion), u (b*oo*k, never as in ukelele), y (pronounced like the Czech i, see above), ž (as in French bon*j*our or English vi*si*on, symbolized in our pronunciation by zh).

A final note on tonal stress—this is practically always on the *first* syllable, as in the English words *coo*ker, *Al*bert, *ba*con.

USEFUL EXPRESSIONS

Hello, how do you do	Dobrý den (dobree den)
Good morning	Dobré jitro (dobreh yitro)
Good evening	Dobrý večer (Dobree vecher)
Goodnight	Dobrou noc (dobrow nots)
Goodbye	Sbohem; Na shledanou (sbohem; Na skhledanow)
Please	Prosím (proseem)
Thank you	Děkuji (dyekuyi)
Thank you very much	Velmi děkuji (velmi dyekuyi)
Yes	Ano (ano)
No	Ne (neh)
You're welcome	Prosím (proseem)
Excuse me	S dovolením (s dovolenyeem)
Come in!	Dále! (dahle!)
I'm sorry	Lituji (lituyi)
My name is . . .	Jmenuji se . . . (menuyi se . . .)
Do you speak English?	Mluvíte anglicky? (mluveete anglitsky?)
I don't speak Czech	Nemluvím česky (nemluveem chesky)
Please speak slowly	Prosím, mluvte pomalu (proseem, mluvte pomalu)
I don't understand	Nerozumím (nerozumeem)
Please write it down	Prosím, napište to (proseem, napishte to)
Where is . . . ?	Kde je . . . ? (kde ye . . .)
What is this place called?	Jak se to (místo) jmenuje? (yak se to/meesto/menuye?)
Please show me	Prosím, ukažte mně (proseem,

ukazhte mnye . . .)

I would like . . .	(Já) bych chtěl; (yah bykh khtyel . . .)
	a woman says (Já) bych chtěla (yah bykh khtyela . . .)
How much does it cost?	Kolik to stojí? (kolik to stoyee?)

SIGNS

Entrance	Vchod (vkhod)
Exit	Východ (veekhod)
Emergency Exit	Nouzový východ (nowzovee veekhod)
Toilet	Toaleta, záchod (toaleta, zahkhod)
men, gentlemen	muži, páni (muzhi, pahnyi)
women, ladies	ženy, dámy (zheny, dahmy)
vacant	volno (volno)
occupied	obsazeno (obsazeno)
Hot	Horká (horkah)
Cold	Studená (studenah)
No smoking	Kouření zakázáno (kowrzhenyee zakahzahno)
No admittance	Vstup zakázán (vstup zakahzahn)
Stop	Stát! (staht!)
Danger	Nebezpečí, Výstraha (nebezpechee, veestraha)
Open	Otevřeno (otevrzheno)
Closed	Zavřeno (zavrzheno)
Full, no vacancy	Obsazeno (obsazeno)
Information	Zprávy (zprahvy)
Bus stop	Zastávka (zastahvka)
Taxi stand	Parkoviště taxíků (parkovishtye taxeekoo)
Pedestrians	Pěší (pyeshee)

ARRIVAL

Passport check	Pasová prohlídka (pasovah prohleedka)
your passport, please	Váš pas, prosím (vahsh pas, proseem)
I am with the group	Já jsem se skupinou (yah sem se skupinow)
Customs	Celnice (tselnitse)
Anything to declare?	Máte něco k proclení? (mahte nyetso k protslenyee?)
Nothing to declare	Nemám nic k proclení (nemahm nyits k protslenyee)
Baggage claim	Výdej zavazadel (veedey zavazadel)
This suitcase is mine	To je můj kufřík (to ye mooy kufrzheek)
A porter, baggage carrier	Nosič (nosich)
Transportation	
to the bus	k autobusu (k autobusu)

to a taxi — taxi (taxi)
to the Hotel . . . , please — k hotelu . . . , prosím (k hotelu . . . , proseem)

MONEY

Currency exchange office — Směnárna (smnyenahrna)
Do you have the change for this? — Máte drobné za to? (mahte drobneh za to?)
May I pay — Smím platit (smeem platyit)
  with a traveler's check? — cestovním šekem (tsestovnyeem shekem?)
  with a voucher? — kupónem? (kupohnem?)
  with this credit card? — tou kreditní kartou (tow kreditnyee kartow?)
I would like to exchange some traveler's checks — Chtěl (a woman says chtěla) bych Vyměnit několik šeku (khtyel (khtyela) bykh vymnyenyit nyekolik shekoo)

THE HOTEL

I have a reservation — Mám zajištěn pokoj (mahm zayishtyen pokoy)
A room with a bath — Pokoj s koupelnou (pokoy s kowpelnow)
  a shower — sprcha (sprkha)
  a toilet — toaleta (toaleta)
  hot running water — teplá voda (teplah voda)
What floor is it on? — V kterém poschodí je to? (v kterehm poskhodyee ye to?)
  ground floor — přízemi (przheezemee)
  second floor — první poschodí (prvnyee poskhodyee)
The elevator — Výtah (veetakh)
Have the baggage sent up, please — Dejte, prosim, poslat nahoru zavazadlo (deyte, proseem, poslat nahoru zavazadlo)
The key to number . . . , please — Klíč číslo . . . , prosím (kleech cheeslo . . . , proseem)
Please call me at seven o'clock — Prosím, vzbuďte mě v sedm hodin (proseem, vzbudte mnye v sedm hodyin)
Have the baggage brought down — Dejte snést dolů zavazadlo (deyte snehst doloo savazadlo)
The bill — Účet (oochet)
A tip — Spropitné (spropitneh)

THE RESTAURANT

Restaurant — Restaurace (restauratse)
Waiter! — Pane vrchní! (pane vrkhnyee!)
Waitress! — Slečno! (slechno!)
Menu — Jídelní lístek (yeedelnyee leestek)
I would like to order (this) . . . — Chtěl (a woman says, chtěla) bych si objednat . . . (khtyel (khtyela) bykh si obyednat . . .)

Some more . . . please	Ještě víc . . . prosím (yeshtye veets . . . proseem)
That's enough	Je to dost (ye to dost)
The check, please	Platit, prosím (platyit, proseem)
Breakfast	Snídaně (snyeedanye)
Lunch	Oběd (obyed)
Dinner	Večeře (vecherzhe)
Bread	Chléb (khlehb)
Butter	Máslo (mahslo)
Jam	Marmeláda (marmelahda)
Salt	Sůl (sool)
Pepper	Pepř (pepezh)
Mustard	Hořčice (horzhchitse)
Sauce, gravy	Omáčka (omahchka)
Vinegar	Ocet (otset)
Oil	Olej (oley)
Bottle	Láhev (lahhev)
Wine	Víno (veeno)
red, white wine	cervené, bílé víno (cherveneh, beeleh veeno)
A bottle of wine	Láhev vína (lahhev veena)
beer	Pivo (pivo)
Water	Voda (voda)
Mineral water	Minerálka (minerahlka)
Milk	Mléko (mlehko)
Coffee (with milk)	Káva (bílá káva); (kahva/beelah kahva)
Tea with lemon	Caj s citrónem (chay s tsitrohnem
Chocolate	Čokoláda (chokolahda)
Sugar (some sugar)	Cukr (tsukr)
Spirits	Slivovice (plum brandy), (slivovitse)

MAIL

A letter	Dopis (dopis)
An envelope	Obálka (obahlka)
A postcard	Pohlednice (pohlednitse)
A mailbox	Poštovní schránka (poshtovnyee skhrahnka)
The post office	Pošta (poshta)
A stamp	Známka (znahmka)
By airmail	Letecky (letetsky)
How much does it cost	Kolik stojí (kolik stoyee)
to send a letter	Poslat dopis (poslat dopis)
a postcard	Pohlednice (pohlednitsi)
Air mail to the United States, Great Britain, Canada?	Letecky do Spojených států, Velké Británie, Kanady? (letetsky do Spoyeneekh stahtoo, Velkeh Britahnyye, Kanady?)
To send a telegram, cable	Poslat telegram (poslat telegram)

LOCATIONS

. . . Street	. . . ulice (ulitse)
. . . Avenue	. . . třída (trzheeda)

. . . Square   . . . náměstí (nahmnyestyee)
The airport   Letiště (letyishtye)
A bank   Banka (banka)
The beach   Koupaliště (koupalishtye)
The bridge   Most (most)
The castle   Zámek (zahmek)
The cathedral   Katedrála (katedrahla)
The church   Kostel (kostel)
The coffee house, café   Kavárna (kavahrna)
The garden   Zahrada (zahrada)
The hospital   Nemocnice (nemotsnyitse)
The movies, cinema   Kino (kino)
  a movie   film (film)
The museum   muzeum (muzeum)
A nightclub   Noční lokál (nochnyee lokahl)
The palace   Palác (palahts)
The park   Park (park)
The post-office   Pošta (poshta)
The station   Nádraží (nahdrazhee)
The theater   Divadlo (dyivadlo)
  a play   hra (hra)
The official travel   Čedok (chedok)
  bureau
The university   Univerzita (univerzita)

TRAVEL

Arrival   Příjezd (przheeyezd)
Departure   Odjezd (odyezd)

The Airplane

Letadlo (letadlo)

I want to reconfirm a reservation on flight number . . . for . . .   Chtěl (a woman says chtěla) bych potvrdit rezervaci na let . . . do . . . (khtyel (khtyela) bykh potvrdyit rezervatsi na let . . . to . . .)

Where is the check-in?   Kde je kontrola? (kde ye kontrola?)

I am checking in for . . .   Letím do . . . (letyeem do . . .)
Fasten your seat belt   Připoutejte se (przhipowteyte se)

The Railroad

Železnice (zheleznyitse)
The train   Vlak (vlak)
From what track does the train to . . . leave?   Z kterého nástupiště odjíždí vlak do . . . ? (z kterehho nahstupishtye odyeezhdyee vlak do . . . ?)

Which way is the dining car?   Kde je jídelní vuz? (kde ye yeedelnyee vooz?)

Bus, Streetcar

Autobus, tramvaj (autobus, tramvay)
Does this bus go to . . . ?   Jede tento autobus na . . . ? (yede tento autobus na . . . /do . . . /?)

trolley bus	trolejbus (troleybus)
I want to get off at . . . Street	Chtěl (chtěla) bych vystoupit na . . . ulici (khtyel/khtyela/bykh vystowpit na . . . ulitsi)
at the next stop	na příští stanici (. . . na przheeshtyee stanitsi)

Taxi

Taxi	Taxi (taxi)
I (we) would like to go to . . . , please	Chtěl (a woman says chtěla) bych (chtěli bychom) jet na . . . , prosim (khtyel (khtyela) khtyeli bykhom/yet na . . . , proseem)
Stop at . . .	Zastavte na . . . (zastavte na . . .)
Stop here	Zastavte zde (zastavte zde)

NUMBERS

1 jeden (yeden)	20 dvacet (dvatset)
2 dva (dva)	25 dvacet pět (dvatset pyet)
3 tři (trzhi)	30 třicet (trzhitset)
4 čtyři (chtyrzhi)	40 čtyřicet (chtyrzhitset)
5 pět (pyet)	50 padesát (padesaht)
6 šest (shest)	60 šedesát (shedesaht)
7 sedm (sedm)	70 sedmdesát (sedmdesaht)
8 osm (osm)	80 osmdesát (osmdesaht)
9 devět (devyet)	90 devadesát (devadesaht)
10 deset (deset)	100 sto (sto)
11 jedenáct (yedenahtst)	200 dvě stě (dvye stye)
12 dvanáct (dvanahtst)	300 tři sta (trzhi sta)
13 třináct (trzhinahtst)	400 čtyři sta (chtyrzhi sta)
14 čtrnáct (chtrnahtst)	500 pět set (pyet set)
15 patnáct (patnahtst)	600 šest set (shest set)
16 šestnáct (shestnahtst)	700 sedm set (sedm set)
17 sedmnáct (sedmnahtst)	800 osm set (osm set)
18 osmnáct (osmnahtst)	900 devět set (devyet set)
19 devatenáct (devatenahtst)	1000 tisíc (tyiseehts)

HUNGARY

FACTS AT YOUR FINGERTIPS

Planning Your Trip

 WHAT WILL IT COST. Despite considerable rises in 1982 in food and transport prices, costs in Hungary are generally low by Western standards. Even in Budapest and the larger tourist resorts prices are reasonable, while away from the larger centers almost everything can seem a bargain, though at the same time facilities may be few and far between. All prices quoted in this chapter are those of mid-1982 and may well have changed both before and during 1983. *$1 = 49,5 1985 1 = 2¢*

The unit of currency in Hungary is the Forint, which is divided into 100 fillérs (abbreviated Ft and f). There are coins of 10, 20 and 50 fillér and of 1, 2, 5 and 10 Forint. There are notes of 10, 20, 50, 100 and 500 Forint.

The tourist exchange rate was about 35 Ft to the US dollar and about 60 Ft to the pound sterling at the time of writing, but again this is almost certain to change both before and during 1983. All the usual credit cards, such as American Express, Diner's Club, Eurocard and Access are widely accepted, as are traveler's checks. Holders of Eurocheque cards can cash personal checks in all banks and in many hotels and stores.

You may bring in any amount of foreign currency, but must declare it on arrival or you will not be allowed to export the balance. The import and export of Hungarian currency in excess of 100 Ft (and then only in coins, *not* notes) is not allowed. Foreign currency may only be exchanged at official exchange agencies such as those in banks, travel agencies, hotels and airports. No foreign currency may be given or sold to individuals in Hungary. There is a black market in foreign currency in Hungary but you will be tempting fate if you try to take advantage of it (you are also likely to be cheated). *yls — warning*

A day's basic costs for two people might be:

Hotel with bath and breakfast	1,350 Ft
Lunch, with beer	240
Transport (2 metro trips, one taxi)	30
Museum entrance	10
Dinner, in Moderate restaurant with half liter wine	400
Total	2,030

In good hotel - Beer 45 (90¢) soup same

Sample Costs. Theater ticket 50 Ft; pack of good local cigarettes 15 Ft; beer in a bar 30 Ft; cup of coffee 6 to 10 Ft; half liter of wine in a restaurant up to 50 Ft; scotch (glass) 45 to 70 Ft (can be much more in places such as the Hilton or in nightclubs).

 HOW TO GO. All foreign travel to Hungary is handled via the offices of IBUSZ, the Hungarian national tourist office. It has many branches in Budapest, including desks in all the major hotels as well as in the more important towns. In Budapest, perhaps confusingly, different brances of IBUSZ deal with different aspects of travel; one with rail or air tickets, for example, another with hotel reservations and so on. The IBUSZ desk at your hotel will be able to help with problems of all kinds and will also exchange foreign currency.

However, the overseas offices of IBUSZ do not actually arrange travel to Hungary. This can only be done by a travel agent accredited by IBUSZ. These, however, include most of the major travel agents such as American Express and Maupintor. IBUSZ offices will be able to supply a complete list of all agents accredited by them in your country. Agents will also be able to arrange visas, as well as making hotel reservations and other travel arrangements.

Apart from IBUSZ, there are other Hungarian agencies, such as Cooptourist and Express, as well as local tourist offices in all major centers.

The addresses of IBUSZ offices overseas are:

In the US: 630 Fifth Ave., New York, NY 10020.

In Canada: Hungarian Embassy, 7 Delaware Ave., K2P 02Z, Ottawa, Ontario.

In the UK: Danube Travel Ltd., 6 Conduit St., London W1.

You can also obtain information from the offices of MALEV, the Hungarian airline. Their offices in New York are at the same address as those of IBUSZ; in the UK, their address is 10 Vigo St., London W1.

TOURS. IBUSZ offers a wide range of inclusive tours. Four tours covering different parts of the country—northwest Hungary, northern Hungary, southwest Hungary and the Great Plain—each lasting 5 days (4 nights), cost around $150 for full board in a double room with bath. In addition, there are numerous hobby tours, including accompanied bicycle tours, photo safaris, anglers' tours, visits to vineyards during the fall, cookery courses, weaving courses, keep-fit courses, agricultural courses and music courses; the choice seems endless. Tours for young people (under 30) are handled by the Express Youth and Students' Bureau.

If you visit Hungary on a pre-paid package tour (both less expensive and less troublesome than independent travel) a sample package tour, arranged by Danube Travel ex London, to cover a 7-night stay in Budapest in a Moderate hotel with breakfast, return flight, a half-day sightseeing tour and visa, costs from £220 in the summer.

WHEN TO GO. From May to September is the best time, though June, July and August are usually hot and crowded. Spring and fall are often delightful and numerous fairs and festivals are held during the season. Winters are cold and the winter sports season lasts from late November through early March.

Average maximum daily temperatures in degrees Fahrenheit and Centigrade

Budapest	Jan.	Feb.	Mar.	Apr.	May	Jun.	Jul.	Aug.	Sep.	Oct.	Nov.	Dec.
F°	34	39	50	63	72	79	82	81	73	61	46	39
C°	1	4	10	17	22	26	28	27	23	16	8	4

SPECIAL EVENTS. The Budapest International Fair takes place in May and September. Among the many musical festivals are the Beethoven Memorial Concerts at Martonvásár, southwest of Budapest, in June and July, the Haydn Concerts at Fertőd, in Western Hungary; and the Open-air

Opera and Drama Festival of Szeged, which runs from late July to late August. The Budapest Musical Weeks are a traditional attraction of the early autumn. Dates of the various events vary from year to year and details of these and many other musical and artistic events can be obtained from IBUSZ, or from its representatives abroad.

Other special events are as follows. **February,** Gypsy Festival (Budapest). **March,** Spring Festival Week (Budapest). **May–June,** Film Festival (Miskolc). **July,** Bartók Choral Festival (Debrecen); Chamber Music Festival (Veszprém); Film Week (Siófok). **August,** Ethnic Folk Festival (Keszthely); National Flower Festival (Debrecen); Summer Music Festival (Békéscsaba); Horse Show (Bugac puszta). **October,** Limestone Cave Concerts (Aggtelek).

National Holidays. Jan. 1; Apr. 4 (Liberation Day); Easter Monday; May 1 (Labor Day); Aug. 20 (St. Stephen's and Constitution Day); Nov. 7 (Anniversary of Russian Revolution; Dec. 25 and 26.

VISAS. In addition to a valid passport, all western Europeans (except Austrians), Americans and Canadians and citizens of all Commonwealth countries require visas to enter Hungary. If you arrive by air or car, you can obtain visas on the border, otherwise you should apply to the Hungarian consulate in your own country or to an accredited travel agent at least 14 days before you wish to visit Hungary. However, even if you are flying or driving to Hungary, it is advisable to get your visa in advance to avoid what can be a tiresome wait as well as an additional charge. To apply for a visa (either at the border or before making your trip) you will need two recent passport photographs. There is a fee of about $6. Visas are valid for about 30 days.

Visas can be extended by applying to the *KEOKH* (Aliens' Registration Office) in Budapest (Népköztársaság Ut 12) and in the provinces. *All visitors must be registered with the police,* but if you are staying at a hotel the porter will do this for you, while if you are staying in a private home booked through a travel agency, the agency will see to the registration.

HEALTH CERTIFICATES. These are not required to visit Hungary from any country.

MEDICAL INSURANCE. There is no reciprocal agreement concerning medical treatment between Hungary and the US. It is advisable, therefore, to take out comprehensive medical insurance before you leave. British subjects are entitled, on showing their passports, to free hospital treatment and to the services of a general medical practitioner, though a nominal charge is made for prescriptions. But in any case, comprehensive medical insurance is strongly recommended.

CUSTOMS. Objects for personal use may be imported freely. If you are over 16, you may also bring in 250 cigarettes or 40 cigars or 200 grs. of tobacco, plus 2 liters of wine and 1 liter of spirits, plus 250 grs. of perfume. In addition, small gifts not exceeding a value (in Hungary) of 1,000 Ft each, to a total value of 5,000 Ft, may also be imported duty-free. If a traveler intends to leave valuable objects, such as cameras and typewriters, with relatives or friends as gifts, this should be stated at the time of entering the country, so as to benefit from a reduced tourist rate of duty.

All personal belongings that have been imported may be freely taken out of the country. So may food for the journey, 2 liters of wine, 1 liter of spirits and 250 cigarettes. Gifts of a non-commercial character may also be freely exported, provided that they have been bought with hard currency or with forints obtained by the legal exchange of hard currency. Goods to any value bought from the Intertourist or Konsumtourist stores (for hard currency) may be exported without license, provided that the bill received at the store is produced at customs.

Remember that the import and export of Hungarian currency is not allowed for sums in excess of 100 Ft (and then only in coins), but that you may export any foreign currency you imported but did not spend provided you declared it on arrival.

Staying in Hungary

LANGUAGE. Hungarian (Magyar) is one of the more exotic languages of Eastern Europe and at first sight looks forbidding. A knowledge of German is most useful. English, and to a lesser extent, French and Russian, are spoken and understood.

HOTELS. Hungarian hotels are graded from 5-stars down to 1-star. These grades correspond closely to our grading system in the lists that follow of Deluxe (L) for 5-stars, Expensive (E) for 4-stars, Moderate (M) for 3- and 2-stars and Inexpensive (I) for 1-star. In practice the Hungarian grading system sometimes appears rather arbitrary, especially in more modest establishments and to be decided by factors not always clear to the visitor.

5-star hotels have every comfort and luxury, including airconditioning throughout. Only one 4-star hotel (the Forum in Budapest) has complete airconditioning, though many have this amenity in the public rooms; however, all 4-star hotels are extremely comfortable. 3- and 2-star establishments are less luxurious, though they are usually well furnished and well run. They are often crowded with package-tour groups, but this fact will rarely affect individual travelers. Single rooms with bath are scarce. 1-star hotels are generally simply furnished with few, if any, private baths; they are rarely recommended to foreign tourists, though in some provincial towns there may be no better accommodations available. The plumbing is satisfactory everywhere. Visitors from the West are made very welcome and service almost everywhere will be both friendly and smooth—though here, as elsewhere in Hungary, a tip can work wonders.

In addition to ordinary hotels, there are also so-called Tourist Hostels. These provide very simple accommodations, usually in rooms with four or more beds.

The table below shows approximate prices for rooms with bath, breakfast and 15% service charge, except for 5-star and some 4-star hotels where the rates do not include breakfast or service. Balaton hotel rates include full board, which is compulsory at most hotels during the high season (June through August). Owing to a shortage of hotel rooms, best book in advance. Hotel rates are considerably lower in many hotels in the low season; in Budapest, this is December through March (with the exception of the New Year holiday); in the Balaton area, where most hotels are only open from May to September, it is May and September.

Two people in a double room will pay approximately:

	Budapest	Balaton	Provinces
Deluxe (5-star)	1,000–1,750 Ft (1)	—	—
Expensive (4-star)	900–1,500 Ft (1)	650–850 Ft	400–500 Ft
Moderate (3-star)	500–800 Ft	550–700 Ft	300–400 Ft
Moderate (2-star)	400–600 Ft	350–450 Ft	200–300 Ft
Inexpensive (1-star)	300–450 Ft	300–350 Ft	150–250 Ft

For single rooms with bath, count on from 100 Ft (1-star) to as much as 1000 Ft (5-star) more per night. Rooms with bath are very rare in 1-star hotels.

Breakfast and service charges are generally not included in the 5-star and most luxurious 4-star hotels. Rates at Balaton hotels include full board.

There are no 5-star, and only a few 4-star, hotels outside Budapest, but the latest 3-star hotels are usually very comfortable and well run.

SELF-CATERING. Bungalows with two rooms, fully equipped for cooking, etc., can be rented at a large number of resorts, particularly on the shores of Lake Balaton. Full details and rates can be obtained from tourist offices in Hungary and abroad, who can also arrange bookings.

PRIVATE ACCOMMODATION. Available almost everywhere, paying-guest accommodation is an inexpensive and excellent way of getting to know the people. In Budapest and in Lake Balaton resorts, the rate per night for a double room (single or double occupancy) is around 60 to 100 Ft (single) to 140 to 380 Ft (double) a night, which includes the use of a bathroom, but not breakfast. A few rooms with private bath are available at higher rates. In provincial towns, the rates are lower. Such accommodation can be booked either through local tourist offices or by travel agents abroad. Applications should be made well in advance.

 **CAMPING.** There are over 80 campsites in Hungary. They are to be found in all the country's chief beauty spots. Most of the sites cater only for campers bringing in their own equipment, but a few provide tents. There are four categories of site, from 4-star to 1-star, depending on the amenities provided and most are open from May through September. Caravans are permitted in all sites that have power points; a parking charge is made for such caravans, as well as for cars, motorcycles and other forms of transport. At the time of going to press, the rates for use of the site vary from approximately 10 to 50 Ft a day, plus a charge for hot water and electricity. Young people between 6 and 16 years of age pay half these rates and there is no charge for children under the age of 6. Camping is forbidden except in the specially designated areas.

Bookings can be made through the *Hungarian Camping and Caravanning Club,* Üllői Út 6, Budapest VIII, or through travel agencies.

 RESTAURANTS. There are many excellent restaurants throughout the country, most, though not all, state-owned. In the large restaurants you will find an impressive bill-of-fare, often in several languages. If you want to eat really well, with famous Hungarian specialties such as goose-liver, and with some excellent Hungarian wine, you should reckon on 300 to 500 Ft a head at the very least in an Expensive (E) restaurant; you could pay much more. In a good Moderate (M) restaurant, with half a bottle of wine, reckon on between 100 and 150 Ft a head. On the other hand, for those with slender means (and not too large an appetite), there is often, even in quite high-class restaurants, an Inexpensive (I) fixed-price meal, called a *menü*, of two or three courses, which can cost as little as 30 to 50 Ft. This *menü* tends to be tucked away at the bottom of the bill-of-fare and to be in Hungarian, or Hungarian and German, only. Needless to say, the waiter will not usually draw your attention to it, but it is worthwhile looking for and often very good value. Drink, of course, is extra. Most of the better places have music in the evening and prices are then correspondingly higher.

There are also many inexpensive self-service restaurants (*önkiszolgáló étterem*), snack bars (*bisztró* or *étel-bár*) and buffets (*büfé*), which serve freshly-cooked meals.

Budapest is no longer a city of great coffee houses in the old Austro-Hungarian tradition, places where people met to discuss the topics of the day. In the capital, and indeed throughout Hungary, their place has been taken by a host of small cafés or coffee bars (*eszpresszó*) and so-called *drink-bárs*. There are also numerous excellent pastry shops (*cukrászda*), where superb pastries are consumed, with or without the accompaniment of tea or coffee. For more details on Hungarian cuisine, see our chapter on Food and Drink.

 TIPPING. Hungarians have always been generous tippers and Communism hasn't affected this in the least. Although your hotel bill usually contains a service charge, tips are expected. You should be generous to the head-porter (*portás*), who in practice supervises your stay. Then there is the chambermaid (who will get laundry done for you in a day), the breakfast waiter and the liftboy. Altogether, reckon to pay out not less than about 15% of your bill.

In restaurants give the head waiter, who presents you with the bill, at least 10%; the money is divided among the staff. If there is a gypsy orchestra, the leader of the band (*primás*) should be given 20 or 30 Ft, but only if he plays for you and your table. In some restaurants he may try to; it is up to you to welcome him—or not! Gas station attendants, taxi drivers and hairdressers all expect a few forints. In fact, if you are in any doubt whether or not to give a tip, do!

 MAIL AND TELEPHONES. Postcards by surface mail to Western Europe (including, of course, the UK) cost 5 Ft, letters 8 Ft; by air to the United States 7 Ft, to western Europe 6 Ft. Letters by air cost 10 Ft to the United States, 9 Ft to western Europe. (There is little advantage in paying the airmail supplement to western Europe.) Stamps may be bought from tobacconists as well as post-offices. In Budapest, the main post-office in Petőfi Sándor Utca, in the Inner City, is open till 8 pm, Mondays through Fridays, and until 3 pm on Saturdays; closed on Sundays. The post-offices at the East and West stations are open day and night.

Telephoning in Hungary is extremely difficult; calls from Hungary to the West are practically impossible to make.

TIME. Hungary is seven hours ahead of Eastern Standard Time and two hours ahead of Greenwich Mean Time. From April to September (dates vary from year to year) the country operates on summer time, which is six hours ahead of Eastern Standard Time and one hour ahead of Greenwich Mean Time.

CLOSING TIMES. There is now a five-day working week in Hungary, from Monday through Friday, though most shops are also open on Saturday till around midday. The usual office hours are 8 to 5, banks 8 to 3; many shops do not open until 10 am.

most good is shipped / abroad.

SHOPPING. The best things to buy in Hungary are peasant embroideries and the exquisite Herend and Zsolnay porcelain. Dolls dressed in national costume are popular and records are of good quality and inexpensive.

Government tourist shops, called Intertourist or Konsumtourist have multilingual assistants and stock the widest choice. They sell only against hard currency, e.g. dollars or sterling.

WINTER SPORTS. There are few capitals in the world where you can take a bus-and-funicular ride or a 15-minute car trip to the nearest ski and toboganning slopes, but Budapest is one of them. The Buda hills cover an area of about 19 by 16 km (12 by 10 miles); the skiing center is the Szabadsághegy, but there are slopes for beginners and experts alike on the neighboring hills. There are many other skiing centers in the mountains of northern Hungary.

Perhaps the most unusual winter sport is to be found on Lake Balaton, which generally freezes over to a depth of 8 to 12 inches. Here ice-sailing is a popular pastime from the end of December to the beginning of March and speeds of up to 96 kph (60 mph) have been reached.

HUNTING AND HORSE RIDING. Hungarians are famous horsemen and their country provides all sorts of facilities for riding and hunting. Hunters can obtain details (and the necessary license) from *MAVAD* (Hungarian Hunting Association), Úri Utca 39, Budapest I. Prices are high and must be paid in hard currency; you pay even if you miss your shot.

Riders will find that there are a large number of special riding holidays. Detailed information can be obtained from travel agencies abroad and from tourist offices in Hungary. There are holidays based on a stay at a stud farm and cross-country tours on horseback. A stay in a stud farm, which includes accommodations, all meals and tuition, ranges from about 650 Ft to around 1,000 Ft a day, according to season and the comfort provided. Cross-country tours, lasting 10 days, with about 6 days' riding, cost from 20,000 Ft upwards, fully inclusive.

SWIMMING AND BOATING. Lake Balaton and the Danube are the main centers. Yachts and rowboats can be hired at lake resorts and sailing courses are organized for beginners. Sailing holidays on Lake Balaton can be arranged through IBUSZ and other tourist offices.

Budapest is dotted with swimming pools, many of them attached to the medicinal baths and mineral springs. Of the many pools the largest and finest is the Palatinus Lido on Margaret Island; this also has a pool with artificial waves and a thermal pool. There is a closed terrace for nude bathers (men and women separate). At certain spots north of Budapest you can swim in the Danube though you must watch the current, which can be very strong. You will find a swimming pool in almost every town.

Getting around Hungary

BY PLANE. Somewhat surprisingly there is no internal air service in Hungary. Budapest airport (Ferihegy) is about nine miles from the city center with regular bus services as well as taxis to and from the city.

BY TRAIN. There is an extensive network of railways. Standards are higher than average in Eastern Europe with buffet car expresses linking Budapest with a number of other cities. Country services are slow and less frequent. On the fastest express trains, seat reservation is obligatory and on others there is a supplementary charge. However, if you have bought your ticket before leaving home, no supplement is necessary. But where seat reservation is required this must still be complied with. IBUSZ are helpful in this direction.

BY BUS. An extensive network of medium and long distance buses operates throughout Hungary. But buses are always crowded and speed is not their greatest asset. Tickets and full information on the services can be obtained from IBUSZ or at the VOLAN long distance bus station in Engels Ter in Budapest. Patience both in getting tickets and in travelling by bus is essential.

BY CAR. Hungarians drive on the right and the usual Continental rules of the road are observed. The speed limit in built-up areas is 60 kph (40 mph), on main roads 80 kph (50 mph) and on highways (motorways) it's 100 kph (65 mph). Horns should be sounded before overtaking, except in towns, where their use is forbidden. Seat belts are compulsory and drinking is absolutely prohibited with no minimum intake of alcohol allowed; penalties for infringement are extremely severe. Any road accidents must be reported to the police within 24 hours. Detailed information on the documents you will need if you're taking your own car into the country is given on page 21.

Gasoline (petrol) is called *benzin* in Hungary. Gas stations are marked on most touring maps. The approximate cost of a liter of Extra Super (96 octane) is 18.50 Ft and of Super (92 octane) 17 Ft.

In case of accident or repair problems, the *Hungarian Automobile Club* operates a breakdown service on all main roads at weekends and permanently on the M1 (Vienna) and M7 (Balaton) highways. Its head office is at Rómer Flóris Utca 4–6, Budapest II, where English-speaking advisers are always available. There are service stations at all towns of any importance throughout the country where you will find skilled mechanics. A small tip will speed the service.

Hungary's main roads radiate from Budapest. There are three motorways (*autopálya*), two of them only partly complete. The M1 now reaches Győr on its way to the Austrian frontier (and Vienna); the M3 will, when it is finished, connect Budapest with Eastern Hungary; while the M7 leads to Lake Balaton. In general the main roads, which have a single number, are excellent, as are many of the secondary roads. Many of the minor country roads, however, are either dusty or muddy, according to the season.

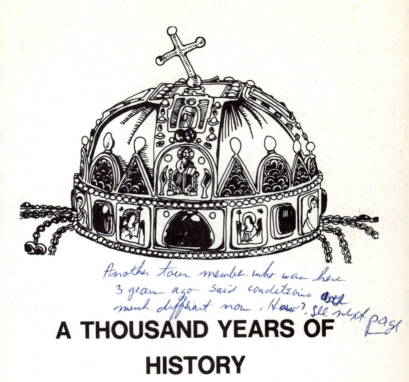

Another town member who was here 3 years ago said conditions were much different now. How? See next page

A THOUSAND YEARS OF HISTORY

Hungary's Past and Present

A visit to Hungary will reward you with an experience unlike anything else in Europe. You'll feel the curious results of, on the one hand, being right in the center of the Continent, whether in the cities or in the provinces, while yet seeming to be curiously out of Europe, because of the language, the food, the music and the people—all different from anything you have seen and sensed elsewhere. The language bears no relation to those of its neighbors, for its nearest relatives are the tongues of the Finns and the Estonians, far away in Northern Europe.

Officially the Hungarian People's Republic, Hungary is a small, mostly flat country; to the west and north there are mountains, to the *3000'* east and south stretches the continuation of the great Hungarian plain. *highest* It covers just over 93,000 sq. km (35,000 sq. miles)—an area about the size of Ireland or Indiana—and has a population of about 10½ million. It is in many ways unique in Eastern Europe; it is more than the equal of its socialist neighbors in the things that appeal to a foreign visitor—a warm welcome from a kindly people with a sense of humor, good hotels, outstanding cuisine and excellent facilities for every kind of sport. Its capital, Budapest, is one of Europe's most handsome cities;

a busy administrative and industrial center of over two million people, it is at the same time a great holiday resort and a famous spa. Budapest is completely oriented on the Danube—with its three islands and eight bridges, the great river skirts an impressive array of castles, churches, forts and monuments on the Buda hilltops. On the opposite, Pest, side of the river, a huge neo-Gothic Parliament building, church domes and spires, art-nouveau edifices and modern hotels line the Danube. It is one of the most splendid panoramic sweeps in Europe.

After Budapest, there's Lake Balaton, Europe's largest warm-water inland sea, with its charming, almost Italianate, hinterland of baroque towns and sunny vineyards on low hills. Then there is the Great Plain, with its alien, un-European air, purely Magyar—an area of small, low towns and villages almost lost amid the vast lowlands stretching endlessly to the horizon. This is a land of splendid horses and their riders, the *csikós,* and of fiery food and strong wine. Eger, in the north of the country, and Sopron, in the extreme west, are two of the loveliest baroque towns in Europe.

Before we delve into Hungary's turbulent history, a word or two about the country's tourist amenities will not be out of place. Enormous advances have been made in recent years and the best hotels are probably the equals of those anywhere in the world. Only in a few of the older establishments are standards sometimes below those customary in the west. Food is almost everywhere good to excellent, though here and there one may come across slow and off-hand service. But things get better year by year, and a visit to Hungary is no longer the adventure it was only a few years ago, although, it should be added, one may still meet with an occasional disappointment.

Before St. Stephen

First in recorded history came the Romans, who built forts and camps for their legions, amphitheaters for their games, and aqueducts for their sumptuous baths. They called Western Hungary Pannonia—but they withdrew from Pannonia when the barbarians besieged their declining empire. Next came Attila, the Scourge of God, with his Huns. (It was at one time thought that the Hungarians derived their Western name from these wiry horsemen; this view is no longer held and the Hungarian Academy derives the word 'Hungar' from an ancient Turkic word 'on-ogur', meaning 'ten tribes'. This dates from the 5th century AD, at a time when the nomadic tribes, which later became the Hungarian and Turkish races, were in close contact in what is now Southern Russia. Their own name has been Magyars, members of the Finno-Ugric division of the Ural-Altaic peoples.) After the Huns came the Avars, of whom little is known. They were vanquished in their turn by Charlemagne.

The Magyars originated from the region of the Ural mountains. They came to present-day Hungary in the 9th century—the generally agreed date of the 'taking of the land' is AD 896. By that time—apart from a few Avar settlements—Svatopluk, King of Moravia, ruled Western Hungary. The picturesque folktales tell the manner in which Árpád, the first chieftain or prince of Hungary, proclaimed his intention of conquering the country. He had been chosen leader by seven tribes; according to the ancient custom they raised him on his shields; then the seven chiefs of the seven tribes each opened a vein in their arms and let their blood spurt into a common vessel to seal their blood-pact.

So the united nation of Magyars was born. When Árpád reached the Verecke pass over the Carpathians, he sent a beautiful white stallion to Svatopluk, King of Moravia, asking him only for some earth, water and grass in return. He saw that the earth was rich, black soil, easy to till; that the water was clear and fresh; that the grass was abundant.

Árpád promptly declared that by giving him these gifts, Svatopluk had ceded the country to the Hungarians; and when the Moravian king protested against such a sweeping interpretation of his intentions, the swift horsemen of the Hungarians routed his army. Within a comparatively short time the Carpathian mountains embraced a country ruled by the Magyars. Their mounted forays ranged deep into Europe, into Germany, France, Switzerland, Italy; the Western princes used them often as allies in their dynastic and internecine warfare. But finally they were beaten and retreated within their frontiers. This, and the fact that in the 11th century they embraced Christianity, saved them from the fate of the Avars.

The Holy Crown

St. Stephen, the first king of Hungary (1000–1038), was born a pagan, but he founded monasteries, built churches and brought Western craftsmen and artisans to his nascent country, and married Gisela, a Bavarian princess. Above all, he created a strong centralized monarchy, crushing a number of bloody revolts. Pope Sylvester II sent him a crown, and he was anointed king of Hungary in a solemn ceremony. He used foreign ideas and institutions but adapted them to suit the Magyars.

Though St. Stephen had no direct heir (his only son, St. Imre or Emery, died young), the Árpád Dynasty endured for three centuries. It was St. Stephen who broke consciously and definitely with the heritage of the East and, for better or worse, linked his country's fate to the West. He also severed all connection with Eastern Christianity, the influence of Byzantium, choosing the Church of Rome.

In the subsequent centuries, Hungary developed as a feudal country on the model of the other monarchies of Europe, with magnates, a landed gentry and a large mass of serfs. Its Magna Carta was called the Golden Bull, issued only 7 years after the signing of the Magna Carta at Runnymede. In the 11th and 12th centuries, the Magyars had to fight many battles to preserve their independence against successive German attacks. The 13th century brought a Mongol invasion that laid the whole land waste. The nation managed to survive, but the monarchy itself was weakened under St. Stephen's successors, and the Magyar equivalents of the English barons and the French *seigneurs* flourished in growing anarchy.

With the extinction of the Árpád Dynasty in 1301, came two kings of the Anjou (Angevin) Dynasty. Charles Robert re-established royal authority and curbed the robber barons. His son, Louis the Great, extended Hungary's frontiers to the Baltic and the Adriatic and was the 'paramount knight' of his age. Princes and savants flocked to his court and bitter international disputes were submitted to his judgment.

The growing power of the Turks with the expansive aims of the Ottoman Empire began to menace Hungary in the 15th century. Sigismund—later Holy Roman Emperor—was crowned king of Hungary in 1387, having eliminated various rival factions. He was far more interested in his German and Czech possessions than in Hungary; his chronic financial difficulties made him pawn 13 Hungarian mining and manufacturing towns in the north. His vacillating reign fatally weakened Hungary. János Hunyadi, who came from Wallachia, attached himself to Hungary and became its most brilliant general. But he tried in vain to stem the Turkish tide, though he had some temporary successes and the noontime ringing of bells in Christendom still commemorates his great victory at Belgrade. Hunyadi was also the father of Hungary's brilliant Renaissance king, Matthias (Matthias Corvinus, 1458–90), the last national monarch of native stock, who was elected by mass acclaim on the frozen Danube.

Matthias and the Turks

Nicknamed 'Matthias the Just', he restored and enlarged the great castle of Visegrád; his Italian architect built 350 rooms, which were filled with glittering treasures. Here he held his dazzling court, and from here he started on his elaborate hunting expeditions. After his death, 'King Matthias is dead, justice is gone!' was a popular saying. His famous library, whose beautifully-bound volumes were called Corvinas (his heraldic emblem was the raven, corvus in Latin), was scattered all over Europe, though a few dozen are still preserved in Budapest. Matthias built up the economic strength and created a short-lived, but nonetheless brilliant Renaissance court. His army, the 'black host', was one of perfectly-trained mercenaries. He was the wielder of considerable power in Central and Western Europe during the 32 years of his reign. But he left only a weak, illegitimate heir, and the series of weak, ineffectual kings (of Czech and Polish origin) who followed gave a free hand to feudal development.

In 1514, when a crusade was proclaimed against the Turks, the peasants rose against the unbearable burden of taxation and corvée. Led by George Dózsa, a member of the minor gentry, they fought the nobles, but lost in the end to superior armament and strategic skill. Dózsa was roasted alive on an iron throne and his followers were forced to eat of his flesh before being broken on the wheel or hanged. Thousands of serfs were massacred; the terror of retaliation caused a fatal split in national unity.

Twelve years later came the decisive Hungarian 'Waterloo', at a place downriver from Budapest, called Mohács, a traumatic, total defeat of the Hungarian Army by the Turks, during which the king, Louis II, was drowned in a stream. Soon Buda itself was taken and the 150-year interval of Turkish occupation began. Hungary was actually split into three parts—the territory ruled by the sultan's satraps, which included the Great Plain, and much of western and southern Hungary;

the rest of the west and north under Habsburg rule; and finally, Transylvania, the beautiful, wooded, mountainous province 'beyond the forests', which survived for a long time, keeping an uneasy balance between Austrian and Turk under its own Hungarian princes. Here at least Magyar culture survived through six generations.

The Habsburgs

The liberation of Hungary came at the end of the 17th century; Buda was recaptured by the Christian forces in 1686, some three years after the vast Turkish armies were defeated under the walls of Vienna. But 'liberation' simply meant exchanging one master for another. The Habsburgs turned Hungary into a province and a colony, and though the degree of oppression changed slightly during the next 150 years, the essential aim of exploiting the country for the benefit of the hereditary Habsburg lands remained the same. Before long, the first of many revolts, all of them doomed to failure, began.

The scattered resistance groups were united by Prince Ferenc Rákóczi II, the richest magnate of the country, who raised the standard of revolt in 1703. He was supported by the French, whose persistent purpose was to weaken the Habsburgs, and for eight years he and his ragged, brave troops were defiantly successful against overwhelming odds. These odds became impossible when, at the end of the War of the Spanish Succession, Vienna was able to concentrate all its forces on suppressing the Magyar fight for independence. Rákóczi ended his life in Turkish exile and the subsequent, smaller risings were usually nipped in the bud.

Slowly, Hungary's economic potential grew, though it was hampered gravely by the stubborn insistence of the nobility on its privileges, which included tax exemption and the unlimited exploitation of the peasant class. Maria Theresa (1740–80) fought a long but fruitless battle to abolish these privileges, and when she failed, found it necessary to protect the other provinces of her empire with high tariffs against Hungarian exports. This led to the country 'drowning in its own fat'; in addition, the Seven Years' War demanded considerable sacrifices from the nascent middle class and the serfs. At one point, the Queen fled to the ancient Hungarian city of Pozsony (now Bratislava, in Czechoslovakia), and appealed to the chivalry of the Magyar nobles who, according to a somewhat colored version, offered their lives and blood to the young and beautiful sovereign. Maria Theresa's successor was Joseph II. He was a free-thinker and follower of Voltaire (he never had himself crowned and was nicknamed 'the King in the hat') and accordingly attempted to end the prerogatives of the Hungarian nobility. But, despite the ambitiousness of his reforms and the apparent liberality behind them, he revoked the majority of them on his death bed.

Maria Theresa's Guard of Hungarian Nobles imbibed the ideas of Enlightenment, and the French Revolution also had a somewhat delayed influence. But the Hungarian Jacobins, led by the prelate Ignatius Martinovics, were betrayed and arrested, and, on May 20 1795, put to death on the Field of Blood (Vérmező) in Budapest. Emperor

Francis I and his successor, the weak-minded Ferdinand, continued the policy of repression and centralization, but the early years of the 19th century brought a great and vigorous rebirth of ideas in Hungary.

In the next decades, two men became the leaders of the struggle for reform and national independence. Their ideas were often opposed, though they were both great and true patriots of genius. To put it in a nutshell, Count István Széchenyi wanted to see Hungary first prosperous and civilized, with freedom to follow; Lajos Kossuth, his adversary, claimed that without liberty, economic progress was impossible. Széchenyi, a great Anglophile, founded the Hungarian Academy of Sciences, initiated the building of the Chain Bridge in Budapest, steamboats on the Danube and Tisza rivers, horse-racing and more scientific agricultural methods. In his great ideological duel with Kossuth, he lost, and ended his life, after years in an asylum, by suicide.

Kossuth and Revolution

Kossuth was the first to publish regular reports about the deliberations of the Diet and, both as a political journalist and a spellbinding orator, fought indefatigably for the national cause. Imprisoned, he used his years in jail to teach himself English from Shakespeare and the Bible. The so-called Reform Age in Hungary culminated in the year of revolutions, 1848, when the February rising in Paris triggered a whole series of liberal and national explosions throughout Europe. Hungary's came on March 15, led by the students and apprentices of Pest, headed by Sándor Petőfi, the great poet, and Maurus Jókai, destined to become the Hungarian Walter Scott. Within a few weeks, much of the past was swept away, the serfs were liberated and a responsible government was installed. But the Habsburgs would not allow Hungary even a modicum of freedom. Rousing the Slav minorities against Kossuth's government, they launched their armies against the national forces. But this led only in 1849 to the dethronement of their dynasty and Kossuth's election as regent or governor.

The Austrians suffered a series of crushing defeats, but the young Emperor Francis Joseph and his cabinet turned to Czarist Russia for help, and the overwhelming Russian superiority in arms and men defeated the Magyar armies. Kossuth had to flee into exile with a small band of his followers. First in Turkey, later in England, France and the United States, and finally, during a long emigration in Italy (he died at the age of 92), he tried with stubborn brilliance, though with little or no success, to rally Austria's enemies to the Hungarian cause. It was, however, during these years that he elaborated a prophetic and comprehensive plan of a Danubian federation—a plan that would have solved the age-old rivalries and hostilities of the Danubian nations and still awaits realization.

The defeat of the Hungarians in their fight for independence was followed by almost two decades of Habsburg repression—executions, deportations, impressment into the Austrian forces and suppression of Magyar institutions were administered by a harsh, bureaucratic, police regime. When, in 1866, Bismarck ejected Austria from the German Reich, she had to turn eastwards. This time she sold out her Slav minorities to the Magyars; in 1867 the Hungarian liberal leader Ferenc Deák, and the ministers of Francis Joseph negotiated the *Ausgleich* (Compromise), which transformed the monarchy into a dual one.

Industrialization and economic expansion then followed, though there was constant constitutional strife and a far from liberal or sympathetic attitude towards the mass of the people and towards the large Slovak, Romanian, Serbian and Croatian minorities under Hungarian rule.

In World War I, Hungary marched with Austria and Germany, though her prime minister, Count István (Stephen) Tisza, had grave misgivings about the wisdom of such an alignment. The chauvinistic, feudalistic policies of the past decades came home to roost in 1918. There was a brief liberal revolution led by the well-meaning, but ineffective, Count Mihály (Michael) Károlyi, and Hungary broke away from Austria. Károlyi played much the same part as Kerensky did in Russia, though for a much shorter time. There followed a Communist régime under Béla Kun, which lasted 133 days; then a Romanian occupation of Budapest and finally a right-wing régime under Admiral Miklós (Nicholas) Horthy, a former aide-de-camp of Francis Joseph and the last commander of the Austro-Hungarian Navy. In the ensuing Treaty of Trianon, Hungary lost those lands inhabited by the Slovak, Romanian, Serbian and Croatian minorities as well as considerable strips of territory which were purely Hungarian; in all she was deprived of two-thirds of her former territories and 50 percent of her population.

For the next three decades, she was a kingdom without a king, ruled by a regent who was an admiral without a navy, a largely peasant country in which 85 percent of the land was owned by five percent of the population: a mock-democracy in which Jewish students were restricted to five percent of the university admittances, and in which irredentist propaganda covered the misery of the over-educated and under-employed middle class. In foreign affairs, Hungary was allied to Mussolini's Italy. István Bethlen, a clever, though not too scrupulous, Transylvanian aristocrat, was premier for 10 long years, but with Hitler's rise, Hungary was drawn more and more into the German orbit, hoping to regain her lost territories through an alliance with the Nazi *Drang nach Osten*. In 1938 and 1940 this policy paid a short-term dividend, when parts of Slovakia, Yugoslavia and Transylvania were temporarily returned to Hungary.

The Scene Today

The war brought endless suffering and devastation to the country. Though Horthy tried to make a separate peace in 1944, this act only led to his arrest and the installation of an extreme right-wing, pro-Nazi Arrow Cross government. Eighty percent of Hungary's half-million Jews perished in the gas-chambers, the ghettos and the forced labor camps. The Hungarian Army was decimated in the Ukraine. Forty percent of Hungary's national wealth was destroyed before the Red Army completed its occupation on April 4, 1945, just about a month before VE Day.

The brief interval of a broad-based democratic government ended with the establishment of a People's Democracy, closely linked, economically, militarily and politically, to the Soviet Union. The Hungarian Communist Party became the ruling force under Mátyás Rákosi. Intensive industrialization, a thorough land reform and the establishment of collective farms were accompanied by a virtual reign of terror.

Stalin's death, the Twentieth (Soviet) Party Congress, the East Berlin rising and the 'Polish October' culminated in the Hungarian Revolution of 1956, which has been called both a counter-revolution (though only by the Soviet Union) and a hopeless revolt against unbearable conditions. 200,000 Hungarians went into exile when it was brutally suppressed after less than two weeks, though a number have returned. The revolution was at least a partial triumph. János Kádár, a popular leader, has been Hungary's Party Secretary since then. Agricultural collectivization was completed in 1961, some private enterprise has been introduced into industry and commerce, and incentives have become more tangible. Today, Hungarians can once again travel abroad, though passports and foreign currency allowances are still restricted. Hungarian writers and artists are given more scope for expressing their individuality, though they must observe the party line.

Under the 'New Economic Mechanism' initiated in 1968, a great many things have changed for the better. Conditions have been stimulated by the encouragement of technical and commercial initiatives, moving the economy with increasing effectiveness towards meeting consumer needs. The results are clearly visible in the well-stocked shops, new cars, better-dressed people and places of entertainment humming with activity. In the last few years, however, this economic progress has slowed noticeably.

In some other ways, too, things have changed. Although Hungary is still a 'police state' and has the closest political and economic ties with the Soviet Union, life is becoming increasingly free; people talk and criticize more openly and no longer feel they need to look over their shoulders before telling a political joke. Hungarians are as courteous as ever and to their courtesy they have now added a sense of enjoying life, which had for many years been noticeably absent. Churches of all denominations are well-attended and relations with the Vatican have been normalized.

Contacts of all kinds with western countries increase steadily. The most striking sign of this was the return to Hungary (January 1978), by the US Secretary of State Cyrus Vance, of the historic 'Crown of St. Stephen', the symbol of Hungarian sovereignty, which had been handed over to American custody at the end of World War II to prevent its falling into the hands of the Russians. President Carter, in an accompanying letter, said that the act of returning the crown expressed the strengthening of the traditional friendship between the United States and Hungary.

There are more Western tourists every year, too. Great new luxury hotels, most of them built with Western capital and know-how help to provide an atmosphere that in places could almost be taken for the West. But almost is the operative word, because wherever he goes the visitor will be struck by the fervent patriotic spirit of the Hungarians, influenced inevitably by recent history. These facts, surely, make this little country, perhaps more than any other, a true meeting point between West and East.

HUNGARIAN CULTURE

Talents Spread Abroad

It has been said that in the sphere of culture there are no large or small nations. All have a significant contribution to make. But the success rate of Hungarians in the world cultural scene is remarkable. Despite being imprisoned at birth behind the bars of a language which none but natives can understand properly—or perhaps because of it—Hungarian artists and writers have become outstandingly successful communicators in the fields of art and entertainment. Like some other small and intensely 'national' peoples, they have emigrated with enthusiasm and transplanted extremely well; especially in Great Britain, the US and France.

Literature

Imre Madách (1823–1864), a strange, solitary figure, produced Hungary's first major work of literature with his epic drama *The Tragedy of Man.* It is available in English translation, as are a few of the works of the literary trio who dominated the later 19th and early 20th centuries. They were Mór Jókai (1825–1904), a prolific and inventive novelist; Kálmán Mikszáth (1847–1910), a campaigner for social justice whose short stories have enjoyed a revival under the present regime;

and Zigismond Móricz (1879–1942), who first illuminated the pathos and humor of Hungarian peasant life.

A near contemporary of these writers, Baroness Emma Orczy, the daughter of an expatriate Hungarian nobleman, wrote only in English. Hungarians like to boast that three of their compatriots were involved in the creation of the film archetype of the English gentlemen, the Scarlet Pimpernel—the Baroness wrote the books, Sir Alexander Korda produced the pictures and Leslie Howard (born Leó Steiner) played the part.

Frigyes (Frederick) Karinthy (1887–1938) was both a humorist and a satirist. His *Journey Round My Skull* is one of several of his works to have been published in English.

Modern Authors

Modern Hungarian writers who have made their reputations abroad include the late Yolanda Földes, whose *Street of the Fishing Cat* won a great international prize in 1936, and Lajos Zilahy, whose *Two Prisoners,* recently reissued in America, is a central European classic of World War I.

Among Hungarian writers living and working abroad, Arthur Koestler has won a world-wide reputation, both with his novels and his philosophical and popular scientific books, ranging from *Darkness at Noon* to *Scum of the Earth,* from *The Yogi and the Commissar* to in-depth exploration of humor, creativity, biology and the space-age. Stephen Vizincey's *In Praise of Older Women* was a widely-acclaimed success. The pages of American and British short-story magazines contain a relatively high proportion of Hungarian names. Very typical of the national capacity for psychological penetration and the mood of cynical realism are the novels (*Rusty Graveyard*), short stories (*Engagement* and others) and film scripts of Endre Fejes (b. 1923).

Returning to Hungary, one must mention Aron Tamási (1897–1966), the poet-novelist of Transylvania, whose almost untranslatable, richly-embroidered prose is like the ornate Székely embroideries of his native land, and above all the late Tibor Déry (1894–1977), whose short story *Niki,* widely translated in the West, gives a deeply moving picture of life in Hungary in the unbearable conditions of the early 1950s; imprisoned briefly after the 1956 Uprising, he lived to become one of the great figures of 20th-century Hungarian literature.

A Poetic Sweep

If you visit Hungary, you will inevitably hear a great deal about poets past and present—and rightly so. They were great and tragic figures. The three greatest—Sándor Petőfi, Endre Ady and Attila József—all died young; Petőfi on the battlefield, Ady of a blood disease, József by suicide.

There had been many considerable poets in Hungary during the 18th century, but a sudden, new blossoming of poetry, a great resurgence, came in the 1820s. Mihály (Michael) Vörösmarty (1800–55), the first great Hungarian epic poet, delved into his nation's past and described the heroic deeds in rolling hexameters. His translations of Shakespeare's *Julius Caesar* and *King Lear* were particularly brilliant. In János (John) Arany (1817–82) the epic qualities of Hungarian poetry reached their highest fulfilment. His ballads were short dramatic masterpieces.

Sándor (Alexander) Petőfi (1823–49), Hungary's most original poet, fulfilled the ideal fate of a burning, restless soul, a patriot and a prophet. At the age of 26 he disappeared in the battle of Segesvár, where the veteran Polish General Bem, who had joined Kossuth, was trying to check the Russian armies. Petőfi's life was short and violent, full of love and hate, triumph and defeat; he was a comet, drawing a fiery trail across the heavens and then vanishing suddenly. His heritage has been inexhaustible and has again and again inspired his country's poets.

Between Petőfi's death and the début of Endre (Andrew) Ady (1877–1919) there were a great many good poets in Hungary—but no great ones. But when Ady arrived, he became the leader of a new renaissance, an almost feverish flowering of Hungarian poetry. He headed the literary group that had founded the important magazine *Nyugat* (West)—a group to which most of the leading writers belonged for the next two generations. This single word marked their aims—to turn to the West instead of the East; to fuse modern Western culture with the traditional heritage of Hungarian poetry.

Attila József

Even the scantiest survey of Hungarian poetry would be incomplete without four final names. Attila József (1905–37) came from a proletarian family—his mother was a washerwoman. A rebel who joined the Communist Party only to be expelled; a lover of the good things of life who dreamed in vain on a monthly pittance—he was only 32 when he threw himself in front of a train on the shores of Lake Balaton.

Miklós (Nicholas) Radnóti (1909–44) was a highly intellectual *poeta doctus,* who was murdered by a Nazi guard after enduring every possible torture and indignity in a death march to a concentration camp. His final poems, written during his slave labor service and in the last weeks of his life, were miraculously preserved and represent a terrible indictment of man's inhumanity to man.

Sándor (Alexander) Weöres is the great eclectician of Hungary; a virtuoso of form and thought, he is always experimenting, often hermetic, burningly sensuous and yet child-like in flashes of simplicity.

Gyula (Julius) Illyés, winner of the Grand Prix de Poésie, is the doyen of living Hungarian poets, a peasant who has imbibed the riches of Latin, and especially French, culture and whose prose is just as vivid as his sensuously beautiful poems. There are translations in English of much he has written, including his most famous prose work *The People of the Puszta.*

English-language selections of the above author's works occasionally appear in anthologies and in publications from Budapest. If you need reminders of the unfamiliar names, look around you! The streets, squares and cafes of Budapest bear the names of all her favorite men and women of letters.

Music

When St. Gellért (Gerard), the first Bishop of Hungary, came to the country almost 1,000 years ago, he rested at a small inn. In the evening he went to bed early, but could not sleep, for outside in the garden a maid was pounding grain and singing. 'The sweet melody of the Magyars', St. Gellért said, and listened intently. Ever since then, 'the sweet melody of the Magyars', though often polluted by the meretricious, has been a constant source of inspiration for Hungarian musicians. Hungarians and violins seem to have been created for one another and the Magyar recruiting dance, the *verbunkos* (from the German word *Werbung,* recruitment) found its way into Beethoven's *Eroica* and Mozart's A-major Violin Concerto; just as the fiery *Rákóczi March* became an integral part of Berlioz' *Damnation of Faust.* Great foreign musicians often came to Hungary—Beethoven and Hummel gave concerts in Buda, and Haydn was for many years the conductor of Prince Esterházy's private orchestra.

Hungarian opera was created by Ferenc (Francis) Erkel (1810–93), who was equally outstanding as pianist, conductor and composer, founder of the Budapest Philharmonic Orchestra and musical director of the National Theater.

Ferenc (Franz) Liszt (1811–86) has often been claimed by Germany, but when, at the age of eleven, he had his first public concert in Buda (before setting off on a foreign tour), he announced: 'I am a Hungarian and I cannot imagine any greater happiness than to offer the first fruits of my training and study to my beloved country'—an unequivocal declaration. Liszt, of course, was not only a great composer but an even greater virtuoso. Though he spent most of his life abroad, he never severed his connections with his native country. He became the first director of the Budapest Academy of Music. His *Hungarian Rhapsodies,* of which he composed 20 and the symphonic poem *Hungaria* proved his unbroken links with the soil that reared him.

Jenő (Eugene) Hubay and Ernő (Ernest) Dohnányi have both been composers of talent and brilliant performers—Hubay on the violin and Dohnányi on the piano.

The two modern Hungarian composers who have found world fame, Béla Bartók (1881–1945) and Zoltán Kodály (1882–1967), have both gone back to the deepest roots of folk music. They explored small villages and tiny settlements, making records of the peasant songs and dances. From these collections, or at least partly within their framework, their astonishing musical creations were born.

Bartók, who spent his last years in the United States, tried to create an independent language of music on the basis of ancient East European folk music. His ballets, *The Wooden Prince* and *The Miraculous Mandarin* show a demonic imagination creating organic life and perfect form; his one-act opera, *Duke Bluebeard's Castle,* his *Cantata Profana* and his amazingly intricate chamber music have earned him a place as the fourth 'B' with the three other geniuses—Bach, Beethoven and Brahms.

Zoltán Kodály's music was perhaps the first in Hungary to merge East and West in a passionate, beautiful union. Kodály was less of a revolutionary than Bartók, as he was often looking into the past. His *Psalmus Hungaricus,* first performed in 1923, composed to the words of a 16th-century poet, with a tenor solo, mixed choir and orchestra, immediately became world famous. It was followed by his folk opera *Háry János,* by his *Dances of Galanta* and his *Te Deum of Budavár,* all equally successful. But Kodály, above all, was the master of composing for the human voice, and especially for children. His method of teaching young, even very young, people to sing is still used in Hungary.

Composers of Today

Among modern Hungarian composers one may also briefly mention Ferenc (Francis) Szabó for his chamber music; László (Ladislas) Lajtha for his research into folk themes; Leó Weiner for *his* research into folk music, and György (George) Ránki, who also sought inspiration in Hungarian folk tales.

A very important group of Hungarian musicians lives outside Hungary. Many of them are indeed household names. Sir Georg Solti has been in charge of many famous orchestras, including the Chicago Symphony Orchestra, Covent Garden and the Paris Opera. Two other Georges, George Sebastian and George Széll, also belong to the major ambulant conductors of our age. Antal Doráti has been commuting for years between Europe and America, while Eugene Ormandy has a secure place among the great masters—and there are many more. The versatile tenor Sándor Konya is equally renowned in the opera houses of America and his native Hungary.

The late Joseph Szigeti has been acclaimed as one of the greatest violinists of all times. Among contemporary virtuosos, Andor Földes, Tamás Vásáry, Péter Frankl and Géza Anda are celebrated names.

Nor have Hungarians lacked eminence in light music. Franz Lehár was a Hungarian and his *Merry Widow* has proved truly immortal. So were Imre Kálmán, Pál Ábrahám and Miklós Brodszky, whose operettas and musical comedies have filled many a theater for years on end. Hungarians have also contributed to international jazz festivals; the pianist Attila Garay, the contrabassist Aladár Pege and the drummer Gyula Kovács (whom American jazz critics have hailed as the best in Europe) are masters of their modern art. Jazz concerts and records are immensely popular within the country and are no longer identified with 'Western capitalism and decay'.

When summer comes to Hungary the sound of music does not die away. Under the stars, within the walls and parks of old palaces and abbeys, choral and orchestral concerts draw large crowds: Beethoven at Martonvásár, Haydn at Fertöd, organ recitals and medieval court music at Tihany and Buda castle, chamber concerts at Kesthely . . . . musical picnics of an elegant kind, in quiet harmony with their surroundings.

Art and Architecture

Successive invasions, the long Turkish occupation and the numerous battles that raged on her soil have left few ancient Hungarian monuments and buildings standing. Nor have Hungarian architects been particularly brilliant; the cathedrals and palaces, the fortresses and magnates' mansions were usually designed and built by foreigners. The great building boom of the last decades of the 19th century produced an eclectic, bastard style, with an almost pathological passion for cupolas; the results can still be seen in Budapest and most provincial cities. The chief exception to this rule was Ödön Lechner (1845–1914), who created a new, short-lived 'Hungarian Art Nouveau' style, perhaps best exemplified by the former Hungarian Foreign Trade Bank in Budapest, in Rosenberg Házaspár Utca, not far from the Parliament.

For the most striking modern buildings, such as the 'stone dustbin' of the Hotel Budapest, foreign architects are again responsible. But one name of native significance is that of Marcell Breuer (b. 1902).

Hungarian sculpture has had its academic representatives of neo-baroque, among them Zsigmond Kisfaludi Strobl (1884–1975), whose G. B. Shaw and Lawrence of Arabia are considerable achievements, and the talented Ferenc Medgyessy (1881–1958), who also followed classical precedents.

Outside Hungary, the best-known Hungarian painter is the ambitious and talented Philip de László (1869–1937), Europe's most fashionable portraitist between the wars. Inside Hungary, no school of original painting developed. Her best domestic artists followed in the train of the French masters. Pál Szinyei Merse's (1845–1920) *Picnic in May* and *Lady in Violet,* which have pride of place in Budapest's National Gallery, derive from Manet. Tivadar Csontváry Kosztka (1853–1919) was a combination of Dali and Rousseau le Douanier. József Rippl-Rónai (1861–1927) introduced his fellow-countrymen to Parisian art-nouveau.

The Hungarian National Gallery in Budapest has the best collection of native artists. The Fine Arts Museum contains some celebrated Italian, Flemish and Spanish artists. Beautiful relics of ecclesiastical art are kept at the Christian Museum in Esztergom and in the Greek Orthodox Collection at Szentendre.

Horror Masks and Brandy Flasks

Delightful combinations of the strands which make up the national artistic temperament—gypsy, Oriental, Teutonic, Slav, classical—occur in the applied arts and crafts. Peasant traditions are powerful and idiosyncratic. Artistically the Hungarians are not all that creative; but they have enormous talent for improvisation, decoration and ingenious contrivances (of the last-named, the Rubik cube is the latest novelty). The Museum of Applied Arts in Budapest is a fascinating compendium of artefacts with the inimitable Magyar stamp.

Cultural shocks await the visitor to Hungary wherever local arts and crafts are strong: in the village museums or *skanzen* which are sprouting everywhere; in the flower-painted town of Kalocsa, where the rich botany of the Danube meadows is reproduced all over the cottage facades; in the carnival 'horror' masks of Villány (you may be invited to help make them); in the clusters of ceramic fountain statuary at Pécs. . . . ceramics are the glory of Hungarian craftwork, milestones on its folk history.

The earliest pottery dates from the 9th century. Progressive improvements in techniques led to the introduction of glazes, at first on insides and rims, afterwards overall. From the 16th century, when much of Hungary was under Ottoman rule, the simple bird-and-flower patterns became more Oriental and geometrical.

In the more peaceful atmosphere of the 17th century a new era began. Craftsmen settled into village communities and organized their guilds. Hungary expanded into an empire, with many foreign trading links, and this greatly benefited her potters. Ceramics of that period are highly decorative, with 'slip trailing' as the predominant technique. Ropes of 'slip,' a colored liquid clay, were squeezed on to the surface of the damp pot, producing a slightly raised pattern, and the colors, usually green, brown and black, were seen through a transparent glaze. Later, in the interests of speedier production, the brush superseded the 'trailer,' giving a flatter design.

Traditional forms, apart from common plates and dishes, were variations on the conventional bottle and pitcher shapes. Water vessels, the korsó with narrow neck and the kanta with a wide one, were often unglazed—the slow evaporation of the contents through the porous clay kept the liquids cool. In Hungarian museums there are fine examples of the bokály, a tall rounded vessel with funnel-shaped neck and handle.

The kulacs, the pilgrim's brandy flask, has small feet and small handles, which allowed it to be stood upright or slung from a shoulder-strap. The pereckulacs is ring-shaped, with a hole in the middle. Brandy flasks also exist in the shape of little kegs and plum stones. Most pieces have an inscription incised in the clay—the owner's name, or a poem, or a guild symbol. Many beautiful examples can be seen at the Ethnographical Museum in Budapest and the Déri Museum at Debrecen.

The folk-art of pottery flourishes still. Many potters work in country districts in the traditional idiom; a few hold the coveted title of 'Master of Folk Art.' The Hungarian potter best-known abroad is Margit Kovács (1902–1977), famous for her bizarre little groups and figurines.

Stage and Screen

In no other field of creative endeavor have Hungarians been as prominent as in the cinema and in the theater. A large number of the Hollywood 'giants' were Hungarians. Adolph Zukor's long life-span covered practically the whole history of the movies; and on the Paramount lot, there is still a signpost showing the exact distance to the tiny Hungarian village where he was born. The Fox in Twentieth Century Fox was William Fox (Fuchs), a Hungarian. We have already mentioned Sir Alexander Korda, who was for long a vital prop of the British film industry and whose screen-hits would fill pages. His two brothers, Zoltan and Vincent, were his constant collaborators, Zoltan as director and Vincent as set-designer. Their lives have been entertainingly described in the recent book *Charmed Lives* by Michael Korda.

Nor has there been a lack of Hungarian filmstars—though some of them have completely sloughed off their Magyar skins. Paul Lukas and Peter Lorre, genuine Hollywood stalwarts, Tony Curtis (born Bernie Schwarz), Cornel Wilde, 'Cuddles' Sakall, Zsa-Zsa Gabor and her sister and many others have all contributed their individual talents to Hollywood's symphony.

Hungary has always been a theater-loving country and Budapest has more theaters than Broadway; but Hungarian playwrights have been less successful in New York and London than on the European continent. Ferenc Molnár, whose wicked wit made him a living legend in his lifetime, was far more than the master of the well-made play. He was a poet of the theater, and although *Liliom, The Guardsman* and a few others are part of the enduring heritage of 20th-century theater, many of his plays, just as good, have suffered from atrocious adaptations.

There have been others to share the limelight since Molnár. Melchior Lengyel is best-known for two such opposite achievements as the story of *Ninotchka* and the libretto of Bartók's *The Miraculous Mandarin.* George Mikes has managed the almost incredibly difficult feat of becoming a true British humorist, whose books, ranging from *How to Be an Alien* to *Milk and Honey,* have made fun out of people and places until hardly any country has escaped his playful and incisive wit.

The events of 1956 were traumatic for the Hungarian cinema, as for other cultural activities, but it has shown signs of an interesting resurgence in the more enlightened political climate of the past four years, and is once more sending films to festivals (chiefly the competitive ones) abroad. One of the Hungarian cinema's chief representatives is Miklós Jancsó, whose main preoccupation is with guilt and courage. His austere and moving films have achieved world acceptance. There are echoes of Dreyer and Bergman in his work, but he has a style and philosophy all his own. Other outstanding Hungarian film directors are Zoltán Fabry, Károly Makk, György Révész, Istvan Szabó, Istvan Gáal, Pal Sándor and Marta Mészáros.

HUNGARIAN FOOD AND DRINK

From Gulyás to Dobostorta

Hungarian cooking is a sophisticated and delicious anthology of color, shape, odor and taste. It has absorbed, though with suitable modifications, the best of Viennese, French, Slav and Oriental traditions. There have been some unjust generalizations about its being too spicy or too heavy. This may be true in some parts of the country, but certainly not in Budapest or other culinary centers.

From Soup to Soup

Hungarian soups are memorable experiences. Perhaps the most fabulous is the Magyar version of *bouillabaisse*. It is called *halászlé* and is best eaten in Szeged or on Lake Balaton, though several Budapest restaurants also serve it. The Szeged version is a thick, rich soup made from giant catfish, carp or sterlet. The Balaton *halászlé* is a clear soup that contains onions, a moderate amount of paprika and is made with bream, pike-perch or shad. In many places cubed potatoes are added and sometimes small pieces of *pasta* (gnocchi-like bits of dough, kneaded with egg) are used to make the mixture richer. There is only one caveat—beware of the bones!

Goulash or *gulyás* is the Hungarian dish that is best known internationally, but in most cases when it is served outside the country, it is not goulash at all. A proper *gulyás* is a soup, though a soup that can be a meal in itself. It will contain slices of green pepper, as well as paprika, tomatoes, onions, *csipetke* (little dumplings) and enough rich gravy to make it completely liquid. Of course, its main ingredient will be pieces of beef (or occasionally pork). Contrary to popular misconceptions, it is not hideously spicy, does not contain any sour cream and is never served with rice. It does sometimes number caraway seeds among its many ingredients.

Other Hungarian soups include a modified version of the Russian cabbage soup known as *káposztaleves*. Particularly good on winter days is *bableves*, made from broad beans and lightly flavored with paprika and with boiled ham, bacon or sausages floating in it. Other very popular soups include potato soup, *rántott leves* (a thick brown soup with croûtons) and *húsleves* (bouillon), with or without a raw egg. Delicious in the summer is *meggyleves*, made from morello cherries and sour cream and chilled to an agreeably cooling temperature.

Main Courses

What *we* think of as goulash—a paprika-flavoured stew in which meat predominates—is known in Hungary as *pörkölt* or *tokány*. This can contain almost any kind of meat or fowl, though mutton and lamb are on the whole rarely eaten in Hungary. It consists of much the same ingredients as the *gulyás* we have referred to, but it is a solid dish and is usually served with sour cream and one of the many variants of dumplings; it is usually accompanied by a cucumber or lettuce salad. A regional variation of this theme is the so-called *székelygulyás*, which originated in Transylvania. It is a tasty combination of cabbage, sour cream, paprika and meat, usually pork. This, of course, is a main dish. As an alternative, you might try *kolozsvári rakottkáposzta* (layered cabbage); this is a very filling dish of sour cabbage, eggs, rice, smoked sausage and pork.

Among the other typical dishes you will find in Hungary are various stuffed vegetables. For instance, *töltött paprika*, green peppers filled with minced (ground) meat and served in a rich tomato sauce and *töltött káposzta*, cabbage leaves similarly prepared. There is also *serpenyős rostélyos*, which is made from sirloin steaks with onions, paprika and potatoes. Even the Hungarian versions of such international dishes as *Wiener Schnitzel*—in Hungarian, *bécsi szelet*—have a surprising and delightful taste of their own.

A favorite meat dish is the *fatányéros* (wooden platter), the Hungarian version of a mixed grill, surrounded by small helpings of salads, vegetables and crowned with bacon.

There is a great variety of excellent freshwater fish in the country— the giant catfish of the Danube, the pike-perch (*fogas*) of the Balaton, the sterlet of the Tisza and the mirror carp. One of the finest fish courses is the *rácponty* (devilled carp) with potatoes, peppers, tomatoes and onions, topped with sour cream.

Turkey is particularly good in Hungary, but chickens, geese and ducks are equally luscious and tasty. *Paprikás csirke* (paprika chicken) is usually served with sour cream poured over it and a side dish of cucumber salad. *Galuska* (small dumplings boiled in water) adds an additional attraction to the rich, golden-red gravy. *Rántott csirke* is the Hungarian version of Southern fried chicken.

Finishing the Meal in Style

Few countries have such variety and enchanting perfection in boiled desserts and cakes. *Túrós csusza* is made of small strips of *pasta* spread with curd cheese, sour cream and scraps of pork crackling. *Barátfüle* (literally, friar's ears) are, in effect, jam pockets and use the same *pasta* as *túrós csusza.* For extra sophistication they are sprinkled with ground nuts.

Hungarian noodles are called *metélt* or *nudli.* They are sprinkled with ham pieces, nuts, or poppy seeds mixed with sugar. The Hungarian pancakes (*palacsinta*) are equally tasty—their fillings can be sweetened curd cheese with raisins, ground walnuts, chocolate, various kinds of jam or poppy seeds.

Hungarian pastry is one of the most varied and tempting in the world, and can be readily sampled in any *cukrászda* (pastry shop). Perhaps the most famous is the *rétes* (the Austrian strudel), a paper-thin flaky pastry, which is filled with fruits, ground nuts, poppy seeds—even sweetened curd cheese and peppered cabbage. The *dobostorta,* a layered fancy cake with a hard burnt sugar top, is widely imitated throughout the world.

What to Drink

After some difficult years, Hungarian vintages have returned to their former excellence. A few of the most famous include: *Tokaji aszú* (Tokay), a dessert wine almost like a sweet, but heart-warming, brandy; *Egri bikavér,* the famous Bull's Blood from Eger (a full-bodied Burgundy); other fine red wines are *Medoc Noir,* also from the Eger district, *Szekszárdi* and *Soproni kékfrankos,* from southern and western Hungary respectively. Among white wines, are *Badacsonyi kéknyelű* (moderately dry) and *Badacsonyi szürkebarát* (sweet), both from the sunny slopes of the long-extinct volcano overlooking the northern shore of Lake Balaton. *Debrői hárslevelű* is an extremely popular white wine from the famous wine district of Gyöngyös. From the extreme south of Hungary come *Villányi hárslevelű* (white) and *burgundi* (red).

There are also large vineyards in the Great Plain, around the area of Kecskemét. Hungarian *barack,* the apricot brandy, is smooth and has a deceptively mild effect, with a fiery aftermath you will remember and wish to experience again. There are other Hungarian liqueurs made from plums, pears, cherries and even green walnuts, though this last is not always easy to find.

For those who prefer not to drink wine with their meals there is an excellent choice of natural mineral waters. Then there are several native brands of beer, the best known probably being *Kinizsi.* Foreign beers, such as Pilsen, are also freely available, while the well-known Danish *Tuborg* lager is produced in Hungary under license. Both Coca Cola and Pepsi Cola are to be found everywhere. Coffee is usually prepared like the *espresso* of Italy (though the coffee served at some of the hotels at breakfast is perhaps an acquired taste!) and tea is usually drunk with sugar and lemon or rum.

BUDAPEST

The Cosmopolitan City

There are many ways to know a city, varying degrees of discovering its essence. You can form a picture of London by visiting Soho, Chelsea and Westminster; you can claim that you know the Paris of Montmartre, Montparnasse and the Faubourg St Honoré or the Vienna of the Naschmarkt, Kärntnerstrasse and the Heuriger—but every capital has many faces, and Budapest is no exception. Twice-battered within 12 years, some houses still pockmarked with bullet-holes, the constant chaos of building and rebuilding enveloping many quarters, you will find in it light and shadow, moving beauty and stark ugliness, baroque elegance and modern utility. But it has also a spirit of its own, a unique blend of *laissez-faire,* biting wit and self-deprecation, cattiness and soaring enthusiasm, ribaldry and hearts-and-flowers sentiment. Hungarians are very articulate indeed, and their nimble tongues leave few secrets untold. Budapest has over two million inhabitants, about 20 percent of the population of the whole country, but news travels amazingly quickly and private affairs seldom remain private for long.

Cities are living beings and sometimes they change so quickly that you barely take eyes off them before finding them totally altered. Budapest is no exception, but here the changes have been forced upon a city that has one of the loveliest situations in Europe, straddling, as it does, one of Europe's most majestic rivers. Both in 1944–45 and in 1956 there

214

was prolonged street fighting within its limits and, as a result of this and of the innumerable battles, sieges and civil wars of earlier centuries, there is not a great deal of distinguished architecture in the city; but there are small details, unexpected corners, sudden delights that reward the pedestrian. It is not a city that you can explore properly in a car. The distances are modest; the more reason to stroll—and to linger.

Castle Hill

Start by taking a taxi or a bus (no. 16 from Engels Tér) up to Castle Hill. Here, around the former royal palace, a true labor of love has been performed. The seven-week siege of 1944-45 turned the whole district into a vast acreage of ruins. The final German stand was made in the palace itself, which was burnt out completely, its walls largely reduced to rubble, with a few scarred pillars and fire-blackened statues sticking out of the devastation. The destruction was incalculable—yet not without unexpected advantages. Archeologists and art historians were provided with a unique opportunity to explore the past, to discover the medieval buildings that had once stood on the site of the baroque and neo-baroque palace. The details of the edifices of the kings of the Árpád and Anjou dynasties, of the Holy Roman Emperor Sigismund, and of the great national king, Matthias Corvinus, have been preserved in about 80 different reports, travelogues, books and itineraries, which spoke with the authenticity and appreciation of contemporaries about the beauty and riches of the Buda royal residence.

The post-1945 rebuilding was slow and elaborately considerate—it tried to restore and enhance the values of the different epochs in their historic and architectural beauty. In some places more than 20 feet (6 meters) of rubble had to be removed, and the remains found on the medieval levels were restored on the original planes. The foundation walls and the medieval castle-walls freed from the tall mounds of rubble were completed and the ramparts surrounding the medieval royal residence were erected again as close to their original shape and size as possible.

The former Royal Palace itself can be reached in a few minutes on foot from Dísz Tér (Square), where you leave your bus or taxi, or you can take bus V from the square at the western end of the Chain Bridge (Clark Ádám Tér) direct to the terrace in front of the Palace. This contains an equestrian statue of Prince Eugene of Savoy, one of the commanders of the army fighting the Turks at the end of the 17th century; from the terrace there is a superb view over Pest. The Palace has been restored to its original splendor and is now a vast museum complex and cultural center. In the northern wing is the Museum of the Hungarian Working Class Movement—here are relics from guilds and from the beginnings of modern industry, as well as an exhibition of Socialist Art in Hungary. The immense center block contains the Hungarian National Gallery, with a wide-ranging collection of Hungarian fine arts throughout the ages, from medieval ecclesiastical paintings and statues to works of the 19th and 20th centuries, which are richly represented. The southern block contains the Budapest History

Museum, while the western block is to be the home of the National Library, with over five million volumes.

The whole of Castle Hill, a long narrow plateau with several streets of miniature palaces and mansions and a few medieval churches, saw bitter fighting in 1944–45, but restoration work is virtually complete. The great 'Coronation Church' or Matthias Church (*Mátyás templom*), officially the Church of Our Lady, has been rebuilt and refurnished. Dating back to the middle of the 13th century, it has suffered many changes and attacks—for almost a century and a half, it was the principal mosque of the Turkish overlords. It was badly damaged in the recapture of Buda in 1686, and was completely reconstructed at the end of the 19th century, receiving an asymmetrical west front with one high and one low spire, and a fine rose window. The south porch is 14th century, and inside there are a number of paintings and sculptures of considerable age and artistic value. The *encolpium*—an enameled casket, containing a miniature copy of the gospel, to be worn on the chest—belonging to King Béla III (1173–1196) and his wife, Anne of Châtillon, is of particular interest; the burial crowns of the royal couple and a cross, scepter and rings found in their excavated graves are to be seen here, too. The Treasury contains renaissance and baroque chalices, monstrances and vestments. High Mass is celebrated here at 10 a.m. on Sundays, with a fine orchestra and choir. It was in this church that the last two kings of Hungary, Francis Joseph and Charles, were crowned.

Outside the church there is a richly convoluted baroque column dedicated to the Trinity. Nearby are the remains of the oldest church of Castle Hill, built by Dominican friars in the 13th century; only the tower and one wall have survived and these have, with considerable skill, been incorporated in to the impressive Hilton Hotel, which manages to combine old and new architecture to form a harmonious whole. Close at hand is the modern romanesque Fishermen's Bastion (*Halászbástya*), which consists of cloisters of white stone whose columns and arches provide perfect frames for the splendid view below. The top is crowned by a round tower, which houses a highly-popular café-restaurant; in front stands a modern bronze equestrian statue of St. Stephen, Hungary's first king.

The town houses that line the narrow streets of Castle Hill are now occupied by offices, restaurants, espresso coffee bars and a few lucky foreign diplomats. In András Hess Square, named after the first Hungarian printer (who started work in 1473), there is the famous House of the Red Hedgehog (*Vörös Sün*), formerly an inn. Throughout Castle Hill, medieval, classical and baroque houses stand cheek by jowl. At no. 9 Táncsics Mihály Street a baroque building masks the dungeons where Lajos Kossuth, Hungary's great national leader, spent more than three years in prison; next door (no. 7) Beethoven stayed in 1800 when he came to Buda to conduct his works. To the north, in Kapisztrán Tér (Square of St. John Capistrano) is all that remains of the Gothic church of St. Mary Magdalene—the tower—which has been carefully restored.

Narrow medieval alleyways connect the main streets of Castle Hill, and in almost each of them there is something of historical interest. There are fine Gothic buildings in Úri Street, which also contains the grave of Abdurrahman Ali, the last Turkish pasha to rule Buda. The buildings at the southern end of the Hill include the recently-rebuilt Castle Theater, where Beethoven once performed. While it retains its original façade, the interior has been planned in accordance with the most modern principles.

Down to the Danube

If you are tired after your explorations, you might have a snack and something refreshing to drink at Ruszwurm (Szentháromsag Utca 7), which is opposite the Matthias church and is perhaps the oldest pastry shop in Hungary. Then you can start your descent towards the Danube. There are many winding paths and roads, but the easiest leads south to the ancient quarter called the Tabán. Though most of the small, sunken houses have been demolished—many in the interests of traffic— here and there a few picturesque buildings remain. At no. 1 Apród Street is the house where Ignác Semmelweis, the great Hungarian physician and the discoverer of the cause of childbed fever, was born in 1818. This is now a museum of medical history. In the narrow strip between Castle Hill and the Danube much of the ambiance of Old Buda is preserved. A broad promenade flanks the river embankment and a single street runs parallel with it. The cross-streets all climb the hill,

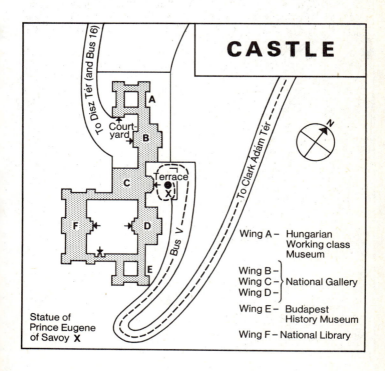

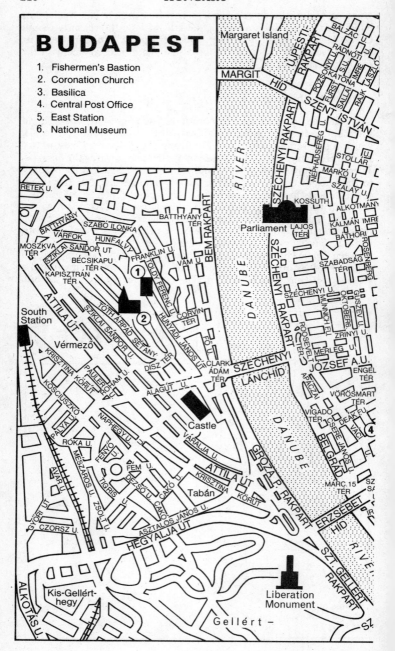

BUDAPEST

1. Fishermen's Bastion
2. Coronation Church
3. Basilica
4. Central Post Office
5. East Station
6. National Museum

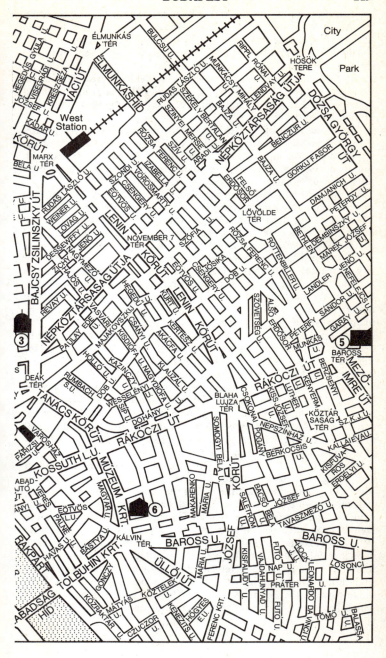

some of them flights of steps rather like the old streets of Montmartre. Fő (Main) Street starts at the Chain Bridge, where a square has been named after the British builder of the bridge, Adam Clark. At the northern end of Fő Street there is a bronze statue of Joseph Bem, the Polish general who led one of the main Hungarian armies in the struggle for freedom in 1848–49. It was at this statue that a great demonstration was held in 1956 in sympathy with the Polish striving for liberal reform—the demonstration which developed into the great and tragic Hungarian uprising.

One of the relics of the Turkish occupation is in the nearby Mecset (Mosque) Street—the tomb or *türbe* of Gül Baba, the 'Father of the Roses', a Dervish and poet. His tomb, built of carved stone blocks with four oval windows, was a place of pilgrimage for several centuries, even after the Turks had been ejected from Hungary.

To the south of Castle Hill rises Gellért Hill. It's only 770 feet (232 meters) high, but from its summit the whole city appears spread out like an unrolling tapestry. Looking down from the hill, which bears an old fortress on its rocky crown, the scenic panorama of one of the most spectacularly-chosen city sites spreads to the horizon. Directly opposite is the vast plain occupied by Pest, the more modern part of the twin city. Spreading on the left or eastern bank of the Danube, the vista is closed by the towering chimney stacks of the distant industrial suburbs. Between the labyrinth of roofs, domes, and spires, it is possible to discern the inner and outer boulevards, the large green oases of the many parks and the occasional squares.

The Danube itself curves through the capital roughly from north to south, dividing repeatedly to embrace islands. In the north, you can see the southern end of large Szentendre Island, with a number of small hamlets on it. Next is a smaller one, once called Szunyog (Gnat) Island, with some shipyards. In the very heart of Budapest lies Margitsziget (Margaret Island), which is occupied by a beautiful park, hotels, restaurants, swimming pools and rowing and athletic clubs. At the southern extremity of Budapest stretches Csepel Island (Csepelsziget), almost 30 miles (48 km) long, with extensive market gardens and a huge industrial complex, the Csepel Iron and Steel Works.

Standing on the top of Gellért Hill, you will see, south of the old fort and rising well above it, the 110-foot (32-meter) high Liberation Memorial, commemorating the end of the 1944–45 siege and the Russian soldiers who fell in the seven-week battle. It is the work of Zsigmond Kisfaludy-Strobl, the veteran Hungarian sculptor. Facing the Danube, you will have, on your left, two other hills—Várhegy (Castle Hill) and Rózsadomb (Hill of Roses). Beyond these, there is a range of higher hills, of which the conical Jánoshegy (John's Hill) is the tallest; its 1,435 feet (435 meters) are topped by a lookout tower. Other Buda hills include the Szabadsághegy (Freedom Hill) and, further to the northwest, the Hármashatárhegy (Hill of Three Borders), both of which have their tourist centers, restaurants and hostels.

The Danube Bridges

Budapest had always been as proud of its bridges as London or Paris. Their total destruction by the retreating Nazi armies was as much of a blow as the wanton blowing-up of the Arno bridges at Florence. For many months, only a pontoon bridge connected the two halves of the city (Pest and Buda became one in 1873 when Óbuda, Old Buda, was also added to the capital), but within 20 years, all of them had been rebuilt. Farthest north is the railway bridge (reopened May 1955), which provides direct transport from the Hungarian coalfields into the heart of Budapest. Then follow the two bridges connecting Margaret Island with the city.

The Árpád Bridge was opened in 1950 and is the longest of all, 1.3 miles (2 km) in length. It connects the northern industrial suburbs of Újpest and Óbuda and is the normal means of access by car to the beautiful island. It is now being widened. The Margaret Bridge, at the southern tip, unusual in shape (it forms an obtuse angle in midstream, from which a short leg leads to the island), also had to be rebuilt, but its original design was retained. The bridge was blown up by the Nazis towards the end of 1944 when it was crowded with rush-hour traffic. Margaret Island contains, within a comparatively small space, the most attractive features of outdoor living in Budapest and lends the character of a holiday resort to the city during the summer months. It is a park, a sports center and a spa and has two excellent hotels.

The oldest of the Danube Bridges is the Chain Bridge (Lánchíd), designed in 1839 by the British engineer William Tierney Clark and finished ten years later by a compatriot, Adam Clark, who also built the 383-yard (350-meter) long tunnel under Castle Hill which connects the Danube Quay with the rest of Buda. The bridge was rebuilt and reopened in 1949, to mark the centenary of its inauguration.

South of the Chain Bridge, the reconstructed Elizabeth Bridge (Erzsébethíd) is another graceful suspension bridge, in a single arch. It was the last of the bridges to be rebuilt and was reopened in 1964. Next is Liberty Bridge (*Szabadsághíd,* formerly named after Francis Joseph), which leads to the foot of Gellért Hill. Then comes the Petőfi Bridge, linking the Pest and Buda sides of the Grand Boulevard and finally a railway bridge.

Belváros, the Inner City

The heart of Pest is the Belváros, or Inner City, which is enclosed by the somewhat irregular semicircle of the Inner Boulevard. Modern Pest, much younger than Buda, has been conceived on a roughly concentric plan. The innermost boulevard was the first to be built and contains the heart of Pest. The second, or Grand, boulevard was built in the 1880s and 1890s and describes a semicircle from the Danube at Margaret Bridge in the north to Petőfi Bridge in the south. The third, outer, boulevard again forms a large semicircle around Pest, with the Danube as its diameter. The big boulevards are intersected by a number of straight main roads, such as Rákóczi Út, which radiate out from the center of the city and lead ultimately to the main national highways.

Crossing the Danube from Buda by the Chain Bridge, you first reach the large oblong of Roosevelt Square. Here the statue of Count István Széchenyi, whom his most determined opponent, Lajos Kossuth, dubbed 'the greatest Hungarian', and the statue of Ferenc Deák, the architect of the Austro-Hungarian monarchy, stand close to one another; both men resided in this square. The large, neo-renaissance building of the Academy of Sciences, on the left, forms a fitting background for Széchenyi, for it was he who donated a year's income to establish it in 1825.

On the far side of the square is the Gresham Building, an interesting art-nouveau structure built for a British insurance company, and to the right stands the large new Atrium-Hyatt hotel.

Strolling southwards from Roosevelt Square, we find the so-called *Korzó*—a promenade reserved for pedestrians. The first building on the Corso is the new Forum Hotel. Then follows Vigadó Square with, on the left, the Vigadó Concert Hall, built in a striking romantic style in the middle of the last century. Liszt, Brahms, Bartók and many other famous artists have given concerts here. It was gravely damaged during World War II, but is again one of the most important centers of Hungarian cultural life.

Soon there follows the Duna-Intercontinental Hotel, a massive modern building in which every bedroom overlooks the Danube. The *Corso* is a favorite strolling-place and the view of Buda and its historic palace and churches across the river affords a delightful panorama. It has several pleasant and popular open-air cafés and restaurants.

Walk down the Corso past the Intercontinental Hotel as far as Március 15 (March 15th) Square and turn left to penetrate the maze of narrow streets and closely-packed houses which lie behind it. This was the old walled city of medieval times; wherever the walls have been uncovered, they are preserved and marked with tablets. In this part of Pest are some of the oldest and finest churches. Two are in March 15th Square, forming a backdrop to the statue of Sándor Petőfi, the greatest 19th-century Hungarian poet. One is a Greek Orthodox church, built at the end of the 18th century, largely remodeled but still preserving some fine wood-carvings and a late 18th-century iconostasis. The second is the Inner City Parish Church (*Belvárosi plébánia templom*), the oldest in Pest; its origins go back to the 12th century. There are hardly any architectural styles that cannot be traced in some part or other. The single nave still has its original Gothic chancel; two side chapels contain beautifully-carved renaissance altar-pieces and tabernacles of red marble from the early 16th century. The 150 years of Turkish occupation are marked by a *mihrab,* a Moslem prayer niche. The organ of the Inner City Church was often played by Liszt who, between 1867 and 1875, lived only a few yards away. In his town house he regularly held 'musical Sundays', at which Richard and Cosima Wagner were frequent guests.

To the east of the Corso, and parallel with it, is Váci Utca, which has Budapest's smartest shops. It is an excellent center for clothes, furs, shoes, books and folk art (the largest folk art shop is here); most of it is closed to motor traffic (as is one of its more attractive side-streets, Kigyó Utca) and it affords a pleasant opportunity for window-shopping, if no more. It has a couple of popular cafés. Just beyond Kigyó Utca, Váci Utca crosses Szabadsajtó Út, a prolongation of Kossuth Lajos Utca, which is another fashionable shopping street. At the point where the roads cross lies Felszabadulás (Liberation) Tér, with an old Franciscan church. A bronze tablet on its wall shows a scene from the memorable flood of 1838, which devastated Pest and claimed many lives. The water rose 3 to 5 feet (1 to 1½ meters) above the pavement.

Beyond the Franciscan church, along Károlyi Mihály Utca (named after Count Michael Károlyi, who headed a short-lived democratic government at the end of World War I), we reach Calvin Square (Kálvin Tér) named after the Calvinist church whose classical façade dominates it. A short distance to the left is one of Budapest's most famous historic monuments, the National Museum. Built between 1837 and 1847, it is a fine example of 19th-century classicism, well proportioned and simple. It was outside this famous building that Sándor Petőfi recited his famous *National Song* (Nemzeti dal) on March 15 1848, calling the people to rise against the Habsburgs; and it is here that the Hungarian Coronation regalia, recently returned to their homeland, are displayed.

Rákóczi Út is the eastern continuation of Kossuth Lajos Utca and is the busiest shopping street of Pest, with several large department stores; it ends at the East Station (*Keleti pályaudvar*).

At the north end of Váci Utca is Vörösmarty Tér, with a statue of one of Hungary's great poets, Vörösmarty, and the famous pastry shop now named after him (it was formerly known as Gerbeaud and is still often so called), where the fashionable (and, nowadays, the not-so-fashionable) world meets for tea, coffee, or rich pastries. In and around this square are the chief airline offices, and not far away to the northeast is Engels Square, which contains the city's long-distance bus terminal. Beyond this is the impressive St. Stephen's basilica, which was built in the second half of the 19th century; its 300-foot (91-meter) high dome dominates the whole of Pest. Planned originally as a neo-classical building, it was completed in neo-renaissance style.

The district lying to the north of Vörösmarty Square is the Westminster and Whitehall of Budapest; most of the ministries are here, as well as the National Bank, the Courts of Justice and the Party Headquarters. Dominating the whole district, however, is the huge neo-Gothic Parliament building; its situation is particularly fine, as it is mirrored in the Danube in much the same way that the British Parliament is mirrored in the Thames. Its vast central dome, crowned by a red star, is well balanced by the arcades and the windows. It is now the center of Hungary's political life, with the offices of the Prime Minister and of the Presidential Council, which is elected by the National Assembly from among its members. The building is probably the city's most famous landmark.

The Grand Boulevard

The Grand Boulevard (Nagykörút) stretches from the two ends of the large loop which the Danube describes at Budapest, forming a wide semicircle. Laid out at the end of the 19th century, it shows the influence of Haussmann's Paris boulevards; an arm of the Danube was covered up, the bed of the river's backwater having been drained and banked, so that a broad thoroughfare, 120 feet (35 meters) wide and almost 3 miles (5 km) long, could be created. The large apartment houses flanking much of its length were all built at about the same time and in the same architectural style.

Most of Budapest's theaters and many of its cinemas are situated on the Grand Boulevard and its sidestreets. Here, too, are several large cafés, a few nightclubs and a number of hotels. The Boulevard starts at the southern end, at Boráros Square; here it is called Ferenc Körút (Francis Boulevard), after the typical old district which it traverses. Then comes the section called József Körút (Joseph Boulevard). The main buildings of Lenin Körút (Lenin Boulevard), which follows, are the famous Hungária café-restaurant, the Hotel Royal and the Academy of Music. Lenin Körút ends at Marx Square, with the West Station. With a typical Hungarian sense of humor (or irony), the next section of the boulevard is named after St. Stephen (Szent István Körút); this ends at the Danube (Margaret Bridge). A stroll along the Grand Boulevard would take about an hour and a half and would be a good introduction to the busier parts of Budapest.

The grandest avenue of Budapest is the almost two-mile (3-km) long People's Republic Avenue (Népköztársaság Útja). It was formerly known as Andrássy Út, after the Hungarian statesman in whose time it was inaugurated, and has changed names several times since; at one time it was, inevitably, Stalin Avenue! It begins near the Basilica and finishes at Heroes' Square (Hősök Tere), at the entrance of the City Park (Városliget). It is lined with neo-renaissance buildings, some of them with ornate but attractive façades. Under it runs Budapest's original underground (subway), the first on the European continent, which was opened in 1896. This, now known as Line 1, connects with the fine new Metro at Deák Tér, in the Inner City.

Not far from the Basilica stands the State Opera House, built between 1878 and 1884, in a neo-renaissance style, by the architect Miklós Ybl. Badly damaged during the siege of 1944-45, it was restored with the same loving care as was Vienna's Staatsoper; with the Ferenc Erkel Theater it is the center of Hungarian opera and ballet. (The Opera House is at present closed for renovation and performances are held at the Erkel theater.) The National Ballet School is conveniently housed just across the avenue in a large French renaissance-style building known as the Drechsler Palace. This is the Shaftesbury Avenue or Broadway district of Budapest, in which half a dozen theaters are situated, including the Municipal Operetta Theater and the Variety Stage (Vidám Színpad).

Vörösmarty Square, in the Inner City, out to the City Park and beyond. It's useful to remember that Lines 1, 2 and 3 all meet at Deák Square (Deák Tér).

There are local electric trains to the suburbs and an electric cogwheel railway as well as a chair-lift to the Buda Hills.

By Taxi. You will find taxis outside hotels, railway stations, theaters and at the principal street corners, or they may be hailed while cruising. When free, they display the illuminated sign 'TAXI'. You can order them by telephone, dialing 222–222 or 666–666. Fares are reasonable; give a tip of around 20%. There are also a number of private taxis with the sign MAGÁN TAXI.

Car Hire. This can be arranged through travel offices in Budapest, for instance the travel desk at your hotel. There is an Avis office at the airport and at Martinelli Tér 8, in the Inner City.

HOTELS. In spite of an ambitious building program, there can still be a shortage of rooms during the tourist season (May to September) and it is highly advisable to book accommodations well in advance. Even in spring and fall, all but the best hotels tend to be overcrowded. In addition, Budapest is becoming increasingly popular as the venue of international congresses and conferences, during which hundreds of rooms are preempted. Single rooms with bath are scarce except in the best hotels. At almost any time of the year the lower grades of hotels tend to be overcrowded with package tour groups and individual travelers wishing for a high standard of service are therefore recommended to use hotels of a higher category.

If you arrive in Budapest without a reservation, there are two places that will do their utmost to help you. These are the IBUSZ office at Petőfi Tér 3, just behind the Intercontinental Hotel and, for travelers arriving by air, the tourist office at Ferihegy Airport.

Deluxe

Atrium-Hyatt, Roosevelt Tér 2, Budapest V (tel. 383–000). Large luxury hotel, opened in 1982, in the Inner City with fine view over the Danube. 357 air-conditioned rooms, all with bath and color television. Large restaurant, cocktail bar, covered swimming pool, sauna and gym. Ballroom; conference-rooms with every modern facility for businessmen.

Duna-Intercontinental, Apáczai Csere János Utca 4, Budapest V (tel. 175–122). On the Danube Quay; its 349 rooms and suites, all with bath, overlook the Danube. Several restaurants, café with terrace overlooking the river, penthouse bar and nightclub. Fully-equipped conference rooms. Garage. Full air-conditioning.

Hilton, Hess András Tér 1–3, Budapest I (tel. 853–500). In a magnificent position on Castle Hill with a splendid view over the city. The hotel incorporates the tower and other remains of a 13th-century Dominican church. 323 rooms and suites, all with bath. Several restaurants, nightclub, fully-equipped conference rooms. Airconditioned throughout. Garage. Casino.

Thermal, Margitsziget, Budapest XIII (tel. 111–000). Opened in 1979, this luxury spa-hotel has 206 rooms, all with private bath; thermal swimming pool and medicinal baths. Medical supervision of any treatment desired; sauna, solarium, gym. Good restaurant, conference-hall and nightclub. Direct bus connection to the city center.

Expensive

Forum, Apáczai Csere János Utca 12, Budapest V (tel. 178–088). New hotel on the Danube Quay, near the Chain Bridge, with splendid view. 408 rooms with bath, airconditioning throughout. Several restaurants, swimming pool, sauna, gym, solarium; conference and ballrooms. Underground garage.

Gellért, Szent Gellért Tér 1, Budapest XI (tel. 460–700). Traditional and famous old hotel in Buda, at the foot of Mount Gellért and overlooking the Danube. 235 elegant rooms, most with bath; some are airconditioned. The hotel's attractions include indoor and outdoor swimming pools and elaborate medicinal baths. Excellent restaurant, nightclub. Warmly recommended.

Novotel, Alkotás Utca 63–67, Budapest XII (tel. 666–756). Hotel opened in 1982 in Buda, with a fine view. 324 rooms, each with bath and television. Public rooms are airconditioned. Covered swimming pool, sauna, tennis court. Several restaurants and bars.

Olympia, Eötvös Utca 40, Budapest XII (tel. 166–450). Situated in the Buda Hills, with easy access to town. 200 rooms, most with bath, restaurant, conference room, bars, nightclub with floorshow; swimming pool, sauna, gym. A few minutes' walk will take you into the Buda woods.

Royal, Lenin Körút 47–49, Budapest VII (tel. 421–120). In the busy heart of Pest. Traditional hotel, recently completely rebuilt; very comfortable and popular, particularly with businessmen. 366 rooms, all with bath. Several restaurants, garden-terrace, cafés and nightclub. Ask for a back room.

Moderate

Aero, Ferde Utca 1–3, Budapest IX (tel. 270–690). Convenient for the airport and useful chiefly to transients. 140 doubles with bath; restaurant, bar.

Astoria, Kossuth Lajos Utca 19, Budapest V (tel. 173–411). At a busy corner in the Inner City, with front rooms correspondingly noisy, but conveniently located and extremely popular. 190 rooms; many doubles, and some singles, with bath. Good restaurant, snack-bar, café and nightclub with floor-show.

Béke, Lenin Körút 97, Budapest VI (tel. 323–000). Near West Station, 141 rooms, many with bath. Restaurant, well-known and popular nightclub. The wine cellar resounds to 'yodel music'.

Buda-Penta, Krisztina Körút 41–43, Budapest I (tel. 153–655). Hotel opened in 1982 in the heart of Buda and near the South Station. 400 rooms with bath and television. All public rooms are airconditioned. Covered swimming pool, sauna, gym; restaurant, café, nightclub.

Budapest, Szilágyi Erzsébet Fasor 47, Budapest II (tel. 153–230). A striking circular building in a pleasant part of Buda, opposite the lower terminus of the cog-wheel railway. 280 double rooms, all with bath. Restaurant, wine cellar, café and roof-top bar with spectacular view; dancing.

Emke, Akácfa Utca 3–5, Budapest VII (tel. 229–814). Centrally located just off busy Rákóczi Út, 70 doubles with bath. Restaurant, café and much frequented nightclub (*Maxim's*).

Európa, Harshegyi Utca 5–7, Budapest II (tel. 164–099). This 13-story hotel is situated high above Buda, with fine views, and is surrounded by woods. 20 single and 138 double rooms, all with bath. Restaurant, tavern, bar.

Expo, Dobi István Utca 10, Budapest X. New hotel adjoining the site of the International Trade Fair, well away from the center. 160 rooms with bath; restaurant. Every conceivable modern facility is provided for the businessmen who provide most of the clientèle.

Grand Hotel Margitsziget, Margitsziget, Budapest XIII (tel. 111–000). Beautifully situated on Margaret Island with 150 rooms, many with bath. Good restaurant and large garden-terrace. This famous old hotel has recently been

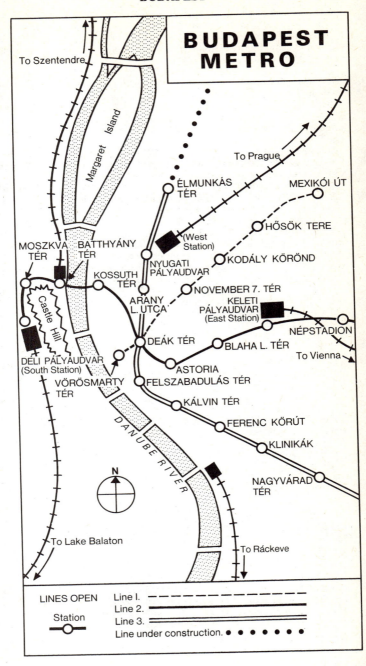

BUDAPEST METRO

To Szentendre

Margaret Island

To Prague

ÉLMUNKÁS TÉR

MEXIKÓI ÚT

HŐSÖK TERE

MOSZKVA TÉR   BATTHYÁNY TÉR

(West Station)

NYUGATI PÁLYAUDVAR

KODÁLY KÖRÖND

KOSSUTH TÉR

Castle Hill

ARANY L. UTCA

NOVEMBER 7. TÉR

KELETI PÁLYAUDVAR (East Station)

NÉPSTADION

DÉLI PÁLYAUDVAR (South Station)

DEÁK TÉR

BLAHA L. TÉR

To Vienna

VÖRÖSMARTY TÉR

ASTORIA

FELSZABADULÁS TÉR

KÁLVIN TÉR

FERENC KÖRÚT

KLINIKÁK

N

D A N U B E   R I V E R

NAGYVÁRAD TÉR

To Lake Balaton

To Ráckeve

LINES OPEN

Station

Line I.
Line 2.
Line 3.
Line under construction.

upstaged by its new and grander neighbor, the *Theraml* (E), whose medicinal waters it shares. Direct bus to the city center.

Metropol, Rákóczi Út 58, Budapest VII (tel. 421–175). Somewhat noisy situation in main shopping street, but very comfortable. 102 rooms, some with bath. Restaurants, café, bar.

Palace, Rákóczi Út 43, Budapest VIII (tel. 136–000). In noisy main shopping street, so ask for back rooms. 93 rooms, some with bath. Good restaurant, bar, night-club.

Park, Baross Tér 10, Budapest VIII (tel. 131–420). Hotel with over 300 beds, many with bath or shower, and more singles with bath or shower than is usual in this category. Conveniently situated opposite East Station. Restaurant, café, bar.

Szabadság, Rákóczi Út 90, Budapest VII (tel. 229–050). A large modern hotel opposite the East Station. 400 single and double rooms, most with bath. Restaurants, confectionery, bars and night-club, Recommended.

Volga, Dózsa György Út 65, Budapest XIII (tel. 290–200). Large hotel with 743 beds; 190 doubles and 116 family rooms, all with bath. Restaurants, bars and night club with floor show. The hotel is some way out of town but there are good bus and tram connections. Extremely popular with groups.

Vörös Csillag, Rege Út 21, Budapest XII (tel. 290–200). Attractive hotel built in the style of a hunting-lodge on a hill in Buda 1,000 feet above the Danube and a few yards from the upper terminus of the cog-wheel railway. 24 doubles, many with bath, and 16 singles, some with bath. Restaurant, bar, open-air terrace with splendid view. The Buda woods are only a few yards away.

Wien, Budaörsi Út 88, Budapest XI (tel. 665–400). In the southwest outskirts, near the junction of the motorways from Vienna and Lake Balaton. 110 double rooms, many with bath. Restaurant, café, bar. Petrol station and repair shop; good spot for motorists.

TOURIST HOSTELS. There are several so-called tourist hostels in and around Budapest, suited above all to young people. They include the **Strand** (Pusztakúti Utca 3, Budapest III), which lies some miles north of the city but is easily reached by electric suburban railway from Batthyány Tér; has a few simple single rooms, some doubles, and dormitory accommodations. There is a similar hostel at **Csúcshegy** (Menedékház Utca 122) in the Buda Hills; dormitory accommodations only. In each case there is a restaurant close by.

Arrangements for these hostels are best made through IBUSZ.

The Express Travel Bureau (Szabadság Tér 16, near the Parliament) can arrange accommodations for young people in university hostels during July and August only.

PRIVATE HOUSES. IBUSZ, at its office at Petőfi Tér 3, as well as the other main tourist offices, can make arrangements for you to stay in private houses. Clean, comfortable bedrooms are provided, with use of bathroom, but no service.

CAMPING. There are two main camp sites in Budapest—**Római Fürdő,** near the Danube, north of the city (open-air baths) and **Hárshegy,** in the Buda Hills, nearly 800 feet (244 meters) up. Details from Budapest Tourist, Roosevelt Square 5, opposite the Chain Bridge, in Pest, or from the Hungarian Camping and Caravanning Club, Üllői Út 6, Budapest VIII (tel. 336–356).

RESTAURANTS. Prices in Budapest restaurants vary quite considerably depending on whether or not an orchestra is playing, so that, for instance, a portion of goose that costs 100 Ft at lunch may cost 125 Ft at dinner. However, a good meal, with half a bottle of wine, can be had for a little over 150 Ft a head and in some of the smaller and more modest places (where the food may be even better) for half that sum. A *menü* (fixed-price menu) of two or three courses can be had at many restaurants for as little as 30 to 50 Ft.

Nearly all restaurants are state-owned but a few, generally small ones, are offered on lease to the highest bidder and are granted licenses to sell food and drink at controlled prices.

Our grading of the restaurants, inns and taverns of Budapest that we list is based not on their official classification, but on reasonable standards of cuisine, comfort, atmosphere and value for money. At the more fashionable places it is generally necessary to book a table; check with your hotel porter. We have divided the restaurants, other than those at the hotels, into three categories: Expensive (E), Moderate (M) and Inexpensive (I), though there are, inevitably, borderline cases. Furthermore, we have separated them into those on the west bank of the Danube (Buda) and those on the east bank (Pest).

A large proportion of Hungarian restaurants have some kind of music, though only in the evening. This can range from a soft lute or piano to a full gypsy orchestra. The music is, of course, part of the Hungarian 'scene' and diners will sit near to, or away from, the music according to their tastes. We have, as far as possible, noted the presence, or absence, of music.

The better hotels (the 5-star and 4-star establishments) all have excellent restaurants. The more luxurious of them have several each. For instance, the Hilton serves Hungarian specialties at the *Kalocsa,* while the *Tower* has an international menu; at the Intercontinental, the *Csárda* is well-known for its Hungarian food and the *Rendezvous* has a wider range of dishes. Restaurants in the better hotels expects their men guests to wear a tie in the evening.

It is important to remember that nearly all restaurants, though not those in the hotels, are closed one day a week, though not all on the same day. Make enquiries of your hotel porter.

Buda

Expensive

Alabárdos, Országház Utca 12 (tel. 160–828). On Castle Hill; small, intimate restaurant in a beautiful old building with period décor. Perhaps *the* restaurant of Budapest. Superb food and wines, with soft lute music. Open in the evening only; booking and suitable dress essential.

Arany Hordó, Tárnok Utca 16 (tel. 361–399). Historic 14th-century building on Castle Hill. Its specialty is the *fogas,* the delicious fish from Lake Balaton. Dining room, beer hall and wine cellar. Open from noon to evening. Gypsy music in the evenings.

Fortuna, Hess András Tér 4 (tel. 160–270). In an ancient palace in the heart of the Castle district. Very good food, a distinguished wine list and, in the evenings, a gypsy orchestra. Open from noon.

Régi Országház, Országház Utca 17 (tel. 160–225). A very old, rebuilt, inn at the northern end of Castle Hill. Seven rooms, each decorated in a different style. Famous for its wines. Open all day; gypsy music in the evenings.

Moderate

Arany Szarvas, Szarvas Tér 1 (tel. 351–305). Below the Castle; a typical small Buda restaurant famous for its dishes of game and venison. Open in the evenings only; gypsy music.

Fehér Galamb, Szent Háromság Utca 9 (tel. 160–809). Attractive restaurant a few yards from the Matthias Church, in the Castle district. Open from mid afternoon. Its specialty is meat roasted on the spit. Gypsy music. Book your table.

Rózsafa, Kacsa Utca 26 (tel. 354–701). Pleasant restaurant near the Danube Bank; typical Hungarian food. Open all day; popular music in the evenings.

Tabáni Kakas, Attila Út 27 (tel. 352–159). A delightful small restaurant to the west of Castle Hill. Specializes in poultry dishes and is famous for its goose. Open evenings only—a pianist plays and sings.

Vadrózsa, Pentelei Molnár Utca 15 (tel. 351–118). In the garden of a private villa. The food, and especially the goose-liver (which is not cheap) is highly praised. Open evenings only during the week, also for lunch on Sundays.

Inexpensive

Márvány Menyasszony, Márvány Utca 6 (tel. 151–229). Charming garden restaurant situated not far from the South Station. Indoor rooms decorated in Hungarian peasant style. Open all day, Music and dancing in the evenings.

Muskétás, Dísz Tér 8 (tel. 161–283). Part restaurant, part snack bar. Situated on Castle Hill, near the northern entrance to the Castle. Simple and very inexpensive.

Pest-Buda, Fortuna Utca 3 (tel. 360–768). Charmingly-decorated little restaurant with good food and very friendly service. Open from noon in the season, otherwise evenings only, when there is old-time music. Warmly recommended.

Sipos Halászkert, Lajos Utca 46 (tel. 686–480). Halfway between the Margaret Bridge and Old Buda (Óbuda). Tasty fish dishes, served both indoors and in the garden. Gypsy music in the evenings, when it is very crowded.

Szeged, Bartók Béla Út 1 (tel. 251–268). Just south of Mount Gellért and a few yards from the Danube bank. Furnished in the style of a typical fisherman's inn. Fish soup a specialty. Gypsy music in the evenings.

Pest

Expensive

Gundel, in the City Park (tel. 221–002). Famous old restaurant. Excellent food and wine; outdoor tables. Gypsy music in the evenings.

Hungária, Lenin Körút 9 (tel. 220–849). Famous café-restaurant, opened in 1894, when it was known as the *New York.* Destroyed in World War II, it has been rebuilt and redecorated in all its original art nouveau splendor. Open for lunch and dinner; in the evening music and dancing. Booking essential.

Kárpátia, Károly Mihály Utca 4 (tel. 173–503). In the heart of the Inner City. Very good food; pleasant outdoor terrace and garden. Gypsy music in the evenings.

Mátyáspince, Március 15. Tér 8 (tel. 180–608). In the Inner City, close to the Elizabeth Bridge. Excellent food and service, always full for lunch. One of Hungary's most famous gypsy orchestras plays in the evenings. Must book.

Nimród, Münnich Ferenc Utca 24 (tel. 116–098). Near the US Embassy. Decorated with hunting trophies and famous for its game dishes. Open for lunch and dinner; gypsy music in the evenings.

Százéves, Pesti Barnabás Utca 2 (tel. 183–608). Just off Váci Utca, in the Inner City. Good food and wine in an 18th-century baroque palace. Charming old-fashioned booths for private eating. In the evening the gypsy music can sometimes be a bit overpowering for so intimate a place.

Moderate

Alföldi, Kecskeméti Utca 4 (tel. 174–404). In the Inner City, not far from Kálvin Tér (Calvin Square). Typical Hungarian restaurant, with very good food.

Apostolok, Kigyó Utca 4–6 (tel. 183–704). Famous beer hall and restaurant in the Inner City pedestrian precinct. Good hot food all day and tasty cold dishes in the evenings. Separate booths, named after the Twelve Apostles. Excellent beer.

Dunakorzó, Vigadó Tér (tel. 186–435). In a delightful position right on the Corso, overlooking the Danube and Buda. Outdoor covered terrace. Good and reasonably-priced food. Open all day; music in the evening.

Opera, Népköztársaság Útja 44 (tel. 328–586). Recently refurbished restaurant and beer hall in the heart of the theater district, with outdoor tables. Italian food specialties. Gypsy music in the evening. Very popular for a meal after the show.

Vigadó, Vigadó Tér (tel. 176–222). Beerhall and restaurant with excellent food in elegant surroundings. It is in the newly rebuilt Vigadó Concert Hall, in the Inner City and a few yards from the Corso.

Inexpensive

Bástya, Rákóczi Út 29 (tel. 130–477). Very popular and often crowded restaurant in the city's main shopping thoroughfare. Quick and friendly service. Open all day. No music.

Erzsébet, Lenin Körút 48 (tel. 223–003). Quiet beer hall restaurant opposite the Royal Hotel and near the theater district. Good food; open all day. No music.

Múzeum, Múzeum Körút 12 (tel. 138–282). Very popular restaurant next to the National Museum, open all day. No music.

Rézkakas, Veres Pálné Utca 3 (tel. 180–038). In the Inner City, just south of the pedestrian precinct. Simple but good; poultry a specialty. Open all day. No music.

Sirály, Bajcsy Zsilinsky Út 9 (tel. 228–864). Small, quiet restaurant near the main long-distance bus terminal. Good food; open all day. No music.

FOREIGN-STYLE RESTAURANTS. There are a good many of these, all of them in the Moderate (M) or Inexpensive (I) categories. Here is a selection:

Bajkál (Russian), at the corner of Semmelweis Utca and Kossuth Lajos Utca, in the Inner City. Excellent tea; open all day.

Bukarest (Romanian), Bartók Béla Út 48, beyond the Hotel Gellért, in Buda. Open all day. Dancing in the evenings.

Havanna (Latin-American), József Körút 46. Open evenings only; Latin-American music.

Karczma Polska-Kis Royal (Polish), Márvány Utca 19, near the South Station. Beer hall open all day, restaurant in the evening only.

Napoletana (Italian), Apáczai Csere János Utca, near the Intercontinental Hotel. Open all day.

Szófia (Bulgarian), Kossuth Lajos Tér, behind the Parliament.

 BEER AND WINE RESTAURANTS. Most of the larger hotels have both a wine cellar *(borozó)* and a beer cellar *(söröző),* so we do not list these separately. We must, however, mention the **Borkatakomba** (Wine Catacombs) at Budafok, a southwestern suburb of Budapest. Here there is a whole series of vaults cut into the limestone. The caves are decorated in Hungarian style and a gypsy band plays Hungarian folksongs. Excellent simple Hungarian food; open in the evening only.

In the center of town, just behind the Hotel Intercontinental, is the **Rondella,** a wine cellar which is also an inexpensive restaurant—though the accent is on the wine, not the food.

Budapest has also numerous wine-tasting establishments *(borkóstoló).*

SNACK BARS *(bisztró* or *ételbár).* These are to be found in almost every street in the busier parts of the city. Those most conveniently situated and most likely to be of use to the visitor include: **Belvárosi,** Szabadsajtó Út 5, near the Elizabeth Bridge; **Gresham,** Roosevelt Tér 5, near the Pest entrance to the Chain Bridge; **Mézes Mackó,** Kigyó Utca 4, in the Inner City pedestrian precinct; **Savoy** and **Abbazia,** Népköztársaság Útja 48 and 49, opposite each other where the avenue crosses the Grand Boulevard.

There are also many self-service restaurants *(önkiszolgáló étterem);* these, however, may present problems if you do not know the language, or recognize Hungarian dishes.

PASTRY SHOPS AND CONFECTIONERS *(cukrászda).* Two of the many are outstanding. They are the very fashionable and crowded **Vörösmarty** (formerly known as Gerbeaud), in Vörösmarty Square, an oasis of peace in the heart of the Inner City and a few yards from all the airline offices, and **Ruszwurm,** Szentháromság Utca 7, on Castle Hill, perhaps the oldest in Hungary, which is tiny and charmingly furnished in Biedermeier style. The **Korona,** in Dísz Tér, nearer the Castle, is also pleasant, as is the smart **Különlegességi,** at Népköztársaság Útja 70. The **Hungária,** already mentioned as an outstanding restaurant, also has a much-frequented pastry-shop and café.

CAFÉS. The famous old cafés of Budapest are no more. Instead, there are innumerable small coffee-bars (in Hungarian *eszpresszó*). Two of these, very conveniently situated for shoppers, are in the Inner City pedestrian precinct; they are the **Anna,** at no. 7 Váci Utca (which turns into a popular night spot when the shops close), and the **Muskátli** at no. 11 (which serves good tea). Both have terraces on the street, where one can see—and be seen.

MUSEUMS. For a country that has been looted so frequently in the course of centuries, Hungary has managed to retain a remarkable quantity of artistic and historical treasures. Visiting hours are normally from 10 am to 7 pm, except on Mondays, when museums are closed. Check details with your hotel porter or a tourist office.

Agricultural Museum (Mezőgazdasági Múzeum), in the Városliget, (City Park). This is probably the most characteristic, and one of the most interesting, museums in Hungary. The group of buildings that constitute the museum are representative of the national architecture throughout the centuries. The museum has five main sections: (1) Hungarian animal husbandry; (2) forestry (in the Gothic part); (3) horticulture; (4) hunting and fishing and (5) recent trophies.

Budapest History Museum (Vármúzeum), in block E of the former Royal Palace. This has on its main floor a permanent exhibition entitled '1,000 Years of Our Capital' which depicts through historical documents and exhibits the medieval history and art of Buda fortress and of the capital as a whole. The beautifully restored Medieval Hall of the Knights is particularly impressive.

Ethnographical Museum (Néprajzi Múzeum), Kossuth Lajos Tér 12, Budapest V. A branch of the National Museum, this contains Hungarian folk art and folklore collections. A collection of the art of Oceania is also housed here. Library.

Fine Arts Museum (Szépművészeti Múzeum), Dózsa György Út 41, at the end of Népköztársaság Útja, at the edge of the City Park. This contains the largest collection of paintings and sculpture in Hungary. It is particularly rich in Flemish, Dutch and Spanish old masters—the latter perhaps the best collection outside Spain, including, as it does, seven fine El Grecos and five beautiful Goyas, as well as paintings by Velázquez and Murillo. The Italian School is represented by two superb paintings by Raphael, and others by Giorgione, Bellini, Correggio and Tintoretto. The Dutch and Flemish masters include three Rembrandts and words by Frans Hals, Rubens, Van Eyck, Memling, Van Dyck and Brueghel the Elder. Dürer and Cranach represent the German School, while the French have excellent pictures by Monet, Renoir, Gauguin and Cézanne. The sculpture collection aims to show the development of this art from the 4th to the 18th centuries; its 'star item' is a small equestrian bronze statuette, attributed to Leonardo da Vinci. There is also a magnificent display of over 150,000 drawings, as well as an Egyptian and a Graeco-Roman exhibition.

Folklore Center (Művelődési Ház), Fehérvari Út 47, Budapest XI. Exhibitions and film-shows on tourism and folklore and performances of folk dances and music by the best Hungarian popular ensembles. It is open in the summer only.

Jewish Museum (Zsidó Gyűjtemeny), Dohany Utca 2. (Open 2 to 6 Mondays and Thursdays, 10 to 1 Tuesdays and Fridays). History of the Hungarian Jews; religious relics and works of art.

Museum of Applied and Decorative Arts (Iparművészeti Múzeum), Ullői Út 33–37, near the southern end of the Grand Boulevard. This is a building in modern Hungarian style. There are two permanent exhibitions: (1) the history of ceramic art from Grecian vases to china from the great contemporary porcelain workshops; (2) the goldsmith's art in Europe from the 16th to the 20th centuries.

National Gallery (Nemzeti Galéria), in the central blocks (B, C and D) of the former Royal Palace on Castle Hill. It contains a representative display of Hungarian fine art throughout the ages, beginning with the work of old masters (medieval panel-paintings, triptychs and wooden statues) and including masterpieces of the 19th and 20th centuries. There is an especially fine collection of the works of Munkácsy, perhaps the best known of Hungarian 19th-century painters, and there are fine paintings by, among many others, the impressionist Szinyei Merse and Csontváry Kosztka, whose work was a strange combination of expressionism and surrealism. There is also a large collection of modern Hungarian sculpture.

National Museum (Nemzeti Múzeum), Múzeum Korut 14–16, Budapest VIII. A monumental building in classical style with a colonnadad portico and built between 1837 and 1847. It is surrounded by a large garden. There are two permanent exhibitions: (1) the pre-history of the peoples of Hungary (on the mezzanine floor; stone, bronze and iron ages plus Roman antiquities and collections of the Great Migrations); (2) history of the Hungarian people from the 9th to the 20th centuries.

Among the most precious and popular of the Museum's exhibits are the Hungarian royal regalia, including the Holy Crown of St. Stephen. These are impressively displayed in the 'Hall of Honor'. The crown, together with the scepter, the orb, the sword and the coronation robe were restored to Hungary in January 1978 by the United States, who had held them since 1945, when the fleeing Hungarian Army handed them over to prevent their falling into the hands of the Russians. The crown, a masterpiece of Byzantine art, is not now thought to be that presented by Pope Sylvester II in the year 1000 and with which Stephen was crowned first king of Hungary, but is believed to date from the 12th century. The regalia are regarded as the legal symbols of Hungarian sovereignty—even by a Communist government—as they provide evidence of unbroken statehood for close on a thousand years.

Stamp Museum (Bélyegmúzeum), Hársfa Utca 37 (open on Sunday, Wednesday and Saturday); contains all Hungarian stamps ever issued.

Transport Museum (Közlekedési Múzeum), in the Városliget (City Park). (Closed on Mondays and Fridays.) Covers the whole field of transport in Hungary.

War History Museum (Hadtörténeti Múzeum), Tóth Árpád Sétány 40, Budapest 1. This contains rich collections of Turkish and Napoleonic periods, documents of Hungarian military history, particularly of the wars of independence. Comprehensive collections of arms and battle pictures.

NIGHTLIFE. Unlike most other Eastern European capitals, Budapest has good nightlife, with a great variety of night spots, from the staid to the near-riotous. The **Troubadour** at the Hilton and the **Starlight** at the Intercontinental are elegant, expensive and somewhat subdued. Among top favorites are **Maxim's**, at the Hotel Emke, and the **Moulin Rouge**, in Nagymező Utca; both have good floorshows, both charge an entrance fee and both are expensive. Best reserve. Avoid whiskey, unless you have money to throw around—this applies to all Hungary. The **Hungária**, in Lenin Körút, and the **Kupola**, at the Hotel Béke, are also very popular, the latter particularly with the younger generation. Many hotels, restaurants and bars have dance bands; fashions alter, so ask your hotel porter.

On Castle Hill the **Old Firenze** is worth a visit, as is the **Casanova**, on the Danube bank. In the Inner City, try the **Anna**, in Váci Utca, or the far-less-sedate **Pipacs**, a few yards away in Aranykéz Utca. You will find it difficult to get in to the **Funko Disco**, at the **Eden**, Széna Tér 7, in Buda. The choice and variety are endless—and the scene is constantly changing.

OPERA, THEATER, CONCERTS. For details of all the events consult the monthly *Coming Events in Budapest,* which is freely available at your hotel. Tickets can be obtained from the Budapest Tourist Board, Roosevelt Tér 5, Budapest V, or from the Central Booking Agency for the Theaters, Népköztársaság Útja 18, Budapest VI. Even simpler, you can ask the information desk of your hotel to get them for you. Prices are remarkably low, and if you go to the various box offices of theaters and concert halls yourself, you will get them even more cheaply.

Opera and theater. There are two opera houses in Budapest, under the same management—the **State Opera House** (on Népköztársaság Útja) and the **Erkel Theater,** Köztársaság Tér 30, Budapest VIII, not far from Rákóczi Út. At present the Opera House is closed for renovation and performances take place at the Erkel Theater. Dress is almost always informal, even on gala occasions.

There are some 20 permanent theaters in Budapest and in summer performances are given on open-air stages, the largest of which is on Margaret Island (closed at the time of writing). Performances usually begin at 7 pm at open-air theaters in the summer at 8 pm.

Concerts. There is a year-round feast for music-lovers in Budapest. Apart from the Erkel Theater, musical life is centered on the **Academy of Music** (Liszt Ferenc Tér 8, near Népköztársaság Útja), which has a large and small concert hall, and the newly reopened **Vigadó,** on the Danube quay.

Hungary has an inexhaustible fund of chamber orchestras. The Tátrai String Quartet and the Budapest Wind Quintet, the Bartók String Quartet, the Weiner String Quartet and the Szécsi String Quartet all give regular performances throughout the country and do a great deal of foreign touring. The Hungarian Chamber Orchestra has a changing number of members, but no conductor.

The Hungarian State Concert Orchestra gives the greatest number of concerts in Budapest, The Symphony Orchestra of the Hungarian Radio and Television has also given a growing number of performances since the early Sixties. Finally, the Philharmonic Orchestra (about 110 years old) of the State Opera House sometimes finds additional time to give concerts.

Choral singing is an old tradition in Hungary, which has been greatly developed by Zoltán Kodály's pioneering work in musical education. Handel's and Bach's oratorios and cantatas are performed annually; many baroque concertos and orchestral compositions are frequently presented.

The Budapest Musical Weeks, started in 1956, have become the traditional attractions of early fall. They have featured competitions for pianists, for singers, for cellists and for chamber music. In the fall of 1962, a Jazz Club was founded for young people in Budapest, which meets weekly; it has more than a thousand members. Excellent church music can be heard at the Matthias or Coronation Church on Castle Hill. Not only are concerts and organ recitals given here, but the High Mass on Sundays at 10 am is sung by a large and well-trained choir, to the accompaniment of an orchestra. There is also good church music at the Basilica and at the Inner City Parish Church, on the Pest side of the Elizabeth Bridge.

Cinema. In addition to Hungarian films, some of which are outstandingly good, cinemas also show foreign films, from both East and West. These are usually, though not invariably, dubbed.

 PARKS AND GARDENS. Budapest is extremely well supplied with large and beautiful parks and gardens— and the Buda Hills themselves are, for the most part, wooded and parklike. Here is a selection of those most worth visiting.

Margaret Island. Almost the whole island is one large park, occupying over 200 acres. It contains vast sports grounds and the National Swimming Pool, as well as Budapest's largest public swimming pool, the Palatinus, with artificial waves, medicinal pools and separate pools for children. This has changing rooms for almost 20,000 visitors. There is also a tennis stadium and open-air stage. A spa hotel, the Grand Hotel Margitsziget, lies towards the north of the island and another, the Thermal, has been opened nearby. There are a number of interesting historic relics, including the remains of a medieval Dominican nunnery and of a 13th-century Franciscan church. Cars and taxis may only enter the island from the north, over Árpád Bridge, but bus 26, starting just off Marx Tér, near the West Station, is permitted to enter from the south.

City Park, (Városliget) in Pest. The largest park in Budapest. It contains the Zoological Garden, a circus and an amusement park. In the center is a large boating lake (where people skate in winter) and, on the shores of the lake, a group of exhibition buildings. The park is easily reached by the subway (underground railway) from the Inner City.

Gellért Hill, in Buda. Though the side facing the Danube is fairly steep, it has been landscaped with stairs, small or large look-out spaces, benches and zigzag paths. The Citadella, or Old Fort, is a pleasant goal with its indoor and outdoor restaurant (closed for alterations at the time of writing).

Youth Park (Ifjúsági Park). This is also in Buda, not very far from the Hotel Gellért, around the large 'Bottomless Lake.' It has tennis courts, a cafe, restaurant, children's playground and a large open air theater.

 SHOPPING. Almost all shops—and all the larger ones —are state-owned, and the variety of goods on sale, although a vast improvement on even the recent past, is generally somewhat limited. The best things to buy are peasant embroideries and the charming Herend and Zsolnay porcelain. The *Intertourist* shops (which accept only hard currency) have the widest choice. Intertourist has branches all over the city as well as kiosks in most of the hotels. Its main shop is at Kígyó Utca 5, in the Inner City pedestrian shopping precinct. There is also an excellent folk art shop at Váci Utca 14, also in the shopping precinct, and smaller, similar shops in all important streets; in these you can pay in Hungarian currency. Records are also an excellent buy as are dolls dressed in peasant costume.

There are first-class, if expensive, fashion shops in Váci Utca and neighboring streets. Hungarian tailors, for both men and women, are also good. There are so-called 'commission shops' (*bizományi boltok*), where such things as antiques and pictures are sold on commission by private persons. You may occasionally find a good piece, but a word of warning! If it is a work of art, you will need a special permit to take it home with you; the shops will advise you on this. But if you buy anything of value from the hard currency shops, you need no such permit; keep the receipt, which will ensure a safe passage through Hungarian customs.

There are a few privately-owned boutiques in the streets between the Váci Utca and the Duna Intercontinental Hotel. Their goods are generally of high quality, with prices to match.

You might like to wander round one of the department stores and here are some of the principal stores of Budapest. Note that service at large stores that are not primarily intended for foreign visitors can at times be offhand. A good rule is that the smaller the store, the more gracious the attention you will receive. The largest is the *Corvin Áruház* (áruház—department store), Blaha Lujza Tér, just off Rákóczi Út. Others are *Luxus Áruház*, in Vörösmarty Tér, in the Inner City, and three new stores called *Skála Áruház*, one not far from the Gellért Hotel in Buda, another in Ó Buda (Old Buda) and the latest opposite the West Station. The *Vásárcsarnok* (Central Market), Tolbuhin Körút, near Kálvin Tér, is a colorful covered fruit and vegetable market. The best bookshops are in Váci Utca (in the Inner City) and in Népköztársaság Útja. The *Antikvárium* (second-hand bookshop) is in Múzeum Körút, opposite the National Museum.

There are first-class, if expensive, fashion shops in Váci Utca and neighboring streets. Hungarian tailors, for both men and women, are also good. There are so called 'commission shops' (*bizományi boltok*), where such things as antiques and pictures are sold on commission by private persons. You may occasionally find a good piece, but a word of warning! If it is a work of art, you will need a special permit to take it home with you; the shops will advise you on this. But if you buy anything of value from the hard currency shops, you need no such permit; keep the receipt, which will ensure a safe passage through Hungarian customs.

There are a few privately-owned boutiques in the streets between the Váci Utca and the Duna Intercontinental Hotel. Their goods are generally of high quality, with prices to match.

You might like to wander round one of the department stores and here are some of the principal stores of Budapest. Note that service at large stores that are not primarily intended for foreign visitors can at times be offhand. A good rule is that the smaller the store, the more gracious the attention you will receive. The largest is the *Corvin Áruház* (áruház-department store), Blaha Lujza Tér, just off Rákóczi Út. Others are *Luxus Áruház*, in Vörösmarty Tér, in the Inner City, and three new stores called the *Skála Áruház*, one not far from the Gellért Hotel in Buda, another in Ó Buda (Old Buda) and the latest opposite the West Station. The *Vásárcsarnok* (Central Market), Tolbuhin Körút, near Kálvin Tér, is a colorful covered fruit and vegetable market. The best bookshops are in Váci Utca (in the Inner City) and in Népköztársaság Útja.

There are several second-hand bookshops (known as *Antikvárium*); the chief of these are in Múzeum Körút, opposite the National Museum, but there is a well-stocked second hand shop in Váci Utca, the main shopping street in the Inner City.

 SIGHTSEEING. There are a number of sightseeing tours by coach, organized by IBUSZ (the state tourist organization) and by Budapest Tourist, which cover all the main sights. Most IBUSZ tours start from the Intercontinental Hotel, the Budapest Tourist trips from their head office at Roosevelt Square 5, not far away. One 3-hour tour covers all the main sights of the city and runs both morning and afternoon. It costs around 150 Ft. There are other tours to the Parliament and the Castle, to museums and galleries, to the Buda Hills and to the Danube Bend. There is also a 5-hour-long *Budapest by Night* program. Full details and prices can be obtained from the travel offices mentioned.

 **USEFUL ADDRESSES.** The main embassies are all in Budapest: *British:* Harmincad Utca 6, Budapest V (off Vörösmarty Square); tel: 171–430. *American:* Szabadság Tér 12 (near the Parliament): tel: 124–224. *Canadian:* Budakeszi Út 55d/P8 (in Buda); tel: 165–858.

IBUSZ Travel Bureau, Tanács Körút 3/c. *Budapest Tourist Board,* Roosevelt Tér 5. *Coopturist,* Kossuth Lajos Tér 13–15. *Volán Travel Bureau,* Október 6 Utca 11–13. *Express Youth and Students Travel Bureau,* Szabadság Tér 16. *Wagons-Lits/Cook,* Pilvax Köz 7. All these are in Pest, in or near the Inner City.

HUNGARY'S HEARTLAND

The Danube Bend

The Danube Bend, where the great river breaks through the Börzsöny and Visegrád mountains, represents a major shift in the flow of the
river. It stretches for 12 to 14 miles (19 to 23 km). But for the tourist
the name means a much larger district, both the immediate vicinity of
the Danube banks, an area stretching from Esztergom to Budapest, first
flowing west to east and then bending around the town of Vác, into a
more-or-less direct north to south line, and the mountains that rise
along both sides. In the north, this stretches to the Czech border and
includes the Börzsöny Mountains; in the south, the hills of Esztergom
and Visegrád.

Scenically, it is a most varied part of Hungary. There is a whole chain
of riverside spas and watering places, bare volcanic mountains and
limestone hills. It is the heartland of Hungary's history. Here the *limes*,
the frontier district of the Roman Empire, was established, here kings
set up their residences, ambassadors came and great international and
national forces met and clashed. The Danube Bend was one of the
celebrated centers of the cultural life of the Hungarian Renaissance; it
contains archeological and historical relics stretching back six or eight
centuries.

The region on the west bank of the Danube is the more interesting,
with three charming and picturesque towns—Szentendre, Visegrád and

Esztergom—all of which richly repay a visit. The district can be covered by car in one day, the total round trip being no more than 67 miles (108 km), but this would allow only a cursory look at the many places of interest. Two days, with a night at either Visegrád or Esztergom (both of which have good hotels), would give the visitor time for a more thorough and more leisurely look at this delightful part of Hungary. The east bank has only one town, and that of only moderate interest, Vác, though it also has many pleasant holiday resorts; but it cannot be compared in its appeal to the tourist with the west bank. There are numerous ferries across the Danube, though no bridges, so that it would be possible to combine a visit to both sides of the Danube if the visitor so wished—and had ample time.

The West Bank

Whether one leaves Budapest by rail (electric suburban train from Batthyány Tér) or road for Szentendre, the nearest and most picturesque town of the Danube Bend, one sees on the right Aquincum, a Roman settlement dating from the 1st century AD and the capital of the Roman province of Pannonia. Little remains of the military settlement, but the civilian city has been well excavated and reconstructed and provides a good example of an important Roman town. The most notable buildings are the basilica, the forum and the public baths.

The Aquincum Museum contains relics of a Roman camp, inscribed stones, mosaics, glass and jewelry. The Hercules Villa, in Meggyfa Utca, just before Aquincum, contains beautiful mosaic floors, with colors as vivid as they were 1,800 or 1,900 years ago.

Just beyond Aquincum is the *Római fürdő* (Roman Bath), one of Budapest's two main camping-sites.

Szentendre, about 12 miles (19 km) from Budapest on a good, though very busy, road, is one of the most charming small towns in Hungary, with a population of about 17,000. It was settled by refugees from Serbia and Greece fleeing from the advancing Turks. They built their own baroque churches, many of them beautifully decorated. The Greek-Orthodox church (often closed) in the main square, and the Serbian-Orthodox Cathedral on a hill just to the north, are well worth visiting. The little cobble-stoned streets, with their picturesque baroque houses have an old-world charm. There are several museums, including one of Serbian ecclesiastical art and another displaying the outstanding ceramic work of the late Margit Kovács. Several restaurants serve Serbian and Greek dishes. Szentendre is the home of one of Hungary's most active artists' colonies.

We continue along the west bank of the Danube, past Leányfalu, a pleasant holiday resort, with a tourist hotel and a camping-site, to Visegrád (27 miles/43 km from Budapest), once the seat of the kings of Hungary. The town now has less than 3,000 inhabitants, but in the 14th century it was both large and important. It was then that the Angevin kings built a citadel here, which became the royal residence.

Later, King Matthias Corvinus (1458–1490) had a palace built on the banks of the Danube. Its entrance is in the main street (Fő Utca).

It was razed to the ground by the Turks and it is only in the last 30 years or so that the ruins have been excavated and much of what must have been a magnificent palace has been restored. Specially worthy of a visit is the red marble well, built by a 15th-century Italian architect, and decorated with the arms of King Matthias. This is situated in a ceremonial courtyard, which has been restored in accordance with authentic contemporary records. Above the courtyard rise the various halls; that on the left has a few fine original carvings, which give an idea of how rich and beautiful the 15th-century palace must have been. Do not fail to walk or drive up to the remains of the citadel (good restaurant and hotel at the top), which not only is interesting in itself, but provides a superb view over the Danube Bend.

Esztergom

A town of some 30,000 inhabitants, Esztergom can be reached either by continuing along the Danube bank from Visegrád (40 miles/64 km from Budapest) or directly from the capital by a good road (bus service) or very slow train (27 miles/43 km). The city, which stands on the site of a Roman fortress, is the seat of the Cardinal-Primate of Hungary and its striking cathedral (built between 1822 and 1869) is the largest church in the country. It lies on a hill overlooking the town. Its most interesting features are the Bakócz chapel (1506–1511), named after a Primate of Hungary who only narrowly missed becoming Pope—it was part of the earlier medieval church and was incorporated in the new edifice—and the sacristy, which contains a valuable collection of medieval ecclesiastical art. According to tradition, Géza, the father of Hungary's first king, St. Stephen, was born in Esztergom and it was here that Stephen was crowned, in 1000. Below the Cathedral Hill lies the so-called Víziváros (Water Town), with many fine baroque buildings, and here, in the Primate's palace, is the splendid Museum of Christian Art (Keresztény Múzeum), which is the finest art gallery in Hungary after that in Budapest and is particularly rich in early Hungarian and Italian paintings and contains, among much else, pictures by Duccio, Memling and Cranach. Fine French tapestries and a French renaissance codex are among the treasures. The same building houses the Primate's Archives, whose oldest document dates from 1187; it contains 40,000 volumes, including several medieval codices and incunabula. To visit the Archives, permission must be obtained in advance. When, in the 17th century, Buda became the political capital of Hungary, Esztergom remained—and still is—the country's ecclesiastical capital.

At Esztergom, the Danube is now the frontier; across the river is Czechoslovakia. The former bridge is no longer in existence, but there is a ferry which, however, may only be used by the local inhabitants.

The East Bank

The only town of importance on the east bank, Vác, is 22 miles (35 km) from Budapest and can be reached by either road or rail; it has some 35,000 inhabitants. Its two chief monuments are its Cathedral, built in 1763–77 by Archbishop Migazzi to the designs of the Italian architect Carnevale, and a triumphal arch, by the same architect, erected to celebrate the visit to the town of the Empress Maria Theresa.

Along the Danube north of Vác lie a whole string of pleasant summer resorts, nestling below the picturesque Börzsöny Hills and stretching as far as Szob, just before the Czechoslovak frontier. One of them, Zebegény, is well known as the resort of painters.

PRACTICAL INFORMATION FOR HUNGARY'S HEARTLAND

WHEN TO COME. 'Szentendre Days' in July include a symposium on art, concerts of baroque and modern music, cookery competition, beauty and dancing contests, camp-fire programs on the Danube embankment. A revival of the traditional market-day theatrical performances takes place in the Main Square (Marx Tér). Throughout July, some newly-discovered classic of Hungarian drama and folk poetry is performed against the background of the old medieval and baroque houses; *commedia dell'arte* productions with close contact between audience and players.

GETTING AROUND. If you have enough time, you should certainly travel by boat from Budapest, a leisurely and pleasant journey, especially in summer and spring. The steamers for Esztergom start from the main Pest landing stage near Vigadó Tér. On summer Sundays and public holidays a hydrofoil service brings Visegrád within an hour, and Esztergom within 1½ hours of Budapest. Timetables available at your hotel. Trains run frequently to Szentendre from Batthyány Tér, in Buda. By car via Szentendre-Visegrád, follow no. 11 highway, which more or less hugs the Buda bank of the Danube.

To reach Vác, go by steamer from Budapest, Vigadó Square, by bus or train from the West Station, or by road via highway no. 2.

HOTELS AND RESTAURANTS

All hotels listed below have restaurants unless otherwise stated.

ESZTERGOM. Fürdő (M), spa hotel, Bajcsy Zsilinszky Utca. Attached to the local spa and swimming-pools; recently enlarged and modernized. Rooms with bath; central heating and bar. **Volán** (M), is in the town center, near the park; several (I) hotels.

Restaurants. Kispipa, corner of Kossuth Lajos Utca and Arany János Utca; **Úszó halászcsárda** (fisherman's inn), on the island.

SZENTENDRE. Danubius (I), between Szentendre and Leányfalu. An attractive modern hotel on Road 11, bordering the Danube. There is also a tourist hostel and camping site plus motels.

Restaurants. Görög Kancsó (Serbian dishes), Görög Utca, near landing stage; **Béke,** in main square; **Teátrum,** north of the town; **Duan.** The **Határcsárda,** on the road to Leányfalu, is popular.

VÁC. No recommended hotel.

Restaurants. Halászkert (fish restaurant) on Danube bank; **Fehér Galamb,** Lenin Út; snack bar in Széchenyi Utca.

VISEGRÁD. Silvanus (M), on top of Mount Visegrád, with a spectacular view; highly recommended, especially for motorists. **Vár,** in the main street, offers simple accommodations. Also Tourist Hostels.

Restaurants. Vár Étterem, in main street; **Diófa, Sirály,** both near Danube.

USEFUL ADDRESSES. The following are the addresses of the local tourist offices. **Szentendre:** near the landing stage; **Visegrád:** Fő Utca (Main Street); **Esztergom:** IBUSZ office, Széchenyi Tér; **Vác:** IBUSZ, Széchenyi Utca.

LAKE BALATON

The Nation's Playground

Lake Balaton is the largest lake in Central Europe. It stretches some 50 miles (80 km) across Western Hungary, within easy reach of Budapest. The 120 miles (193 km) of its shoreline are almost completely occupied by a continuous chain of summer resorts. The southern shore is generally flat, with long sandy beaches and only an occasional steep hill rising from the lake, as at Fonyód; the northern shore is marked by a chain of long-extinct, eroded volcanoes, of which the Badacsony is the largest and the most remarkable. The peninsula of Tihany sweeps deep into the lake and brings the two shores quite close. The water of the southern shore is very shallow and warms up to a remarkable degree; you can walk for almost a mile before it deepens, and thus it is ideal for children. On the northern shore it shelves more abruptly and the swimming is better, though the water is also pleasantly warm even in autumn and spring.

In recent years much has been done to develop the lake into a mass recreation area. Most of the private villas and hotels have been nationalized and turned into trade union and factory holiday homes. (Hungarian writers, for instance, have an attractive literary retreat at Szigliget.) At the same time, new hotels have been built and more are being planned, with tourist hostels, students' homes and large camping sites in many places. During the three summer months, the whole lakeshore is extremely crowded. The wise visitor will choose either the late spring or the often incredibly beautiful fall for his stay, when prices are somewhat lower and he will find much more elbow room. If he is gregarious and likes crowds, of course, he will stick to June, July and August.

The Balaton has much to offer in water sports. Swimming, sailing, wind surfing and water-skiing are all catered for—you can hire boats, yachts and water-skiing equipment. Motorboats are forbidden, however. There are numerous cottages for anglers. (From April 25 to May 25, however, it is a closed season for fishing and angling.) During the winter, skating, ice-sailing and ice-fishing are especially popular. There is a special sled used on the Balaton ice known as the *fakutya* (wooden dog). Among the non-aquatic sports, motor-racing and various ball games are the best catered for. International fencing championships are held every year near the lake.

The Balaton is extremely well provided with both road and rail communications. In the summer, frequent fast trains run from Budapest and there are through trains from most parts of Hungary. On summer Saturdays there is a through express from Vienna to Siófok and back. Long-distance bus services connect it with every part of the country. The new M7 motorway runs from Budapest to Zamárdi, west of Siófok; it bypasses some major resorts, but is connected to them by link-roads. The lake is crisscrossed by frequent ferry-boats, which provide the most leisurely and pleasant way of exploring its shores.

The Southern Shore

Along the whole of this shore, from Balatonaliga in the east to Balatonberény in the west, there is a practically unbroken chain of summer resorts. Here are the 'mass', popular, crowded beaches which attract most local and foreign visitors. But there are smaller, quieter, places, too, with an unpretentious informality of their own. It is on this shore that the family hotels and the children's holiday homes have largely been developed.

The nearest resorts to Budapest are Balatonaliga and Balatonvilágos, on the easternmost corner of the lake. Like all the places on the southern shore, they are served by the Budapest-Nagykanizsa railway, while the M7 motorway approaches the lake at Balatonvilágos, which is connected to it by a link-road. There are no hotels at either place, but ample paying-guest accommodations are available, as well as a camping site; there are plenty of snack bars and cafés.

Siófok

Siófok is the largest and by far the most popular community on the southern shore, with a population of some 22,000; it has a well-developed tourist organization and a long row of comfortable and pleasant modern hotels, all overlooking the lake. Its history stretches back a long time; the Romans had already settled here and had built locks to regulate the level of the lake at the mouth of the river Sió. None the less, there is little to see in the town itself. The Beszédes József Museum

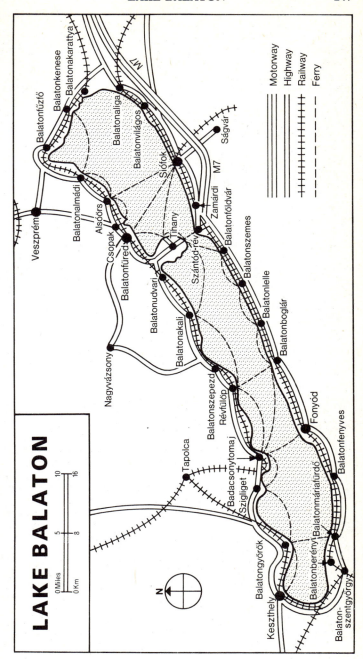

in Sió Utca contains displays of the history of Balaton shipping and there is a library and a large open-air theater, which seats 1,800. But the main attraction is the long, sandy beach, where most of the 'action' is, and the pleasant, shady gardens with their open-air restaurants.

There is one excursion of interest to be made from Siófok; along highway 65 we can reach Ságvár (6 miles/9 km), which has Roman remains, those of the fortified camp of Tricciani (AD 284–305). In the clay soil of the surrounding hills, traces of primitive man's occupation 17,000 years old have been found.

Zamárdi, a few miles further on, is a quiet resort. It is here that the M7 motorway reaches the lakeside, having passed just south of Siófok. The village has restaurants and cafés. To the west of it, towards the neighboring resort of Szántód-Rév, there is a camping site for motorists with its own 800-yard (731-meter) long beach, snackbar, general store and a pleasant garden-restaurant within walking distance. The camping site is well-equipped and has rowing-boats for hire. Zamárdi village has a few fine old peasant houses and there are ancient wine-cellars among the nearby vineyards. The baroque church dates from 1771–74. A walk of less than three hours takes us to Balatonendréd, a small village with some striking Roman remains; the community is known for its exquisite lace-making.

Szántód-Rév is at the narrowest point of Lake Balaton; the ferries to Tihany, on the northern shore, start here, taking only eight minutes. At the ferry-landing stands the old Rév (Ferry) Inn, recently and lovingly restored, with a wine-room and a nearby snack-bar. Close by is Szántódpuszta, with its restaurant, horse-riding and trips on ox-drawn carts.

Balatonföldvár

Balatonföldvár is one of the oldest-established resorts on the southern shore of the lake. Designed and laid out around the end of the 19th century, it has a large park, promenades, many picturesque villas and excellent bathing beaches. The Fenyves (Pine) Park has an open-air theater. Two miles (3 km) or so to the south (there is a bus service) lies the village of Kőröshegy, which has a 15th-century single-naved Gothic church, restored in the 20th century but retaining many of its original features. Recitals of music by Bach, Liszt and Kodály are given in the church in the summer.

Balatonszárszó is another of the quiet, peaceful resorts, with a few charming little inns, restaurants and cafés. There is a good beach and a camping site near the railway station. It was here that Attila József, one of Hungary's greatest modern poets, killed himself in 1937 by throwing himself in front of a train. There is a memorial museum in the street called after him and the park contains a bronze statue of him.

Balatonszemes is another old-established lakeside resort, situated partly on the shore and partly on the hillside. The former Hunyady mansion (built in the second half of the 18th century), the Gothic church (15th century) and the so-called Bagolyvár (Owl's Castle), which stands on the site of an old Turkish fort, are all worth visiting.

Balatonlelle is one of the busiest resorts on the southern shore. There are well-appointed beaches and much traffic at the ferry-boat pier. In the village there are one or two fine old houses. The annual meeting of Hungarian folk artists takes place here.

Balatonboglár, now administratively united with Balatonlelle under the name of Boglárlelle, was mentioned as a community as early as the 13th century. There are good beaches and much ferry traffic, with a direct line to Révfülöp on the northern shore. There is a wine research station in the village, which has a number of picturesque old houses.

Fonyód

Fonyód is the furthest from Budapest of the major resorts on the southern bank of the lake. It consists of several different settlements, stretching some 4½ miles (7 km). It is growing rapidly and is being developed as the most important bathing resort on the southern shore after Siófok. It is an ancient settlement; historical discoveries include late Stone Age and Bronze Age implements and there are Roman ruins. Fonyód began to be developed around 1890; since the 1930s it has been one of the most popular places on the lake's southern side; its steep wooded hills and its altogether charming situation, combined with its excellent beaches, are ensuring an ever-greater influx of visitors. There are good accommodations of every kind, as well as pleasant restaurants and cafés. An interesting excursion can be made to Buzsák, some 10 miles (16 km) to the south, a village famous for its colorful folk art and for its fine carvings, mostly done by shepherds.

Balatonmáriafürdő is another small, quiet resort, set among vineyards; its excellent beach stretches along six miles (10 km) of the lake shore. There are good accommodations, as well as a restaurant and nightclub.

At Balatonberény, the last resort on the southern shore, the lake narrows and there is a fine view of the Keszthely Hills, on the opposite side. The village was settled under the Árpád dynasty and Bronze Age and Roman relics have been found here. The Roman Catholic church dates from the 15th century; its original Gothic design was remodeled into baroque in the 18th.

The Northern Shore

This is different in many ways from the southern shore of the lake. The geographical structure is less uniform and the outlying spurs of the Bakony Hills and the extinct volcanoes of the Tapolca Basin make it a romantic, often dramatic, landscape. The almost flat southern shore provides little beyond one continuous sandy beach and caters for large crowds; the northern shore, on the other hand, is more 'select', more fashionable; it, too, has several fine beaches, but it has also many other attractions and many interesting objectives for excursions into the hinterland, with its ruined castles, charming valleys, forests and springs.

The water of the Balaton is just as soft and enticing as on the opposite shore, but the beaches shelve much more sharply and are, on the whole, less suitable for children, demanding swimming rather than playful splashing about. Here and there the bottom is sandy, but in places it is pebbly and stony.

The resorts on the northern side all lie on or near highway 71, which branches off the M7 motorway shortly before the Balaton is reached. The railway branches off the line serving the southern shore soon after leaving the interesting town of Székesfehérvár (see chapter on Western Hungary).

Balatonakarattya and Balatonkenese are the first resorts on the northern shore to be reached by a traveler from Budapest. They lie on gentle hill-slopes covered with vineyards and have camping sites, bungalows, restaurants and cafés, as well as several good beaches.

Balatonfűzfő, on the northernmost corner of the lake, is surrounded on the landward side by hills and woods. Though it has a beach, it is now above all an industrial community, with paper mills and a chemical factory.

Balatonalmádi has developed into a town of some size, with many good shops, restaurants and places of entertainment. It has two hotels (one of them of a high standard), as well as a tourist hostel and a camping site; the excellent beach is one of the best on the northern shore of the lake. Buses ply to neighboring resorts and to the picturesque town of Veszprém (see chapter on Western Hungary), and there is a boat pier.

The next resort is Alsóörs, a quiet, beautifully-situated village at the foot of the wooded Somló Hill. It has a camping site, bungalows and an inn. At Felsőörs, a few miles to the north, is the finest romanesque church of the Balaton uplands, as well as an 18th-century priory.

Csopak is situated on the hillside, the resort stretching down to the lake. It lies in fine wine-growing country; the beach is well supplied with all the usual holiday amenities. Paying-guest accommodation is available and there are two pleasant inns. The former Ranolder castle, dating from the middle of the 19th century, now houses the Institute for Plant Protection.

Balatonfüred

Balatonfüred is the oldest, most distinguished and most internationally famous health resort of this shore of the lake. It has every amenity of a lakeside holiday resort and is, in addition, a spa of the first class. Above the beaches and the promenade the twisting streets of the old town (some 12,000 inhabitants) climb the hillsides, which are thickly planted with vines. The hills protect the town from cold northerly winds. This is one of the most celebrated wine-growing districts of Hungary and it frames an old-established spa for cardiac diseases. Great plane and poplar trees provide shade as we arrive by boat at the always-busy landing-stage.

The center of the town in Gyógy Tér (Spa Square), where the waters of the volcanic springs bubble and rise under a slim, colonnaded pavilion. The springs have a strong carbonic content. In the Square is the Cardiac Hospital, where hundreds of patients from all over the world are treated. Two excellent large hotels have recently been built and a third is planned.

Balatonfüred has 11 medicinal springs and they have a stimulating and highly-beneficial effect on the heart and nerves. There is plenty of sunshine but also pleasant shade. It was here that Rabindranath Tagore, the great Indian poet and Nobel Prize winner, recovered from a heart attack. He planted a tree to commemorate his stay, a tree which still stands in a little park of its own. Another Nobel Prize winner, the Italian poet Salvatore Quasimodo, planted his own tree near Tagore's in 1961.

There is much to see in and around Balatonfüred and an excursion to Tihany (described later on) should on no account be missed. There is a classical Round church (Kerek templom), built in 1841–46, near the center of the town and there are many picturesque old houses as well as an attractive ensemble of neo-classical villas around Gyógy Tér.

There are several beaches, a motel, a camping site and excellent restaurants, pastry shops and cafés.

The most interesting longer excursion, apart from that to Tihany, already mentioned, is to the small town of Nagyvázsony, about 12 miles (19 km) to the northwest. Its castle was built in the 15th century and owned by Pál Kinizsi, one of the generals of King Matthias Corvinus and known for his great physical strength. During the season a colorful equestrian pageant in medieval costumes is held in the grounds of the former Zichy Castle in the town. There is a hotel and a pleasant restaurant.

Tihany

The small peninsula of Tihany, surrounded on three sides by the lake, is a rich open-air museum as well as a very popular holiday resort. There are geological and botanical rarities; the Celtic walls of the Óvár (Old Castle), the ruins of the Roman watchtower on Csúcshegy (Mount Peak), the traces of churches dating back to the Árpád dynasty, the squat romanesque columns of the 900-year-old Abbey crypt—all bear witness to human faith and human hate.

From the ferry on the lakeside the road climbs between poplars to the range of hills which form the peninsula; these are barely 650 feet (200 meters) high and are covered with acacia copses. Only a few hundred yards beyond the two hotels, the modern motel and the multicolored tents of the hillside camping area, nature appears primitive and undisturbed. In the middle of the peninsula, framed in waving green reeds, is the smooth Belső (Inner) Lake. Around it are bare, yellowish-white rocks; volcanic cones rise against the sky. The whole area, so rich in rare flora and fauna, is a national park, where all building and agriculture is carefully controlled.

Between the Inner Lake and the eastern shore of the peninsula lies the village of Tihany, with, as its crowning glory, the famous Abbey. Its foundations were laid by King Andrew I some nine centuries ago. Only the crypt, in which the king is buried, and a priceless historical document have survived the ravages of time. This document, the Abbey charter, dating from 1055, contains in its Latin text many Hungarian words and phrases—one of the earliest surviving documents to do so. It is kept at Pannonhalma; see Western Hungary chapter. The present Abbey church is in a baroque style and was built between 1719 and 1737; it is magnificently ornate, with silver-gilt altars and, on the large ceiling fresco, pink floating angels. The Abbey has a famous organ, on which recitals are given in the summer. It also houses a museum and is visited each year by over 100,000 people. In the village there are many beautiful old houses, the finest of which have been formed into an open-air museum. Tihany has a Biological Research Institute and an Institute of Geophysics, with an observatory.

There is no railway station at Tihany, but it is easily reached by a regular bus service from Balatonfüred or by one of the frequent ferry boats.

Going westwards along the northern shore of the lake, we come to Örvényes, a quiet resort with an 18th-century watermill, which holds an exhibition of folk art, and a baroque Roman Catholic church. A few miles further on is Balatonudvari, with a breeding-station for Balaton fish. The beach is at Kiliántelep, about a mile (1.6 km) to the west; here there is a large camping site with a self-service restaurant, a motel and a supermarket.

Révfülöp is a traditional crossing point of the southern basin of the lake; there are around eight ferry boats a day to and from Balatonboglár, on the southern shore, as well as ferries to most of the other lakeside resorts. There is a camping site here, and a small hotel, as well as paying-guest accommodation and a restaurant. One of the prettiest villages of the Balaton is Kővágóörs, a few miles inland. Another camping site is a few miles further along the shore, at Pálköve, near the railway station of Balatonrendes. This, together with the adjoining Ábrahámhegy, forms one of the quieter resorts of the northern Balaton. It has excellent local wines. There is a small motel and a pleasant restaurant.

The Badacsony

Along the volcanic, cone-shaped peaks of the Balaton Uplands, the broad-beamed, flat-topped Badacsony is one of the most striking. The masses of lava that coagulated here created bizarre and beautiful rock formations. At the upper edge there are 180- to 200-foot (52- to 61-meter) high basalt columns in a huge semicircle. The land around has been lovingly tilled for centuries and everywhere there are vineyards and in every inn and tavern there is splendid wine. The Badacsony is now a protected area.

Badacsonytomaj is a holiday resort with a tourist hostel, a camping site and several restaurants and cafés, as well as a well-known wine-tasting bar (the Borkóstoló). On the top of the mountain is the Kis-faludy House, named after the Hungarian poet Sándor Kisfaludy (1772 –1844), who lived here. It has a fine view. The picturesque baroque wine-press house belonging to the poet's wife, Róza Szegedi, is now a museum. There is also a wine museum, illustrating the history of local wines and of Hungarian wines generally.

Szigliget is a small village at the foot of the Várhegy (Castle Hill), which rises more than 600 feet (183 meters) above the lake. The resort lies to the south of the hill and has a good beach, a camping site and a ferry landing-stage. In the baroque former Esterházy castle, standing in a beautiful park, there is a holiday home for Hungarian writers.

Tapolca

Tapolca lies some miles from the lakeside, in the center of the Tapolca Basin, which is surrounded by a ring of volcanic hills. Its most interesting attraction is its system of caves, of which the Lake Cave (Tavasbarlang) is open to visitors. Discovered in 1902, the caves stretch for some 1000 yards (914 meters) and, as the cave has a brook flowing through it, can be traversed by boat. Tapolca has a tourist hostel, which is a converted watermill.

Keszthely

Keszthely is the second-largest town on the Balaton (21,000 inhabitants). It has a municipal charter dating from 1404; its romanesque Roman Catholic parish church was built in 1386; and its famous agricultural college, the Georgikon, was established in 1797 and was the first on the continent of Europe. The town offers the rare combination of a historical center of culture and a restful, relaxing summer resort.

The magnificent baroque Festetics Palace, begun around 1750, is one of the finest in Hungary. Concerts are held in the fine music room or, in the summer, in the courtyard. The palace is surrounded by a beautiful park. The Helikon Library, in the south wing of the palace, contains over 50,000 volumes, as well as precious incunabula, a collection of etchings and valuable paintings. The Georgikon, now the Agricultural University, has become the agricultural headquarters of southwestern Hungary. The Balaton Museum contains rich and varied exhibits of local history, ethnography, folk art and painting.

Keszthely has excellent hotel accommodations in all categories, a camping site for 1,000, good restaurants, cafés and pastry shops; it has several good beaches and opportunities for every kind of sport.

The Little Balaton (Kis-Balaton)

The largest river feeding the Balaton, the Zala, enters the lake at its southernmost point. On either side there is a swamp of several thousand acres, formerly part of the lake. This is now a vast protected area and the home of many rare birds. Among the most famous visitors are the great heron and the black ibis. The area can be visited only by special permission, obtainable from the National Office for the Protection of Nature (*Országos Környezetés Természetvédelmi Hivatal*), Költő Utca 21–23, Budapest XII.

PRACTICAL INFORMATION FOR LAKE BALATON

WHEN TO COME. If you like crowds and the best of the summer sun, choose June, July and August. Spring or fall are less crowded and prices are lower. Winter is the time to go for skating, ice-sailing and ice-fishing.

Southern Shore

GETTING AROUND. All the resorts on the southern shore are either on, or just off, the M7 highway or its continuation Highway 7. By rail, they all lie on the main Budapest-Nagykanizsa line, most of the trains of which leave the South Station (Déli pályaudvar) in Budapest. Regular ferry connections link main resorts on the lake itself.

HOTELS AND RESTAURANTS

All hotels listed below have restaurants unless otherwise stated.

BALATONBOGLÁR. Hullám (I), opposite station. **Platán Motel,** Hunyadi Utca. Camping-site and paying-guest accommodations.
　Restaurants. Kinizsi beerhall, Vörösmarty Tér. Several snack bars.

BALATONFÖLDVÁR. Neptun (M), Széchenyi Sétány. **Express** (I), József Attila Utca. Camping-sites and paying-guests accommodations.
　Restaurants. Balatongyöngye, Szentgyörgyi Út; **Kukorica Csárda,** Budapesti Út. Self-service restaurant, **Hősök Útja.**

BALATONLELLE. For hotel, see Balatonboglár, above. There is a camping-site.
　Restaurants. Vörös Csillag, Köztársaság Útja; **Becsali csárda,** Rákóczi Út. Many others in beach areas; self-service restaurant on beach.

BALATONSZÁRSZÓ. Tourist hostel and bungalows, plus a camping-site.
　Restaurants. Véndiófa, Kossuth Utca; **Balaton csárda,** Szóládi Utca; **Tóparti,** on beach.

FONYÓD. Sirály (I), above the town, in Bartók Utca. There are tourist hostel, bungalows and camping-sites at Alsóbélatelep, west of the town.
　Restaurants. Panoráma, Kossuth Erdő; **Présház csárda,** wine-bar with food. Several self-service restaurants.

SIÓFOK. Balaton, Europa, Hungária and **Lido,** all (M) hotels on the lakeside. **Napfény** (I), also overlooking the lake. **Venusz** (M), in the town. There is a motel by the lakeside; the town also has tourist-hostels, camping-sites and paying-guest accommodations.
　Restaurants. A large choice; we recommend **Fogas,** in the main street, with garden; **Csárdás,** also in the main street, with gypsy music in the evenings; and

Matróz, near the pier. Among the numerous night haunts the **Pipacs,** the **Eden,** the **Maxim** and the **Delta** all offer local wines and a live show.

USEFUL ADDRESSES. The following are the addresses of the local tourist offices. **Balatonboglár:** Dózsa György Utca 13; **Balatonföldvar:** Spur István Utca 1; **Balatonlelle:** Szent István Utca 1; **Fonyód:** next to the station; **Siófok:** adjoining station and in main street (Fő Utca).

Northern Shore

GETTNG AROUND. Highway 71 runs the whole length of the northern shore; it branches off the **M7** motorway from Budapest some miles to the east of the lake. By rail, there is a good direct service to all the resorts on the north of the lake from Budapest South. Tihany and Hévíz have no railway stations; for Tihany one must get out at Balatonfüred and for Hévíz at Keszthely; in both cases there are frequent buses. Regular ferry connections link main resorts on the lake itself.

HOTELS AND RESTAURANTS

All hotels listed below have restaurants unless otherwise stated.

BADACSONY. Egri József Tourist Hostel, Badacsonytomaj. Camping-site. **Restaurants. Hableány,** near the harbor; **Halászkert Garden Restaurant** (fish), in the park; **Bormúzeum,** Hegyalja Utca, wine-tasting.

BALATONALMÁDI. Auróra (M), Bajcsy Zsilinszky Út. **Tulipán** (M), Marx Tér. **Kék Balaton** Tourist Hostel. Motel, bungalows and camping-site, west of the station. **Restaurants. Aranyhíd.** Self-service restaurant on the beach.

BALATONFÜRED. Annabella and **Marina,** both (M), are two fine modern hotels on the lakeside. **Arany Csillag** (I), old-fashioned hotel in town center with no private baths. Bungalows and splendid camping-site. Paying-guest accommodations. **Restaurants. Balaton,** in the park, praised. **Baricska, Hordó** and **Tölgyfa,** not far from the lake. Self-service restaurants. The **Kedves** pastry-shop, in Blaha Lujza Utca, serves excellent tea, coffee and cakes.

HÉVÍZ. Thermal (E), large new spa hotel. **Gyöngyvirág,** simple, no private baths. Paying-guest accommodations. **Restaurants. Debrecen,** Rákóczi Utca; **Béke,** Szabadság Utca, and many others.

KESZTHELY. Helikon (E), large new hotel on the lakeside. **Amazon** (I), in town center. Motel near the lake; also tourist hostel and paying-guest accommodations. **Restaurants. Halászcsárda** (fish), on the lakeside; **Béke,** Kossuth Utca, simple but good; the **Helikon Tavern,** 5 miles (8 km) out on the road leading east (Highway 71), occupies a neo-classical building erected in the early 19th century by Prince Festetics; open evenings only, all the year round, with a good choice of wines and a gypsy band.

NAGYVÁZSONY. Kastély (I), in former Zichy Palace; some private baths; a motel is attached to the hotel. Riding-school.

Restaurant. Vázsonykő, Kinizsi Utca.

TAPOLCA. Gabriella (I), in town center; it was formerly a water-mill. Tourist hostel, simple.

Restaurants. Balaton, Deák Ferenc Utca; **Tavasbarlang,** with garden, Arany János Utca.

TIHANY. Tihany (M), large hotel near the landing-stage. **Kis Tihany** (M), small but comfortable; all rooms with bath in both hotels. Motel nearby, also bungalows and paying-guest accommodations, and camping-site.

Restaurants. Fogas, near the terminus of the bus from Balatonfüred; **Halász-tanya** (fish), and others; good pastry-shop **(Rege)** near Abbey.

USEFUL ADDRESSES. The following are the addresses of the local tourist offices. **Badacsony:** near the landing stage; **Balatonalmádi:** Lenin Utca and at railway station in summer; **Balatonfüred:** at railway station and in town center; **Hévíz:** Rákóczi Utca; **Keszthely:** Fő Tér. **Tapolca:** Deák Ferenc Utca; **Tihany:** near the landing stage.

NORTHERN HUNGARY

Small Mountains, Great Beauty

Northern Hungary is the region which stretches from the Danube north of Budapest to the northeastern borders of the country, to Czechoslovakia and the Soviet Union. It is a clearly defined area, marked by several mountain ranges of no great height but considerable scenic beauty; these form the southernmost outcrops of the Carpathians. Most of them are limestone hills with some volcanic rocks. Few of the peaks reach 3,000 feet (914 meters) and most of them are thickly wooded almost to their summits. Oak, beech, and hornbeam are the main forest trees, with comparatively few patches of pine and fir. Naturalists, botanists, geologists, ethnographers and folklorists find much of interest in the hills. In the state game reserves herds of deer and wild boar roam freely; the eagle and the rare red-footed falcon still survive.

Within this region most of Hungary's mineral wealth is concentrated —iron, some copper, and rich (though inferior) coal deposits.

The Northern Hills

Historically, the valleys of Northern Hungary have always been of considerable strategic importance, as they provided the only access to the north. Eger, renowned in Magyar feats of arms as one of the guardians of these strategic routes, is in this region, while many ruined

257

castles sit picturesquely on the hilltops. The Mátra mountains, easily reached from Budapest, have been developed into an important winter sports area. Last but not least, this is one of the great wine-growing districts of Hungary, with Gyöngyös and Eger contributing the 'Magyar nectar' and (most famous of all) Tokaj producing the 'king of wines'.

We have already mentioned the Börzsöny Hills in our 'Danube Bend' section; they contain many of the most delightful country resorts near Budapest, most of which can be easily reached by the Budapest-Vác-Szob railway line or by bus. Dotted throughout the region are the ruins of many old castles. Nógrád Castle was originally built under the Árpád dynasty; its ancient tower is still a landmark. In the Nógrád valley, which runs between the Nógrád and Mátra Hills are the Palóc villages, representing one of the most interesting and individual ethnic groups of Hungary. In their villages, Hungarian national costumes have been preserved and are still occasionally worn; Hollókő is the most picturesque of these.

The Mátra, a volcanic mountain group, rises with dramatic suddenness above the Palóc world. Its capital is Gyöngyös, famous for the excellent wine produced round about—do not miss *Debrői hárslevelű*, a magnificent white wine—and, more recently, for its new industrial importance. Early in the 1960s huge lignite deposits were discovered and the large-scale mines and power-stations established since then have changed the character of the whole region. Among the chief sights of the town are the 14th-century church of St. Bartholomew (Szent Bertalan) and the Mátra Museum, which exhibits folk art of the region. To the north of Gyöngyös lie many beautiful resorts, popular in summer for their invigorating mountain air and in winter for their skiing and other seasonable sports. The most famous is Mátrafüred (1,312 feet/400 meters). Bus services connect the resorts with Gyöngyös and Budapest. The highest peak is Kékestető (3,300 feet/1,006 meters), the highest point in Hungary, with a sanatorium.

Highway 3 (a motorway—M3—for the first part of the journey) is the main road link between Budapest and Northern Hungary.

Eger

The famous and picturesque city of Eger lies on the line where plain and mountain meet, between the Mátra mountains and their eastern neighbor, the Bükk. It bears within its limits much of the history, the heartbreak and the glory of Hungary's past and should on no account be missed. Eger was settled very early in the Hungarian conquest of the country and one of the five bishoprics founded by King Stephen was here. Eger castle was built after the devastating Tartar invasion and the cathedral, originally romanesque, was rebuilt in Gothic style in the 15th century, though few vestiges of this structure now remain.

In 1551 the city was attacked by the Turks, but the commander, István Dobó, held out against vastly superior forces. It fell in 1596 and was until 1687 one of the most important northern outposts of Moslem power. The main aspects of present-day Eger were developed in the 18th century and it is now a splendid example of a baroque city. The imposing Cathedral was completely rebuilt, in Classical style, early in the 19th century; it is the second largest church in Hungary. Opposite the Cathedral is the former Lyceum, an impressive baroque building which is now a teachers' training college and includes an observatory.

The most picturesque street of Eger is Kossuth Lajos Utca, which consists almost entirely of baroque and rococo buildings. No. 4 is the Minor Canons' residence and one of the most beautiful rococo palaces in Hungary. Further on, the County Council Hall dates from 1749–56; it has exquisite wrought-iron gates. To the north, in Dobó István Square, stands the fine baroque Minorite Church. Continuing northwards we reach one of Eger's landmarks, the Turkish minaret. The Castle is best reached along Kossuth Lajos Street, turning to the left at the end; the original casemates survive and much excavation is being carried out. The Castle Museum is worth a visit. Eger is also a spa, with valuable therapeutic waters and bathing facilities of all kinds; the water is recommended for rheumatic ailments.

Eger wine is famous and perhaps the best known is *Bikavér* (Bull's Blood), a full-blooded red wine; *Leányka,* a delightful white wine, and the Eger version of *Medoc Noir,* a heavy, sweet dessert wine, are also outstanding.

A particularly pleasant excursion from Eger is to Szilvásvárad, a charming small resort deep in the wooded Bükk Mountains, some 17 miles (28 km) north of Eger and easily reached by train or bus. Its streams are full of trout and there are many small waterfalls.

Mezőkövesd, about 10 miles (16 km) to the southeast, is famous for its folk art, examples of which are on display in the village museum; many of them are for sale.

Miskolc

East of the picturesque Bükk Mountains lies Miskolc, the second largest town in Hungary and one of its chief industrial centers. A vast conurbation with a population of some 200,000, it is surrounded by beautiful country. It contains some interesting buildings, many of them baroque, and, in a western suburb, the medieval castle of Diósgyőr. South of the city is the spa-suburb of Miskolc-Tapolca, with the town's best hotels.

Beyond Miskolc lie two objectives of the greatest interest to the visitor; the vast cave system of Aggtelek and the famous vineyards of Tokaj.

Aggtelek

One of the most extensive cave systems in Europe lies at the extreme northern end of Hungary, right on the Czechoslovak border. The caves are spectacular in the extreme and have been ranked with such natural monuments as the Grand Canyon or the Niagara Falls. The largest of the caves, the Baradla, is over 15 miles (24 km) long, with stalactite and stalagmite formations of great beauty and extraordinary size, some more than 80 feet (45 meters) high. A full tour of the caves takes five hours, but there are shorter tours taking one to two hours, which will give the visitor a very good overall impression of the majesty of this underground marvel of nature. In one of the chambers of the cave a concert-hall has been created; it can hold 1,000 people and concerts and operas are given here. Further caves are being discovered and opened to the public. There are two entrances, at Aggtelek and at Jósvafő, near both of which there are comfortable hotels.

Sárospatak, some 45 miles (70 km) to the northeast of Miskolc, is the cultural center of this part of Hungary. It is a picturesque old town, with many fine old houses. Its ancient castle was begun in the 11th century and contains a museum of old furniture. Its Calvinist College was founded in 1531 and for many years had close links with Britain. Many famous Hungarians were educated here. It is now a state school.

Tokaj

Tokaj, the home of Hungary's most famous wine, lies about 30 miles (48 km) east of Miskolc. The countryside round it is beautiful, especially in October, when the grapes hang from the vines in thick clusters. Tokay, the 'king of wines', as it has been called, is golden yellow with slightly brownish tints and it has an almost oily texture. It has been cultivated for over 700 years. Other countries—France, Germany and Russia—have tried to produce the wine from Tokaj grapes; all failed. It would seem that the secret of the wine lies in a combination of the volcanic soil and the climate. The little town of Tokaj is built on the slopes and contains many wine-cellars and a first-class international camping site. In the Museum of Local History objects connected with the history of the production of the wine are on display.

PRACTICAL INFORMATION FOR NORTHERN HUNGARY

WHEN TO COME. Spring and summer are the best seasons for the hill resorts. The traditional and extremely colorful wine festivals are held in the fall, when the weather can also be quite delightful.

GETTING AROUND. There are good rail connections from Budapest (East Station). Local trains and buses complete the network. Otherwise, traveling by car gives you the greatest freedom.

HOTELS AND RESTAURANTS

All hotels listed below have restaurants unless otherwise stated.

AGGTELEK. Tengerszem (I), **Cseppkő** (I), both near an entrance to the caves. Also, Tourist Hostel, paying-guest accommodations and camping-site.
Restaurants. At the two hotels and at the ÁFÉSZ (Co-op) at Jósvafő.

EGER. Eger (M), Park (M), both close together near town center. The Eger is modern, but short on charm, the Park is elegant, but rather old-fashioned. Both have rooms with bath. **Unicornis** (I). Also, Tourist Hostels, Motel, camping-site and paying-guest accommodations.

Restaurants. Széchenyi, Marx Utca; **Belvárosi,** in Bajcsy Zsilinszky Utca; **Vörös Rák halászcsárda** (fish restaurant), Alkotmány Utca, and many others. Eger (see above) has many wine-tasting bars and shops.

GYÖNGYÖS. Mátra (M), in town center. **Avar (M)** at Mátrafüred, in the hills to the north of the town. Here too is a Tourist Hostel, a camping-site and paying-guest accommodations.

Restaurants. Kékes and **Kedves,** both in town center; **Bacchus** wine-bar. There are restaurants and snack-bars in all the Mátra hill resorts.

MISKOLC. Juno (M) and **Park (M),** new, both in spa suburb of Tapolca, south of the town. In the town itself there are only (I) hotels: **Arany Csillag, Széchenyi** and **Pannónia,** all centrally situated; some rooms have baths. Tourist hostels and luxury camping-site in the Tapolca suburb. Paying-guest accommodations.

Restaurants. Alabárdos and **Bükk** in town center; **Kisvadász** at Tapolca (recommended).

SÁROSPATAK. Bodrog (M), Borostyán (M). Paying-guest accommodations.

SZILVÁSVÁRAD. Lipicai (I), some private baths. Paying-guest accommodation.

TOKAJ. Tokaj (M). Camping-site and paying-guest accommodations.

Restaurants. Rákóczi, Tiszavirág Halászcsárda and many other fish restaurants and snack-bars. The **Rákóczi Cellar,** which may be visited, contains 20,000 hectoliters (nearly 450,000 gallons) of wine.

 USEFUL ADDRESSES. The following are the addresses of the local tourist offices. **Aggtelek:** at the entrance to the Baradla cave; **Eger:** Bajcsy-Zsilinszky Street and at the Castle; **Gyöngyös:** Szabadság Ter; **Miskolc:** Széchenyi Street; **Sárospatak:** Town Council Office, Kádar Kata Street; **Tokaj:** in town center.

THE GREAT PLAIN

Magyar to the Core

The Great Plain, which stretches from Budapest as far as the borders of Romania and Yugoslavia and covers an area of some 20,000 sq. miles (51,800 sq. km), is what most people think of as the typical Hungarian landscape. Almost completely flat, it is the home of shepherds and their flocks and, above all, of splendid horses and the *csikós,* their riders. The plain has a wild, almost alien, air; its sprawling villages consist mostly of one-story houses, though there are many large farms and up-to-date market gardens. The Plain, which is divided into two almost equal parts by the River Tisza, also contains several of Hungary's most historic cities.

Three main road routes link Budapest with the Great Plain. The first leads east to Szolnok, Debrecen, Nyíregyháza and the Soviet frontier-point of Záhony; the second southeast to Kecskemét and Szeged; the third, hugging the Danube, south to Kalocsa and Baja.

The most northerly part of the region is known as the Nyírség; it borders on the Soviet and Romanian frontiers and its chief town is Nyíregyháza. This will hardly detain the visitor, who, however, will find a famous medicinal spa, Sóstó, only 4 miles (6 km) away and easily reached by bus. From an architectural point of view the most interesting place in the district is Nyírbátor, 24 miles (39 km) east of Nyíregyháza and easily reached by train or bus; it has a very fine

15th-century Gothic Protestant church; a musical festival is held in the church in August.

Debrecen and the Hortobágy

Thirty miles (48 km) south of Nyíregyháza is Debrecen, one of the largest and historically most important towns of Hungary, with a population of some 200,000. It is the economic and cultural center of Eastern Hungary and a town with a character all its own—its inhabitants have called it 'the Calvinist Rome' and most of its people are Protestants. Its University has always been famous as a center of learning and its predecessor, the Calvinist College, was founded more than 400 years ago. In its Great Church Hungarian independence from the Habsburgs was proclaimed by Kossuth in 1849. Here, too, in 1944, the anti-Nazi coalition government met, bringing the hope of peace to the war-ravaged country.

Debrecen has been inhabited since the Stone Age. It was already a sizable village by the end of the 12th century and by the 14th century it was a privileged and important market town. After the Reformation it became—and has remained—the stronghold of Hungarian Protestantism.

The street leading from the railway station to the Great Church contains many of Debrecen's most interesting buildings. The Old County Hall was built in 1912 in what is known as the 'Hungarian style', with majolica ornaments. In the neo-classical Town Hall, farther on, Kossuth lived in 1849. The Great Church, which faces a tree-lined square, is the largest Protestant place of worship in Hungary; it was built early in the 19th century in an impressive neo-classical style. Near it are the original Calvinist College, already referred to, and one of Hungary's best-known hotels, the art nouveau Arany Bika (Golden Bull), whose cuisine is famous. In the northern part of the city lies the Nagyerdő (Great Forest), a large park with thermal establishments and every facility for water sports.

Just over 12 miles (19 km) south of Debrecen lies Hajdúszoboszló, one of Hungary's oldest and most famous medicinal spas.

Stretching for many miles to the west of Debrecen is the Hortobágy, the most typical and most romantic part of the Great Plain, a grassy *puszta* or prairie covering over 250,000 acres (100,000 hectares). Though much of it has, in recent years, become agricultural land, there is still enough of its unique atmosphere left to attract the foreign visitor. The center of the Hortobágy is where highway 33 crosses the Hortobágy river on a famous nine-arched bridge dating from the beginning of the 19th century. Near it is the Nagycsárda (Great Inn), built in 1699; there are guest rooms, a restaurant and a café. 'Equestrian Days' are arranged here every summer.

The road (highway 4) from Budapest to Debrecen passes just north of Cegléd and through Szolnok, two towns which are chiefly of importance as road and railway junctions and as the economic centers of important agricultural districts. Cegléd has a neo-classical Protestant church of some interest. Szolnok lies on the River Tisza and is the geometrical center of the Great Plain. It has several fine old churches, among them the high-baroque Franciscan church near the river bank. In addition it houses a well-known artists' colony and has good facilities for swimming and other water sports. It is now an important industrial center.

Kecskemét

Taking the road (highway 5) leading southeast from Budapest we soon reach Kecskemét, one of the most characteristic of Hungarian towns, with a population of around 100,000; it is an important railway junction and the center of a large and rich agricultural district. Here is one of the most valuable fruit-growing areas in the country; it produces the delicious Hungarian apricots, from which the famous *barack,* the fiery yet smooth apricot-brandy is made.

The heart of the sprawling town is formed by two vast squares which join each other: Szabadság (Liberty) and Kossuth Squares. In Szabadság Square is a remarkable double Synagogue, recently restored and housing some public collections. A fine, Hungarian-style art nouveau building called the Cifrapalota (Ornamental Palace) stands opposite; today it is the home of the local trade union council. In Kossuth Square is the Town Hall, built in 1893–96 by Ödön Lechner in the Hungarian art nouveau style which he created. There are several interesting churches in Kecskemét, including the baroque 'Old Church' (1772–1805), just north of the Town Hall; the oldest and most important building in Kossuth Square is the Church of St. Nicholas (Szent Miklós templom), on the south side, originally built in a Gothic style in the 15th century but rebuilt in a baroque style in the 18th. Kecskemét has an artists' colony and was the birthplace of the composer Kodály. An excursion can be made to Kiskőrös, 30 miles (48 km) to the southwest along road 54; here Sándor Petőfi, one of Hungary's most famous poets and a leading spirit of the 1848 revolution against the Habsburgs, was born. The tiny house—his father was the village butcher—is now a memorial museum. Kiskőrös can also be reached from Kalocsa on the east bank of the Danube.

About 20 miles (32 km) south of Kecskemét and easily reached by road lies Bugac *puszta,* the center of a large sandy area, which has provided poets and artists with inexhaustible material. It has a famous inn (the *Bugac csárda*), with excellent food, drink and music, as well as an open-air museum. While much of the region has now been brought under cultivation, the landscape has kept its character. In the summer there are horse shows (the Hungarian version of rodeos) and festivities with gypsy music. There is also good pheasant-shooting in the woods.

Szeged

Szeged, with around 180,000 inhabitants, is the traditional economic and cultural center of the southern part of the Great Plain. Its great tourist attraction is its open-air festival (July–August each year), but it has many other features to interest the visitor. It was almost completely rebuilt after a great flood in 1879; and constructed on a concentric plan, not unlike that of Pest. There is an inner boulevard, now named after Lenin, and an outer ring, whose sections, named after Rome, Brussels, Paris, London, Moscow and Vienna, recall the international help given in the reconstruction of the city. Avenues connect these two boulevards like the spokes of a wheel.

The heart of the Inner City is the large Széchenyi Square, full of trees and surrounded by imposing buildings, among them the Town Hall and the largest hotel, the Tisza, which has a fine concert-hall. The most striking building in Szeged is the Votive Church, or Cathedral, a neo-romanesque edifice built between 1912 and 1929 in fulfillment of a municipal promise made after the great flood. It is one of Hungary's largest churches and has a splendid organ with 12,000 pipes. The church forms the backdrop to the open-air festival, held in Dóm (Cathedral) Square. The Festival started in 1913 and has been held ever since, though with occasional gaps. The stage is huge—600 sq. yards (502 sq. meters)—and the square can hold an audience of 7,000. Outstanding performances are occasionally given of Hungary's great national drama, *The Tragedy of Man,* by Imre Madách. The program contains a rich variety of theatrical pieces, operas and concerts.

Dóm Square is impressive, with arcaded buildings, among them scientific institutes and a theological college. In the center of the Square stands an isolated romanesque tower, which was formerly part of the 11th-century Church of St. Demetrius (Dömötör). Other interesting sights are the baroque Greek Orthodox Church, in the Inner City, built between 1743 and 1745, and the so-called Lower-City Church (Alsóvárosi templom), in the southwest part of the town. This was built in the 15th and 16th centuries, but much of it is now in a baroque style.

Szeged is famous for its paprika, an important ingredient of Hungarian cuisine. It has two universities and good hotels and restaurants. Újszeged (New Szeged), on the opposite side of the river, is something of a holiday resort, with every facility for water sports and an open-air theater.

To the northeast of Szeged and near the Romanian border there are several places of interest. One of them, Gyula, has recently developed into a spa of some importance. It has an interesting medieval castle and plays are performed each summer in the castle courtyard. There are comfortable accommodations for visitors.

There is much of this vast central part of the Great Plain that we have not touched on, but a visitor with time to spare—and, if possible, a slight knowledge of Hungarian—will find in many of its small towns things of interest which reflect, perhaps more accurately than anywhere else in Hungary, the genuine life and customs of Hungarian country people.

The East Bank of the Danube

Highway 51 leads due south from Budapest, never far from the east bank of the Danube. Apart from the town of Ráckeve, on the Danube island of Csepel, where there is a museum in the former palace of Prince Eugene of Savoy as well as an interesting Serbian Orthodox church, there is little to detain the traveler until he reaches Kalocsa. This is a town unusually rich in architectural beauty and in memorials of Hungarian cultural history. It was formerly on the Danube, but now, because of a change in the river's course, lies 4 miles (6.5 km) away from it. Kalocsa is rich in charming baroque buildings. The cathedral, the seat of a Roman Catholic archbishop, was built between 1735 and 1754. The archbishop's palace is another fine baroque edifice; the archiepiscopal library is one of the most valuable in Hungary, with over 100,000 volumes and many rarities. Kalocsa is famous, too, for its richly colored embroideries, created by its 'painting women', examples of whose exquisite work can be seen in a permanent exhibition in the town and can, of course, be bought. Kalocsa can also, though not without inconvenience, be reached by train; the walls of its railway station are covered with examples of this beautiful form of decoration. Kalocsa is, like Szeged, famous for its paprika.

Highway 51 brings us in another 27 miles (43 km) to the pleasant town of Baja, built on an arm of the Danube. It contains several interesting baroque churches. Béke (Peace) Square, on the river bank, is lined with fine old houses. A bridge from the square leads to Petőfi Island, where there is a pleasant beach and a large stadium. Baja boasts a considerable artists' colony.

PRACTICAL INFORMATION FOR THE GREAT PLAIN

WHEN TO COME. Spring, summer or fall are best, especially as the most interesting events and festivals are held in July and August.

GETTING AROUND. There are good rail connections from Budapest (East and West Stations); local trains and buses complete the network. Otherwise traveling by car gives you the greatest freedom.

HOTELS AND RESTAURANTS

All the hotels listed below have restaurants unless otherwise stated.

BAJA. Duna (I), Béke Tér. Tourist Hostel, camping-site and paying-guest accommodations.
Restaurant. Halászcsárda (fish), on Petőfi Island.

CEGLÉD. Kossuth (I). Paying-guest accommodations.
Restaurants. Magyar, Zöld Hordó, Alföld.

DEBRECEN. Arany Bika (M), a historic hostelry famous for its food. **Főnix** and **Debrecen** (I). Camping-site and paying-guest accommodations.
Restaurants. Hungária, Szabadság and **Gambrinus,** all in town center. **Újvigadó** and several others in Nagyerdő (Great Park), to the north of the town.

GYULA. Komló and **Park,** both simple (I). Tourist-hostel, motel, camping-site.

Restaurants. Otthon, in town center, and **Strand,** near swimming-pool.

HAJDÚSZOBOSZLÓ. Délibáb (M). **Gambrinus** and **Szabadság,** both (I), Tourist hostel, camping-site, paying-guest accommodations.

Restaurants. Alföldi, Hősök Tere, Szigeti Halászcsárda (fish), near the thermal baths.

HORTOBÁGY. Csárda Inn (I). Tourist Hostel and good restaurant.

KALOCSA. Piros Arany (I). Paying-guest accommodation.

Restaurant. Kalocsai Csárda, István Utca.

KECSKEMÉT. Aranyhomok (M). Camping-site, paying-guest accommodations.

Restaurants. Hirös, Rákóczi Út; **Park,** in the park; **Halászcsárda** (fish) in the outskirts of the town.

NYÍRBÁTOR. Paying-guest accommodations.

NYÍREGYHÁZA. Szabolcs (M). **Béke** (I). Paying-guest accommodation. (see also under SÓSTÓ).

RÁCKEVE. Motel, camping-site, paying-guest accommodations.

Restaurant. Fekete Holló, a good restaurant in a well-restored old house.

SÓSTÓ. Krúdy (M). **Svajci Lak** (I). Tourist hostel, paying-guest accommodations.

SZEGED. Hungária (M). **Royal** and **Hungária,** both (M). Several (I) hotels and inns. Motel, camping-site, paying-guest accommodations.

Restaurants. Hági, Kelemen Utca, well spoken of; **Alabárdos,** Oskola Utca; **Szeged,** Széchenyi Tér; **Tiszagyöngye,** across the river. Many fishermen's inn and snack-bars.

SZOLNOK. Pelikán (M). **Tisza** and **Touring,** both (M). Camping-site on river bank and paying-guest accommodations.

Restaurants. Nemzeti, Ságvári Utca; **Múzeum,** Kossuth Tér; **Aranylakat,** in park.

USEFUL ADDRESSES. The following are the addresses of the local tourist offices. **Baja:** Béke Tér; **Cegléd:** Szabadság Tér; **Debrecen:** next to **Arany Bika** Hotel; **Gyula:** Kossuth Lajos Utca; **Hajduszoboszlo:** in spa quarter; **Hortobágy:** in the village; **Kalocsa:** in town center; **Kecskemét:** Kossuth Tér; **Nyíregyháza:** Dózsa György Út; **Szeged:** Klauzál Tér; **Szolnok:** Kossuth Lajos Utca.

WESTERN HUNGARY

Civilized and Mellow

Western Hungary—often known as 'Transdanubia' (*Dunántúl* in Hungarian)—is that part of Hungary south and west of the Danube, stretching to the Czech and Austrian borders in the north and west and to Yugoslavia in the south. It is an undulating country, with several ranges of hills and outposts from the Alps. The part of the region around Lake Balaton we have already described in an earlier chapter.

Western Hungary's climate is rather more humid than that of the rest of the country; most of its surface is covered with farmland, vineyards and orchards. It presents a highly picturesque landscape with many attractions for the tourist.

The Romans called the region Pannonia; for centuries it was a frontier province and it is richer in Roman remains than the rest of Hungary. The towns are mostly old and have highly civilized traditions. Some industrial complexes have recently developed, the most important of them being at Dunaújváros, a large iron and steel town on the west bank of the Danube.

Győr and Pannonhalma

Entering Western Hungary at Hegyeshalom, on the Austrian border, the first important town one reaches is Győr, with 130,000 inhabitants.

It lies exactly halfway between Vienna and Budapest and is both an ancient city and a modern industrial community. It was known to the Romans as Arrabona and here they built a fortress on what is now Káptalan (Chapter) Hill, in the heart of the Old Town. Most of the streets below the hill are built in a regular, checkboard pattern, dating from the 16th century, and many of them are extremely picturesque. The most beautiful baroque church is the Carmelite church (1721–1725) in Köztársaság (Republic) Square, whose eastern side is lined with fine baroque houses. The Castle district on Káptalan Hill contains Győr's oldest church, the Cathedral, whose foundations are believed to go back to the time of St. Stephen (11th century). It has been frequently rebuilt and is now largely baroque, though with a neo-classical façade. In the Héderváry chapel (15th century) is a masterpiece of medieval Hungarian goldsmith's art, the reliquary of King St. Ladislas (1040–1095).

Altogether the streets and squares of the Old Town present one of the most delightful baroque townscapes of Hungary. They include the Bishop's Castle, opposite the Cathedral, the Diocesan Library and Museum, the house at 4 Alkotmány Street in which Napoleon stayed in 1809 (now a museum) and many other interesting buildings too numerous to mention.

About 13 miles (21 km) southeast of Győr lies the great Benedictine Abbey of Pannonhalma, which dates back a thousand years. In the Middle Ages it was immensely powerful and, though, of course, it no longer exerts any political influence, it still pursues its tasks of religion and learning and has a large and important grammar school.

The present abbey was rebuilt in baroque style on 13th-century foundations. Its cloisters are the sole surviving monument of monastic architecture of the Árpád dynasty. The abbey church is the only early Gothic church in Hungary, but there have been many later additions, including a 165-foot (52-meter) high tower in a classical style built early in the 19th century. The library, which contains 300,000 volumes, is one of the most important in Hungary. The archives contain priceless 11th- and 12th-century documents, including the foundation deed of the abbey at Tihany, on Lake Balaton, dating from 1055 and the first Hungarian document to contain a large number of Hungarian words inserted into its Latin text. The abbey also contains a superb collection of ecclesiastical plate and vestments.

Tata and Tatabánya

Continuing eastwards from Győr towards Budapest we reach Tata, another of Hungary's interesting old towns; it is also a spa and well-known equestrian center. On the shores of the large lake, which is in the middle of the town, stands the Castle, medieval in origin but rebuilt at the end of the last century. It contains a museum of local history. Most of the town is baroque, designed by the architect Jakab Fellner on the instructions of Count József Esterházy between 1751 and 1787. The Hungarian Olympic training camp is at Tata, which is one of the country's leading sports centers. At Remeteségpuszta nearby there are opportunities for riding.

Tatabánya, a few miles further on, is a fast-growing industrial town, with important coal mines, factories and power-stations, but little to detain the tourist.

Sopron and Szombathely

Sopron lies on the Austrian frontier, between Lake Fertő (in German *Neusiedlersee*) and the Sopron Hills. It has a population of 56,000 and is one of the most picturesque towns in Hungary. It has many historical and cultural monuments and it enjoys a sub-alpine climate—cooler than the sultry lowlands in summer and sheltered by its hills from the harsh western winds in winter.

The chief sights of Sopron, mostly medieval and baroque, are to be found in the horseshoe-shaped inner town, which was formerly enclosed by the city walls. Széchenyi Square—not far from the main railway station—links the two ends of the boulevard that follows the horseshoe line of the city. The former Dominican church, on the south side of the square, is a fine example of baroque (1719–1725). Petőfi Square lies to the west and two curving streets lead from this square to Lenin Boulevard, a long, busy shopping street and promenade, built on the site of a former moat. On the odd-numbered side of the boulevard are a whole row of interesting baroque, rococo and classical houses. Near the Előkapu (Outer Gate), leading into the inner town, stands the baroque St. Mary Column (1745).

Further on along the boulevard we find several outstanding buildings; the Patika-ház (no. 29) has been the home of the Arany Sas (Golden Eagle) pharmacy since 1724; no. 55 was formerly the Fehér Ló (White Horse) Inn, where Haydn often stayed and where Johann Strauss composed part of his *One Night in Venice*. The Előkapu (referred to above) is a short street, with medieval houses, leading to the spacious Fő Ter (Main Square) through a passage under the 180-foot (56-meter) high Várostorony (City Tower). The tower—the symbol of the city—was begun not later than the 12th or 13th century, though it has clearly-marked romanesque, renaissance and baroque additions.

The square contains many fine buildings, varying from Gothic, through baroque, to the late 19th-century Town Hall. The Benedictine church was built between 1280 and 1300; its 144-foot (43-meter) high steeple dates from the 14th century. In the interesting Gothic interior five national assemblies were held between 1553 and 1681 and three kings and queens were crowned. The Storno house, near the City Tower, is Sopron's most beautiful baroque building; still in private ownership, it houses a fine collection of furniture, porcelain and paintings. The 1701 baroque statue of the Trinity in the middle of the Square is the oldest such monument in Hungary. The baroque Fabricius House, in the same Square, contains some of the exhibits of the Ferenc Liszt Museum, the main building of which is situated just west of the inner town, in Május 1. (May 1st) Square.

Templom (Church) Street leads to the south. Here the former Esterházy Palace, part medieval, part baroque, contains a Mining Museum. Most of the other houses in this street are officially-protected Gothic or baroque monuments. Új (New) Street, to the east, in spite of its name one of Sopron's oldest streets, contains several interesting buildings, including a medieval synagogue, unique in Hungary, now a religious museum. The former Erdődy Palace, in Szent György (St. George) Street, close by, is the finest rococo building in Sopron. Almost all of the narrow and picturesque streets of the inner town and those just outside it offer views of historic and picturesque buildings.

The most interesting excursion from Sopron is to Fertőd, 17 miles (27 km) to the southeast, where the largest and finest baroque palace in the country, the Esterházy Palace, stands. It is easily reached by bus. Though badly damaged in World War II, it has been painstakingly and beautifully restored. It attracts some 100,000 visitors annually, partly because of the celebrated concerts held here each summer and of the Haydn Memorial Museum. Haydn was from 1761 to 1790 the court conductor of the great Esterházy family. The palace contains 126 rooms and was built between 1760 and 1770; it is horseshoe-shaped and is surrounded by splendid gardens. The house in which Haydn lived and a comtemporary baroque inn are also fine buildings.

Another worthwhile trip is to Nagycenk, 8 miles (13 km) southeast of Sopron. Here is the former home of the Széchenyi family, where the great Hungarian statesman, Count István Széchenyi, lived for many years and is buried. The beautiful baroque mansion is now the Széchenyi Memorial Museum. There is also a toy railway, with a steam engine and signal equipment that are 100 years old.

Another interesting town, also not far from the Austrian border, is Szombathely, with about 83,000 inhabitants. It was the Roman Savaria and has for centuries been an important economic center. It has several sights which will appeal to the tourist. Two important squares lie in the town center—Köztársaság (Republic) Square and Berzsenyi Square. Köztársaság Square, formerly the market-place, is still the business center of the city. In Berzsenyi Square are the baroque cathedral and Bishops' Palace, which, with adjoining buildings, form a harmonious whole. To the south lie the remains of the Temple of Isis, which are believed to date from the 2nd century AD. Here devotees of a cult which originated in Egypt used to worship. The Savaria Festival takes place in the grounds each summer.

Several interesting excursions can easily be made from Szombathely. Kőszeg, 10 miles (16 km) to the north, is reached by frequent trains in about half an hour. It is one of Hungary's most fascinating small towns, with some 12,000 inhabitants. It lies higher than any other town in the country (855 feet/270 meters above sea-level), among the eastern outcrops of the Alps, and is very rich in medieval monuments; indeed, its appearance can have changed little since the Middle Ages. It is, too, important historically; the stand of a few hundred Hungarian troops here in 1532 forced the Turkish Army of almost 200,000 to abandon their attempt to capture Vienna. A gate in Jurisich Square (Jurisich was the Hungarian commander) was erected in 1932 to commemorate the historic event. The square leads to the heart of the old town, in which medieval churches, houses and public buildings alike preserve their ancient appearance. The Castle contains an interesting museum.

Ják, 7 miles (11 km) south of Szombathely, has the finest romanesque church in Hungary, dating from the period of the Árpád Dynasty, with two fine towers, crowned with spires, and a magnificently ornate west door. It is best reached by road.

Veszprém and Székesfehérvár

These two historic towns lie not far from Lake Balaton, in the eastern part of the region. Both are important traffic centers—Veszprém lying on the main road and railway routes from Szombathely to Budapest, and Székesfehérvár being one of the most important traffic junctions in all Hungary. Here the routes from the northern and southern shores of Lake Balaton meet and these themselves are crossed by the main traffic links between the northwest and the south of Hungary.

Veszprém, a town of 55,000 inhabitants, is not only a picturesque center of cultural and economic life, but also unique in Hungary in that it is built on five hills and in the intervening valleys. Its traffic center is Szabadság (Liberty) Square, on which is situated the baroque Town Hall.

The most interesting quarter of the town lies to the north and is approached along Rákóczi Road; this ends in Vöröshadsereg (Red Army) Square, at the top of the Castle Hill (Várhegy). Here is the southern entrance to the Castle, which rises on a dolomite rock 100 feet (30 meters) above its surroundings. The Hősi kapu (Heroes' Gate), at the entrance to the Castle, contains the Castle Museum. On the left a short cul-de-sac leads to the Tűztorony (Fire Tower), which is partly medieval and partly baroque; its gallery offers a fine panorama of the town and its environs. Continuing along Tolbuhin Street we pass the fine baroque Bishop's Palace; the 13th-century Gizella chapel adjoining it is one of Hungary's most famous early Gothic buildings, with contemporary murals.

The road ends in a spacious square where, on the left, stands St. Michael's Cathedral, one of the most precious architectural features of Veszprém. The city was an episcopal see under King St. Stephen and the cathedral was begun in the 11th century in a romanesque style; in the 14th century Gothic details were added. It was remodeled along baroque lines in the 18th century, after destruction by the Turks, while in the 20th century it was recast in a neo-romanesque style. Its baroque and classical altars are exceedingly fine and there is a large collection of plate and vestments in the sacristy. The new town of Veszprém is being developed in and around Rákóczi Square, east of the traditional center, while the university district lies to the south of the town.

About 10 miles (16 km) to the west of Veszprém lies Herend, the Hungarian Sèvres or Nymphenburg. The porcelain works were founded early in the 19th century and its products are world famous. A museum showing some of the best examples of Herend work is open to the public.

Székesfehérvár lies some 25 miles (40 km) east of Veszprém and is one of the most interesting and important provincial towns of Hungary, with a population of 105,000. Known to the Romans as Herculia, its neo-Latin name of Alba Regia was bestowed on it during the Middle Ages. Under King St. Stephen it was already an important place and it was he who built its first cathedral and royal palace. The royal seat was later transferred to Esztergom, then to Óbuda and finally to Buda, but Székesfehérvár long preserved its royal links—until 1527 Hungarian kings were crowned here and many were buried here. The town has played an important rôle throughout Hungarian history and latterly it has become a very busy industrial center.

Szabadság (Liberty) Square is the hub of the city and almost all the sights lie close by. In the square itself lies the Town Hall, a baroque building, with beautiful gates at its eastern end, and the Bishop's Palace begun in 1790 in an Empire and Biedermeyer style. To the south of the square, in Arany János Street, stands the baroque Cathedral, built in 1758–78 on the site of an earlier medieval church. King Bela III, who ruled from 1174 to 1196, and his consort were buried in the crypt. At the eastern end of Szabadsag Square is the Garden of Ruins (Romkert) on the site of the former cathedral and royal palace, both of which have been extensively excavated. There are many fine baroque buildings all over the old town, and pleasant cafés and restaurants, together with shady gardens, so that a stroll will prove both interesting and agreeable.

Only a few miles away and just south of the road from Székesfehérvár to Lake Balaton lie Tác and the recently-excavated ruins of the Roman city of Gorsium. A restaurant and café have been opened here.

Not far to the east of Székesfehérvár lies Lake Velence, with a number of popular summer resorts; part of the lake is a protected haunt of water birds. Still further to the east, on the way to Budapest, lies Martonvásár, with the picturesque Brunswick Palace, built in 1773–75 but rebuilt in an 'English' Gothic style a century later. Beethoven often stayed here and Beethoven Memorial Concerts are held here each year in June and July.

Pécs and Southwest Hungary

Southwest Hungary, the district lying south of Lake Balaton, is a smiling, fertile region. Its climate is much milder than elsewhere in Hungary and in the extreme south of the region there are some fair-sized hills. The chief city of the entire region is Pécs, the third largest provincial town in Hungary, with over 170,000 inhabitants. It was the Roman Sopianae, the capital of southern Pannonia, and here several Roman commercial and military roads met. Its great four-towered cathedral rests on Roman foundations. Pécs has always been a prosperous town and was an important staging-post for German and Italian merchants on their way to Byzantium. Hungary's first university was founded here in 1367. During the 143 years of Turkish rule (1543–1686), Pécs acquired a new architectural image, some of which remains to this day.

The center of the town is Széchenyi Square. This contains, among many other old buildings, one dating from the time of the Turkish occupation; the Gazi Kassim Pasha mosque, the largest Turkish monument in Hungary, is now a parish church. Built in the 16th century, it still has its mihrab, the Muslim prayer-niche facing Mecca. Along Janus Pannonius Street, to the northwest, we reach the ecclesiastical center of the city, Dóm (Cathedral) Square, itself a fine piece of architectural planning. The entire northern side of the square is taken up by the Cathedral, one of the most splendid medieval monuments in Hungary. It was begun by King Stephen, but has been rebuilt and remodeled several times. Of its four great, spire-capped towers, two date from the 11th and two from the 12th century. Both externally and internally, the cathedral is both impressive and beautiful. On the west side of the square is the Bishop's Palace, whose garden façade is perhaps the finest baroque monument in Pécs. Nearby there are some early Christian catacombs.

Other buildings of note in the city include several Turkish monuments. One is the Jakovali Hassan mosque, in Rákóczi Street, southwest of the town center, built late in the 16th century; this is the only Turkish building in Hungary to have survived intact and it still has its minaret. Another is the *türbe* (tomb) of Idris Baba, northwest of the inner city; there are also many fine baroque churches and houses in and around Széchenyi Square.

Pécs is famous for the Zsolnay porcelain produced here since 1851. The Zsolnay Museum, in Káptalan (Chapter) Street, which links the Cathedral Square with the northern part of the town center and which is lined with fine old houses, each an 'ancient monument', contains valuable examples of Zsolnay ware. Pécs is also a university city and is rapidly developing into an important industrial town. Nearby lie large coal mines and Hungary's only uranium mine.

Two towns well worth visiting from Pécs are Szigetvár and Siklós, both of which have interesting medieval castles. The castle at Szigetvár played an important rôle in the fight against the Turkish invaders of Hungary in 1566, when a handful of soldiers held out against the army of Sultan Soliman II. There is a Turkish mosque in the castle courtyard. At Siklós, about 20 miles (32 km) due south of Pécs, the castle has been continuously inhabited since the Middle Ages and now houses a comfortable hotel. The town lies in the center of a rich wine-producing district at the foot of the Villany Hills.

The West Bank of the Danube

There remains to be mentioned the country along the west bank of the Danube. Mohács, 25 miles (40 km) to the east of Pécs, lies on the river and is famous above all for the disastrous battle fought there in 1526, in which the defending Hungarians were routed by the Turkish army of Sultan Soliman II. It contains a number of pleasant baroque churches, but nothing of special interest. Szekszárd, 27 miles (43 km) further north, lies some miles to the west of the present course of the Danube. The former County Hall, built in 1780 on the site of a Benedictine abbey, and a late baroque Roman Catholic church are its chief sights. Liszt spent much of his time here and gave several concerts. Szekszárd is the center of notable vineyards, famous from Roman times; and the Gemenc forest nearby is a well-known game reserve.

Finally we must mention Dunaújváros, almost exactly halfway between Szekszárd and Budapest. It is Hungary's greatest purely industrial city, with about 60,000 inhabitants. Until the Fifties, it was no more than a small village. It has no buildings of historical importance, but it will interest those—and they amount to over 100,000 visitors a year—who wish to see how a small country has, in little over 30 years, transformed a sleepy country hamlet into an industrial complex, with vast iron and steel works. A museum illustrates the development of the town.

PRACTICAL INFORMATION FOR WESTERN HUNGARY

 WHEN TO COME. Spring, summer and fall are all delightful times to visit western Hungary. Most of the more interesting festivals and popular events are held in July and August.

 **GETTING AROUND.** There are good rail connections from Budapest (South and East Stations). There are also fast through trains from Vienna to Győr. Local trains and buses are adequate. Needless to say, touring by car provides you with the greatest freedom.

HOTELS AND RESTAURANTS

All the hotels listed below have restaurants unless otherwise stated.

DUNAÚJVÁROS. Aranycsillag (M). Tourist-hostel, camping-site, paying-guest accommodations.
Restaurants. Béke, Kohász.

FERTŐD. Kastély, Udvaros Ház, both tourist-hostels.
Restaurant. Haydn, in the village.

GYŐR. Rába (M). Motel, camping-site, paying-guest accommodations.
Restaurants. Hungária, Lenin Út; **Kristály,** Bartók Béla Út; **Vaskakas,** Köztársaság Tér, and many others, including a fishermen's inn (**Halászcsárda**), Rózsa Ferenc Utca.

KŐSZEG. Írottkő (M), in town center. **Panoráma** (M), on hills to west of town. **Strucc** (I), historic hostelry in main square dating from the late 17th century. Two Tourist Hostels, one in the ancient castle and one on a hill outside the town; paying-guest accommodations.
Restaurants. Kulacs; Turista; snack-bar in castle.

MOHÁCS. Csele (M). **Béke** (I). Paying-guest accommodations.
Restaurants. Pannonia, in the town; **Halászcsarda,** fisherman's inn on the island.

PÉCS. Pannonia (M). **Nádor** (M), a famous old house in the main square. Four (I) hotels, motel, camping-site, paying-guest accommodations.
Restaurants. Borostyán and **Hullám** are both in town center; **Tettye** is on the hill to the north of the town.

The great medieval cathedral at Pécs, one of Hungary's finest buildings.

The ornate 15th-century altarpiece by Wit Stwosz in the church of St. Mary, Cracow.

An open-air concert on the grounds of the Lazienki Pal-ace, home of Poland's last king, Stanislas Poniatowski.

The modern statue in Warsaw of Poland's most famous son, Chopin.

Polish hunters roast some of their catch at the end of a boar—and fox—hunt.

A Romanian wooden church in a remote region near the Apuseni mountains.

A popular beach at Eforie, on the sunny Black Sea coast of Romania.

TOURIST VOCABULARY

Hungarian is very different from the languages of the West and at first sight looks forbiddingly difficult. It has many double consonants and accented vowels and it is not easy to represent its pronunciation accurately in a way easily understandable by the ordinary traveler. We have listed below what we consider to be the most important words and phrases for the visitor and we have tried to help him (or her) to pronounce them.

There are three important 'keys' to the imitated pronunciation we have used. **1** *Every* word, without exception, is strongly accented on the *first* syllable and, to draw attention to this, we have *italicized* this syllable in the imitated pronunciation. **2** The letter *'o'* in the imitated pronunciation is pronounced like the short English 'o' in the word 'on'; the letters *'oh'* represent the longer sound of 'o', as in the English word 'home'. **3** The sign *'u[r]'* represents roughly the *vowel* sound in the English word 'hurt', but *the 'r' is not pronounced*.

USEFUL EXPRESSIONS

Hello, how do you do?	Jó napot? (*yoh* nopp oht?)
How are you?	Hogy van? (*hohdge* von?)
Good morning	Jó reggelt (*yoh* reg-gelt)
Good evening	Jó estét (*yoh* esh-teht)
Goodnight	Jó éjszakát (*yoh* eysokaht)
Goodbye	Viszontlátásra (*vissohnt*-lahtahshro)
Please	Kérem [szépen] (*keh*rem [*seh*pen])
Thank you	Köszönöm (*ku*[r]su[r]nu[r]m)
Thank you very much	Köszönöm szépen (*ku*[r]su[r]nu[r]m *seh*pen)
Yes	Igen (*i*gen)
No	Nem (nem)
You're welcome, don't mention it	Nincs mit; szívesen (ninch mit; *see*veshen)
Excuse me	Bocsánat (*boh*chahnot)
Come in!	Szabad! (*sob*od!)
I'm sorry	Sajnálom (*shahee*-nahlohm)
My name is . . .	. . . vagyok (. . . *voj*ohk)
Do you speak English?	Beszél angolul? (*bess*ehl *ong*-gohlul?)
I don't speak Hungarian	Nem tudok magyarul (nem *too*dohk *moj*orool)
I don't understand	Nem értem (nem *ehr*tem)
Please speak slowly	Kérem beszéljen lassan (*keh*rem *bess*-ehyen *losh*-shon)
Please write it down	Kérem, írja le ezt (*keh*rem, *eer*-yo lay ezt)
Where is . . . ?	Hol van . . . ? (hohl von . . . ?)
What is this place called?	Hogy hívják ezt a helyet? (*hodge heev*yahk ezt o *hey*et?)

Please show me	Megmutatná nekem (*meg*moototnah nekem)
I would like . . .	Szeretnék . . . (*serret*nehk . . .)
How much does it cost?	Mennyibe kerül? (*men*yibe *kere*wl?)

SIGNS

Entrance	Bejárat (*bey*ahrot)
Exit	Kijárat (*kee*yahrot)
emergency exit	vészkijárat (*vehss*-keeyahrot)
Toilet, lavatory	Toalet, W.C. (*twah*let; *veh*-tseh)
men; gentlemen	férfiak; urak (*fehr*fiok; *ooro*k)
women; ladies	hölgyek; nők (*hu*[r]*l*jek; nu[r]k)
vacant	szabad (*sob*od)
occupied	foglalt (*foh*glolt)
Hot	Meleg (*mel*leg)
Cold	Hideg (*hidd*eg)
No smoking	Dohányozi tilos (*doh*ahnyozni *till*osh)
No admittance	Tilos a bemenet; nem bejárat (*till*osh o *bemm*enet nem *bay*ahrot)
Stop	Stop (stohp)
Danger	Veszély (*ves*say)
Closed	Zárva (*zahr*vo)
Full, no vacancy	Megtelt (*megg*-telt)
Information	Információ (*in*fohrmahtsioh)
Bus stop	Autóbusz megálló (*ow*tohboos *meg*ahl-loh)
Taxi stand	Taxi-állomás (*tok*si-*ahl*-lohmahsh)
Pedestrians	Gyalogjárók (*joll*ohg-yahrohk)

ARRIVAL

Passport check	Útlevélellenőrzes (*oot*levehl-*ell*enu[r]rzehsh)
Your passport, please	Kérem az útlevelét (*keh*rem oz *oot*leveleht)
I am with the group	A csoporttal vagyok (o *chohp*pohrt-tol *vo*johk)
Customs	Vám (vahm)
anything to declare?	van elvámolni valója? (von *el*vahmohlni *volo*hyo?)
nothing (to declare)	semmi nincs (*shemm*i ninch)
Baggage	Poggyász (*pohj*-jahss)
baggage ticket	Poggyászjegy (*pohj*-jahss-yedge)
Transportation	
to the bus	az autóbuszhoz (oz

owtohbooss-hohz)

to a taxi — egy taxihoz (edge *tok*si-hohz)

To the Hotel . . . , please — Kérem, a szállóhoz (*keh*rem, o *sahl*-loh-hohz)

MONEY

Money — Pénz (paynz)

The currency exchange office — A pénzváltás (o *paynz*vahltahsh)

Can you change this? — Fel tudya ezt váltani? (fel *tood*-yo ezt *vahl*toni?)

May I pay . . . — Fizethetek . . . (*fizet*-hetek . . .)
  with a travelers' check? — csekkel? (*check*-kel?)
  with this credit card? — evvel a kreditkártyával? (*ev*vel o *kred*itkahrtyahvol?)

I would like to exchange some travelers' checks — Szeretnék beváltani néhány csekket (*serr*etnayk *be*vahltoni nay-hahn *check*-ket)

THE HOTEL

A hotel — Egy szálló (edge *sahl*-loh)

I have a reservation — Foglaltam egy szobát (*fohg*lahltom edge *soh*baht)

A room with bath — Szoba fürdőszobával (*fewr*du[r]-*soh*bahvol)

  a shower — egy zuhany (edge *zoo*-hon)

  hot running water — meleg víz (*mel*leg veez)

What floor is it on? — Melyik emeleten van? (*may*-ik *emm*eleten von?)

  ground floor — földszint (*fu*[r]*ld*-sint)

  second floor — első emelet (*el*-shu[r] *emm*elet)

The elevator — A lift (o lift)

Have the baggage sent up, please — Kérem a poggyászt felküldeni (*keh*rem o *pohj*-jahst *fel*-kewldeni)

The key to number . . . , please — Kérem a kulcsot a . . . es szobához (*keh*rem a *kool*choht o . . . esh *soh*bah-hohz)

Please call me at seven o'clock — Kérem hétkor felkelteni (*keh*rem hayt-*kohr* *fel*-keltenee)

Have the baggage brought down, please — Kérem a poggyászt lehozni (*keh*rem a *pohj*-jahst *leh*-hoznee)

The bill — A számla (o *sahm*-lo)

A tip — Egy borravaló (edge *bohr*-ro-voloh)

THE RESTAURANT

The restaurant — A vendéglő, az étterem (o *ven*dehglu[r], oz *eht*-terem)

Café — Kávéház, eszpresszó

	(*kah*vayhahz, *e*spressoh)
Menu	Étlap (*ayt*-lop)
Waiter!	Pincér! (*pin*-tsair)
Waitress!	Pincérnő! (*pin*-tsairnu[r]!)

(Both are more likely to respond to the request Kérem – *keh*rem = Please!)

I would like to order this	Kérem ezt (*keh*rem ezt)
Some more . . . , please	Még néhány . . . , kérem
	(Mehg *nay*-hahn . . . , *keh*rem)
Enough	Elég (*elle*hg)
The check, please	A számlát kérem; fizetek (o
	*sahm*laht *keh*rem; *fi*zetek)
Breakfast	Reggeli (*reg*-gellee)
Lunch	Ebéd (*eb*-ehd)
Dinner	Vacsora (*votch*-ohro)
Bread	Kenyér (*ken*-yehr)
Butter	Vaj (voy)
Jam	Lekvár (*lek*vahr)
Salt	Só (shoh)
Pepper	Bors, paprika (bohrsh,
	*pop*riko)
Mustard	Mustár (*moosh*tahr)
Sauce, gravy	Mártás (*mahr*tahsh)
Vinegar	Ecet (*et*set)
Oil	Olaj (*oh*loy)
A bottle	Egy üveg (edge *ew*veg)
Wine	Bor (bohr)
red, white wine	vörös, fehér bor (*vu*[r]ru [r]sh,
	*f*ehehr bohr)
Beer	Sör (shu[r]r)
Spirits (apricot brandy)	Barackpálinka
	(*b*orotsk-*pah*lingko)
Water	Víz (veez)
Mineral water	Kristályvíz, Ásványvíz
	(*kirsh*tahee veez, *ahsh*-vahn
	veez)
Milk	Tej (tay)
Coffee	Kávé (*kah*vay)
Tea with lemon	Tea citrommal (*tay*-o
	*tsit*rohmmol)
Sugar	Cukor (*tsoo*kohr)
Lemonade	Limonádé (*limoh*nahday)
(Fruit) juice	(Gyümölcs) lé (*jew*-mu(r)lch) lay

Further Hungarian restaurant hints are given in the chapter on food and drink.

MAIL

A letter	Egy levél (edge *leve*hl)
An envelope	Egy boríték (edge *boh*reetehk)
A postcard	Egy levelező lap
	(edge *leve*lezu[r] lop)
A mailbox	Egy postaláda (edge
	*pohsh*to-lahdo)

The post office	A posta (o *pohsh*to)
A stamp	Egy bélyeg (edge *bay*-yeg)
By airmail	Légi postával (*lay*gi *pohsh*tahvol)
How much does it cost to send a letter, a postcard, airmail to the United States Great Britain, Canada?	Mennyibe kerül egy levelet, egy levelező lapot, légi postával az Egyesült Államokba, Angliába, Kanadába küldeni? (*men*-nyibeh *ker*ewl edge *lev*elet, edge *lev*elezu[r] lopoht, *lay*gi *pohsh*tahvol oz *Edge*-eshewlt *Ahl*-lomohkbo, (*Ong*-gliahbo, *Kon*odahbo) *kewl*deni?
To send a telegram, cable	Egy táviratot küldeni (edge *tah*virotoht *kewl*deni)

LOCATIONS

. . . Street	. . . Utca (. . . *oot*so)
. . . Avenue	. . . Út (. . . ooht)
. . . Square	. . . Tér (. . . tayr)
The airport	A repülőtér (o *rep*ewlu[r]-tayr)
A bank	Egy bank (edge bongk)
The beach	A strand (o shtrond)
The bridge	A híd (o heed)
The castle	A kastély (o *kosh*-tay)
The cathedral	A székesegyház (o *say*kesh-edgehahz)
The church	A templom (o *temp*lohm)
The garden	A kert (o kairt)
The hospital	A kórház (o *kohr*-hahz)
The movies, cinema	A mozi (o *moh*zi)
a movie	Egy film (edge film)
The museum	A múzeum (o *moo*-zayoom)
A nightclub	Egy mulatóhely (edge *moo*lotoh-hay)
The palace	A palota (o *poll*ohto)
The park	A park (o porrk)
The post office	A posta (o *pohsh*to)
The restaurant	A vendéglő, az étterem (o *ven*dehglu[r], oz *eht*-terem)
The station	A pályaudvar, a vasúti állomás (o *pah*-yo-oodvor, o *vosh*ooti *ahl*-lomahsh)
The theater	A színház (o *seen*-hahz)
a play	Egy színdarab (edge *seen*-dorob)
Travel bureau (IBUSZ)	IBUSZ (the official travel agency) (*ib*booss)
in general	Utazási iroda (*oot*ozahshi *eer*ohdo)
The university	Az egyetem (oz *edge*-etem)

TRAVEL

Arrival	Érkezés (*ehr*-kezehsh)
Departure	Indulás (*in*-doolahsh)

The airplane:

| | A repülőgép, a gép (o *repp*ewlu[r] gehp, o gehp) |

I want to confirm a reservation on flight number . . . for . . .

Szeretnék érvenyesíteni egy rezervációt a . . . járatszámon . . . ba. (*serr*etnehk *ehr*ven-yesheeteni edge *rez*ervahtsioht o . . . *yah*rot-sahmohn . . . bo.)

Where is the check-in?

A jegykezelés hol van? (o *yedge*-kezelehsh hohl von?)

I am checking in for . . .

Megyek . . . ba (*medge*-ek . . . bo.)

Fasten your seat-belt

Kösse össze a biztonságövet (*ku*[r]sheh *u*[r]sse o *biz*tohnshahg-u[r]veht)

The railroad:

A vasút (o *vosh*oot)

From what track does the train to . . . leave?

Melyik vágányról indul a . . . -i vonat? (*mey*ik *vah*gahn-rohl *ind*ool o . . . -i *voh*not?)

Which way is the dining-car?

Merre van az étkezo-kocsi? (*mehr*-re von oz *eht*kezu[r]-*koh*chi?)

Bus, streetcar, subway:

Autóbusz, villamos, metró (*owt*ohbooss, *vill*amohsh, *met*ro)

Does this bus go to . . . ?

Megy ez az autóbusz . . . felé? (medge ez oz *owt*obooss . . . *fel*eh?)

Trolleybus

Trolibusz (*trohl*ibooss)

I want to get off at . . . Street

Szeretnék leszállni . . . utcánál (*ser*etnehk *leh*sahl-ni . . . *oot*sahnahl)

at the next stop

a legközelebbi megállónál (o *leg*ku[r]zeleb-bi *meg*-ahl-lohnahl)

Taxi:

Taxi (*Tok*si)

Please go to . . .

Kérem . . . -ba menni (*Keh*rem . . . -bo *men*ni)

Stop at . . .

Álljon meg . . . -nál (*Ahl*-yon meg . . . -nahl)

Stop here

Álljon meg itt (*Ahl*-yon meg itt)

NUMBERS

1 egy (edge)	9 kilenc (*kil*ents)
2 két, kettő (keht, *ket*-tu[r])	10 tíz (teez)
3 három (*hah*rohm)	11 tizenegy (*teez*enedge)
4 négy (naydge)	12 tizenkét, – kettő (*teez*enkeht, – *ket*-tu[r])
5 öt (u[r]t)	
6 hat (hot)	13 tizenhárom (*teez*enhahrom)
7 hét (hayt)	14 tizennégy (*teez*en-naydge)
8 nyolc (nyohlts)	15 tizenöt (*teez*enu[r]t)

16 tizenhat (*teezen*hot)
17 tizenhét (*teezen*hayt)
18 tizennyolc (*teezen*-nyolts)
19 tizenkilenc (*teezen*-kilents)
20 húsz (hooss)
25 huszonöt (*hoss*ohnu[r]t)
30 harminc (*horr*-mints)
40 negyven (*nedge*-ven)
50 ötven (*u[r]t*-ven)
60 hatvan (*hot*-von)
70 hetven (*het*-ven)
80 nyolcvan (*nyohlts*-von)

90 kilencven (*kil*ents-ven)
100 száz (sahz)
200 kétszáz (*keht*-sahz)
300 háromszáz (*hahr*ohm-sahz)
400 négyszáz (*naydge*-sahz)
500 ötszáz (*u[r]t*-sahz)
600 hatszáz (*hot*-sahz)
700 hétszáz (*heht*-sahz)
800 nyolcszáz (*nyohlts*-sahz)
900 kilencszáz (*kil*ents-sahz)
1000 ezer (*ezehr*)

POLAND

FACTS AT YOUR FINGERTIPS

Planning Your Trip

WHAT WILL IT COST. Despite considerable rises in many basic commodities, not least food, Polish prices are still extremely reasonable by Western standards, though you may find some services unpredictable. The least expensive, and in many ways most convenient and sensible, way of visiting Poland is on a package tour with all expenses pre-paid before you leave home. This will also exempt you having to exchange the minimum $15 per day, which must be done at the official rate of exchange. Though you can also buy a series of pre-paid vouchers before you leave which exempt you from having to change this minimum sum. Even if you travel independently, with or without pre-paid vouchers, you will still find costs low. Holders of Polish passports resident abroad need exchange only $8 per day.

Foreign currency may be exchanged at all border points (ie air, sea and road), in most hotels and at any Orbis exchange counter. Exchange of foreign currency anywhere else is strictly forbidden and subject to penalties. Remember also that the import and export of foreign currency is not permitted. You may, of course, bring in any amount of foreign currency.

The unit of currency in Poland is the złoty which is divided into 100 groszy, though the latter are rarely seen. There are coins of 1, 2, 5, 10 and 20 zł; bank notes are in denominations of 50, 100, 500 and 1,000 zł.

The official rate of exchange at the time of writing (mid-1982) was about 80 zł to the dollar and about 150 zł to the pound. But these rates are almost certain to change both before and during 1983. It is very important therefore to check the latest rate when planning your trip.

Major credit cards, such as American Express, Carte Blanche, Diner's Club, Master Card, etc., are accepted at all principal hotels and restaurants, night-clubs, selected stores in larger towns and for Orbis services. Holders of Euro-cheque cards may also cash personal checks.

All prices quoted in this chapter are those of mid-1982.

A day's basic costs for two people might be:

Hotel, Moderate, with breakfast	5,200	zł
Lunch, in Moderate restaurant	1,000	
Transportation (4 tram rides, 1 taxi)	150	
Museum entrance	50	
4 coffees, 2 beers	600	
Dinner, in Moderate restaurant including wine	2,000	
Total	9,000	zł

Sample Costs. Cigarettes (best local) 28zł., (imported) 50zł; glass Scotch whiskey 100zł., glass vodka 50 zł.; opera ticket from 200 zł., theater or concert ticket from 150 zł.; movie from 100 zł.; short coach tour with guide about 400 zł.

HOW TO GO. ORBIS, the official Polish Travel Bureau, though not actually able to arrange travel to Poland themselves, have a number of officially accredited travel agents overseas, of which the principal agent is Polorbis. They will organize travel to and from Poland, whether by plane, train, ship or bus and can also book hotels and organize visas. They can also supply pre-paid vouchers for hotels, camping sites, gasoline and the like. For independent travelers this last can be extremely useful. However, the many other travel agents who organize travel to Poland (Thomas Cook, Maupintour and American Express among them) can also help in many of these areas.

Within Poland itself, you will find that all the major hotels are owned and operated by Orbis. They have offices in all main towns and cities.

The addresses of Polorbis offices overseas are:

In the US: 500 Fifth Ave., New York, NY 10110.

In the UK: 82 Mortimer St., London W1.

Apart from package holidays in one town or center, a number of tours of Poland are also available. For example, there is a *Tatra Mountains Spectacular* or a tour from the Baltic to the Tatra Mountains or a *History and Landscapes of Southern Poland* tour, all at extremely competitive rates and all organized by Polorbis. Polorbis also organize special interest holidays such as hunting, fishing, sailing, winter sports, parachuting, etc., as well as fly drive holidays. *Swan's Art Treasures Tours* (237–238 Tottenham Court Rd., London W1) and *Serenissima Travel Ltd.* (140 Slaone St., London SW1) organize much more expensive but nonetheless excellent art tours of Poland.

 WHEN TO COME. Spring and summer, frequently very warm though the spring can be windy, are the best periods for sightseeing. Fall sees most of the major cultural events, which mostly take place in the cities. The Tatra mountains are at their best in the fall, which can be long and sunny. The winter sports season lasts from December to March.

Summer, being the high season, is the most expensive time to visit, especially the seaside resorts of Gdansk, Gdynia and Sopot. The mountain resorts, as might be expected, are most expensive in winter. You will also find that hotel prices in particular go up when special events take place, such as the Poznan International Fair in June. However, in Warsaw and Cracow hotel prices remain fixed all year long.

Average maximum daily temperatures in Fahrenheit and centigrade:

Warsaw	Jan.	Feb.	Mar.	Apr.	May	June	July	Aug.	Sept.	Oct.	Nov.	Dec.
F°	34	36	46	55	66	72	75	73	68	57	45	39
C°	1	2	8	13	19	22	24	23	20	14	7	4

 SPECIAL EVENTS. January, 'Golden Washboard' Traditional Jazz Meeting (Warsaw). **February,** Highland carnival in the Tatra Mountains (Bukowina Tatrzańska); Festival of Modern Polish Music (Wrocław); 'Jazz on the Odra' Student Festival (Wrocław); Festival of Polish Art (Wrocław). **March,** National Review of Professional Variety Theaters (Szczecin). **April,** National Student Song Festival (Cracow). **May,** International Chamber Music Festival (Lańcut, near Rzeszów); Festival of Contemporary Polish Plays

(Wrocław); International Book Fair (Warsaw); 'Apple Blossom Days' folk festival (Łack, near Sacz); 'Neptunalia' Student Festival (Gdańsk and Szczecin); 'Juvenalia' Student Festival (Cracow).

From **May to October,** Sunday Chopin recitals take place in Łazienki Park (Warsaw). **May–December,** Symphonic and chamber music concerts in Wawel Castle courtyard (Cracow). **June,** Folk Festival (Kazimierz Dolny); International Short Film Festival (Cracow); International Poster Biennale (even-numbered years, at Wilanów, just outside Warsaw); 'Cepeliada' Folk Art Fair (Warsaw); International Trade Fair (Poznań); Chamber and Organ Music Festival (Kamień Pomorski, Szczecin Bay); Polish Song Festival (Opole, between Wrocław and Katowice); International Graphic Art Biennale (Cracow); Polish Days of the International Highland Folklore Festival (Zywiec in the Beskidy Mountains); International Puppet Theater Festival (Bielsko-Biala, south of Katowice); Folklore Festival (Ostrołeka, north of Warsaw and at Płock and Olsztyn); Midsummer 'wianki' celebrations on June 23 throughout Poland, when small flower garlands carrying lit candles are thrown on the river, an echo of a pagan Slavonic tradition.

June–September, Chopin recitals at composer's birthplace (Żelazowa Wola just outside Warsaw). **July,** 'Fama' Student Festival (Świnoujście); 'Jazz Jantar' (Sopot, Olsztyn, Szczecin, Kołobrzeg, Koszalin). **August,** Chopin Festival (Duszniki-Zdrój, in the mountains of Lower Silesia); Dominican Fair, a commercial fair that draws on local traditions, with a good flea market (Gdańsk); Dymarki (Old Smelting Furnaces) Festival with demonstrations of 2,000-year-old smelting methods (Nowa Słupia in the Świetokrzyskie Mountains); International Song Festival (Sopot); Folk Art Fair (Cracow).

September, 'Wratislavia Cantans' Oratorio and Cantata Festival (Wrocław); International Festival of Highland Folklore (Zakopane); 'Warsaw Autumn' International Festival of Contemporary Music, Feature Film Festival (Warsaw); Musica Antiqua Europae Orientalis (Bydgoszcz); International Festival of Song and Dance Ensembles (Zielona Góra, west of Poznań); International Old Music Festival (Toruń). **October,** Jazz Jamboree (Warsaw). **November–December,** Presentation of year's most outstanding dramas (Warsaw). **December,** Competition for the best Christmas Crib (Cracow); 'Sylwester' New Year's Eve celebrations everywhere.

National Holidays. Jan. 1; Easter Monday; May 1 (International Labor Day); Corpus Christi; July 22 (Independence Day); Nov. 1 (Remembrance Day); Dec. 25 & 26.

 VISAS. In addition to a valid passport, visitors resident in all Western European countries, North and South America and all Commonwealth countries require a visa to enter Poland. These are available from Polish Consulates, Polorbis offices and many travel agents. To apply for a visa your passport must be valid for at least nine months from the date of your application. You must also have two passport size photographs and copies of any pre-paid services which you have already booked. The fee for a visa is approximately $12. Children under 16 traveling on their parents' passports do not require visas. It is advisable to apply a few weeks in advance of your departure date.

MEDICAL INSURANCE. Medical insurance is strongly recommended for visitors to Poland from North America, as charges are made for all medical treatments and medicines. However, visitors to Poland from Great Britain are entitled to free treatment in emergencies upon presentation of an NHS medical card.

HEALTH CERTIFICATES. These are not required to enter Poland unless arriving within five days of leaving any country where cholera exists.

CUSTOMS. You may import duty free into Poland all personal belongings. Those over 17 may also import duty free 250 cigarettes or 50 cigars or 250 grs. of tobacco; plus one liter of wine and one liter of other alcoholic drink.

You may export duty free from Poland any Polish goods worth less than 2,000 zł. You may also export duty free goods bought with no more than 50% of the foreign currency exchanged during your stay, but you must have both receipts of exchange and receipts for the goods. However, the duty imposed on certain goods may be as high as 100% of their Polish market value. It is not always clear which goods are liable for this extra duty, so check carefully with Orbis and tourist shops. Goods bought with foreign currency are not liable for duty, but again make sure you have valid receipts with you.

You may also export any foreign currency you brought into Poland but did not spend, provided you have changed the daily minimum amount of foreign currency ($16). No Polish currency can be either imported or exported. No works of art or books of any kind published before 1945 may be exported.

Staying in Poland

LANGUAGE. Polish is a Slavonic language. Unlike Russian, it uses the familiar Roman alphabet, but with many additional accents. German, Russian, English and French are spoken by members of the travel industry, in hotels and are understood in the larger cities.

HOTELS. Hotels in Poland are reasonably plentiful, though quite expensive by the standards or other Eastern European countries. All the top hotels are owned and operated by Orbis and, though other hotels exist outside the Orbis ambit, it is unlikely that Western visitors will come into contact with them. Certainly, if you have pre-paid hotel vouchers or have booked your hotel in advance through Polorbis, you will stay in one of the Orbis hotels. However, non-Orbis hotels are considerably less expensive, though at the same time you may well find difficulty making reservations. You can also be sure that Orbis hotels will have the best food supplies, and, if for no other reason than this, they are definitely the best bet for Western visitors.

However, of the other hotels, the best are Municipal Hotels, usually run by local authorities. There are also a number of PTTK hotels (run by the Polish Tourist Association); these are frequently called *Dorn Turysty*. There are also a number of inexpensive roadside inns known as *zajazdy*, but these are most likely to suffer from erratic food supplies. Information on all Polish hotels is available from Polorbis, and Orbis within Poland.

Polish hotels are graded from luxury through 4- to 1-star. These categories correspond closely to our gradings of Deluxe (L), Expensive (E), Moderate (M) and Inexpensive (I). 3- and 2-star hotels are graded as Moderate in our listings. Most Orbis hotels come within our Expensive category.

Rates quoted below are for Orbis hotels. They include bed and breakfast and all taxes and service charges. A number of hotels, especially the larger ones, often have rooms in more than one category. Rates are in US dollars.

Two people in a double room will pay:

	Warsaw	Provincial centers
Deluxe	$110–120	—
Expensive	85–105	60–70
Moderate	65–85	40–50
Inexpensive	—	30–40

YOUTH HOSTELS. The Polish Youth Hostels Association operates about 1,200 hostels, which are open to all. It is best to join the Association or belong to any other similar association of the International Youth Hostels Federation, thus entitling you to reductions. A list is included in the IYHF international register (see also Youth Hostels in Planning Your Trip).

CAMPING. There are over 200 campsites in Poland, nearly 75% of which are fitted with 220 volt power points and most with 24 volt points for caravans. Facilities also include washrooms, canteens and nearby restaurants and food kiosks.

RESTAURANTS. The selection of restaurants is wide, but it should be noted that food supplies are currently erratic and that it is advisable to book meals in top-class hotel restaurants as they receive the best ingredients. A meal in an expensive (E) restaurant will cost around 1,500 zł., moderate (M) 1,000 zł., inexpensive (I) from around 600 zł., but can even be less.

Roadside inns *(zajazdy)* are inexpensive and serve traditional Polish cuisine. Self-service snack and coffee bars are to be found in larger centers; cafés *(kawiarnia),* a way of life in Poland, serve delicious pastries.

TIPPING. A service charge is usually added to restaurant bills, but if not, add 10%. Tipping for other services is not obligatory, but is readily accepted. Cab drivers get 10% and expect to be tipped.

MAIL. An airmail letter to the US or a European country costs 27 zł., a postcard 17 zł. Post offices are open from 8 to 8 and there is usually one main post office in major towns that is open 24 hours a day.

TELEPHONES. In public phone booths (for local calls), you'll need a 1 zł. coin; there are also some newer machines which take 1, 2 and 5 zł coins. Long distance calls can be placed from your hotel or post office. Be sure to check the surcharge if placing the call from your hotel; this can sometimes double the basic price of the call. Telephoning in Poland, especially if you are making a long-distance call, can be both frustrating and time consuming.

TIME. Poland is six hours ahead of Eastern Standard Time and one hour ahead of Greenwich Mean Time. In the summer, clocks are put forward by one hour so that the country is seven hours ahead of Eastern Standard Time and two hours ahead of Greenwich Mean Time.

 CLOSING TIMES. Food shops are open from 7 or 8 to 7, others from 11 to 7. Department stores are open from 9 to 7 and 'Ruch' newspaper kiosks from 6 to 9. Offices and banks are generally open from 8 to 3 or 9 to 4. Local tourist information centers can advise on up-to-date opening times of historic monuments and museums.

 **SHOPPING.** The wide range of store chains specializing in different items, makes shopping in Poland relatively easy, though not necessarily cheap. Glassware, ceramics, woodcarvings, articles of amber, silver and other metals, embroideries and pictures all make good gifts to take back home.

Some of the best souvenirs can be bought from Cepelia (Folk Arts and Crafts Cooperative) with stores all over Poland. They sell a wide range of genuine folk art from all regions. Desa stores stock tapestries, paintings, sculptures and porcelain, while branches of Orno specialize in handmade silver work. All these accept local and foreign currency. The Pewex stores accept only hard currency. They sell local and imported items such as imported spirits (very reasonable vodka), imported chocolate, coffee and clothing.

 SPAS. There are several dozen spas and health resorts scattered throughout Poland, the largest of which is Ciechocinek. Orbis takes care of all the arrangements. A high season stay in a spa starts at $51 per person per day, in a double room with bath. This includes full board and treatment. 10 percent discount is granted for groups consisting of 10 or more people; 20 percent is given on groups of 20 or over.

 WINTER SPORTS. The most popular resorts are Zakopane in the Tatra Mountains and Krynica (also a well-known spa) in the Beskidy Mountains. Skiing from November through May. You'll find good Orbis hotels and boarding houses, ski-runs, restaurants, lots of après-ski, and cable railways and lifts to nearby peaks. Ski-jumping competitions are frequently staged. In Lower Silesia, holiday resorts with good skiing facilities include Karpacz, Szklarska Poreba, Szczawno, Polanica, Kudowa, and Duszniki. Beginning to rival Zakopane as Poland's winter capital is Szczyrk in the Beskid-Ślaski Mountains; good facilities, but snow cannot be guaranteed.

 WATER SPORTS. Main sailing regions in Poland are the Mazurian Lakes and the nearby Suwałki and Augustów Lakes, a natural continuation of the waterways. Zegrzyńskie Lake not far from Warsaw offers splendid facilities. In winter there is ice-boating on many of Poland's frozen waterways.

No special qualifications or documents are required for tourists entering Poland with their own yachts or motor boats, but you must have life-saving equipment on board. Many Polish waters have 'quiet zones' where motor-powered boats are banned; these areas include many of the Mazurian Lakes, as well as (on Sundays and holidays) Warsaw's Zegrzyńskie Lake.

Canoeing enthusiasts have many good river routes to choose from, but especially recommended are the Krutynia river in the Mazury region, the Dunajec Gorge (skilled canoeists only), the Pilica river, and of course, the Vistula.

There are swimming pools in most cities; sandy beaches along the Baltic coast and Mazurian Lakes. Avoid swimming in the rivers as pollution is high.

HUNTING. Poland is definitely a hunting country, but fairly expensive. After hard winters, hunting can be cut back severely for some time to allow game to recover. In a number of reserves, fallow deer, roe deer, elk, wild boar, lynx, wolf, and fox are to be found and you get a run for your money. Game birds include wood-grouse, blackcock, woodcock, pheasant, and partridge. The best hunting can be found in the Bieszczady and Carpathian Mountains, Białowieża Forest, Mazury, Augustów, and Koszalin.

Full details of gun licenses and rates for organized hunting trips can be obtained from Orbis.

ANGLING. The best places for quiet fishing in lovely surroundings are Western Pomerania (Białogard and Kołobrzeg), and the Mazurian Lakes in the neighborhood of Giżycko (Kamień, Stare Jabłonki, Paławki, Wegorzewo). There are over 47 kinds of fish to choose from—salmon, trout, chub, roach, sheatfish and pike. A crayfish hunt can be great fun, as can ice-hole angling in winter.

Foreign tourists will need to buy a fishing license valid for 14 days. There are also 7-day licenses for special angling grounds reserved for foreign tourists. Full details are available from Orbis.

RIDING. Poland has a stirring and ancient tradition of riding and horse-breeding (it even supplies the Arabs with Arabs) and a good way of seeing the countryside is from a saddle. It's becoming a very popular form of holiday, so riding centers tend to get booked up early. Biały Bór near Koszalin is situated in wooded, hilly country and also has indoor facilities. Racot near Poznań is set amid forests and lakes. It is one of the oldest studs in the country and has 800 Arab horses. Many riding holidays can be spent in old manor houses and palaces, as at Czerniejewo, Dłusko, Ptaszkowo, Sieraków, Iwno and Podkówka Leśna. The end of the riding season is marked by the traditional St. Hubert's Races (usually held in early November), which are only open to advanced riders as the courses are fairly tough.

Traveling in Poland

BY PLANE. LOT, the state airline, flies into 11 cities and towns in the country, as well as into Warsaw, whose airport Okecie is about ten miles south of the city and handles both international and domestic traffic. There are bus services into the city, as well as taxis. If your are intending to travel by internal flights, book as far in advance as possible, even before you arrive in the country.

BY TRAIN. Polish State Railways (PKP) suffered very badly during World War II and even now are still being rebuilt and modernized. Steam engines are widely used, but all the expresses are now either diesel or electric. As in most Comecon countries, the trains are well-patronized and provide the main method of long-distance travel. Seat reservation is mandatory on all expresses, but is advisable also for fast trains, especially at the peak holiday times, the 1st, 15th and 31st of July and August. Cost of reservation is 30 zł. To reserve your seat, go to the Polres office at the railway depot, or make use of any Orbis office. Remember lines are a Polish way of life—especially for rail tickets, so if you have not pre-booked and reserved your seat, turn up well in advance of departure time.

The *Polrail Pass* is an excellent buy and costs $20 for 8 days, $30 for 15, $40 for 21 and $50 for 30 (subject to change). First class travel is 50% more expensive and well worth the extra cost. Seats have to be reserved on express trains but Polrail Pass holders are not charged for this. The Pass can be purchased at Polish Tourist Offices overseas, or at Orbis exchange counters when entering Poland.

BY BUS. The state-run bus service *(PKS)* operates several long distance routes, but mainly as a feeder service for the railway system. It is cheap, always very crowded and probably best suited to the adventurous.

BY CAR. Poles drive on the right and the usual Continental rules of the road are observed. There is a speed limit of 90 kph (55 mph) on the open road and 50 kph (31 mph) in built-up areas. Drinking is absolutely prohibited and carries heavy penalties. In built-up areas, horn blowing is also prohibited.

Detailed information on the documents you will need if you're taking your own car into the country is given on page 21. Foreign tourists can only buy gasoline in exchange for gasoline coupons bought in foreign currency at the frontier only in batches of 40 liters. At presstime the cost was uncertain. Coupons are available for 94 and 78 octane, the first low, the second terrible. There is no limit on the amount of gasoline you can buy and unused coupons are refundable. Gas stations are situated in towns and along major routes, usually open from 6 to 10, but some are open 24 hours a day.

In case of accident or repair problems, contact the Polish Motoring Association, *PZM* (*Polski Zwiazek Motorowy*), ul. Krucza 14, Warsaw (tel. 29 62 52). PZM can also supply you with a list of gas stations, service centers and road maps; they have branches all over Poland. It is sensible to carry a spare parts kit with you.

A number of main European (E) routes cross Poland. They include E12 from West Germany through Prague to Wrocław, Łódź, Warsaw and Białystok; the E14 from Austria, through Czechoslovakia to Świnoujście and on to Ystad in Sweden; and the E8 from East Germany through Poznań, Warsaw and on to the USSR.

The main roads are maintained in good condition and motor traffic is sparse. But away from main routes, the roads tend to be narrow and cluttered with horse-drawn carts on country roads. Nevertheless, visitors find them acceptable and much more interesting than the main roads.

Car Hire. Cars are available for hire from *Avis* at Okecie international airport or through *Orbis* offices. High-season rates are from $15.40–$28.60 per day, according to car model, plus insurance and 16–22 cents per km, or $230 to $354 one week with unlimited mileage. Fly-drive arrangements are also available ex-UK through *Magic of Poland* and *Polorbis.*

BY TAXI. Taxis are cheap, starting at 27 zł and increasing by about 13 zł per km. Fares double after 11 P.M. They operate only from special taxi ranks and you sometimes have to wait a fairly long time.

HITCHHIKING. Poland is one of the few countries that does not frown on this method of travel. Hitchhikers can buy special books of coupons at border points, tourist information centers, etc., and, on obtaining a lift, give drivers the appropriate coupons covering the distance they plan to ride. Drivers who collect the largest number of coupons during the year actually receive prizes. A system of inexpensive accommodation for hitchhikers has also been evolved. Directing this unusual aspect of travel is the Hitchhiking Committee *(Komitet Autostopu),* ul. Narbutta 27a, Warsaw.

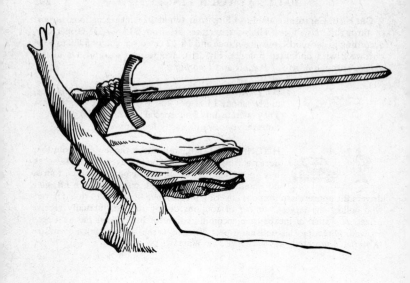

POLAND'S TROUBLED HISTORY

A Fierce Independence

Poland's geographical position between Eastern Germany and the Soviet Union has given it a history of almost continual war. It is roughly square in shape and about the size (312,700 square km./ 150,572 square miles) of New Mexico or the British Isles. As a result of the territorial changes and loss of life caused by World War II (over 6,000,000 Poles died, half of them Jews), the present population of 35,000,000 consists predominantly of Polish-speaking Roman Catholics; and, since the War was followed by an extended baby boom, over half are under 30—making Poland one of the most youthful countries in Europe. Every one of its major cities, with the exception of Cracow, had to be rebuilt after the wholesale destruction of the war. Particularly splendid restoration work has been done on Warsaw's Old Town and in Gdansk on the Baltic coast.

The Long Road to Independence

The modern Polish state emerged in the 10th century, when one of the Slavonic tribes, the Polanie, began to lord it over the other Slavs between the Vistula and Oder rivers. Their ruler, Mieszko I, who waged an almost life-long battle against the Germans, was the first Polish ruler to embrace Christianity (in 966). Thereafter, the borders of the Polish state advanced and receded under a succession of feudal rulers. Under Casimir the Great in the 14th century she became a major power, and subsequently under the Jagiellonian dynasty expanded to become one of the largest states in Europe. The 16th century was the golden age of economic and cultural development. After the death without heir of Sigismund II Augustus in 1572, there was a period of elective monarchy, the rulers including those of the Swedish Vasa dynasty, during which successful military campaigns were conducted against the strengthening power of Muscovy.

In 1683 John III Sobieski defeated the Turks at the gates of Vienna and rescued Christian Europe from the Ottoman onslaught. Christianity remembers the debt of gratitude it owes the Poles for this victory, although at the time Poland's neighbors repaid it by taking advantage of her internal weakness, the result of an over-progressive democracy in which any one member of the Diet could break up the sitting by the use of the famous *liberum veto*. By 1795, despite the rich revival of its economic and cultural life under Stanislaus August Poniatowski, the last of her kings, Poland had been more or less wiped off the map of Europe as Russia, Prussia and Austria carved it up between themselves in the First, Second and Third Partitions.

Polish patriotism burned hot beneath the surface however. Love of freedom drove many to fight in other countries' wars for freedom. Polish military commander Kazimierz Pułaski gave his life for the colonial cause in the American Revolution, while General Tadeusz Kościuszko, who distinguished himself in the American Revolution, later returned to lead an abortive but heroic uprising in his native Poland.

During more than a century of political oblivion, when economically the country began to poke its head out of the Middle Ages, the Poles tried repeatedly to regain their independence in a series of uprisings culminating in the abortive January Uprising of 1863–64. Thereafter the Poles abandoned the armed struggle, biding their time and positively trying to resist the Russification and Prussification of their dismembered country. But the outbreak of World War I saw them ready—armed Polish legions had been formed to take up the struggle again.

Independence finally did come, in 1919, but it was not to last for long. On September 1 1939 the Nazi invasion began, triggering off World War II, during which Hitler turned Warsaw into a martyred city, exterminated over 6,000,000 Polish citizens, deporting 2,000,000 to Germany as forced labor and devastated huge areas of the country. During the war Polish legions fought with remarkable bravery on many fronts abroad (Monte Cassino, Battle of Britain, Narvik, Tobruk, Alamein and scores of others).

But when the smoke of war cleared, it rapidly became apparent that the independence Poland had enjoyed in the inter-war years had been little more than a temporary interlude and that nearly all her extraordinary sufferings had been in vain. Under the none too deft prompting of her Russian 'liberators', the Polish Committee of National Liberation proclaimed Poland a 'People's Republic' and Soviet-style Communism was imposed throughout the country.

Devastated Poland in the years immediately after the war faced enormous difficulties. Chief among them was the problem of finding food and shelter for her 28,000,000 inhabitants as well as rebuilding towns and industries from scratch. Industry and agriculture were nationalized on a large scale under the new Communist government while at the same time the affairs of the Church, an institution of central importance both spiritually and morally to the country's deeply Catholic population, came increasingly under government scrutiny. Discontent became widespread and in 1956 the government was forced to retreat in the face of vocal recriminations from under paid workers, over-collectivized peasants and hitherto largely muzzled intellectuals. A short-lived two-day demonstration against the government in Poznan in June 1956, followed by the decisive October Days of the fall, resulted in the collapse of the government and the elevation of Wladyslaw Gomułka to First Secretary.

His arrival in power saw a measure of liberalization, particularly in the affairs of the Church. But during the sixties, it became clear that the new era many had hoped for was very much more apparent than real and that the actual nature of the government was fundamentally unchanged. Events came to a head when highly unpopular and sudden food price increases just before the 1970 Christmas holidays inflamed the populace. Demonstrations and riots took place in some cities with heavy loss of life, particularly in Gdansk. The government was again forced to step down, to be replaced by that led by Edward Gierek. Further liberalization of a sort followed, accompanied by a massive program of foreign borrowing designed, rather optimistically, to boost the country's almost wholly moribund economy. But as the early years of liberalization under Gomułka were followed by increasing oppression and food price rises, so too the apparently reformist government of Gierek became steadily more repressive. By 1976 demonstrations against further rises in the price of food flared again and small pockets of political opposition to the government began to form, albeit somewhat clandestinely.

It was from these sources that the Solidarity movement was born, formed in the Gdansk shipyards in the heady days of August 1980 and heralding a popular upheaval unprecedented in post-war Eastern Europe. However, its hey-day was shortlived, and following the steadily rising alarm of the Soviet Union at the growing demands of—and obvious popularity enjoyed by—Solidarity, Martial Law was declared by the Polish Government in December 1981. Solidarity was promptly disbanded and its leaders imprisoned.

Poland Today

During both the period when Solidarity was at its height and following the imposition of Martial Law, the Polish economy continued to slump disastrously, and no amount of Western aid has been able to reverse its decline. This economic malaise, coupled to the inevitable atmosphere of tension that accompanied the events of December 1981, have conspired to deaden the natural gregariousness of many Poles. They are a people who love to eat and drink, as the bustling cafes and restaurants of Warsaw once eloquently attested. In recent years, discos and nightclubs also became popular. But legal restrictions and the continuing fall in living standards have made these activities the preserve of a tiny elite.

But in many ways, preconceptions one may have regarding Eastern European countries have to be drastically revised in the case of Poland. There are some successful private enterprises in the form of shops, restaurants and light industries, for example, as well as a sort of semi-private compromise by which a Pole can rent premises from a State company and is then entirely responsible for its operation and profits. However, it would be a mistake to imagine that operators of these *Spolem,* as they are known, are rich men.

As in other Eastern European countries, the Poles are avid culture-vultures. They pack theaters to watch productions of Molière, Shaw, Beckett, Miller, and Albee. Theaters, opera, and the cinema are subsidized by the government, resulting in comparatively low ticket prices. Concert halls and art exhibits attract crowds in the big cities. Poets are pointed out at parties as VIPs, and their work widely quoted by waiters, taxi-drivers and fellow-poets.

In the province of sex, too, Poles have wandered a little from the well-beaten Socialist path. Polish pictorials and posters go in for more well-displayed curves, and their films lean towards more socialistically taboo subjects than in other Communist countries.

Urban life is, however, by no means the whole story, as anyone traveling through Poland in a car or by train will soon realize. The Polish peasantry is religious, conservative, and now mostly uncollectivized, with 80 percent of the land in private hands. Rural life remains centered on the home, and work in the fields and the raising of animals is still done in fairly traditional—not to say hidebound—ways. Working horses, in the fields and as a means of transportation, are seen to an extent now unknown in much of the rest of Eastern Europe.

In the day-to-day frame of present Polish existence, there are several bright spots of which Poles generally approve; vacation facilities are provided for workers; free medical care is universal. With more than one-third of the population under 15 years of age, Poland devotes much of her effort to education. Today there is virtually no illiteracy. Free education prevails to university level, with students in institutions of higher learning receiving accommodations and, frequently, grants.

Nurtured on Western culture, the Poles still regard themselves as a link between East and West, their strong belief in their bond with Western Christianity being given a great moral boost by the election of the first Polish Pope in history.

POLISH CULTURE

Not Only Chopin

Polish culture is the product of one thousand years of tradition, the country's geographical position and its turbulent, often tragic, history. Her Slavonic origins combined with strong Western and Oriental influences have contributed to making Polish culture unique in its richness among the Eastern European nations.

In the early days of the Polish state, Christianity (brought to Poland in 966) and Western thought represented by foreign clergy, had to fight to reach people who continued to live in tribal communities, holding on to their old religious beliefs and Slav rituals.

The political expansionism of Poland in the Middle Ages turned it into a virtual empire with the highest level of civilization in Eastern Europe. It also made her subject to cultural influences from the Czechs, Germans, French and Italians, as well as Tartars and Turks. Some of these have continued throughout Poland's history. Italian tradition, for example, is clearly visible in Polish architecture, especially of the Renaissance and baroque periods. Education and science in 18th-century Poland owed much to France, as later did the Polish legal system. In the 19th century close links developed with Germany and France in the field of literature and music.

Although often acting as a defender of the Roman Catholic faith, Poland was also a pioneer of religious tolerance at a time when many European nations were persecuting dissidents.

However, the most distinguishing feature of Polish culture is its national character. Foreign influences were never strong enough to prevent the simultaneous development of individual Polish forms and ideas, and this can be seen in the architecture, as well as in the visual arts, literature, theater and music. Poland retained her language and cultural identity despite more than a 100 years of intensive Russification and Prussification during the 19th century; and she also survived the outrages of World War II when the Nazis set out to destroy the Polish people and their cultural heritage.

Music

Polish music does not begin or end with Chopin, although for many people his art represents the very symbol of Poland. Chopin's piano compositions take their roots and inspiration from Polish folk music with its characteristic dance rhythms of the krakowiak, mazurek, oberek and polonaise. These rhythms have been incorporated in the works of many Polish composers, ever since the nationalist movement began in Polish 18th-century art as a reaction against the political enslavement of the country.

Folk music influenced the 19th-century composer, Stanisław Moniuszko, generally recognized as the father of Polish national opera (*Halka, Hrabina* and *Straszny Dwór*). It was also an inspiration to the virtuoso violinist and composer Henryk Wieniawski (1835–1880), and for the most outstanding Polish composer of the first half of the 20th century, Karol Szymanowski.

The reputation of contemporary Polish music is very high indeed, and Polish composers enjoy a large following abroad. Among the leading figures in the world of music are Witold Lutosławski, who often conducts his own compositions in concert halls the world over, Krzysztof Penderecki, the creator of monumental oratorios; *St. Luke's Passion, Dies Irae, Cosmogony* and *Utrenja,* and Tadeusz Baird, who has composed symphonic music, works for voice and instruments and an opera, *Tomorrow,* based on a story by Joseph Conrad.

Poland has also produced a number of outstanding musicians—pianists, violinists, singers and conductors. Among the best known are Ignacy Paderewski and Artur Rubinstein, but there is a whole generation of young and exceptionally gifted musicians led by the most brilliant of them all—Krystian Zimmerman, who at the age of 18 won the first prize at the 1975 International Chopin Piano Competition.

Universality is a major feature of Polish musical life today when state patronage allows music to extend beyond the metropolis to the small towns and rural areas. A wide network of musical institutions covers the whole country. Every major Polish city has its own Philharmonic Orchestra (there are 12 in all), and seven symphony orchestras tour the remaining larger towns. There are also three excellent radio orchestras and some 20 permanent opera and operetta theaters. A visitor to Warsaw should not miss the Grand Opera Theater. This splendid neo-classical building was destroyed by the Germans and has been faithfully reconstructed since the war.

Poland takes an avid interest in international musical life and has long been a meeting place for musicians from other countries. Four major international events traditionally take place in Poland. These are the Frederic Chopin International Piano Competition (held in Warsaw every five years), The Henryk Wieniawski International Violin Competition (held in Poznań every five years), The International Festival of Contemporary Music 'Warsaw Autumn' (held annually in Warsaw), and The International Jazz Jamboree Festival (held in Warsaw every October).

Art and Architecture

When the war ended in 1945, the whole of Warsaw and a large part of the rest of Poland lay in ruins. Previous wars—and Polish history is full of foreign invasions, uprisings and struggles for independence—had also contributed to the cumulative destruction of much of the country's art and architecture.

To find the best preserved of Poland's architecture, one should visit the old city of Cracow with its medieval and Renaissance buildings and a splendid royal castle—the Wawel. In other cities—for example Warsaw, Gdańsk, and Poznań—a program of extensive and painstaking reconstruction has brought some of their finest monuments back to life.

Certainly stately homes and palaces have survived almost intact (Łańcut is a good example) and most of them now serve as museums and art galleries. Others, like the neo-classical Łazienki Palace in Warsaw and the early baroque Palace in Wilanów, just outside the capital, both destroyed in the last war, have been completely rebuilt in their original styles. Apart from a remarkable collection of old Polish and foreign paintings and furniture, the Wilanów Palace houses a poster museum, unique in Poland and one of very few in Europe. Posters, which cover all aspects of political, cultural, and social life of the country, are one of the most interesting forms of Polish contemporary graphic art. They are also an art form most easily accessible to the general public.

20th-century Poland has produced a number of notable avant-garde and traditional painters. Their works can be seen in the National Museum in Warsaw and Poznań, and in the Museum of Contemporary Arts in Łódź. The greatest Polish modern sculptor, Xavery Dunikowski, has his own museum in Warsaw called Królikarnia, and there are also sculpture galleries in the Łazienki and Wilanów Parks.

In addition, numerous art galleries in cities and large towns specialize in exhibitions of modern painters, graphic artists, and sculptors. The best known of them is Zachęta Gallery in Warsaw, where the International Poster Biennale and other events are held.

Folk Art

Despite the urbanization and industrialization that has taken place since 1945, Poland has retained a rich and lively tradition of folk art, which is second to none in Europe. Hand-woven tapestries, wood carvings, pottery, paper cutouts, embroidery, and paintings on glass, are still produced by artists and artisans, not only for collectors and the state-owned chain of CEPELIA shops, which specialize in traditional Polish arts, but for everyday use by ordinary people.

Polish folk costumes, known to millions from the dazzling performances by the Mazowsze and Śląsk Song and Dance Ensembles, are still part of the wardrobe of many Polish peasants. The town of Łowicz in central Poland and, above all, the highland villages in the south, take on a festive look on Sundays and other holidays when streets are full of men, women and children dressed in their colorful traditional costumes.

Polish authorities make considerable efforts to protect the finest examples of folk art around the country and wherever possible to preserve them in their natural environment. This applies equally to traditional architecture and decorative arts, to furniture making and pottery and to the extremely rich Polish musical folklore.

There is an abundance of subsidized song and dance companies devoted to preservation of old musical traditions. Festivals and competitions are organized to keep alive the interest in Polish folklore. A visitor to Zakopane in early autumn should not miss a chance to see one such event—the annual Tatra Autumn Festival—which brings together folk musicians, singers, dancers, artists and craftsmen from many regions of the country.

Theater

Several things come to mind when one considers the Polish theater today. Compared with that of, let's say, Britain or the USA, Polish theater maintains a unique balance between national and foreign works and between its classical and avant-garde repertoire.

The second characteristic feature is the high status and popularity which the theater enjoys in society. There are more than 70 professional dramatic companies 26 of which go on tour. Their productions, which average about 400 a year, are seen by some 8,000,000 spectators, including viewers of Poland's acclaimed TV drama slot.

The third feature that distinguishes contemporary Polish theater is the exceptionally high standard of its stage design. On the whole, Polish stage designers make an equal and sometimes greater contribution to theatrical productions than that made by directors, playwrights or actors. Some designers take on a dual or even triple rôle, perhaps designing, directing, and writing. Jósef Szajna is one example of this versatility, since as well as being a painter, he is stage designer, director, and manager of his own theater, the Teatr Studio in Warsaw. Tadeusz Kantor—also a painter, as well as an actor, founder and the soul of his own avant-garde theater Cricot in Cracow—is another.

However, an artist who has gained the highest international reputation for his work in the theater is Jerzy Grotowski, creator and director of the Polish Laboratory Theater of Wrocław. Following in the footsteps of Stanisławski, the great Russian theoretician, Grotowski places the actor at the heart of theatrical spectacle. His austere and serious theater, often described as 'poor' and 'essential', places enormous demands on actor and public alike, but it gives them in return a unique spiritual and artistic experience. Few of the spectators who were lucky enough to see the Laboratory Theater in Grotowski's *Apocalypsis cum Figuris* or *The Constant Prince,* will ever be able to forget the powerful imagery, unique use of sound, superbly controlled acting, and the almost religious atmosphere which Grotowski created.

Because of its severe discipline and intellectual emphasis the Laboratory Theater of Wrocław has never aimed at mass audiences. The companies with the largest following are those who regularly reach out for great romantic repertoire without neglecting good contemporary plays.

Among the most outstanding theater companies in Poland, are Teatr Narodowy (The National Theater) in Warsaw, which is the oldest public theater in Poland (first opened in 1764) and under the directorship of Adam Hanuszkiewicz has presented some of the most memorable productions of great Polish romantic authors—Mickiewicz (*Forefathers' Eve*), Słowacki (*Beniowski, Kordian*), and Krasiński (*Un-Divine Comedy*). Teatr Współczesny (Contemporary Theater) in Warsaw, directed by Erwin Axer, has made its name with such productions as *Who's Afraid of Virginia Woolf?* by Albee, *Inadmissible Evidence* by Osborne, and *Ubu Roi* by Jarry. Teatr Stary of Cracow, the second oldest public stage in Poland (established 1799) became the leader of the Polish theater in the 1960s, thanks to its exceptional actors and directors, particularly Jerzy Jarocki and Konrad Swinarski.

Jarocki was the most successful interpreter of plays by Witkacy, a long-neglected Polish writer, artist, and philosopher of the between-the-wars era, who only now begins to be recognized as a forerunner of the theater of the absurd. Jarocki was also the first director of most new works by Tadeusz Różewicz, leading Polish contemporary poet and playwright (*The Card-Index, Witnesses or Our Little Stabilization,* and others).

The art of Konrad Swinarski, who died tragically in a plane crash in 1975, has often been compared with that of Peter Brook. Swinarski was, among others, the creator of such outstanding productions as *A Midsummer Night's Dream* by Shakespeare and *Marat-Sade* by Peter Weiss.

More recently, Andrzej Wajda, internationally known for his films, has joined Teatr Stary as a guest director and produced acclaimed stage adaptations of works by Dostoyevsky (*The Possessed* and *The Idiot*).

At least two other leading Polish companies should be mentioned here. Teatr Wielki in Lódź and Teatr Wybrzeże in Gdańsk. The director of the Teatr Wielki, Kazimierz Dejmek, has been equally successful in producing a Polish medieval mystery play (*The Story of the Glorious Resurrection of Our Lord*) and staging avant-garde plays, including comedies by Sławomir Mrożek, perhaps the best known and most frequently performed contemporary Polish playwright (*Tango, The Emigrés, The Police*).

Teatr Wybrzeże, situated in Gdańsk on the Polish coast, has rediscovered for the theater a number of unjustly forgotten Polish authors. In doing so, it has made headlines with the world premiere of the stage adaptation of Joyce's *Ulysses* and the extraordinary interpretations of *Waiting for Godot* by Beckett and *Tiny Alice* by Albee.

Last but not least there is Poland's chief theatrical export—the Pantomime Theater of Wrocław, directed by Henryk Tomaszewski. It's outstanding because of its artistic qualities, its technique and dramatic contents.

Cinema

The fortunes of Polish cinema have waxed and waned as in other countries. There has been an active film industry in Poland since 1909, but although early Polish films, particularly those in the '30s, were popular at home, they achieved little artistic success abroad. The outbreak of World War II interrupted Polish film-making for six long years and later, during the Stalinist era, it was crippled by strict censorship and artistic and ideological stereotypes. With few exceptions (*The Last Stage, Boys from Barska Street*) it wasn't until the mid-'50s that the Polish cinema erupted with an unprecedented wealth of talent.

Andrzej Wajda's heroic trilogy—*A Generation, Canal,* and *Ashes and Diamonds*—was the first in a series of films that gained world-wide recognition for Polish cinema. Apart from becoming a must for every film addict, *Ashes and Diamonds* made an international star of the late Zbigniew Cybulski, the most popular actor Poland has ever produced.

Among other outstanding film-makers of this period were Andrzej Munk (*Eroica, Bad Luck, Passenger*) and Wojciech Has (*Farewells, Eve Wants to Sleep*) who were joined in the '60s by younger graduates of the now famous State Film School in Łódź—Roman Polański and Jerzy Skolimowski. After a very successful debut in Poland, Polański and Skolimowski decided to pursue their careers in the West, as did another successful Polish director, Walerian Borowczyk.

By the early '70s, the impetus of Polish cinema weakened, although Andrzej Wajda did make several films (*Landscape after the Battle,* and *The Wedding*). His most recent works—*Man of Iron, Man of Marble,* and *Without Anaesthetic*—as well as the prize-winning films of the younger directors, particularly Krzysztof Zanussi (*Structure of Crystal, Family Life, Camouflage*), suggest that Polish cinema is entering a new period of revival.

POLISH FOOD AND DRINK

Fish, Mushrooms and Herbs

Poland's shifting borders and history of foreign domination have, not unnaturally, left their mark on the Polish cuisine. But though there are Austrian, French, Italian, and Russian echoes in some of their dishes, the Poles have managed to produce a specifically Polish cuisine characterized by the use of certain typical ingredients such as dill, marjoram, caraway seeds, and wild mushrooms (gathered in enormous quantities and varieties by large family contingents during the autumn months). The mushrooms (*grzyby*) are dried or pickled for winter use, used fresh as a garnish for soups and meat dishes or as a vegetable in their own right. Sour cream, which is inexpensive, is another hallmark of Polish cooking, being frequently added to soups, sauces, and braised meats.

In Poland, as in many countries, there is a sharp distinction between the food you get in a restaurant and what the ordinary people eat; the closest you'll get to the latter is in villages and market towns, where delicious *barszcz* (beetroot soup) is served, along with sausages, cabbage, potatoes, sour cream, *czarny chleb* (rye bread) and beer.

Starters

Polish meals start with przekąska, which, if you're in a smart restaurant might include marinated fish in sour cream, pike in aspic, stuffed

306

carp, herrings (*śledźiki*) in various guises, pig's knuckles (*nózki*), Polish sausage (*kiełbasa*)—like the long, thin and highly spiced *kabanos* or the hunter's sausage (*myśliwska*) made with pork and game—cheese spreads garnished with chives (a good one is *bryndza,* made of ewe's milk and not unlike Greek *feta*), various kinds of pâtés (*pasztety*) and galantines, as well as tasty Polish smoked bacon and ham (*szynka*). Good hot appetizers to try are *kołduny* (beef or lamb turnovers served in hot bouillon) and *kulebiak* (a large mushroom and cabbage pasty).

To a Pole a meal without soup *(zupa)* is almost unthinkable, and a Polish soup can be an awesomely rich and filling knife-and-fork affair, thickened with sour cream or made even more substantial by the addition of pearl barley, Cracow groats, noodles *(łazanki),* dumplings *(uszka),* stuffed with mushrooms or meat, suet balls *(pulpety)* and potato dumplings of various kinds *(pyzy* and *kopytka).* Apart from the ubiquitous *barszcz* (one form of which is traditionally served during the Christmas Eve supper with mushroom-stuffed *uszka),* the soups you're most likely to come across are *kapuśniak* (sauerkraut), *kartoflanka* (potato), *grochówka* (pea soup, often served with croutons), *krupnik* (pearl barley), *grzybowa* (mushroom) and *jarzynowa* (vegetable).

Clear soups, such as *barszcz* or *rosół* (beef bouillon), are often served in cups, accompanied by small hot pasties stuffed with meat or cabbage *(paszteciki* and *kapuśniaczki).* In restaurants specializing in Old Polish cookery (currently springing up all over the place) you'll find traditional *żur* (sour rye or oat soup), *czarnina* (literally, 'black soup', made with fresh blood, bones, giblets and dried prunes or cherries!), *zupa piwna* (beer soup) and *zalewajka* (onion soup). *Chłodnik,* which literally means 'cooler', is a delicious cold sour-cream soup with crayfish. In summer, sorrel soup *(szczawiowa),* garnished with hard-boiled eggs, is very popular, as are the rather unusual cold summer soups made with puréed fruits such as strawberries, raspberries, apples, cherries or blueberries, and thickened with sour cream.

Meat Dishes

Supplies of meat (*mieso*) tend to be rather erratic in Poland; the best goes to the first-class hotels, so cheaper restaurants have been forced to institute one meatless day a week. Pork (*wieprzowina*) and beef (*wołowina*) are used a great deal, as is game (*dziczyzna*), which the Poles are very fond of, in particular wild duck with apple (*kaczka*), hare in sour cream (*zajac*) and roast venison (*sarnina*). Roast pork loin (*pieczony schab*) is a great treat, generally served with pickled plums and sauerkraut and apple salad.

Other popular Polish dishes are *zrazy zawijane* (mushroom-stuffed beefsteak rolls in sour cream served with boiled rice or *kasza*—buckwheat groats), *golabki* (cabbage leaves stuffed with minced beef and rice) and Polish-style *flaki,* a far cry from English tripe and onions, being seasoned with ginger, nutmeg, marjoram and garnished with Parmesan cheese.

The menu will invariably include *bigos,* which must rank as the national dish of Poland. Made with sauerkraut, fresh cabbage, onions and a variety of leftover meats (pork, game, sausage and smoked bacon) it was once traditionally served at hunt meetings and allegedly improves with each reheating (optimum flavor is supposedly reached the seventh time round).

Homegrown Vegetables

Frozen or packaged foods are not popular in Poland, so ingredients are usually fresh and not ruined by chemical additives. Typical vegetable accompaniments (*jarzyny*) and salads (*sałatki*) include sauerkraut garnished with caraway seeds (*kiszona kapusta*), pickled dill cucumbers (*ogórki kwaszone*), grated beets with horseradish (*ćwikła*) and sliced fresh cucumbers garnished with dill and served in sour cream or yogurt (*mizeria*). Grated potato pancakes (*placki kartoflane*), smothered in sour cream, are absolutely gorgeous—a meal in themselves. *Pierogi* (pockets of noodle dough stuffed with meat, cabbage or cheese and potatoes) can be a bit heavy, but are consumed in vast quantities by every Pole worth his salt.

The Ubiquitous Herring

Poland is a great country for fish (*ryba*), particularly the freshwater variety, which is prepared in a way Westerners may find rather unusual. Try *karp w galarecie* (carp served in a sweet and sour jellied sauce) and *szczupak po Polsku* (poached pike with horseradish and sour cream sauce). Crayfish (*raki*), boiled and served in a green dill and sour cream sauce, are also extremely popular. The Baltic Sea provides the Poles with cod (*dorsz*) and, of course, the herring (*śledź*), which they serve in every way imaginable. Salted herring fillet, rolled up tight and served with pickles and onions, features as a starter on most menus, and is traditionally associated with Lent (the high point of the last carnival dance on Shrove Tuesday is marked by the bringing in of a mock herring on a stick).

Refreshing Desserts

Most full-scale Polish meals are best rounded off with a refreshing stewed fruit *kompot,* but if you're feeling adventurous (and not counting the calories) the things to try are fruit or milk *kisiel* (a very popular dessert thickened with potato starch giving it the consistency of a jelly), *knedle* (dumplings stuffed with plums or apples), *pierożki* (dumplings with blueberries, cherries or prunes), *naleśniki* (pancakes with fruit or cheese), *racuszki* (sour-milk pancakes) and *leniwe pierogi* (poached cheese dumplings, which can also appear as a light main course for lunch). *Kutia* is a traditional Christmas Eve dessert made with whole wheat grains, ground poppy seeds and honey.

A Necessary Accompaniment

The national drink of Poland is undoubtedly vodka *(wódka),* which is drunk chilled in staggering quantities before, during and after virtually every meal. *Wyborowa* is the best standard vodka, but you shouldn't leave the country without trying some of the many flavored varieties, such as *żubrówka* (bison grass), *tarniówka* (sloe-plum), *śliwowica* (prune), *jarzębiak* (rowan berry) and *pieprzówka* (vodka with ground white pepper—apparently the local cure for an upset stomach). *Krupnik,* vodka with honey and spices, and *miód* (mead) are extremely popular, as are cherry cordials, such as *wiśniówka* (sweet) and *wiśniak* (dry), which the Poles often make at home on a base of 96° spirits.

Western drinks, such as whiskey, gin or brandy, can be had in most bars, but are extremely expensive. Wine *(wino)* is drunk, but again is imported and expensive. The best bottled beer *(piwo)* is *Żywiec,* a fairly strong lager-type beer.

Chief among the non-alcoholic beverages, apart from Pepsi-Cola and Coca-Cola which the young are fairly hooked on, is tea *(herbata).* But it's usually drunk black or with lemon—the Poles don't really understand how anyone could possibly drink tea with milk. A close second is coffee *(kawa)* which is generally served with rich delectable cakes and pastries *(torty* and *ciastka).*

Traditional Pastries

Don't leave Poland without trying delicious *pączki* (jam doughnuts sold in most coffee shops and much in evidence on the last Thursday before Lent—appropriately enough named 'Fat Thursday'). Though available all year round, many cakes and pastries are traditionally associated with either Christmas or Easter—*makowiec* (poppy seed roll), *sernik* (cheese cake), *babka wielkanocna* (Easter yeast cake with raisins), *mazurki* (flaky finger biscuits) and *chrusty* (twiggy Shrove Tuesday cookies fried like doughnuts and sprinkled with vanilla sugar).

[handwritten annotations] 1,200,000 pop. 800,000 were Jewish

[handwritten] I stretch Synagogue only / over 300 churches etc / altars organs / relics

[handwritten] The only section not destroyed was where Nazis had their headquarters — so old 19th cent. architecture now surfaces / Bullet holes / 200 acre park / Roses & Chopin

[handwritten] LKB / July 6 '89 / 1st Prime min of Poland 1918 / Paderewsky died '41 buried in Arlington

WARSAW
The Phoenix City

In January 1945, Warsaw—Poland's capital since the early 17th century—was a heart-breaking, barren, depopulated desert of ruin and rubble, a prostrate victim of systematic Nazi destruction. Only a third of its pre-war population remained; of its 500,000 Jews, some 200 were still alive. But Warsaw's survivors, determined to rebuild their ancient city, set about the task so energetically that today the hollow shells of buildings have disappeared and there is a new Warsaw of a million-plus inhabitants. Across what was once a giant construction site, stretch wide avenues, bright new pastel apartment houses, handsome buildings, broad parks, and painstakingly accurate replicas of Warsaw's old quarters. Historically, Warsaw is a relatively new city, as you will be told by an ultra-conservative Cracovian, who will dismiss the 13th-century city's inhabitants as nouveau-riche, wheeler-dealers; all in strictly friendly rivalry of course. The capital of the Duchy of Mazovia until 1526, Warsaw was in that year incorporated into the Kingdom of Poland when the last duke died without an heir. From then on its prosperity was assured and in 1611, after Wawel Castle in Cracow had burnt down and the king transferred his court here, it became the capital (the king also found that it was a much better place from which to keep a wary eye on the Swedes marauding on the Baltic Sea).

[handwritten] Warsaw old city — the largest reconstruction in EUROPE

300 sq mecha *170' tall* *(? in Moscow?)*

With ironic humor, Warsaw citizens will tell you that the best vantage point from which to admire their rebuilt city is from the top of the 37-story Palace of Culture and Science on pl. Defilad (Parade Square). Why? Because it's the only spot from which you can avoid looking at the Palace of Culture and Science—a wedding-cake-skyscraper gift from Stalin. Built in 'Stalin-Gothic' style, it houses an impressive number of theaters, museums, swimming pools, libraries, restaurants, a cellar nightclub and, of course, the Academy of Science. From this ~~68~~-foot (234-meter) pinnacle you can see the river Vistula to the east, with two of its bridges, the Ślasko–Dabrowski and the Poniatowskiego, crossing to the Praga side of the city.

790

Praga was the poor quarter of Warsaw up until the war, housing the working and artisan classes. In the massive changes that followed the war the area was completely rebuilt, and despite the introduction of new industry and housing estates it has managed to retain a specific character of its own. If you cross into Praga by the bridge near Rynek Starego Miasta, you come to the Zoological Gardens; cross by the Poniatowskiego bridge to get to the giant Zieleniecka stadium. While on the subject of bridges, get a look at the 'Łazienki Thoroughfare', a freeway system of loops, twirls and curlicues connecting left and right bank Warsaw, its edges blurred with banks of trees and flowers. The people of Warsaw are inordinately proud of it and speak of it with a curious degree of affection.

city is 700 yr old — not oldest in Poland.

14 colleges + universities/y

The Old Town

Visit on foot —

The rebuilding of the historic Old Town district of Warsaw, situated on an escarpment on the left bank of the Vistula, is a real phoenix-risen-from-the-ashes story. Post-war architects, determined to get it absolutely as it was before, turned to old prints, photographs in family albums and paintings, in particular the detailed views of the 18th-century Bernardo Bellotto (the nephew of Canaletto). This eliminated some of the later, less attractive buildings, but resulted in a curious back-to-front situation, since some of Bellotto's views were painted not from real life but from sketches of projects that were never realized. Whatever your feelings about reproduction architecture—and there's an awful lot of it in Warsaw—it seems to have worked here. The warm, pastel colors have 'aged' attractively, and the atmosphere is further enhanced by the fact that the Old Town is closed to all traffic except horse-drawn cabs and electric buggies.

The narrow houses, little winding streets and numerous churches cluster round a living replica of the city's old market place—the cobble-stoned Rynek Starego Miasta—with its pretty house fronts, wrought-iron grillwork and steep tiled roofs, all charmingly uneven. The old Town Hall that once stood in the middle of the square was pulled down in the early 19th century; it was not replaced and today the square is full of open-air cafés, tubs of flowering plants, and earnest guided tourists. The whole is a sort of cleaned-up version of Montmartre, with the inevitable art students displaying their talents in and around the square throughout the summer.

1971 1st reconstruction started.

August II of Saxon dynasty had 280 children he recognized as his

Fiats manufactured in Poland — Cheapest $1500 U.S. Gas is rationed 10-15 gal/month.

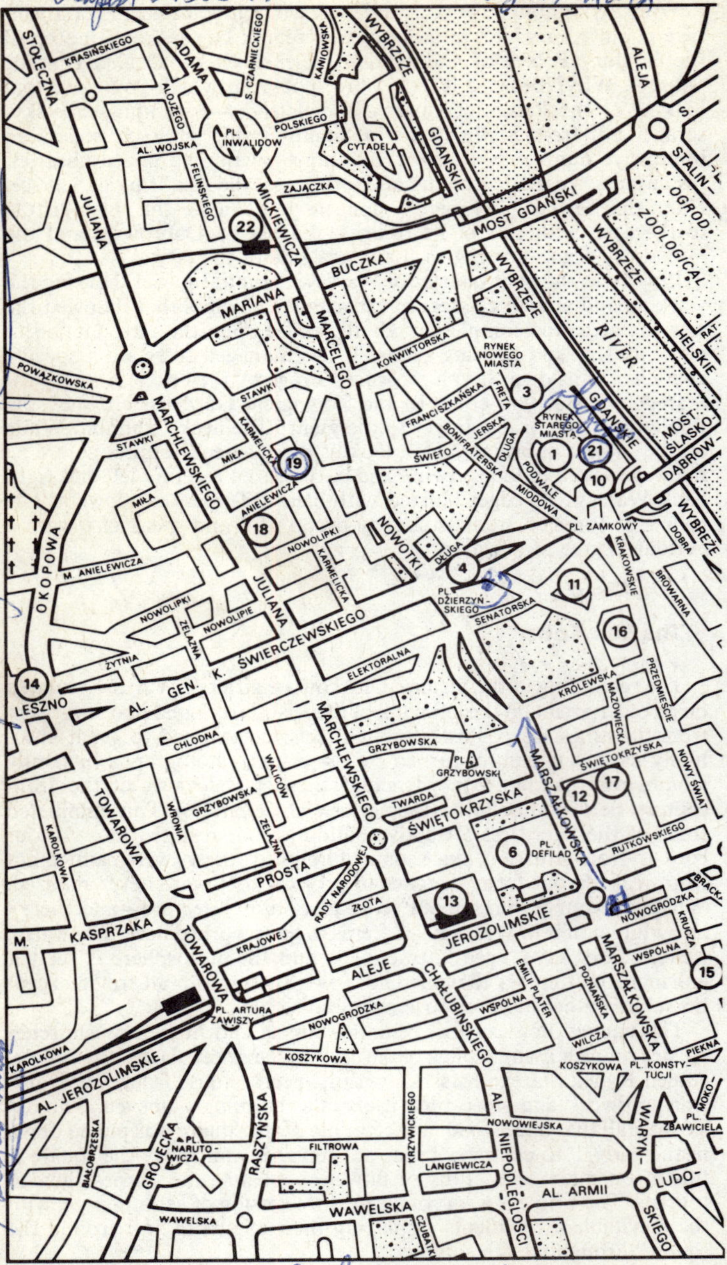
STOŁECZNA
KRASIŃSKIEGO
ADAMA
ALOJZEGO
S. CZARNIECKIEGO
KANIOWSKA
WYBRZEŻE
GDAŃSKIE
PL. INWALIDÓW
AL. WOJSKA
POLSKIEGO
CYTADELA
FELIŃSKIEGO
ZAJĄCZKA
J.
MICKIEWICZA
JULIANA
MOST GDAŃSKI
ALEJA
STALIN-
OGRÓD ZOOLOGICAL
BUCZKA
MARIANA
MARCELEGO
WYBRZEŻE
RIVER
HELSKIE
POWĄZKOWSKA
KONWIKTORSKA
RYNEK NOWEGO MIASTA
FRETA
STAWKI
FRANCISZKAŃSKA
RYNEK STAREGO MIASTA
GDAŃSKIE
MOST ŚLĄSKO-DĄBROW-
KARMELICKA
BONIFRATERSKA
JERSKA
DŁUGA
ŚWIĘTO-
MIŁA
PODWALE
MIODOWA
MARCHLEWSKIEGO
ANIELEWICZA
PL. ZAMKOWY
WYBRZEŻE
DOBRA
NOWOLIPKI
NOWOTKI
DŁUGA
KRAKOWSKIE
BROWARNA
OKOPOWA
M. ANIELEWICZA
PL. DZIERŻYŃSKIEGO
SENATORSKA
NOWOLIPIE
ŻELAZNA
JULIANA
ŚWIERCZEWSKIEGO
ŻYTNIA
ELEKTORALNA
PRZEDMIEŚCIE
LESZNO
AL. GEN. K.
KRÓLEWSKA
MAZOWIECKA
CHŁODNA
GRZYBOWSKA
ŚWIĘTOKRZYSKA
NOWY ŚWIAT
PL. GRZYBOWSKI
MARSZAŁKOWSKA
WALICÓW
TOWAROWA
WRONIA
TWARDA
ŚWIĘTOKRZYSKA
KAROLKOWA
ŻELAZNA
PL. DEFILAD
RUTKOWSKIEGO
PROSTA
RADY NARODOWEJ
ZŁOTA
BRACKA
KASPRZAKA
TOWAROWA
JEROZOLIMSKIE
NOWOGRODZKA
KRUCZA
M.
KRAJOWEJ
ALEJE
CHAŁUBIŃSKIEGO
EMILII PLATER
POZNAŃSKA
WSPÓLNA
PL. ARTURA ZAWISZY
WSPÓLNA
NOWOGRODZKA
KAROLKOWA
WILCZA
PIĘKNA
KOSZYKOWA
KOSZYKOWA
PL. KONSTYTUCJI
AL. JEROZOLIMSKIE
MOKO-
RASZYŃSKA
KRZYWICKIEGO
AL.
WARYŃSKIEGO
PL. ZBAWICIELA
BIAŁOBRZESKA
PL. NARUTOWICZA
GRÓJECKA
NOWOWIEJSKA
FILTROWA
LANGIEWICZA
NIEPODLEGŁOŚCI
AL. ARMII LUDO-
WAWELSKA
WAWELSKA
CZUBATKI
1
3
4
6
10
11
12
13
14
15
16
17
18
19
21
22

Hotel on main St of city — across from church

Jewish community here just in front of Belgian embassy

Jewish museum directly beside building under construction that was forced to stop

because [illegible]

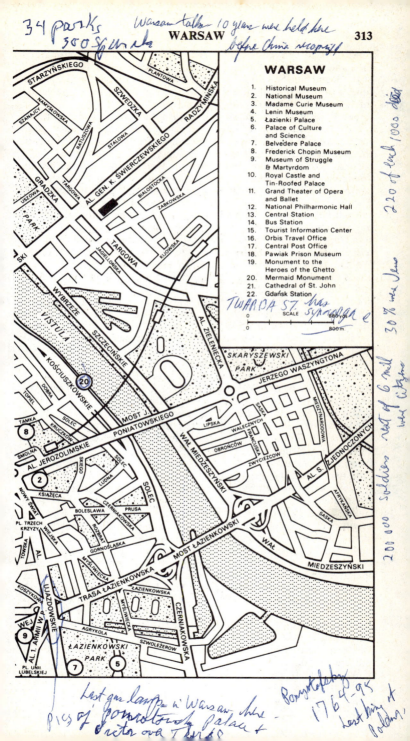

WARSAW

1. Historical Museum
2. National Museum
3. Madame Curie Museum
4. Lenin Museum
5. Łazienki Palace
6. Palace of Culture and Science
7. Belvedere Palace
8. Frederick Chopin Museum
9. Museum of Struggle & Martyrdom
10. Royal Castle and Tin-Roofed Palace
11. Grand Theater of Opera and Ballet
12. National Philharmonic Hall
13. Central Station
14. Bus Station
15. Tourist Information Center
16. Orbis Travel Office
17. Central Post Office
18. Pawiak Prison Museum
19. Monument to the Heroes of the Ghetto
20. Mermaid Monument
21. Cathedral of St. John
22. Gdańsk Station

SCALE

0 _____ 800 m

Handwritten annotations:

34 parks
380 Sq m de

Warsaw talks 10 years were held here
before China recognize

220 of each 1000 dead

30% are Jews and citizens

rest of 6 mill
were citizens

200 000 soldiers

TWARDA ST has synagogue

Last gas lamps in Warsaw here —
Pics of Poniatowski Palace +
Orator over Twist

Poniatowski
1764–95
Last king of Poland

Leon Uris Mila 18 headquarters of ghetto –

At night the Rynek is romantically floodlit and if you're after good food and atmosphere this is definitely the place to head for. Try duck at the Kamienne Schodki, tripe Polish-style or game at the Bazyliszek (one of the best restaurants in Warsaw) or a glass of wine in the period interior of Fukier's 300-year-old wine cellar.

For those with time to stop and stare, however, the frescoes and architectural details on the late Renaissance and baroque façades round the square will be a delight. For legend-lovers there are the vaults of the Bazyliszek restaurant where, the story goes, there used to live a basilisk with a literally deadly glance. Undeterred, an enterprising young shoemaker's apprentice got himself a suit of many mirrors to confront the Terror of Warsaw. The monster saw himself—and died. The 'Negro House' at no. 36 ('Pod Murzynkiem') has a fine Renaissance doorway and a sculpted negro's head on the wall (not difficult to guess that the former occupants of the house were engaged in 'overseas trade'). During the war the building miraculously survived and today, together with the seven adjoining houses, it is the home of the Warsaw Historical Museum (chamber concerts here every Tuesday; also a moving 15-minute documentary film showing Warsaw 'before' and 'after'). The stuffed croc in the Krokodyl restaurant at no. 21 is not an indication of what you might expect to find on your dinner plate, but a gift from Fidel Castro, who once ate here. 'The House of the Mazovian Dukes' or St. Anne's House (no. 31), is one of the oldest in the square and has the greatest number of surviving Gothic details. For the life and times of Poland's greatest Romantic poet, visit the Adam Mickiewicz Museum of Literature at no. 20.

Poland is a land of churches, and in your wanderings through the narrow streets of old Warsaw, you'll see a fair selection. The most important is the Cathedral of St. John, on the right of ul. Świętojańska as you walk towards Rynek Starego Miasta. Destroyed like everything else in the area, it has been completely rebuilt, but in its original late 14th-century Gothic form, thus removing later accretions. Two Polish kings were crowned here and the crypts contain the tombs of famous Poles, among them Henryk Sienkiewicz, whose story of life in early Christian Rome, *Quo Vadis?*, won the 1905 Nobel Prize for Literature. It was here that the historic Third of May Constitution, the first written constitution in Europe and the second in the world (after that of the United States), was confirmed by oath in 1791. There is also a legend—a figure of the crucified Jesus in one of the chapels miraculously grew hair, which every year had to be cut by a Warsaw virgin.

Next to the cathedral, separated by a narrow lane, is the Renaissance Jesuit Church which was built in 1608 over the foundations of burgher houses that had been destroyed in the fire of 1607 (the cellars are open to the public). On the other side of the cathedral is the narrow ul. Dziekania, where you can still see the arcaded gallery that once connected the cathedral with the Royal Castle. This was built to protect King Sigismund III Vasa after an attempt had been made on his life. The would-be assassin was disposed of in a fairly thorough manner: he was torn apart by horses, his body burnt and the ashes shot out of a gun. Further on, embedded in the south wall of the cathedral, is a relic of World War II: the crawler-chain of a self-propelled 'Goliath' mine.

July 22, 42 extermination started

Most to Treblinka Book 3 pics 300,000 killed in 1 yr. in TREBLINKA

[handwritten: 30% 1,300,000 Pop. priv of letter will have]
[handwritten: were fewy (3 mill will all of Poland)]

For a stroll down Old Warsaw's most picturesque street, cross over into medieval ul. Piwna, running parallel to ul. Świętojańska.

The surviving remnants of the 15th- and 16th-century fortifications that once circled the Old Town have been partially restored, and in summer are often bedecked with modern pictures, which you are earnestly invited to buy. On the northern side is the Barbican, a carefully restored and fairly rare example of medieval defensive architecture, leading through into Warsaw's 'New Town'—which was actually founded at the turn of the 14th and 15th centuries! The name of the area's main street, ul. Freta, is supposed to come from the German *freiheit,* meaning 'open market' (outside the town gates). This part of Warsaw was rebuilt after the war in 18th- and 19th-century style, so has a more elegant and spacious feel about it than the Old Town. Of interest are: the Marie Curie-Skłodowska Museum at ul. Freta 16, where the Polish discoverer of radium and polonium was born; the baroque Church and Convent of the Blessed Sacrament Sisters in the Rynek Nowomiejski (New Town Market), founded in 1688 by Queen Marysieńka Sobieska to commemorate her husband's victory over the Turks; and the Gothic Church of the Visitation on an embankment overlooking the Vistula, the oldest church in the New Town, with a 16th-century belfry that survived the war remarkably undamaged.

At the intersection of Długa and Miodowa streets is a manhole cover with a trail of black basalt cobblestones leading to it. On a nearby building is a plaque with the following inscription: 'By way of this canal, after the heroic defense of the Old Town, 5,300 insurgents of the North Group got through to the City Center and Żoliborz. 1944—2 September—1974'. Anyone who has seen Wajda's shattering film *Canal* won't need reminding of the horrors of this journey through the sewers.

[handwritten: Statue of Chopin was destroyed but a copy was found in a basement so was re made.]
[handwritten: He left Poland 1830 & never returned.]

Castles and Columns

[handwritten: Died & buried in Paris - his heart in a church in Warsaw.]

Warsaw's most instantly recognizable monument stands in the center of Plac Zamkowy (Castle Square); it is also its oldest and most famous. The tall, slender column carrying a statue of King Sigismund III Vasa (the one who made Warsaw his new capital in the late 16th century) shares the honor of being Warsaw's symbol with the Mermaid. Symbolically, it was the first monument to be rebuilt when the people of Warsaw began to trickle back into their devastated capital (the bits and pieces of the shattered column have, in a typically romantic Polish gesture, been put on display in nearby Mariensztat Market Square).

The cleared site in front of the statue—the site of the Royal Castle—stood empty for more than 25 years however. Today the rebuilt castle once again dominates the escarpment on the left bank of the Vistula. The decoration and furnishing of the interior, which was a mammoth task, involving relearning of traditional skills, matching of ancient woods and fabrics, and even reopening disused quarries to find just the right kind of stone.

[handwritten: Jews moved here from other places. 1/2 mill people 3¼ mill survived by 10]

Next to the castle, on a lower terrace, stands the quaintly named Pałac pod Blachą (Tin-Roofed Palace), now the offices of the city architect.

Down the Royal Road

All towns with kings had their 'Royal Routes' and in Warsaw it stretches south from Castle Square for 2 miles (4 km), running through busy Krakowskie Przedmieście, along Nowy Świat and al. Ujazdowskie (a sort of Embassy Row), and on to the Belvedere Palace and Łazienki Park. Lots of 'architecture' along this route, lined as it is with some of Warsaw's finest churches and palaces, but if it's people you want you'll find the names of famous Poles at every turn. Marie Curie-Skłodowska carried out her first experiments in Krakowskie Przedmieście, in the building adjoining St. Anne's Church; further on is a statue of Adam Mickiewicz; Tadeusz Kościuszko, national hero of Poland and the United States, received his military education at the famous Knights' School in the Casimir Palace in the second half of the 18th century. In front of the neo-classical Staszic Palace, which closes the perspective at the southern end of the street, is a statue (1830) of the great astronomer Nicolaus Copernicus by the famous Danish sculptor Bertel Thorvaldsen. But it's with the name of Frederick Chopin that the street is most intimately linked. As a child he played in the Casimir Palace gardens, gave his first concert in the Radziwiłł Palace and then moved with his family to No. 5 Krakowskie Przedmieście, now the Academy of Fine Arts. Here you can visit the Chopin Family Drawing Room, the reconstructed interior of Chopin's last home before he went abroad. He was never to see the land of his birth again, but his heart returned and is immured in a pillar in the Holy Cross Church a short distance away.

The famous name in Nowy Świat is Blikle—though you may have never heard of him. Mr Blikle's confectionery business has been baking doughnuts here for over 100 years, and still does. On the last Thursday before Lent (a kind of Polish 'Pancake Tuesday'), a collective doughnut-mania hits Warsaw and every last one of these calorific concoctions disappears off the shelves. Those who know their doughnuts will however tell you that it's the instantly recognizable Blikle bag that has the cachet and that you can buy bigger, better, and cheaper elsewhere.

Turn off Nowy Świat to visit the Ostrogski Palace in ul. Tamka 41, one of several buildings in Poland by Tylman van Gameren, from where the Frederick Chopin Society organizes the International Chopin Competition every five years. At the bottom of ul. Tamka on the banks of the Vistula stands Warsaw's other symbol—the silver Mermaid Monument, sword and shield in hand. Legend has it that the city owes its existence to the beautiful mermaid, who rose out of the Vistula and commanded two children playing on the shore to found a city; the children's names were Wars and Szawa and so the city came to be called 'Warszawa' (the Polish name for Warsaw).

Further down Nowy Świat, turn off into al. Jerozolimskie for the National Museum. You'll never get round everything in its 100 halls,

Bullet holes — _Joseph Conrad house_

so make a beeline for the famous Faras frescoes, which were recently discovered by Polish archeologists in the Sudan.

Al. Ujazdowskie, Warsaw's fashionable 'Corso', which in the 19th century was thronged with smart carriages and riders eager to be 'seen', is now a favorite with Sunday strollers, taking us on to beautiful Łazienki Park and the white wedding-cake Palace on the Lake, the private residence of Stanisław August Poniatowski, last king of Poland. The palace, a gem of Polish neo-classicism built towards the end of the 18th century, stands on an island in the middle of a park dotted with pavilions—the White House (Biały Domek), where the future Louis XVIII of France holed up when he was in exile, and the Theater in the Orangery, one of the few surviving court theaters in Europe. Take a short stroll across the park to the impressionistic Chopin Monument for a well-deserved rest. Open-air Chopin concerts are given here throughout the summer.

Heroes of Warsaw

Poniatowski - last king was a Marshall of Napoleon
Nap. residents here - Big love + had a son -

Behind the old city in pl. Teatralny, facing the monumental Grand Theater of Opera and Ballet (1826–33), stands the Monument to the Heroes of Warsaw. Known as the Warsaw _Nike,_ it was erected in 1964 in memory of the men, women and children who died for Warsaw during the years 1939–45. The simple Monument to the Heroes of the Ghetto, a slab of dark granite with a bronze bas-relief, stands on ul. _Pic_ Zamenhofa in the Muranów district, the historic heart of the old pre-war Warsaw ghetto where the Nazis concentrated the entire Jewish population of Warsaw. The armed revolt that broke out in April 1943 was put down with unbelievable ferocity and Muranów was flattened. Now there are only bleak gray apartment blocks here. _Good Mdll of_

The Tomb of the Unknown Soldier stands in the Saxon Gardens, _end_ which were laid out in the 18th century on the French system of _pic_ geometric walks and flower beds. Pause here for a while—the eternal _pic_ light still glows beneath the triple colonnade and there is always a guard on duty. A moving changing of the guards ceremony takes place here every Sunday around noon. _pic_ _+ meaning is here_

Wilanów—from Baroque to Biennale
Opera house largest in Europe 2500 seats
opposite to Nike statue

The Royal Route extends along the poplar-lined al. Belwederskie to Wilanów, some 6 miles (10 km) from the center of town. This was where King Jan Sobieski (the one who defeated the Turks at the gates _A c_ of Vienna) betook himself every summer with his pretty French wife Marysieńka. The palace is still used for important state occasions; in fact President Carter stayed here when he visited Poland in 1977. Lots to see here, from period furniture and china to old clocks and original coffin portraits (hexagonal or octagonal paintings nailed to the coffin before burial and found only in Poland). For a different—and painless —way of learning about Jan Sobieski and his lovely baroque palace, wait till dusk falls to take part in the dramatic _son et lumière_ spectacle 'Return to Wilanów' that is staged beneath the rustling linden trees. It's

Great restaurant here

all in Polish, but you can hire portable tape recorders to follow the action.

In the grounds, on the site of a former court riding school, stands a modern pavilion housing the Poster Museum (Muzeum Plakatu), the first of its kind in Europe. During the International Poster Biennale you can see poster art from all over the world.

Folk Fairs and Chopin Preludes

Around Warsaw the Mazovian plain stretches flat and monotonous as far as the eye can see. Regional architecture is disappearing fast, but here and there you may still see traditional thatched cottages with giant sunflowers and hollyhocks in the garden, and perhaps a stork nesting on the roof.

There are pleasure steamers cruising downriver to Młociny (4 miles/ 7 km) and its Museum of Folk Culture housed in a small baroque palace. Further along (78 miles/116 km) is Płock, an old town dating back to the 10th century, picturesquely situated on a high bluff overlooking the river. In June Płock turns the clock back and plays host to the National Festival of Folklore and Folk Art which attracts folk dancers, artists, poets, and story tellers from all over the country. If you time your visit to coincide with the 'Płock Fair', which takes place during the festival, you can buy all the wooden sculptures, clay figures, pots, woven and embroidered goods, paintings on glass, wickerwork, and cut-outs that you want.

Łack, 7 miles (12 km) from Płock on the other side of the river, is a forest-cum-lake holiday resort. There's horseriding here, and a famous state stud farm. At the confluence of the rivers Bug and Narew is Zegrzińskie Lake, where you will find half the population of Warsaw on hot summer afternoons. There are facilities for water-sports as well as beaches, and jetties; and in winter there's ice-yachting.

Mecca for all Chopin lovers is the composer's birthplace at Zelazowa Wola, some 30 miles (50 km) west of Warsaw. The small country manor, overgrown with creepers and set in a dreamy flower-scented garden, is definitely the place to listen to Romantic music. Each Sunday (11 to 2) from June through to September the world's best pianists play Chopin here.

Arcadian Gardens

For a bit of rustic simplicity try Łowicz, about 12 miles (20 km.) from Zelazowa Wola, the center of a region famous for its colorful rainbow-striped regional costume. You're not very likely to see people wearing their costumes for everyday use any more, so the best time to come is Corpus Christi day (first Thursday after Trinity Sunday) when the townsfolk dress up to take part in religious processions. The regional museum—in a small 17th-century palace—will fill you in on local folk arts and crafts.

Southeast of Łowicz, on the former Radziwiłł estates, are two charming places: Arkadia (2 miles/4 km), a landscape park laid out in 1778 with pavilions, temples, and neo-Gothic ruins galore, and Nieborów

(3½ miles/6 km further on), a 17th-century mansion by Tylman van Gameren set in one of the finest baroque gardens in Poland.

Kampinos Forest

On your way back to Warsaw, drive through the Kampinos National Park (130 sq. miles/340 sq. km of pine forests, marshes, peat bogs, and sand dunes, some of them as high as 100 feet/30 meters). Parts have been fenced off as natural elk reserves and here you can also see wild boar, stag, badgers, and many different species of birds. Permits for restricted areas of the reserve can be got from the park administration offices at Izabelin, and they also provide guides.

The remote and inaccessible areas of the Kampinos forests and marshes have seen much fighting down the centuries. At Palmiry, on the eastern edge of the forest, the Nazis organized mass executions of Polish hostages during the occupation. On the entrance gate to the cemetery is a moving inscription found on a cell wall in Gestapo headquarters: 'It is easy to talk of Poland, more difficult to work for Poland, still more difficult to die for her, and most difficult of all to suffer for her.'

The American Connection

The Vistula valley south of Warsaw has many links with Tadeusz Kościuszko and Kazimierz Pułaski, the Polish national heroes who also distinguished themselves in the American War of Independence. The Polish Motor Union has even organized a 9-day excursion to take in the most important places connected with the two. Warka, 37 miles (60 km) from Warsaw, on the Pilica river, is where Kazimierz Pułaski was born in 1747. Unable to save Poland's freedom, he died for that of the emergent United States in 1779. The beautiful old 17th-century manor house where he was born is now the home of the Pułaski Museum. Maciejowice, on the other side of the Vistula river, is the site of the famous battle fought by Kościuszko against overwhelmingly superior Russian forces in 1794. Kościuszko, already a seasoned campaigner having fought on the colonists' side during the American revolution, was wounded and taken prisoner.

On your way back to Warsaw, watch out for the impressive ruins of a large 14th-century castle at Czersk, once the home of the powerful Dukes of Mazovia.

Kazimierz Dolny

However short your stay in Warsaw, you must try and see Kazimierz Dolny, only an hour out along the Vistula on the fringes of the Lublin Upland. It's a pretty place, overlooking the river from high sandy banks overgrown with clumps of willows and criss-crossed by ravines, though during the summer rather tends to get taken over by tourists and the artistic fraternity.

The richly ornamented façades of the houses round the market square date back to the time when Kazimierz Dolny, situated at the junction of two trade routes and the center of the corn trade, was at the height of its prosperity. Don't miss the arcaded Przybyła houses (1615), the early 17th-century Celej house (now a regional museum), the ruined castle dominating the town, the 18th-century synagogue turned movie house, and the many Renaissance granaries along the Vistula.

On your way back to Warsaw, stop over at Puławy, the residence of the powerful Czartoryski family in the 18th and early 19th centuries, who made it into a kind of cultural and scientific capital of Poland. The much-rebuilt palace is now neo-classical (circa 1800) and is set in a large 'English' park dotted with follies. There is an attractive beach in the town where canoes are hired out, and there is also a regular passenger boat service to Cracow, Sandomierz, Warsaw and Toruń.

Biatowitża Bisons

To the east of Warsaw, 158 miles (255 km.) away, is the largest and last primeval forest in Central Europe—the Bialowieza National Park. Its 480 square miles (1,250 square km.) straddle the Polish–USSR border; 220 square miles (580 square km.) being Polish territory. These are no tame well-manicured woods for Sunday strollers, but a dense tangle of ancient oaks, pines, spruces, treacherous morasses and sudden danger as some centuries-old giant crashes unexpectedly to the ground. The best way to see these virgin forests is to take advantage of the four-hour horse-drawn excursions through the most interesting parts. Rare animals such as bison, moose, lynx, and wild tarpan forest pony now feel safe in this vast, unspoiled, state-protected reserve. Even bears have been known to wander across the border from Bielorussia. Driving through these fairy-tale woods, you may also get a glimpse of less exotic creatures such as foxes, deer, and wild boars, not to mention a great variety of game birds. Orbis organizes big-game hunting as well as pheasant and water-fowl shoots.

PRACTICAL INFORMATION FOR WARSAW

WHEN TO COME. Warsaw is best visited from May through mid-October when it's warm and dry. Winters are likely to be severe or dreary, though it's a fairly lively time for cultural events.

GETTING AROUND. By Tram and Bus. City transport is still cheap, although rush hours are as bad as anywhere in the West. Fares are 2 zł. for trams and 3 zł. for buses. Express buses (distinguished from regular services by having letters rather than numbers on the front) are 6 zł. or more, depending on the number of zones you cross. Tickets must be bought from 'Ruch' kiosks (the buses have no conductors) and must be canceled in a special punch machine situated on the vehicles. Plain-clothes inspectors make frequent spot-checks and there are heavy fines for those who haven't canceled their tickets. Fares are doubled after 11 P.M.

By Taxi. Taxis are cheap, starting at 27 zł. and increasing by about 13 zł. per additional km, but very scarce. You can either line up at a taxi rank, or, if there isn't one around you can hail a passing driver. Warsaw cab drivers (many of whom speak English) love to gossip. They're a sure source of political jokes and intimate social news. Tipping is obligatory. The short ride from Okęcie airport should cost you no more than 150 zł. maximum, with the tip included.

 HOTELS. Most of the better hotels in Warsaw are operated by Orbis, though there are also a number of other, non-Orbis hotels in the city; all these hotels are so indicated. In all Orbis hotels there are exchange bureaus and information desks. Be careful to check whether rates quoted by hotels include breakfast, service charges and taxes. This applies particularly to non-Orbis hotels. If your accommodations have not already been booked as part of a package deal, it is advisable to make them in advance to avoid both frustration and potential disappointment.

Deluxe

Victoria Intercontinental, ul. Krolewska 11 (tel. 278 011). Modern hotel in ideal location; 370 rooms with bath, TV and airconditioning. Several restaurants, plus nightclub, indoor pool, sauna and garage.

Expensive

Europejski, Krakowskie Przedmiescie 13 (tel. 265 051). Best for food and service; 279 spacious rooms, most with bath. Restaurant with dinner dancing, nightclub.

Forum, ul. Nowogrodzka 24 (tel. 210 19). Completely air-conditioned; 271 rooms with bath. Cocktail lounge and good food.

Grand, ul. Krucza 28. All 430 rooms with bath, radio and telephone. The rooftop restaurant, with its glass-enclosed terrace, offers jazz bands, dancing and variety shows, plus of course the great view.

Metropol, ul. Marszalkowska 99a (tel. 294 001). Non-Orbis hotel; 192 rooms, most with bath. Many facilities, including restaurant.

Novotel, ul. 1-go Sierpnia 1 (tel. 464 051). 153 rooms, all with bath. Restaurant and outdoor pool.

Polonia, al. Jerozolimskie 45 (tel. 287 241). Non-Orbis hotel; 240 rooms, only a few with bath. Restaurant.

Solec, ul. Zagorna 1 (tel. 259 241). 150 rooms, all with bath; bar and restaurant.

Vera, ul. Wery Kostrzewy 16 (tel. 227 421). 300 rooms; large and comfortable Orbis hotel.

Moderate

Dom Chlopa, pl. Powstancow Warszawy 2 (tel. 279 251). 320 rooms, most with bath; bar and restaurant. Non-Orbis hotel.

MDM, pl. Konstytucji 1 (tel. 282 526). Non-Orbis hotel; 190 rooms, some with bath. Restaurant and bar.

Nowa Praga, ul. B. Brechta 7 (tel. 195 001). 143 rooms, about half with bath. Restaurant and bar. Non-Orbis hotel.

Saski, pl. Dzierzynskiego 7 (tel. 204 611). 106 rooms. Bar and restaurant. Non-Orbis hotel.

Syrena, ul. Syreny 23 (tel. 321 257). 150 rooms, most with bath. Bar and restaurant. Non-Orbis hotel.

Warszawa, pl. Powstancow (tel. 269 421). 243 rooms, all with bath. Bar and restaurant. Non-Orbis hotel.

RESTAURANTS. Warsaw has a wide range of restaurants, though the current food shortages mean that the best ingredients go to the first-class hotels. There are several very nice atmospheric places that you might try along Rynek Starego Miasta.

Expensive

The best hotel restaurants are the Victoria's **Canaletto,** which serves Polish specialties, and the restaurant in the **Forum.**

Klimczok, Leszno 32. An attractive restaurant specializing in regional food.

Retman Gdański, ul. Bednarska 9. Frequented by lots of locals, this charming restaurant in the Mariensztat district also specializes in regional food.

Bazyliszek, Rynek Starego Miasta 7/9. Best for game (boar, venison, and duck) and fruit (try their cold fruit soup).

Moderate

Kamienne Schodki, Rynek Starego Miasta 26. Has candlelight, good wines, and duck specialties.

Fukier, Rynek Starego Miasta 27. A popular wine-cellar cum coffeehouse.

Staropolska, Krakowskie Przedmieście 8. A small, informal restaurant serving Old Polish cuisine with a well-deserved reputation for fish dishes.

Centralna Rybna, pl. Zbawiciela, ul. Marszałkowska. Another good seafood restaurant on the mezzanine floor.

Murzynek, Rynek Starego Miasta. Excellent for quick, light meals.

Other good Moderately priced restaurants, some with regional cuisine, include: **Hortex,** Rynek Starego Miasta; **Kameralna,** Foksal 16; **Ambassador,** ul. Piękna, opposite the US Embassy; **Rarytas,** ul. Marszałkowska 15, with floorshow; **Kaukazka** (Georgian specialties, floorshow and dancing); **Łowicka** (regional cuisine); **Gościniec Opolski,** ul. Puławska 102; **Karczma Słupska,** ul. Czerniakowska 127; **Suwalska,** ul. Spokojna 4; **Zalipie,** ul. Filtrowa 83; **Kurpiowska,** Ciołka 20; and **Zywiecka,** ul. Marszałkowska 66.

There is also a selection of restaurants serving cuisine from other parts of the world, all of which are Moderate. **Ha-Long,** pl. Grzybowski 4 (Vietnamese); **Cristal-Budapest,** ul. Marszałkowska 21/25 (Hungarian); **Trojka,** Palace of Culture (Russian, Bielorussian and Ukrainian); **Sofia,** pl. Powstańców Warszawy 3/5 (Bulgarian); also on Marszałkowska are **Havana** (Cuban) and **Szanghaj** (Chinese).

CAFÉS. Warsaw teems with cafés (*kawiarnia*), which move outdoors in summer. They're a way of life with the Poles, places where everybody meets. Most cafés have cloakrooms where you are asked to leave your overcoat. Coffee, tea, and those luscious cakes can be found at the following.

Krokodyl, Rynek Starego Miasta 21; **Gong,** al. Jerozolimskie 42, has a marvelous selection of imported teas; **Alhambra,** al. Jerozolimskie 32, for Turkish coffee; **Teatralna,** ul. Corazziego 12; **Telimena,** Krakowskie Przedmieście; **Trou Madame,** Łazienki Park, in a beautiful setting. At Wilanów, just outside Warsaw, try the **Kuźnia Królewska,** ul. Wiertnicza 2, in a converted blacksmith's forge.

MUSEUMS. These are open daily except on Monday and the day after a public holiday; best to check opening times with Orbis. There is usually a small entrance fee. Of Warsaw's many museums, the following perhaps are of most interest to out-of-town tourists.

Adam Mickiewicz Museum of Literature, Rynek Starego Miasta, 18/20.

Frederick Chopin Society, Ostrogski Palace, ul. Okólnik 1, with branches at the Chopin Salon, ul. Krakowskie Przedmieśćie 5, and the Manor House in Żelazowa Wola, 22 miles (35 km) from Warsaw. Here, in the house where he was born, Chopin concerts are held every Sunday throughout the summer.

Folk Art Museum, al Na Skarpie 8.

Lowicz Ethnographic Museum. Collection of folk costumes and a gallery of 19th-century paintings, 31 miles (50 km) from Warsaw.

Madame Curie Museum, ul. Freta 16. In the house where she was born and lived for many years.

National Museum, al. Jerozolimskie 3. Poland's main collection of ancient, classical and modern art. See in particular the famous Faras frescoes.

Pawiak Prison Museum, ul. Dzielna 22/26.

Warsaw Historical Museum, Rynek Starego Miasta 48. Don't miss the historical film *Warsaw Prevails,* graphically showing the destruction of the city in the last war.

Wilanów Palace. The former royal summer residence built by King Jan III Sobieski, with beautiful antiques and a gallery of contemporary posters in the grounds; only 6 miles (10 km) from Warsaw.

In the city's lovely **Lazienki Park,** there are several former royal summer residences, including that of Poland's last king, Stanislaus August Poniatowski in the 18th century, now a museum of palace interiors.

ART GALLERIES. These are usually open the same times as museums, also charging a small entrance fee. A full list can be obtained from Orbis offices.

Artists' House, ul. Mazowiecka 11a.

Foksal Gallery, ul. Foksal 1/4.

Kordegarda Gallery, Krakowskie Przedmieście 15/17.

MDM Art Gallery, ul. Marszałkowska 34/50.

Modern Art Gallery, Rynek Starego Miasta 2.

Sculpture Gallery, ul Marchlewskiego 38.

Zacheta Art Gallery, pl. Małachowskiego 3. Contemporary painting, sculpture and graphics.

NIGHTLIFE. Disco fever has arrived in Warsaw, although not on the same scale as in the West; the discos at ul. Marszałkowska and ul. Polna are both fairly mediocre. Apart from those hotels with nightclubs, you might try **Akwarium,** a two-story jazz nightclub just behind the Palace of Culture.

Two good music clubs are **Wanda Warska's Modern Music Club,** which is a very popular candle-lit jazz club (must book) and **Amfora,** on the East Wall, an intimate redecorated club with good food.

The place for satire is the **Pod Egida** cabaret on Nowy Świat, which has a ready-made source of jokes by being in the basement of the building housing the censor's office and across the square from the Central Committee of the Polish United Workers (Communist) Party.

Favorites among the younger clientele are the inexpensive student clubs, in particular: **Hybrydy,** ul. Koniewskiego 7/8; **Riviera-Remont,** ul. Waryńskiego 12; **Stodoła,** ul. Batorego 2; and **Proxima,** ul. Żwirki i Wigury 95.

 CONCERTS, THEATER, CINEMA. Warsaw reflects the strong theatrical and musical traditions of Poland, with many important drama, music, and film festivals taking place throughout the year.

The **National Philharmonic,** ul. Sienkiewicza 12, puts on excellent concerts. International Chopin Competitions and ᴵWarsaw Autumn festivals of modern music are held here. Poland's 13 opera companies stage frequent operas and operettas. The famous folk dance troupes, **Mazowsze** and **Ślask,** perform to full houses and often travel abroad. Each Sunday, from June to September there are midday concerts at Żelazowa Wola, Chopin's birthplace, near Warsaw.

There are 17 theaters in Warsaw, many with bold and original stage sets and excellent acting. Those which visitors might enjoy include:

Ateneum, ul. Stefana Jaracza 2; traditional and contemporary drama.

Dramatyczny and **Teatr Studio,** both in the Palace of Culture and Science; contemporary plays.

Syrena, ul. Litewska 3; revues.

Teatre Wielki (Grand theater of Opera and Ballet), pl. Teatralny; superb operatic stage—one of the largest in Europe, seating for 1,900.

Thatr Narodowy (National Theater), pl. Teatralny.

Współczesny, ul. Mokotowska 13; contemporary works.

Concerts are held in the summer at the open-air theater in **Lazienki Park.**

There are many cinemas showing both Polish and foreign films, though the English and American ones tend to concentrate on the seamier aspects of the 'decadent' West. September is the month for Polish films, while in October there are a large number of Russian films on view.

 **SHOPPING.** Beautiful handicraft items and specialties are plentiful. Shop along Rynek Starego Miasta, Nowy Świat, Krucza, and Marszałkowska for all sorts of attractive local craftwork. Don't forget to take home some Polish *Żubrówka* (flavored vodka), or the standard *Wyborowa*-brand vodka.

Try the Cepelia stores for a wide range of Polish folkcraft, such as glass and enamelware, amber, and lovely hand-woven woolen rugs; Orno shops for silverware and hand-made jewelry; and Desa stores for works of art, ornaments, and objets d'art. These accept local and foreign currency. Pewex hard-currency shops sell local and imported items, such as cigarettes, imported spirits, and especially vodka at very low prices, as well as imported chocolate, coffee, and a range of clothing.

Junk-hunters might like to visit Warsaw's flea market in ul. Wolumena in the Bielany district to see what Poles collect, and throw out.

USEFUL ADDRESSES. The main embassies are all in Warsaw: *British,* al. Róż 1; *American,* al. Ujazdowskie 29; *Canadian,* ul. Katowicka 16 or 25.

Listed here are the main travel offices, which are all in Warsaw. Regional offices of Orbis and PZM are given under individual centers. *Orbis,* ul Bracka 16 and ul. Stawki 2. *PZM* (Polish Motoring Association), ul Krucza 14. *PTTK* (Polish Tourist Association). ul. Świętokrzyska 36. *Sports-Tourist,* ul. Moliera 8. *Almatur* (Student Travel Office), ul. Ordynacka

9. *LOT* (Polish Airlines), al. Jerozolimskie 44, ul. Waryńskiego 9 and ul. 17 Stycznia 39. *British Airways*, ul. Krucza 49.

In Warsaw, telephone 997 (police), 998 (ambulance). Other areas of the country have different numbers which are given in every telephone booth.

LUBLIN AND ITS ENVIRONS

Icons and Oil Wells

In the middle of the wooded Lublin Upland, stands Lublin, the most important cultural center in eastern Poland, some 102 miles (164 km) from Warsaw. Its five universities include the Lublin Catholic University, the only one of its kind in Poland. The Old Town is full of magnificent churches, delightful houses, secretive nooks, vaulted archways, and romantic courtyards. The wine cellar at Rynek 8 (in the market square) is worth visiting for its 16th-century wall paintings; and at no. 12 look out for the ornate sculptural details on the first and second storeys. The castle, which was remodeled in 'Mock Gothic' in the 19th century, houses a gallery of Polish painting (including the famous *Lublin Union* by Jan Matejko), as well as historical and ethnographical exhibits. Its Gothic Holy Trinity Chapel is decorated with unique Ruthenian–Byzantine murals dating back to 1418.

Reminders of World War II are never far away in Poland, and on the outskirts of the town stands the Majdanek Museum of Martyrology, the site of a former Nazi concentration camp where 360,000 people were killed.

Zamość (54 miles/87 km southeast of Lublin) is the best-preserved renaissance architectural complex in Poland. Recently the town was given a complete face lift in readiness for the 400th anniversary of its founding, celebrated in 1980, and there is new plasterwork everywhere,

326

shoddy conversions and buildings have been removed, and the town's massive defense walls are in the process of being restored. Zamość was built between 1580 and 1610 by the enterprising chancellor Jan Zamoyski in a 'barren field' on his estates, which stood on the trade route connecting the Black Sea with northern and western Europe; and as you will see, much of the town has not changed since then. Dominating the market square is the impressive 16th-century town hall, with a spire that reaches 164 feet (50 meters) high. You almost expect characters in period costume to come sweeping down its grand entrance staircase. The 16th- and 17th-century arcaded houses round the square and side streets, none of them more than two storeys high, are a salutary example of human-scale architecture. The renaissance St. Thomas Collegiate Church houses a library of manuscripts and rare books.

In Łancut, some 10 miles (17 km) east of Rzeszów, visit the 17th-century palace of the Lubomirski family, which has been turned into a museum and picture gallery. Built in a square around an inner courtyard, the palace contains lovely historical furniture, clocks, and Gobelins. In the park is an old coach-house converted into a coach museum; excursions in horse-drawn carriages to explore the surrounding countryside can be arranged.

Right down in the southeastern corner of Poland, in Sanok's History Museum, you'll find Poland's largest collection of icon paintings and other liturgical items. On the other side of the river is an enormous open-air Folk Museum, including among its exhibits an 18th-century Orthodox church, an old mill, and a peasant cottage from 1681. Krosno (about 31 miles/50 km from Sanok) has a Museum of Kerosene Lamps (which were invented in Poland in 1853), and just outside is Bóbrka, which has its very own oil well, dating back to 1854, which is now open to the public.

PRACTICAL INFORMATION FOR LUBLIN

WHEN TO COME. Any time of year for Lublin, though summers are obviously warmer. Spring or summer for the Bieszczady Mountains in the southeast. This area is a real paradise for ramblers with miles of ancient forests and lakes.

GETTING AROUND. There is a direct air link from Warsaw to Rzeszów, but not to Lublin, which is only a short distance by road from Warsaw (route E81). Lublin is included in Orbis tours from Warsaw, as is Rzeszów. Rail and bus networks cover the region.

HOTELS AND RESTAURANTS

All hotels listed below have restaurants unless otherwise stated.

ŁANCUT. *Zamkowy* (I). Set at the back of Lancut Castle, the hotel is in Poland's most beautiful 'English' park; single and double rooms; riding facilities.

LESKO. *Motel* (M), ul. Bieszczadzka 4. A 16th-century castle converted into a delightful 120-bed hotel.

LUBLIN. *Orbis-Unia* (M), al. Racławickie 12; *Victoria* (M), ul. Narutowicza 58/60; *Lublinianka* (M), ul. Krakowskie Przedmieście 56; *Motel,* ul. Prusa 6.

ZAMOŚĆ. *Renaissance* (M), ul. Grecka 6.

USEFUL ADDRESSES. There are Orbis offices in most of the main towns. The principal tourist offices for Lublin, who can supply information for the surrounding region, are: *Orbis,* ul. Krakowskie Przedmieście 25; *PZM,* ul. Prusa 8; *Central Tourist Information Office,* ul. Narutowicza 56.

CRACOW

Gleaming Spires

Cracow, the seat of Poland's oldest university and until 1611 the capital of Poland (before it was transferred to Warsaw) is the only major city in the country that escaped devastation during the last war, (Hitler's armies were driven out before they had a chance to demolish it). Today it is once again a major city, with a lively theatrical, musical, and cultural life, and its fine ramparts, towers, dungeons, and churches illustrate seven centuries of Polish architecture. Unfortunately, the increasing amount of tourists and motorized traffic, in what was once just a backwater of the Austro-Hungarian Empire, has meant that Cracow is quite literally beginning to crack. The Cracovians however have in recent years taken to the scaffolds with a vengeance, perhaps belying the close-fistedness Varsovians traditionally accuse them of.

The best time to come here is in June, when everything seems to be happening at once: the International Biennale of Graphic Arts (even-numbered years); the Polish and International Short Film Festival; a Folk Art Fair, where you can buy your souvenirs; the Juvenalia festival, when weirdly garbed students take over the running of the city for a few days; and the colorful Lajkonik Pageant, celebrating the day a young Cracovian raftsman successfully drove back a Tartar invasion, with a little help from his friends, and returned triumphantly into Cracow wearing the clothes of the defeated Khan.

Wawel Hill

Top of your sightseeing agenda will be Wawel Castle and Cathedral, the see of the former Cardinal Wojtyla, Archbishop of Cracow, who as Pope John Paul II (the first Polish Pope in history and the first non-Italian in 455 years) returned triumphantly to his native country in 1979. The eight-day pilgrimage took on great religious and patriotic significance and attracted huge crowds of Poles, many of whom had traveled miles, often on foot, to catch a glimpse of 'their' Pope.

Dominating the old part of the city, this impressive complex of Gothic and renaissance buildings stands atop Wawel Hill, a rocky limestone outcrop on the banks of the Vistula, which was fortified as early as the 8th and 9th centuries. The castle itself is largely in the renaissance style (the arcaded courtyard is probably the best example of its kind in Europe), though there are surviving traces of Gothic and pre-romanesque (10th-century rotunda of the Virgin Mary). The castle's 71 restored rooms are filled with works of art and historical relics, but the best of them are the priceless 16th-century Flemish tapestries that were specially made for King Sigismund Augustus (of the original 356, only 136 survived the war, having been smuggled across to Canada); the famous jagged sword 'Szczerbiec' used by the kings of Poland as a coronation sword since 1320; and a unique collection of embroidered four-room Turkish tents, glittering with small appliqué mirrors, captured at the Battle of Vienna in 1683.

Wawel Cathedral, across the courtyard from the castle, was begun in the 14th century on the site of two earlier romanesque cathedrals. Polish kings were crowned and buried here until the 18th century, though the capital had transferred to Warsaw in the 17th century (a mistaken move according to some Cracovians even now!). Of the 18 chapels opening out onto the nave the most splendid, with its perfectly proportioned and graceful gilt dome, is undoubtedly the Sigismund Chapel. See also the Holy Cross Chapel with its Gothic sarcophagus of Casimir by Wit Stwosz (1492) and the 15th-century Ruthenian–Byzantine frescoes. In the center of the cathedral stands the silver tomb of Poland's patron saint, St. Stanislaus, who was murdered by his king in the 11th century for alleged high treason. In 1979 the Poles celebrated the 900th anniversary of his death, and invited Pope John Paul II—who as Archbishop of Cracow had been largely responsible for organizing the event—to lead the celebrations.

Down in the crypt are the tombs of kings, as well as those of Poland's great poets and national heroes, among them Tadeusz Kościuszko, hero of Polish and American resistance. In fact you'll find a statue of him on the slopes of Wawel, greeting you as you go in. The statue suddenly disappeared several years ago, but it was only so that a copy could be made for the American Bicentennial. Kościuszko is well remembered in Cracow, for it was here in the market square that he swore allegiance to the Polish nation and began the national uprising of 1794.

From the cathedral tower there is a magnificent view over the city, and you can also have a look at Poland's largest bell, the 'Sigismund', which has a circumference of 26 feet (8 meters). Sigismund was cast from enemy cannon in 1520, and is rung only on very important occasions.

No ancient monument would be complete without a legend, and Wawel Hill is no exception. It has its very own fire-breathing Dragon (a modern stand-in) down in the Dragon's Den (Smocza Jama) over-looking the Vistula. Legend has it that after many years of decimating Cracow's virgin population the damsel-devouring dragon was finally disposed of by a local cobbler who tricked it into eating a ram stuffed with tar and sulphur. The thirst-crazed dragon rushed into the Vistula and drank and drank until he burst into a 1,000 pieces. Needless to say the cobbler then married Prince Krak's lovely daughter.

Some of Cracow's finest old architecture can be found in the small streets clustering at the foot of Wawel Hill, particularly in Kanonicza, Senatorska and Poselska streets, where you'll see picture-postcard buildings, cloisters and inner courtyards, all in almost pure renaissance style.

Cracow's 'Drawing-Room'

The heart of the city has for centuries been the Main Market Square, a magnet for tourists and locals alike, a place to sit and watch the world (and pigeons) go by in one of its many open-air cafés; every hour on the hour four short bugle calls, each ending on a sudden high note, come drifting down from the spire of the Church of the Virgin Mary. Everyone always momentarily stops what they're doing to stare up-wards as the plaintive notes, sometimes touchingly off-key, re-enact a centuries-old tradition in memory of the original trumpeter whose call was cut short when a well-aimed enemy arrow pierced his throat as he was warning his fellow citizens of an impending Tartar attack. (The bugle call—known as the 'Hejnał Mariacki'—is broadcast every day at noon on Polish radio.)

Cracow's 'drawing-room' (as it's often called) is reputedly the big-gest and most splendid market place in Europe, a bit like the Piazza San Marco in Venice. In the center stands the 328-foot-long (100-meter-long) covered market known as Sukiennice (Cloth Hall), which was built in the 14th century but largely remodeled during the renais-sance. In front of its symmetrical arcades women sell flowers as they did centuries ago and horse-drawn cabs ply for hire. The ground floor is still in business—but now selling trinkets and folk-art souvenirs—while the first floor, with its beautiful renaissance attic decorated with quaint masks, has been converted into a gallery of Polish paintings of the 18th and 19th centuries. Next door stands the 14th-century Town Hall Tower, all that is left of the Town Hall which was pulled down in 1820. It is now the home of a branch of the Cracow History Museum and the cellars have been turned into an attractive candle-lit café. But the gem of the market-place is the Church of the Virgin Mary with its two unequal spires. Legend has it that when the two brothers who were building the church quarrelled and one was killed, the steeple of the murdered brother miraculously grew and overtook the other (the knife the brother was supposedly killed with hangs on chains in the Cloth

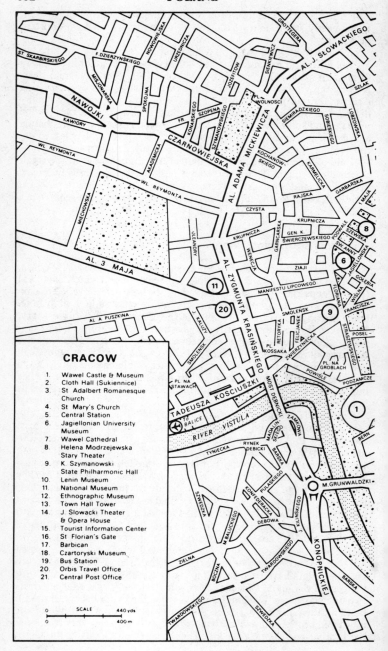

CRACOW

1. Wawel Castle & Museum
2. Cloth Hall (Sukiennice)
3. St Adalbert Romanesque Church
4. St Mary's Church
5. Central Station
6. Jagiellonian University Museum
7. Wawel Cathedral
8. Helena Modrzejewska Stary Theater
9. K. Szymanowski State Philharmonic Hall
10. Lenin Museum
11. National Museum
12. Ethnographic Museum
13. Town Hall Tower
14. J. Slowacki Theater & Opera House
15. Tourist Information Center
16. St Florian's Gate
17. Barbican
18. Czartoryski Museum
19. Bus Station
20. Orbis Travel Office
21. Central Post Office

SCALE
0 — 440 yds
0 — 400 m

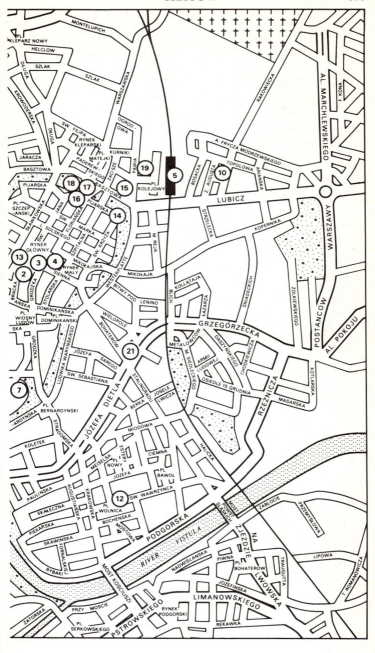

Hall). Inside the church you can see one of the most magnificent altarpieces in Europe. Carved by Wit Stwosz in the 15th century, the gilded and painted polyptych is 36 feet (11 meters) high and 42 feet (13 meters) across when fully open.

The Green Belt

The medieval town walls and moats of Cracow have now largely gone, pulled down in the mid-19th century to make room for an admittedly beautiful 2-mile (4-km) long green belt of gardens and tree-lined walks known as the Planty. How the Barbican (1499) and the St. Florian Gate (1300) at the top of ul. Floriańska were saved is another story—and probably apocryphal. A zealous burgher is reputed to have argued that without these bastions ul. Floriańska (part of the former royal route that ran down through the market place, up ul. Kanonicza and on to Wawel Castle) would become a wind tunnel, blowing the skirts of the good wives of Cracow over their heads.

Walking down ul. Floriańska, stop off at no. 45, an old coffee-shop known as Michalik's Den (Jama Michalikowa), where the 'Green Balloon' satirical cabaret attracted prominent Polish artists and writers at the turn of the century; and at no. 41, where Jan Matejko, the creator of Polish historical painting, was born in 1839. And while on the subject, the Czartoryski Museum in ul. Św. Jana (parallel to ul. Floriańska) contains two of Cracow's most famous and priceless paintings, Leonardo da Vinci's 'Lady with the Ermine' and Rembrandt's 'Landscape with the Good Samaritan'.

The Collegium Maius, the seat of the Jagiellonian University (Poland's oldest, founded in 1364), is on ul. Św. Anny. The red-brick Gothic building with its beautiful arcaded courtyard is now a museum where you can see the famous Jagiellonian Globe (c. 1510, the first globe on which the American continent was shown), as well as the astronomical instruments belonging to Nicolaus Copernicus, who must be Cracow University's most famous graduate.

Woods and Mounds

Just outside Cracow are the beautiful Wolski Woods, Cracow's favorite recreation spot; and the Kościuszko Mound (111 feet/34 meters high), which was raised in 1820 by the townspeople in honor of their national hero. There's a wonderful view of the city from the top, and on a clear day you can even see the snowy caps of the Tatra Mountains.

If you take a guided tour, you won't be allowed to miss Cracow's model industrial suburb of Nowa Huta, with the largest steelworks in western and central Europe. But the real triumph of Nowa Huta, the people will tell you, is the building of the ultra-modern, ark-shaped Church of the Queen of Poland to serve Nowa Huta's 200,000 inhabitants. The foundation stone was laid by the then Archbishop of Cracow (now occupying the Holy See in Rome) after local demands for a church were finally met. A good view of the two faces of Cracow— dreaming spires on the one hand and industrial chimneys on the other —can be had from the top of the Wanda Mound, an 8th- and 9th-century barrow or site of a pagan cult named after the legendary Wanda who drowned herself in the Vistula rather than marry a German.

Down the Salt Mines

The hilly countryside round Cracow offers many tourist attractions. At Tyniec, to the southwest, is a small village with some interesting ancient wooden buildings. Its magnificent Benedictine Abbey, founded in 1044, perches on a rocky limestone outcrop on the right bank of the Vistula. To the east, from the center of Cracow, at the village of Niepołomice, you will find the beginning of the Niepołomice Forest, once a favorite royal hunting ground abounding in bison and elk. Worth visiting are the renaissance hunting lodge of the Polish kings and the Gothic Church of the Virgin Mary (good medieval paintings). About one mile north of the village is a mound, 46 feet (14 meters) high, which was built in 1910 to commemorate Poland's victory over the armies of the Teutonic Knights near Grunwald in 1410. Niepołomice Forest is a shadow of its former self, but still has tracts of primeval forest, sheltering a herd of protected bison.

The last vestiges of old Polish architecture can be seen in Lipnica Murowana, 38 miles (61 km) east of Cracow. In spite of its name (Murowana means 'brick-built' in Polish), most of the houses in the area are in fact made of wood. The late 15th-century Church of St. Leonard, made of larchwood, is the village's most precious relic.

But the main magnet is the small town of Wieliczka, which lies about 8 miles (13 km) southeast of Cracow in the sub-Carpathian foothills. The Wieliczka salt mine, one of the biggest and oldest working salt mines in Europe, still produces about 700 tons of pure salt a day, but it is estimated that there is only enough left in the ground to keep the mines open for between 10 and 20 years. 20 worked-out chambers have been opened to the public along a one and a half mile route, which descends through three levels to a depth of 442 feet (135 meters). The mine was recently declared a historical monument of world-wide importance by UNESCO, and an extensive program of restoration has been undertaken to save its cracking props and liquefying statues.

The most breath-catching chamber in the mine is the enormous 180-foot (55-meter) long Chapel of St. Kinga, hewn out of the rock salt and illuminated by salt-crystal chandeliers. Lovely salt statues and reliefs are everywhere. Below, on a second level, are two chambers with small lakes leading through to the huge Staszic Chamber (137 feet/42 meters high) in which the Germans manufactured spare parts for aircraft during World War II, and the Warsaw Chamber, with a stage, bar and even sports facilities for the miners. But the most interesting section is undoubtedly at the deepest level, containing the air-conditioned museum of Polish salt mining, complete with lecture hall, library and small coffee bar. The museum's historic documents, wooden treadmills, wagons and mining tools go back to the 13th century when mining began at Wieliczka. Other exhibits however indicate that man was producing salt in the vicinity (by the evaporation process) as early as 3,500 BC. The geological exhibits are particularly fascinating. There are salt crystals with embedded corals, fossilized dates, pine cones and nuts, going back some 20 million years, when the area was covered by the warm waters of a Miocene ocean.

This remarkable underworld has been exploited in yet another way. The micro-climate is such that in 1964 a sanatorium for respiratory illnesses located 735 feet (224 meters) underground was opened (patients only go below for treatment). Another sanatorium, taking 1,000 patients at a time, is to be opened soon.

The town of Wieliczka itself offers some interesting sightseeing; if time allows visit the 16th-century wooden Church of St. Sebastian.

Auschwitz

A grim reminder of man's truly appalling inhumanity to man is Oświęcim, better known by its German name of Auschwitz, which lies 34 miles (54 km) west of Cracow. Between 1940 and 1945 4,000,000 human beings were gassed or shot here by the Nazis and then burnt. The camp has been turned into an eloquent museum, sparing you none of the ghastly detail, dedicated to the men, women and children from 29 countries who died here.

On the Trail of the Eagles' Nests

Northwest from Cracow is the beginning of one of Poland's prettiest scenic routes, crossing the Cracow–Częstochowa Upland (popularly known as the Cracow Jura), and winding down into the Prądnik valley and the ravines, limestone caves, and woods of the Ojców National Park. The medieval castles (nicknamed eagles' nests) that you see everywhere, strategically perched on limestone cliffs, once defended the route from Cracow to Silesia. Most of the 14 castles are now picturesquely ruined, but Pieskowa Skała (Dog's Rock) has been restored to its former renaissance splendor and is open to the public.

For something completely different, make a detour into the Błedowska Desert—12 sq. miles (32 sq. km) of shifting sand dunes, here and there overgrown with sharp-bladed grass—the only true desert in Europe. Sand storms have been known to occur here, as well as (or so people say) the optical phenomenon of 'fata morgana'. So like the deserts of North Africa is it that Rommel trained troops of the Afrika Korps here during the occupation.

The Black Madonna

Probably the holiest shrine in a country that is over 90 percent Roman Catholic is Jasna Góra (Hill of Light) in Częstochowa, a Pauline monastery founded in 1382 and converted in the early 17th century into an impressive stronghold. It was here that the advancing Swedish armies were halted in 1655 and finally driven out of the country. Among the monastery's priceless treasures is the famous Black Madonna, a painting of Our Lady of Częstochowa attributed by legend to St. Luke. The painting is said to have miraculous powers and has been the object of veneration for centuries; the two slashes in the cheek were reputedly inflicted by an enraged Tartar who found the picture getting heavier and heavier as he was trying to steal it. The image wears a cloak covered with military honors (the Poles don't find this in the least bit odd) and a protective cover is drawn up in a twice-daily ceremony in front of a large congregation. On Assumption Day (15 August) Poles in their hundred thousands converge on Częstochowa, many of them on foot as a sign of penance.

PRACTICAL INFORMATION FOR CRACOW

 WHEN TO COME. Any time of year for theater events. In June there is the International Biennale of Graphic Arts (even-numbered years), the Polish and International Short Film Festivals, the Folk Art Fair, and Lajkonik Pageant. In December the Christmas Crib Competition is held in the main Market Square. This is a magnificent display of intricate and colorful cribs made by amateurs in a variety of architectural styles, some with miniature stages and equipment for shadow theater. The best ones are chosen to go into the Cracow Historical Museum.

 GETTING AROUND. There are direct and easy connections from Warsaw to Cracow by air, train, and bus. Orbis organize morning and evening tours of Cracow (June 1 to September 30; departure from Orbis-Cracovia and Orbis-Francuski hotels) as well as scheduled coach excursions to Wieliczka salt mine, Ojców–Pieskowa Skała, Zakopane and Oświęcim.

HOTELS AND RESTAURANTS

All hotels listed below have restaurants unless otherwise stated.

Expensive

Orbis-Cracovia, Al. Puszkina 1 (tel. 286 66). 430 rooms, all with bath.

Orbis-Holiday Inn, ul. Koniewa 6 (tel. 750 44). 308 rooms, all with bath. Many facilities. This was the first Holiday Inn to be built in Eastern Europe.

Moderate

Europejski, ul. Lubicz 5 (tel. 209 11). 54 rooms.

Orbis-Francuski, ul. Pijarska 13 (tel. 251 22). 59 rooms, most with bath. Recommended for those in search of atmosphere. Good restaurant and cafe.

Korona, ul. Pstrowskiego 9/15 (tel. 618 00). Small hotel, most rooms with bath.

Kotwica, ul. Szpitalna 30 (tel. 210 44). Medium-sized hotel, about half the rooms with bath.

Monopol, ul. Warynskiego 6 (tel. 276 26). About half the rooms with bath in this medium-sized hotel. No restaurant.

Pod Kopcem, Al. Waszyngtona (tel. 222 58). Most rooms with bath. No restaurant.

Polonia, ul. Basztowa 24 (tel. 216 61). 73 rooms, most with bath.

Polski, 60 rooms, most with bath.

There are also three student hostels, which will also take in guests if they are unable to find accommodations elsewhere. These are the Hotels **Olimp** (ul. Nawojki 23, tel. 720 22), **Czyzny** (ul. Skarzynskiego 3, tel. 850 06), and **Rumcajs** (ul. Skarzynskiego 3, tel. 838 13).

 RESTAURANTS. The best in town are at the hotels: **Holiday Inn** and **Francuski,** also **Kaprys,** Florianska 32. All (E). Others recommended are: **Wierzynek,** Rynek Główny 16, in beautiful historic buildings, very popular and full of atmosphere, try their wild boar and special cakes; **Balaton,** Grodzka 37 (Polish and Hungarian food); **U Wentzla,** Rynek Główny 18, quite elegant; **Dniepr,** 18 Stycznia 55; **Staropolska,** Sienna 4; **Kurza Stopka;** all (M).

 CAFÉS AND CABARETS. Kaprys, ul Floriańska 32; **Noworol,** rather elegant café in the old Cloth Hall; **Feniks,** ul. Św. Jana 2; **Jama Michalikowa,** ul. Floriańska 45, cabaret, has 19th- and 20th-century wall paintings; **Piwnica pod Baranami,** Rynek Główny 27, an ancient palace vault, cabaret weekends only, late evening; **Pos Jaszczurami,** Rynek Główny 8, student club with good jazz; **Wieża Ratuszowa,** in Town Hall tower, Rynek Główny.

 MUSEUMS. Outstanding is the **Wawel Castle Museum** with its 71 rooms of treasures including superb Flemish tapestries and lovely furnishings. **National Gallery of Polish Painting** (Cloth Hall), Rynek Główny. Historical collection of Polish canvases; **Czartoryski Museum** (Collection of the Princes Czartoryski), Pijarska 9. Canvases of old European masters, including some works of Rembrandt and a beautiful Da Vinci; **History Museum,** Sw. Jana; **Ethnographical Museum,** Pl. Wolnica, an excellent folk museum.

 USEFUL ADDRESSES. All the information needed during your stay in Cracow may be got from *Wawel Tourist Information and Advertising Center,* ul. Pawia 8. Other tourist offices are: *Orbis,* al. Puszkina 1; *PZM,* ul. Sławkowska 4.

*Eagle + cross — Poland symbol
also Romania?*

POZNAŃ

*No more Jewish
community here
60% destroyed w[?]*

The Fair City

July 9 '87

Situated halfway between Warsaw and Berlin, in the middle of the
monotonously flat Polish lowlands, Poznań has been an east-west market place for over 1,000 years. During medieval times, merchants made
a great point of bringing their wares here on St. John's Day (June 24),
and the annual tradition has continued. The markets have now been
superseded by the important International Trade Fair, which has been
held here since 1922 and has become a major trading point between the
communist and capitalist worlds. The fair is held twice a year—June
for industrial and technical goods; September for consumer goods—
and regularly attracts British and American participation.

Up until the 13th century, Poznań was (on and off) the capital of
Poland, and in 968 the first Polish bishopric was founded here by
Miezko I. It still remains the capital of the Wielkopolska ('Great
Poland') region. Poznań is a sedate and quiet town, very conscious of
its historical role as the cradle of the Polish state. Architecturally,
there's lots to see here, from romanesque right through to neo-classical
and even Romantic-Byzantine. Start your sightseeing in the Old Market Square (Rynek Starego Miasta), with its superb Italian-style town
hall. Best time to be here is around noon, which is when you can watch
the three famous Poznań goats appear over the town hall clock. The
old pillory outside is only a copy, but you can see the original in the

History Museum of the City of Poznań inside the town hall; don't miss the renaissance Chamber on the first floor with its fine coffered ceiling dating back to 1555. The tiny arcaded shopkeepers' houses by the town hall date back to the mid-16th century, when they were built to replace the herring stalls that had been erected here since the middle of the 13th century. At no. 45 is an interesting Museum of Musical Instruments, containing exhibits from all over the world.

Poznań's many historical churches and palaces had to be either rebuilt or greatly restored after the war, since 55 percent of the town was destroyed during the fighting. Of particular interest are: Działyński Mansion, now a Dom Turysty hotel; Przemysław Castle, former seat of the great Dukes of Poland and now a Museum of Arts and Crafts (particularly interesting is their collection of woven sashes worn by Polish noblemen in the 18th century); the Franciscan church with a richly decorated stucco interior in the baroque style; the Raczyński Library, built in the 19th century with the Paris Louvre as its model; Górki Palace, a unique renaissance structure, with a roof-garden-cum-fishpond; the state ballet school (a former 18th-century Jesuit school), with a lovely baroque arcaded courtyard; a baroque parish church with 17th-century stuccos and wall paintings; Church of the Virgin Mary, with fine stained-glass and contemporary polychromy; and Poznań's oldest brick structure, the Church of St. John, built in about 1187 by the Knights Hospitallers of St. John of Jerusalem.

Ostrów Tumski (Cathedral Island), an islet in the Warta river, is the historic cradle of the town. This is where the Polanie tribe built their first fortified settlement and their first basilica in the 10th century. The present cathedral was rebuilt after the war in 15th-century Gothic, but 10th- and 11th-century remains can be seen in a special crypt, (a baptismal font and the supposed tombs of Poland's first kings—Mieszko I and Bolesław Chrobry). The Golden Chapel, containing the sarcophagi of these two kings, is worth seeing for the sheer opulence of its 'Romantic-Byzantine' style (1840), an extraordinary contrast with the stark bricks of the nave.

Music features large in Poznań. It is the home of the famous Poznań Boys' Choir—'Słowiki' (nightingales)—the State Philharmonic and the Henryk Wieniawski International Violin Competition, which is held here every five years. There are a dozen theaters and cinemas, a number of dancing spots, many restaurants and cafés and, of course, the large permanent fair ground.

Parks and Ancient Oaks

For nature lovers and the sports-minded, the Wielkopolski National Park southwest of Poznań, is a marvelous place for a day trip out of town. It has 16 lakes set in pine forests full of many different types of birds and game. Lake Rusałka and Lake Strzeszynek have long beaches, tourist accommodations and water sports equipment for hire. Kiekrz is the place for sailing enthusiasts. Splendid legends abound here. At the bottom of Lake Góreckie, for example, there is supposed to be a submerged town, and on still nights if you're very lucky you can hear the faint ringing of the town bells, although it's probably nothing more eerie than water birds calling.

The old town of Kórnik, 12 miles (20 km) southeast of Poznań, is worth visiting for its moated medieval castle housing a museum of old furniture, pictures, and hunting trophies, as well as an enormous library of incunabula and rare books (over 150,000 volumes). Watch your feet—you'll be walking on some really magnificent wooden inlaid floors. The castle, remodeled in the 19th century in English 'Mock Gothic', stands in Poland's largest arboretum.

In Rogalin, 8 miles (12 km) from Kórnik, you'll find an 18th-century palace containing a folkcraft collection and paintings by French Impressionists. Some of the oaks in the park around the palace are said to be over a 1,000 years old; and three hoary old giants, measuring about 30 feet (9 meters) around the middle, have been christened 'Lech', 'Czech' and 'Rus', the three legendary founder-brothers of the Slavic nations.

Along the 'Piast Route' to 'Pompeii'

For a trip along Poland's folk memory lane, take the 'Piast Route' from Poznań to Kruszwica, 65 miles (105 km) away in the northeast. First stop is Gniezno, residence of the first Polish rulers. According to legend it was here that Lech, one of the three Slav brothers, decided to build his city when he found white eagles nesting on the site. The white eagle was adopted as the new nation's symbol, which it has been ever since, and the settlement was named 'Gniezno', meaning nesting-site in Polish. The most important monument in Gniezno is the cathedral, restored to its basic Gothic after the war (traces of a late 10th-century, romanesque cathedral were uncovered during rebuilding). Many of the cathedral treasures were plundered during the occupation, but luckily not the amazing 'Gniezno Door', an enormous pair of 12th-century romanesque doors cast in bronze and covered with intricate bas-relief scenes from the life of St. Adalbert (the doors are now kept in the chapel behind the presbytery).

On now to Biskupin (18 miles/29 km northeast of Gniezno), where you can visit the largest, best preserved, prehistoric fortified swamp settlement in Europe. This 100 acre (40-hectare), 2,500-year-old 'Polish Pompeii' was discovered by archaeologists at the bottom of a lake near Biskupin village. Parts of it have been reconstructed and you can take yourself back into the Stone Age by wandering along the wood-paved streets and peering into the small wooden huts.

Kruszwica, a small town on Lake Gopło, 65 miles (105 km) from Poznań, is the final stop on the Piast Route. The place has legends galore about the Piast dynasty and the founding of the Polish state, probably reflecting the tribal battles fought by the Polans and Goplans for supremacy. The most popular centers on Mysia Wieża (Mouse Tower), the only surviving part of a brick castle built in 1320 by Casimir the Great. This is where the cruel king Popiel is said to have made his exit, pursued not by a bear but by hordes of ravenous, vengeful mice (Popiel had in a fit of pique poisoned his dinner party guests, who were casting envious eyes on his throne, and thrown them in the lake; mice had emerged out of the bodies, besieging Popiel in his tower until he starved to death).

The other legend is of course about Piast, the humble cartwright, and how he became king. Piast's son was having his hair cut for the first time on his seventh birthday to mark his passage from the nursery into his father's strict care, when two beautiful strangers knocked on the door. Piast welcomed them and asked them to perform the rite of cutting the boy's hair. They did so, baptized the child and prophesied that Piast would one day found a dynasty. In 1966, when Poland celebrated 1,000 years of Christianity, the Lake Gopło area was designated a landscape reserve.

On your way back to Poznań, stop by at an 18th-century working windmill at Lednogóra, where the resident miller will sell you a small bag of flour together with a recipe for a delicious old-Polish *zurek* (a sort of sour soup).

PRACTICAL INFORMATION FOR POZNAŃ

WHEN TO COME. The main event of the year is the International Trade Fair in June, which has been held annually for over 50 years. Summers are warm, with water sports on the nearby lakes, set among pine forests.

GETTING AROUND. There are regular connections by air from Warsaw, which are more frequent during the Trade Fair. Fast train connections also exist, though traveling by car gives you more freedom. Poznań lies on two main routes, E8 and E83 and is also included in Orbis tours from Warsaw.

HOTELS AND RESTAURANTS

All hotels listed below have restaurants unless otherwise stated. During the fair, accommodations can be very hard to find. It is advisable to book well in advance if you plan to visit Poznan during this period.

Expensive

Orbis-Merkury, ul. Roosevelta 20 (tel. 408 01). 351 rooms, 42 suites; every comfort.

Orbis-Novotel, ul. Warszawska 64 (tel. 700 41). 154 double rooms with bath.

Orbis-Polonez, ul. Stalingradzka 54/68 (tel. 699 141). 408 rooms, most with bath.

Orbis-Poznan, ul. gen. Dabrowskiego 1 (tel. 332 081). 425 rooms, 20 suites.

Moderate

Orbis-Bazar, al. Marcinkowskiego 10 (tel. 512 51). 89 rooms, all with bath.

Dom Turysty, Stary Rynek 91 (tel. 588 93). 41 rooms, about half with bath.

Wielkopolski, ul. Czerwonej Armii 67 (tel. 576 31). 106 rooms, most with bath.

RESTAURANTS AND CAFÉS. Poznań eating places are apt to be very crowded during the fair. Apart from those in the hotels mentioned above, you can eat and dance at the following (all M-E). **Magnolia,** ul. Głogowska 40; **Adria,** ul. Głogowska 14; **Pod Koziolkami,** Stary Rynek 63; **Moulin Rouge,** ul. Kantaka 8/9; **Smakosz,** ul. 27 Grudnia 8 and **Arkadia,** pl. Wolności 11.

USEFUL ADDRESSES. The two main tourist offices are: *Orbis,* ul. Głogowska 10 and *PZM,* ul. Ratajczaka 44.

WROCŁAW AND THE SOUTHWEST

Youth and Health

Situated midway between Cracow and Poznań on the Odra river, Wrocław, the capital of Lower Silesia, dates back to the 10th century when Ostrów Tumski islet on the Odra became a fortified Slav settlement. There are now some 100 bridges spanning the city's 56-mile (90-km) network of slow-moving canals and tributaries, giving it its particular charming character. The other overwhelming impression you will get is of the extraordinary preponderance of young people—almost half the population is under 30 years old—something which is reflected in the large number of institutions of higher learning in the city.

Although it suffered tremendous losses during the last war, Wrocław has gone to great effort to restore its old buildings. Sightseeing should start in the market square, which is almost as grand as the one in Cracow. The dominant feature here is the Town Hall, basically Gothic with a dash of renaissance and baroque. Of the many old houses around the square, with their characteristic steep gables, particularly appealing are the two little 'Hansel' and 'Gretel' houses, coyly holding hands over a linking arcade.

Ostrów Tumski (Cathedral Island—though it's no longer an island) is the cradle of Wrocław and one of its most charming olde-worlde quarters. Dominating it is the impressive Gothic cathedral, with a high altar that has been ascribed to the workshop of Wit Stwosz, the famous 15th-century master sculptor. On the other side of the river are two fine baroque buildings: the University on pl. Uniwersytecki (occupying a former Jesuit Academy built in 1728–42) has a magnificent assembly hall—the Aula Leopoldina—with some rather lush frescoes that somehow managed to survive the war; close by in ul. Szewska is the Ossolineum National Institution, which houses the biggest collection of manuscripts and old prints in Poland.

Wrocław buzzes with culture, which is reflected in the many artistic festivals held here each year and its flourishing experimental theater groups, particularly the world-famous Jerzy Grotowski Laboratory Theater and Henryk Tomaszewski's Pantomime Theater.

Surrounding Sights

The countryside around Wrocław is particularly rich in architecture, and every small town and hamlet seems to have its four-star monument. The following are all within 50 miles (80 km) of Wrocław and worth visiting, perhaps on your way to the Karkonosze Mountains. Lubiąż (famous Cistercian Abbey); Henryków (an equally fine Cistercian Abbey); Świdnica, the medieval capital of the Piast dukes (Gothic church); Bolków (13th-century castle); Bolesławiec (baroque houses and town hall, defense walls); Legnica, the site of the famous battle against the Tartar hordes in 1241 (baroque church with magnificent murals); Oleśnica (14th-century castle); Trzebnica (romanesque-Gothic basilica rebuilt in the 18th century, with two surviving tympana from about 1230–40); Opole (14th-century Piast Tower); Paczków, a magnificent little town, a kind of 'Polish Carcassonne', completely ringed by medieval walls with towers and bastions.

Into the Valley of Health

Wrocław is a good jumping-off point for touring the holiday resorts and spas in the southwest of the country, and in the Kłodzko valley you'll find some of Poland's most famous spas. Kudowa-Zdrój ('zdrój' means 'spa' in Polish by the way) was once visited by Winston Churchill; situated in a deep, sheltered valley it was a popular health resort as early as the 17th century. In July it plays host to the Moniuszko Festival, celebrating the creator of the Polish opera style. The ghoulish might like to visit the Skull Chapel in Czermna (1 mile/2 km to the north), which is lined with thousands of human skulls and bones. Behind Kudowa-Zdrój, sheltering it from the north wind, stretch the Stołowe (Table) Mountains, a labyrinth of gorges, ravines, and really extraordinary rock formations.

Of the other spas in the area—Lądek-Zdrój, Polanica-Zdrój and Duszniki-Zdrój—the last is perhaps the most famous. It was here that the 16-year-old Chopin came for treatment and gave two public concerts to raise money for some orphaned children. An annual Chopin festival (mid-August) takes place in the small spa theater in which Chopin gave his two concerts in 1826.

Skiing Country

Further west is the Jelenia Góra valley, with its main ski resorts of Karpacz and Szklarska Poręba situated on the thickly wooded slopes of the Karkonosze, the highest range of the Sudety Mountains. The climate is fairly severe here, with heavy snowfalls, so skiing conditions are exceptionally good. Karpacz has a bob-sleigh track and a ski lift up the slopes of Mount Śnieżka, (5,257 feet/1,602 meters). While you're up here try and see the local curiosity in Bierutowice (in upper Karpacz). This is a 13th-century wooden church that originally stood on Lake Wang in Norway. In 1841 Frederick William IV of Prussia brought it over lock, stock, and altar and erected it on the present site. Even now after more than a 100 years, the romanesque-cum-Viking elements carved on the doorpost look strangely alien here.

PRACTICAL INFORMATION FOR THE
SOUTHWEST

 WHEN TO COME. From August through September, the 'Wratislavia Cantans' Festival of Oratorio and Cantata Music is held in Wrocław. From November to May, there are excellent winter sports facilities in the southwest. The spas are open year round.

 GETTING AROUND. There are regular connections by air from Warsaw to Wrocław; trains and buses complete the network. Four international road routes run through this region—E14, E22, E83, and E12.

HOTELS AND RESTAURANTS

All hotels listed below have restaurants unless otherwise stated.

DUSZNIKI-ZDRÓJ. Pod Muflonem (chalet), ul. Górska 14; private accommodation office is at Rynek 14.

JELENIA GÓRA. Europejski (I), ul. 1 Maja 16; PTTK Tourist Hostel, ul. 1 Maja 88.
Two good restaurants are Karczma Staropolska (M) and Pod Lipami (M), which is just outside the town.

KARPACZ. Orbis Skalny (E), ul. Obrońców 3; Orlinek (M), ul. Olimpijska 9; private accommodation office is at ul. 1 Maja 8.

KŁODZKO. Astoria (I), pl. Jedności 1 (also handles all private accommodation).

KUDOWA-ZDRÓJ. Kosmos (I), ul. Buczka 8a.

SZKLARSKA POREBA. Chalet, on the Hala Szrenicka; **Karkonosze,** ul. Sikorskiego 2; private accommodation office is at ul. 1 Maja 4.

ŚWIDNICA. Two good restaurants (both M) are **Zagłoba,** a tavern serving Old Polish dishes, specialty of spiced hot mead, and **Stylowa,** with Hungarian interior and food (try their *halasle* fish soup).

WROCŁAW. Novotel-Orbis (E), ul. Wyścigowa 35. New hotel with 154 rooms, restaurant, outdoor swimming pool; **Orbis-Panorama** (M), pl. Dzierżyńskiego 8; **Orbis-Monopol** (M), ul. Modrzejewskiej 2, has good restaurant; **Grand** (M), ul. Świerczewskiego 102; **Europejski** (M), ul Świerczewskiego 88.

 RESTAURANTS AND CAFÉS. Stylowa, pl. Kościuszki 1/4, **Lotos,** ul. Grabiszyńska 9 (both E); **Bieriozka,** ul. Nowotki 13 (Russian food) and **Lajkonik,** ul. Nowowiejska 102 (both M); **Herbowa,** Rynek 19, is a tearoom-café.

 USEFUL ADDRESSES. Most main towns have Orbis and PZM offices. The main tourist offices for Wrocław are: *Orbis,* Rynek 29 and ul. Świerczewskiego 62; *PZM,* pl. Solny 15.

THE BALTIC BEACHES

Beaches and Châteaux

A dip in the Baltic Sea is a rugged but rewarding experience, which you can enjoy at a wide choice of resorts scattered along Poland's 311-mile (500-km) coastline. There is fine soft sand for sunbathing, but the exposed coast is often very windy. You can however rent a special windproof beach device, half tent, half chair, to ward off the chill north wind. Thick fragrant pine forests begin at the beach edge, their inviting paths lined with little refreshment stands selling strawberries, raspberries, and blueberries, which you can take back to the sand and eat with thick fresh cream. Mosquitoes also like these woods, so take along your insect repellent.

Tri-City

Sopot, with its 1-mile (2-km) sandy beach, concert pier, and the romantically situated open-air Forest Opera, used to be the most elegant seaside resort in Poland. But its popularity has caught up with it; it tends to get very crowded and is beginning to look a bit down-at-heel. Its position, squeezed between the two large ports of Gdynia and Gdańsk, forming part of a stretch of built-up coastline known as 'Tri-City', has inevitably meant that the sheltered bay is beginning to show signs of pollution. Nevertheless, it has retained its Riviera-like atmosphere, which is reflected in its mid-summer international festival of pop music and annual election of 'Miss Polonia'. There is an excellent racecourse on the southern outskirts of the resort.

The Kashubian Lakes, set amid wooded hills, are a welcome change from Sopot's sun and sand. The area, popularly known as the 'Kashubian Switzerland', is easily reached by road (about 25 miles/40 km southwest) and is well worth visiting for its strong local culture and folk art; Kashubian ceramics are particularly famous and can be bought at Chmielno, the center of Kashubian pottery. Interestingly, the Kashubs speak a dialect which is the most far removed of any from written Polish.

Gdynia is to the Poles a proud example of what they were able to achieve after regaining their independence. In 1924 it was only a tiny fishing village, but by 1939 it had grown into one of the biggest ports on the Baltic. Unless your taste runs to modern cargo-handlers and shipyards however, you won't find that much to see here, apart from a few fishermen's cottages that have been 'preserved' and two good museums (the Oceanographic Museum and the Polish Navy Museum).

Gdańsk—formerly the 'Free City' of Danzig—is altogether different. It has changed hands many times in its 1,000 years of history, the Poles taking turns with the Teutonic Knights, the Prussians, and finally the Nazis. The first shots of World War II were fired here, and at Westerplatte, jutting out into the mouth of Port Canal, stands the monument to the Defenders of the Coast. Here a small Polish garrison bravely resisted German attacks from 1 to 7 September 1939. The old town was 90 percent destroyed but has been completely rebuilt. Your sightseeing list should include the Church of the Virgin Mary, one of the largest Gothic brick churches in Poland reputedly able to hold some 25,000 people; the Golden Gate (1612); a Gothic town hall, now housing a branch of the Pomerania Museum; Długa Street, lined with beautifully restored renaissance houses; Gothic Artus Court; the 17th-century Neptune fountain; the late Gothic St. George Fraternity Mansion; and the Old Crane (1443) on the Motława river, which has an inbuilt wooden elevator. The medieval Dominican Fair, held in Gdańsk since the 12th century, was revived several years ago, so it's worth being in town during the early part of August to join in the general merrymaking—and buy your souvenirs.

Oliwa, now a Gdańsk suburb on the road to Sopot, you must visit. Its 13th- to 15th-century cathedral (a former Cistercian abbey) houses one of the most amazing rococo organs you're ever likely to hear—and see. It has nearly 8,000 pipes and when a special mechanism is activated wooden angels ring bells and blow trumpets, and a wooden star climbs up a wooden sky. There are daily organ recitals here, and an annual organ festival takes place in August.

Go to Hel

Sopot tends to be overrun in the summer months, so for a change of pace you can try Hel. This beautiful forested peninsula of sandy beaches curves far out into the Gulf of Gdańsk, threatening to cut off Puck Bay completely and form a coastal lake, a characteristic feature of Poland's seaboard. Jastarnia is a quiet fishing village, a favorite with 'artists', while Jurata is the most modern and fashionable. Władystawowo, another popular resort, is soon to have an open-air folk museum, featuring a 200-year-old fisherman's cabin where you will be able to examine old fishing gear and the arts and crafts of the Kashubs. Rozewie lighthouse (the northernmost point on Poland's coastline), very near Władystawowo, houses mementoes of Stefan Żeromski, a 19th-century Polish writer who often stayed here. Hel village at the tip of the peninsula has an ancient tradition of folk art and architecture and is well worth visiting; the Gothic church has been turned into a Fishing Museum, and there's a lighthouse and some early 19th-century fishermen's cottages.

Forever Amber

Fishermen finding large quantities of amber washed up by the sea in this area called it the 'Amber Coast'. It's a lovely part of the Baltic seaboard, stretching for 35 miles (56 km.) between Gdańsk and the tip of the Vistual Spit; an area of sandy beaches and wooded slopes. A splendid way of seeing it, particularly if you have children, is to take a 'toy-train' ride on the Amber Route narrow-gauge railway line, which consists of a little steam engine pulling several brightly painted open cars along a 2-mile (20-km) route from Jantar to Sztutowo.

Taking over from Sopot as *the* place to spend one's summer holidays is the tiny fishing village of Krynica Morska, which is about 12 miles (20 km) from Sztutowo, in the middle of the Vistula Spit, with sandy beaches and forests all round.

The Polish Riviera

The many resorts strung out along Poland's 'Riviera' cater for all tastes, ranging from busy Kołobrzeg, one of the most fashionable resorts and spas on the open coast, to the quieter fishing villages of Ustronie Morskie, Mielno, Unieście, and Jarosławiec. Ustka and Łeba are also popular, particularly the latter with its famous shifting dunes of white quartz sand (often used by the Polish film industry for desert scenes). Świnoujście, situated on the eastern headland of Uznam Island (the rest of the island belongs to East Germany by the way), is a fishing port and popular health resort, with a ferry service to Ystad in Sweden and a hydrofoil down into Szczecin. Międzyzdroje on Wolin Island (which is the other island at the entrance to the funnel-shaped bay of Szczecin) is the warmest of all Polish sea resorts; it has a vast sunny beach, backed by magnificent walks in the beechwoods of the Wolin National Park, where you might be able to catch a glimpse of the rare sea eagle. Other attractions on offer include the famous thermal springs, varied sports facilities, and a busy social life.

The best place on the mainland is the lovely old town of Kamień Pomorski. Its late-romanesque cathedral (with Gothic conversion) has a splendid baroque organ on which recitals are given every Friday throughout the summer; there is also ar annual festival of organ and chamber music in June.

Szczecin, on the mouth of the Odra (Oder) river, is the largest port on the Baltic, for all that it lies some 37 miles (60 km) from the open sea. Like Gdańsk it has changed hands many times down the centuries, and, like Gdańsk, it has had to rebuild its many war-damaged historic buildings and architectural monuments. The city was remodeled in the 19th century on the Parisian system of radiating streets and is particularly pretty in spring when the avenues along the Odra glow with flowering magnolias.

Knights and Castles

Avid sightseers might find it rewarding to visit Poland's chateau country on their way to the Baltic. Toruń, birthplace of Nicolaus Copernicus, is a most interesting medieval city, with remarkable architecture, several Gothic churches and well-preserved granaries. Chełmno, one of the most attractive ancient towns in Poland, perches on a promontory, its 13th-century ramparts almost intact. It was from this town, leased to them in 1228 by the Duke of Mazovia, that the Teutonic Knights launched their conquest of Prussia. The once fortified town of Grudziądz has centuries-old grain storehouses along the river—still in use.

Next stop is Gniew, which also has a 13th-century castle belonging to the Teutonic Knights, as well as arcaded Gothic houses in the market square. Malbork, 58 km. (36 miles) from Gdańsk, is also well worth a visit. The hugh Castle of the Teutonic Knights, the residence of the Grand Masters between 1308 and 1457, was one of the most impressive strongholds in medieval Europe. Tucked away in the castle is the intriguing Amber Museum, where you'll see some magnificent examples of this fossil resin—lumps as big as a human head, in colors ranging from palest yellow through to golden-orange, red and bronze. Some pieces contain perfect specimens of imprisoned prehistoric plants and insects, while others hold inorganic bodies such as grains of sand or bubbles of water. Amber has been used to make decorative items since time immemorial and the museum's collection ranges from Neolithic times to the present day. While in Malbork see also the small, beautifully maintained cemetery for British and American heroes who fell in defense of this town during World War II.

PRACTICAL INFORMATION FOR THE BALTIC BEACHES

WHEN TO COME. June through September is the time for a good suntan. However, this is also the time when the Baltic beaches will be crowded with Poles and Scandinavians taking their own summer vacations, though there are still many less-frequented villages and beaches strung out along the coast.

GETTING AROUND. There are direct rail and air connections from Warsaw to Gdańsk, Koszalin, Słupsk, and Szczecin. Traveling by car gives you greater freedom and roads are well maintained.

HOTELS AND RESTAURANTS

All hotels listed below have restaurants unless otherwise stated.

GDAŃSK. Orbis-Novotel (E), ul. Pszenna 1, 154 rooms, all with bath; the **Orbis-Hevelius** (E), ul. Heweliusza, 250 rooms.
Restaurants and Cafés. Gedania (M), ul. Dluga 75; **Pod Zurawiem,** ul. Dlugie Pobrzeze; **Cristal,** ul. Grunwaldzka 105; **Kameleon,** ul. Armii Radzieckiej 10. A very popular café that is always overflowing is **Marysieńka,** ul. Szeroka 29, with dancing.

GDAŃSK-JELITKOWO. Orbis-Posejdon (E), ul. Kapliczna 33.

GDYNIA. Bałtyk (M), ul. Kielecka 2a.
Restaurants and cafés. Polonia, ul. Świętojańska 92; **George,** ul. 3 Maja 21; **Sim,** ul. Świętojańska 21; **Myśliwska,** ul. Abrahama 18 (all M). Two good cafés are **Arkadia,** ul. Władysława IV 7/15 and **Grand Café,** ul. Świetojańska 27.

KOŁOBRZEG. Orbis-Solny (M), ul. Fredry 4; **Skanpol** (M), ul. Dworcowa 10, 188 rooms, at the edge of a sandy beach. A good restaurant is **Fregata** (M-E), ul. Dworcowa 12.

KOSZALIN. Jałta (I), ul. Zwycięstwa 20/24; **Turystyczny** (I), ul. B. Głowackiego 7/9.
Restaurants. (All M) **Bryza,** ul. Morska 15 (Kashubian cuisine); **Fregata,** ul. Krótka 6 (nightclub, too); **Neubrandenburg,** ul. W. Wasilewskiej 1 (German cuisine).

SŁUPSK. Zamkowy (I), ul. Dominikańska 9; **Gryf,** pl. Jedności Narodowej 5; **Piast,** pl. Jedności Narodowej 1.
Restaurants. Two very good ones here renowned throughout Poland, serving regional specialties: **Karczma Słupska,** ul. Wojska Polskiego 11 and **Pod Kluką,** ul. Kaszubska 22 (both E).

SOPOT. Orbis-Grand (E), ul. Powstańców Warszawy 8/12, 154 rooms, many with bath; **Maryla** (I), al. Sępia 22; **Irena** (I), ul. Chopina 36; **Bungalow** (I), al. Sępia 50; **Dom Turysty** (M), al. Sępia 51, with camping site at Kamienny Potok.
Restaurants and cafés. Ermitage, ul. Bohaterów Monte Cassino 23; **Alga,** ul. Bohaterów Monte Cassino 62 (both M); an inexpensive café is **Złoty Ul,** ul. Bohaterów Monte Cassino 17.

ŚWINOUJSCIE. Bałtyk (I), ul. Armii Czerwonej 4: **Albatros** (I), ul. Kasprowicza 2; **Atol,** ul. Orkana 3; **Orbis-Alga** pension, ul. Zeromskiego 2.
Restaurants Both (M) are: **Albatros,** ul. Powstańców Ślaskich 1 and **Bałtyk,** ul. Armii Czerwonej 5.

SZCZECIN. Orbis-Arkona (M), ul. Panieńska 10; **Orbis-Reda (M),** ul. Cukrowa 1; **Orbis-Continental (M),** ul. 3 Maja 1; **Gryf (M),** al. Wojska Polskiego 49; **Piast (M),** pl. Zwycięstwa 3; **Pomorski (I),** Brama Portowa 4; **Sportowy (I),** ul. Unisławy 29.

Restaurants and cafés. Kaskada (E), ul. Obrońców Stalingradu 28; **Balaton (M),** pl. Lotników; **Atlantycka (M),** ul. Niepodległości 30; **Ryska,** ul. Piastów 16; **Chief,** pl. Grunwaldzki. Four lively cafés are: **Jubilatka,** al. Wojska Polskiego 39; **Zamkowa** (in the castle); **Kaprys,** ul. Krzywoustego 5 and **13 Muz,** Zołnierza Polskiego 2.

TORUŃ. Orbis-Helios (M), ul. Kraszewskiego 1/3; **Orbis-Kosmos (M),** ul. Portowa 2; **Pod Orłem (I),** ul. Mostowa 17; **Polonia (I),** pl. Armii Czerwonej 5; **Pod Trzema Koronami (I),** Rynek Staromiejski 21.

 USEFUL ADDRESSES. Most towns and resorts have Orbis and PZM tourist offices. The main Orbis offices for the region are as follows. **Koszalin:** ul. Zwycięstwa 20; **Gdańsk:** pl. Gorkiego 1; **Słupsk:** ul. Wojska Polskiego 1; **Szczecin:** pl. Zwycięstwa 1.

THE NORTHEAST

Land of a Thousand Lakes

In the northeast of Poland—formerly part of East Prussia—lies a land of a 1,000 lakes, 1,000-year-old forests; and thousands of mosquitoes. Hardly known to western tourists, the Mazurian and Augustów-Suwałki lakes form an intriguing labyrinth of interconnecting lakes, rivers, and canals, set amid ancient forests teeming with birds and wild animals. Whatever you're looking for—a 'back to nature' type of holiday, sailing, canoeing, hunting with a gun or camera, foraging for mushrooms (the national pastime), fishing, or even ice-sailing on the frozen Mazurian lakes in winter—you'll find it here.

The area's 90 nature reserves are a paradise for both birds and animals, some of them now extremely rare and found only in zoos elsewhere in Europe. In the Borecka Forest, 15 miles (25 km) northeast of Giżycko, lives a wild herd of European bison, some 300 strong, while at Popielno on Lake Śniardwy there are wild tarpan ponies, the smallest forest ponies in the world, which until recently were on their way to becoming extinct. The largest herd of elk (300 head) in Europe can be spotted in the Czerwone Bagno (Red Swamp) reserve, 8 miles (12 km) southeast of Rajgród, not far from Augustów. Other less exotic animals include lynx, roe-deer, foxes, and beavers (particularly on the Pasłęka river). Shoots are organized for wild goose, duck, wood grouse, and black grouse, but you'll need a permit. Take along your camera to take shots of the area's protected eagles circling the sky, nesting grey herons on Lake Śniardwy and the largest concentration of mute swans in Europe on Lake Luknajno. Ostrów Wysoki island on Lake Mamry is the place for cormorants.

So large are some of the lakes that they're known as the 'Mazurian seas'; there's no pollution as yet since the Poles very sensibly don't let motor boats into some of the waterways (good news, too, for those who don't like the constant whine of outboard motors). Fish thrive here and anglers can hook salmon, trout, miller's thumb, European whitefish, eel, pike, and many other fish characteristic of foothill and lowland regions. A special treat is hunting for crayfish by torchlight and fishing with nets for delicious bleak and lavaret on Mamry and Wigry lakes in depths of up to 131 feet (40 m).

This sparsely populated area also has its ethnic oddities, in the form of a sect of Russian Old Believers who settled in these parts in the 17th century. In several of their close communities people still speak an archaic form of Russian and keep to their religious practices. They intermarry and the men are not allowed to shave their beards.

The Mazurian lakes are synonymous with sailing, however. Here the wind can almost always be guaranteed, averaging 3–5 on the Beaufort scale for about 70 per cent of the time. For canoeists the chains of interconnected lakes and rivers offer some of the finest routes in the country. Best are the Łyna and Krutynia rivers and the Czarna Hańcza, perhaps the prettiest and most winding river in the country. While in the Augustów area take a trip down the Augustów Canal, built in 1824–39 to link the Vistula and Niemen basins. The old canal buildings and locks have been carefully preserved.

Olsztyn is the principal city, and Giżycko, Mikołajki, Ruciane-Nida, Węgorzewo, and Augustów are among the main resorts. In addition to inexpensive hotels and boarding houses, self-catering cottages can be rented through the Mazur Tourist Enterprise, who also arrange all kinds of special interest facilities, such as boat or bicycle hire, photo-safaris, and sailing holidays. Try their 'Baked Potato Holiday' in mid-September, which includes a ride on a horse-drawn farmer's wagon, ending in bonfire-side tastings of the region's culinary specialties.

Copernicus Country

In this part of Poland every other town—Lidzbark Warmiński, Olsztyn, Malbork, and Frombork—seems to have some connection with the great Polish astronomer who was born in Toruń over 500 years ago. As befitted a renaissance man Copernicus was able to turn his hand to most things and in the years 1516–21 successfully directed the defense of Olsztyn castle against the Knights of the Teutonic Order. In Frombork, where he spent 30 years of his life, Copernicus was elected canon of the cathedral. This meant lifelong financial security, enabling him to make some of his most famous discoveries. Adjoining the massive Gothic cathedral that dominates the town is the Nicolaus Copernicus Museum, where you can see a Mercator atlas of 1595 and a 1617 copy of Copernicus's *De Revolutionibus Orbium Coelestium* (On the Revolutions of the Celestial Spheres) explaining his theory of a heliocentric universe. Lidzbark Warmiński, where Copernicus was employed by the bishop of Warmia as a personal-cum-medical secretary, has a monumental Gothic castle which survived the war only because the local population refused to help the Germans demolish it. It is one of the best preserved examples of secular medieval architecture in Poland and has been turned into a museum.

The Wolf's Den

In Gierłoż Forest, about 5 miles (8 km) from Kętrzyn, stand the ruins of a massive concrete bunker known as the 'Wolf's Den', the headquarters of Hitler's general staff during World War II, which the Nazis themselves blew up in 1945. An unsuccessful attempt on Hitler's life was made here on 28 August 1944.

Two places worth stopping off at between Kętrzyn and Lidzbark Warmiński are Święta Lipka, a beautiful 17th-century baroque church built with donations collected from all over Poland, and Reszel, with its Gothic parish church, Gothic bridge, and old houses and granaries. But if you're more interested in regional folk architecture, the place to go is the Olsztynek open-air folk museum, featuring a small Mazurian thatch-roofed church, inn, mill, forge, old windmills, and thatched cottages, some of which have been furnished period-style.

For a wolf of another order, take a detour to the Grunwald Battlefield several kilometers west of Olsztynek and the E81, the site of the greatest battle of the Middle Ages. Here, on 15 July 1410, Władysław Jagiełło and his Polish-Lithuanian army annihilated the Grand Master of the Teutonic Order, Ulrich von Jungingen, and thousands of his knights. A small museum on the site (open summer only, 10 to 10) graphically explains the course of the battle.

PRACTICAL INFORMATION FOR THE
NORTHEAST

 WHEN TO COME. The main season of interest is summer, but Orbis organizes winter-break holidays that include sleigh-rides, skiing, sledging, skating, and ice-hole angling.

 GETTING AROUND. There are direct rail and road connections with Warsaw. Passenger steamers through the lakes operate from Giżycko and boats and canoes may be hired through Orbis. You can tour the forest by coach or private car. Orbis also organize a Copernicus sightseeing tour from Warsaw.

HOTELS AND RESTAURANTS

All hotels listed below have restaurants unless otherwise stated.

AUGUSTÓW. Stara Poczta (I), ul. 1 Maja 73; **PTTK Tourist Hostel,** ul. Sportowa 1.

BIAŁYSTOK. Turkus (I), ul. Zwycięstwa 54; **Cristal** (I), ul. Lipowa 3.

ELBLAG. Dworcowy (I), al. Grunwaldzka 49; **Żuławy** (I), al. Armii Czerwonej 126.
Restaurant. Słowiańska (M).

FROMBORK. PTTK Tourist Hostel (I), in cathedral precincts.

GIŻYCKO. Wodnik (I), ul. 1 Maja 7; **Mazurski** (I), pl. Grunwaldzki 17. Two good restaurants, both (M) are: Centralna and Wodnik (in the hotel of the same name).

LIDZBARK WARMIŃSKI. PTTK Tourist Hostel (I), in the High Gate.

OLSZTYN. Orbis-Novotel (M), ul. Sielska 4, new hotel with 98 rooms and swimming pool; **Gromada-Kormoran** (I), ul. Kościuszki 6; **Warmiński** (I), ul. Głowackiego 8.
Restaurants. Nowoczesna (E); Pod Żaglami (M).

SUWAŁKI. Hańcza (I), ul. Wojska Polskiego 1; **Motel,** ul. Mazurska 1.

USEFUL ADDRESSES. All in Olsztyn: *Mazur-Tourist Enterprise,* ul. Staromiejska 6. Arranges everything from standard holidays to Foto-Safari events and scuba-diving; also rents out private cottages. Orbis, ul. Dąbrowszczaków 1; PZM, ul. Pstrowskiego 28.

ZAKOPANE AND THE DUNAJEC RIVER

High Paradise

Poland's 'winter capital', 2,626 feet (800 meters) high in the dramatic Tatra Mountains along the Czechoslovakian border, is Zakopane, the top winter-sports resort in the country. Real skiers, both native and foreign, mix with a fair sprinkling of dedicated après-skiers, who tend to be more interested in smart anoraks and the town's fairly sophisticated nightlife than anything else. Nevertheless the old town hasn't quite vanished, and you'll still see plenty of traditional mountain chalets with their carved gables and steeply sloping roofs. It's probably tourism that is keeping folk traditions and costumes alive here, but it means that you can enjoy splendid sleigh rides and bonfire evenings where highlanders clad in white woolen trousers perform the dramatic Zbójnicki Robbers Dance (a sort of souped-up version of the Highland Fling).

Skiing conditions are excellent, the season lasting from November right through to May. There is a funicular to the top of Gubałówka just above the town, and a cable car (be prepared for a long wait in the season unless you have prebooked) to the top of Kasprowy Wierch (nearly 6,514 feet/1,985 m), the most famous skiers' mountain in Poland, with a mountain-top restaurant right on the border with Czechos-

358

lovakia. The whole Zakopane area is well equipped with chair and trapeze lifts, and there are four ski jumps.

Room to Breathe

The deep alpine pastures, clear mountain streams and waterfalls of the Tatras draw thousands of visitors in the summer, too. Marked trails provide pleasant walks, catering for all degrees of physical fitness, and since the whole area has been declared a national park, you're likely to see eagles, chamois, marmots, lynxes, and even bears. In spring there are flowering fields of protected wild crocus, particularly in the Chocołowska valley. The lovely 5-mile (8-km) long Kościeliska valley is where most people head for however, and in the height of summer it's a bit like Grand Central Station. Well worth a visit is Morskie Oko (Eye of the Sea), a crater-like lake nestled among soaring snow-capped peaks.

If you want to find some really untouched nature, stop off at the Gorce Heights, to the left of Nowy Targ as you go towards Zakopane, and try a climb up the thickly forested Mount Turbacz. It's not for the faint-hearted, the undergrowth hasn't been kept in check and there are rotting tree trunks everywhere, but you won't meet a soul and the reward is a magnificent view from the mountain-top shelter.

Rivalling Zakopane are the two fast-developing resorts of Wisła and Szcyrk in the forested Beskid-Śląski mountains to the west. When there's snow, and it can't always be guaranteed in this particular area, there are excellent skiing conditions and numerous ski lifts on the slopes of Mount Skrzyczne (4,125 feet/1,257 meters) and a funicular up Szyndzielnia. For those who prefer their skiing fairly primitive however, the Beskid-Żywiecki mountains (main resort Zwardoń) will offer none of the trappings, but guarantees snow.

Down the Dunajec

Not far beyond the Tatras lie the picturesque Pieniny, a small range of limestone mountains, sliced through by the magnificent Dunajec river gorge, its sheer cliff faces rising up to 985 feet (300 m). For a different type of thrill, take the nerve-twisting, half-day raft ride down the sinuous, turbulent river from Czorsztyn to Szczawnica.

The Podhale region, between Zakopane and Czorsztyn, is noted for its quaint wooden villages and colorful costumes. It's certainly worth a visit, particularly the mountain village of Dębno (23 miles/38 km from Zakopane), which boasts one of the oldest and loveliest specimens of wooden folk architecture you're likely to see. The small 15th-century church, shingle-covered and built of larchwood, is inside entirely covered with geometrical, floral, and figural paintings, which even after all this time still look remarkably fresh.

Winter Sports

Krynica, in the nearby Beskid Sądecki mountains further east, is also an important winter sports resort. There is snow here from December through to March and plenty of sunny days. On Góra Parkowa you'll find a mountain-top restaurant with beautiful views, skiing grounds, a toboggan run, ski-jump, and a funicular to take you there. But its main claim to fame is as a spa, Krynica waters being regarded as some of the best in Europe. The secluded south-facing valley, protected from the freezing north wind by high wooded slopes, is a marvelous sun-trap, making Krynica one of the warmest places in the area. In spring a charming 'Apple Blossom Days' festival, attended by dozens of regional folk troupes, takes place in this region of orchards.

PRACTICAL INFORMATION

WHEN TO COME. Winter lasts six months with good skiing well into May in the Zakopane region. Summer offers pleasant mountain and river excursions. Many cultural and sports events throughout the year, particularly the 'Tatra Autumn', the main event of which is the International Festival of Highland Folklore in early September.

GETTING AROUND. Zakopane is linked to the Dunajec region and to the rest of the country by efficient rail and bus networks. Orbis organize half-day raft excursions down the river Dunajec during summer.

HOTELS AND RESTAURANTS

All hotels listed below have restaurants unless otherwise stated.

KRYNICA. Rzymianka Tourist Hostel, ul. Dabrowskiego 15. The private accommodations office is at ul. Pułaskiego 4/1.

Restaurant. Góra Parkowa (M), right on top of Park Mountain and reached by funicular; great views from the terrace.

NOWY SĄCZ. Orbis-Beskid (M), ul. Limanowskiego 1, 145 rooms, some with bath or shower. The private accommodation office is at Rynek 15. A recommended restaurant is **Imperial** (M), ul. Jagiellońska 14.

ZAKOPANE. Orbis-Kasprowy (L), Polana Szymoszkowa, 300 double rooms with bath, restaurant, nightclub, indoor pool, sauna, ice rink, minigolf, overlooks the resort from a fine position on the outskirts; very central is the **Giewont** (M), ul. Kościuszki 1, 52 rooms and suites; **Gazda** (M), ul. Zaruskiego 1; **Dom Turysty,** ul. Zaruskiego 5, attractively decorated, with accommodations ranging from dormitories to rooms with bath; **Morskie Oko** (M), ul. Krupówki 30.

Restaurants and cafés. (Some with dancing and open late). **Jedruś,** ul. Świerczewskiego 5 (until 2 AM); **U Wnuka** (regional dress); **Gubałówka,** Gubałówka; **Watra,** ul. Zamoyskiego 2 (until 2 AM); **Wierchy,** ul. Tetmajera 2 (all M-E). **Kmicic** is a nice café. **Siedem Kotów** (Seven Cats) and **Obrochtówka** both have a good local atmosphere and are inexpensive.

USEFUL ADDRESSES. All in Zakopane: Orbis, ul. Krupówki 22; IT Tourist Information Center, ul. Chramcówki 33; accommodation in private houses is organized at the reception office, ul. Kościuszki 23a; PZM, Rondo (Roundabout), ul. Droga na Bystre. Nowy Sacz: Orbis, ul. Limanowskiego 1.

TOURIST VOCABULARY

Polish spelling is to a great extent phonetic, one letter corresponding to one sound. However, some sounds are marked by a combination of two letters, e.g. cz, dz, sz, while others are indicated by letters with diacritical marks. The letters b, d, f, k, l, m, n, p, s, t and z are pronounced as in English. The others are as follows (the corresponding English sound is italicized in brackets): a (*cut*), a (nasal o, as in French *on*), c (ra*ts*), ć and ci (very soft *ch*), ch and h (*h*alf), cz (*ch*urch), dz (car*ds*), dź and dzi (bu*dg*et), dż (*j*ump), e (*red*), e (nasal e as in French *vin*), g (*get*), i (ma*ch*ine), j (*y*oung), ł (*w*indow), ń and ni (o*ni*on), o (*pot*), ó (r*oo*k), r (clearly trilled), rz (plea*s*ure or softer as in *sh*op), ś and si (very soft *sh*), sz (*sh*op), u (c*oo*k), w (*v*ine), y (r*i*ch), ż (*g*endarme), ź and zi (very soft *s* as in plea*s*ure).

In words of more than one syllable the stress falls on the last syllable but one.

USEFUL EXPRESSIONS

Hello, how do you do	Dzień dobry (dgen do-bri)
Good morning	Dzień dobry (dgen do-bri)
Good evening	Dobry wieczór (do-bri vye-choor)
Goodnight	Dobranoc (do-bra-nots)
Goodbye	Do widzenia (do vee-dze-nya)
Please	Proszę (pro-she)
Thank you	Dziękuję (dgen-koo-je)
Thank you very much	Bardzo dziękuję (bar-dso dgen-koo-je)
Yes	Tak (tak)
No	Nie (nye)
You're welcome	Proszę bardzo; Nie ma za co (pro-she bar-dso; nye-ma za tso)
Excuse me	Przepraszam (pshe-pra-sham)
Come in!	Prosze! (pro-she)
I'm sorry	Bardzo mi żal (bard-dso mee zhal)
My name is . . .	Nazywam się . . . (na-zi-vam sh-ye)
Do you speak English?	Czy pan mówi po angielsku (chi pan moo-vee po an-gyel-skoo)
I don't speak Polish	Ja nie mówię po polsku (ya nye moo-vye po pol-skoo)
Please speak slowly	Proszę mówić wolno (pro she moo-veech vol-no)
I don't understand	Nie rozumiem (nye ro-zoo-myem)
Please write it down	Proszę to napisać (pro-she to na-pee-sach)
Where is . . . ?	Gdzie jest . . . ? (gdge yest)
What is this place called?	Jak się nazywa ta miejscowość? (yak sh-ye na-zi-va ta myeys-tso-voshch)
Please show me	Proszę mi pokazać (pro-she mee po-ka-zach)

I would like . . .	Chciałbym . . . (a woman says chciałabym) (hcha-w-bim, hcha-wa-bim)
How much does it cost?	Ile to kosztuje? (ee-le to kosh-too-ye)

SIGNS

Entrance	Wejście (vey-sh-che)
Exit	Wyjście (viy-sh-che)
Emergency exit	Wyjście zapasowe (viy-shche za-pa-so-ve)
	Drzwi zapasowe (dzhvee za-pa-so-ve)
Toilet	Toaleta, Ustep (to-a-le-ta, oos-temp)
men, gentlemen	panowie; dla panów; dla mężczyzn (pa-no-vye; dla pa-noof; dla mezh-chizn)
women, ladies	panie; dla pań; dla kobiet (pa-nye; dla pani; dla ko-byet)
vacant	wolny (vol-ni)
occupied	zajęty (za-yen-ti)
Hot	Gorąca (go-ron-tsa)
Cold	Zimna (zhee-mna)
No smoking	Palenie wzbronione (pa-le-nye vzbro-nyo-ne)
	palić nie wolno (pa-leech nye vol-no)
No admittance	Wejście wzbronione (vey-sh-che vzbrno-nye-ne)
Stop	Stój (stooy)
Danger	Niebezpieczeństwo (nye-bez-pye-cheny-stvo)
Closed	Zamknięte (zam-knyen-te)
Full, no vacancy	Zajete (za-yen-te)
Information	Informacja (een-for-ma-tsya)
Bus stop	Przystanek (pshi-sta-nek)
Taxi stand	Postój taksówek (po-stooy tak-soo-vek)
Pedestrians	Piesi (pye-shee)

ARRIVAL

Passport check	Kontrola paszportów (kon-tro-la pash-por-toof)
your passport, please	proszę o paszport (pro-she o pash-port)
I am with the group	Jestem z grupą (yes-tem zgroo-pon)
Customs	Kontrola celna; Komora celna (kon-tro-la tsel-na; ko-mo-ra tsel-na)
Anything to declare?	Czy jest coś do oclenia? (chi yest tsosh do ots-le-nya)
Nothing to declare	Nic nie ma do oclenia (neets nye-ma do ots-le-nya)

Baggage claim	Dostawa bagażu (do-sta-va ba-ga-zhoo)
A porter	Bagażowy (ba-ga-zho-vi)

Transportation

to the bus	do autobusu (do a-oo-to-boo-soo)
to a taxi	do taksówki (do tak-soof-ki)
to the Hotel . . . ,	do hotelu . . . (do ho-te-loo, pro-she)
please	proszę

MONEY

Currency exchange office	Wymiana walut (vi-mya-na va-loot)
Do you have the change for this?	Czy pan (pani) to może zmienić? (chi pan (pa-nee) to mo-zhe zmye-neech)
May I pay	Czy mogę płacić (chi mo-ge pwa-cheech)
with a traveler's check?	czekiem? (che-kyem)
with a voucher?	kuponem? (koo-po-nem)
with this credit card?	tą kartą kredytową? (ton karton kre-di-to-von)
I would like to exchange some traveler's checks	Chciałbym (chciałabym) zmienić kilka czeków (hcha-w-bim, hcha-wa-bim, zmye-neech keel-ka che-koof)

THE HOTEL

A hotel	Hotel (ho-tel)
I have a reservation	Mam zarezerwowany pokój (mam za-re-zer-vo-va-ni po-koo-y)
A room with a bath	Pokój z łazienka (po-koo-y zwa-zhen-kon)
a shower	prysznic (prish-neets)
a toilet	toaleta (to-a-le-ta)
hot running water	gorąca woda (go-ron-tsa vo-da)
What floor is it on?	Na którym piętrze? (na ktoo-rim pyen-tshe)
ground floor	parter (par-ter)
second floor	pięrwsze piętro (pyer-fshe pyen-tro)
The elevator	Winda (veen-da)
Have the baggage sent up, please	Proszę mi posłać bagaż do pokoju (pro-she mee pos-wach ba-gash do po-ko-yoo)
The key to number . . . please	Proszę klucz do pokoju numer (pro-she klooch do po-ko-yoo noo-mer)
Please call me at . . . o'clock	Proszę mnie obudzić o siódmej godzinie (pro-she mnye o-boo-dgeech o shood-mei go-dgee-nye)
Have the baggage brought down	Proszę mi przynieść bagaż (pro-she mee pshi-nyeshch ba-gazh)

The bill	Rachunek (ra-hoo-nek)
A tip	Napiwek (na-pee-vek)

THE RESTAURANT

Waiter!	Proszę pana! (pro-she pa-na)
Waitress!	Proszę pani! (pro-she pa-nee)
The menu	Spis potraw (spees po-traf)
I would like to order (this)	Chciałbym (chciałabym) zamówić (to) (hcha-w-bim, hcha-wa-bim, za-moo-veech to)
Some more . . . , please	Proszę jeszcze . . . (pro-she yesh-che)
That's enough	Dosyć tego (do-seech te-go)
The check, please	Rachunek, proszę (ra-hoo-nek pro-she)
Breakfast	Śniadanie (shnya-da-nye)
Lunch	Obiad (ob-yat)
Dinner	Kolacja (ko-lats-ya)

(Remember that the main meal in Poland is *obiad,* while *kolacja* may be substantially smaller and not necessarily hot.)

Bread	Chleb (hlep)
Butter	Masło (mas-wo)
Jam	Dżem (jem)
Salt	Sól (sool)
Pepper	Pieprz (pyep-sh)
Mustard	Musztarda (moosh-tar-da)
Sauce, gravy	Sos (sos)
Vinegar	Ocet (o-tset)
Oil	Oliwa (o-lee-va)
Bottle	Butelka (boo-tel-ka)
Wine	Wino; wina (vee-no; vee-na)
red, white wine	wino czerwone, białe (vee-no cher-vo-ne; bya-we)
A bottle of wine	Butelka wina (boo-tel-ka vee-na)
beer	piwo; piwa (pee-vo; pee-va)
Water	Woda; wody (vo-da; vo-di)
Mineral water	Woda mineralna (vo-da mee-ne-ral-na) wody mineralnej (vo-di mee-ne-ral-neyi)
Milk	Mleko; mleka (mle-ko; mle-ka)
Coffee (with milk)	Kawa (z mlekiem) (ka-va, zmle-kyem) kawy (ka-vi)
Tea with lemon	Herbata z cytryną (her-ba-ta, stsi-tri-no) herbaty (her-ba-ti)
Sugar (some sugar)	Cukier (tsoo-kyer) cukru (tsoo-kroo)

(Further Polish menu hints are given in the chapter on food and drink.)

MAIL

A letter	list (leest)
An envelope	koperta (ko-per-ta)

A postcard	pocztówka (poch-toof-ka)
A mailbox	skrzynka pocztowa (skshin-ka poch-to-va)
The post office	poczta; urząd pocztowy (poch-ta; oo-zhond poch-to-vi)
A stamp	znaczek pocztowy (zna-check poch-to-vi)
By airmail	pocztą lotniczą (poch-ton lot-nee-chon)
How much does it cost	Ile kosztuje opłata (ee-le kosh-too-ye op-wa-ta)
to send a letter	za list (za leest)
a postcard	pocztówkę (poch-toof-ke)
air mail to the United States (Great Britain, Canada)?	pocztą lotniczą do Stanów Zjednoczonych (Wielkiej Brytanii, Kanady)? (poch-ton lot-neech-on do Sta-noof Zyed-no-cho-nih, Vyel-kyej Bri-tan-yee, Ka-na-di)
To send a telegram, cable	Nadać telegram (na-dach te-le-gram)

LOCATIONS

. . . Street	Ulica . . . (oo-lee-tsa)
. . . Avenue	Aleja . . . (a-le-ya)
. . . Square	Plac . . . , rynek . . . (plats, ri-nek)
The airport	Lotnisko (lot-nees-ko)
A bank	Bank (bank)
The beach	Plaża (pla-zha)
The bridge	Most (most)
The castle	Zamek (za-mek)
The cathedral	Katedra (ka-ted-ra)
The church	Kościół (kosh-choow)
The coffee house, café	Kawiarnia (ka-vyar-nya)
The garden	Ogród (o-groot)
The hospital	Szpital (shpee-tal)
The movies, cinema	Kino (kee-no)
a movie	film (feelm)
The museum	Muzeum (moo-ze-um)
A nightclub	Nocny lokal (nots-ni lo-kal)
The palace	Pałac (pa-wa-ts)
The park	Park (park)
The post-office	Poczta, urząd (poch-ta; oo-zhond) pocztowy (poch-to-vi)
The station	Stacja, dworzec (stats-ya, dvo-zhets)
The theater	Teatr (te-atr)
a play	sztuka (shtoo-ka)
The official travel bureau	Orbis (Orbees)
The university	Uniwersytet (oo-nee-ver-si-tet)

TRAVEL

Arrival	Przyjazd (pshee-yazd)

Departure	Odjazd (od-yazd)

The airplane — Samolot (sa-mo-lot)

I want to reconfirm a reservation on flight number . . . for . . . — Chciałbym potwierdzić rezerwację na lot numer . . . do . . . (h-cha-w-bim pot-fyer-dzeech re-zer-va-tsye na lot noo-mer do)

Where is the check-in? — Gdzie jest kontrola biletów? (gdge yest kon-tro-la bee-le-toof)

I am checking in for . . . — Lecę do . . . (le-tse do)

Fasten your seat belt — Proszę zapiąć pas (pro-she za-pyonch pas)

The railroad — Kolej (ko-ley)

The train — Pociąg (po-chong)

From what track does the train to . . . leave? — Z którego peronu odjeżda pociag do . . . ? (sktoo-re-go pe-ro-noo od-yezh-dga po-chong do)

Which way is the dining car? — Gdzie jest wagon restauracyjny? (gdge yest va-gon res-taw-ra-tsiy-ni)

Bus, Streetcar — Autobus, tramwaj (a-oo-to-boos, tram-vai)

Does this bus go to . . . ? — Czy ten autobus jedzie do . . . ? (chi ten a-oo-to-boos yedge do)

trolley bus — trolejbus (tro-lei-boos)

I want to get off at . . . Street — Chciałbym wysiąść przy . . . ulicy (hcha-w-bim vish-onshch phshi oo-li-tsi)

at the next stop — przy następnym przystanku (pshi na-ste-priim pshi-stan-koo)

Taxi — Taksówka (tak-soof-ka)

I (we) would like to go to . . . , please — Proszę jechać do . . . (pro-she ye-hach do)

Stop at . . . — Proszę stanać przy . . . (pro-she sta-nonch pshi)

Stop here — Proszę stanąć tutaj (pro-she sta-nonch too-tai)

NUMBERS

1 jeden (yeden)	12 dwanaście
2 dwa (dva)	13 trzynaście
3 trzy (chǐ)	14 czternaście
4 cztery (chtérǐ)	15 piętnaście (pyentnashche)
5 pięć (pyench)	16 szesnaście
6 sześć (sheshch)	17 siedemnaście
7 siedem (shedem)	18 osiemnaście
8 osiem (oshem)	19 dziewiętnaście (dgevyetnashche)
9 dziewięć (dgevyench)	20 dwadzieścia (dvadgeshcha)
10 dziesięć (dgeshench)	
11 jedenaście (yedenashche)	

25 dwadzieścia pięć
30 trzydzieści
   (tshidgeshchi)
40 czterdzieści
50 pięćdziesiąt
   (pyenchdgeshont)
60 sześćdziesiąt
   (sheshchdgeshont)
70 siedemdziesiąt
   (shedemdgeshont)
80 osiemdziesiąt
   (sohemdgeshont)
90 dziewięćdziesiąt
   (dgevyendgeshont)
100 sto

200 dwieście
    (dvyeshche)
300 trzysta (tshista)
400 czterysta
500 pięćset
    (pyenchset)
600 sześćet (sheiset)
700 siedemset
    (shedemset)
800 osiemset
    (oshemset)
900 dziewięćset
    (dgevyenchset)
1000 tysiac (tíshonts)

ROMANIA

FACTS AT YOUR FINGERTIPS

Planning Your Trip

WHAT WILL IT COST. Prices in Romania are under strict government control, so inflation, in theory at any rate, is less of a problem here than in western countries. However, the country does have substantial economic difficulties and food prices, for example, rose by 25 to 30% in 1982. Nonetheless, prices are still very reasonable by western standards, and you will be able to have a pretty comfortable holiday for relatively little outlay.

The unit of currency in Romania is the leu (plural lei) which is divided into 100 bani. There are coins of 5, 10, 15 and 25 bani and 1, 3 and 5 lei; banknotes are in denominations of 1, 3, 5, 10, 25, 50 and 100 lei.

You may bring in any amount of foreign currency, including travelers' checks, and exchange them at branches of the National Bank of Romania, most border crossings and major hotels. The import and export of Romanian currency is not permitted. All exchanges, beyond the minimum daily exchange rate (see below) can be refunded in hard currency on your departure.

The tourist exchange rate was about 11 lei to the US dollar and 19 lei to the pound sterling at the time of writing, but will certainly change during 1983. Travelers' checks and credit cards, such as American Express, Carte Blanche, Eurocard and Barclaycard may be used to exchange currency and are accepted in most major hotels and restaurants. There is an active blackmarket in foreign currency which you are strongly advised to avoid, both on legal and moral grounds (you are also likely to be cheated). It is hoped to clean up the unattractive presence of currency dealers in many tourist haunts.

It is important to note that visitors to Romania *must* exchange a sum of $10, or its equivalent, per adult per day for the number of days for which they have requested a visa. Children under 14 years are exempt from this. If you have booked on a pre-paid tour (see below for details), you will already have met this requirement, as is also the case if you hold any other pre-paid vouchers (eg for camping or hotel accommodations). If you have no pre-paid services, you will be required to exchange the minimum sum on arrival in Romania.

A day's basic costs for two people might be:
(for hotel rates see *Hotels* in Staying in Romania)

Lunch, in Moderate restaurant excluding drinks	120 lei
Transport (3 tram trips, 1 taxi)	34
Museum entrance	14
4 coffees, 2 beers	26
Dinner, in Moderate restaurant with wine	180
Total	374

Sample Costs. Taxis 5 lei on starting plus 6 lei per km.; bus 1.75; trolleybus 1.50; metro 1; tram 1; museum entrance 4–12; opera tickets 8–18; concert tickets 8–18; theatre 10–20; circus 8–20; Romania cigarettes 5–11; American/British cigarettes 30; bottle of wine, from a shop, starts at 30; bottle of beer, from a shop, 8 (Romanian), 12–15 (imported).

Note. All the prices we quote in this chapter are those for 1982. You should therefore allow for a slight increase for 1983.

HOW TO GO. All foreign travel to Romania is organized by the Romanian National Tourist Office, which is run by the Ministry of Tourism. They have a number of offices overseas (see below for addresses), but tours to Romania cannot be booked through them but must be made via a travel agent accredited by the National Tourist Office. There are a good many of these, however, so booking your vacation should prove no problem, and a list of all officially-approved agents is available free from the National Tourist Office. When you apply for the list, make a point of specifying any special interests you may want to follow in Romania as some agents make a point of featuring activities such as motoring, walking, birdwatching, archeology and so on.

In Romania itself, there are two offices of the National Tourist Office, one at Carpaţi-Bucuresti, 7 Magheru Blvd., Bucharest 1; the other is at Litoral, Bucuresti Hotel, Mamaia. These offices, also known by the abbreviation ONT, give out information and handle most tourist services within the country. There are also ONT offices in most towns and resorts, and in addition there are also often country tourist offices known as OJT.

The addresses of Romanian National Tourist Offices overseas are:
In the US: 573 Third Ave., New York, NY 10016; and Romanian Commercial Office, 575–577 Third Ave., New York, NY 10016.
In Canada: Embassy of Romania and Consular Office, 655 Rideau St., K1N 6A3, Ottawa, Ontario.
In the UK: 98–99 Jermyn St., London SW1.

As a general rule, and this is especially true for independent travelers, you'll find that the best way to arrange your holiday is by buying a series of pre-paid vouchers for things like hotels, restaurants, gasoline (which you can *only* buy with vouchers, though some pre-paid systems do include a free daily allowance of gasoline) etc. Once in Romania these will save time and frustration; the tourist industry revolves around vouchers and they will smooth your way enormously. Note also that those without pre-paid vouchers must also exchange $10 per day for the number of days for which they have asked for a visa during their stay.

If you prefer to visit the country on an all-in package, sample costs are likely to be as follows: two weeks at a Black Sea resort in a good hotel with full-board and return flight is £185 to £250 per person according to season. Another tour, also lasting two weeks, combines a first class hotel on the Black Sea with a Dracula coach tour through Transylvania. This runs from around £235 to £255 with return flight and full board. These prices and tours are all from London.

 CLIMATE. If you're a beach-and-swimming enthusiast, opt for a summer visit to the Black Sea; the resorts don't start coming alive until mid to late May. The best time for touring the interior is any time from late spring to fall, with fine summer hiking or winter sports facilities in the Carpathian resorts. Bucharest, like Paris, is at its best in the spring, though its rich cultural life is year round.

Romania's climate is of the temperate-continental type, and is generally mild and free of extremes. Beach resorts average 12 hours of sunshine a day during the summer.

Average maximum daily temperatures in Fahrenheit and centigrade:
Bucharest

	Jan.	Feb.	Mar.	Apr.	May	June	July	Aug.	Sept.	Oct.	Nov.	Dec.
F°	34	39	50	64	73	81	86	86	77	64	50	39
C°	1	4	10	18	23	27	30	30	25	18	10	4

SPECIAL EVENTS. The folkloric tradition is still very much alive in Romania, not only as part of the every day life of country folk, but as represented by a number of festivals or traditional customs of a more local nature. First, there are the annual ceremonies connected with various mountains once considered holy, a few of which survive today, the best known being the Celebration of Mount Ceahlău at Durău, Moldavia, on a Sunday in August. The Fair of the Girls on Mount Găina, Transylvania, in July is another regular colorful event; as is The Hora at Prislop on the Transylvanian-Moldavian border. Some regions also go in for big winter festivals and one of the biggest is at Sighetu Marmației in Maramureş over the Christmas period, when folk masks feature prominently. And there are many other folkloric song and dance festivals, parades, contests and crafts fairs worth investigating if you are in the right area at the right time. The Ministry of Tourism publish an annual calendar of such events.

Other celebrations are less specifically timed and you need luck on your side to coincide with them. Many are connected with the rhythm of the rural calendar: for example, harvest time, or the departure of the sheep to mountain pastures in spring and their return in autumn. In some regions (notably Maramureş and Bucovina), Easter brings everyone out in their finest costumes, and on the previous Sunday the custom of taking willow branches to church to be blessed is still widely maintained; but remember Easter dates are usually different according to the Orthodox calendar.

VISAS. In addition to a valid passport, all western Europeans, Americans and Canadians and citizens of most Commonwealth countries require visas to enter Romania. These are available at border crossing points, but you can also obtain them in advance from Romanian Embassies abroad. Travel agents officially accredited by the Romanian National Tourist Office will also be able to help in obtaining visas. Within Romania itself, visas can be extended by local police authorities.

Visas are issued free to Americans; for Canadian and British citizens there is a small fee.

HEALTH CERTIFICATES. These are not required to enter Romania from any country.

INSURANCE. Both personal insurance and insurance against loss (see also Medical Treatment) are always a wise precaution. The Romanians have many admirable qualities, but personal possessions left unattended are liable to disappear, so take extra care. A small word of warning: attempts to obtain the usual written confirmation (for insurance purposes) that a loss has been reported to the police have been known to fail. In such situations, there is little you can usefully do.

CUSTOMS. Personal belongings may be brought in without declaration including the following: a reasonable amount of jewelry, two cameras and 24 cassettes or 10 rolls of film, one small movie camera and 10 rolls of movie film, binoculars, tape recorder, portable radio, portable typewriter, camping and sports equipment. Some other items may need to be declared at the border so if in doubt check. You may also bring in 2 liters of liquor, 5 liters of wine, 300 cigarettes or 300 gr. tobacco, and gifts up to the value of 2,000 lei. Purchases up to 1,000 lei in value may be exported, as can items bought for foreign currency in the special Comturist shops, so keep your receipts. Antiques, rare books, etc., may only be exported with special authorization.

Remember that the import and export of Romanian currency is not allowed, but that you may export any foreign currency you imported but did not spend.

Staying in Romania

LANGUAGE. Romanian is a Romance language with some Slavonic, Turkish, Magyar and French additions. German, Russian and Hungarian are also spoken in some areas. French is widely spoken and understood; English is spoken by members of the travel industry, so in major resorts at least you should have few difficulties communicating. Romanian schoolchildren are required to study two widely-spoken foreign languages, choosing between German, English, French or Russian.

HOTELS. Nearly all hotels marketed overseas and used by western visitors belong to the Ministry of Tourism. It is worth noting, however, that there are others belonging to Consumer Cooperatives or city or local councils, some of them excellent. It is highly advisable to make advance reservations, but if you have not done so, bookings can be made through local ONT or ACR offices, or direct with the hotel. In this case, should you want to pay in lei, you must have proof of official money exchange.

Romania is in the process of changing over to the international star system of hotel classification. This will take some time and the old system of Deluxe, 1st class, 2nd class, etc., is still liable to be encountered. This can be misleading as 1st class is sub-divided into categories from (a) to (f), the differences being quite considerable.

We have graded hotels in our lists in four categories (based on price). These are Deluxe (L), approximating to 5-star, Expensive (E), approximating to 4-star, Moderate (M), approximating to 3-star, and Inexpensive (I), approximating to 1- or 2-star. See table below for prices.

Remember that quoted rates often do not include breakfast, and that standards of service are not always comparable with those in western hotels. Plumbing, for example, that long-time bane of so many Eastern European hotels, is often erratic. Many hotels also have rooms in more than one category.

Two people in a double room will pay:

	Bucharest*	Black Sea resort**	Carpathian resorts*** and inland cities
Deluxe (5-star)	$80–94	$52–54	$70–72
Expensive (4-star)	$54–88	$30–44	$40–44

Moderate (3-star)	$38–48	$20–28	$26–36
Inexpensive			
(1- or 2-star)	$24–38	$14–18	$18–24

* breakfast included except in Deluxe
** breakfast included only in Deluxe
*** breakfast included

In addition to the above accommodations, there is a growing network of motels and inns run by the Union of Consumer Cooperatives. These are indicated on the tourist maps revised annually by ACR and will eventually be brought into the system of star classification.

Private accommodations are only available in a limited number of places where hotel accommodations are lacking or are insufficient and can only be arranged through local tourist offices. However, these types of accommodations are likely to increase in the future.

There are a number of student hostels, usually open from July through August. The locale varies from year to year, but the rate is about $5.75–$8.50 per person per night. Bookings can be made through the Carpați National Tourist Office on arrival in Bucharest.

CAMPING. There are well over 100 camp sites in Romania, and all main towns and resorts have one. The best appointed sites are the ones for which the Romanian Automobile Club (ACR) issues pre-paid coupons (valid May through September). Some sites also have bungalows or chalets for hire. Details from the Romanian National Tourist Office.

RESTAURANTS. Romanian restaurants have enjoyed a great improvement in both standard and choice of late. The bulk of restaurants that foreign visitors are likely to encounter are in hotels, and quite a few of these now make a point of offering regional specialties, sometimes with attractive displays from which to make your choice. The chapter on Food and Drink describes a number of dishes to watch for. But in some restaurants the choice is still limited and you may also find that there is no printed menu. In these cases it is a good idea to check prices when you order.

Despite persistent increases in food prices, meal costs remain reasonable, and you'll have a hard time paying more than 150 lei per person in even the most expensive restaurants, including tip and a bottle of wine. We have divided restaurants in our listings into three categories; Expensive (E), up to 150 lei, Moderate (M), 80 to 90 lei, Inexpensive (I), 60 to 80 lei. All these prices are per person.

For inexpensive snacks, try a *bufet express* or *lacto vegetarian* snack bar. Excellent cream cakes are available at the better *cafeteria* establishments (which rarely, however, serve coffee; soft drinks are the norm).

TIPPING. A 12% service charge is added to meals at most restaurants. Elsewhere, tipping is discouraged but the practice persists, although nowhere is it obligatory. You might want to leave about 10% if service has been exceptionally good. Give porters and taxi drivers about 5 to 10 lei.

MAIL AND TELEPHONES. An airmail letter to the US costs 16 lei, a postcard 10 lei; to destinations in western Europe an airmail letter is 11 lei and a postcard 8 lei. But check prices before mailing as they are quite likely to change both before and during 1983.

Telephone calls in Romania, either internally or externally, are not something to undertake lightly. Though you can make calls from both post offices and hotels, the process is frustrating and time consuming at best. Language problems and unreliable equipment only conspire to exacerbate the difficulties. If you do make a call from your hotel, aside from making sure you have a good book with you, bear in mind that the hotel will probably add 300 to 400% onto the price of the call.

TIME. Romania is seven hours ahead of Eastern Standard Time and two hours ahead of Greenwich Mean Time. From the first Sunday of April to the last Sunday of September, the country operates on summer time, which is eight hours ahead of Eastern Standard Time and three hours ahead of Greenwich Mean Time.

CLOSING TIMES. Shops are generally open from 9 or 10 A.M. to 6 or 8 P.M., though some food shops open much earlier but close for some hours in the middle of the day. Supermarkets are open daily from 8 A.M. to 8 P.M., and on Sundays from 8.30 A.M. to 1 P.M. Opening times of museums, art galleries and other historic monuments are best checked with local tourist offices; most are closed on Mondays.

Public holidays are January 1 and 2, May 1 and 2, August 23 and 24.

SHOPPING. The best bet for foreign visitors hoping to bring back a souvenir or two from Romania is to go to one of the many Comturist shops, the official outlet for souvenirs and the like. There are over a dozen in Bucharest alone and numerous others elsewhere, most of them in hotels. Hard (ie western) currency only is accepted. But there are also many small arts and crafts shops which belong to the Union of Plastic Artists. In particular, those marked *Galerie de Artă* are well worth investigating. Prices here will be higher, but so will the quality of the worksmanship. For inexpensive buys, the big department stores in main cities are recommended.

Romania's peasant art is still very much alive and includes pottery from Bucovina as well as woodcarvings and woven goods from Maramureş and ceramics and textiles from many regions, and all are available from Comturist. But even in the rural areas they're not particularly cheap. There is also an excellent range of cosmetic products.

For further information on shopping in the capital, see Practical Information for Bucharest.

MEDICAL TREATMENT. Emergency treatment is free. Otherwise medical assistance is provided by hospitals and health units all over Romania at charges comparable with average European rates. It makes sense to take out a health insurance before traveling. See page 16 for details.

SPAS. The spas and health resorts of Romania are known all over the world, particularly for their 'anti-aging' compounds, *Gerovital* and *Aslavital,* and for their sapropel mudpackings, *Pell-Amar.* Treatment is available in Bucharest at the Otepeni Sanatorium and Parc and Flora hotels. Outpatient treatment is also available at the Geriatric Institute. (In fact the emphasis on the term geriatric is perhaps a little unfortunate since the treatment has been used beneficially by many who would certainly not welcome and, in many cases, not qualify for the description.)

Of the 160 spas in the country, the following is a selection of the most important available to overseas visitors: on the Black Sea coast; Eforie Nord, Mangalia, Neptun; inland at Călimănești-Căciulata, Felix, Herculane, Sovata, Covasna, Slănic Moldova, Vatra Dornei, Tușnad. Generally Romania can claim to have one of the widest ranges of health resources in Europe and has invested a great deal in exploiting these. About 1½ million Romanians follow either curative or preventative treatment in spas every year and the facilities at the best of them are being widely promoted abroad.

Most spas are open year round. An example of prices for a 14-night stay at the Flora Hotel in Bucharest, ex-London and including top class accommodations, full board, medical examinations and treatments is from £624 per person (low season) to £767 (high season). In Felix, the range is about £240 less. Otherwise, costs vary widely, depending on the type of accommodations and treatment. Full details can be obtained from the National Tourist Office.

SPORTS AND SPECIAL INTERESTS. There are good facilities for water sports, tennis, mini-golf, cycle hire, and horse riding at the Black Sea resorts. The main winter sports resorts are Sinaia, Predeal and Poiana Brașov. The Carpathians also offer marvellous hiking possibilities and some specialist tours for walkers are arranged from the UK as also are birdwatching tours to the Danube delta.

Within Romania, the Carpați National Tourist Office offers a range of special interest vacations including folklore, art and architecture, botany, cave explorations, walking, horse riding and gastronomy, though these are mostly suitable for small groups rather than individuals.

Getting Around Romania

BY PLANE. Tarom, the state airline, operates several internal services linking Bucharest with cities such as Constanza, Cluj, Craiova and Arad. Most internal services go from the domestic airport at Bucharest (Banea-sa) although one or two operate from the International Airport at Otopeni. The former is about five miles from the city center, the latter about 12 miles. Be certain you know which one your flight leaves from. Buses and taxis serve both. Air fares in Romania are about the equivalent of first class by rail and are accordingly lower than in western Europe. But book as far ahead as possible. Be prepared too for overbooking. If you are caught out, make a fuss—and demand the aid of the Carpati Tourist Official at the airport. It works.

BY TRAIN. Although the railway system is quite extensive, because of the curious geography of the country (high mountains alternating with plains) the routes tend to wander (other than the near straight route from Bucharest to the Black Sea at Constanza). Electrification is progressing but with its own oil supply at hand diesel-hauled trains are in the majority. Many long- and medium-distance day trains carry restaurant or buffet cars. Overnight expresses have both sleeping cars and second class couchettes. Supplements are required on main expresses unless you hold tickets purchased outside Romania. But on some trains reservation is obligatory. Always check on this.

The Inter-Rail Card (for under 26 year olds) is valid in Romania.

BY BUS. Except for group tours, there's no long range bus travel. But it's a cheap way of travel for short excursions.

BY CAR. Romanians drive on the right and the usual Continental rules of the road are observed, except that speed limits are based on the size of engine, but for all ordinary cars are 60 kph (40 mph) in built-up areas and 80–100 kph (50–65 mph) on all other roads. No minimum alcohol intake is allowed. Extra care should be taken on country roads.

Detailed information on the documents you will need if you're taking your own car into the country is given on page 21. *Important:* All foreign motorists must purchase gasoline coupons for hard currency at the equivalent of 70 cents per liter (high octane). These are available at border points, tourist offices and main hotels. Gas stations (PECO) are generally open from 7 A.M. to 10 P.M.; some stations in cities and on major highways are open 24 hours a day.

You obtain a free road map from tourist offices, though you'll find it better to travel on main highways as secondary roads are mostly unsurfaced and poorly signposted. It's sensible to carry a spare parts kit with you.

The *Romanian Automobile Club* (ACR) has its headquarters in Bucharest and also maintains branches all over Romania. Local office telephone numbers for breakdown emergencies are shown on road signs. To members of affiliated automobile clubs, such as AAA, AA and RAC, it offers a variety of services, including free breakdown service, information on weather and road conditions and general tourist information. ACR also handle fly-drive arrangements from London, full details of which can be obtained from the NTO.

Car Hire. Self-drive car hire is available through *Avis* in association with the Romanian Automobile Club. Avis have offices at Otopeni Airport and at Strada Cihoski 2 and you can also hire a car self-drive or chauffeured from the main tourist offices. Weekly rate, unlimited mileage, for the ubiquitous little Dacia 1300 is $260. Note also the fly-drive arrangements already mentioned, some of which include a free daily gasoline allowance.

INTRODUCING ROMANIA

A Latin Island

There is much about Romania that is extremely unusual. Its culture, most especially its peasant culture (the product of a turbulent history allied to considerable remoteness), is unique. It is easy enough to get to Romania today and though once there you will encounter many of the industrial and urban landmarks common to any European state, away from these you will find in many regions a way of life that barely survives outside folk museums elsewhere in Europe. Additionally, both internal and external influences have endowed the country with a fine miscellany of monuments. And to all this you can add much splendid scenery.

To deal first with the vital statistics, Romania has an area of 91,700 sq. miles (237,500 sq. km), and is the twelfth largest country in Europe, similar in size to Yugoslavia, Great Britain, West Germany and Oregon.

The 'Latin island' is bounded by two seas, one actual and the other metaphorical. The first is, of course, the Black Sea, to which Romania contributes about 150 miles (245 km) of coastline. The other is the 'sea' of non-Latin countries that hem in Romania on every side—Bulgaria to the south, Yugoslavia to the west, Hungary to the northwest and the USSR to the north and northeast.

Geographically, the country is almost equally divided into mountains, plains, hills and plateaus. Apart from a stretch of tableland near the Black Sea, all Romania's mountainous sector is part of the Carpathian chain. Though rugged, the Carpathians are not particularly high; the loftiest peak, Moldoveanu, is only 8,344 feet (2,543 meters) high. This means there is more arable land and none of those barren wastes above the timber line characteristic of higher countries. Much of the upland area has been cleared for farming and the remainder is used for grazing sheep.

This high percentage of fertile land, combined with a favorable climate and navigable river system, makes Romania the breadbasket of Eastern Europe. She is a leading producer of wheat, corn, sugar beet, livestock, fruit, vegetables, potatoes and wine grapes. But though 62% of Romania's land is agricultural, this doesn't mean that industry is neglected. Petroleum plays a large part in Romania's economy, as do other minerals such as natural gas, iron ore, lignite, copper, gold and silver. The most important manufacturing activity is in the areas of heavy industry, food processing, textiles, metals, chemicals, wood and paper.

The Regions of Romania

In the following chapters, Romania has been divided into the three traditional historic regions of Wallachia, Transylvania and Moldavia, plus a separate section for the Black Sea coast and immediate hinterland (Dobrudja, as well as a chapter on Bucharest). In the interests of simplicity, certain smaller regions whose historical course has been somewhat different, have been incorporated into the most appropriate of the three regions (e.g. Banat with Transylvania, Bucovina with Moldavia).

Broadly speaking, Wallachia is the area bounded by the Banat at its western extremity, the south Carpathians to the northwest, Moldavia to the northeast and Dobrudja to the east. Moldavia is bound on the east and north by the Soviet border, on the west by the main watershed of the Carpathians and to the south by an imaginary line running from the eastern extremity of the Carpathians to the last bend of the Danube before it empties into the Black Sea. Transylvania is easy to define. The Carpathians, semi circular in shape, form a natural amphitheater. Transylvania is all the territory contained within it.

Though a wealth of tours and trips around the country are available, the important thing is not to try and fit too much in to the time available. Romania's charm lies not simply in scenic beauty and historic interest, but in the incredible variety and vitality of its folk culture, reflected in architectural styles, costumes, crafts and customs, that vary from region to region. With the march of progress, this folk culture will inevitably be affected. As standards of living improve, a good deal of the 'color' of the more human aspects of Romania's countryside will gradually give way to the uniformity of better but duller housing, and the attractive costumes will slowly vanish. For the moment, though, there is probably a greater presence of living peasant culture in Romania than anywhere else in Europe. It would be a pity merely to rush by.

Latin Roots

It is quite astounding how, despite countless invasions and migratory movements, the Romanians have tenaciously clung to their Latin heritage. Of a population of nearly 22 million, 88.1 are ethnic Romanians, a strain that will be discussed more fully in the historical section of this chapter. Of the minorities, 7.9% are Hungarian, 1.6% German and the remainder are Slavs, Jews, gypsies, Tartars and Turks.

Romania's Latin connection is linguistic and cultural as well as ethnic. Modern Romanian is primarily based on the popular Latin spoken in the eastern portion of the Roman Empire. Though foreign elements are present (Magyar, Slavic, German, Turkish and Greek), the language is about threequarters of Romance origin. Also, it has few of the regional variations characteristic of other languages. Those with a grounding in the three leading Romance languages (French, Italian, Spanish) will have a head start in picking up a working knowledge of Romanian.

Romanians are nothing if not unique. They are the only Latin people ← in Eastern Europe yet, unlike other Latins, they are mostly Orthodox in religion. Paradoxically, they are the only predominantly Orthodox country to use the Latin alphabet! And irony is further heightened by the fact that many neighboring Slavs and Magyars, though lacking the Romanians' Roman heritage, are Catholic. This uniqueness has certainly contributed to the individualism Romanians have displayed over the centuries.

Early Days

Archeological finds from neolithic times (5,500–2,500 BC) include items showing a high degree of artistry of which examples are the beautiful statuette *The Thinker* from the Hamangia Culture of Dobrudja and painted ceramics of the Cucuteni Culture of southeast Transylvania and southwest Moldavia. The subsequent arrival of Indo-European tribes and the gradual fusion of cultures, skills and social structures eventually led, about 2,000 BC, to the emergence of a compact group of Thracian tribes in the Carpathian-Danube-Balkan area. Among these were the Dacians, also known as Getae, later described by Herodotus as 'the most valiant and righteous of the Thracians.'

The first centralized Dacian state was ruled by a remarkable personality, Burebista, from 70–44 BC, whose capital was Sarmizegetusa in southwest Transylvania. However, he was murdered, and his territory thereafter divided into several political units. Nonetheless the Dacians continued to flourish and their inroads south of the Danube opened a long chapter of Dacian-Roman wars. They were ruled by kings whose chief advisers were high priests, and they enjoyed an advanced civilization, being well versed in the fields of music, astronomy and medicine.

The Romans finally conquered Dacia in AD 106, during the reign of the Emperor Trajan. But it was no easy victory. The Dacians, who had defeated Rome in AD 88, fought stubbornly and didn't yield until their king, Decebal, committed suicide to avoid capture. Celebrations of the victory went on for 30 days in Rome and the event is commemorated there in the monumental Trajan's Column (you can see a replica of it in the History Museum of Romania in Bucharest). Once conquered, Dacia was subject to intense colonization. Dacians and Romans fused into a new Daco-Roman race and this prosperous region —known as Dacia Felix—became the most Romanized of the Empire's provinces.

This influence lingered even after Rome's official withdrawal in AD 275. A high proportion of the soldiers and colonists simply stayed on. Resisting barbarian influence culturally as well as militarily, they tenaciously clung to the Latin language and Roman ways. Thus, through the refusal of stubborn Daco-Romans to accept assimilation into other cultures, was born the 'Latin island,' and from it emerged the Proto-Romanians, ancestors of the Romanians of today.

After the Romans

From the 4th to 9th centuries, barbarian invasions came so thick and fast that the main concern of the Romanians was to maintain their identity and avoid being engulfed altogether. But gradually small political units were formed (dukedoms, or voivodeships) in the 10th and 11th centuries. But at about the same time, there began the gradual penetration of Transylvania by the Hungarians which eventually resulted in Hungarian, Turkish and, later, Habsburg rule (which was to last until 1918), though numerically the Romanians continued to predominate overwhelmingly. Romania had also to withstand, in the 13th century, the great Tartar invasion, which came and went. Despite this, however, to the south and east of the Carpathians (Wallachia, Moldavia, Dobrudja), Romanian society continued its feudal evolution. At times, varying degrees of Romanian unity were achieved, especially against common enemies—Hungary to the west and Turkish expansion from south of the Danube.

In fact, Romania's mammoth struggle against the Turkish Ottoman Empire began in the late 14th century and the seesaw conflict dragged on for the next five centuries. Sometimes the Turks had the upper hand, sometimes the Romanians, and there were periods of compromise when the Turks received an annual tribute in return for local autonomy. With considerable justification, the Romanians point out that in their own tussle for freedom, they acted as an effective buffer, delaying the Turkish advance into central Europe which, in the end, the Turks only accomplished by taking the longer route across Bulgaria and Yugoslavia into Hungary.

Turbulent Centuries

The period from the late 14th to the 17th century produced a number of great military leaders, and you will come across their names many times as you visit the historic sites of Romania. Among them was Mircea cel Bátrîn (Mircea the Old, 1386–1418) of Wallachia who won notable victories against the Turks, and Iancu of Hunedoara (János Hunyadi in Hungarian history), prince of Transylvania, who halted the advance of the Turks by successfully defending Belgrade in 1456. His son Matei Corvin became the popular King Matthias Corvinus of Hungary.

One of the most colorful and controversial characters of these times was Vlad Țepeș, prince of Wallachia (1456–1462, 1476). The son of Vlad Dracul, he became known as Vlad the Impaler because of his habit of impaling his foes, and waged numerous battles against the Turks. He became the subject of many legends, some of them of a less than flattering nature, originating from his enemies, who depicted him as a monster of depravity engaged in savage ritual practices. It was from this lurid but unsubstantiated material that the 19th-century novelist Bram Stoker created his fictional *Dracula*.

The achievements of Ștefan cel Mare (Stephen the Great, 1457–1504) were cultural as well as military. In 1475 he dealt the Turks a bloody defeat near the Moldavian town of Vaslui. Coming shortly after the Turkish conquest of Constantinople, the victory at Vaslui was a much-needed tonic to the Christian world. Plaudits rained down on Stephen from all over Europe and the Pope styled him Atleta Cristi— 'Athlete of Christ.'

Nevertheless, Stephen had to compromise in the end by paying tribute to the enemy in return for non-interference in Moldavia's internal affairs. But he had succeeded in creating a climate of stability in which economic and cultural development flourished. Remarkable witnesses to this are the superb painted monasteries dating from the late 15th and 16th centuries, though their defensive walls are also a measure of the times.

By a series of splendid victories against the Turks at the end of the 16th century, Mihai Viteazul (Michael the Brave, 1593–1601) regained Romania's independence for a time. His outstanding place in his country's history, however, is marked by his achievement of the first-ever union, albeit short-lived, of Wallachia, Transylvania and Moldavia in 1600. But it was not long before the Turks re-established control and the struggle then shifted to the diplomatic arena, with such rulers as Matei Basarab of Wallachia (1632–54) and Vasile Lupu of Moldavia (1634–53) negotiating more liberties for their subjects under Turkish suzerainty.

The struggle for emancipation continued throughout the 17th century, and produced leaders such as Șerban Cantacuzino (1678–1688) and Constantin Brîncoveanu (1688–1714) in Wallachia. The latter has also left his indelible stamp on Wallachia in the form of churches and monasteries whose distinctive Brîncoveanu (Brancovan) style combines not only Renaissance and Byzantine elements, but a liberal injection of native Romanian folk traditions. In 1691, neighboring Transylvania came directly under Habsburg rule and increasingly subject to Austrian centralism. During the course of the shuffling power politics of the 18th century, further areas were amputated from Romanian territory, notably Oltenia (Wallachia) and Bucovina (north Moldavia) which, for varying periods, came under Austrian rule.

Despite these setbacks, the Romanians continued to yearn for complete freedom. In 1721, Dimitrie Cantemir, Prince of Moldavia, led an unsuccessful rising against the Ottomans. He retired in exile to Russia after his defeat, where he became a noted historian. From then until 1821, the Turks ruled Wallachia and Moldavia through puppets known as Phanariots since they were all from the Phanar district of Constantinople. While a few Phanariots were Romanian, the majority were Greek. Meanwhile, in Transylvania, Austrian rule provoked a massive peasant revolt in 1784. Though it failed, the rebellion served as an inspiration of sorts for the French Revolution.

In 1821 a Wallachian army officer, named Tudor Vladimirescu, led a revolt against the Phanariot regime. Through a curious and tragic irony he was killed not by Turks but by a rival commander. But a number of his goals were attained. The Romanian lands were once more governed by native-born rulers and Phanariots were removed from civil, military and ecclesiastical offices.

Tudor Vladimirescu's revolt coincided with a war between Turkey and Russia, won by the latter. The treaty of Adrianople (1829) eliminated many of the Turks' prerogatives in Romania, but resulted in a five-year Russian occupation. During this period Wallachia and Moldavia received their first modern constitution, known as the Règlement Organique. Though aristocratic in tone (favoring landlords over peasants), the Règlement pleased many Romanian patriots because it called for a new state based on union of the Wallachian and Moldavian principalities.

In 1848, a near Europe-wide revolution was waged against established regimes. But the embattled oppressors buried mutual differences and successfully stemmed the revolutionary tide. In Romania, as in other countries, liberation movements were crushed by the military might of sultan, tsar and Habsburg emperor. After 1848, Transylvania was ruled directly from Vienna and in 1867 it was annexed by Hungary.

A United Romania

The principalities were a Russian protectorate from 1848 until 1858, two years after Russia's defeat in the Crimean War. At that time they reverted to nominal Turkish rule, with the Romanians' political rights guaranteed by the great European powers. The Règlements Organiques were replaced by more democratic assemblies known as the Ad Hoc Divans.

In 1859 Colonel Alexandru Ioan Cuza, head of the army, was elected ruling prince by the elective chambers of Moldavia and Wallachia and thus, at last, the two principalities were united. This move is known in Romanian history as the Union of the Principalities.

Prince Cuza, a dynamic reformer, centralized the administration and strengthened the army. Both the Ottoman Empire and Tsarist Russia were displeased with the emergence of a more powerful state, and threatened to invade the country should the two principalities maintain the union. In 1866 Cuza abdicated in favor of a foreign prince (Carol of Hohenzollern-Sigmaringen), a move which placed the united Romania under the protection of central European powers and thus discouraged any attempted intervention in Romanian affairs.

Though the new state had considerable local autonomy, it was still officially part of the Ottoman Empire. This artificial relationship ended in 1877, when Russia and Turkey again went to war and Romania entered the conflict on Russia's side. The Treaty of Berlin (1878) recognized Romania's full independence and re-established Romanian state authority over the province of Dobrudja. Only Transylvania remained outside the new state.

Into the 20th Century

Prince Carol, who was crowned King Carol in 1881, died in the opening months of World War I. A kinsman of the Kaiser, he had tried to bring Romania into the war on the German side. King Ferdinand I, his nephew and successor, was less susceptible to German pressure and his wife, English-born Queen Marie, was openly against the Central Powers. Romania entered the war, but her military difficulties were complicated by the October Revolution of 1917 and Russia's withdrawal from the war. In May 1918, she was forced to sign a harsh peace. However, all this was canceled out by the Allied victory in November. Transylvania was united with Romania on December 1 1918, marking the formation of the Romanian state within its present-day boundaries.

The Interwar Years

But the years between the wars were not happy ones. Economic crises, bitter political strife, the rise of fascism—all three left scars on the fledgling nation.

In 1925, Crown Prince Carol was forced to renounce his rights to the throne for personal reasons related to his less than discreet private life. A regency was set up with his son, 5-year-old Michael, recognised as heir apparent. Ferdinand died in 1927 and Carol began to have second thoughts about his decision. He began a successful movement for his return, which resulted in his being crowned as Carol II in 1930.

This period saw the rise of a rightwing terrorist organization, usually referred to as the Iron Guard. In the interwar period, however, Romania generally followed an anti-fascist foreign policy, supporting the League of Nations and opposing Italy's 1935 invasion of Ethiopia, Hitler's 1936 occupation of the Rhineland and annexation of Austria in 1938.

But the internal situation remained chaotic, and in 1938 King Carol dissolved all political parties and set up a royal dictatorship. Realizing the precariousness of Romania's position, he tried to play both sides against the middle. He first visited London and Paris in an unsuccessful attempt to obtain Franco-British aid, then went to Germany for conversations with Hitler and Goering. Though he accepted the idea of economic cooperation, he rejected Hitler's demand that he take Iron Guardists into his cabinet. Carol, far from wishing to share power with the Iron Guard, was in fact committed to its destruction. Corneliu

Codreanu, the Guards' leader, was arrested in April 1938 and brought to trial. He and 12 of his top followers were executed in November.

During the war itself, Polish civilians and soldiers were granted asylum in, or free passage through, Romania after the German invasion, including help to ship the Polish treasury to England. Nor did Romania give in to the demands of the Nazis to surrender her Jews for the 'final solution.'

The Rise and Fall of the Iron Guard

Romania's fortunes took a disastrous plunge in 1940. Suffering territorial dismemberments that wiped out a century of gains, she lost Bessarabia and northern Bucovina to the USSR, southern Dobrudja to Bulgaria and one-third of Transylvania to Hungary. Carol was forced to abdicate in September; replacing his royal dictatorship was an Iron Guard-backed military one under pro-Nazi Marshal Antonescu. Carol was again succeeded by his son, Michael, who took the throne as a puppet ruler.

In January 1941 the Iron Guard tried to oust Marshal Antonescu and seize sole power. But Antonescu rallied the army and crushed the revolt and led Romania into the war on Germany's side. On August 23 1944, when the tide had turned against Hitler, he was overthrown by a broad coalition including King Michael and a number of anti-fascist elements, both Marxist and non-Marxist. Romania entered the war on the Allied side and Antonescu, following a trial, was executed in 1946. Transylvania, the largest lost territory, was restored to Romania.

The Modern State

King Michael abdicated at the end of 1947 and as a result of her 'liberation' by the armies of the USSR Romania became a Marxist republic. The country today is nominally an independent communist state. In reality, however, she is, along with all the other countries of Eastern Europe, an integral part of the Warsaw Pact and as such answers to Moscow in all matters of foreign and domestic policy.

Since the end of the war, progress has been made in the fields of education, medicine, industrialization, housing and so on. But massive foreign debts and an increasingly unsound economy have conspired to halt progress in the last few years. These fundamental economic problems, frequently allied to problems of distribution, often for example lead to shortages in shops and long lines whenever distributions are made (the two eternal curses of life in post-war Eastern Europe). However, handicaps of this type are unlikely to affect the western visitor, who inevitably receives preferential treatment, though it is hard not to be aware of them. Similarly, the vagaries of a mysterious bureaucracy and the frustrations these can cause are also conspicuous. Even touristic services might appear to lack a certain polish or sophistication to some. But as a visitor to Romania, however strongly one might feel that her fight for freedom remains to be won, it is important to approach the country with an open mind, for there is much here that is fascinating and beautiful.

ROMANIAN CULTURE

Kaleidoscopic Styles

by
LESLIE GARDINER

If you enter a Romanian museum—and there are hundreds, 46 in Bucharest alone—you will have an impression of diverse cultural activities throughout the ages in a land which is really three lands: Transylvania, Moldavia, Wallachia. The exhibits reflect local traditions; but outside pressures have shaped them too. Admiration of the Gothic, the Byzantine, Impressionism, above all Roman classical ideals is evident. Yet when Romanian genius breaks out, as it has occasionally done, the result is fascinatingly (sometimes outrageously) original. Sculptors like Brancuşi, musicians like Enescu, playwrights like Ionesco . . . they are wayward and isolated figures, they do not fit into schools. Even Ilie Nastase played tennis in a manner peculiar to himself.

Language and Literature

Romanian literary aspirations were first expressed in unwritten songs, ballads, proverbs and fairy-tales, all within the framework of folklore. The first printed book was a Lutheran catechism (1544), the result of a Reformation demand that services be conducted in the language of the people. After church literature came history. In the 17th and 18th centuries many weighty tomes asserted the Latin origins and Roman pride of the Romanians. One of the important names from this period is that of Dimitrie Cantemir (1673–1723), author of a history of the Ottoman empire and of a book of travels, *Description of Moldavia*.

In the so-called Transylvanian School, cultural and political writers urged national awareness and produced scientific evidence for the Roman connection. Later writers of that School, the poet Ion Radulescu (1802–1872) and the historian Nicolae Balcescu (1819–1852), helped lay the foundations of higher education and a nationwide press. Vasile Alecsandri's (1821–1890) collections of folk poetry made some stir when they appeared in translation in Paris and London.

Around 1863 two literary groups began to give literature its direction. First came *Junimea* ('Youth'), with the Byronic figure of Mihai Eminescu (1850–1889). His precocious, diffuse but always romantic work included some early science fiction. His *Memento Mori* is a time-warping odyssey across lost civilizations and his *Povestea Magului Calator in Stele* ('Tale of the Magic Star-Traveler') a journey among the plants. Eminescu is regarded as Romania's national poet.

The second literary circle, called *Contemporanul* ('Contemporary'), embraced Symbolism and *Poporanismul* ('Folkism'), launched lyric poetry and experimental drama and published a magazine *(Contemporanul)* which survives to the present day. Tristan Tzara (1896–1963) is claimed as the father of Dadaism; another follower of the group, Eugen Ionescu (born 1909) exploited a private fantasy world which gave rise to the Theatre of the Absurd. Ionescu, known in the West as Ionesco, is the one Romanian writer everyone has heard of, but he has been long established in Paris and his fellow-countrymen rarely mention him.

Up to 1940, literature was dominated by the prolific talents of Mihail Sadoveanu (1880–1961). His massive epic on the making of the nation ran to more than 100 volumes. Respectful tributes are paid to Sadoveanu in the works of George Calinescu (1899–1965), critic, historian and a better writer, who successfully spanned the decades on either side of the political transformations of the 1940s.

Popular in both the old regime and the new were Lucian Blaga (1895–1961), poet, philosopher and playwright, and Zaharia Stancu (1902–1974), novelist. These authors' works may be read in English. Stancu's novel *Barefoot* has appeared in 140 foreign translations.

Of the present generation of writers, the majority incline to the safe and conventional mainstream of national literature. The epic and lyrical poets and poet-dramatists continue to proliferate. Chief among them, after Nicolae Labis (1935–1956)—perhaps once Romania's most promising modern poet—are Nichita Stanescu (born 1933), Adrian Paunescu (born 1943) and Marin Sorescu (born 1936). The novelists Marin Preda (born 1922) and Eugen Barbu (born 1924) have become respected abroad.

No survey of modern literature can overlook the contributions the minority writers have made—especially the Hungarians who live within Romania's borders. Three outstanding poets and prose writers are István Nagy (1904–1977), Jósef Méliusz (born 1909) and Andras Sütö (born 1927).

According to the latest figures there are more than 21,000 public libraries in Romania. Including journals in Hungarian, Russian and Serbo-Croat, the nation has 59 newspapers and 430 periodicals. Last year the State Publishing House and the Academy of Romania published more than 7,000 books and booklets; and every Romanian, on average, read five books.

Art and Architecture

A native style in architecture, a blending of local forms with Byzantine elements, was first seen in the 10th and 11th centuries: in the churches of Moeşti, Biharia and Basarabi and in a few rustic buildings of Transylvania. Later, in the Middle Ages, the style incorporated late-Roman and Gothic influences. The great Gothic example is the Black Church in Braşov, built between 1385 and 1477.

In Wallachia, notably in the Princely Church at Curtea de Argeş (1352) and the Cozia monastery (1388), Byzantine influences are more pronounced. The so-called Muntenian style superseded them: elaborate constructions with open sculpture, arches and friezes. Brebu and Cornetu monasteries and the Mihai Voda monastery in Bucharest (1589) are typical Muntenian structures. Then came the florid and ambitious churches and palaces of the Brancoveanu period, with lavish decorations inspired by Oriental embellishment and topped with baroque froth. The larger buildings, Hieraşti palace (1650), Hurez and Vacareşti monasteries (around 1700) and many more, are distinguished by their richly-colored murals and stucco work.

The painted churches of the Bucovina ('birch country') region are the architectural glory of Moldavia. This north-eastern compartment of Romania was for centuries a princely state and its 14th- and 15th-century fortresses and monasteries are adorned with stone sculptures, glazed ceramics and mural paintings of a sumptuous kind. In the 16th century, Eastern Orthodoxy imposed its restraint and elegance and brought at the same time the most original artistic productions in Romania: exterior murals covering the entire facades of several large churches, of which Voroneţ, Moldoviţa, Suceviţa and Arbore are the most dazzling examples. They were done by self-taught local painters, illustrating Bible stories, and for scale and chromatic richness they were unrivalled in Europe at the time.

Much of the country's large-scale, richly-ornamented, centuries-old architecture is done in wood. Ancient monuments everywhere proclaim the abundance of wood as a building material, and the lack of stone and metals.

In the past two centuries, nothing architecturally memorable has arisen. Romania declined in her troubled post-Ottoman era into a land of shacks and tin roofs. The 'royal palace' to which the first monarch, Prince Carol of Hohenzollern-Sigmaringen, was directed was a shabby one-storyed building on a mean street of Bucharest, back-to-back with a pig-sty. The most admired new constructions of Carol's long reign (1866–1914) was the hybrid extravaganzas of Peleş and Pelişor at Sinaia, an architectural stew in which every European style was stirred.

Ion Mincu (1852–1912) is credited with having founded the national school of architecture. A more functional approach was adopted by Horia Creanga (1893–1943) and Duiliu Marcu (1885–1966). More recently Octav Doicescu (born 1905) and Nicolae Porumbescu (born 1919) have contributed to various cultural, industrial and residential projects in the well-known socialist-heroic manner. Romanian architects, town planners and civil engineers have achieved some impressive public works, using color to startling effect . . . but a harsh critic would deny the existence of any really worthwhile modern architecture.

Painting as a separate art began barely 100 years ago with the influential Nicolae Grigorescu (1838–1907), a painter of mildly impressionistic peasant scenes. Ştefan Luchian (1868–1916) combined folk traditions with experiments in Symbolism. The post-Impressionists or 'Colorists' flourished after 1919 with Gheorghe Petraşcu (1872–1949), Theodor Pallady (1871–1956) and others. More modern schools appear unadventurous, flirting with Cubism, Constructivism and other -isms but reluctant to abandon traditional forms of representational art for the abstract.

Painters whom you will see represented in museums and at modern art exhibitions include Gheorghe Popescu (1903–1975), Braduţ Covaliu (born 1924), Grigore Vasile (born 1935) and Horia Bernea (born 1938). A distinguishing quality of Romanian artists ancient and modern is their fondness for bold bright colors.

Music

As a nation, Romania is fairly small and very young. Literacy came late, and one hardly expects solid cultural accomplishment of international renown. Yet in George Enescu (1881–1955) this land produced a composer and instrumentalist who ranked with the best of his time; and since then most concert-goers have learned the names of Dinu Lipatti (1917–1950) the pianist, and of Constantin Silvestri (1913–1969) and Sergiu Celibidache (born 1912), both conductors.

The Romanian musical tradition stems from folk melodies and ritual songs of uncertain origin. The old-time 'singing monks'—Eustatie of Putna, Filotei of Bucharest and others—integrated those melodies into their hymns and canticles in the 16th and 17th centuries. After the Conservatoires of Bucharest and Iaşi had been established (1864), composers such as Gavriil Musicescu (1847–1903) and Dimitri Kiriac (1866–1928) set the pattern for a national school of music which continued to base its compositions on folk and Byzantine tunes and rhythms.

Bucharest has had its Opera since 1864; and the soprano Elena Teodorini (1857–1926) became famous far beyond her country's bounds.

The early 1900s saw the bright sun of George Enescu (sometimes called Enesco in the West) rising amid dim stars. A pupil of both Massenet and Fauré, he gave his first public recital at the age of 13. He played violin and piano brilliantly, but his chief contribution to world music was in composition, especially the Romanian rhapsodies and orchestral suites which introduced music-lovers to the strange and complex harmonies of country and gypsy songs. His opera *Oedipus,* a lyric tragedy in a classical setting, may sometimes be seen at the Romanian Opera of Bucharest and heard on the radio. Enescu was also a popular conductor who boasted that he never needed a score. As a teacher of the violin he had both Yehudi Menuhin and Christian Ferras as pupils.

Modern Romanian composers who began where Enescu left off are Sabin Dragoi (1894–1968), Mihail Jora (1891–1971) and Ion Dumitrescu (born 1913). The young school is represented by Theodor Grigoriu (born 1926), Anatol Vieru (born 1926) and Miriam Marbé (born 1931) among others. These musicians strive to reconcile folk traditions with modern developments in what is known as the 'open form,' involving variational and improvisatory techniques.

A more recent generation—Cornel Taranu (born 1934), Nicolae Branduş (born 1935) and Liviu Glodeanu (1938–1978) are typical of it—moved into experimental areas of electronic music and 'total art' with a freedom and enthusiasm one does not usually associate with cultural institutions in eastern Europe.

Folksong and dance have many devotees. The National Festival 'Song to Romania' has its finals in Bucharest every odd-numbered year, but the qualifying competitions take place in provincial centers all the time. The finalists of 1981 were drawn from an entry of more than 130,000 choirs and music groups.

Light music is extremely popular. Romania admires western styles and has some bright and innovative composers of rock and jazz. The annual Jazz Festival at Sibiu attracts big crowds every year.

Woodcraft and Sculpture

'When this oak came from the forest he was cold and lonely,' the wood-carver says. 'With my chisel I gave him a sun for warmth. Then I cut in some flowers to remind him of his youth. Now I open his ribs a little, to let him breath. . . . '

The wood-carver is making a gatepost. His approach typifies the anthropomorphic views of Romanian craftsmen whose work is spread over the living museums of Transylvania's towns and villages. And their products are stamped with the Romanian trade-mark: bright and garish colors, applied to cheerful and melancholy subjects alike. The Merry Cemetery of Sapinţa in Maramureş and the sampler-patterned houses of Ciocaneşti in Suceava are remarkable sights.

Polychromatic decoration and elaborate designs, spiralling and angular, are features of the craftwork, from the black and red Cucuteni pottery to the multicolored icons painted on glass; from the embroidered sheepskin vests of the Nasaud region and carnival marks to the slim geometry of the wooden churches and vigorously carved gateways and porches; especially in the Gorj and Maramureş districts. Even the wooden kitchen utensils in a rural tavern will merit examination.

This environment nurtured Constantin Brancuşi (1876–1957), arguably one of the greatest sculptors, along with Henry Moore, of our century. Born in Gorj county, he began life as a shepherd boy, carving flutes and staffs. At nine, as errand boy to a carpenter of Tirgu Jiu, he was copying the rippling effects his master achieved on rafters and wellheads. Forty years on he was a cult figure in Paris and New York, forging ahead of Epstein. Strength, simplicity and the flowing line were his hallmarks. On his controversial *Bird* the New York Customs levied duty, classing it as a 'piece of metal' instead of a 'work of art.' Brancuşi appealed successfully.

His best work is at his home-town of Tirgu Jiu, in the public park: wood and stone groups which include the *Kissing Gate, Table of Silence* and, in the city center, the *Endless Column.* The last is, technically at any rate, a display of 'bilateral symmetry on four vertical and two horizontal planes'; to most of us a totem-pole of polished rhomboidal wood-blocks climbing skyward in imitation of the well-known Transylvanian motif, the 'pillar of heaven.'

After Brancuşi, the sculptors Cornel Medrea (1889–1964) and Oscar Han (1891–1976) grappled like him with problems of harmony and balance in wood, stone and metal. Vida Gheza (born 1913) has produced some interesting, heavy and tormented bronze groups.

Ştefan Popescu (1872–1948) pioneered a national school of engraving, nowadays a prestigious subject for Romanian arts and graphics students. In fabrics, interior decoration and ceramics, the present generation gives old folk themes a new twist. Look out for the work of Geta Bratescu (born 1926), Ana Lupaş (born 1940), Ion and Ariana Nicodim (born 1932, 1935) and Costea Badea (born 1940).

The National Gallery and National History Museum in Bucharest are the places for native arts, artefacts and costumes. The Village & Folk Art Museum, also in Bucharest, surveys peasant life and crafts over three centuries.

Theater and Cinema

There are only 45 drama theaters in Romania (compared with 6,000 cinemas) and statistics indicate that the average citizen sees a play once in eight years; the country-dweller hardly ever. Drama is the Cinderella of the arts, but it ought not to be ignored. It has a venerable history.

The traditional theatrical entertainments—masques and monologues, courtly buffoonery and puppetry—developed from archaic rites brought in by the Greeks from the Black Sea coast and the Romans from south of the Danube. Up to the late 18th century an anonymous passion or morality play—like *Herodes* or *The Birth of Jesus*—vied for popularity with rough comedies about the *haidouks* (freebooters) in which the outlaws were depicted as heroes. Theater was essentially a winter-festival entertainment.

Bucharest's Dramatic Conservatoire started training professionals in 1836. Some decades later the father of a well-known theatrical family, Costache Caragiale (1815–1877) encouraged community drama throughout the nation; and two actors revered as pioneers today, Matei Millo (1814–1896) and Mihail Pascaly (1830–1882) formed companies for the Great Theater—afterwards the National Theater—of Bucharest. Up to the date of Romania's entry into World War I the playwrights I.L. Caragiale *(A Lost Letter)* and Barbu Ştefanescu-Delavrancea *(Sunset)* and several actors had made their mark. Aristizza Romanescu (1854–1918), a notorious author of memoirs, and Agatha Barsescu (1857–1939) are among the actresses remembered today. The famous actors were Grigore Manolescu (1857–1892), Constantin Nottara (1859–1935) and Petre Liciu (1871–1912)—famous in Romanian eyes, at least.

Between the two World Wars drama blossomed in several centers: Bucharest, Cluj, Timişoara, Iaşi, Oradea, Craiova and Cernauţi (now Cernovsty in the USSR). All had their State-subsidized theaters and resident companies. Romania's version of the matinee idol emerged with Aristide Demetriade (1871–1930), Lucia Sturdza Bulandra (1873–1961) and George Calboreanu (born 1896). Lucian Blaga (1895–1961) as a playwright and Ion Sava (1900–1947) as director had something of a reputation abroad.

Pay a speculative visit to a Romanian theater and the chances are that you will see classical drama by Sophocles, Shakespeare or Racine rather than the stilted, old-fashioned domestic product. Whatever it is, you will probably feel the acting and production are 60 years behind the times. But this is what Romanians like, and a small avant-garde battles in vain against both this and the post-1945 emphasis on didactic celebrations of the nation's struggles for self-determination.

Prominent present-day producers include Liviu Ciulei (born 1923) and Andrei Şerban (born 1942). Among leading players are Dina Cocea (born 1918), Radu Beligan (born 1918), Mircea Albulescu (born 1934) and Irina Petrescu (born 1940). The last-named is also the darling of motion-picture audiences.

The principal playhouse is the I.L. Caragiale theater in Bucharest. In the same city are two new theaters, named after C.I. Nottara and Lucia Sturdza Bulandra respectively. The Hungarian minority theaterland is in Cluj, with the Cluj-Napoca National theater and the Magyar theater. There is a German State theater in Timişoara.

The first movie show took place in the offices of a Bucharest newspaper in May 1896. For the next 50 years the medium was restricted almost entirely to newsreels and documentaries; though film buffs now regard the animated cartoons of Aurel Petrescu (1897–1949) with nostalgic affection.

The current regime has studios for feature films (Bucureşti), documentaries and popular science films (Alexandru Sahia) and cartoons (Animafilm)—all in Bucharest. In subject-matter there is still a preoccupation with the nation's struggles: Romania's few contributions to the international movie scene *(The Dacians, The Uprising, The Forest of the Hanged)* deal with this theme.

The best-known directors are Liviu Ciulei (born 1923), an actor and Cannes Film Festival prize-winner; Sergiu Nicolaescu (born 1930) and Elizabeta Bostan (born 1931). The leading motion-picture actors and actresses often come from the theater, but cinema has itself produced stars in Ilarion Ciobanu (born 1931), Florin Piersic (born 1936) and Carmen Galin (born 1946).

The national plan, 1981–1985, calls for a big expansion of film-making, probably 50 to 60 long-feature films, along with a development of the radio network and the introduction of color television.

ROMANIAN FOOD AND DRINK

Corn Mush and Wine

As befits one of Europe's richest agricultural countries, Romania's cuisine is distinctive, and its recipes have won over many a discerning palate both at home and abroad. Until fairly recently, it has not been that easy to find places serving Romanian as opposed to run-of-the-mill international dishes. But there has lately been a marked improvement in the variety and standard of food available, with particular emphasis on national or regional specialties. It is impossible to generalize, however, for while menus still offer rather limited choices in some places, in others—and not necessarily in obvious tourist haunts—you find excellent displays of dishes from which to make your selection. In fact, Romanians are great meat eaters, despite the frequent shortage of this in the shops (though not in the hotels), and there have been moves recently to encourage the populace to a greater appreciation of other home grown products of farm and market garden.

Starters

Romania's most celebrated pre-prandial or cocktail snack is the ubiquitous *mititei,* short skinless sausages hot from the grill and moderately well-spiced. Mititei are found at all levels of society from the most luxurious restaurants to humble kiosks near the market place. Also popular as pre-meal snacks are the *brinze,* or cheeses; a much sought-after variety is the Telemea from Dobrudja.

Other cold starters come in a great variety, sometimes eaten on their own or as part of a more extensive hors d'oeuvre. There are all kinds of thick vegetable purées—for example of spinach or white beans—some of them combining several ingredients such as eggplant, tomato, onions and peppers, subtly flavored with herbs. Sometimes, a vegetable is scooped out and filled with a delicious stuffing of other finely chopped mixed vegetables. Beetroot or eggplant come in for this kind of treatment. A variation on this theme is egg stuffed with spinach *(ouă umplute cu pîre de spanac),* popular throughout Romania. Various kinds of meat roll in pastry also feature on the list. *Piftie,* which is either pork or chicken in aspic decorated with chopped pepper or other vegetable, is another tasty starter. Some of these dishes may be beautifully decorated with radishes, onions or tomatoes 'sculptured' into pretty flower shapes.

Soups

These can almost be meals in themselves. They fall into two main categories, *sopa* and *ciorbă,* the latter being made with sour cream. Ingredients are practically limitless, but some popular ones are: *ciorbă de pui* (chicken), *ciorbă de perişoare* (with meatballs), *ciorbă de potroace* (giblet), *ciorbă teraneasca* (with meat and vegetables) and *bors pescaresc* (a mixed fish soup, mainly from the Danube Delta). In addition, there are many regional variations, such as *supa gulaş* (meat and potatoes) which is popular in Maramureş.

Main dishes

Probably the best known staple is *mamaliga,* a kind of corn mush that is eaten everywhere and with almost everything. It comes in various guises ranging from the rather leaden to the really good and tasty. In a Maramureş version *(balmoş),* it is cooked in sour cream and served with ewe's milk. Potatoes also come in for interesting treatment, as in *cartofi Bucovinei* in Moldavia; these are baked and stuffed with cheese, egg and butter and served with a slice of egg and olives.

Some dishes will seem familiar if you have visited other parts of the Balkans. There is *sarmale*—rice, usually with minced meat, wrapped in cabbage leaves. In Maramureş they use corn rather than rice *(sarmale cu păsat),* and add chopped mushrooms. Another Balkan favorite is *musaka:* eggplant, minced meat, potatoes, topped with a batter, but using other vegetables according to season.

Many dishes feature meat stuffed with a variety of ingredients. *Muşchi ciobanesc* (shepherd's delight) consists of pork stuffed with ham and cheese, covered with cheese and served with mayonnaise, cucumber and herbs. In *muşchi poiana,* beef is stuffed with mushrooms, bacon, pepper and paprika and served with a delicious sauce of veal stock, tomato and vegetable purée. Chicken comes in for similar treatment, as in the case of *pui Cîmpulungean,* sampled in the Moldavian mountains; in this case, the stuffing is often of smoked bacon, sausage meat and vegetables, flavoured with garlic. Another Moldavian dish—*rasol Moldovenesc cu hrean*—features boiled chicken, pork or beef, with a sauce of sour cream and horse radish. Across the mountains in Maramureş again, you may well be introduced to *rotogol Maramureşean:* veal meat (can also be pork) and mushrooms, fried with onions, cheese, smoked bacon, then rolled and dipped in egg, breadcrumbs and cheese before frying. The result is usually delicious.

Devotees of stew will enjoy *tocana.* This is composed of small pieces of meat (usually pork) in a stock strongly flavored with garlic or onions and served with *mamaliga.* Vegetarians will be drawn to *ghiveci,* a mélange of many vegetables, cooked in oil, which can also be served cold.

Among the fish specialties of the Black Sea coast, in addition to a great variety of fish soups, there is *nisetru la gratar* (grilled sturgeon, and rather expensive), *raci* (crayfish), *scrumbii la grater* (grilled herring) and *saramură de peşte* (grilled fish which is then skinned and put briefly into hot water with seasoning and spices).

Desserts and Cakes

Plăcintă cu brinza (cheese pie) and *plăcintă cu mere* (apple pie) are popular, as are pancakes with various fillings. A Maramureş variation is *mîr în foietaj*—apple stuffed with raisons, baked in pastry and served with a sprinkling of sugar. *Papanaşi,* a very superior form of doughnut, comes with cream, a touch of cheese and dusting of flour, and melts in the mouth. Indeed, cheese is a frequent ingredient of desserts, as in *ruladă rarău* a kind of Moldavian Swiss roll with cheese. Of oriental origin are *baclava,* soaked in syrup, and *cataif cu Frisca,* crisp pastry topped with whipped cream.

The Romanians are great cake eaters and you will find many establishments called *cafeteria* entirely devoted to cream cakes, pastries and biscuits; the best of them are luscious. The Moldavians make a tasty brioche called *cozonac,* while in almost any home you are likely to be offered *gogoşi,* a kind of doughnut.

Drinking

Romania is truly Latin in her devotion to the grape. Listen to the accolade paid to a great Moldavian Cotnari by a vintner at the court of Stephen the Great, 'This princely wine should not be drunk as water, to hear it gurgle down your throat, but you must receive it on your tongue like a string of beads, so that you may catch its strength and fragrance.'

Romania's best-known vineyards are at Murfatlar, near the Black Sea coast. One of the most popular excursions for Black Sea tourists is a wine tasting at Murfatlar. Murfatlar's wines, which have won gold medals in international competitions, include a Riesling, Muscat, Pinot Noir and Chardonnay. Cotnari, so beloved of Stephen the Great's vintner, produces the noted Grasa and Feteasca brands. Other popular regional selections are the Segarcea cabernet, Sadova rosé, a cabernet from Dealu Mare, Pinot Gris and Aligoté from Iaşi, Galbena from

Odobesti, Furmint from Panciu and Frincuşa and Nicoreşti. Wine is not always obtainable by the glass and, when it is, it is usually white wine only.

Romania's most highly-recommended beer comes from Azuga, a town in the Carpathians between the ski resorts of Sinaia and Predeal. Good beers are also brewed in the Black Sea province of Dobrudja.

Turning to stronger spirits, Romania's national drink is *ţuica,* a fruit brandy made mainly from plums. Because of its distinctive flavor, ţuica is best taken neat, either before or after your meal. Another plum drink, even fiercer than ţuica, is *rachia.* This is not to be confused with *rachiu,* made from grapes.

Among soft drinks, there are some splendid locally-made fruit juices, though they are not easily obtainable in hotels which more usually serve local or imported (and expensive) versions of international soft drinks that are not nearly as good!

BUCHAREST

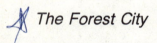 *The Forest City*

Some thousands of years ago, great forests covered the plains from the Carpathian mountains down to the shores of the Danube. A major trading route crossed these forests from north to south and, in due course, small settlements developed in clearings along the way. One of these became Bucharest and that old trading route is now the main artery through the city: a chain of broad boulevards—Bulevardul 1848, Blvd. N.Bălcescu, Blvd. Magheru, Blvd. Ana Ipătescu. The first Princely Court or palace was built just west of the southern stretch of these modern thoroughfares; at that time it was just one of several main centers of medieval Wallachia. Around it grew the bustling trading area that is now the Lipscani district, with narrow streets radiating from it, linking with another major street, Calea Victoriei on or near which are most of the main hotels and shops of the city.

Though there is a mention of 'a citadel on the Dimbovița' (the river that flows through Bucharest) in documents as early as 1368, the name Bucharest was first used officially by Prince Vlad Țepeș, the historic Dracula, in 1459. The name itself is said to derive from a shepherd named Bucur who was attracted to the region. For two centuries Bucharest alternated with Tirgoviște as the Wallachian capital. It has been the sole capital of Wallachia, and later Romania, since 1659.

Though the most lasting visual impression of Bucharest is of broad *he* boulevards, verdant parks, neoclassical 19th-century and monumental 20th-century architecture, the old core of the city is around Lipscani, and to get a true perspective of the capital, this is where your tour should begin. *Ours did not.*

The Old Core

The Old Princely Court is now a museum and, as you wander through its substantial ruins, it is possible to trace its development from the 15th century onwards. You can clearly see, for example, the rounded river stones used in the earlier construction, later alternating with red brick and then, in the 17th to 18th centuries, in brick only. In due course, the lower levels of the complex became the cellars of merchants' premises and craftsmen's workshops. Even today, the cellars spread far beyond the limits of the museum itself, and you will come upon them in the form of cellar restaurants in several of the surrounding streets. A number of the more famous of the Wallachian princes mentioned in our chapter on history were associated with the Old Princely Court, incidentally. Vlad Ţepeş was one; another was Brîncoveanu, the last to add to the construction of the palace.

As time went on, churches were founded and inns built to accommodate the many travelers and traders who came to do business in the growing town. Curtea Veche church, founded in the 16th century, is just next door to the Old Princely Court and, should you happen to be here on a Tuesday, you will see the astonishing sight of many hundreds of worshippers—mainly women—filing into the church to pray for some favor or express thanks for one that has been granted. Opposite the Old Princely Court is Hanul Manuc, perhaps the most attractive hotel in Bucharest; it also has a good restaurant. It was built in the early 19th-century by a rich Armenian, but incorporates older walls and is arranged in traditional style round an open courtyard. The Russian-Turkish Peace Treaty of 1812 was signed here.

Lipscani's traditional role as a bustling center for trade lives on. Private enterprise may be a thing of the past, but there are innumerable small shops, artisan workshops and open-air stalls, mostly belonging to consumer cooperatives or craft unions and all combining to create a bazaar atmosphere humming with activity. Among them is the complex of Bazarul Hanul cu tei in which boutiques and art galleries have their premises in a restored former inn. Several of the more attractive restaurants and taverns listed under *Practical Information* are also to be found in this area. Another church well worth visiting in the vicinity is that of Stavropoleos. It was built in 1724 in Brîncoveanu style combining late-Renaissance, Byzantine and Romanian folk art elements. It includes some superb wood and stone carving, not least the remarkable and richly-decorated iconostasis that separates the nave from the altar.

Calea Victoriei

You are now a stone's throw from Calea Victoriei, Bucharest's most famous street, which winds from Piaţa Natiunile Unite (and the Ope-

By the gardna of the Imperial Court in VIENNA

BUCHAREST

1. The Museum of the History of the Communist Party, of the Revolutionary and Democratic Movement in Romania
2. Museum of Natural History
3. Bucharest Circus
4. H. Coanda Museum
5. North Railway Station
6. St Elefterie Church
7. Romanian Opera House
8. Museum of Folk Art
9. Art Museum
10. Carpati, Bucharest National Tourist Office
11. National Theater
12. Museum of Bucharest
13. Tarom Agency
14. Stavropoleos Church
15. Domnita Bălaşa Church
16. Military Museum

Scale 0 — 440 yds
       0 — 400 m

TO THE AIRPORT

PIATA VICTORIEI
PIATA ROMANĂ
PIATA UNIRII
CIŞMIGIU
GRADINA BOTANICĂ
PARCUL SPORTIV DINAMO
PARCUL SPORTIV PROGRESUL
STADIONUL REPUBLICII
PARCUL LIBERTĂTII

BULEVARDUL 1 MAI
SOSEAUA KISELEFF
CALEA GRIVITEI
CALEA PLEVNEI
SPLAIUL INDEPENDENTE
CALEA VICTORIEI
B-DUL MAGHERU
B-DUL BALCESCU
B-DUL ANA IPATESCU
B-DUL ILIE PINTILIE
B-DUL GH. GHEORGHIU-DEJ
CALEA FLOREASCA
CALEA DOROBANTILOR
EROILOR

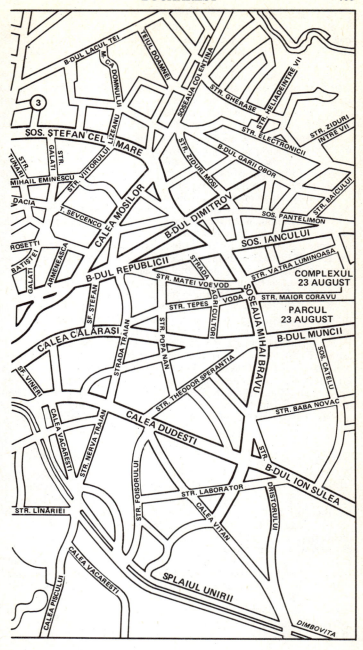

retta Theater) in the south to Piața Victoriei in the north, passing
several major monuments and buildings on the way. Near its southern
end (and Stavropoleos Church) is one of the most important: the History Museum of Romania, housed in the former Post Office. Its collections are magnificent and range from prehistoric to modern times, but
the most stunning of all are contained in the Treasury which you can
visit (and pay for) separately. The exhibits are changed from time to
time, but the emphasis is on objects of gold and precious stones and
spans Romania's history from the 4th millenium BC to the 20th century. The result is a staggering array of ornaments, weapons, vessels,
jewelry, medals, religious and royal paraphernalia. The most famous
of all is the Pietroasa treasure 'The Hen with Golden Chickens' (5th
century) composed of 12 pieces in gold weighing about 19 kilos; but be
prepared to be dazzled at every turn. The most massive item in the
whole museum is a full size replica of Trajan's Column (the original
is in Rome) commemorating his victory over Dacia in the 2nd century
AD. You pass the lower end of it as you enter the Treasury.

Did Not See

As you continue northwards along Cala Victoriei, you pass several
of the older hotels, main stores and a theater or two. The next point
of sightseeing interest is on the left just before you enter the wide
expanses of Piața Gh.Gheorghiu-Dej: the pretty little red brick Crețu-
lescu Church. It was originally built in 1722 and subsequently rather
badly renovated. But it was restored more or less to its former state in
the 1930s, as were some of the original frescoes.

Title Changed Analysis

The church overlooks a small park surrounded by very large and
more modern buildings, the contrast adding to its appeal. Immediately
to the north is the huge complex of the former Royal Palace, today the
Palace of the Republic and which also houses the National Art Museum. The latter contains fine collections of medieval and later
Romanian art as well as a good foreign section. You are now in Piața
Gh.Gheorghiu-Dej, the east side of which, opposite the Palace, is taken
up by the headquarters of the Romanian Communist Party and in front
of which, incidentally, you may not walk. Just beyond it is the fine
neoclassical concert hall of the Romanian Athaeneum with its gardens.

Parisian Aspects

Bucharest has often been described as the Paris of Eastern Europe.
It would be absurd to pretend that it has the *chic* of the French capital,
but there are quite a few features that bear comparison. Among them
are the broad boulevards that are characteristic of modern Bucharest,
including the continuous chain referred to at the beginning of this
chapter, which runs more or less parallel with Calea Victoriei until the
two converge at Piața Victoriei. It is on this chain of boulevards that
you find the Intercontinental Hotel (Blvd. Bălcescu) next to the ultra
modern National Theater; some distance north of it is the main office
of Carpați National Tourist Office (Blvd. Magheru), hub of all tourist
comings and goings in the city center. Colțea Church, a pretty little
early 18th-century building, is another edifice worth visiting just south
of the National Theater.

Reminiscent of Paris, too, are the terrace restaurants and brasseries, which are packed on a summer's evening. The similarities become even more marked as you continue north along the wide avenue of Şoseaua Kiseleff and come to the Arc de Triomphe or Triumphal Arch. It was built in 1922 to celebrate the Allied victory in World War I and to honor Romania's war dead. Originally constructed in wood and stucco, it was rebuilt in stone in the 1930s. It was designed by the gifted Petru Antonescu and carved by some of Romania's most talented sculptors. Beyond it, the lake-laced park of Herăstrău stretches away on your right, a true playground for the city's inhabitants who come here to fish or take boat trips on the several lakes, to stroll along the extensive network of paths, to eat and drink in the several restaurants, or to visit one of the top sights of the capital. This is the Village Museum (entrance from Şoseaua Kiseleff), one of the best of its kind anywhere.

The Village Museum is truly 'Romania in a nutshell.' It consists of about 70 structures, brought here from all over Romania and representing every kind of folk architecture, most of them furnished in original style. The majority are peasant houses from regions as wide-ranging as the Danube Delta, Moldavia, Maramureş and the Banat, but there are also windmills, watermills, artisans' workshops, a couple of churches, and a whole range of equipment used in rural areas from the 18th to early 20th century.

Şoseaua Kiseleff ends at the Piaţa Scînteii, dominated by Scînteia House, the State publishing enterprise. To the left of it Blvd. Poligrafei leads to several hotels, including the modern Flora with its full facilities for gerovital and other anti-aging treatments. To the right of Scînteia House, Şoseaua Băneasa is the main thoroughfare leading north out of town. The interesting Minovici Museum of Feudal Art is just along here on the left, and before very long you come into another verdant area, that of Băneasa Forest (near the airport for domestic flights) and also the setting for the main camp site and a number of pleasant restaurants. With every impression of being in the heart of the countryside, you are still only about 6 miles from the city center.

City Oases

In addition to the considerable expanses of Herăstrău Park, the heart of the city is dotted with smaller areas of greenery where you can interrupt your sightseeing and join the citizens of Bucharest in the ever-popular pastime of watching the rest of the world go by. Cişmigiu Gardens, just west of Calea Victoriei, are big enough to contain a lake of their own; they were created in 1850. Popular with students and artists, they also contain a small zoo.

Further west still, beyond the Opera House, are the Botanical Gardens. These were created in 1884 and contain some 10,000 plants, including tropical ones. South of the center is popular Liberty Park and the nearby and larger Tineretului (Youth) Park, with more lakes.

The final oasis on our list is rather further afield: about 22 miles north of Bucharest, in fact, but well worth the trip. This is Lake Snagov which, as well as being well endowed with camp sites, restaurants, sports facilities and a lot of attractive elbow room, is also of some historical significance. One of its main features is a large lake and on an island in it is the Snagov Monastery, which was founded by Vlad Tepeş in the 15th century. Indeed, it is here that this highly controversial gentleman has his last resting place after being killed by Boyars in the nearby forest, according to one of several versions of his death. It was also at the monastery that one of Wallachia's first printing presses was established in the latter part of the 17th century.

PRACTICAL INFORMATION FOR BUCHAREST

 WHEN TO COME. Like all capitals, Bucharest is a year-round city, but spring is probably the best time when the many parks and tree-lined avenues come to life again.

 GETTING AROUND BUCHAREST. By Subway. The first two lines of the new subway system are now ready. Cost is 1 leu for any distance; you insert the coin into a machine which opens a barrier.

Tram and Bus. Trams cost 1 leu (pay as you enter); tickets for trolley buses (1.50 lei) and buses (1.75) can be bought at kiosks.

By Taxi. Taxis are very reasonable, starting at 5 lei, plus 6 lei per Km.

 HOTELS. Bucharest hotels are often heavily booked during the tourist season, so if you haven't a reservation, go to the Carpaţi Tourist Office. The list below is a selection taken from the wide range available, from deluxe to unpretentious hostelries. All establishments have restaurants unless otherwise stated. Remember that many hotels have rooms in more than one category.

Deluxe

Intercontinental, Blvd. Bălcescu 4–6. Centrally located, with top class amenities; 423 rooms; night club.

International, opposite the Athenée Palace. New.

Expensive

Ambassador, Blvd. Magheru 10. Very central; all facilities; 233 rooms.

Athenée Palace, Str. Episcopiei 1–3. Old-fashioned, gracious and comfortable with all the facilities of a top hotel, very central; night club.

Dorobanţi, Calea Dorobanţi 5–9. Modern, fairly central; 298 rooms.

Flora, Poligrafiei Blvd.1. Modern, on outskirts of center, near Herăstrău Park. Top amenities, pool and full facilities for geriatric (anti-aging) treatment.

Lido, Blvd. Magheru 5. Very central, less plush but good value; 121 rooms, pool.

Manuc Inn, Str. 30 Decembrie 62, opposite the Old Princely Court Museum. One of the most attractive hostelries in the city, dating from early 19th-century and built round courtyard. Belongs to the city authorities; 30 rooms.

National, 33 Republicii Blvd. Good downtown location.

Nord, Valea Griviței 143. Near the Nord railway station, so away from center; 245 rooms.

Moderate

Capitol, Calea Victoriei 29. Central; 80 rooms.
Minerva, Str. Lt.Lemnea 2–4. 83 rooms.
Modern, Blvd. Republicii 44. 184 rooms.
Palas, Brezoianu 24. 160 rooms.
Parc, Blvd. Poligrafiei 3. 272 rooms.
Union, Str.Decembrie 11. 221 rooms

Inexpensive

Banat, Piața Rosetti 5. 40 rooms
Central, Brezoianu 13. 64 rooms
Muntenia, Str. Academiei 21. 123 rooms.
Negoiu, Str. 13 Decembrie 16. 93 rooms
Tranzit, Str. Miliției 4. 107 rooms
Veneția, Piața Mihail Kogălniceanu 2. 46 rooms

Restaurants

Expensive

Berlin, 4 C. Mille Str. Excellent food
București, 34 Calea Victoriei. One of the best in town, plush and with *belle époque* atmosphere.
Cina, 1 C.A. Rosetti St. Pleasant and next to the Athenaeum.
Marul de Aur, 163 Calea Victoriei. Reached through courtyard, a little less central.
Miorița, Șoseaua Kiseleff. Attractive situation in Herăstrău Park.
Monte Carlo, nicely placed in Cismigiu Gardens.

Moderate

Bucur, 2 Poenaru Bordea St.
Carul cu Bere, 5 Stavropoleos St. Traditional late 19th-century beer house, former meeting place of the artist set; lots of atmosphere. The ground floor tavern specializes in spicey sausages and there's a cellar restaurant below.
Crama Domnească, 13 Șelari St. Very attractive setting in ancient cellars adjoining those of the Old Princely Court; from the restaurant's terrace you overlook the latter.
Doina, 4 Șoseaua Kiseleff. With garden terrace; on the way to Herăstrău Park.
Hanul Manuc, 30 Decembrie St. 62. Good atmosphere in the courtyard and adjoining rooms of this old inn, now hotel, opposite the Old Princely Court.
La Doi Cocoși, 6 Șoseaua Străulești.
Pădurea Băneasa in Băneasa Forest, towards the airport. Pleasant setting, folkloric shows.
Rapsodia, 2 Șelari St. Another attractive cellar restaurant near the Old Princely Court, decorated with old folk masks.

Establishments marked *Cofeteria* serve rich, creamy cakes and pastries; the best of them are delicious.

MUSEUMS. Check the opening times, but Monday is the usual closing day.

Art Collections Museum, 111 Calea Victoriei. Romanian and foreign art.

The Art Museum of Romania, 1 Ştirbei Voda St. Housed in part of the former Royal Palace (now Palace of the Republic). Ground floor: feudal art with icons and copies of monastery frescoes from all over Romania; first floor: Romanian art; second floor: foreign art.

Folk Art Museum, Calea Victoriei.

Grigore Antipa Natural History Museum, 1 Şoseaua Kiseleff.

History Museum of Romania, 12 Calea Victoriei. A vast and interesting collection from neolithic to modern times. The Treasury (which can be visited separately) has a superb and changing collection of objects in gold and precious stones from pre-Dacian times to 20th-century Romanian royalty. Near the entrance to the Treasury is the base of a full-size replica of Trajan's column (the original is in Rome) commemorating the Roman victory over Dacia.

Minovici Museum of Feudal Art, 3 Dr.Minovici St., near Herăstrău Park. A villa furnished mainly in 18th- and 19th-century style. Next door is the small but interesting **Minovici Folk Art Museum.**

Museum of the City of Bucharest, 2 Anul 1848 Blvd.

Old Princely Court Museum, 30 Decembrie St. 31. In the heart of the oldest part of the city, these are the fascinating ruins of the first Princely Court in Bucharest and part of a very extensive site dating from the 15th century onwards and extending beneath the surrounding buildings.

Railway Museum, 193B, Calea Griviţei.

Romanian Music Museum, 141 Calea Victoriei. The collection is devoted to the renowned composer and musician George Enescu.

Theodor Aman Museum, 8 C.A. Rosetti St. Devoted to the well-known Romanian painter.

Tudor Arghezi Museum. Contents detail the life of the well-known Romanian poet.

Village Museum, 28–30 Şoseaua Kiseleff, in Herăstrău Park. A marvellous collection of ancient buildings of all kinds from all over Romania, furnished in original style. One of the best of its kind anywhere.

 NIGHTLIFE. Nightlife in Bucharest is surprisingly lively, though everything closes by about 1 A.M. Discos are quite popular and there are also nightspots with entertainment and live music for dancing. Among these are the **Melody, Bucureşti, Athenée Palace** and **Atlantic Bar.** In line with Bucharest's Parisian quality you'll also encounter a number of popular cafés and brasseries. Among the more widely patronized in the evenings are the **Tosca, Tic-Tac, Ciresica** and **Tomis** on Boulevard Gheorghiu-Dej, the **Turist** on Magheru, the **Unic** on Bălcescu and the **Corso** brasserie at the Hotel Intercontinental. There are also folkloric shows in many restaurants.

 OPERA, CONCERTS, THEATER. The magnificent Romanian Athenaeum at Str. Franklin 1 regularly plays host to two distinguished Romanian symphony orchestras and many noted foreign performers. For opera lovers, there is the **Opera House** at Blvd. Gheorghiu-Dej 70 or the **Operetta House,** 1 Piaţa Natiunile Unite. Don't miss the fine folkloric show at the **Rapsodia Romana Artistic Ensemble Hall** at Str. Lipscani 53.

Theatrical performances range from serious drama at the **Caragiale National Theater,** Blvd. Bălcescu 2, to lighter entertainment at the **Comedy Theater** on Str. Mandinesti, but these of course are in Romanian so may be somewhat baffling if your command of the language is limited. Of more international appeal are the charming shows at the **Tandarica Puppet Theater** at Calea

Victoriei 50. Of ethnic and cultural interest are Yiddish-language performances offered at the **State Jewish Theater,** Str. Barasch 15.

Bucharest has many cinemas that frequently run old American and English films; they are rarely dubbed.

 **SHOPPING.** In addition to hotel shops there are a number of outlets in Bucharest where you can pay with freely convertible (that is, hard) currency. *Comturist* (the international agency for the sale of imported and Romanian products) has many branches in the city including in several main hotels. *Artizanat,* Str. Academei 25, specializes in handicrafts.

Should you be paying in Romanian currency, the leading department stores are *Unirea,* Piaţa Unirii 1; *Cocor,* Blvd. 1848 33; *Bucur,* Şoseaua Colentina 2; *Romarta,* Calea Victoriei 60–68; *Victoria,* Calea Victoriei 17; *Bucureşti,* Baraţiei 2; *Tineretului,* Calea Dorobanţi 10. The following are some of the best shops specializing in various items. **Foreign books:** *Dacia Bookshop,* Calea Victoriei 45; *M. Sadoveanu,* Magheru 6. **Jewelry:** *Bijuteria,* Calea Victoriei 25. **Handicrafts:** *Artă Populară,* Calea Victoriei 118; *Săteanca,* Calea Victoriei 91; *Hermes,* Şepcari 16; *Meşteri Făurari,* Strada Gabroveni 6. **Glassware:** *Stirex,* Calea Victoriei 88. **Woolens:** *Electa,* Calea Victoriei 95. **Stamps:** *Filatelia,* 13 Decembrie 25. **Records and Music:** *Muzica,* Calea Victoriei 41.

Keep an eye open, too, for *Galerie de Artă* shops run by the Union of Plastic Artists *(Fondul Plastic),* specializing in various kinds of arts and crafts of high standard, though probably at fairly high prices. *Horizont* is one of the main ones; it is almost opposite the Intercontinental Hotel. Other small specialist shops are run by consumer cooperatives.

The traditional shopping area is the Lipscani district of the old part of the city, where there are many picturesque, varied and old-style small shops within walking distance of central hotels. In this area is *Bazarul Hanul cu tei,* a complex of small shops and galleries in the courtyard of a restored early 19th century inn. Here, too, is the *Consignaţia,* a kind of vast warehouse of second hand and antique items of all kinds.

Finally, the Romanians do some good lines in cosmetics; you can check these out in *Parfumerie* shops.

 SIGHTSEEING. The Carpaţi National Tourist Office arrange a wide variety of tours from half-day city sightseeing to 12-day packages ranging across the country. Some city sightseeing tours are of general interest, others concentrate on particular aspects such as folk, art, architectural monuments, etc. There are also day trips into the areas round the capital, or two-day arrangements to the mountains, the coast, the monasteries or the Danube Delta.

 USEFUL ADDRESSES. The main embassies are all in Bucharest: *British,* Strada Jules Michelet 24; *American,* Tudor Arghezi 7–9; *Canadian,* Nicolae Iorga 36.

Carpaţi National Tourist Office, Blvd. Magheru 7, Bucharest. *Litoral National Tourist Office,* Hotel Bucharest, Mamaia. *Romanian Automobile Club* (ACR), Blvd. Poligrafiei 3 (tourist services), Beloianis St. 27 (club and technical assistance). *Youth Tourist Bureau* (BTT), Strada Onesti 4–6, Bucharest. *Tarom* (Romanian Airlines), Athenée Palace, Calea Victoriei 96, and Strada Brezoianu 10. *Navrom* (Danube river boat travel), Blvd. Dinicu Goleseu 58.

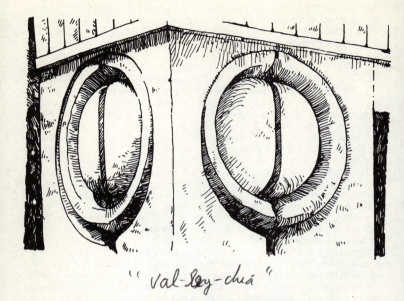

" Val-lay-chá "

WALLACHIA

Mountains and Plains

check this

A high proportion of Wallachia is made up of plains—those flat lands, once covered with forests, that stretch from the Carpathians down to the Danube. Today they are largely fertile farmlands; even the great marshy tracts created by the Danube and its tributaries have to a large extent been drained and replaced in due season by a sea of waving corn or the bright blaze of sunflowers. And where farmland ends, industry takes over. In the middle of the plains sits Bucharest, the focal point from which main roads radiate in all directions.

The Danube

It is a mere 40 miles from the capital south to Giurgiu on the Danube and the Bridge of Friendship that leads across it into Bulgaria. Romania has a 600-mile share in the Danube, much of it forming a border with Yugoslavia and Bulgaria until, near Calaraşi, it eases northwards to become wholly Romanian. The Wallachian Danube, however, is not particularly interesting. By far the most fascinating or dramatic stretches lie in the west (covered by the chapter on Transylvania) or to the northeast (described in conjunction with the Black Sea coast). The most likely circumstance in which you might be traveling the intervening stretches would be on a Danube cruise ship en route from Vienna to the Black Sea.

The Valleys

The most scenically and culturally rewarding regions of Wallachia lie in the southern parts of the Carpathians or the river valleys boring into them. Several of these rivers are pursued by main roads, leading eventually north into Moldavia or Transylvania, and the best plan if you intend touring the region would be to combine two of them in a circular trip beginning and ending in Bucharest. Though there are, of course, other routes, the three principal ones follow the valleys of the Prahova, the Olt and the Jiu.

Whichever route you decide to take from Bucharest into the Carpathians, it would be difficult to miss one of two major oil cities: Ploieşti and Piteşti. Neither is worth detailed investigation unless you have an interest in the oil business, but they do have their own curious appeal, especially if you happen to approach them at dusk when the massive petro-chemical works (and all their attendant paraphernalia), billowing smoke and flames into the sky, acquire a dramatic aura of their own.

The Prahova valley leads eventually to Braşov via Predeal, Romania's highest town and located on the watershed which acts as the border with Transylvania. It is one of Romania's busiest roads but a lovely one nevertheless once you have shaken off Ploieşti and the plains, and begun the long climb into the Carpathians. But the greatest attractions lie at the upper end of the valley where a number of winter sports centers cluster beneath the towering Bucegi mountains.

The best known of these is Sinaia, so called because of the monastery of the same name built in the 17th century by Mihail Cantacuzino in memory of his visit to Mount Sinai. The monastery now has two churches, the original one from the late 17th century and to which the indefatigable Brîncoveanu added a porch, and another from the 19th century whose frescoes include a portrait of King Carol. Near the monastery are a great many villas that used to belong to the Romanian aristocracy and are now used as holiday accommodations. The other architectural sight of Sinaia is the former royal summer palace of Peleş Castle, an exotic hybrid of Renaissance, baroque and rococo styles from the late 19th-century. Sinaia is a lively resort with some excellent hotels and plenty of entertainment facilities, but the ski slopes are not exactly on the doorstep. For these, you take the two-stage cable car leading up into the mountains where there are fine ski runs for all levels of skier. Equally, there are excellent opportunities for summer hiking.

The Olt Valley, which takes you through to Sibiu, is reached via Piteşti and joined at Rimnicu Vilcea, itself of no great interest. The Olt has been subjected to a great deal of construction of a hydro-electric nature of recent years and it is worth checking whether the road is open to motorists before including it in your plans. Scenically, it is a fine road, much of it winding through steep rocky or thickly-wooded mountains. It also links a number of popular small spas, of which the best known and perhaps the nicest is Călimaneşti Căciulata. About three miles to the north of it, you reach one of Romania's prettiest monasteries: Cozia, dating from the 14th century. The church was built by Mircea the Old and has changed little over the centuries except for the addition of an open porch by Brîncoveanu in the 18th century. The frescoes are from the late 14th to early 18th century.

The Jiu valley is the most westerly of the three and eventually leads to Deva. For much of the way, it is a steep narrow gorge with some evidence of coal mining. The main town is the valley is Tîrgu Jiu, an industrial center whose main claim to the visitor's attention is an unusual collection of sculptures. These are the works of Constantin Brăncuși (d. 1957), one of Romania's best known sculptors. He was born in a nearby village. Three sculpture groups in all were created by him in the 1930s as monuments to those who fell in World War I. Two of them—the *Kissing Gate* and *Table of Silence*—are in the town park; the third—the *Endless Column*—raises its slender silhouette above the town center. The design of these works is very simple yet full of symbolism; the *Table of Silence* for example is surrounded by twelve stools representing both the continuity of the months and the traditional number of seats at a funeral feast.

Historic Centers and Folklore

The several main routes that cross the Carpathians are, in turn, linked by a network of other roads, usually of a more minor nature, that serve the communities in the southern foothills. They are usually well worth taking, for as soon as you leave the main roads you are back amongst the predominantly folk architecture that characterizes much of rural Romania. The houses quite often carry the year they were constructed, but don't be misled if some of them appear to be of recent date for in many cases they have been built in just the same style as the houses they replaced. They are charming and colorful, usually with a porch or verandah (called *prispa*) that may run the length of the building beneath the jutting eaves of the roof; at higher altitudes, this verandah will be enclosed as protection against the elements. Roofs of wooden tiles are another common feature of rural areas. In these mountain regions, land is privately owned, fragmented into small fields or orchards or grazing land. It is all very lovely and unspoilt, and a far cry from the undoubtedly efficient but large scale state or cooperative farms only a short drive away down in the plains. You need to drive carefully though, for the farming folk, their livestock and their non-motorized transport are all totally unpredictable.

Such a road is the one that links the Olt and the Jiu valleys. This also provides an opportunity to visit a monastery of particular interest at Horezu. This is another of the creations of Constantin Brîncoveanu, that Prince of Wallachia who probably contributed more than any other individual to the architectural awareness of his people. The monastery was built in the late 17th century and you can pick out quite well the Renaissance, Byzantine and Romanian folk elements whose combinations were the hallmark of the Brîncoveanu style, whether in the heart of Bucharest or in the depths of the countryside. There are some beautiful examples of carved wood and stonework and plenty of frescoes. Those inside the church are rather dark for, when the Turks briefly sojourned here, it served as the quarters for their slaves who lit fires to keep warm; but elsewhere, for example in the nuns' refectory, the pure colors of the original frescoes are untarnished. Part of the church exterior is also decorated, including the usual picture of the *Last Judgement* showing the frightful things that will happen to sinners. Within the monastery is an excellent small museum whose exhibits include the oldest bible in Romanian (late 17th century).

Horezu Monastery is a delightfully peaceful place and, as is the case of some other monasteries in Romania, it has a few guest rooms, though foreigners will need special permission to stay there and this is not always easily obtained. Initial enquiries should be made through Carpaţi. The nearby village of Horezu is known for its pottery. There is still a strong tradition of special feasts held during the weeks following a funeral at which each guest keeps his or her plate as a kind of keepsake of the departed. Victor Vicsoreanu, who has his pottery on the outskirts of the village, is a third generation craftsman in this particular skill and is creating a small museum to display this type of ware.

In the Argeş valley to the east of the Olt, one of the early capitals of Wallachia, Curtea de Argeş, is another point of interest. Its most striking sight is the Episcopal Church, built in the early 16th century by Prince Neagoe Basarab, a most exotic structure combining a melange of oriental influences. The story goes that the prince was so determined no other building should be the equal of this, that when it was completed he left its skilful mason Manole trapped on the roof without any possibility of getting down. Manole jumped to his death and, according to legend, a fountain appeared where he fell.

Like every historic town in Wallachia, Curtea de Argeş had a Princely Court and its 14th-century ruins can be seen by the Princely Court Church, one of the oldest in Wallachia.

Another former capital of Wallachia lies much closer to Bucharest. This is Tirgovişte, about 1½ hours drive from the capital, roughly half way between Piteşti and Ploieşti. There is quite a lot of interest to be seen here, especially round the museums associated with yet another Princely Court, in this case built in the reign of Mircea the Old, though subsequently added to by later princes, including Brîncoveanu. The Chindia Tower, though since rebuilt, also dates from the 15th century and now houses a museum dedicated to the legendary Vlad Ţepeş. The Princely Church was built a century later. Also worth visiting in the vicinity of Tirgovişte is Dealu Monastery (late 15th century) in whose crypt is kept the head of one of Wallachia's greatest rulers, Michael the Brave, the first to achieve, albeit briefly, the union of the Romanian people. It was here also that Romania's first printing press was installed in the early 16th century, and there is a museum of Printing and Old Romanian Books in the town.

PRACTICAL INFORMATION FOR WALLACHIA

 WHEN TO COME. Apart from Bucharest itself, the most attractive parts of Wallachia are the southern areas of the Carpathians and the deep valleys that penetrate them, so spring, summer, and early fall are the best times for touring. The area also includes some excellently-equipped winter sports resorts.

 GETTING AROUND WALLACHIA. There are organized excursions from Bucharest to some main points of interest. Otherwise travel by car gives the greatest freedom. There are regular passenger boats on the Danube. Details from Carpaţi.

HOTELS AND RESTAURANTS

All hotels listed below have restaurants unless otherwise stated.

BRĂILA. Traian (M), 110 rooms
Main sights. The activities of a busy river port; this is the head of navigation on the Danube for ocean-going vessels.

CĂLIMANESTI-CĂCIULATA. Spa attractively situated in the Olt valley. **Vîlcea** (M), 120 rooms. **Căciulata** (M), 205 rooms.
Main sights. A few miles away is lovely Cozia Monastery (founded 14th century).

CURTEA DE ARGEŞ. A former capital of Wallachia. **Posada** (M), 53 rooms.
Main sights. 14th century Princely Church and ruins of the Princely Palace. Exotic 16th-century Episcopal Church.

PITEŞTI. Major oil town. **Muntenia** (M), 275 rooms

PLOIEŞTI. Major oil town. **Prahova** (E), 126 rooms

SINAIA. Winter sports town. **Montana** (E), 180 rooms. Central, modern and near cable car station. **Palas** (E), 148 rooms. **Sinaia** (E), 248 rooms. Modern, also central. **Alpin** (M), 56 rooms. Many attractive villas offer Inexpensive accommodations, though without food which is available in nearby restaurants.
Main sights. Sinaia Monastery with 17th- and 19th-century churches. Peleş Castle in ornate German Renaissance style.

TÎRGOVISTE. A former capital of Wallachia. **Dimbovita** (M), 107 rooms. **Turist** (M), 29 rooms.
Main sights. 15th-century ruins of Princely Court and 16th-century Princely Church. 15th-century Chindia Tower housing Vlad Tepeş (Dracula) Museum.

TÎRGU JIU. Gorj (M), 235 rooms.

Main sights. The Sculpture Group by Constantin Brăncuşi.

 USEFUL ADDRESSES. Carpaţi or ONT have offices in most towns and resorts, as does the Romanian Automobile Club (ACR). In addition there are County Tourist Offices (OJT) as follows: **Brăila,** 58 Republicii St.; **Piteşti,** 1 Muntenia St.; **Sinaia,** 19 Carpaţi Blvd.; **Slatina,** 2 23 August St.; **Tîrgu Jiu,** 6 Eroilor St.

TRANSYLVANIA

Folklore, History and High Places

Transylvania is a region of enormous beauty and variety, not the least of which is the extremely vital peasant culture surviving in many areas. Contributing to this variety are the substantial national minority groups (especially German and Hungarian) reflecting the region's long, if often reluctant, association with the Habsburg empire.

Topographically it consists of the Transylvanian Plateau, with an average altitude of 1,300–2,000 feet. This is bounded by the sickle-shaped Carpathian Mountains, the inner ranges of which also form part of Transylvania. The plateau in turn is divided by the Mureș river flowing down through the less substantial western Carpathians into the Banat before eventually joining the Tisza river in Hungary. The Banat Mountains (that part of the Carpathians lying between the Danube and the Mureș) contribute to probably the most spectacular stretch of the entire Danube on its approaches to the Iron Gates. In the far northwest of Romania, Maramureș concludes the list of regions associated with Transylvania, and in many respects it is the most enchanting of all.

Braşov and Sibiu

Two of Romania's most interesting towns are to be found on the Transylvanian plateau: Sibiu, more or less half way along its southern

416

fringes, and Braşov, at its upper end, tucked in at the foot of the eastern
Carpathians. Both are linked to Bucharest and each other by good
roads, and both can boast very beautiful old districts of Gothic, Renaissance and Baroque houses reflecting in style the predominantly Germanic influence on the area of those times. Sibiu is the more attractive
of the two, but Braşov has the best and most rapid access to Romania's
best winter sports facilities. 2nd largest in Romania

We'll begin with Braşov, this being the nearest town to Bucharest in
the area. It is reached by the Prahova valley (described in the chapter
on Wallachia). You enter Transylvania at the ski resort of Predeal
(Romania's highest town) straddling the heights which divide the
Prahova and Timiş valleys. Its situation gives it good access to the
skiing and hiking facilities of both the Bucegi and Baiu Mountains.
From here it is only about 15 miles into Braşov.

Today, Braşov is a busy industrial center, but the old core of the
town, founded back in the 13th century, still survives in many aspects
despite fires and battles. The History Museum in the attractive former
Town Hall is one place where you can trace local history, though of
greater interest still is the Museum in Braşov Citadel and housed in the
medieval Weavers Bastion, to the south of the town center. To the
north of it, Cetăţuia is a small fortress rebuilt in the 17th century and
offering good views of the city as well as a pleasant complex of restaurants. But Braşov's most famous sight by far is the Black Church in
the heart of the old city, so called because it still bears the marks of
the fire caused by the Austrians in 1689. Though largely reconstructed,
it is a fine Gothic building, especially noted for its collection of old
oriental carpets and its massive organ (which dates from 1839). Other
nearby traces of the old fortifications are the Ironsmiths' Bastion and
Ecaterina's Gate. A little away from the center, look out for the charming 16th-century St. Nicolae Church—unusual because it is an Orthodox church built in what was at the time a predominantly Roman
Catholic town; it was funded by ruling Orthodox families in Wallachia.

Only about 7 winding miles up through the forests is Poiana Braşov,
in some ways the most appealing of Romania's winter sports resorts.
Its situation on a small plateau beneath Postăvarul mountain means
that you can ski from your hotel doorstep. But you can also take
advantage of the cable cars, gondola lifts and other skiing facilities to
reach greater altitudes. There are about a dozen hotels in all categories,
several folk-style restaurants and also summer sports facilities, including a riding school. Easy access to the town is not its least attraction.

In complete contrast is another highly popular excursion from Braşov: Bran castle, this of Dracula fame and about 20 miles to the southwest along a narrowing valley. The connection with Vlad Ţepeş (the
original Dracula of legend) is, in fact, very tenuous, but the castle is
well worth visiting anyway. It dates from 1377 when it was built by the
citizens of Braşov to guard the narrowest point of the valley and its
border with Wallachia (a remnant of the frontier wall is still to be seen)
and though there have been many changes since then, Bran remains a
most satisfying castle, both in its situation and its construction with its
courtyards, galleries and narrow passages. One of its early owners was
the grandfather of Vlad Ţepeş, and a further connection with this

* 1456-1462
Period he ruled

enigmatic Wallachian prince (see the chapter on history) is that he is said to have been imprisoned here by Matei Corvin (King Matthias Corvinus of Hungary) in 1462 on his way to Buda—though technically the castle was not on his route. The castle today is a museum and contains medieval and later furnishings and weaponry. Its last owner was Queen Marie (the English-born wife of King Ferdinand).

About 90 miles separate Braşov from Sibiu. It is worth pausing at Făgăraş on the way to glimpse the restored 16th-century citadel, which contains a museum as well as a hotel and restaurant. It is also worth the detour to take in the Monastery of Sîmbăta de Sus, another of Brîncoveanu's creations from the late 17th-century and surrounded by orchards and beautifully-framed by the highest peaks of the south Carpathians. The monks here specialize in painting icons on glass and have a fascinating exhibition of these, some dating back to the monastery's earliest days though it was deserted for a long period after destruction by the Austrians (its reconstruction was completed in 1936). It is a splendidly peaceful place, and the countryside in these parts has an unchanging quality emphasized by the sight of horsedrawn ploughs and carts powered by black water buffalo. *June 25 1985*

Sibiu is a lovely town and a great deal of its medieval past survives. There are substantial sections of the old defensive walls and three of the original bastions. These date from the 14th century when the town was divided into guilds, each with its own defence system (at one time there were as many as 40). The old town is built on two levels which adds to its visual appeal, for steep stairways link the small squares and narrow streets of the two. Many of the houses are colorful and charming, a characteristic being the small windows, like sleepy eyes, peering out from the middle of their ancient roofs. The hub of the old town is Republic Square and close to it is the Brukenthal Museum, one of the best ethnographic collections in Romania. This is a must if you have any interest in the development of folk art of all kinds—pottery, textiles, furnishings and many other crafts—from different parts of the country, many also reflecting the influences of other nationalities. Brukenthal, incidentally, was Governor of Transylvania in the the 18th century at the time of Maria Theresa mother of Marie Antoinette, and created the building for his collections which have since been expanded. It also features a gallery of fine Romanian paintings and a number of other European works including a couple of pictures by Rubens and a Van Dyck.

To the south of Sibiu is the fine oak forest of Pădurea Dumbrava, setting for a zoo and an open air museum. You pass through this on your way to the delightful village of Răşinari, about 12 miles away—a gem of a place with colorful houses and courtyards tucked away behind high walls. It is a village of shepherds, craftsmen and artists, many of the inhabitants combining all three skills. It may be possible to arrange a visit to one of them, such as Vasile Frunzete who paints on glass while his wife and parents produce superb hand-embroidered leatherwork. At the same time you will learn a good deal about a way of life which has changed little, for transhumance (the seasonal movement of livestock) is still a governing feature of this village from which 25,000 sheep leave for the summer pastures each May and return in the fall.

About 10 miles beyond Rǎşinari, the road comes to an end at the developing winter sports resort of Pǎltiniş.

Along the Mureş River

About 45 miles to the northwest of Sibiu on the Mureş river is Alba Iulia. This was not merely a Roman town, as you might guess from the name, but was at one time the capital of Roman Dacia. Its main sights, however, are of more recent date. The present Citadel is of Italian design and dates from the early 18th century though with later restoration and additions. The Orthodox church for example was built in the 1920s and it was here that the coronation of King Ferdinand and Queen Marie took place. There are also a number of 19th-century buildings, one of which contains a particularly well-planned History Museum. Opposite the History Museum is a place of special significance in Romanian history. This is the Museum of the Union—the very spot where the Unification of Transylvania with the rest of Romania took place in 1918.

Follow the Mureş river for 48 miles downstream and you come to Deva, associated with an earlier attempt to unite the Romanian states by Michael the Brave. He was briefly successful in this effort at unification at the end of the 16th century, but soon afterwards, alas, the new 'king of the three Romanian countries' was defeated in a battle here. You can hardly miss Deva's most significant monument—the Citadel—for its ruins crown a hill rising almost out of the city center. It's quite a slog to the top, but worth it for the view. Only a few miles south of Deva is Hunedoara which has not only one of Romania's biggest and earliest steel works but, more or less engulfed by it, an astounding castle. It was first built in the 14th century, but every subsequent century has added something to it, giving it both a massive and a flamboyant presence. Much of it is due to Iancu de Hunedoara who, in the 15th century, turned it from a stronghold into a sumptuous castle, and some of those details—such as the Renaissance loggia—you can see today. Iancu fought and beat the Turks in Belgrade in 1456 and his son Matei Corvin was to become King (Matthias Corvinus) of Hungary. Though there have been many alterations since those days and a major fire caused much damage in 1854, a great deal has been restored to its original condition.

The road south into the Carpathians from Deva leads eventually into the Jiu valley described in the chapter on Wallachia. On the way, a minor road leads to Densuş and one of the many delightful and more remote monuments that Romania has to offer: a remarkable little 13th-century church (with 15th century frescoes), largely built of Roman stones and bricks excavated from Sarmizegetusa. The latter was the capital of Dacia before and during the Roman period and is one of several interesting archeological sites to be found in the surrounding mountains.

Nearly 100 miles west of Deva along the Mureş river is Arad, close to the Hungarian border. Its main points of interest are the Citadel, the St. Simion Stîlpnicul Monastery and the Chapel St. Florian, all dating from the 18th century.

Other Transylvanian Centers

Several other towns in more northern parts of the Transylvanian plateau should be mentioned and could be incorporated into your itinerary according to your direction and inclination. Three of them are linked, for example, by the main road from Braşov which eventually leads to Oradea and Hungary. The first is Sighişoara which has a particularly impressive hill top citadel whose features include a 14th-century clock tower, now containing the History Museum. Not far from this, a yellow house announces itself to be the birthplace of the inescapable Vlad Ţepeş. Tîrgu Mureş on the Mureş river also has a citadel with a number of bastions, and a late Gothic church.

Over in the northwest, Cluj-Napoca, where the western Carpathians meet the Transylvanian plains, is a major educational and economic center. The city was known as Napoca in Roman times, hence its double name, but its main development came in the 15th century when it was powerfully fortified by Matei Corvin (Matthias Corvinus) King of Hungary. His equestrian statue is one of the landmarks of the city. Many of the inhabitants of Cluj are Hungarians, and much of its architecture is reminiscent of other central European cities of the Habsburg empire. The great church of St. Mihail—the largest Roman Catholic church in Romania—was founded in the 14th century and rebuilt following a fire in 1698. The Art Museum is located in an 18th-century baroque palace built by local Hungarian rulers, the Banffy family. There is also a good Ethnography Museum in the Empire-style Reduta Palace, with an openair section in Hoia forest.

Oradea, close by the Hungarian border, is a pleasant town, with a ruined citadel and good access to the Apuseni mountains of the western Carpathians. It is also close to several of Romania's many spas, the best known being Băile Felix, only 5 miles away.

Maramureş

Tucked away close to the Soviet border in northwest Romania is one of this area's most charming regions. Despite industrial development around one or two main towns, much of Maramureş is blessedly untouched by the more garish aspects of the 20th century. The deep-rooted traditions reflected in its rural architecture, its peasant costumes, its crafts and customs have remained intact to a remarkable degree, and it is infinitely worthwhile taking the time to wander through its villages at leisure.

Baia Mare is the main town of the area. Its extensive modern districts and industrial developments seem to offer an unpromising start, but there are a number of interesting sights in or near Liberty Square, the old core of the town. One of the several ancient buildings round the square, for example, contains the Mineral Exhibition with quite stunning geological specimens in exotic shapes and colors. The History Museum, in a restored 17th-century building on the square, is interesting too, and there are also a number of surviving remnants from the medieval town such as parts of the 15th-century citadel and St. Stephen's tower. The Cathedral is 18th century, with original furnishings and stained glass.

There is a very active artists' colony in the town which developed its own school of painting in the 19th century. Some of the modern architecture is quite impressive too and, in front of the new City Hall, there is a particularly charming sculpture group by Vida Gheza, depicting the infinite patience of old age. But above all this is a good place to get an introduction to the very rich folkloric traditions of the region; the place to go is the well-planned Ethnographic Musem.

The outstanding attraction of Maramureş, as we have said, is its peasant culture, and there are any number of places where you will find evidence of it. The following route, which will eventually lead you east into Moldavia, is one suggestion for getting the best from your visit. The route first heads northwest to Sighetu Marmaţiei. Your first stop should be the village of Sat Şugatag. Maramureş is famous for its old wooden churches and this is the oldest of them all (from 1642), complete with original frescoes and altar gate. From Sighetu Marmaţiei (good Ethnographic Museum with folk masks) follow the Soviet border westwards for a few miles to Sapinţa, which boasts one of Europe's strangest cemeteries, and certainly its jolliest. Indeed, it is known as the 'Merry Cemetery' and was the creation of one man, Stan Pătraş who, until his death in 1977, carved the incredible range of wooden memorials which fill the graveyard, each vividly describing in pictures and words the life or character of the person buried beneath it. His house is now a museum and the work is being continued by one of his students.

You will need now to return to Sighetu Marmaţiei. Beyond it, take the road which follows the Iza valley southeast towards Moisei. There are two roads, so be careful to take the one that links the villages of Rozavlea and Bogdan Vodă, if possible including a short detour to Ieud. In the villages along this road you will see all that is most typical of Maramureş: the beautiful folk architecture of the houses with their open verandahs, wooden-tiled roofs, colorful decoration and, most typical of all, the ornately carved gateways leading into their courtyards. Several of the villages have beautiful examples of the old wooden churches of the region, notably the three villages already mentioned. You will see, too, to what a remarkable degree the delightful traditional costumes are still worn—especially by the women—not as a tourist attraction, but as part of every day life. Particularly striking are the woven aprons with their broad horizontal stripes of black alternating with a bright color, and the exquisitely embroidered blouses or waistcoats. Distinctive, too, are the soft moccasin-type shoes, bound round the lower leg with a long leather thong. The country people can be extremely welcoming and you are quite likely to be invited to watch some handicraft in progress, such as spinning, weaving, embroidery or wood carving. (Some of these handicrafts may be bought, but don't expect them to be particularly cheap). Or you may be invited into a home.

From Moisei you begin the steady climb into the eastern Carpathians which culminates at the Prislop Pass, the watershed which divides Maramureş from Moldavia. It is a magnificent road scenically and on the way you will pass the little mountain resort of Borşa, a good place for an overnight stop—or longer if you want to take advantage of the marked mountain trails for some rewarding exercise.

The Banat and the Iron Gates

Our final region in this section is the most southwesterly corner of Romania, the plains of the Banat and that part of the Carpathians that stretches down to the Danube. In the plains, the town of Timişoara is arguably one of the loveliest in the country, with some very fine 18th-century architecture (Old Town Hall, Hospital and Church of the Order of Mercy, Unirii Square and Roman Catholic Cathedral, Serbian Cathedral, Episcopal Palace, etc.), and the 14th-century castle of Iancu de Hunedoara. The latter contains the excellent Banat Museum.

The other outstanding sight of the area is the spectacular narrow gorge which the Danube has carved on its passage through the Carpathians. Along this stretch, the river forms the border with Yugoslavia and flows through an almost continuous series of deep gorges. In a massive collaboration between the two countries, the level of the river has been considerably raised and its power harnessed to feed the great hydro-electric works of the Iron Gates. River traffic overcomes this obstacle by means of a huge double lock. Human history along these banks goes back a long way and the Romans in particular have left substantial traces of their presence. On the Romanian bank, these are best seen at Drobeta-Turnu Severin, the main town just east of the Iron Gates, where there are impressive traces of a great bridge built by Apollodorus for Trajan in the early 2nd century AD, as well as of a Roman camp and baths. The town has an exceptionally good archeological and ethnographic museum, as well as a 13th-century citadel.

Only a short drive into the mountains, there is more evidence of the Romans in the spa of Băile Herculane, founded by them in AD 153. It has been used continuously ever since and is one of Romania's most famous watering spots. The town's name comes from the legend that it was here that Hercules slew the Hydra, healing himself afterwards in the mineral springs. Two points of interest are the Historical Museum, devoted to Roman objects, and a room in the Hotel Cerna which was occupied by the Austrian Emperor Franz Josef on his many visits.

PRACTICAL INFORMATION FOR TRANSYLVANIA

WHEN TO COME. Spring (for orchard blossom) and summer for walking and hiking, and touring the region's many splendid historic sites and beauty spots. There are especially colorful events in Maramureş at Easter and folkloric festivals in several mountain regions in summer. The fall is good for trips to the vineyards and the winter for the growing sports facilities in the Carpathian resorts. Spa treatment is available all year round.

GETTING AROUND TRANSYLVANIA. Carpaţi organize tours ranging from one- or two-day trips concentrating on specific areas or incorporating them in more extensive tours of Romania up to 12 days long. Traveling by car gives the greatest freedom. Several of the main centers are linked by air with Bucharest, and rail and bus connections complete the network.

HOTELS AND RESTAURANTS

All hotels listed below have restaurants unless otherwise stated.

ALBA IULIA. Cetate (M), 128 rooms. Modern, near entrance to Citadel. **Transilvania** (M), 83 rooms. Central, a short walk from the Citadel. **Apullum** (I), 26 rooms. Central.

Restaurant. Crama Cetate, wine tavern in walls of Citadel.

Main sights. Citadel (largely 18th century), excellent History Museum of the region. Museum of Union, commemorating historic unification of Transylvania with Wallachia and Moldavia.

ARAD. Astoria (E), 155 rooms. **Parc** (E), 80 rooms.

Restaurant. Zarand in typical Romanian style.

Main sights. 18th-century Citadel. Baroque St. Simion Stîlpnicul Monastery and St. Florian Chapel. Early 19th-century Old Arad Theater.

BAIA MARE. Mara (E), 120 rooms. New in 1983 in newest part of city, near sports hall. **Carpaţi** (M), 114 rooms. By river in the modern part of town. **Bucureşti** (M), 74 rooms. In modern center of town; has prize-winning chef and particularly good food. **Minierul** (M), 48 rooms. Turn-of-century building on main square of old Baia Mare.

Restaurants. Păstrăvul (M), with fish specialties, and **Birt "Igniş"** (M), both in older part of town; **Maramureşul** (M), in newer district. All (M).

Main sights. Libertăţii Square, the old center of town with attractive buildings, including remarkable collection of exotic specimens in the Mineral Exhibition. Ethnographic Museum, with fine displays of Maramureş folk culture. Restored History Museum (due to open 1984). 15th-century Ştefan Tower. Baroque Cathedral.

BĂILE FELIX. Well-equipped spa. **Belvedere** (E), 220 rooms. **Lotus** (E), 200 rooms, and **Termal** (E), 180 rooms. **Nufărul** (M), 78 rooms. **Felix** (M), 153 rooms.

BĂILE HERCULANE. Well-equipped spa. **Afrodita** (E), 210 rooms. **Diana** (E), 210 rooms. **Roman** (E), 182 rooms. **Hercules** (M), 280 rooms. **Cerna** (M), 81 rooms.

BISTRIŢA. Coroana de Aur (E), 117 rooms.

BORŞA. Cascada (M), 58 rooms. Lovely mountain setting on the western approach to Prislop Pass. Walking center with developing winter sports facilities.

BRAŞOV. Carpaţi (L), 312 rooms. Top facilities; central. **Capitol** (E), 180 rooms. Central. **Parc** (M), 38 rooms. Short stroll from the center. **Postăvarul** (M), 167 rooms. Restored late 19th-century building; near center.

Restaurants. Cerbul Carpatin (E). Popular cellar restaurant in 17th-century merchant's house, with excellent folk show: a great favorite with visitors. In **Cetăţuia** fortress, complex of restaurants, including in Transylvanian style, also tavern, coffee shop, disco.

Main sights. The famous Black Church (14th to 15th centuries) with notable collection of carpets and monumental organ. Cetăţuia, 17th-century fortress on hill north of the center with fine views. Excellent Braşov Citadel Museum, south of the center. 16th-century St. Nicolae Church. 16th-century Ecaterina's Gate. The whole of the old town center, around the Black Church, has many charming corners and buildings, largely from the 18th century.

CLUJ-NAPOCA. Belvedere (E), 153 rooms. **Napoca** (E), 159 rooms. **Continental** (M), 51 rooms. **Astoria** (I), 100 rooms.

Main sights. Ethnographic Museum, especially the open air section in Hoia forest, with collection of buildings characteristic of Transylvania. History of Pharmacy Museum in 16th-century pharmacy. St. Mihail Cathedral. Gothic and restored in 17th century. Fragments of old defensive walls. Fine Botanical Gardens.

DEVA. Cetate, due to open in 1983. **Sarmis** (M), 124 rooms. Modern, central.

Main sights. The ruined Citadel, crowning hill dominating the town, with splendid views; worth the stiff climb.

DROBETA-TURNU SEVERIN. *Parc* (E), 138 rooms.

Main sights. Various Roman remains (camp, baths, ruins of massive bridge over Danube). Citadel. Portile de Fier Museum with excellent archaeological and ethnographic sections, and aquarium.

FĂGĂRAŞ. Restaurant is restored 16th-century Citadel, which is the town's impressive main monument.

HUNEDOARA. Rusca (M), 106 rooms.

Main sights. Fabulous castle (14th to 19th centuries) rubbing shoulders with one of Romania's biggest steel works.

ORADEA. Dacia (E), 177 rooms. **Transilvania** (M), 71 rooms.

Main sights. Ţara Crişurilor Museum in baroque palace. Citadel. 18th-century Canons' Row.

POIANA BRAŞOV. Alpin (E), 141 rooms. Best and quietest. **Teleferic** (E), 149 rooms. Closest to the cable car station. **Sport** (M), 122 rooms. Simple rooms but good value and nearest to the nursery slopes. There are several other Expensive hotels near the Alpin; all have good views to the mountains surrounding this popular resort which has excellent and growing winter sports facilities. In summer, there's swimming, tennis, horse riding.

Restaurants. Several in typical local style, with attractive décor, include **Şura Dacilor, Coliba Haiducilor** and **Vînătorul** (game specialties). **Capra Neagră** is a night bar.

PREDEAL. Cioplea (E), 162 rooms. **Orizont** (E), 157 rooms. **Bulevard** (M), 43 rooms. There is a wide choice of accommodations in all categories in this popular skiing resort and busy town.

REŞIŢA. Semenic (lower M), 110 rooms. **Bistra** (lower M), 27 rooms.

SATU MARE. Aurora (M), 108 rooms. **Dacia** (lower M), 48 rooms.

SIBIU. Continental (E), 180 rooms. Modern, near old town. **Bulevard** (E), 129 rooms. Older, but comfortable, at entrance to old town. **Împăratul Romanilor** (E), 96 rooms. Attractively restored 18th-century building in heart of old town. **Pădurea Dumbrava** (lower M), 65 rooms, out of town in oak woods, near camp site.

Restaurants. Butoiul de Aur (Golden Barrel) (M), charming tavern in the old town. **Sibiul Vechi** (Old Sibiu) (M), tavern in the old town in Romanian folk style. **Bufnita** (M), tavern style in the old town. **Dunarea** (I), old town. **Unicum** (I), old town.

Main sights. The old core of the city is lovely, with several ancient bastions, towers, defensive walls and many 15th to 18th-century buildings. 18th-century Brukenthal Palace and museum of the same name, with outstanding ethnographic displays (among the best in the country) and good collection of 15th to 18th-century paintings. Open-air Ethnographic Museum and zoo in the oak woods outside the city.

SIGHIŞOARA. Steaua (M), 54 rooms

Restaurants. Vlad Dracul House, in the citadel.

Main sights. Imposing 14th to 17th-century Citadel crowning hill, including History Museum in 14th-century clock tower and 17th-century wooden Gallery of 175 Stairs. 14th to 15th-century Biserica din Deal (Church on the Hill).

TIMIŞOARA. Continental (E), 167 rooms. **Timişoara** (E), 242 rooms. **Central** (E), 87 rooms.

Main sights. 14th-century Iancu of Hunedoara's Castle, housing Museum of Banat. Many 18th-century buildings including Bastion of the Citadel, the House of the Prince of Savoya, the Old Town Hall and the Hospital and Church of the Order of Mercy.

USEFUL ADDRESSES. There is a Carpaţi or ONT Office in all towns and resorts. In addition County Tourist Offices (OJT) are maintained in the following centers. **Alba Iulia,** 22 1 Mai Sq.; **Arad,** 72 Republicii Blvd.; **Baia Mare,** 1 Culturii St.; **Bistriţa,** 14 Petru Rareş Sq.; **Cluj-Napoca,** 2 Gheorghe Şincai St.; **Drobeta-Turnu Severin,** 41 Decebal St.; **Deva,** 1 Unirii Sq.; **Predeal,** 74 Gh. Gheorghiu-Dej Blvd.; **Satu Mare,** 11 Libertăţii Sq.; **Sibiu,** 4 Unirii Sq.; **Timişoara,** 6 Republicii Blvd.; **Tîrgu Mureş,** 31 Trandafirilor Sq.

The Romanian Automobile Club (ACR) also maintain offices in many centers.

MOLDAVIA

Mountains and Monasteries

Moldavia fills the northeastern corner of Romania, bounded by the Soviet Union to the north and east, rising into the Carpathians to the west and spreading southwards down the valleys of the Siret and its tributaries to merge into the Wallachian plains. It has many of the attributes of other parts of Romania, not least its fine mountain areas and its colorful peasant culture. But to these it can add the unique attraction of its painted monasteries, high on the list of the art treasures of Europe.

To reach it by road, you take one of Romania's main highways north through Buzău and Focșani (formerly on the Wallachian-Moldavian border) to Bacău. It is a tedious stretch of about 200 miles across the plains on which, in due season, you are likely to encounter vast armies of agricultural machinery moving from one district to another. As there is usually a lot of livestock and non-motorized traffic as well, you may need to drive with special care and patience. By the time you reach Bacău, the foothills of the Carpathians are gradually closing in to the west and you now have a choice of routes: the main highway continuing north to Suceava, and another road branching north west up the Bistrița valley.

The Bistriţa Valley

The upper reaches of the Bistriţa form one of the lovely untouched regions of Romania and this route is highly recommended. First you come to the sizeable town of Piatra Neamţ, a good place to pause and get your bearings. It has some Princely Court ruins from the time of Stephen the Great, an Archeology Museum and the Museum of the Carpathians devoted to the natural history of the mountains. From here, carry on to Bicaz beyond which lies the great man-made Bicaz lake formed by the waters of the Bistriţa.

While you are in this area, you might consider a worthwhile detour if you have time. Southwest of Bicaz, a road brings you through the fabulous Bicaz gorges to the developing little mountain resort of Lacu Rosu. From here you could take a minor road northwards with Durău as your destination. This is another small mountain resort, with an attractive new hotel as well as other accommodations, and a restored but interesting monastery almost next door (striking modern frescoes). Durău is overlooked by one of Romania's most distinctive mountains, Ceahlău. Like many, it was once considered holy and innumerable legends have been woven round its craggy presence. These holy mountains were traditionally the scene of annual celebrations when people flocked to the summit to greet the sun to the accompaniment of feasting, folkloric events and religious ceremonies. The practise still survives in several mountain areas, Ceahlău being the most celebrated on a Sunday in August.

Durău can more easily be reached by road from the northern end of Bicaz lake. It is northwest of the lake that the Bistriţa valley is at its best. It is a superb valley carved out through richly wooded mountains and peppered with farming and timber communities whose folk architecture and culture has, as yet, made few concessions to the jet age. Thatched or shingled roofs and color-washed façades, sometimes decorated with delicate floral motifs, reflect a quiet evolution that has grown out of generations of continuity. In the old days, the river was used for floating timber.

The road eventually brings you to the little town and spa of Vatra Dornei and a few miles beyond this it divides. To the left it pursues the Bistriţa still further before clambering up to the Prislop pass and on into Maramureş (see the chapter on Transylvania). To the right it brings you to Cîmpulung Moldovenesc, a center for the timber industry, nestling in the mountains. Here it is well worth seeking out the Museum of Wooden Spoons, the quite astonishing private collection of Ioan Ţugui containing 5,400 different spoons in 100 different kinds of wood from every corner of Romania and many parts of the world. Some are purely utilitarian, others are true works of art, and many combine both qualities. They range from historic spoons from the time of Maria Theresa to a modern contribution from New York inscribed 'kissin' don't last, cookin' do!'

Cîmpulung Moldovenesc is on the threshold of painted monastery country centered on or near the Moldava valley. However, most visitors are likely to approach these from Suceava, so we will first turn our attention to this modern hub of Moldavia.

Suceava

The first impression of Suceava is of an extremely modern town, but you need only glance up at the high plateau to the east of it to realise its history goes back a long way. Up there are the substantial ruins of the Citadel, first mentioned in documents in 1388, subsequently strengthened, especially by Stephen the Great in the 15th century. In the following centuries, it suffered sieges by the Turks, featured in numerous battles and was occupied briefly by the Poles. At last, in 1675, the Turks ordered its destruction, a process further aided by an earthquake later in the 17th century. Today, it is a fine ruin offering panoramic views over the city.

Other points of interest in the town are the ruins of the Princely Court, the New St. George Church which is a monument to Moldavian art from the 16th century, other remnants from medieval times and several museums, of which the Regional Museum gives an excellent idea of court life in the times of Stephen the Great.

It was during his reign in particular that Moldavia prospered, both economically and culturally, despite constant battles with the Turks. Some of the superb monasteries and churches you are about to visit stand as witnesses to and evidence of his victories. Before you set off for these, though, you might go and see the fortified monastery of Dragomirna a few miles north of Suceava. Though it is not one of the painted monasteries, it is an interesting building from the early 17th century, with an ornate tower and curious interior columns. The museum of the monastery contains some exquisitely carved wooden crosses and some illuminated manuscripts.

The Painted Monasteries

All built in the 15th and 16th centuries and usually fortified, Moldavia's painted monasteries combine Byzantine and Gothic elements, but their unique and most characteristic feature are the frescoes which cover not only the interior but also the exterior walls, many of them of a vividness that is quite breathtaking. Of the 14 with external frescoes that still survive, we shall concentrate on five. There are plenty of organized excursions to these, but there is much to be said for an independent visit at a quiet time of day with leisure to stop and ponder.

If you have followed our route through to Cîmpulung Moldovenesc, you could quite easily take in three of the monasteries on the way to Suceava by taking a slightly devious route. Otherwise it is easy enough to visit one or more of them on a circular trip out of Suceava.

The first on the list is Moldoviţa, founded in this case not by Stephen the Great, but by his son Petru Rareş. The exterior frescoes on one side of the church have been destroyed by the passage of time but on the other they are in superb condition and repay careful examination—remembering that their original purpose was to bring the Bible alive to the illiterate populace who were not allowed, in any case, to go beyond the portico of the church. Most of their themes are common to several or all of the churches: scenes from the life of Christ, historic scenes such as the Siege of Constantinople, the Tree of Jesse with its branches entwined round an array of prophets, and a kind of portrait gallery of philosophers amongst which such familiar names as Aristotle and Socrates stand out (if you can decipher the Cyrillic alphabet!). The interior walls are divided into 365 squares, representing the days of the year, each depicting a saint or martyr from the Orthodox calendar. No one knows precisely the techniques of those anonymous painters of long ago, but the effect is quite startling with the rich deep blue of the background predominating against the soft purples, reds and yellows of the scenes imposed upon it.

Moldovița, now a convent, is still an active religious center. It also houses a museum whose exhibits include the chair of Petru Rareș, old manuscripts and icons, and remnants from an earlier 15th-century church destroyed by a landslide.

Voroneț was founded by Stephen the Great in 1488, but the paintings date from the time of Petru Rareș and those inside the church include a portrait of Stephen himself, holding a model of the building. The outer frescoes feature a magnificent Last Judgment; note the hand protruding from the Throne of Justice, holding the scales with devils hanging to one side and angels to the other. Against the background of an Eternal Fire there are gruesome portrayals of what can happen to sinners, while angels run their spears through vicious little black devils and the shrouded dead arise from their graves to be rescued by the angels, saints and bishops waiting by the Door of Paradise.

The monastery of Humor dates from 1530 and its church is one of the simplest in design. There is another fearsome Last Judgment scene (in the portico) and a stirring representation of the Siege of Constantinople on the south wall. The interior frescoes are well-preserved and there is also a finely carved iconostasis.

The furthest of the monasteries from Suceava, and only a few miles from the Soviet border, is Putna, another of the creations of Stephen the Great which is also his last resting place. It is revered for this reason especially, since it has no external frescoes and has suffered damage by fire, pillage and earthquake on several occasions, the present building being the result of extensive restoration in 1968.

Sucevița is the 'newest' of our selection, built in the 1580s and painted in the first years of the 17th century; its defensive walls and towers are particularly well preserved. Today a convent, its frescoes include a massive composition of the Ladder of Heaven, each rung representing a mortal sin with winged devils waiting to snatch any luckless sinner who transgresses. Near Sucevița, the village of Marginea is worth visiting not only for its characteristically decorated wooden houses, but also for the black pottery produced here, achieved by smoking and polishing the pot before the clay hardens.

Last on our list is Arbor, similar in style to Humor and built by one of Stephen the Great's officers. The prevailing color here is green and the best known paintings, on the west wall, portray Genesis and scenes from the lives of saints.

Eastern Moldavia

Close to the eastern border with the Soviet Union is a town considered by some to be the most attractive in Romania: Iris Iaşi, the former capital of Moldavia. Its history has been turbulent from the plunderings of Tartar and Turk and attacks by the Poles to the ravages of fire and plague. But still much of great interest and beauty remains from the 15th to 19th centuries. One of the most beautiful buildings is the Trei Ierarhi Church (1639), its façade a veritable lacework of stone. Among many other churches and monasteries in the town is the Golia Monastery dating from the 17th century and surrounded by thick walls.

Iaşi got its start as an intellectual center in the 17th century when Prince Vasile Lupu founded the Vasilean School. Another Moldavian ruler, Dimitrie Cantemir, was a leading historian in his own right, and the town has produced Romania's national poet, Mihai Eminescu, as well as other literary greats. The Palace of Culture in attractive Gothic style houses museums of history, art, science and ethnography. Among others are the Museum of Old Moldavian Literature and the Museum of Union (of Moldavia and Wallachia). A number of statues, from Stephen the Great to several literary figures, reflect Iaşi's glorious past as the political and cultural hub of Moldavia.

PRACTICAL INFORMATION FOR MOLDAVIA

 WHEN TO COME. Spring, summer and early fall are the best times for touring the mountain areas and visiting the magnificent monasteries.

 GETTING AROUND MOLDAVIA. There are many organized tours from Bucharest or the Black Sea to the famous painted monasteries of Moldavia. Otherwise traveling by car gives the greatest freedom and possibilities to explore little known valleys not easily accessible by public transport. Peasant culture is still very much alive in some of these remoter valleys.

Hotels and Restaurants

All hotels listed below have restaurants unless otherwise stated.

CÎMPULUNG-MOLDOVENESC. Zimbrul (M), 90 rooms; modern.
Main sights. Museum of Wooden Spoons, astonishing private collection of thousands of spoons from all corners of Romania and many parts of the world.

DURĂU. Durău (M). Modern attractive building in beautiful mountain setting, in interesting and unspoilt area.

IAŞI. Traian (M), 137 rooms. **Unirea** (M), 183 rooms.

Main sights. Trei Ierarhi Church (1639) with exquisitely carved exterior stonework. History, Ethnographic and Art Museums in the neo-Gothic Palace of Culture. St.Neculai Domnesc Church (1492). 16th-century Golia Monastery, late 19th century National Theater. Museum of the Union. Museum of Old Moldavian Literature. Many charming corners and buildings in one of Romania's loveliest towns.

PIATRA NEAMŢ. Ceahlău (E), 146 rooms. **Central** (E), 132 rooms.
Restaurants. Colibele Haiducilor, in typical Romanian style.
Main sights. 15th-century ruins from the time of Stephen the Great include the Princely Court and St.Ioan Church. Archaeology Museum. Museum of the Carpathians with wild life exhibits.

SUCEAVA. Arcaşul (E), 100 rooms. **Bucovina** (E), 130 rooms. **Central** (M), 89 rooms.
Main sights. 14th-century Citadel, enlarged and strengthened by Stephen the Great, offers fine views of city. 15th-century ruins of the Princely Court. New St.George Church, 16th-century monument to Moldavian art. 14th-century Mirăuţi Church. This is also a main launching point for the spectacular painted monasteries of Moldavia.

 USEFUL ADDRESSES. Carpaţi or ONT have offices in most towns and resorts, as do the Romanian Automobile Club (ACR). In addition there are Country Tourist Offices (OJT) as follows: **Bacău** 10 Calea Mărăşeşti; **Focşani,** 3 Unirii Sq.; **Iaşi** 12 Unirii St.; **Piatra Neamţ,** 38 Republicii St.; **Suceava** N. Bălcescu St., Block 2A.

THE DANUBE DELTA AND
THE BLACK SEA COAST

Sun and sand—and a Watery Wilderness

The Dobrudja region of eastern Romania contains the historic port of Constanţa, the Romanian Riviera pleasure coast, the celebrated Murfatlar vineyards, fine Roman (and earlier) remains and the Danube Delta, one of Europe's leading wildlife sanctuaries. From any of the coastal resorts you can easily make excursions to all of these places, but do allow enough time to do them full justice.

A Natural Paradise

Even faced with its impressive vital statistics, it is difficult to imagine the vastness of the Danube Delta: 1,676 sq. miles or 4,340 sq. km of watery wilderness sprawling from the Soviet border to a series of lakes north of the popular Black Sea resorts. As it approaches the delta area, the great Danube river divides into three. The northernmost branch forms the border with the Soviet Union, the middle arm (to a large extent canalized) leads to the busy port of Sulina, and the southernmost arm meanders with a marvellous lack of urgency to the little port of Sfîntu Gheorghe. Between these three main arms lie huge tracts of

432

marshes, reed beds and smaller pockets of lush forest, laced with lakes and labyrinthine minor waterways in which the uninitiated could lose themselves for weeks.

The central Sulina channel is the main shipping lane for the ocean-going vessels, passenger ships and smaller craft which also ply the waters of the southern Sfîntu Gheorghe channel. Ocean-going vessels can go as far upstream as Brăila, but the main town of the Delta is Tulcea, a busy river port from which you can take a passenger boat or hydrofoil to the Black Sea and back, or join one of many excursions into remoter parts of the Delta. The sight of the big ships manoeuvring the twists in the river at Tulcea is fascinating. Here, too, is the excellent Danube Delta Museum which provides a very good introduction to the flora, fauna and way of life of the communities in this remote corner of Europe.

Many of the inhabitants of the area are Ukrainians, but there are also descendants of a Russian religious minority known as Lipovans who came here long ago to escape religious persecution in Russia. Fishing, of course, is a major occupation and it is quite common to see a long line of fishing boats strung together being towed out to their fishing grounds in some remoter part of the Delta by motor boat which will come and pick them up again at the end of the day. In several of the smaller communities, these same fishing boats can be hired by visitors to take them out on excursions—by far the best way of experiencing the region. Murighiol, which has a big camp site, is a particularly popular center for tourists since, unlike many others, it is accessible by road. Crişan, on the Sulina channel, is another main tourist center. A certain amount of livestock is also reared in the Delta, and the reeds are harvested for cellulose, roofing and a variety of other purposes.

But the great attraction of this watery wilderness is the incredible bird life. There are over 300 species here, including several colonies of pelican and spectacular numbers of herons, egrets, glossy ibis and many kinds of wader. Birdwatching enthusiasts will find themselves in paradise. Mammals include wild cat, wild boar and deer, and marine life ranges from caviar-bearing sturgeon, sheatfish and catfish to the more plebian perch and carp, most of them adding to the variety of the Delta's gastronomy.

From Tulcea there are good roads to the Black Sea resorts, taking you first through the strange, eroded Macin hills to Babadag. Further south, make a point of visiting Istria, an impressive archeological site combining both Greek and Roman remains. It was actually founded in the 7th century BC. The site is extensive and includes Greek baths and a temple of Aphrodite, as well as more substantial traces of the commercial and residential districts of the Roman and Byzantine city.

Mamaia and Constanţa

The resort strip of the Black Sea coast stretches from Mamaia in the north almost to the Bulgarian border in the south. Mamaia is the largest of the resorts and has the greatest choice of facilities, as well as the advantage of proximity to the archeological treasures of Constanţa, only a few miles to the south.

Mamaia itself has a 5-mile stretch of beach and lies between the Black Sea and Siutghiol, a freshwater lake. It has facilities ranging from modern high rise blocks to neat villas, from garden restaurants to night clubs and swinging discos and from camp sites to shopping centers and beer halls. Though you could hardly call Mamaia typically Romanian, any more than you could any of the other beach resorts, it is a completely self-contained community offering all that's necessary for a seaside holiday, plus plenty of excursions into the surrounding countryside and beyond.

From here it's only a short trolley ride into Constanţa, Romania's second largest city as well as one of its most ancient. If you like rummaging about in the distant past, you'll be in your element here, for traces of Constanţa's long history are scattered all over the city. It has, too, that polyglot flavor so characteristic of port communities.

Founded by the Greeks in the 6th century BC, Constanţa was known as Tomis until the 4th century AD, when it was renamed in honor of Constantine the Great. Ovid, the Roman poet, lived here in exile from AD 8 until his death nine years later and spent much of his time writing letters of complaint back to Rome for which he was passionately homesick. However, although he was apparently oblivious to the region's charms, the city has named a square after him, erecting in the middle of it a statue to his memory. The statue (1887) is the work of Etorre Ferrari, incidentally, the sculptor who also created Lincoln's statue in New York. Behind it, in what was formerly the Town Hall, is the really splendid National History and Archeological Museum, one of the top museums of Europe. Exhibits range from neolithic right up to modern times, but the most outstanding are from Greek, Geto-Dacian, Roman and Daco-Roman cultures. If you have time for nothing else, don't miss the Treasury whose unique exhibits include some stunning Greek statuettes from the 2nd and 4th centuries BC, the Glykon serpent (antelope's head, serpent's body, lion's tail and some human elements) and the Goddess of Fortune, protector of the city of Tomis, both from the 2nd to the 3rd centuries AD. Some of the treasures were found in the course of building new blocks of apartments in the area—just where they had been hidden to conceal them from the barbarians so many centuries ago. Two other items not to be missed among the neolithic finds are the exquisite statuettes of *The Thinker* and *Seated Woman* from the Hamangia culture of 4,000 to 3,000 BC.

Near the museum is another of Constanţa's major sights: a Roman complex of warehouses and shops from the 4th century AD, incorporating a magnificent mosaic floor over 2,000 meters square. Not far from this complex are remains of Roman Thermae from the same period. Yet another archeological site is the Openair Archeological Museum by the new Town Hall right in the town center, and there are several other foundations or remnants of ancient buildings or walls in other parts of the city. From Turkish times there is the Mahmudiye Mosque and, close to it, the relatively modern Orthodox Cathedral.

And there is still plenty more to see: a fine aquarium on the sea wall opposite the Casino restaurant, the dolphinarium with displays by trained dolphins, a naval museum and several folk art and art exhibitions.

The Mythology Belt

South of Constanța is a string of seaside resorts which, between them, attract a very high proportion of Romania's visitors from both east and west. Most have the sandy Black Sea shore on one side and easy access to one of a string of freshwater lakes on the other. The lakes—especially that of Techirghiol—are known for their healthgiving sapropel mud, highly recommended for rheumatic ailments. A number of centers offer thermal establishments and full treatment facilities. Best-equipped is Eforie Nord which has an up-to-date treatment center dispensing a wide range of therapy to sufferers. This is the northernmost of the resorts only a short distance from Eforie Sud on the shores of lake Techirghiol. To the south of this are a series of new resorts begun in the 1960s, all bearing names echoing the coast's Graeco-Roman past: Neptun, Jupiter, Venus, Saturn. They are not so much towns as tourist complexes consisting of modern hotels, villas, camp sites, shopping centers, restaurants and various sports facilities and all set in pleasant gardens. Again, they are hardly typically Romanian, but they do offer good amenities for a relaxed holiday by the sea.

The southernmost resort is the old port of Mangalia, formerly the Greek city of Callatis as evidenced by its Archaeological Museum and Graeco-Roman remains. Attached to it are several modern hotels.

Inland Excursions

A popular excursion from any of the resorts is to the famous Murfatlar vineyards whose wines were discussed in the chapter on food and drink. There's usually plenty of opportunity to sample the products, too!

On the same or different occasion, you can continue further west to a village called Adamclisi, near which is one of Romania's most famous Roman monuments. This is Tropaeum Traiani, a massive circular triumphal monument, 102 feet (31 meters) in diameter, 131 feet (40 meters) high and built in AD 109 to celebrate Emperor Trajan's victory over the Dacians. Over the centuries of invasions and neglect it fell into considerable disrepair, but in 1977 the most recent reconstruction took place and today the monument soars again out of the landscapes of Dobrudja. Though the present structure is modern, it follows as closely as possible the design of the original as far as it is known. The actual original pieces of carved stonework are kept in a special museum in Adamclisi itself. Traces of the adjoining Roman citadel can also be seen.

PRACTICAL INFORMATION FOR THE COAST

WHEN TO COME. Though a handful of hotels stay open in winter and spa treatment is available year round, the Black Sea resorts don't begin to come alive until the middle or end of May. By high summer, they are packed with people and buzzing with activity. The wild life that haunts the watery wilderness of the Danube Delta is best seen during spring and early fall (the times of the migrations); you'll be spared the worst of the mosquitoes then too!

GETTING AROUND THE COAST. The Litoral National Tourist Office arranges a variety of sightseeing tours of the region; also a number of packages further afield to other parts of the Balkans, Italy, Turkey and so on. There are air links between Bucharest and Constanţa and Tulcea; rail and bus connections complete the network. Otherwise traveling by car gives the greatest freedom. Car hire can be pre-booked or arranged on the spot. Regular passenger boats ply the central and southern arms of the Danube through the Delta and there are plenty of sightseeing boats as well. Tulcea is the main center, but fishermen will take you out from a number of small communities scattered about this vast watery labyrinth.

HOTELS AND RESTAURANTS. All hotels listed below have restaurants unless otherwise stated. The frenzy of hotel building has eased off recently, and attention is being concentrated on the renovation of older hotels and the provision of greater camping, villa and sports facilities.

CONSTANŢA. Palace (E), 132 rooms. Near the Casino, with terrace overlooking the sea and tourist port of Tomis. **Continental** (M), 139 rooms. Central, near Town Hall.

Restaurants. Casino (M), in ornate early 20th-century style with night bar, by the sea. **Casa cu Lei** (M), with rooms in Romanian, Spanish and Venetian style.

Main sights. National History and Archeological Museum, with outstanding collections from prehistoric to modern times, and superb Treasury containing unique statues, pottery, etc. Roman complex including fabulous Mosaic, over 2,000 sq. meters, from 4th century AD. Openair Archeological Museum in city center park. Roman Thermae, near the Mosaic. Aquarium, opposite the Casino, excellent of its kind. Dolphinarium with shows by trained dolphins. Mahmudiye Mosque. Several other archeological remains are scattered about the city.

EFORIE NORD. Europa (L), 242 rooms. High rise building in small park near sea. There are hotels of all categories, but most of the buildings immediately overlooking the beach are villas. The **Delfin, Meduza** and **Steaua de Mare** (all E), are linked to the excellent facilities of the treatment center of this important spa for rheumatic complaints, but these hotels are also available to holidaymakers.

Restaurants. Nunta Zamifirei, folk architecture and décor, with Romanian specialties and folk shows. **Acapulco,** nightclub.

EFORIE SUD. Flamingo, Măgura, Gloria, Excelsior, Cosmos, Capitol, all (E-M). The resort is scattered along a narrow strip of land between the Black Sea and Lake Techirghiol with its health-giving mud.

Restaurants. Haiduc Han, bar with folk show. **Complex, Central** and **Vienez,** all with dancing.

JUPITER. Atlas, Capitol, Cozia, Olimpic, Scoica, Tismana all (E). A little inland is the extensive holiday village **Zodiac** (E) in a natural park.

Restaurants. Paradis, night club, near beach. **Orizont,** garden restaurant.

MAMAIA. Largest of the resorts on isthmus between Black Sea and Mamaia lake; has the most extensive facilities. **International** (L), 204 rooms. **Amiral, Bucharest, Condor, Dacia, Orefu, Parc, Perla, Victoria** are among the (E)s. **Caraiman I, Histria, Midia** are (M)s.

Restaurants. Insula Ovidiu, rustic style on island on lake Mamaia. **Miorița,** Romanian food and attractive setting on lake shore. **Orient,** with night club. **Melody,** night club and music hall. **Cherhana,** fish specialties served in Danube-delta style building on lake shore. **Vatra,** garden restaurant in resort center.

MANGALIA. Romania's southernmost resort and spa. **Mangalia** (E). **Scala** and **Zefir,** both (M)s.

Main sights. Archaeological complex in resort's central park, with many Greek relics.

NEPTUN. Many modern hotels, shops, restaurants, set in attractive gardens by Neptun Lakes. Hotels include **Doina** (E), with balnealogical treatment facilities. Other (E)s are **Callatis, Romanța, Tomis.** In the adjoining resort of *Olimp,* **Amfiteatru** and **Belvedere** are (L); **Oltenia** and **Panoramic** are (E)s.

Restaurants. Calul Bălan, attractive setting in nearby Comorova forest, with folkoric shows. **Neptun,** in typical Romanian style, also in Comorova forest. **Insula,** on island in Neptun lake, serving fish specialties. **International,** with night club and beer house.

SATURN. High rise blocks interspersed with shopping complexes, restaurants and gardens. **Aida, Balada, Cleopatra, Hora, Sirena** are (E)s. **Alfa, Beta, Gama, Prahova, Siret** are (M)s.

Restaurants. Pelican in unusual and attractive building serving fish and other Romanian specialties. **Cleopatra Tavern,** with folk and music hall shows.

TULCEA. Main center of the Danube delta. **Delta** (M), 117 rooms; by the Danube. **Egreta** (M), 116 rooms.

Main sights. Museum of the Danube Delta, excellent introduction to the flora, fauna and way of life of this unique watery wilderness. Ocean-going ships and other vessels passing through this busy river port.

VENUS. Modern hotels and resort facilities amidst gardens. **Cocorul, Favorit, Lidia, Raluca, Silvia** are (E)s. **Corina, Dana, Egreta, Rodica, Veronica** are (M)s. The adjoining resort of *Aurora* rises in a series of pyramid-shaped hotels including **Agat, Coral, Cristal, Granat, Onix, Opal, Safir, Topaz,** all (E)s.

Restaurants. Cătunul, folk-style complex of restaurant, pastry shop and coffee house. **Calipso,** with music hall show; **Aladin.**

SPORTS. All the Black Sea resorts have facilities for tennis, mini golf, water skiing, boat and bicycle hire. There is a riding school at Mangalia.

USEFUL ADDRESSES. The main body dealing with all tourist aspects of the coast is the Litoral National Tourist Office whose head office is Hotel Bucharest, **Mamaia** (branches in Constanța and most resorts). In addition there is a County Tourist Office (OJT) at 2 Isaccea St., **Tulcea.**

TOURIST VOCABULARY

Of the five languages which appear in this book Romanian is the easiest for an English-speaking person to handle. Not that Romanian is all that easy a language, but since it is related to the Romance languages, Spanish or Italian, it is more immediately recognizable. It stems from the Latin spoken along the Danube by the Roman colonists and has survived countless conquests.

Here a few pronunciation rules—'e' at the beginning of a word is pronounced 'ye'; 'e' and 'i' before another vowel is 'y', consonant; 'i' at the beginning of a word 'yi'; 'i' at the end of a word 'y' as in 'yellow'; 'o' and 'u' before another vowel is 'w'; consonants are much as English except that 'c' is 'k', except before 'e' and 'i' when it is 'ch'; 'che' and 'chi' are 'ke' and 'ki'; 'g' is hard, but pronounced as 'j' before 'e' and 'i'; 'j' is 'zh' as in French; 'ş' is 'sh'; 'ţ' is 'ts'; stress is usually on the penultimate syllable, but on the last if the word ends in a consonant or a dipthong.

USEFUL EXPRESSIONS

Hello; how do you do	Bună ziua
Good morning	Bunădimineaţa
Good evening	Bună seara
Goodnight	Noapte bună
Goodbye	La revedere
Please	Vă rog
Thank you	Mulţumesc
Thank you very much	Vă mulţumesc foarte mult
Yes	Da
No	Nu
You're welcome	Cu plăcere
Excuse me	Scuzaţi-mă
Come in!	Intraţi
I'm sorry	Îmi pare rău
My name is . . .	Mă numesc . . .
Do you speak English?	Vorbiţi engleză?
I don't speak Romanian	Nu vorbesc românește
I don't understand	Nu înţeleg
Please speak slowly	Vorbiţi rar, vă rog
Please write it down	Scrieţi, vă rog
Where is . . . ?	Unde este . . . ?
What is this (place) called?	Cum se numește acest (loc)?
Please show me	Indicaţi-mĭ-mĭ, vă rog
I would like . . .	Aș vrea
How much does it cost?	Cît costă?

SIGNS

Entrance	Intrare
Exit	Ieșire
Emergency exit	Ieșire in caz de pericol
Toilet	Toaletă
men, gentlemen	domni, bărbaţi
women, ladies	doamne, femei
vacant	liber
occupied	ocupat

Hot	Cald
Cold	Rece
No smoking	Fumatul Oprit
No admittance	Intrarea Oprită
Stop	Stop
Danger	Pericol
Open	Deschis [deskis]
Closed	Inchis
Full, no vacancy	Complet
Information	Informaţii
Bus stop	Staţie de Autobus
Taxi stand	Staţie de taxi
Pedestrians	Pietonĭ

ARRIVAL

Passport check	Controlul paşapoartelor
Your passport, please	Paşaportul, vă rog
I am with the group	Sînt cu grupa
Customs	Vama
Have you anything to declare?	Aveţĭ ceva de declarat?
Nothing to declare	Nimic de declarat
Baggage claim	Primirea Bagajelor
A porter	Un hamal

Transportation

to the bus	La autobus
to a taxi	La un taxi
to the Hotel . . . please	La Hotelul . . . , vă rog

MONEY

Currency exchange office	Banca
Do you have the change for this?	Aveţĭ mărunţiş?
May I pay	Pot plăti [plûti]
with a traveler's check?	cu un traveler's check?
with this credit card?	cu acest credit card?
I would like to exchange some	Aş vrea sa schimb nişte traveler's
traveler's checks	checks
What is the exchange rate?	Care-i cursul?

THE HOTEL

A hotel	un hotel
I have a reservation	Am o cameră rezervată
I would like a room	Aş vrea o cameră
with a double bed	cu pat dublu
with a bath	şi baie
with a shower	cu duş
with a private toilet	cu toaletă separată
without a bath	fără baie
What is the rate per day?	Cît costă pe zi?
Is breakfast included?	Este micul dejun inclus?
What floor is it on?	La ce etaj este?
ground floor	parter
second floor	etajul unu
Is there an elevator?	Are ascensor?

Have the baggage sent up, please   Vă rog să trimeteţi bagajul sus
The key to number . . . please   Cheia camerei numărul . . . , vă rog
Please call me at seven o'clock   Sculaţi-mă la şapte, vă rog
Have the baggage brought down   Vă rog sa duceţi bagajul jos
The bill   plata
A tip   bacşiş

THE RESTAURANT

A restaurant	Restaurantul
café	cafeneá
Waiter!	Ospătar!
Waitress!	Domnişoară!
Menu	Meniul, lista
I would like to order this	As vrea să comand acesta
Some more . . . please	Înca puţin . . . , vă rog
That's enough	Destul
The check, please	Plata, vă rog
Breakfast	micul dejun
Lunch	dejun, prînz
Dinner	masa de seară
Bread	pîine
Butter	unt
Jam	gem
Salt	sare
Pepper	piper
Mustard	muştar
Sauce, gravy	sos
Vinegar	oţet
Oil	untdelemn
The wine list	lista vinurilor
red wine	vin roşu
white wine	vin alb
rosé wine	vin roz
Bottle	o sticlă
A carafe	o garafă
A beer	o bere
Some water	nişte apă
A bottle of mineral water	o sticklă de apă minerală
carbonated	gazosă
non-carbonated	negazosă
Some ice	nişte gheaţă
Some milk	nişte lapte
Lemonade	limonată
Coffee (with milk)	cafeá (cu lapte)
Tea (with lemon)	ceai (cu lămîie) [chai cu lûmiye]
Chocolate	cacao
Juice	suc
Sugar	zahăr

(Further Romanian restaurant hints are given in the chapter on food and drink.)

MAIL

A letter	o scrisoare
An envelope	un plic

A postcard	o carte poştală
A mailbox	o cutie de scrisori
The post-office	poşta
A stamp	un timbru
Airmail	un avion
How much does it cost to send a letter (a postcard) air mail to the United States (Great Britain, Canada)?	Cît costă o scrisoare (o carte poştală) cu avionul în Statele Unite? (Marea Britanie, Canada)?
To send a telegram, cable	a trimite o telegrammă

LOCATIONS

. . . Street	strada . . .
. . . Avenue	calea . . .
. . . Square	piaţa
The airport	aeroportul
A bank	o bancă
The beach	plaja
The bridge	podul
The castle	castelul
The cathedral	catedrala
The church	biséri
The garden	grădina
The hospital	spitalul
The movies, cinema	cinema
a movie	un film
The museum	muzéul
A nightclub	un bar
The palace	palatul
The park	parcul
The post-office	pŏsta
The station	gara
The theater	teatrul
a play	o piesă
The travel bureau	Oficiul National de Turism ONT [oneté]
The university	universitatea

TRAVEL

Arrival	Sosire
Departure	Plecare

The airplane	Avionul
I want to reconfirm a reservation on flight number . . . for . . .	Aş vrea să reconfirm o reservă, zborul numărul . . . spre . . .
Where is the check-in?	Unde se face controlul?
I am checking in for . . .	Plec la . . .
Fasten your seat belt	Puneţi centura de siguranţă

The railroad	Calea ferată
The train	trenul
From what track does the train to . . . leave?	De la ce peron pleacă trenul spre . . . ?
Which way is the dining car?	Pe unde este vagonul restaurant?

Bus, streetcar, subway — Autobus, tramvai, metro
Does this bus go to . . . — Acest autobus merge la . . .
   trolley bus —   troleibuz
I want to get off at . . . Street — Doresc să cobor la . . . strada
   at the next stop —   la staţia următoare

Taxi — Un taxi
I (we) would like to go — Aş vrea să merg (Am vrea să
   to . . . please —   mergem) la . . . vă rog
Stop at . . . — Opriţi la . . .
Stop here — Opriţi aici

NUMBERS

1	unu, una	20	douăzeci
2	doi, două	25	douăzecisicinci
3	trei	30	treizeci
4	patru	40	patruzeci
5	cinci	50	cincizeci
6	şase	60	şasezeci
7	şapte	70	şaptezeci
8	opt	80	optzeci
9	nouă	90	nouăzeci
10	zece	100	o sută
11	unsprezece	200	două sute
12	doisprezece	300	trei sute
13	treisprezece	400	patru sute
14	paisprezece	500	cinci sute
15	cincisprezece	600	şase sute
16	şaisprezece	700	şapte sute
17	şaptesprezece	800	opt sute
18	optsprezece	900	nouă sute
19	nouăsprezece	1000	o mie

LANGUAGE/30
For the Business or Vacationing International Traveler

In 22 languages! A basic language course on 2 cassettes and a phrase book . . . Only $14.95 ea. + shipping

Nothing flatters people more than to hear visitors try to speak their language and LANGUAGE/30, used by thousands of satisfied travelers, gets you speaking the basics quickly and easily. Each LANGUAGE/30 course offers:

- up to 2 hours of guided practice in greetings, asking questions and general conversation
- special section on social customs and etiquette

Order yours today. Languages available:

ARABIC	GERMAN	JAPANESE	RUSSIAN
CHINESE	GREEK	KOREAN	SERBO-CROATIAN
DANISH	HEBREW	NORWEGIAN	SPANISH
DUTCH	INDONESIAN	PERSIAN	SWAHILI
FRENCH	ITALIAN	PORTUGUESE	TAGALOG
	TURKISH	VIETNAMESE	

To order send $14.95 per course + shipping $2.00 1st course, $1 ea. add. course. In Canada $3 1st course, $2.00 ea. add. course. NY and CA residents add state sales tax. Outside USA and Canada $14.95 (U.S.) + air mail shipping: $8 for 1st course, $5 ea. add. course. MasterCard, VISA and Am. Express card users give brand, account number (all digits), expiration date and signature. SEND TO: FODOR'S, Dept. LC 760, 2 Park Ave., NY 10016-5677, USA.

INDEX

INDEX

In this index **E** indicates Entertainment (theater, opera, ballet & concerts), **H** indicates Hotels & other accommodations, **M** indicates Museums and art galleries, **R** indicates Restaurants

CZECHOSLOVAKIA
Practical Information
(see also Practical Information at the end of each chapter in section)

Geographical

HUNGARY
Practical Information

(see also Practical Information at the end of each chapter in section)

Geographical

POLAND
Practical Information

(see also Practical Information at the end of each chapter in section)

ROMANIA
Practical Information
(see also Practical Information at
the end of each chapter in
section)

Geographical

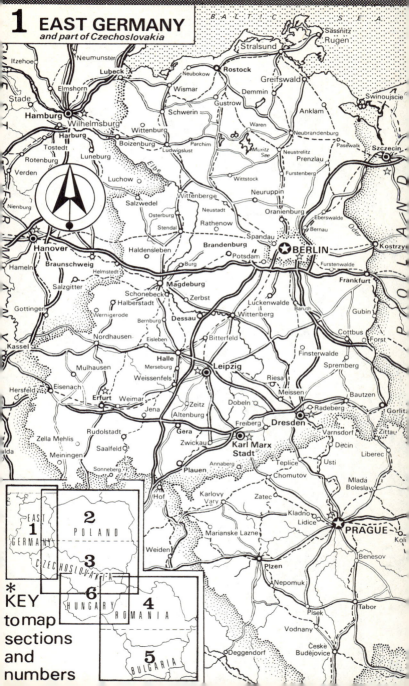

EASTERN EUROPE

1 EAST GERMANY
and part of Czechoslovakia

KEY to map sections and numbers

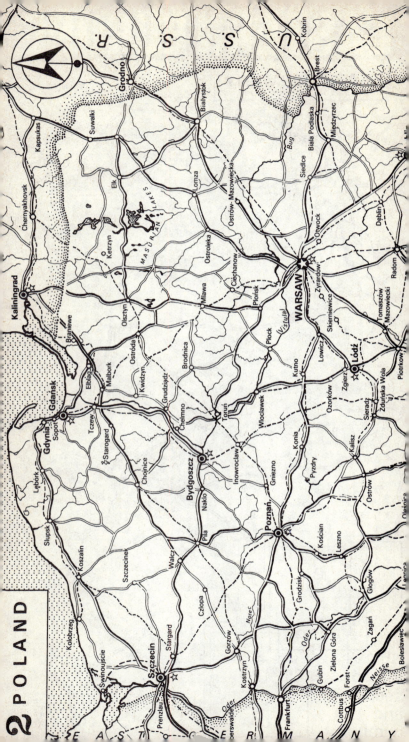

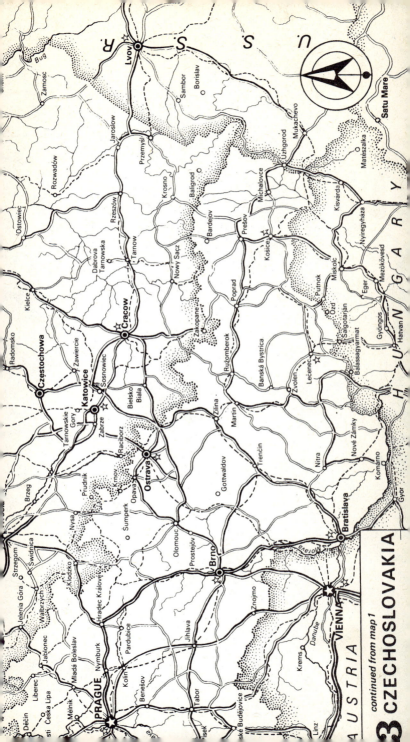

continued from map 1

3 CZECHOSLOVAKIA

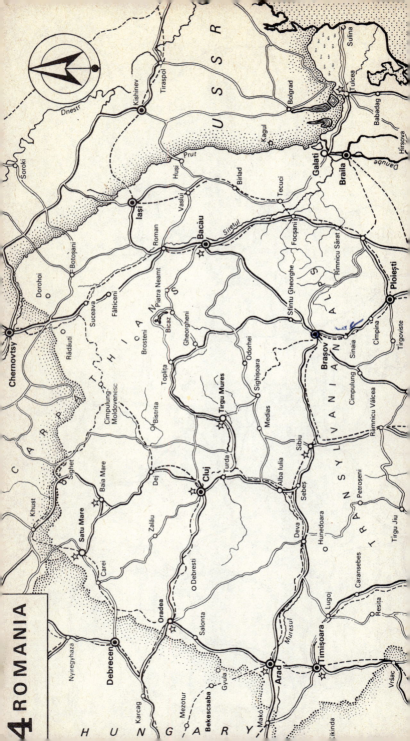

5 BULGARIA

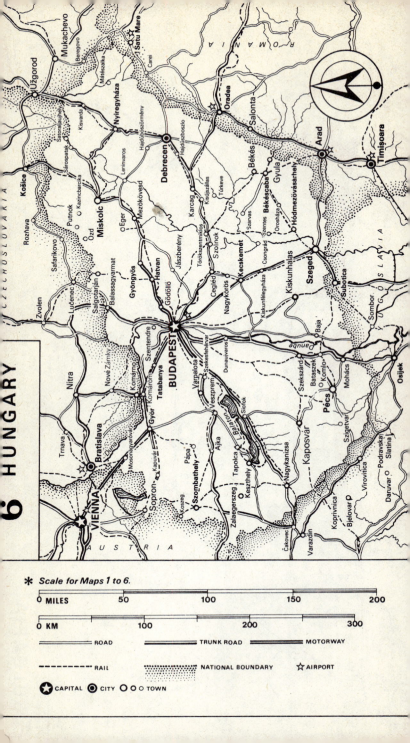

6 HUNGARY

Scale for Maps 1 to 6.

MILES				
0	50	100	150	200

KM			
0	100	200	300

═══ ROAD   ═══ TRUNK ROAD ═══   ═══ MOTORWAY

--- RAIL   ···· NATIONAL BOUNDARY   ☆ AIRPORT

★ CAPITAL   ◉ CITY   ○ ○ TOWN